D1519132

SAGE was founded in 1965 by Sara Miller McCune to support the dissemination of usable knowledge by publishing innovative and high-quality research and teaching content. Today, we publish over 900 journals, including those of more than 400 learned societies, more than 800 new books per year, and a growing range of library products including archives, data, case studies, reports, and video. SAGE remains majority-owned by our founder, and after Sara's lifetime will become owned by a charitable trust that secures our continued independence.

Los Angeles | London | New Delhi | Singapore | Washington DC | Melbourne

Financial Management

Financial Management
A Contemporary Approach

Rajesh Kothari

Director, R. A. Podar Institute of Management, and Dean,
Faculty of Management Studies, University of Rajasthan, Jaipur

Los Angeles | London | New Delhi
Singapore | Washington DC | Melbourne

First published in 2017 by

SAGE Publications India Pvt Ltd
B1/I-1 Mohan Cooperative Industrial Area
Mathura Road, New Delhi 110 044, India
www.sagepub.in

SAGE Publications Inc
2455 Teller Road
Thousand Oaks, California 91320, USA

SAGE Publications Ltd
1 Oliver's Yard, 55 City Road
London EC1Y 1SP, United Kingdom

SAGE Publications Asia-Pacific Pte Ltd
3 Church Street
#10-04 Samsung Hub
Singapore 049483

Published by Vivek Mehra for SAGE Publications India Pvt Ltd, typeset in Stone Serif 9.5/11.5 pts by Zaza Eunice, Hosur, Tamil Nadu, India and printed at Sai Print-o-Pack, New Delhi.

Library of Congress Cataloging-in-Publication Data Available

ISBN: 978-93-515-0821-2 (PB)

SAGE Team: Amit Kumar, Indrani Dutta, Vandana Gupta, Derrick Samuel and Ritu Chopra

To all the students, researchers, scholars, practitioners, and fellow colleagues who have a keen desire to study and understand financial management.

Thank you for choosing a SAGE product!
If you have any comment, observation or feedback,
I would like to personally hear from you.
Please write to me at **contactceo@sagepub.in**

Vivek Mehra, Managing Director and CEO,
SAGE Publications India Pvt Ltd, New Delhi

Bulk Sales

SAGE India offers special discounts
for bulk institutional purchases.

*For queries/orders/inspection copy requests
write to* **textbooksales@sagepub.in**

Publishing

Would you like to publish a textbook with SAGE?
Please send your proposal to **publishtextbook@sagepub.in**

Get to know more about SAGE

Be invited to SAGE events, get on our mailing list.
Write today to **marketing@sagepub.in**

This book is also available as an e-book.

Brief Contents

Detailed Contents

Preface

Financial Management: A Contemporary Approach is a humble effort to appreciate the emerging significance of subject of financial management in a very intense competitive market situation where every penny spent needs to be reflected in good returns. Gone are the days when financial management was seen as reactive. It is now proactive for students and readers including practitioners and professionals in search of a lucid, compact, and handy title on financial management out of many titles available on the subject.

It may be recalled that the last 10 years have been very turbulent, vibrant, and dynamic as far as the Indian corporate sector, in general, and the financial sector, in particular, are concerned. This book acknowledges all major changes: consolidation and growth in the corporate sector; opening of capital market to FIIs; transparent and well-connected market structure, new instruments, revolutionary changes in regulatory framework, and attempts to introduce the GST, GAAR, IFRS, and FDI in insurance sector for integrating with the global economy. In addition, the subject assumes greater significance when India is the "Bright Spot" as per IMF.

The contemporary environment has underlined how to grow against the odds. Every corporate is focused on making the organization viable, sustainable, and growth-oriented, especially when the external environment is competitive. Keeping all the micro and macro changes in focus, the converge of the book is extensive.

Every chapter includes a prelude, learning objectives, test yourself, key terms, summary, assess yourself, case studies, student activities, and practice problems. Due care has been taken to ensure that the book is lucid and simple. It avoids complex numerical and complicated calculations in light of the various customized software applications available, thanks to the rapid advancement in technology. The focus is to "read in between the lines" and "interpret and infer" rather than calculating and solving hypothetical problems. While preparing the text, published sources in the form of textbooks, articles, web resources, and relevant reports have been used extensively and referred to. The author does not claim any of these published works to be his creativeness; the objective is to solely use them for the academic interest of the fraternity. It is expected that the book shall meet aspirations and inspirations of readers who are keen to learn financial management in a lucid way.

Acknowledgments

At this point, I wish to acknowledge the kind cooperation received from fellow colleagues, peers, critics, and students from across the country. My warm thanks is due to my colleagues Professor Kailash Sodani (VC, Maharshi Dayanand Saraswati [MDS] University, Ajmer), Professor Deepak Gupta (Vikram University, Ujjain), Professor Anil Kothari (Mohan Lal Sukhadia University [MLSU], Udaipur), Professor Karunesh Saxena (MLSU, Udaipur), Professor Manoj Kumar and Professor Satish Agrawal (MDS University, Ajmer), Professor S.K. Vyas, Bikaner, Professor Y.S. Thakur, Dr Hari Singh (Gour University, Sagar, Madhya Pradesh), Professor Hemant Dangi (Faculty of Management Studies [FMS], Delhi), Professor Anil Mehta (University of Rajasthan [UOR], Jaipur), Professor Meenakshi Malhotra (University Business School [UBS], Chandigarh), Professor Kamal Vagrecha and Professor Nawal Kishor (Indira Gandhi National Open University [IGNOU], New Delhi), and my research scholars—Bobby Dutta, Sonal Jain, Roopam Kothari, Anamika Sharma, Bhavya Soni, Vidhu Mathur, Saket Mathur, just to name a few, for their immense help and cooperation.

I would also like to thank the reviewers for their valuable comments on the manuscript, especially Dr P.S.S. Murthy, former director (Advanced Studies) at the Hyderabad Center of Excellence, Institute of Cost Accountants of India; Dr Sulagna Mukherjee, TA Pai Management Institute, Manipal; Dr Pawan Kumar Avadhanam, Institute of Public Enterprise, Hyderabad; and Dr Shubhra Aanand, Symbiosis International University, Pune.

I express my gratitude to my family members for their support, without which this book would not have been possible. I wish to acknowledge the professional support extended by the team at SAGE India and record my special thanks to Amit and Indrani of SAGE Publications for their help in publishing the book.

About the Author

Rajesh Kothari is Director, R.A. Podar Institute of Management and Dean, Faculty of Management Studies, University of Rajasthan, Jaipur. He has had an engaging tenure as a teacher, consultant, and trainer for the last 32 years and has also served in administrative capacity as Director of R.A. Podar Institute of Management, Jaipur, from 2007 to 2010. Over the years, he has also been engaged in teaching assignments and research projects in association with private universities and government enterprises such as Small Industries Development Bank of India (SIDBI), Industrial Finance Corporation of India (IFCI), Institute of Labour Development, and others. He has also acted as an honorary advisor to the likes of *Dalal Street Journal*, IFCI, Mewar University, among various others.

Dr Kothari has guided and supervised more than 30 PhD scholars and has been associated with various universities across India as a member of their Board of Studies. The main subject areas of his interest are management accounting, financial management, financial services, investment management, international finance, and finance for strategic decisions. So far, he has authored five published books and over 40 articles published in various well-acclaimed journals apart from presenting papers and lectures at various seminars and conferences. Some of his published titles include *Financial Services in India: Concepts and Applications* (2010), *Management Accounting: Concepts & Applications* (2007), and *Contemporary Financial Management* (2005).

PART I
An Overview of Financial Management

CHAPTER 1

Introduction to Financial Management: A Contemporary Approach

- To understand the concept, scope, and goals of financial management in the present business scenario.
- To understand the contemporary business environment and to address the issues and challenges in financial management.
- To highlight the changing role of a finance manager through outlining finance function in the organization.
- To discuss the problem of trust.

PRELUDE

Imagine that you were to start your own business. Irrespective of the nature of the business, you need to address the following key financial questions:

(i) **Investment:** Will you require to run the business? In which assets should you invest, that is, what sorts of assets?

(ii) **Financing:** How should the chosen investments be financed? Will you borrow the money or provide whole of the required capital yourself?

(iii) **Operating:** How will you manage your daily financial activities such as managing inventory or collecting from your customers or paying your suppliers?

(iv) **Growth and Value Creation:** How should the investors and stakeholders be rewarded? How much of the profits will you distribute and how much will you retain?

Such decisions may be termed as financial implications of management, popularly known as financial decisions, which may have investment, operations, financing, and reward as their nature. These decisions form the very essence of financial management and collectively they indicate the scope of the financial management of any organization. In fact, financial management is common to all functional areas of management. It is "be-all and end-all" of the enterprise.

Introduction to Financial Management

The word **finance** stands for provision of money as and when required. Finance or provision of money is needed for **as** (purpose) and for **when** (time). Why does an organization need money? The organization needs money for assets' acquisition, for working and operations, and for contingencies and growth. These purposes eventually become the focus of a finance manager. So far "when" is concerned, the time factor is duly recognized. In simple words, money is needed for short term, medium term, and long term. Interestingly, the time is not defined in respect of days or months or years.

Short term, for example, is a duration (specific time is undefined) where either supply or demand of money is constant or fixed. If demand is fixed, an increase in money supply will ensure reduction in the interest rate. The Indian economy in the recent past may prove the point. For the last couple of years, there has not been effective demand for money and the supply kept increasing, resulting in lowering the rate of interest. If supply of funds is constant and demand increases, it may result in an increase in the rate of interest. This is currently happening in India, and there is pressure on the Reserve Bank of India (RBI) to reduce key rates of such as repo and reverse repo for providing momentum to the economy.

Long term is defined as a time frame in which both demand and supply are volatile and flexible. In such a situation, there is no standard rate of interest; rather, every rate of interest is optimum and is volatile.

Financial management may also be defined as: "the ways and means of managing money." More formally, it can be defined as **planning, acquisition, allocation, and utilization** of financial resources with the aim of achieving objectives of the firm.

Financial management starts with realizing financial needs, and it includes analyzing financial situations, making financial decisions, setting financial objectives, formulating financial plans, and providing effective systems of financial control to ensure the progress of organization by achieving some preset objectives.

The Financial Management Process

Financial management is a *dynamic* decision-making process involving a series of interrelated activities as follows:

1. Financial planning.
2. Financial decision-making.
3. Financial analysis.
4. Financial control.

Financial Planning

While the financial objectives set out *what* has to be achieved, the financial plans will discuss how the financial objectives are to be achieved. The essence of financial planning is to ensure that *the right amount of funds are available at the right time and at the right cost for the level of risk involved* to enable the firm's objectives to be achieved. Financial plans will, therefore, show the volume and timing of funds requirements needed to achieve the firm's objectives.

Budgeting is a key financial planning tool. The whole financial planning process is likely to be summarized in a few key budgeted or forecast financial statements: a budgeted balance sheet, a budgeted profit and loss account, and a budgeted cash flow statement. These budgets or forecasts will then provide the reference point against which progress can be monitored and controlled.

The efficiency and effectiveness of the financial planning process will be greatly aided by the application of computerized financial modeling. Proprietary software packages (e.g., MS Excel, SPSS, E Views) can be used to create a range of possible financial plans and to evaluate the financial effects of any changes in plans.

Financial Decision-making

It includes strategic investment decisions, such as investing in new production facilities or the acquisition of another company, and strategic financing decisions, for example, the decision to raise additional long-term loans. Alternatively, the financial review may dictate that disinvestment or "downsizing" is necessary. This may involve the closure or relocation of an unprofitable production facility or subsidiary. In any event, financial decision-making will include a range of strategic options for the business as a whole. The financial manager will be involved in the financial evaluation and assessment of the options presented; in determining their respective *costs*, *benefits*, and *risks*.

The decision-making phase will include the determination of the firm's financial objectives. In the context of the financial review, specific financial objectives will be set, while the primary financial objective is the maximization of shareholder value, if possible, else optimize value. This nevertheless requires specific subsidiary and more pragmatic objectives to be determined, so that the primary objective can be achieved. In general terms, these subsidiary financial objectives will normally be related to:

1. **Profitability:** For a business enterprise, the objective of making a profit is important to ensure the survival and growth of the business in the long run. The firm's investment decisions should yield a rate of return commensurate with the level of risk involved. The management task is to continually seek to improve profitability, and specific objectives for growth in earnings and return on investment (ROI) levels are likely to be set.
2. **Liquidity:** This means ensuring that sufficient cash is always available to pay the bills when they fall due and the business should remain solvent. The importance of adequate liquidity for management cannot be overemphasized.
3. **Capital Structure:** A firm's capital structure refers to the relationship between debt and equity finance in its long-term funds arrangements. *Debt finance* refers to external resources such as long-term loans, whereas *equity finance* refers to the funds provided by the shareholders.

From a purely practical point of view, the financial manager should ensure that the firm maintains a healthy balance between the proportion of debt and equity finance in its capital structure. This relationship between debt and equity finance is also referred as the level of **financial gearing** or **financial leverage**. While it may make financial sense for a firm to use borrowed money if other things are favorable, the firm may not be dependent on borrowed money as this increases its financial risk. Debt finance is often regarded as a cheaper source of capital than equity because the interest payments on borrowings are mandatory and tax allowable expense. The more money a firm borrows, the more it is committed to repaying in the form of interest and principal, whether it is making a profit or not. As these commitments increase, so does the risk to the ordinary shareholders, who are rewarded by way of dividend only after all other financial obligations have been met.

Financial objectives are *measurable* and *quantifiable*, such as the volume of profits and cash flows. However, objectives are also likely to include some qualitative objectives, such as the financial image (e.g., a conservative or entrepreneurial image), which the company wishes to project. Financial objectives will also be defined for achievement within a specified time frame. They may be categorized as being of a short-, medium-, or long-term nature. For example, management may be seeking to achieve a 30% growth in earnings per share (EPS) or ROI over the next five years or to substantially reduce gearing levels.

These are clearly long-term strategic financial objectives, but they must be broken down and phased into short-term (e.g., annual/quarterly/monthly) objectives to serve as benchmarks against which periodic progress can be measured.

Financial Analysis

This is the preliminary diagnostic stage to assess the current financial performance and condition of the business; and an analysis of financial strengths, weaknesses, opportunities, and threats (SWOT). Financial analysis will help management to take realistic view of resources, risk, return, and opportunities attached to the organization.

Financial Control

The final stage of the process will require effective management reporting and control systems to be set in place throughout the organization. This is to ensure that plans are properly implemented that progress is continually reported to the management, and that any deviations from plans are clearly identified.

Effective control systems, by providing a continual comparison of actual performance with planned performance, will alert management about deviations on time. If things are not progressing as planned, for example sales and profits are lower than expected, then remedial action can be taken to bring plans back on track. Alternatively, plans and objectives may need to be modified, if this is considered appropriate. This final control stage will inevitably review and analyze the financial performance—which, in turn, will lead to new decisions being made, objectives and plans being modified, and so forth.

Test Yourself

1. What is finance and financial management?
2. What are key steps in financial management process?

Contemporary Business Environment

Indian economy opened up its economic frontiers to the rest of the world in the early 1990s. Consequently, what was a closed-door economy became an open-door economy. The undercurrent of this open economy is now intense competition (Table 1.1).

A competitive economic environment results in the following:

1. Tremendous pressure on resources.
2. Increase in supply is more than the market demand. The market is now turned into buyers' market. Product life is very short as exact replacements are available at the competitive price.
3. A paradigm shift in consumer's perception so much so that his erstwhile loyalty for a product or company is sacrificed. As competing products are identical in respect of price, utility, and after-sales service, that is, whether you buy for example, a Wagon R or a Santro Car,

TABLE 1.1

SHIFT FROM STATIC TO A DYNAMIC STATE

Traditional Business Environment	Contemporary Business Environment
Profit maximization	Profit optimization
Wealth maximization	Value creation
Sellers' market	Buyers' market
Focus on dividend per share	Focus on earnings per share
Avoid risk	Confront risk
Bottom-line approach	Top-line approach
Scarcity of supply	Abundance of supply
Single demand	Multiple demand

Source: Author.

Head & Shoulders or Clean & Clear, Pepsodent or Colgate, the difference between these two is more of cosmetic in nature rather than real.

4. Also the market, by and large, is driven by volume. In other words, it is now a volume-driven market instead of value-driven market. Business is now "top line" one. Costs seem to be inflexible and this puts the margin under squeeze. Once margin is under squeeze, profit becomes the first casualty and the company finds it difficult to survive.

5. There has been an exemplary thrift in the growth strategies adopted by companies which have survived after the global meltdown and worldwide crisis. Companies today operate in a dynamic environment. Growth through diversification strategy governs the whole business scenario.

6. The current global market presents a mix scenario. The economy of the USA seems to be recovering, whereas EURO Zone and China are facing this recession. To add fuel to fire, China has devalued its currency three times in succession. The crude oil price is at rock bottom and India is seen as a hope of destination for the world.

7. The new regime in India is seen pro-industry, pro-economic growth where the focus is on "Sabka Saath, SabkaVikas."

In view of the changes experienced due to shift from static to the dynamic milieu, the focus is now on survival of the firm in such hostile and competitive situation. For the survival, the firm has to undertake "slimming and trimming" program, whereby all inefficient loss making or less profitable, nonperforming assets are disposed off even at a loss. The exercise aims at losing undesired weight of the firm and acquiring slim and trim shape. After "slimming and trimming" exercise of the firm, the consolidation process would start. Consolidation would mean "tie them together" that is, whatever is leftover, weave them into logical and sequential fabric. Now, the objective would focus on growth from consolidation. As in the present competitive environment, "size" is very crucial. To add to size quickly, the growth mechanism that is usually adopted is through mergers and acquisitions. The wave of mergers and acquisitions in all the core sectors of the economy such as financial services, pharmaceuticals, information technology, telecommunications, and entertainment indicates the realization of the need for growth.

To imbibe the contemporary scenario excerpts from an interview of Mr Deshawar, Chairman, ITC Ltd., may prove the point.

NO SMOKE, ALL FIRE IN THE BELLY: *THE ECONOMIC TIMES*

June 16, 2011

Tobacco-to-hotels major ITC has set its sights on being India's top non-cigarette FMCG company. Deveshwar tells ET's Sutanuka Ghosal his successor will in all probability be an insider, a safe pair of hands. Excerpts:

It's been more than 10 years since you began your current wave of diversification. What have been your successes and failures?

My first challenge was how to resuscitate our paper and hotels business, especially since our paper business had nearly gone sick. It was a separate company, which nearly defaulted on payments to financial institutions (FIs). Our hotels business was also small. The challenge was how to get these businesses to become growth engines. The other challenge was how to get rid of those businesses that were not going to create value for us, like financial services. We ultimately had to get rid of financial services and international trading.

We started with greeting cards. The idea was to add value to pulp, brand it and market it. Subsequently, we found that because of the digital revolution, there was no growth in the paper-based greetings business. We ultimately had to wind up that business. But during that period we had to deploy some artistic and creative talent, which we are now using to grow our stationery and education segment, which is a 500-crore business.

The other one was starting up lifestyle business. Since we were into promoting golf, one of the first things we did was Wills Sport. But we found it too limiting, so we created Wills Lifestyle.

The next was foods. Then we got into packaged "atta", biscuits, and confectionery. In fact, we got into every conceivable item progressively. We are somewhat different, as we have competitors in all segments. Perfetti is a competitor, Pepsi is our competitor in the snacks category, we've got pasta and noodles competing with Nestle, we've had competition from Britannia, Parle, Danone, and now Kraft has come in with Cadbury. We have a range of food products and this is going to continue to grow. There are still a number of items. The whole dairy business is still open.

Why have you not followed the strategy of acquiring brands and companies?

First, we need to see what is available in India. Is it worthwhile? Second, if you see those who've built there businesses through M&A route, they've got a collection of brands, which for the rest of their lifetime they've tried to resolve, by saying "these are my power brands, so I will now shrink it".

We don't have those issues. We can set our brand architecture. We've chosen to keep the purity of our brand architecture intact and then build it for the long term. If we go in for M&A, we will do it for acquiring technology. ITC will always be a company with an Indian soul. Right? We want to invest and grow to create sustainable livelihood for Indians. That's what we want to do.

What about going global? Is that not an aspiration?

It's not an aspiration now. The aspiration is to continue to support the growth engines in India and by competing in India and by creating local brands so that we don't have to pay royalty to anybody. If any Indian consumer is using an international brand, the first thing on the top line goes as royalty payment.

Ultimately, we have to build Indian brands. Nothing goes out, everything remains here. I know it is a tough challenge, an audacious task to fight well-established international players, but it can be done. If you name me some top companies in the world, are they still there? They have all disappeared. By the fifth year from now, our plan is to have. 1,500 crores profit from the FMCG business. Before I give up my executive role, I want this to happen.

To read more: http://itcportal.mobi/Newsroom/Media-Reports/2011/pr-16-june-11a.asp (accessed on April 14, 2016).

To sum up, contemporary business environment has opened new set opportunities in India such as E-commerce and online space. The success of Flipkart, Snapdeal, Ola, Askme, Oyo to name a few, has created new mind-set for business causing and creating unconventional financial structure and deal. As such physical space has been replaced by virtual and convenience having deep financial implication.

Goals of the Firm

In financial management theory, the goal of the business firm is to create the maximum value for its shareholders and this goal is commonly expressed as the maximization of shareholder wealth and value.

There are two broad goals of the firm:

1. Maximizing profit.
2. Maximizing wealth.

Maximizing Profit

The first and foremost goal of a finance manager is to maximize the profit. Profit maximization is a twofold approach which results from the following:

1. First, efficiency in investment decisions leading to capacity creation and assets building.
2. Second, operating efficiency with which assets should be utilized and revenue should be generated.

Profit maximization stands for efficient working, cost control, revenue generation, and better realization. It is the result of efforts in managing the business in the competitive environment (Figure 1.1).

Is Goal of Profit Maximization Relevant?

Although business cannot survive without profit, profit maximization is not an appropriate goal as it ignores the following factors: (1) the timing of returns, (2) cash flows, and (3) risk, all of which are key elements in determining shareholders wealth.

1. Timing of Returns
One of the shortcomings of profit maximization is that it tends to focus on the absolute amount of returns and ignores their timing by simply seeking to select those investments, which yield the greatest total amount of profits. Look at the investment choice presented in Illustration 1. Which investment is of greater value, Project A which yields profits of ₹200,000 a year for the next three years, or Project B which yields ₹660,000 of earnings in three years' time?

Figure 1.1
Process of Profit Maximization

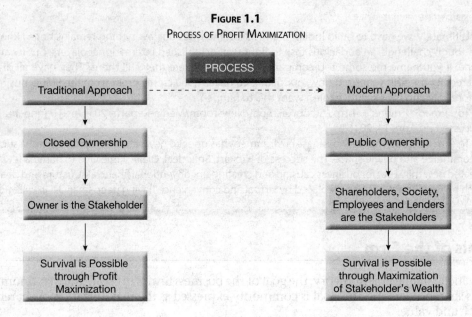

Source: Author.

Illustration 1. Profit Maximization Versus Value Maximization

Year	Cash Flow (in ₹)	
	Project A	**Project B**
1	200,000	0
2	200,000	0
3	200,000	660,000

Profit maximization would dictate the choice of Project B, as it has the greater amount of total profits. However, this may not be the value maximizing decision. With Project A, the firm has the opportunity to reinvest the funds earned in years 1 and 2, and possibly accumulate even greater total returns in the future. This is so because money has time value. Most people prefer to receive funds sooner than later, as they then have the ready opportunity to invest the funds thus accumulate more wealth. Therefore, to make value or wealth maximizing decisions, we need to take into account not only the amounts but also the respective timings of investment returns.

2. Cash Flows

Profits do not represent cash flows. Although profits may be used as the traditional accounting measure of a firm's financial performance and a firm may report healthy profits in its annual accounts, it does not necessarily mean that cash is actually available to pay for the liabilities and finance its investment activities. For example, depreciation and other provisions are included in a profit and loss account but they are noncash items.

Despite the existence of company law and professional accounting standards, firms still have enough "flexibility" in the reporting of profit figures to give the most favorable impression of financial performance.

3. Risk

The objective of profit maximization also ignores the concept of risk, which, for our purposes here, may be defined as the chance that the actual outcome of a decision may differ from the expected outcome.

In comparing the respective returns of the two projects in Illustration 1, we did not consider their relative risks. For example, Project A may be the expansion of an existing product line, whereas Project B may involve launching a new product in the market.

Clearly, Project B, in this case, would contain higher risk investment therefore its cash flows would be subject to a greater degree of uncertainty. If Project B is considered more risky than Project A, then it will be expected to yield a higher return.

By focusing solely on returns, the goal of profit maximization is only looking at "one side of the coin". We cannot make a valid comparison between investments unless we consider the respective risk and return of each investment.

This is the **risk—return trade-off** *that forms the cornerstone of financial decision-making.* Investors can only earn higher returns by accepting higher levels of risk. If a low-risk investment is preferred, then a commensurate low level of return is expected. It is this combination of risk and return that determines a firm's share value.

It is, therefore, advocated that other objectives such as EPS, or CEPS (cash earnings per share), is considered as more appropriate objective.

Maximizing Wealth

The maximization of shareholders wealth, or value, means the maximization of the firm's total market value, that is, maximizing ordinary share price in the long run. In the case of a listed company, shareholders wealth is measured by the share price in the financial markets. For a private company, which does not have its shares quoted on a stock market, shareholders' wealth maximization remains a valid goal, but measuring the market value of the shares in the absence of an active market is a difficult task.

The goals of an organization may even be expressed in the form of a "mission statement." A mission statement sets out an organization's ethos, its beliefs, and value systems which underline its operation.

However, from a purely financial point of view, shareholders' wealth maximization or value creation is a dominant goal because the firm operates in a competitive financial market. Investors have alternative investment opportunities and limited funds to invest. If the firm wants to attract funds for investment, then it must provide investors (both existing and potential) with a fair return for the risk involved. If it does not, then attracting essential financing will become extremely difficult, if not impossible.

Conventionally, main goals of the firm have been profit maximization and wealth maximization besides numerous subgoals such as enhancing EPS, strengthening book values, and strengthening cash flows. It is to be remembered that goals and functions of the firm are greatly influenced by contemporary business environment. When there was complacency in the economy and virtual control over supply, the profit could be infinite or maximum. But when economic environment changed, the goals were reset. Moreover, the word "maximum" represents infinity or "what cannot be quantified." So what cannot be quantified, cannot be achieved. Thus, the first change in resetting of objective was the replacement of "maximum" by "optimum," that is, what is most appropriate with given level of constraints, has to be achieved. At times even meager return of 5% on investment is better than 50%, if warranted by extreme difficult and hostile business environment. Thus, in the competing business environment, the objectives of the firm are survival, consolidation, and growth. Growth through mergers and acquisitions is the fastest way of growth. Reliance Industries Limited (RIL) is the classic example following the growth strategy of "Merger-Demerger-re Merger."

Test Yourself

1. What is profit maximization concept?
2. What is wealth maximization concept?
3. In a competitive environment, which goal will enable the organization to survive?

Mission Statement of the Organization and the Goal of Finance

The fundamental purpose of existence of a firm is reflected in its mission statement. If we consider that maximization of shareholders wealth is the objective of an organization, then the mission statement of an organization should reflect the same. However, vision statement provides a snapshot of the framework of the strategies in future. Although the fundamental objective of an organization remains the maximization of shareholders wealth, in practice, the other factors too play a dominant role in determining the mission, vision, and objectives of a firm. Customer satisfaction becomes the core objective of an organization while drafting the strategic moves related to products and services rendered by the organization. The following mission and vision statement of Coca Cola may highlight the point.

THE COCA COLA COMPANY

Mission

Our Roadmap starts with our mission, which is enduring. It declares our purpose as a company and serves as the standard against which we weigh our actions and decisions.

1. To refresh the world,
2. To inspire moments of optimism and happiness,
3. To create value and make a difference.

Vision

Our vision serves as the framework for our Roadmap and guides every aspect of our business by describing what we need to accomplish in order to continue achieving sustainable, quality growth.

1. **People:** Be a great place to work where people are inspired to be the best they can be.

2. **Portfolio:** Bring to the world a portfolio of quality beverage brands that anticipate and satisfy people's desires and needs.
3. **Partners:** Nurture a winning network of customers and suppliers, together we create mutual, enduring value.
4. **Planet:** Be a responsible citizen that makes a difference by helping build and support sustainable communities.
5. **Profit:** Maximize long-term return to share owners while being mindful of our overall responsibilities.
6. **Productivity:** Be a highly effective, lean and fast-moving organization. (*Source:* http://www.the-coca-colacompany.com/ourcompany/mission vision_values.html)

The contemporary approach has tried to redefine the objective of financial management that beside profit and wealth, social good, go-green and environment preservation should also guide to operation & objective of financial management.

Test Yourself

1. Differentiate between mission and vision.
2. How is the goal of customer satisfaction related with the shareholder's wealth maximization goal?

What Does Financial Management Involve in Contemporary Environment?

The critical activity of the financial management process is that of financial decision-making, specifically decisions aimed at creating maximum value for the stakeholders. Decisions about spending, investing, or borrowing money, for example, are important financial decisions. The main aim of the finance manager is to manage financial resources while performing these financial functions. The financial manager is concerned with the following types of interrelated decisions:

1. Investment decisions.
2. Financing decisions.
3. Dividend decisions.

Investment Decisions

Investment decisions are very crucial decisions as they involve allocation of funds for the long term and they determine the earning capacity of The organization. A sound and careful investment decision will help the organization to take on competitions and gain competitive advantage. Investment decision requires capital expenditure and is generally known as capital budgeting decisions. The investment decisions can be of two types:

1. Long-term or strategic investment decisions.
2. Short-term or tactical and operational investment decisions.

Long-term or Strategic Investment Decisions

These are concerned with investing in the long-term, wealth-creating assets of the business, such as investments in fixed tangible assets (e.g., land and buildings) or the acquisition of other businesses. Strategic investment decisions involve investment of substantial amount of money to selected projects for long periods. Such decisions are taken in the face of considerable risk and uncertainty. Strategic investment decisions have the potential for creating real value for the business, and thus value for its stakeholders. Accurate Strategic investment decisions are crucial to the long-term success of a business. The two important parameters for evaluating investment decisions are (a) estimating future benefits from the investment proposal and (b) measuring the cutoff rate against which the perspective return of new investment could be compared. It means that investment in future must earn required rate of return. The required rate of return is the expected return that a firm could earn by investing its money in long-term projects.

Short-term or Tactical and Operational Investment Decisions

Short-term investment decision relates to investment in medium- to short-term current assets of the firm such as stocks, debtors, bank, and money market deposits. These are the assets, which are essential to manage firm's day-to-day operations. Management of current assets affects short-term liquidity and profitability of the firm. Lack of liquidity can lead a firm to insolvency. If the level of current assets is large in a firm, profitability is adversely affected. There should be a trade-off between liquidity and profitability. The finance manager has to estimate about the investments to be made in current assets and make sure that funds must be made available to meet the payments when needed.

Financing Decisions

Financing decision is the second important finance functions. It deals with when, from where, and how to acquire funds to meet the investment needs. There are two major sources of funds: debt and equity. Mix of debt and equity creates levered capital structure of the firm. The main thrust is to determine appropriate proportion of debt and equity. Optimum capital structure is that when market value of shares gets maximized.

The use of debt in capital structure affects the return and risk of shareholders. The debt in capital structure may increase EPS up to a certain extent but it increases the financial risk as well. The finance manager has to understand the relationship between employment of debt and its impact on shareholder's return. The change in shareholder's return caused by change in profit due to employment of debt is known as leverage. Therefore, the manager has to strike a balance between risk and return to calculate appropriate proportion of equity–debt mix. Once, best proportion of debt–equity is determined, the finance manager must take efforts to decide the available resources of funds considering controls, loan covenants, legal aspects, controlling power, and others restrictions.

Dividend/Reward Decisions

Dividend refers to rewarding the shareholders for undertaking risk by supplying capital to the firm and includes management of profit and dividend decisions. Dividend decision involves deciding how much of the firm's earnings should be distributed to shareholders in the form of dividends and how much should be retained to finance the firm's future growth and investment plans. The proportion of profit which is distributed among shareholders is known as dividend payout ratio and the balance which is retained in business is known as retention ratio. The finance manager has to design the dividend policy of the firm which has significant bearing on the shareholder's value. The optimum dividend policy is one which maximizes the market value of shares. The managers must decide the form in which dividend is to be paid, such as cash dividend or bonus shares. Bonus shares are shares issued to existing shareholders without charging anything. It is referred as capitalization of profit, though it may not be free of cost to the company. Further, a dividend is paid on paid-up capital. Nowadays, dividend decision has become slightly insignificant because all capital issues are made at premium.

Test Yourself

1. What is optimal capital structure?
2. What are the two important parameters that have significant bearing on the long-term strategic investment decision? Explain.

The Role of a Finance Manager

The most important role of the finance manager of a commercial venture is now to optimize the wealth of the shareholders. In a nonprofit organization (NPO), it should be the optimization of value for an identified client group. In particular, the financial manager will be responsible for the effective management of the finance function.

The finance manager, while being a *financial specialist,* is also expected to be an effective *team player* as he will be a key member of the senior management team. This team will require effective interpersonal as well as technical skills in contributing to the overall management of the organization.

In large organizations, the various functions and responsibilities of the financial manager are likely to be shared among a number of specialist staff whereas in small enterprises the finance manager is expected to be a "jack of all trades," being responsible for the conventional financial and management accounting functions.

Specifically, the finance manager will be intimately involved, and be expected to bring his specialist skills to bear in all the stages of the financial management processes, viz., financial planning, financial decision-making, financial analysis, and financial control. The main functions of a finance manager are as follows:

1. Funds Management
This is the primary responsibility of the finance manager and includes the effective and efficient acquisition, allocation, and utilization of funds. **Acquisition** involves ensuring the availability of adequate funds and acquiring the right amount of funds from the right source at the right cost for the risk involved to meet the organization's financing needs. **Allocation** involves the effective allocation of the acquired funds to projects and services in line with stated objectives and agreed priorities. **Utilization** means ensuring that funds are used efficiently and effectively in the pursuit of organizational objectives.

2. Financial Networking
This involves the management of the firm's financial image and its relationships with the financial community. It will mean promoting an appropriate brand for the firm through

conservative, entrepreneurial, or aggressive approach and cultivating good relations with the existing and potential investors.

In large organizations, some of these responsibilities will be delegated to the specialist in finance departments or sections. Taxation, for instance, may fall within the ambit of a specialist taxation department in a large multinational corporation (MNC), whereas funds and risk management may be the responsibility of a centralized treasury department.

The internationalization, integration, and deregulation of financial markets (e.g., capital and money markets), FIs (e.g., banks and insurance companies), and financial instruments (e.g., shares and bonds), and the extensive range of options which they now offer for investing and financing arrangements make it essential for the financial manager to understand, appreciate, and operate in the wider international financial environment.

For example, the finance manager may scan the international marketplace in search of the cheapest source of financing for the business. Similarly, when funds have to be allocated across national borders to subsidiaries, the financial manager will need to be aware of the respective risks (e.g., currency exposure), costs, and tax implications of investing in the relevant countries.

3. Provision of Financial Information
The financial manager is also responsible for the provision of effective financial information and sound professional advice to facilitate the decision-making of the management team. The financial manager will be particularly skilled in the understanding and application of the key financial management concepts in creating value for the business. The financial decisions taken by the financial manager and the management team in general will affect the value of the firm as Figure 1.2 illustrates.

FIGURE 1.2

FINANCIAL DECISIONS AND THE VALUE OF THE FIRM

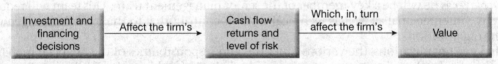

Source: Author.

4. Treasury Management
The structure of the finance function outlined in Figure 1.3 presents a separate treasury function. The Chartered Institute of Management Accountants (CIMA), London, defines treasury management as: "The corporate handling of all financial matters, the generation of external and internal funds for business, the management of currencies and cash flows, and the complex strategies, policies and procedures of corporate finance." Wherever separate treasury function exists, its key responsibilities include:

(a) Risk Management: This will include the identification of risks and formulation of policies and procedures for hedging (which means reducing or minimizing) the different types of risk to which the firm is likely to be exposed. A firm may be exposed to one or more of following financial risks:

    (i)   *Business risk:* It is related to the operations of the firm. Business risk is a type of risk that is largely outside the control of the company's managers. It is the risk which is inherent in the operations of the firm. Once a firm decides to be in a particular economic system (e.g., India, or USA or China) and a particular industry, it will be governed by the parameters affecting the economic system (e.g., inflation) and industry (e.g., logistics, demand and supply conditions, competition, etc.). A business risk

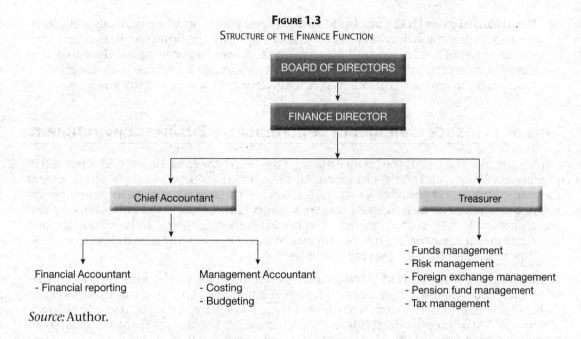

Figure 1.3
Structure of the Finance Function

Source: Author.

affects operating margin of the firm and it represents variation in the level of earning because of variation in the level of quantity produced and sold due to operations.

(ii) *Financial risk*: It refers to the level of debt in relation to equity finance in a firm's capital structure. Financial risk is a type of risk, which is largely within the control of the company's managers. Financial risk is the risk that a company incurs when it uses borrowed funds. The greater a company's reliance on borrowed money, that is, on debt financing, the greater the risk that it will be unable to meet its financial commitments (e.g., loan interest and principal payments, and leasing payments).

A common measure of financial risk is *financial gearing or leverage ratio*. The financial gearing ratio measures the proportion of debt in relation to equity finance in a firm's capital structure—for this reason the ratio is also frequently called the *debt-equity ratio*. Generally speaking, the higher the gearing ratio, the higher a firm's financial risk.

(iii) *Credit risk*: The risk that a debtor or borrower may not pay what they owe. It arises out of credit sale, that is, failure to pay the bill on time.

(iv) *Exchange rate risk*: It refers to the risk of loss or gain from exchange rate fluctuation when a firm has the international exposure being an importer or exporter.

(v) *Technological risk*: A technological risk refers to less productivity due to sudden change in technology, making products and services to be more time-consuming and lengthy. Example, floppy has been replaced by pen drive, and so on.

(b) Pension Fund Management: The treasury function may also include the efficient investment and portfolio management of employee pension schemes. Alternatively, this task may be outsourced from a specialist asset management organization, such as the asset management arm of a leading investment bank.

(c) Tax Management: The aim will be to minimize the firm's overall tax liabilities and this will require specialist knowledge not only of domestic tax regimes but also those of other countries in which the firm operates.

(d) Relationships with Financial Stakeholders: The treasury function is also concerned with maintaining and developing good relationships with the firm's financial stakeholders such as shareholders, lenders, and tax authorities. In very large companies, there may be a specialist investor relations department which is responsible for dealing with shareholders, institutional investors, credit rating agencies, investment bankers, and stockbrokers.

Role of a Finance Manager in Contemporary Business Environment

Conventionally, the role of the finance manager has been type caste. He has been involved in treasury, regulatory, and control function. All these functions have lost their significance as they are routine ones because of far-reaching changes that have taken place in contemporary business environment such as globalization, speedier cross-border transactions, vibrant and volatile exchange rate mechanism, newer technology ensuring speedy and accurate data and information management; the role of a finance manager is now more demanding.

Some of the new focused roles are as follows:

1. **Maintain Flexi-Capital Structure:** The interest rate mechanism is now flexible, vibrant, and dynamic. Gone are the days when interest rate structure was fixed and valid for a fairly long period of time. If at all, any revision was there, it was always on the increasing side. Today, there is a flexi interest rate structure, and because of that the capital structure should assume flexible character, that is, replacement of high cost of debts by low cost of debts if interest rate goes down by using a technique called "swap," loan takeover, refinancing, and so on. This role clearly emphasizes on "maintaining" affordable leverage. The leverage is a double-edged sword. If used judiciously, it would enhance value and if it is used illogically, it might lead to technical insolvency or erosion in profit, consequently erosion in value to the shareholders.

   In recent times, many well-known Indian companies reported losses despite increased turnover. One of the explicit reasons was unmanageable financial cost, that is, cost of debts. It is a known fact that rate of interest was coming down across the board. A company, which took loan at 15% p.a. in the year say 1999, would continue to pay the same rate of interest against the current rate of 10% p.a. Sensing the implication of severe interest burden on profit, companies such as Industrial Development Bank of India (IDBI) and IFCI, resorted to buy back of bonds by invoking the call option. But now interest rates are firming up, making borrowing a costly affair. So, the finance manager would need to be vigilant on the flexi interest rate structure. Also, the finance manager should ensure flexi-capital structure by changing the quantum of loan in view of taking maximum advantage of the situation.

2. **Tax Planning:** An efficient finance manager is one who is truly good at tax planning. By tax planning, it is meant that the firm should avail of fiscal, monetary, and investing opportunities to adjust profit. India's largest private sector company RIL did not pay tax over several years because of effective management of profit by availing investment incentives and fiscal benefits.

3. **Exposure to Global Financial Market:** The globalization has strengthened the flow of funds from low return to high return. Developing economies offer high rate of ROI to resources suppliers. Such resources are cheaper than domestic resources. The finance manager should take note of such a situation and should replace high cost funds with low cost of funds.

Similarly, he should ensure that exposure to forex should not affect the profit. For example, if the company imports, then the finance manager should manage forex exposure. He should take all necessary steps such as 'swap', 'hedge' or adopt suitable measures. Not only this, the modern finance manager needs to be conversant with E-Commerce and should be technology savvy. He should make the best of such opportunities to achieve the objectives.

Figure 1.3 illustrates the structure of the finance function for a large company. It divides the finance role into two separate functions. One is the control function which is managed by the chief accountant and provides the traditional financial and management accounting services to the business. The second is the treasury function, which is normally concerned with funds acquisition, liquidity management, risk management, and investors' relations.

Test Yourself

1. Explain any four major functions of the finance managers.
2. What is profit planning function of the finance manager? Explain.
3. Differentiate business risk from financial risk.

The Problem of Trust

In the beginning of this chapter, it was stated that the most important goal of the finance manager, like all other managers of a commercial venture, is to maximize the wealth of the shareholders. Is this the case in practice? Do company directors and managers, who are in fact trustees of the shareholders, consistently act in the best interests of the shareholders, or do they tend to act in their own best interests?

In an incorporated enterprise, the ownership and management are separated. The separation of *ownership* and *control,* gives rise to a potential conflict between the objectives of the individual managers and the objectives of the shareholders on whose behalf the managers operate the firm. This is known as the **trusteeship issue**—that the managers may place their personal goals and objectives above those of the firm's owners and act accordingly.

The trusteeship problem implies a potential for conflict in objectives of the shareholders and managers. In the corporate finance world, the principals are the shareholders who provide the equity finance for the firm and managers act on their behalf. As a result of pursuing such personal goals, the decisions and actions of the managers will be "satisfying" (a compromise between satisfying and maximizing behavior), rather than maximizing. This will lead to a less than a maximum return for the firm and thus less wealth for its shareholders.

Managers may be more concerned with maximizing their personal wealth through generous salaries, pension, and remuneration packages, their status, job security, and perquisites (executive cars, luxurious offices, and exclusive golf club memberships) than they are with the interests of nondirector shareholders. For example, many CEOs have become millionaires through generous stock options and other incentives when the actual shareholders wealth kept on depleting. Many companies such as Enron, WorldCom, and Tyco gradually became hollow from inside and ultimately became extinct while their CEOs kept on reaping rich rewards.

Each time, managers give precedence to their own personal best interests over those of the shareholders, and the result is **trusteeship costs** which have a negative effect on the owners' wealth. Trusteeship costs are the additional costs incurred by a principal when acting through an agent rather than dealing directly with another party. The trusteeship costs arise as a consequence of:

(i) **Managerial Rewards:** Managers have a considerable degree of discretion and freedom when it comes to determining their own rewards—financial and nonfinancial. They can typically vote themselves for huge pay increases, bonuses, pension, and other benefits and often these are not even related to the firm's actual performance. The costs of excessive and unjustified managerial rewards are clearly borne by the shareholders.

(ii) **Information Asymmetry:** Managers possess intimate inside knowledge of the firm's operations. As insiders, they have access to more information about the firm than the shareholders. They can share this information with shareholders and other stakeholders, for example, lenders, or withhold it if they believe that it is in their best personal interests to do so. This unequal access to, and distribution of, information between managers and owners is known as information asymmetry, and it is a cost borne by the shareholders.

(iii) **Managers' Risk Profile:** The risk profile of managers may be different from those of their principals, the shareholders. Managers may maintain a very low-risk profile and only invest the firm's funds in low-risk, low-return projects fearing that in case the venture fails, they might lose their jobs. Alternatively, managers may have a high-risk profile and expose the firm to inordinately high levels of risk, which are not in the owners' best interests, for example, to be rewarded with high bonuses.

(iv) **Managers' Short-Sightedness:** Managers may make decisions which maximize returns in the short-term at the expense of the firm's longer-term wealth, particularly if their rewards are related to short-term performance. For example, important expenditures on repairs and maintenance, and investments in new fixed assets, may be deferred so as not to depress short-term performance measures such as ROI. These decisions and actions would not be in the best interests of shareholders who are seeking to improve the firm's longer-term value.

How to Solve the Problem?

There are a number of strategies which shareholders can adopt to deal with the trusteeship problem, all of which increase the firm's operating costs but should reduce trusteeship costs:

1. **Monitoring and Control Arrangements:** Shareholders can introduce systems and procedures (e.g., management audit and internal control systems) to limit the satisfying and minimal risk behavior of the managers.

2. **Insurance Arrangements:** A third party (e.g., an insurance company) may be asked, in return for a premium, to underwrite the risk of loss to the firm of arising from defalcation or dishonesty by the managers.

3. **Incentive Arrangements for Managers:** The objective here is to secure better goal harmony between owners and managers, through directly linking the rewards of managers to their performance; which is usually measured by the achievement of specific objectives and targets as set by the owners.

External Influences and Constraints on Management Behavior

In addition to the measures which the shareholders of an individual firm can take to alleviate the trusteeship problem, there are also certain external influences and constraints on managerial behavior. These mainly take the form of market constraints and legal constraints.

1. **Market Constraints:** The external threat of a hostile takeover is always present, particularly where the predator (the acquiring company) considers the target company to be badly managed and undervalued. If a hostile takeover is successful, the existing management of the newly acquired company, which was seen as inefficient, will be replaced. This threat of a job-loss should influence the managers to be more attentive and alert to their shareholder and market expectations concerning value creation. This threat is frequently referred to as the **market for corporate control**.

2. **Legal Constraints:** Shareholders elect the board of directors of a company in a general meeting. The company management is governed by the Companies Act, 1956, which lays down the duties and responsibilities of the directors or managers. These laws act as a constraint on the managers' behavior. However, despite so many rules and regulations, there have been many instances of misconduct by the managers which have resulted in a loss to the shareholders, for example, Global Trust Bank (GTB) bear testimony to this statement where shareholders of GTB ultimately suffered a loss.

Test Yourself

1. What is trusteeship issue? Examine.

Who Are the Shareholders?

At this point you may well be asking, who are the shareholders in companies? And are they really concerned about the behavior of the managers?

If we look at the shareholding pattern of the companies listed on the National Stock Exchange, we will find that a major chunk of the shares is held by the promoters and their business associates and of the remaining shares, FIs hold major stake. Retail investors own only a miniscule percentage of the outstanding shares. According to a study by the Society for Capital Market Development and Research, the number of retail investors in the Indian market has been gradually declining since 1997. Further, the retail shareholders are scattered far and wide across the length and breadth of the country. They seldom attend the annual general meetings (AGMs). As a result, they are not able to exercise what little control they can. Neither are they able to question the activities of the management.

By and large, **shareholder apathy** does exist, but, on occasional protests by the shareholders at what are perceived to be some of the more controversial actions and decisions of the managers, can be very damaging to the company's image and public reputation. Individuals with relatively small shareholdings in a company can simply sell their shares if they are not happy with the way in which the company is run. Institutional investors, with usually very significant shareholdings, are better placed to influence management and board policies and decisions—usually behind closed doors. Now regulators such as Securities and Exchange Board of India (SEBI) and Department of Company Affairs are keen to protect the interest of minority shareholders as such they should not become the victim of big investors.

Stakeholder Theory

Stakeholder theory takes a much broader perspective and looks beyond the two central stakeholder groups—shareholders and managers—to include other groups. These would include groups, such as employees and the local community, who are considered to have a legitimate interest, or even a direct share, in the goals of the firm and who will benefit or suffer according to the fate of the firm. Stakeholder theory applies equally well to public sector and NPO.

In the private sector, the shareholders are the primary **stakeholders**. Citizens are the primary stakeholders in the public sector. Employees, lenders (other than creditors), and any other with a *direct economic interest* in the entity are secondary stakeholders, while potential investors, stockbrokers, tax authorities, members of the public, and other users of the published accounts are classified as tertiary stakeholders.

Organizations which follow stakeholder theory consider it to be part of their "social responsibility" to encourage and actively promote good stakeholder relationships. They strongly believe that it is vital for the long-term benefit of the firm.

For example, providing good value for the customers enhances customer loyalty and improves competitiveness, which, in turn, creates value for the firm, allowing it to create even greater value (wealth) for its other stakeholders such as its employees. Stakeholder theory is reflected in the "partnership" approach taken by many organizations in their relationships with suppliers, customers, and community groups.

The stakeholder approach to management is an all-inclusive or "holistic" one as it recognizes the rights of all the diverse interest groups rather than just the rights of the shareholders. Consequently, multiple organizational goals are likely to emerge, of which the maximization of shareholder value becomes just one, and maybe not even the dominant one!

Is Stakeholder Theory Practical?

Does the stakeholder theory guarantee success? The opinions are divided. One school of thought believes that by taking care of all the relevant interest groups, the company builds a good social image which ultimately helps in getting a bigger market share. Because after all who are the consumers? Of course, the society.

Managing a modern business enterprise is a complex affair, and as is the case for so many other issues, there is no definitive answer as to whether stakeholder theory is right or wrong. The approach taken will be intimately bound up with the culture and value systems of the individual organization, and the contemporary financial manager must be aware of the issues involved.

To conclude, the stakeholder theory requires the interests and objectives of diverse groups or constituencies to be reflected in the activities and goals of the entity. The interests of these various stakeholders will frequently compete and conflict. The task of trying to reconcile the respective interests of such divergent groups is clearly a complex management issue for any organization, yet it is one which is vital for the future success.

Test Yourself

1. What is stakeholder theory?
2. Does stakeholder theory hold good in practical life?

The Fundamental Concepts

The fundamental concepts are core to the subject of financial management. These concepts are as follows:

(1) Cash flow,
(2) Risk and return,
(3) Time value of money,
(4) Opportunity cost, and
(5) Value.

These concepts are the essential characteristics of financial management and the aim here is simply to introduce each one of them as they will recur constantly throughout the text. They serve to guide and direct the financial manager in the task of making business decisions which contribute to shareholder value.

Cash Flow

"Cash generation is the foundation of creating value for the shareholders." There are two dimensions to cash flow, cash inflows and cash outflows, and cash flow management involves the effective management of both. An organization's cash flows will arise as a result of:

(1) Operating Activities: These are the cash flows that arise from core business activities, such as the cash received from customers for goods/services sold and the cash paid for supplies and operating expenses.

(2) Investing Activities: These cash flows arise from non-trading, investment-related activities such as cash actually received from the disposal of assets and investments and conversely, cash actually paid to purchase assets and investments.

(3) Financing Activities: These are cash flows related to raising new capital, such as issuing new ordinary shares or long-term debt and the cash outflows associated with, for example, repayments of loans and finance leases.

Profit Versus Cash Flow

Profit is an accounting concept, whereas cash is a financial management concept; cash is "the real thing." As we have seen, cash is needed to pay creditors, employees, investors, and to run the operation. Cash flow is considered as the most important measure of a firm's performance. A healthy cash flow is essential for any organization' s survival. Shortage of cash is the root cause of the failure of many organizations.

Profit figures, however, while measurable according to legal and professional standards, can still be manipulated by a firm to its best advantage under the garb of "creative accounting."

Reporting profits in a profit and loss account do not necessarily mean that the corresponding amount of cash is available for investment. Thus, compared with profits, cash flow is an unambiguous measure of a firm's financial performance.

Measuring Cash Flow

A cash flow is measured as

Cash flow = Operating profit + Depreciation ± Other noncash items, or
Cash flow = NP after tax + Depreciation

Depreciation represents the loss in the value of an asset over a period of time. It is an expense associated with ownership of the asset and as such must be deducted from revenues in calculating a firm's operating profit.

However, the important point is that *depreciation is not a cash expense.* Therefore, it is added back to the operating profit figure to give an estimate of the cash generated by the firm. Any other noncash items (e.g., profits or losses on the sale of fixed assets) that have been included in the profit and loss account would need to be adjusted accordingly.

Many financial analysts take this calculation a stage further and prefer an estimate of **free cash flow (FCF):**

Free cash flow = Cash flow – (Investment expenditures + Dividends + Taxes)

This measurement of cash flow shows the ***discretionary cash remaining*** after making the necessary investments in fixed assets, rewarding shareholders with dividends and paying tax obligations. FCF then represents the amount of cash available for discretionary purposes such as reducing debt levels, increasing dividends, repurchasing shares, or providing for some other strategic purposes, for example, acquisitions and mergers.

Test Yourself

1. What is the difference between profit and cash flow?
2. What do you understand by free cash flow?

Risk and Return

The motivation for undertaking an investment is the expectation of gaining an expected return commensurate with risk. But the return from an investment, particularly a business investment, is not certain. The actual return may be more than, less than, or equal to the return expected on the investment. Investment decisions are made in not so perfect knowledge of the future which is uncertain. This uncertainty leads to the origin of risk. The actual returns may differ from the expected returns, and in finance, a risky investment is one whose potential returns are expected to have a high degree of variation or volatility. Returns are measured in terms of expected future cash flows—not profits, and risk is the degree of volatility surrounding expected future cash flow returns.

In assessing the risk of an investment, a decision-maker clearly does not know what the actual outcome will be. However, the financial decision-making process can be aided by the application of some statistical techniques. Using these techniques, the decision-maker can quantify the risk inherent in any investment.

Time Value of Money

Not only is the concept of measuring returns in terms of cash flows important but also the timing of cash flow returns. It is the timing of cash flows, as well as their size, which determines their value.

You may have heard the expression: "A bird-in-hand is worth more than two in the bush." If offered the choice between receiving ₹100 today or ₹100 one year from now, most of us would prefer to receive the cash now. We would then have the option to invest it, say at 10% interest, so that in one year's time it would be worth ₹110. Most people prefer to receive cash sooner rather than later, and to spend cash later rather than sooner, because most of us realize, at least intuitively, that *money has a time value.*

Cash flows which are to be received at some point of time in the future, say, one or two years from now, have less value than the equivalent cash flows to be received today because of the changing value of money. The value of money changes because of inflation when the same utility is purchased by spending more with in future, It can be very well argued that value of has gone down these may be value or future value of money. Cash received today can be reinvested in other investments to generate more cash flows. They could at least be placed in a deposit account to earn interest, thereby increasing their future value.

Opportunity Cost

The concept of opportunity cost is very significant in financial management. To attract finance for its investment plans, a firm must offer potential investors an attractive rate of return, a rate of return which is competitive with the rate an investor could obtain elsewhere on an alternative investment of equal risk.

Investors have a number of investment opportunities open to them, and probably limited funds to invest. Rational investors would only invest their available funds in a particular investment avenue, if they perceived the level of return to be at least equal to what they would expect to earn from an alternative investment of equal risk.

When limited funds are available, investors will have to make choices between competing investment alternatives. From an investor's perspective, the opportunity cost of investing in a particular investment option would be the return given up or sacrificed by not investing in another comparable investment.

Thus, to attract funds for its investments, the company would have to earn a rate of financial return which at least matches with competing alternative investments of equal risk. This rate of return which Investors require to earn is the company's *opportunity cost of capital.* If the company's investments earn less than this rate of return, then investors are likely to take their funds elsewhere.

The *firm's* opportunity cost of capital is the rate of return the firm must pay to the investors to induce them to part with their money. Thus, the cost of capital to the firm is the opportunity cost of the next best investment alternative of equal risk available to the investors. In simple terms, potential investments which are expected to earn less than this rate of return should be rejected. Those which are expected to earn an equal or higher rate of return should be accepted.

Value

The process of value creation is the driving force behind financial management, and that creating wealth for shareholders by increasing the value of their investment in the business is now the primary goal of financial management. This goal is the focus of all financial decisions.

It would not be possible for the financial manager to create value for the shareholders without a proper understanding of how a potential investment's expected cash flow returns, their timings, and their riskiness contribute to its value.

When making investment and financing decisions, the financial manager clearly cannot assess their impact on the shareholder value without first analyzing their effects on the firm's cash flows, their timings, and on its risk.

If value-enhancing investment and financing decisions are made, this will be reflected in an increase in the firm's value. In the case of a public company, shareholders can expect to see their wealth increase through an increase in the market value of the company's shares.

For a public limited company, maximizing the shareholder value in essence means maximizing the market value of the firm as reflected in its *long-run* share price and a shareholder's wealth at any point in time is measured by the market value of the shares held.

The market value of the firm can be defined as:

$$MV = MVD + MVE,$$

where

MV = Market value of the firm
MVD = Market value of debt
MVE = Market value of equity.

This is assuming that all the relevant debt and equity instruments are regularly traded in the financial markets. There are various factors affecting the value of the firm. The two most important factors are performance of the company and market sentiments which in turn are ably aided by future of the company, its growth, and expansions vis-à-vis competitors. A good performance is always reflected in higher value if there is favorable stock market, conducive economic environment, and stable political conditions.

Test Yourself

1. What is time value of money? Explain.
2. What do you understand by opportunity cost concept?

SUMMARY

1. Financial management may also be defined as: "the ways and means of managing money."
2. Financial management deals with planning, acquisition, allocation, and utilization of financial resources with the aim of achieving value maximization objectives of the firm.
3. Scope of financial management covers investment decision, financial decision, and dividend decision.
4. The role of the finance manager is to make proper utilization of financial resources that leads to overall value maximization of all the stakeholders.
5. Financial management has direct interface with production, marketing, and other disciplinary functions of the business organizations.
6. Shareholder's wealth maximization goal holds the supreme importance over the other objectives of an organization.
7. The relationship between shareholders and the managers is that of principal and agent. In practice, conflict may arise between the interest of the two, which is known as the problem of trust.

KEY TERMS

- Dividend payout ratio
- Leverage
- Working capital
- Debt/equity ratio
- Required return
- Value maximization
- Subprime
- Retention ratio
- Business risk
- Optimum capital structure
- Earnings per share

- Variable cost
- Bonus share
- Planning
- Gearing ratio
- Financial risk
- Episodic financing
- Return on investment
- Value
- Tax shield
- Owner's equity

Learning Outcomes

Students will get to know financial management and its various aspects in contemporary environment.

ASSESS YOURSELF

Concepts Review and Critical Thinking Questions

1. What is the financial management process? Outline its various stages.
2. Elaborate the scope of financial management.
3. Describe the main responsibilities of a treasury department in a company and explain the benefits which might accrue from the establishment of a separate treasury function.
4. Discuss the changing role of finance manager in competitive market structure.
5. How does financing decision affect the overall value of the firm? Explain.
6. What are the fundamental concepts that form the core of financial management?
7. "Wealth Maximization may reflect the most efficient use of society's economic resources thus lead to a maximization of society's economic well-being." In the light of this statement, do you consider shareholder wealth maximization to be a valid objective for a commercial firm? Give reasons for your answer.
8. "Profit maximization is not a valid goal in financial management." Discuss.
9. The primary goal of financial management is said to be wealth maximization. Is this objective realistic in a world where corporate ownership and control are often separated? Discuss.

STUDENT ACTIVITIES

Collect the mission and vision statements of few companies and try to relate them with the financial objective of shareholder's wealth maximization.

CHAPTER 2

Contemporary Financial Environment

Learning Objectives

- To understand the financial system.
- To know how the financial system, market, intermediaries, and instruments are regulated and operated.

PRELUDE

The 1990s was a "decade of consolidation" for the Indian economy. Although the "opening up" of Indian economy in 1991 was more by compulsion than by choice, yet during the last 24 years Indian economy in general and the Indian financial system in particular have made significant strides in the direction of moving toward the developed economic systems of the world. The focus of economic reforms was primarily on the financial sector. A lot of legal, institutional, and technological developments have taken place in Indian financial system which have been causing a change in the role of the finance manager as discussed in Chapter 1. To act satisfactorily in the new role, it is important for a finance manager to be well aware of the contemporary financial environment which has new mandate in the form of "Go Global, acquire size and internationalize operation." It may be appreciated that companies such as Airtel, Sun Pharma, and Lupin have become Indian born and grown MNC out of contemporary financial environment, spreading acumenship of Indian entrepreneurship. This chapter discusses in detail the contemporary financial environment including financial markets, institutions, instruments, and the regulatory framework.

An economic system consists of various economic participants such as households, producers, government, and consumers. These economic participants undertake various economic activities such as production, exchange, and consumption for the purpose of sustaining themselves. These economic activities result into mobilization, allocation, utilization, and generation of funds. But at any particular point of time, all the units may not be generating surplus funds. Some units in the economic system might be facing deficit of funds. In the absence of any flow of funds between these types of units both will suffer a loss. The surplus units will not be able to invest their surplus funds and hence their profitability will decline. However, the deficit units will be compelled to either forego certain economic activities completely or reduce the scale of their operations for lack of funds.

However, as we know, "necessity is the mother of all inventions." So this need for a mechanism, which could facilitate the flow of funds between surplus and deficit units in an economic system, led to the invention of, what is known as, financial system. A financial system comprises of various FIs, markets, instruments, and regulatory bodies which help in the flow of funds from the areas of surplus to the areas of deficit. By making funds available, the financial system helps in the growth of modern economies and the increase in the standard of living of its citizens. Figure 2.1 depicts a financial system.

FIGURE 2.1
THE FINANCIAL SYSTEM

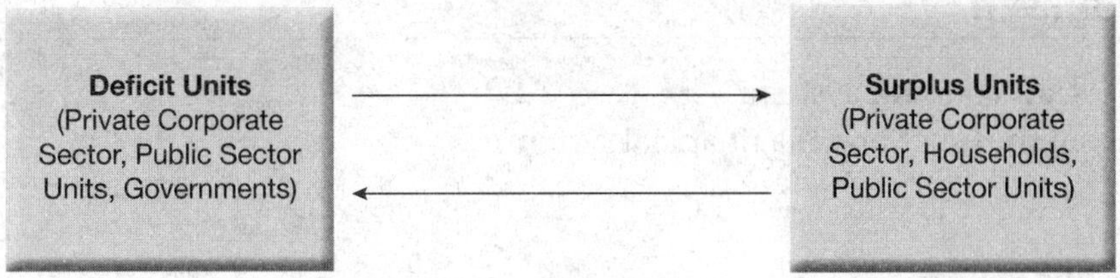

| **Deficit Units** (Private Corporate Sector, Public Sector Units, Governments) | → ← | **Surplus Units** (Private Corporate Sector, Households, Public Sector Units) |

Source: Author.

A financial system helps in discovering the cost of credit, that is, the cost to be borne by the borrowers of funds. By doing so, it also regulates the volume of credit generated in the economic system. If the cost of funds is high, it adversely affects the consumption, production, employment, and growth of the economy. However, a reduction in the cost of credit can enhance all the above factors in the positive direction.

Generally speaking, a financial system performs the following functions:

1. Facilitates Savings
Financial system helps in mobilization of savings from households, public sector, and private sector units and makes them available to the producers. This is done through issuing various financial instruments in the money and capital markets. Mobilization of savings and their utilization has a direct impact on the investment activity in the economy. If industry has plans to make fresh investments, it needs funds, and inadequate availability of funds may hamper the industrial activity and also increases the cost of funds, thereby making production less remunerative.

2. Provides Liquidity
Money is the most liquid financial asset. Money has got time value and inflation erodes its value. That is why one always prefers to store the funds in financial instruments such as stocks and debentures. However, these instruments are relatively more risky and less liquid. Financial markets provide an opportunity to the investor to liquidate the investments if he so desires. This also has an impact on the development of the primary market for these instruments. This ultimately affects the cost of funds and profitability.

3. Facilitates Exchange
The financial system facilitates exchange by offering a very convenient mode of payment for goods and services. Checks, demand drafts, and credit and debit cards are easy and convenient methods of payments. They help in reducing the cost and time of transactions and consequently lessen the risk. The recent advent of Real Time Gross Settlement (RTGS) system will further enhance the efficiency of the payment system and reduce the risks of settlement.

4. Manages Risk
Risk is a realistic concept and is inevitable. It cannot be avoided but has to be managed. A well-developed financial system helps in managing risk by making available various instruments, tools, and techniques of risk management.

5. Regulates Markets

Regulation is essential for nurturing and developing any system. Regulation assumes more importance when we are dealing with financial transactions. In fact, given the number of participants, multiplicity of markets, and variety of instruments, inadequate regulation may lead to chaos. Thus, a financial system invariably has regulators which take on themselves the responsibility of controlling and developing the financial markets in a systematic manner. In the Indian financial system, we have regulators like RBI, SEBI, IRDA, Board of Financial Supervision, PFDRA, and so on.

Test Yourself

1. What is an economic system?
2. What are the functions of a financial system?

Financial Markets

A financial market can be defined as the market in which financial assets are created or exchanged for a consideration. Financial assets represent a claim to the payment of a single sum of money at some point of time in the future and/or multiple payments in the form of interest, profit, appreciation, or dividend spread over many time periods. Depending on whether the market deals in newly issued instruments or instruments issued earlier, financial markets can be classified as:

(i)   Primary market (market for capital issue by corporate). It can be an initial public offer (IPO) or follow on public offer (FPO), and

(ii) Secondary market (market for subsequent trading in issued securities at stock exchange).

Financial markets can also be classified as:

(i)   Money market and
(ii) Capital market.

Money Market

The market which deals with short-maturity instruments (with a period of maturity of 1 year or less) such as treasury bills, commercial paper (CP), bills of exchange, and so on, is called the Money market.

Money Market Players

Money market is wholesale market. The transactions that take place in the money market are of high volumes and amounts of money. Hence, the following large institutional players participate in the market:

 (i)   Government
 (ii) Central bank
(iii) Commercial banks

(iv) Financial institutions

(v) Corporate

Government is an active money market player and it constitutes the biggest borrower in the money market. The government needs funds to meet the fiscal deficit or for certain short-term adjustments like borrowing against the expected advance tax receipts.

The central bank of the country, RBI, operates on behalf of the government. It issues government securities, also it underwrites the issues of the government. Besides, RBI also acts as the apex regulatory body. It issues guidelines to regulate the money market operations and prudential norms for the money market players.

Commercial banks form the most important segment of the money market players and act as borrowers and lenders in the money market. Banks are required to maintain statutory liquid reserves and cash reserves with RBI. Before going for credit creation, they are required to ensure the adequacy of these reserves. In case of any shortfall, they can borrow from the money market for short term to make up the shortfall. If they have any surplus funds, they can lend these funds in the money market.

Financial institutions and banks such as LIC, IDBI, and ICICI also act both as borrowers and lenders in the money market depending on the requirements. In addition to these institutions, mutual funds, foreign institutional investors (FIIs) also participate in the money market as investors or lenders. The level of participation of these players is mainly dependent on the limits prescribed by the RBI. For instance, FIIs can participate in the Indian money market by way of investment in government securities only.

Corporate participate in the money market as borrowers of fund for working capital requirements. They use the organized as well as unorganized segments of the money market for their requirements.

In addition to these players, there are some specialized institutions such as Discount and Finance House of India (DFHI) and primary dealers (PDs) which also participate in the money market. DFHI provides the much needed liquidity by acting as a financier, whereas primary dealers act as market makers by providing two-way quotes for the instruments traded in the money market, thus enhancing the liquidity in the market.

Money Market Instruments

Call Money/Notice Money Market[1]

The money market is a market for short-term financial assets that are close substitutes of money. The most important feature of call money market instrument is that it is liquid and provides an avenue for equilibrating the short-term surplus funds of lenders and the requirements of the borrowers. The call/notice money market forms an important segment of the Indian money market. Under call money market, funds are transacted on overnight basis. Under notice money market, funds are transacted for the period between 2 and 14 days.

Participants in call/notice money market currently include banks, primary dealers (PDs), development finance institutions, insurance companies, and select mutual funds. Of these, banks and PDs can operate as both borrowers and lenders in the market. Non-bank institutions, which have been given specific permission to operate in call/notice money market can, however, operate as lenders only (Table 2.1). Eligible participants are free to decide on interest rates in call/notice money market.

---

[1] Master Circular, RBI, www.rbi.org.in.

TABLE 2.1

ELIGIBLE FOR TRANSACTIONS IN CALL/NOTICE MONEY MARKET

Borrowing	Lending
1. Scheduled commercial banks	1. Scheduled commercial banks
2. Co-operative banks	2. Co-operative banks
3. Primary dealers	3. Primary dealers
	4. Select all-India financial institutions
	5. Select insurance companies
	6. Select mutual funds

Source: Author.

Treasury Bills (T-Bills)

T-Bills are issued by the RBI on behalf of Government of India (GOI) to meet the short-term funds requirements of the government. T-Bills also help RBI to perform open market operations which help in regulating the money supply in the economy.

T-Bills can be issued in physical form or credited to investors' subsidiary general ledger (SGL) account in electronic form. They are issued for a minimum amount of ₹25,000 and in multiples thereof. They do not carry any coupon rate and are issued at a discount to their face value and redeemed at par.

Earlier, RBI used to issue 14-day, 91-day, 182-day, and 364-day treasury bills. However, as per the monetary and credit policy of April 2001, the 14-day T-bills have been discontinued.

Types of T-bills

Ad hoc T-bills: These T-bills were issued in favor of RBI, whenever GOI needed cash. They were neither issued nor available to the public. These bills were purchased by RBI and were held in its Issue Department. Ad hoc T-bills had a maturity period of 91 days and carried a discount rate of 4.6%. However, subsequent to an agreement between the GOI and RBI in March 1997, ad hoc T-bills were replaced by ways and means advances (WMA) for financing the government deficit.

On Tap T-bills: These T-Bills were issued on all working days and there was no limit on the amount of investment in these securities. The maturity period was 91 days and a discount rate was 4.6%. They were redeemable at par value on maturity. State governments, banks, and provident funds used these T-Bills (Ad hoc and on Tap T-bills) as a liquidity management tool. However, these were also discontinued w.e.f. April 1, 2001.

Auctioned T-bills: The 91-day T-Bills and 364-day T-Bills are auctioned since January 1993. Whereas 91-day T-bills are auctioned every week on Wednesdays, 182-day and 364-day T-bills are auctioned every alternate week on Wednesdays. RBI announces the date and the notified amount of auction in advance. Bidders who participate in these auctions can be competitive or non-competitive. Non-competitive bidders like state governments submit only one bid. These bids are accepted at the weighted average of the successful bids if the notified amount is not fully subscribed (Table 2.2).

TABLE 2.2
AUCTION DAYS OF T-BILLS

Type of T-bills	Day of Auction	Day of Payment[a]
91-Day	Wednesday	Following Friday
182-Day	Wednesday of non-reporting week	Following Friday
364-Day	Wednesday of reporting week	Following Friday

[a] *If the day of payment falls on a holiday, the payment is made on the day after the holiday.*
Source: www.rbi.org.in

Competitive bidders submit multiple tenders at different prices. Successful competitive bids are accepted up to the minimum determined price called the "cut-off" price. Bids above the cut-off price are accepted in full and other bids are rejected.

Commercial Paper (CP)

Commercial paper (CP) is an unsecured promissory note. It was introduced in India in 1990 with a view to enable high-rated corporate borrowers to diversify their sources of short-term borrowings and to provide an additional instrument to the investors. Subsequently, PDs, satellite dealers, and all-India FIs were also permitted to issue CP to enable them to meet their short-term funding requirements.

Eligibility

Corporate, PDs and all-India FIs which are permitted to raise short-term resources under the limit fixed by the Reserve Bank of India (RBI) are eligible to issue CP.

A corporate would be eligible to issue a CP provided: (a) the tangible net worth of the company, as per the latest audited balance sheet, is not less than ₹4 crore; (b) the company has been sanctioned working capital limit by bank(s) or all-India FIs; and (c) the borrower account of the company is classified as a Standard Asset by the financing banks institutions.

Rating

All eligible participants shall obtain credit rating for issuance of CP either from the Credit Rating Information Services of India Ltd (CRISIL) or the Investment Information and Credit Rating Agency of India Ltd (ICRA) or the Credit Analysis and Research Ltd (CARE) or the FITCH Ratings India Pvt Ltd or such other credit rating agencies as may be specified by the RBI from time to time, for the purpose.

Maturity

Minimum maturity period is seven days and the maximum is one year from the date of issue. The maturity date of the CP should not go beyond the date up to which the credit rating of the issuer is valid.

Denominations

CP can be issued in denominations of ₹5 lakhs or multiples thereof. Amount invested by a single investor should not be less than ₹5 lakhs (face value).

Certificate of Deposit (CD)

CDs is a negotiable instrument issued for funds deposited at a bank or other eligible FI for a specified time period. Guidelines for issue of CDs are presently governed by various directives issued by the RBI from time to time.

Eligibility

CDs can be issued by (i) scheduled commercial banks excluding Regional Rural Banks (RRBs) and Local Area Banks (LABs); and (ii) selecting all-India FIs that have been permitted by RBI.

Aggregate Amount

Banks have the freedom to issue CDs depending on their requirements. An FI may issue CDs within the overall umbrella limit fixed by the RBI.

Minimum Size of Issue and Denominations

Minimum amount of a CD should be ₹1 lakh, that is, the minimum deposit that could be accepted from a single subscriber should not be less than ₹1 lakh and in the multiples of ₹1 lakh thereafter.

Subscribers

CDs can be issued to individuals, corporations, companies, trusts, funds, associations, and so on. Non- Resident Indians (NRIs) may also subscribe to CDs, but only on non-repatriable basis which should be clearly stated on the Certificate. Such CDs cannot be endorsed to another NRI in the secondary market.

Maturity

The maturity period of CDs issued by banks should be not less than 7 days and not more than 1 year. The FIs can issue CDs for a period not less than 1 year and not exceeding 3 years from the date of issue.

Discount/Coupon Rate

CDs may be issued at a discount on face value. Banks/FIs are also allowed to issue CDs on floating rate basis provided the methodology of compiling the floating rate is objective, transparent, and market-based. The issuing bank/FI are free to determine the discount/coupon rate. The interest rate on floating rate CDs would have to be reset periodically in accordance with a pre-determined formula that indicates the spread over a transparent benchmark.

Reserve Requirements

Banks have to maintain the appropriate reserve requirements, that is, Cash Reserve Ratio (CRR) and Statutory Liquidity Ratio (SLR), on the issue price of the CDs.

Transferability

Physical CDs are freely transferable by endorsement and delivery. Demat CDs can be transferred as per the procedure applicable to other demat securities. There is no lock-in period for the CDs.

Test Yourself

1. Differentiate between money market and capital market.
2. What are T-bills?
3. Explain certificate of deposits.

Repurchase Agreements (REPO)

Repurchase agreements or repos are transactions involving sale of government securities (including T-Bills) with an agreement to buy back the securities at a pre-specified date in future at a pre-specified price. The maturity period varies from 1 to 14 days. As these are collateralized transactions unlike call money transactions, the interest rate on these deals is relatively less. These transactions can be undertaken only among the banks to meet their borrowing needs or between banks and RBI to control the liquidity in the system. When it is an inter-bank repo, the interest rate depends on the needs of the participating banks and is not controlled by the RBI. For example, Bank A may sell the government securities to Bank B with an agreement to buy back the securities 7 days later at a specified price. For Bank B, the same transaction turns out to be purchase of securities with an agreement to sell back these securities after 7 days at a specified price and is referred to as reverse repo. In case of repo deals between the RBI and the banks, the interest rates are fixed by the RBI. RBI uses this route to suck out excess liquidity from the system or to provide liquidity adjustment facility (LAF) to the banks. Thus, in these transactions, the repo rate is the rate at which RBI borrows from the banks. This rate thus affects the bank rate, that is, the rate at which RBI lends to the banks, which in turn will affect the entire gamut of interest rates in the system starting with prime lending rate (PLR). The maturity period of such repos may be 1 day or 7 days or 14 days and the interest rate is fixed by the RBI. This repo rate also acts at the support level of call money rates because if call rates fall below this rate, there is an arbitrage opportunity for banks which can borrow in the call money market and lend to the RBI in the repo market.

Gilt-edged Securities

"Gilt-edged" securities (G-Secs) are those where payment of principal and interest is guaranteed by the Government. They are 100% safe. The securities issued by the central or state governments, semi-government organizations like municipal corporations, autonomous institutions like port trusts, public sector units, and other quasi-government agencies are referred to as G-Secs.

G-Secs have a maturity period ranging from 1 to 30 years and they carry a coupon rate which is paid semi-annually. They are issued both in demat and physical form. These securities can be classified into three categories depending on their maturities, namely, long-dated, medium-dated, and short-dated. Long-dated securities have maturities exceeding 10 years from the issue date, medium-dated securities have maturities ranging from 5 to 10 years, and short-dated securities are those, which mature within 5 years.

Government securities can be held in three forms, namely,

1. Stock certificates,
2. Promissory notes, and
3. Bearer bonds.

Normally in the money market, government securities are held in the form of promissory notes. Besides these principal forms of government securities, there are other types of securities which are floated by the government from time to time. For example, national defense/national savings/national deposit certificates, deposit certificates, annuity certificates, and social security certificates.

Types of G-Secs

□ **Dated Securities:** They have fixed maturity and fixed coupon rates payable half-yearly and are identified by their year of maturity.
□ **Zero-Coupon Bonds:** These bonds are issued at discount and redeemed at par.
□ **Floating Rate Bonds:** They are bonds with variable interest rates with a fixed percentage over a benchmark rate. There may also be a cap and a floor rate attached, thereby fixing a maximum and minimum interest rate payable on it.
□ **Capital Indexed Bonds:** They are bonds where the interest rate is a fixed percentage over the wholesale price index. Redemption is linked to the wholesale price index.

Trading of G-Secs

Both primary and secondary markets exist for G-Secs. The primary market caters to the needs of the banks, FIs, provident funds, insurance, pension funds, and PDs. These are actively traded in the secondary market by the above participants as well as corporate and individuals. Quotes are available daily in the newspapers. An investor who wants to buy or sell a security can do so directly from or to a PD or Banks. Two-way quotes for buying and selling are given by the PD and the banks and these quotes or rates are market determined. Investors can buy and sell securities in demat form as well.

The Settlement Process

Investors desirous of trading in securities in demat form can open a Constituent SGL (CSGL) account with the RBI through a PD or a bank. The CSGL account will hold the securities in demat form. When an investor buys or sells, his CSGL account is credited or debited. Investors could also trade among themselves through CSGL or through the delivery of physical scripts. The procedure for physical scripts would be a bit taxing for retail investors and hence is being ignored.

To ensure a smooth settlement process for demat trading, the RBI has introduced the delivery versus payment system where on submission of the SGL form, payment is made and the SGL account debited or credited with the securities.

Money Market Mutual Funds (MMMFS)

Money market being a wholesale market requires a large amount of sum to participate in the market, the minimum being ₹10 lakh. As a result, the market was beyond the reach of the individual investors. MMMFs were set up to make available the benefits of investing in the money markets to small investors.

MMMFs are mutual funds that invest primarily in money market instruments of very high quality and of very short maturities. MMMFs can be set up by commercial banks, public FIs and so on either directly or through their existing mutual fund subsidiaries. The guidelines with respect to mobilization of funds by MMMFs provide that only individuals are allowed to invest in such funds.

These funds that were regulated by the RBI till March 7, 2000 are thereafter governed by SEBI. The guidelines on MMMFs specify a minimum lock-in period of 15 days during which the investor cannot redeem his investment. The guidelines also stipulate the minimum size of the MMMF to be ₹50 crore and this should not exceed 2% of the aggregate deposits of the latest accounting year in the case of banks and 2% of the long-term domestic borrowings in the case of public FIs.

There is utmost need to regulate financial market for orderly growth and protection of interest of stakeholders. Recently, the GOI has constituted Financial Stability and Development Council (FSDC), apex-level autonomous body to deal with macro-potential and financial regularities in the whole of financial sector of India. FSDC is to strengthen and institutionalize to mechanics of maintaining financial stability, financial sector development, inter-regularity coordination beside spreading financial literacy and financial inclusion.

Regulatory Framework for Money Market

The RBI, established on April 1, 1935, under the RBI Act, is the apex regulatory authority in the Indian Monetary System. Since its inception, the RBI is guiding, monitoring, regulating, promoting, and controlling the Indian financial system. The apex bank has been given the powers to regulate the issuance of notes, act as banker to the Government, maintain price stability, and maintain a control over money supply in the country. It also has been allowed to carry out open market operations. All the powers were given to the RBI, like any other central bank in the world, to promote economic development.

One of the main functions of the central bank in any country is monetary management, that is, regulation of the quantity of money, and the supply and availability of credit to business and industry.

According to Section 21 of the RBI Act, the RBI has been given the power of selective credit control. It is empowered to determine the policy in relation to advances to be followed by banks in general or by any bank in particular. It is also authorized to issue directions to banks as regards the purpose of the advances, the margins to be maintained for secured advances, and also prescribe the interest rate.

The RBI exercises the selective credit control through the following instruments:

- Bank rate
- Open market operations
- Variable reserve requirements

The Bank Rate

It is the rate at which the RBI re-discounts the first-class commercial bills of exchange. The effect of change in bank rate will make the cost of securing funds either cheaper or costlier than the central bank. Whenever the volume of bank credit is to be expanded, RBI reduces the bank rate and vice versa. However, the efficacy of the bank rate depends on the extent of integration in the money market and also on commercial banks' borrowings from the RBI. In today's financial market, the bank rate has become the reference rate, as the interest rates have been deregulated, and they are determined by demand and supply of funds in the market. Thus, the bank rate has a signaling value.

Open Market Operations

The RBI can influence the reserves of commercial banks, that is, the cash base of commercial banks, by selling and buying the government securities in the open market. If the RBI buys government securities from commercial banks in the market, the cash transfer will be from RBI to banks and hence, there is an increase in the cash base of the commercial banks enabling them to expand credit and converse is the effect if it sells. Usually, the success of the open market operations depends on the size of the government securities available, their range, and variety. Most importantly, the prices quoted by RBI should be attractive when compared with the market prices.

Reserve Requirements

The central bank regulates the liquidity of the banking system through two complementary methods such as CRR and SLR. CRR is the average daily balance with RBI, the percentage of CRR will be specified by RBI from time to time on Net Demand and Time Liabilities (NDTL). It is the cash that banks deposit with Reserve Bank as a proportion of their deposits. In addition to the CRR, the banks are required to maintain specified reserves in the form of government securities, specified bonds, and approved securities.

Test Yourself

1. What is repo and reverse repo transaction?
2. Collect the recent repo and reverse repo rates announced by the RBI and study trend.

Capital Markets

It deals with transactions related to long-term instruments (with a period of maturity of above 1 year such as corporate debentures and government bonds) and stock (equity and preference shares) is called the Capital Market. Whereas the money market provides resources to the corporate primarily for working capital needs, capital market provides the resources needed by medium- and large-scale enterprises for investment purposes. This difference in the nature of funds provided translates into a difference in the nature of instruments traded in these markets. Whereas money market deals in short-term sources of funds (maturity period of which is less than or up to 1 year), capital market deals in long-term sources of funds (with maturity more than 1 year).

Market Structure

The capital market consists of the primary market and the secondary market. The primary market is used to create long-term instruments through which corporate can raise capital or loans from the capital market. However, secondary market provides liquidity and marketability to these instruments. An active and buoyant secondary market attracts investors as to the market that more instruments are available in the secondary market for subsequent trading (Figure 2.2).

FIGURE 2.2
STRUCTURE OF THE INDIAN CAPITAL MARKET

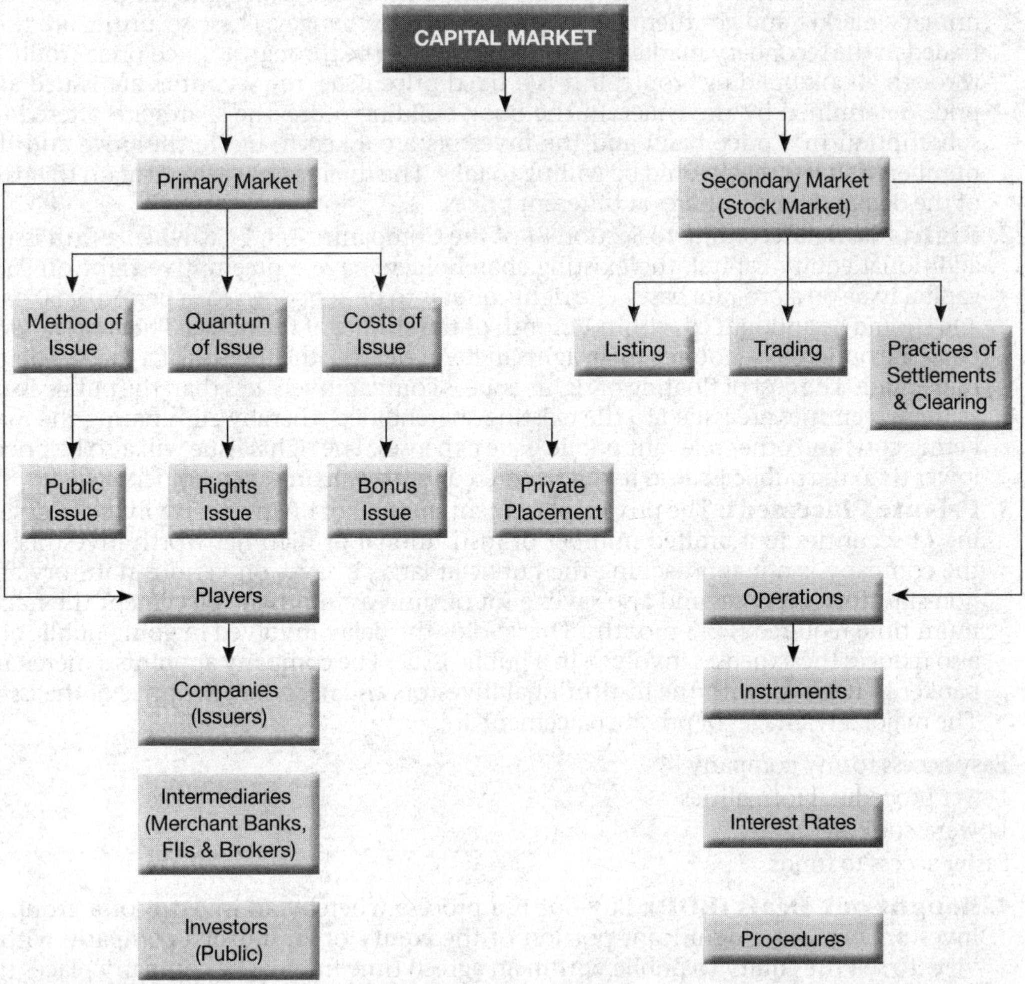

Source: Author.

Primary Market

Primary Market deals with IPO) and FPO for rating long-term sources of capital and loan from the market.

Types of Issue

A company can raise its capital through the issue of shares and debentures by means of:

- Public issue
- Rights issue

- Private placement
- Bought-out deal
- Euro issue.

1. **Public Issue:** Public issue is the most popular method of raising capital and involves raising of funds directly from the public. Companies issue securities to the public in the primary market and get them listed on the stock exchanges. These securities are then traded in the secondary market. The public issue can be through a "fixed price" route or through "book-building" route. If it is a fixed price issue, the securities are issued at a price determined by the issuer. In the book-building route, the shares are offered for subscription in a price band and the investors are asked to quote the price and the number of shares they would be willing to take. The final price is arrived at on the basis of the demand for the shares at different prices.

2. **Rights Issue:** According to Section 81 of the Companies Act, 1956, when a firm issues additional equity capital, the existing shareholders have a preemptive right on such capital issue on a pro-rata basis. The rights offer is to be kept open for a period of 60 days and should be announced within 1 month of the closure of the books. The shareholders have the option to renounce their rights in favor of any other person at a market-determined rate. The cost of floating of rights issue is comparatively less than the public issue, as these securities are issued to the existing shareholders, thereby eliminating the marketing costs and other relevant public issue expenses. The rights issue will also be priced lower than the public issue as it will be offered to the existing shareholders.

3. **Private Placement:** The private placement method of financing involves direct selling of securities to a limited number of institutional or high net worth investors. As the company is not approaching the public at large, it saves on various statutory and non-statutory expenses and also saves a lot of time, as in private placement the maximum time required is 2–3 months. This avoids the delay involved in going public and also reduces the expenses involved in a public issue. The company appoints a merchant banker to network with the institutional investors and negotiate the price of the issue. The major advantages of private placement are:

- Easy access to any company
- Fewer procedural formalities
- Lower issue cost
- Faster access to funds

4. **Bought-out Deals (BOD):** Buy-out is a process whereby an investor or a group of investors buy-out a significant portion of the equity of an unlisted company with a view to sell the equity to public within an agreed time frame. The company places the equity shares, to be offered to the public, with a sponsor. At the right time, the shares will be off-loaded to the public through the OTCEI route or by way of a public issue. The bought-out deal route is relatively inexpensive; funds accrue without much delay (in a public issue funds reach the company only after a period of 2–3 months from the date of closure of the subscription list). In addition to this, it offers greater flexibility in terms of the issue and matters relating to off-loading with the sponsor or the Merchant Banker involved. BOD may be very useful for small projects, which may find it very costly to go for a public issue. Major advantages of entering into a bought-out deal are:

  (i) Companies, both existing and new, which do not satisfy conditions laid down by SEBI for premium issues, may issue at a premium through the BOD method.
  (ii) Fewer procedural complexities, faster access to funds and lower issue costs.

5. **Euro-issues:** Indian companies have been permitted to float their stocks in foreign capital markets. The Indian corporate, which face high rates of interest in the domestic

markets, are now free to tap the global capital markets for meeting resource requirements at less costs and administrative problems. The instruments, which the company
can issue, are global depository receipts (GDRs), American depository receipts (ADRs),
Euro-convertible bonds (ECBs), and foreign currency convertible bonds (FCCBs).

GDRs (Global Depository Receipts)

A negotiable financial instrument issued by a bank to represent a foreign company's publicly
traded securities is called a depository receipt. The depository receipt trades on a local stock
exchange. Depository receipts make it easier to buy shares in foreign companies because the
shares of the company do not have to leave the home state. When the depository bank is in the
USA, the instruments are known as American depository receipts (ADR), European banks issue
European depository receipts, and other banks issue global depository receipts (GDR). Thus, in
other words, GDR is a bank certificate issued in more than one country for shares in a foreign
company. The shares are held by a foreign branch of an international branch. The shares trade
as domestic shares, but are offered for sale globally through the various bank branches.

Usually, a GDR is denominated in US dollars, whereas the underlying shares would be denominated in the local currency of the Issuer. GDRs may be—at the request of the investor—converted
into equity shares by cancellation of GDRs through the intermediation of the depository and the
sale of underlying shares in the domestic market through the local custodian. GDRs, per se, are
considered as common equity of the issuing company and are entitled to dividends and voting
rights since the date of its issuance. The company effectively transacts with only one entity—the
Overseas Depository—for all the transactions. The voting rights of the shares are exercised by the
depository as per the understanding between the issuing company and the GDR holders (Table 2.3).

TABLE 2.3
SOME OF THE INDIAN COMPANIES WHICH ISSUED ADR AND GDR

Company Name	ADR	GDR
Bajaj Auto		√
Dr. Reddys	√	√
HDFC Bank	√	√
Hindalco		√
ICICI Bank	√	√
Infosys Technology	√	√
ITC		√
L&T		√
MTNL	√	√
Patni Computers	√	
Ranbaxy Laboratories		√
Tata Motors	√	
SBI		√
VSNL	√	√
WIPRO	√	√

Source: Author.

American Depository Receipts

Introduced to the financial markets in 1927, an ADR is a stock that trades in the USA but represents a specified number of shares in a foreign corporation. ADRs are bought and sold on American markets just like regular stocks, and are issued or sponsored in the USA by a bank or brokerage.

There are three different types of ADR issues:

(i) Level I: This is the most basic type of ADR where foreign companies either do not qualify or do not wish to have their ADR listed on an exchange. Level I ADRs are found on the OTC market and are an easy and inexpensive way to gauge interest for its securities in North America. Level I ADRs also have the loosest requirements from the Securities Exchange Commission (SEC).

(ii) Level II: This type of ADR is listed on an exchange or quoted on NASDAQ. Level II ADRs have slightly more requirements from the SEC but they also get higher visibility trading volume.

(iii) Level III: The most prestigious of the three, this is when an issuer floats a public offering of ADRs on a US exchange. Level II ADRs are able to raise capital and gain substantial visibility in the US financial markets.

The advantages of ADRs are twofold. For individuals, ADRs are an easy and cost-effective way to buy shares in a foreign company. They save considerable money by reducing administrative costs and avoiding foreign taxes on each transaction. Foreign entities like ADRs because they get more US exposure, tap into the wealthy North American equity markets. In return, the foreign company must provide detailed financial information to the sponsor bank.

Capital

Capital is foundational resources with which a company is incorporated. All resources, cash or kind, to act as foundation are called capital.

Types of Share Capital

A share is a fraction of a whole number. Therefore, share capital is a fraction capital or capital shared by an equal value fraction. Suppose, the capital of the company is ₹10 lakhs and we propose to keep 1 lakh shares (fractions); then, the value per share is ₹10. Now "A" holds 1,000 shares or "B" holds 50 shares, the value per share (fraction) will be equal.

Companies can issue three types of share capital:

 (i) Equity share capital,
 (ii) Preference share capital, and
(iii) Cumulative convertible preferences shares (CCPS).

These two types of share capital differ from each other in terms of their risk profile, returns offered, and ownership pattern.

Equity Share Capital

Equity shareholders are the first to contribute to the capital and the last to receive any return, say dividend. In addition, even the declaration of dividend is not mandatory. However, equity shareholders enjoy voting rights and because of voting rights, they elect the management of any company, that is, Board of Directors who in turn make policy and ensure operation of the company. Equity shareholders are the main investors in the business. In practice, shareholders are the main supplier of capital. Equity shareholders have maximum risk as neither dividend is assured nor there is any redemption of capital as equity share is undated investment or investment for "sine die." Investors in equity shares primarily invest for capital appreciation, that is, market price is more than the issue price for dividends. Their liability is restricted to the amount of share capital they contributed to the company. As dividend payment is not mandatory, equity capital provides the issuing firm the advantage of not having any fixed obligation but offers permanent capital with limited liability for repayment. However, the equity capital is a costlier source of finance as it is relatively more risky, the equity dividends are not tax-deductible and costs of issue is also relatively high.

What Is the "Equity" in Equity Shares?

Interestingly, the word "equity" is derived from the word equality, that is, absence of discrimination among the shareholders. For example, "S" has been a shareholder of XYZ Ltd since 1990 and "R" became a shareholder in the year 2003. The equality would confer the same status to both S and R and both would receive dividend at the same rate irrespective of time, investment size of holding, and purchase price. A blue chip company rewards its shareholders by liberal dividend, which is paid on paid-up capital. The other name of equity share is ordinary share and common stock. The equity share capital is different from equity, which stands for net worth, or shareholders fund composing of paid-up share capital plus reserves and surplus.

Preference Capital

Preference shareholders enjoy "preference" over equity shareholders on the post-tax earnings in the form of dividends; and assets in the event of liquidation. In other words, if directors decide to pay dividends to the shareholders first, it will be paid to the preference shareholders and if any profits are left after that, then only equity shareholders are paid. Thus, there is no obligatory payment to the preference shareholders and the preference dividend is not tax deductible. However, the preference shareholders earn a fixed rate of return for their dividend payment. However, they do not confer any voting rights on the preference shareholders. The Companies Act, 1956 restricts the issue of preference shares with voting rights only in the following cases:

 (i)   There are arrears in dividends for 2 or more years in case of cumulative preference shares;
 (ii) Preference dividend is due for a period of 2 or more consecutive preceding years; or
(iii) In the preceding 6 years including the immediately preceding financial year, if the company has not paid the preference dividend for a period of three or more years.

   Preference shares can be of the following types:

(iv) Cumulative or non-cumulative preference shares;
 (v) Redeemable or perpetual preference shares; and
(vi) Convertible or non-convertible preference shares.

For cumulative preference shares, the dividends will be paid on a cumulative basis, in case they remain unpaid in any financial year due to insufficient profits. The company will have to pay up all the arrears of preference dividends before declaring any equity dividends. However, the non-cumulative shares do not enjoy such a right to dividend payment on cumulative basis.

   Redeemable preference shares will be redeemed after a given maturity period, whereas the perpetual preference share capital will remain with the company forever. However, now with amendments in the Companies Act, only redeemable preference shares with a maximum maturity of 20 years can be issued.

Cumulative convertible preference shares are issued as cumulative preference share with 10-year maturity from the sixth year onward, so 20% of a CCP share would be converted into equity share every year. CCP share carries 10% rate of the dividend.

Interestingly, "preferential share" is different from preference share. A preferential share is an out-of-turn allotment of share, may be equity or preference share.

Who Owns a Company?

Theoretically, no one owns a company. As the company is an artificial legal person, it owns everything. In practice, promoters or shareholders enjoying majority of shares do control the company. But they are not the owner of the company. As existence of the company is independent of its promoters, the Supreme Court (*Bucha F Guzdar vs. CIT, Bombay,* AIR 1956) upheld that shareholders are not the owner of the company. They are not even part owner. They hold interest arising out of subscribing capital.

Loan

A loan is a contractual obligation in which the company agrees to pay a fixed rate of interest and repayment of principal on a fixed date. What a "share" is to capital, a "debenture" is to loan.

A debenture is a marketable legal contract whereby the company promises to pay its owner a specified rate of interest for a defined period of time and to repay the principal at the specific date of maturity. Debentures are usually secured by a charge on the immovable properties of the company. However, the charge so created is not on certain specific assets but a floating charge.

The interest of the debenture holders is usually represented by a trustee and this trustee (which is typically a bank or an insurance company or a firm of attorneys) is responsible for ensuring that the borrowing company fulfills the contractual obligations embodied in the contract. If the company issues debentures with a maturity period of more than 18 months, then it has to create a Debenture Redemption Reserve (DRR), which should be at least half of the issue amount before the redemption commences. The company can also attach call and put options. With the call option, the company can redeem the debentures at a certain price before the maturity date and similarly the put option allows the debenture holder to surrender the debentures at a certain price before the maturity period.

Types of Debentures

Debentures can be classified on the basis of conversion and security.

Nonconvertible Debentures (NCDs)

These debentures cannot be converted into equity shares and will be redeemed at the end of the maturity period. During the life of the debenture, the investors receive semi-annual interest payments at a pre-specified rate.

Fully Convertible Debentures (FCDs)

These debentures are converted into equity shares after a specified period of time at one stroke or in installments. These debentures may or may not carry interest till the date of conversion. In the case of a fully established company with an established reputation and good, stable market price, FCDs are very attractive to the investors as their bonds are getting automatically converted to shares which may at the time of conversion be quoted much higher in the market compared with what the debenture holders paid at the time of FCD issue.

Partly Convertible Debentures (PCDs)

In these debentures, a portion is converted into equity share capital after a specified period, whereas the nonconvertible (NCD) portion of the PCD will be redeemed as per the terms of the issue after the maturity period. The non-convertible portion of the PCD will carry interest right up to redemption, whereas the interest on the convertible portion will be only up to the date immediately preceding the date of conversion.

Secured Premium Notes (SPNs)

This is a kind of NCD with an attached warrant that has recently started appearing in the Indian Capital Market. The warrant attached to the SPN gives the holder the right to apply for and get allotment of one equity share for ₹100 per share through cash payment. This right has to be exercised between one and one-and-half year after allotment, by which time the SPN will be fully paid-up. For example, TISCO issued SPNs aggregating ₹346.50 crores to existing shareholders on a rights basis.

Besides, shares and debentures as described earlier, there are following new instruments available as depicted by Exhibit 2.1.

EXHIBIT 2.1: NEW FINANCIAL INSTRUMENTS

- **Non-voting Shares:** Useful for companies seeking to bolster net worth without losing management control. Similar in every respect to equity, the sole exception being the absence of voting rights.
- **Detachable Equity Warrants:** Issuable with NCDs or other debt or equity instruments. Ideal for firms with growth prospects, which would prefer equity coupons to convertible debentures (CDs).
- **Participating Debentures:** These are unsecured corporate debt securities which participate in the profits of a company. Potential issuers will be existing dividend-paying companies. Could appeal to investors willing to accept risk for higher returns.
- **Participating Preference Shares:** Quasi-equity instrument to bolster net worth without loss of management control. Pay-outs linked to equity dividend, and also eligible for bonus. Will appeal to investors with an appetite for low risk.
- **CDs with Options:** A derivative of the CDs with an embedded option, providing flexibility to the issuer as well as the investor to exit from the terms of the issue. The coupon rate is specified at the time of the issue.
- **Third Party Convertible Debentures:** Debt with a warrant allowing the investor to subscribe to the equity of a third firm at a preferential price vis-á-vis the market price. Interest rate here is lower than pure debt on account of the conversion option.
- **Mortgage-backed Securities:** A synthetic instrument, otherwise known as the asset-backed security (ABS), for securitization of debt. An ABS is backed by pooled assets like mortgages, credit card receivables, and the like.
- **Convertible Debentures Redeemable at Premium:** CD issued at face value with a "put" option entitling investors to sell the bond later to the issuer at a premium. Serves a similar purpose as that of convertible debt, but risks to investors are lower.
- **Debt–equity Swaps:** An offer from an issuer of debt to swap it for common stock (equity). The risks: it may dilute earnings per share in the case of the issuer; the expected capital appreciation may not materialize in the case of the investor.
- **Zero-coupon Convertible Note (ZCCN):** A ZCCN converts into common stock. If investors choose to convert, they forgo all accrued and unpaid interest. The risk: ZCCN prices are sensitive to interest rates.
- **Dutch Auction Note:** Where the interest rate is fixed and re-fixed at every 35 days.

Strategic Debt Restructuring (SDR)

SDR—It allows lenders to ultimately take shareholding control of a "Sick" company by converting its outstanding debt (Principal plus unpaid interest) into 51% or more of the company equity.

Test Yourself

1. What is meant by equity in equity share capital?
2. What is partly convertible debenture? Explain.

Secondary Market

The secondary market is that segment of the capital market where the outstanding securities are traded. The secondary market imparts liquidity to the long-term securities held by the investors. The secondary market operates through stock exchanges. The stock market is a pivotal institution in the financial system. A well-ordered stock market performs several economic functions such as translating short-term and medium-term investments into long-term funds for companies and directing the flow of capital in the most profitable channels.

Benefits of Well-developed Securities Market

A well-developed securities market benefits the national interest in following ways:

  (i) A securities market makes a country's financial system and its economy more stable. Securities markets, rather than banks, have traditionally been the principal source of finance for long-term investment.

 (ii) A securities market helps promote growth and employment.

(iii) A securities market expands the range of financial instruments, offering the investor different combinations of risk and reward. This, in turn, helps raise the total volume of domestic savings and investment.

(iv) A securities market can also provide finance for small business, both directly in its large, more regulated markets and indirectly by making venture-capital operations more feasible. Recently, National Stock Exchange (NSE) has started exclusive platform for SMEs.

 (v) A securities market increases economic efficiency. A formal securities market helps allocate capital more efficiently by establishing fair prices for securities and by minimizing the costs of buying and selling them. By properly supervising new issues and by requiring full disclosure of relevant financial information, a securities market protects investors against insider trading and other unfair practices.

(vi) A securities market helps promote "democratic capitalism." By distributing the ownership of securities more widely among the public, a securities market ensures that the ownership of business is not confined to a small number of wealthy families or to big industrial-financial conglomerates.

(vii) A securities market makes access to international capital easier. Foreign investors (both direct investors and portfolio investors) will be encouraged by an efficient and liquid domestic securities market. This is because they generally prefer to invest in countries where their funds are complementing, rather than replacing, domestic savings.

India has a long tradition of trading in securities going back to more than 200 years. The first Indian Stock Exchange established at Mumbai in 1875 is the oldest Exchange in Asia (even older than the Tokyo Stock Exchange which was established in 1878). Ever since the decade of 1980s, there has been an unprecedented growth of the stock markets. The number of stock exchanges in the country has increased from 8 in 1980 to 23 in 2004 including Over the Counter Exchange of India (OTCEI), National Stock Exchange (NSE) and The Integrated Stock Exchange of India (ISE). However, BSE and NSE are only operative stock exchanges now.

The stock market in India is regulated by the central government under the Securities Contracts (Regulation) Act, 1956. Under this Act, the Government has the powers to supervise and control the stock exchanges and also keep a check on the governing body and supersede it if any irregularities are found to have been committed. To regulate the development of the stock market further, Securities and Exchange Board of India (SEBI) was established in 1988 and was subsequently made a statutory body in 1992. SEBI is presently the apex regulatory body for stock markets.

Regulatory Framework for Capital Market

The four main legislations governing the Indian capital market are: (a) the Companies Act, 1956, which sets out the code of conduct for the corporate sector in relation to issue, allotment and transfer of securities, and disclosures to be made in public issues; (b) the Securities Contracts (Regulation) Act, 1956, which provides for regulation of transactions in securities through control over stock exchanges; (c) the SEBI Act, 1992 which establishes SEBI to protect investors and develop and regulate securities market; and (d) the Depositories Act, 1996 which provides for electronic maintenance and transfer of ownership of demat securities.

Legislations

Capital Issues (Control) Act, 1947: The Act had its origin during the war in 1943 when the objective was to channel resources to support the war effort. It was retained with some modifications as a means of controlling the raising of capital by companies and to ensure that national resources were channeled into proper lines, that is, for desirable purposes to serve goals and priorities of the government, and to protect the interests of the investors. Under the Act, any firm wishing to issue securities had to obtain approval from the central government, which also determined the amount, type, and price of the issue. As a part of the liberalization process, the Act was repealed in 1992 paving way for market-determined allocation of resources.

Companies Act, 1956: It deals with issue, allotment, and transfer of securities and various aspects relating to company management. It provides for standard of disclosure in public issues of capital, particularly in the fields of company management and projects, information about other listed companies under the same management, and management perception of risk factors. It also regulates underwriting, the use of premium and discounts on issues, rights and bonus issues, payment of interest and dividends, supply of annual report, and other information.

Securities Contracts (Regulation) Act, 1956: It provides for direct and indirect control of virtually all aspects of securities trading and the running of stock exchanges and aims to prevent undesirable transactions in securities. It gives central government/SEBI regulatory jurisdiction over (a) stock exchanges through a process of recognition and continued supervision, (b) contracts in securities, and (c) listing of securities on stock exchanges.

As a condition of recognition, a stock exchange complies with prescribed conditions of the central government.

SEBI Act, 1992: The SEBI Act, 1992, was enacted to empower SEBI with statutory powers for (a) protecting the interests of the investors in securities, (b) promoting the development of the securities market, and (c) regulating the securities market. Its regulatory jurisdiction extends over corporate in the issuance of capital and transfer of securities, in addition to all intermediaries and persons associated with securities market. It can conduct enquiry, audits, and inspection of all concerned and adjudicate offences under the Act. It has powers to register and regulate all market intermediaries and also to penalize them in case of violations of the provisions of the Act, Rules, and Regulations made there under. SEBI has full autonomy and authority to regulate and develop an orderly securities market.

Depositories Act, 1996: The Depositories Act, 1996, provides for the establishment of depositories in securities with the objective of ensuring free transferability of securities with speed, accuracy, and security by (a) making securities of public limited companies freely transferable subject to certain exceptions; (b) dematerializing the securities in the depository mode; and (c) providing for maintenance of ownership records in a book entry form. To streamline the settlement process, the Act envisages transfer of ownership of securities electronically by book entry without making the securities move from person to person. The Act has made the securities of all public limited companies freely transferable, restricting the company's right to use discretion in effecting the transfer of securities, and the transfer deed and other procedural requirements under the Companies Act have been dispensed with.

Rules and Regulations

The Government has framed rules under the SCRA, SEBI Act, and the Depositories Act. SEBI has framed regulations under the SEBI Act and the Depositories Act for registration and regulation of all the market intermediaries, and for the prevention of unfair trade practices, insider trading, and so on. Under these Acts, Government and SEBI issues notifications, guidelines, and circulars, which need to be complied with by the market participants.

Regulators

The responsibility for regulating the securities market is shared by Department of Economic Affairs (DEA), Department of Company Affairs (DCA), the RBI and SEBI.

A High Level Committee on Capital Markets coordinates the activities of these agencies. The orders of SEBI under the securities laws are appealable before a Securities Appellate Tribunal. Most of the powers under the SCRA are exercisable by DEA while a few others by SEBI. The powers of the DEA under the SCRA are also concurrently exercised by SEBI. The powers in respect of the contracts for sale and purchase of securities, gold-related securities, money market securities, and securities derived from these securities and RBI, exercises ready forward contracts in debt securities concurrently. The SEBI Act and the Depositories Act are mostly administered by SEBI. The rules under the securities laws are framed by government and regulations by SEBI. All these are administered by SEBI. The powers under the Companies Act relating to issue and transfer of securities and non-payment of dividend are administered by SEBI in case of listed public companies and public companies proposing to get their securities listed (Table 2.4).

TABLE 2.4
PROFILE OF MARKET INTERMEDIARIES

SEBI-Registered Market Intermediaries

Particulars	2000	2005	2010-2011	2011-2012	2012-2013	2013-2014	April 14 to December 14
Stock exchanges (cash market)	23	22	19	19	19	16	14
Stock exchanges (derivatives market)	2	2	2	2	3	3	3
Stock exchange (currency derivatives)	—	—	4	4	4	4	3
Brokers and sub-brokers (cash segment)	14,867	22,745	9,235	9,307	10,128	9,411	7,306
Sub broker (cash segment)			1,722	1,765	1,757	1,710	
FII	506	685	5,686	6,322	6,335	6,344	
Custodians	15	11	19	19	19	19	19
Depositories	2	2	2	2	2	2	2
Depositories participants	191	477	805	854	865	857	858
Merchant bankers	186	128	192	200	199	197	198
Bankers to an issue	68	59	55	56	57	59	60
Underwriters	42	59	3	3	3	3	2
Credit rating agencies	4	4	6	6	6	6	6
Venture capital funds	—	50	184	207	211	207	201
Foreign venture capital investors	—	14	153	175	182	192	201
Registrar to an issue & share transfer agent	242	83	73	74	72	71	71
Portfolio managers	23	84	267	250	241	212	193
Mutual funds	38	39	51	49	52	50	49
Collective investment schemes	0	0	1	1	1	1	1
Approved intermediaries (stock lending schemes)	6	3	2	2	2	2	2

Source: Handbook of Statistics on the Indian Securities Market, 2009 & 2014 (SEBI).

Forex Market

Let us consider a transaction involving supply of bed sheets and cotton skirts from India to Germany. The Indian exporter will price the bed sheets and skirts in such a manner that he would make profit in terms of Indian rupees. He would like the customer abroad to pay him in terms of rupees only. The purchasing power available with the German buyer is in the form of German Marks and thus, he would like to know how many German Marks he has to part with, to buy the bed sheets and/or cotton skirts.

There is a possibility that both seller and the buyer may agree to settle the transaction in third currency, say, US dollar. In that case, the buyer first needs to convert his currency into US dollars. On receipt of the payment, the seller would again convert the dollars into rupees. The market, which facilitates such transactions, is called the forex market. The rate at which one currency is converted into another currency is the rate of exchange between the two currencies concerned. The exchange rate between the two currencies can be obtained from quotation in foreign exchange rate market.

According to Section 2(b) of the Foreign Exchange Regulation Act (1973), Foreign Exchange is defined as:

(i) All deposits, credits, balance of payments in foreign currency and any drafts, travelers' checks, letters of credit, and bills of exchange expressed or drawn in Indian currency and payable in foreign currency;

(ii) Any instrument payable at the option of the drawee or holder thereof or any other party thereto, in Indian currency or in foreign currency or partly in one and partly in the other.

The international foreign exchange market geographically extends from Tokyo and Sydney through Hong Kong, Singapore, Bahrain, the European centers, New York to the West Coast of the USA. This is the world's largest market and is operational for virtually 24 hours a day as different countries are in different time zones. However, there is no physical location for this market where traders can get together and exchange currencies. The traders sit in their dealing rooms and communicate with each other through telephones, computer terminals, telexes, and other information channels.

Participants in the Forex Market

Anyone who exchanges currency of a given country for other, or who needs such services, is a participant of the forex market. Commercial banks are the main participants of the forex market in any country. The large corporate with investments abroad or foreign trade activities, exporters and marketers also participate in the forex market.

Commercial Banks

Commercial banks deal with international trade transactions and offer services of converting one currency into another. Usually, the commercial banks act as intermediaries between importers and exporters who are situated in different countries. A commercial bank, which offers services, would sell foreign currencies to importers and buy foreign currencies from exporters.

Corporate

Large corporate may participate either as exporters or as importers. Exporters may require the services of banks to convert their foreign currency receipts into domestic currency (which they obtain by means of selling the goods and services). Importers requiring to pay for the goods imported by them may utilize the services of banks for converting the local currencies into foreign currencies (which they need to make payments for the goods and services they have imported).

Brokers

The forex brokers bring the seller and buyer banks together without disclosing the name of the counterparty bank before the deal is finalized. The forex brokers are governed by the rules framed by the Foreign Exchange Dealers Association of India (FEDAI). Brokers also render their services by giving market information to the banks. The foreign exchange brokers in India are prohibited to deal on their own account which means they cannot acquire any position.

Central Bank

The central banks in most of the countries have the responsibility of maintaining external value of the currency of the country. If a country is following a fixed exchange rate system, then the central bank has to take necessary steps to maintain the rate. Even if the country is following a floating exchange rate system, the central bank needs to ensure orderliness in the movement of exchange rates by intervening in the forex market.

In India, the responsibility and authority of administration of foreign exchange is vested with the RBI under FEMA. Due to the vast geography and foreign exchange received and required by large number of importers and exporters, it would be impossible for the RBI to deal with everyone individually. Therefore, a provision was made in the Act enabling the RBI to delegate its power or functions to authorized dealers or money changers, with prior approval of the central government.

Authorized Dealers in Foreign Exchange

The institutions which have been authorized by the RBI to deal in foreign exchange are called authorized dealers. For example, authorizations have been granted to banks, certain FIs to undertake specific types of foreign exchange transactions incidental to their main business, certain state co-operative/urban co-operative banks, and scheduled commercial banks to open and maintain ordinary non-resident rupee accounts (NRO accounts) and non-resident (external) rupee accounts (NRE accounts) on behalf of Non-Resident individuals of Indian nationality or origin.

Authorized Money Changers

To facilitate the encashment of foreign currency to visitors from abroad, especially foreign tourists, RBI has granted licenses to certain established firms, hotels, and other organizations permitting them to deal in foreign currency notes, coins, and traveler's checks subject to directions issued to them from time to time. These firms and organizations are known as "authorized money changers." The money changers can be of two types:

 (i) Full-fledged money changers, who are authorized to undertake both purchase and sale transactions with the public.
(ii) Restricted money changers, who are authorized only to purchase foreign currency notes, coins, and traveler's checks, subject to the condition that all such collections are surrendered by them in turn to an authorized dealer in foreign exchange.

Regulatory Framework in the Forex Market

With a view to facilitating external trade and promoting orderly development of foreign exchange market in India, a new Act called the Foreign Exchange Act, 1999 (FEMA) came into force from June 1, 2000. With FEMA coming into force, the Foreign Exchange Regulation Act, 1973 stands repealed.

Under FEMA, foreign exchange transactions have been divided into two broad categories—current account transactions and capital account transactions. Transactions that alter the assets and liabilities of a person residing in India or a person residing outside India have been classified as capital account transactions. All other transactions would be current account transactions.

Under FEMA, only the GOI in consultation with the RBI would be empowered to impose reasonable restrictions on current account transactions. Accordingly, GOI has notified the Rules governing the current account transactions vide its Notification No. G.S.R381(E) dated May 3, 2000, as amended vide S.O. No. 301(E) dated March 30, 2001. As per the GOI Rules, remittances of only eight types of current account transactions are prohibited, 11 types of transactions need GOI's prior approval, whereas 17 transactions need prior permission from the RBI in case the amount of remittances exceeds the prescribed limit for such remittances.

RBI has notified comprehensive simple and transparent regulations under the FEMA, 1999 governing various capital account transactions. The new regulations clearly indicate the types of permissible capital account transactions, leave very few individual transactions to be dealt in by the RBI, simplify procedures, reduce the number of forms to a bare minimum, and grant more powers to the authorized dealers, that is, banks.

Derivatives Market

The word "derivative" means something which has been derived from the other. A financial derivative is a product derived from the market of another product. Hence, derivative market has no independent existence without an underlying asset. The price of derivative instrument is dependent on the value of its underlying asset.

Derivatives are designed to manage risks. The derivative markets enable institutional investors, bank treasurers, and corporate to manage their risk more efficiently and allow them to hedge or speculate on markets.

Participants in the Derivatives Market

Generally, banks, corporate, FIs, individuals, and brokers are seen as regular participants. The derivative markets allow the participants to hedge, speculate, or arbitrage in the markets. The participants can be classified into three categories based on the motives and strategies adopted.

Hedgers

Hedging is an act whereby an investor seeks to protect a position or anticipated position in the spot market by using an opposite position in derivatives. The parties, which perform hedging, are known as hedgers. In the process of hedging, parties such as individuals or companies owning or planning to own, a cash commodity (such as corn, pepper, wheat, treasury bonds, notes, and bills) are concerned that the cost of the commodity may change before either buying (or selling) it in the cash market. They want to reduce or limit the impact of such movements, which, if not covered, would incur a loss.

Speculators

Speculators are basically traders who enter the contract, with a view to make profit from the subsequent price movements. They do not have any risk to hedge; in fact, they operate at a high level of risk in anticipation of profits. The speculators also perform a valuable economic function of feeding information, which is not readily available elsewhere, and help others in analyzing the derivatives markets.

Arbitrageurs

The act of obtaining risk-free profits by simultaneously buying and selling similar instruments in different markets is known as "arbitrage." The person who does this activity is referred to as an "arbitrageur." For example, one could always sell a stock on NSE and buy on BSE. The arbitrageurs continuously monitor various markets, and whenever there is a chance of arbitraging, they buy from one market and sell it in the other and make risk less profit. They keep the prices of derivatives and current underlying assets closely consistent, thereby performing a very valuable economic function.

Types of Derivative Instruments

Derivatives can be classified into two categories based on the nature of the contract:
  (i) Futures and
 (ii) Options.

Futures

A futures contract is a contract which conveys an agreement to buy or sell a specific amount of a commodity or financial instrument at a particular price on a stipulated future date. A futures contract obligates the buyer to purchase the underlying instrument, and the seller to sell it, unless the contract is sold to another before settlement date, which may happen to take a profit or limit a loss.

Futures contracts are highly uniform and well-specified commitments for a carefully described commodity to be delivered at a certain time and in a certain manner. It also specifies the quantity and quality of the commodity that can be delivered to fulfill the futures contract. The quality specifications become less relevant in case of futures on interest rates or currencies. The futures contracts are always traded on an organized exchange with standardized terms of contract. The trading is usually done through the brokers. A trader can trade on his own account also. However, most of the traders act as brokers, and trade on behalf of the clients.

The clearing house ensures smooth and effective functioning of the futures market. It guarantees that all the traders in the futures market honor their obligations. Although it does not take any active position in the market, it interposes itself between all parties to every transaction. It insists on margin and daily settlement for safeguarding the interests of both the parties to perform their contractual obligations.

Options

Option is a contract that confers the right, but not an obligation to the holder to buy (call option) or to sell (put option) an underlying asset (the asset may be a stock, currency, commodity, financial instrument, or a futures contract) at a price agreed on a specific date or by a specific expiry date. The seller or writer of the option has the obligation to fulfill the contract if the holder wishes to exercise the option, for which a premium is paid.

Every exchange-traded option is either a call option or a put option. Options are created by selling and buying and for every option there is a seller and a buyer. The seller of an option is also known as option writer. In option contracts, all the rights lie with the option buyer.

As is obvious from Figure 2.3, the seller always acquires an obligation and the buyer always acquires a right. Hence, the buyer pays the seller a certain amount upfront, which is known as premium.

FIGURE 2.3

SELECT INDIAN COMPANIES HAVING ISSUED ADR AND GDR

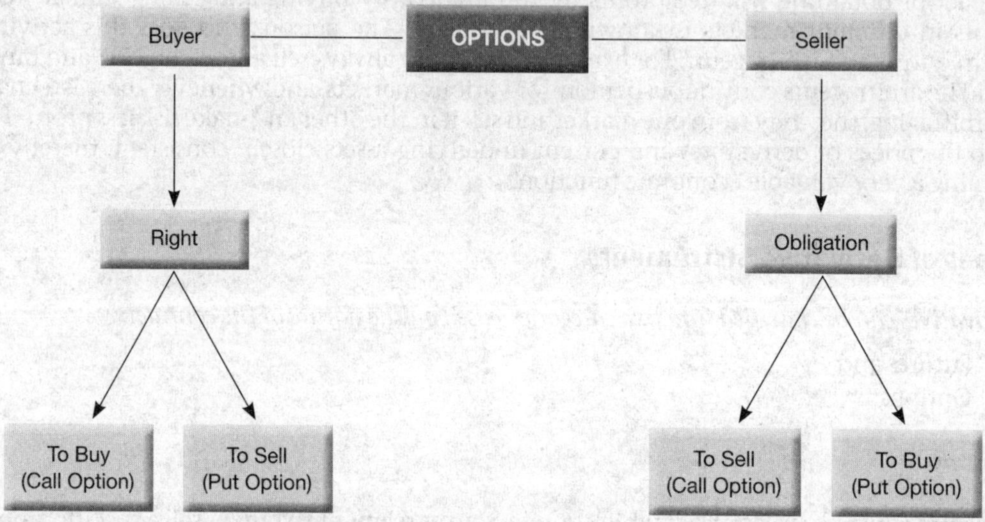

Source: Author.

Besides financial derivatives marked, commodity derivatives market is available in India as well. There are 24 commodity exchanges in India of which the following are national-level commodity exchanges (Table 2.5).

TABLE 2.5

COMMODITY EXCHANGES IN INDIA AS OF 2011

National Multi-Commodity Exchange (NMCE)
Multi Commodity Exchange (MCX)
National Commodity & Derivatives Exchange (NCDEX)
Commodity derivative market is regulated by Forward Market Commission (FMC). It is expected that FMC may merge with SEBI

Source: Author.

Developmental FIs

All-India Development Banks

Industrial Development Bank of India (IDBI)

IDBI was established in 1964 as a subsidiary of the RBI by an Act of the parliament and was made a wholly owned GOI undertaking in 1975. It was established with the main objective of serving as an apex FI to co-ordinate the functioning of all other FIs. IDBI provided financial assistance for the establishment of new projects as well as for expansion, diversification, modernization, and technology upgradation of the existing industrial enterprises. IDBI was vested with the responsibility of coordination the working of institutions engaged in financing, promoting, and developing industries. It had evolved an appropriate mechanism for this purpose. IDBI also undertook or supported wide-ranging promotional activities including entrepreneurship development programs for new entrepreneurs, provision of consultancy services for small and medium enterprises, upgradation of technology and programs for economic upliftment of the underprivileged. IDBI has been merged with its subsidiary IDBI Bank.

Industrial Finance Corporation of India (IFCI)

At the time of independence in 1947, India's capital market was relatively underdeveloped. Although there was significant demand for new capital, there was a dearth of providers. Merchant bankers and underwriting firms were almost nonexistent. And commercial banks were not equipped to provide long-term industrial finance in any significant manner.

It is against this backdrop that the government established IFCI on July 1, 1948, as the first Development FI in the country to cater to the long-term finance needs of the industrial sector. The newly established DFI was provided access to low-cost funds through the central bank's SLR which, in turn, enabled it to provide loans and advances to corporate borrowers at concessional rates.

This arrangement continued until the early 1990s, when it was recognized that there was need for greater flexibility to respond to the changing financial system. It was also felt that IFCI should directly access the capital markets for its funds needs. It is with this objective that the constitution of IFCI was changed in 1993 from a statutory corporation to a company under the Indian Companies Act, 1956. Subsequently, the name of the company was also changed to "IFCI Limited" with effect from October 1999.

Industrial Credit and Investment Corporation of India (ICICI)

ICICI was established in 1955 with the objective of providing finance to the industries in the private sector. It was incorporated under the Companies Act. Although the IFCI was existing at that time, the need was felt for a separate FI to provide finance to the private sector, especially in foreign currency. ICICI was started as a private sector FI unlike the IFCI. However, as the banks and insurance companies that were holding the shares were nationalized, the central government came to own a substantial holding in the company through them.

ICICI is widely known for its flexible approach in financing. It has been merged with the ICICI Bank in May 2002.

Industrial Investment Bank of India (IIBI)

IIBI first came into existence as a central government corporation with the name Industrial Reconstruction Corporation of India in 1971. Its basic objective was to finance the reconstruction and rehabilitation of sick and closed industrial units. Its name was changed to Industrial Reconstruction Bank of India and it was made the principal credit and reconstruction agency in the country in 1985 through the IRBI Act, 1984. The bank started coordination with similar work of other institutions and banks, preparing schemes for reconstruction by restructuring the liabilities, appraising schemes of mergers and amalgamation of sick companies, and providing financial assistance for modernization, expansion, diversification, and technological upgradation of the sick units.

In March 1997, in line with the ongoing policies of financial and economic reforms, IRBI was converted into a full-fledged Development FI. It was renamed as IIBI Limited and was incorporated as a company under the Companies Act, 1956. Its entire equity is currently being held by the GOI. Its activities include providing finance for the establishment of new industrial projects as well as for expansion, diversification, and modernization of the existing industrial enterprises. It provides financial assistance in the form of term loans, subscription to debentures or equity shares, and deferred payment guarantees. IIBI is now also active in Merchant Banking and its services include, inter alia, structuring of suitable instruments for public or rights issues, preparation of prospectus or offer documents and working as lead manager. It also offers its services for debt syndication, and the entire package of services for mergers and acquisitions.

Infrastructure Development Finance Corporation (IDFC)

IDFC, established in 1997, is a specialized financial institution, set up to provide credit enhancement to infrastructure projects and to extend long-term loans and guarantees that existing institutions may not be able to provide.

IDFC has also broadened its initial focus on power, roads, ports, and telecommunications to a framework of energy, telecommunications and information technology, integrated transportation, urban infrastructure, health care, food and agri-business infrastructure, education infrastructure, and tourism.

The Asian Development Bank and the International Finance Corporation are shareholders in the IDFC. A comprehensive funding package for infrastructure projects has been developed by the IDFC and the Power Finance Corporation (PFC). At the state level, the PFC is primarily focused on public sector projects, whereas the IDFC concentrates on the private sector. In the recent budget, the government proposed giving IDFC incentives and benefits available to other public FIs.

Small Industrial Development Bank of India (SIDBI)

What IDBI is for the large corporate, SIDBI, which has been carved out of IDBI in 1990, is for small and medium industries.

Specialized FIs

The Export–Import Bank of India (EXIM Bank)

The Exim Bank is a public sector FI created by an Act of Parliament, the Export-Import Bank of India Act, 1981. The business of Exim Bank is to finance Indian exports that lead to continuity of foreign exchange for India. The Bank's primary objective is to develop commercially viable relationships with a target set of externally oriented companies by offering them a comprehensive range of products and services, aimed at enhancing their internationalization efforts.

Exim Bank provides a range of analytical information and export related services. The Bank's fee-based services help identify new business propositions, source trade and investment-related information, create and enhance presence through joint network of institutional linkages across the globe, and assists externally oriented companies in their quest for excellence and globalization. Services include search for overseas partners, identification of technology suppliers, negotiating alliances, and development of joint ventures in India and abroad. The Bank also supports Indian project exporters and consultants to participate in projects funded by multilateral funding agencies.

State-level FIs

State Financial Corporations (SFCs)

At the beginning of the 1950s, the government found that for achieving rapid industrialization, separate institutions should be set up that cater exclusively to the needs of the small and medium sectors. Consequently, legislation was promoted by the GOI for the setting up of financial corporations, and the State Financial Corporation Act 1951 came into force on August 1, 1952. The SFCs were closely modeled on the line of IFCI, but were intended to serve the financial requirements of small- and medium-sized enterprises. The SFCs provide finance in the form of term loans, by underwriting issues of shares and debentures, by subscribing to debentures, and standing guarantee for loans raised from other institutions and from the general public.

State Industrial Development Corporations (SIDCs)

The SIDCs have been set up to facilitate rapid industrial growth in the respective states. In addition to providing finance, the SIDCs identify and sponsor projects in the joint sector with the participation of private entrepreneurs. For example, RIICO in Rajasthan, GIDC in Gujarat, PIDC in Punjab are SIDCs, and are promoting industrial development in respective states.

Investment Institutions

Life Insurance Corporation of India (LIC)

The LIC was established in 1956 by amalgamation and nationalization of 245 private insurance companies by an enactment of the parliament. The main business of the LIC is to provide life insurance. With the opening up of the insurance sector, some private sector life insurance companies, such as Birla Sun Life, ICICI Prudential, Bajaj Alliance, Birla Sunlife, Met Life, and Max New York have been set up and the monopoly which LIC enjoyed earlier has ended.

General Insurance Corporation of India (GIC)

The entire general insurance business in India was nationalized by General Insurance Business (Nationalization) Act, 1972 (GIBNA). The GOI through Nationalization took over the shares of 55 Indian insurance companies and the undertakings of 52 insurers carrying on general insurance business. GIC was formed in pursuance of Section 9(1) of GIBNA. It was incorporated on November 22, 1972, under the Companies Act, 1956 as a private company limited by shares. GIC was formed for the purpose of superintending, controlling, and carrying on the business of general insurance.

On April 19, 2000, when the Insurance Regulatory and Development Authority Act, 1999 (IRDAA) came into force, it introduced amendment to GIBNA and the Insurance Act, 1938. An amendment to GIBNA removed the exclusive privilege of GIC and its subsidiaries carrying on general insurance in India. Now many general insurance companies in the private sector are there such as Allianz Bajaj, Tata AIG General Insurance, and ICICI Lombard General Insurance.

With the GIBNA 2002 (40 of 2002) coming into force from March 21, 2002, GIC ceased to be a holding company of its subsidiaries. Their ownership were vested with the GOI.

Unit Trust of India (UTI)

The impetus for establishing a formal institution came from the desire to increase the propensity of the middle and lower groups to save and to invest. UTI came into existence during a period marked by great political and economic uncertainty in India. With war on the borders and economic turmoil that depressed the financial market, entrepreneurs were hesitant to enter capital market. The already existing companies found it difficult to raise fresh capital, as investors did not respond adequately to new issues. Earnest efforts were required to canalize savings of the community into productive uses to speed up the process of industrial growth. The then Finance Minister, T.T. Krishnamachari set up the idea of a unit trust that would be "open to any person or institution to purchase the units offered by the trust. However, this institution as we see it, is intended to cater to the needs of the individual investors, and even among them as far as possible, to those whose means are small."

The UTI was founded in 1964 under the Unit Trust of India UTI Act, 1963. Initially, 50% of the capital of the trust was contributed by the RBI, whereas the rest was brought in by the State Bank of India and its associates, LIC, GIC, and other FIs. In 1974, the holding of the RBI was transferred to the IDBI making the UTI an associate of the IDBI. In January 2003, UTI was split into two parts—UTI-I and UTI-II. UTI-I has been given all the assured return schemes and Unit Scheme 64, and it is being administered by the central government. UTI-II is entrusted with the task of managing NAV-based schemes. UTI-II is being managed by the State Bank of India, Punjab National Bank, Bank of Baroda, and Life Insurance Corporations (Table 2.6).

TABLE 2.6
DEVELOPMENT OF FINANCIAL INSTITUTIONS (YEARS OF ESTABLISHMENT)

All-India Development Banks

IDBI (1964)

ICICI Bank (Formerly ICICI; 1955)

SIDBI (1990)

IIBI (1997)

IFCI (1948)

IDFC (1997)

Specialized Financial Institutions

EXIM Bank (1982)

ILFS Venture Cap (1988)

ICICI Venture (1988)

TFCI (1989), IDFC (1997)

Investment Institutions

UTI (1964)

LIC (1956)

GIC and Subsidiaries (1972)

Refinance Institutions

NABARD (1982)

NHB (1980)

Other Institutions

Export Credit Guarantee Corporation of India (ECGC) (1957)

Deposit Insurance

Credit Guarantee Corporation (DICGC) (1962)

Source: Indian Finance Review, BSE Publication, 2003.

Mutual Funds

Mutual funds serve the purpose of mobilization of funds from various categories of investors and channelizing them into productive investment. Apart from UTI, mutual funds sponsored by various bank subsidiaries, insurance organizations, and private sector FIs have come up. These mutual funds operate within the framework of SEBI regulations which prescribe the mechanism for setting up of a mutual fund, procedure of registration, its constitution and duties, and functions and responsibility of the various parties involved. Currently, there are 44 mutual funds operating in India.

Banking System

Banking in India has its origin as early as the Vedic period. It is believed that the transition from money lending to banking must have occurred even before Manu, the great Hindu Jurist, who has devoted a section of his work to deposits and advances and laid down rules relating to rates of interest. During the Mogul period, the indigenous bankers played a very important role in lending money and financing foreign trade and commerce. During the days of the East India Company, it was the turn of the agency houses to carry on the banking business. The General Bank of India was the first Joint Stock Bank to be established in the year 1786. The others which followed were the Bank of Hindustan and the Bengal Bank. The Bank of Hindustan is reported to have continued till 1906, whereas the other two failed in the meantime. In the first half of the 19th century, the East India Company established three banks: the Bank of Bengal in 1809, the Bank of Bombay in 1840, and the Bank of Madras in 1843. These three banks, also known as Presidency Banks, were independent units and functioned well. These three banks were amalgamated in 1920 and a new bank, the Imperial Bank of India, was established on January 27, 1921. With the passing of the State Bank of India Act in 1955, the undertaking of the Imperial Bank of India was taken over by the newly constituted State Bank of India. The RBI which is the central bank was created in 1935 by passing RBI Act, 1934. In the wake of the Swadeshi Movement, a number of banks with Indian management were established in the country, namely, Punjab National Bank Ltd, Bank of India Ltd, Canara Bank Ltd, Indian Bank Ltd, the Bank of Baroda Ltd, and the Central Bank of India Ltd. On July 19, 1969, 14 major banks of the country were nationalized, and on April 15, 1980, 6 more commercial private sector banks were also taken over by the government. Today the commercial banking system in India may be distinguished into:

1. Public Sector Banks

(a) State Bank of India and its associate banks called the State Bank group
(b) Twenty nationalized banks
(c) RRBs mainly sponsored by the Public Sector Banks

2. Private Sector Banks

(a) Old generation private banks
(b) New generation private banks
(c) Foreign banks in India
(d) Scheduled Co-operative Banks
(e) Non-scheduled Banks

Scheduled banks are those, which are included in the Second Schedule of The Banking Regulation Act, 1949; others are non-scheduled banks. To be included in the Second Schedule, a bank (a) must have paid-up capital and reserve of not less than ₹5 lakhs; (b) it must also satisfy the RBI that its affairs are not conducted in a manner detrimental to the interests of its depositors. Scheduled banks are required to maintain a certain amount of reserves with the RBI; they, in return, enjoy the facility of financial accommodation and remittance at concessional rates from the RBI (Figure 2.4).

FIGURE 2.4
STRUCTURE OF THE BANKING SYSTEM IN INDIA

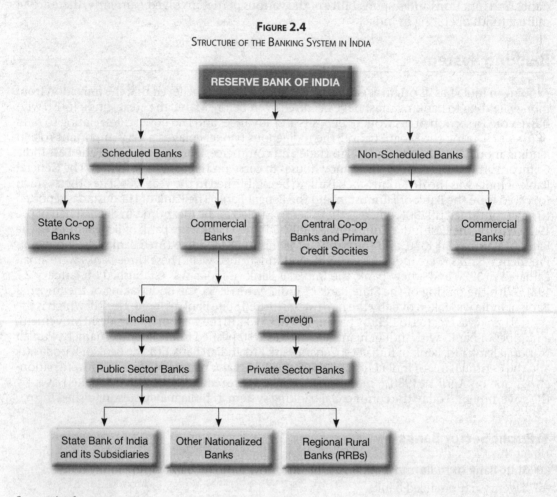

Source: Author.

Regional Rural Banks

Regional rural banks (RRB) were set up under an act of Parliament in 1976 with the objective of developing rural economy through the promotion of agriculture, trade, commerce, industry, and extending credit particularly to small and marginal farmers, agricultural laborers, kisans, and small entrepreneurs. The authorized capital of a RRB is ₹5 crore and issued or paid-up capital minimum of ₹25 lakhs and maximum of ₹100 lakhs contributed in the ratio of 50:15:35 by the central government, state government, and the sponsoring commercial bank, respectively. As at the end of March 1995, the GOI raised the issued share capital of 176 RRBs to ₹75 lakhs each whereas the same for 20 RRBs was raised to ₹100 lakhs. The RRBs are scheduled commercial banks having been included in the second schedule of the RBI Act. The total number of RRBs functioning in the country as at the end of June 1999 was 196 covering 451 districts spread over 23 states with the network of 14,467 branches.

The banking sector is witnessing revolutionary changes. Some new banks such as Bandhan Bank, Bhartiya Mahila Bank, IDFC Banks, and Mudra Bank are taking shape, so is the concept of Payment Bank by Airtel, Sun Pharma, and so on. Recently, the RBI has accorded in principal approval for 10 small finance banks that will focus on small geographies for operations but with strong capital base (*The Economic Times*, September 17, 2015).

Non-banking Financial Companies (NBFCs)

NBFCs can be classified as follows:

   (i) Investment trusts or investment companies
  (ii) Nidhis or mutual benefit funds or mutual benefit finance companies
 (iii) Merchant banks
  (iv) Hire-purchase finance companies
   (v) Lease finance companies or leasing or equipment leasing companies
  (vi) Housing finance institutions (companies)
 (vii) Venture capital funds
(viii) Factors or factoring companies
  (ix) Insurance companies

Investment Trusts or Investment Companies

Investment trusts are close-ended organizations, unlike UTI, and they have a fixed amount of authorized capital and a stated amount of issued capital. Investment trusts provide useful services through conserving and managing property for those who, for some reasons or other, cannot manage their own affairs. Investors of moderate means are provided facilities for diversification of investment, expert advice on lucrative investment channels, and supervision of their investment. From the point of view of the economy, they help to mobilize small savings and direct them to fruitful channels. Most of these companies are not independent; they are investment holding companies, formed by the former managing agents, or business houses. As such, they provide finance mainly to such companies as are associated with these business houses.

Nidhis

Mutual benefit funds or nidhis, as they are called in India, are joint stock companies operating mainly in South India, particularly in Tamil Nadu. The sources of their funds are share capital, deposits from their members, and the public. The deposits are fixed and recurring. Unlike other NBFCs, nidhis also accept demand deposits to some extent. The loans given by these institutions are mainly for consumption purposes. These loans are usually secured loans, given against the security of tangible assets such as house property, gold, jewelry, or against shares of the companies and LIC policies. The terms on which loans are given are quite moderate. They are incorporated bodies and are governed by the directives of the RBI.

Merchant Banks

Merchant banks mainly offer financial advice and services for a fee unlike commercial banks, which accept deposits and lend money. When merchant banks do function as commercial banks, they function essentially as wholesale bankers. They provide a range of services such as management, marketing, and underwriting of new issues; project promotion services and project finance; syndication of credit and other facilities; leasing, including project leasing; corporate advisory services; investment advisory services; bought-out deals; venture capital; mutual funds and offshore funds; investment management including discretionary management; assistance for technical and financial collaboration and joint ventures; investment services for non-resident Indians; and management of and dealing in CP. In India, the merchant banking services are provided by the commercial banks, All-India FIs, Private Consultancy Firms, and Technical Consultation Organizations. Apart from these institutions, professional merchant banking houses are slowly coming up in India.

Hire-purchase Finance Companies

Hire-purchase involves a system under which term loans for purchases of goods and services are advanced to be liquidated in stages through a contractual obligation. The goods whose purchases are thus financed may be consumer goods or producer goods or they may be simply services such as air travel. Hire-purchase credit may be provided by the seller himself or by any FI. Hire-purchase credit is available in India for a wide range of products and services such as automobiles, sewing machines, radios, refrigerators, TV sets, bicycles, machinery and equipment, other capital goods, industrial sheds; services such as educational fees, and medical fees. However, unlike in other countries, the emphasis in India is on the provision of installment credit for productive goods and services rather than for purely consumer goods. Suppliers of hire-purchase finance include retail and wholesale traders, commercial banks, IDBI, ICICI, NSIC, NSIDC, SFCS, SIDCS, Agro-Industries Corporations (AICs), and so on. In the recent past, banks also have increased their business in the field of installment credit and consumer loans.

Lease Finance Companies

Lease finance companies provide finance to acquire the use of assets for a stated period of time without owning them. The user of the asset is known as the lessee, and the owner of the asset is known as the lessor. Lease financing organizations in India include non-bank financial companies such as Infrastructure Leasing and Financial Services Ltd. (IL&FS), ICICI, certain SIDCs and SIICs, and other organizations.

Housing Finance Companies

These companies provide finance for construction or purchase of land and buildings. Housing finance is provided in the form of mortgage loans, that is, it is provided against the security of immovable property of land and buildings. Basically, housing finance loans are given by the Housing and Urban Development Corporation (HUDCO), the apex Co-operative Housing Finance Societies, and Housing Boards in different States, central and state governments, LIC, commercial banks, GIC, and a few private housing finance companies such as HDFC, Deewan Housing Finance, and nidhis.

Venture Capital Funding Companies

Venture capital is the money provided by the professionals who invest alongside management in young, rapidly growing companies that have the potential to develop into significant economic contributors. Venture capital is an important source of equity for the start-up companies. Professionally managed venture capital firms generally are private partnerships or closely held corporations funded by private and public pension funds, endowment funds, foundations, corporations, wealthy individuals, foreign investors, and the venture capitalists themselves. The mushroom growth of the IT companies in Silicon Valley in USA was the result of funding by VC companies.

VC funding in India in the calendar year 2003 was in the $500–600 million range, a sharp drop from $1.1 billion in 2002 and $900 million in 2001. More than 80% of new VC investment in India is in profitable companies rather than startups, with Internet companies clearly out of favor and BPO, media, entertainment, and health care emerging as the new stars.

Factoring Companies

Factoring is a financing technique in which a business sells invoiced receivables at a discount to a bank or a financing house or to an internal finance company. The factor may or may not accept the incumbent credit risk. This is a service offered by a factoring company that enables companies to sell their outstanding book debts for cash. Factoring is an ongoing arrangement between the client and the Factor, where invoices raised on open account sales of goods and services are regularly assigned to "the Factor" for financing, collection, and sales ledger administration. Usually, it an arrangement used when the buyer and the seller have long-term relationships. At times, even the whole turnover of the company may be assigned to the factor. In India, factoring business is still in its nascent stage. Some of the firms offering factoring services include CanBank Factor, SBI Factors, HSBC Factor, and so on.

Insurance Companies

Insurance companies play a decisive role in financial market in India. There are two types of Insurance companies—life insurance companies (24 companies are in operation) and non-life insurance companies (28 non-life insurance companies are operative in India). Insurance Companies are regulated by Insurance Development and Regularities Authority (IRDA).

SUMMARY

1. An economic system consists of various economic agents such as households, producers, government, and consumers. These economic agents undertake various economic activities such as production, exchange, and consumption for the purpose of sustaining themselves.

2. A financial system performs various functions such as facilitating savings, exchange of funds, risk management, and market regulation.

3. Financial markets may be categorized into primary and secondary markets on the basis of instruments issued. On the basis of maturity, the markets are classified into money market and capital market.

4. Government, central bank, commercial banks, financial institutions, and corporate are the major players in the money market.

5. T-Bills are issued by the RBI on behalf of the GOI to meet the short-term funds requirements of the government. T-Bills also help the RBI to perform open market operations which help in regulating the money supply in the economy.

6. CP is an unsecured promissory note. CP was introduced in India in 1990 with a view to enable highly rated corporate borrowers to diversify their sources of short-term borrowings.

7. CDs is a negotiable instrument issued for funds deposited at a bank or other eligible financial institution for a specified time period.

8. Repurchase agreements or repos are transactions involving sale of government securities (including T-Bills) with an agreement to buy back the securities at a pre-specified date in future at a pre-specified price.

9. "Gilt edged" securities mean securities of the best quality. The securities issued by central or state governments, semi-government organizations such as municipal corporations, autonomous institutions such as port trusts, public sector units, and other quasi-government agencies are referred to as gilt-edged securities.

10. MMMFs are mutual funds that invest primarily in money market instruments of very high quality and of very short maturities. MMMFs can be set up by commercial banks, RBI, and public financial institutions either directly or through their existing mutual fund subsidiaries.

11. Bank Rate is the rate at which the Reserve Bank rediscounts the first-class commercial bills of exchange.

12. The capital market consists of the primary market and the secondary market. The primary market is used to create long-term instruments through which corporate can raise capital/loans from the capital market. However, secondary market provides liquidity and marketability to these instruments. There are NBFC, banking, insurance, and mutual funds are also in operation in India.

KEY TERMS

- Primary market
- Secondary market
- Money market
- Capital market
- Call money
- Notice money
- T-Bills commercial paper
- Coupon rate
- Repo rate
- Reverse repo
- Guilt edged securities
- Bank rate
- Open market operations
- CRR
- SLR
- SEBI
- Public issue
- Right issue
- Private placement
- Bought-out deal
- Euro issues
- GDR
- ADR
- Non-convertible debentures
- Partly convertible debentures
- Fully convertible debentures
- Secured premium notes
- Hedgers
- Speculators
- Arbitragers
- Futures
- Options
- Venture capital

Learning Outcomes

The outcome of this chapter will be to appreciate the financial environment consisting of various institutions, regulators, and instruments helping in financial decision-making.

ASSESS YOURSELF

Concept Review and Critical Thinking Questions

1. What is a financial system? What are its various functions?
2. What is a primary market? What are the various instruments issued in primary market?
3. Secondary market cannot exist without a well-developed primary market. Discuss with reference to an emerging market like India.
4. Differentiate between ADR and GDR.
5. Discuss the development of banking sector in India over the last decade.
6. Discuss the role of Commodity derivatives in the Indian Financial System.

STUDENT ACTIVITIES

1. Collect the data of Initial Public offer (IPO's) in the years 2012, 2013, 2014, and 2015. Perform the comparative analysis.
2. Find out the price of selected public issue at IPO launch and after 6 months.

SUGGESTED READINGS

Brealey, R.A. and Myers, S.C. (2002), *Principles of Corporate Finance*, 7th edn., McGraw-Hill.
Ross, S.A., Wasterfield, R.W. (2002), *Fundamentals of Corporate Finance*, 6th edn., Tata McGraw-Hill.
Horne, J.C.V. (2002), *Financial Management & Policy*, 12th edn., Singapore: Pearson Education.
Kothari, Rajesh (2010), *Financial Services in India: Concept & Application*, SAGE India.

CHAPTER 3

Financial Statement Analysis

Learning Objectives

- To understand the concept and types of financial statements.
- To learn how these statements can be analyzed and interpreted.

PRELUDE

The initial stage in the financial management process is financial analysis and review of the enterprise. Financial analysis is an essential step toward gaining an in-depth understanding of a business. It helps in doing the financial SWOT analysis of the business.

Financial analysis involves the quantitative evaluation of a firm's past, present, and expected future financial performance and financial conditions.

However, financial analysis is not a mere number crunching exercise. The results need to be interpreted in the light of the overall industry scenario supported by a thorough qualitative analysis to assess the future strategic potential as well as evaluating the past performance.

In this chapter, you will learn the various tools and techniques of financial statement analysis. Read on…

A financial statement is a compilation of financial and accounting data, which is logically and consistently organized according to some generally accepted accounting principles. Its purpose is to convey an understanding of financial aspects of a business firm. It may show the financial position at a particular moment of time, in the form of a balance sheet, or may reveal the financial flow over a given period of time, in the form of an income statement. Financial statements are major tools through which an enterprise presents its financial performance and financial condition to the various interested parties such as shareholders, creditors, bankers, managers, and investors. Majority of the firms include extensive financial statements in their annual reports, which reflect the performance of the company over a period of time.

The Nature of Financial Statement Analysis

Financial statement analysis consists of the application of analytical tools and techniques to financial data to derive meaningful measurements and relationships that are useful for decision-making.

Financial analysis can be used as a preliminary screening tool in the selection of stocks in the secondary market. It can be used as a forecasting tool of future financial performance. It may be used as a process of evaluation and diagnosis of managerial, operating, or other problem areas. Financial analysis does not lessen the need for judgment but rather establishes a sound and systematic basis for its rational application.

Sources of Financial Information

There are various sources of the data needed in the financial analysis. The financial data is provided by the firm itself in its annual report. The annual report comprises directors' report income statement, the balance sheet, and the statement of cash flows, as well as footnotes/schedules to these statements. Besides, information such as the market prices of securities of publicly traded corporations can be found in the financial press and the electronic media daily. The financial press also provides information on stock price indices for industries and for the market as a whole. In addition, other information about the company may be obtained from various sources such as magazines, industry associations, and websites.

Analytical Tools for Financial Analysis

In the analysis of financial statements, a variety of tools are available to the finance manager. The following are the important tools of analysis:

1. Ratio analysis

    i. Comparative analysis
    ii. Du Pont analysis

2. Funds flow analysis (now irrelevant)
3. Cash flow analysis

Ratio Analysis

Ratio analysis is the most widely used tool of financial analysis. A ratio gives the mathematical relationship between two variables. In financial analysis, a particular ratio represents the relationship between two financial variables. One variable is dependent and the other variable is independent. The relationship is user defined. The analysis of a ratio can disclose relationships as well as basis of comparison that reveal trends which cannot be detected by an analysis of the individual components of the ratio. Although the computation of ratios is fairly simple, more important is their interpretation. The ratio analysis technique yields better results if interpretation is done intelligently and skillfully.

Ratios are used by different people for different purposes. For example, shareholders are more interested in knowing about the profitability and the value of the firm, whereas the creditors are interested in liquidity and long-term solvency of the firm. Different ratios are available to cater to the needs of these different user groups.

Considering this, financial ratios can be broadly classified into four groups:

- Liquidity ratios
- Activity ratios
- Profitability ratios
- Leverage ratios

    - Capital structure ratios
    - Coverage ratios

Relationship between the Ratios

Liquidity stands for short-term solvency and solvency stands for long-term liquidity. Liquidity means the ability to pay as and when payments become due. Payments may relate to routine and operational activities and also payments of any term loan becoming due for the day. Solvency would mean the ability to pay off long-term liability. Activity relates to operational side such as debtors, creditors, and inventory, whereas profitability refers to ability to make profit.

In these four categories, liquidity and profitability are inverse to each other. Liquidity demands availability of funds, whereas profitability demands sacrifice of funds as profit is the result of investment.

To understand the computation and interpretation of financial ratios, we shall consider the financial statements of a hypothetical company, Lifeline Pharma. The financial statements of Lifeline Pharma are as given in Table 3.1.

TABLE 3.1
INCOME STATEMENT OF LIFELINE PHARMA

		2015	2014	2013	2012	2011
		₹ in million				
Income						
A.	Sales turnover	522.00	428.82	362.58	311.16	263.88
B.	Other income	27.82	28.40	19.36	12.78	25.62
C.	Total income (A + B)	549.82	457.22	381.94	323.94	289.50
Expenditure						
D.	Raw materials	244.84	194.08	150.10	133.34	132.92
E.	Power and fuel cost	33.44	28.52	26.82	19.92	17.96
F.	Employee cost	52.24	42.42	38.98	32.04	27.00
G.	Other manufacturing expenses	33.68	29.28	27.04	23.20	21.88
H.	Excise duty	61.48	52.94	48.72	44.44	36.20
I.	Selling and administration expenses	31.96	20.30	18.46	14.18	11.70
J.	Miscellaneous expenses	17.06	15.66	10.66	10.22	8.00
K.	Operating profit (C – D – E – F – G –H – I – J)	74.62	74.02	61.16	46.60	33.84
L.	Interest	19.16	21.42	27.14	22.84	15.30
M.	PBDT (K – L)	55.46	52.60	34.02	23.76	18.54
N.	Depreciation	12.98	12.74	9.52	9.12	4.82
O.	Profit before tax (M – N)	42.48	39.86	24.50	16.64	13.72
P.	Tax	10.60	10.00	7.20	6.00	5.40
Q.	Net profit (O – P)	31.88	29.86	17.30	10.64	8.32

Source: Author.

Liquidity Ratios

Liquidity implies a firm's ability to pay obligation debts in the short run. The obligation may be due to routine operations or payment of financial charges. This ability can be measured by the use of liquidity ratios. Short-term liquidity involves the relationship between current assets and current liabilities. If a firm has sufficient net working capital (excess of current assets over current liabilities), it is assumed to have enough liquidity. The two ratios, which directly measure liquidity, are

1. current ratio (CR) and
2. quick ratio (QR).

Current Ratio (CR)

$$\text{The current ratio is defined as: } \frac{\text{Current Assets}}{\text{Current Liabilities}}$$

Current assets include cash, marketable securities, debtors, inventories, loans and advances, and prepaid expenses. Current liabilities include loans and advances taken, trade creditors, accrued expenses, and provisions.

From the balance sheet data given in Table 3.2 for the year 2015, the CR for the 2015 can be calculated as

$$\text{Current ratio} = \frac{92.60 + 99.70 + 3.70 + 46.20}{64.72 + 8.48}$$

$$= \frac{242.20}{73.20} = 3.31$$

As the CR measures the ability of the enterprise to meet its current obligations, a CR of 3.31:1 implies that the firm has current assets that are 3.31 times the current liabilities. Normally, CR of 2:1 is recommended. But because of tough market conditions, CR of 2:1 and above (as in the case of above company) is a sheer luxury. A CR of 1:1 is highly desirable as it will ensure possible liquidity.

Quick Ratio (QR)

QR is defined as

$$= \frac{\text{Quick Assets}}{\text{Current Liabilities}}$$

$$= \frac{\text{Current Assets} - \text{Inventories}}{\text{Current Liabilities}} + \text{Prepaid Expenses}$$

TABLE 3.2
BALANCE SHEET OF LIFELINE PHARMA

		2015	2014	2013	2012	2011
		₹ in million				
Sources of Funds						
A.	Share capital	23.30	23.30	19.26	15.88	15.88
B.	Reserves total	142.72	119.00	74.10	40.28	33.78
C.	Total shareholders' funds (A+B)	166.02	142.30	93.36	56.16	49.66
D.	Secured loans	97.24	82.50	120.90	106.86	61.16
E.	Unsecured loans	51.40	38.68	21.02	23.00	29.00
F.	Total debt (D+E)	148.64	121.18	141.92	129.86	90.16
G.	Total liabilities (C+F)	314.66	263.48	235.28	186.02	139.82
Application of Funds						
H.	Gross block	220.10	207.78	181.80	150.54	113.62
I.	Less: Accumulative depreciation	104.04	100.04	88.92	80.52	73.76
J.	Net block (H–I)	116.06	107.74	92.88	70.02	39.86
K.	Capital work-in-progress	13.76	11.02	9.54	7.52	16.00
L.	Investments	13.26	6.06	5.78	5.78	5.30
M.	Current assets, loans, & advances (N+O+P+Q)					
N.	Inventories	92.60	80.96	69.74	71.06	82.40
O.	Sundry debtors	99.70	74.60	75.50	61.06	63.72
P.	Cash and bank balances	3.70	3.24	2.20	3.24	2.52
Q.	Loans and advances	46.20	29.76	22.32	20.46	13.80
R.	Less: Current liabilities & Provision (S+T)					
S.	Current liabilities	64.72	43.06	38.34	49.26	79.98
T.	Provision	8.48	6.84	4.34	3.86	3.80
U.	Net current assets (M–R)	169.80	138.66	127.08	102.70	78.66
V.	Misc. expenses not written off	2.58	0.00	0.00	0.00	0.00
X.	Total assets (J+K+L+U+V)	314.66	263.48	235.28	186.02	139.82

Source: Author.

The QR is a more stringent measure of liquidity because inventories, which are least liquid of current assets, are excluded from the ratio. The QR is so named because it measures the abilities of a firm to pay its liabilities without relying on the sale and recovery of its inventories.

QR of Lifeline Pharma for the year 2015 is calculated as

$$\text{Quick ratio} = \frac{242.20 - 92.60}{73.20} = 2.04$$

The QR for the industry (Pharmaceuticals) is 2.26. Normally, a QR of 0.75:1 is highly advisable for two reasons: one, if ₹1 is to be paid, and 75p is available. It is more than satisfying. Two, all payments scheduled for the day do not take place as scheduled. Also, all payments scheduled for the day do not take place as scheduled.

Limitations of the Liquidity Ratios

The CR is a static concept. It tells us about the resources that are available at a given point of time to meet the current obligations. The ratio suffers from the following limitations:

1. Measuring and predicting the future fund flows.
2. Measuring the adequacy of future fund inflows in relation to outflows.

Liquidity depends on the availability of adequate cash in the present as well as future to pay off the obligations. However, the existing funds do not give any indication about the future funds. Yet it is the future flows that are to be examined to assess the liquidity. These flows depend on various factors such as sales, cash, costs and expenses, profits, and changes in business conditions that are not considered in the calculation of this ratio.

Activity Ratios

Activity ratios indicate about the utilization of assets to generate sales. Efficient utilization of assets depends on various managerial decisions relating to current as well as fixed assets. Two important activity ratios that measure the liquidity of a firm are receivables, turnover ratios, and inventory turnover ratios (ITRs).

Receivables Turnover Ratios

Two ratios are used to measure the liquidity of a firm's account receivables. They are

1. accounts receivables turnover (ART) ratio and
2. average collection period (ACP).

Accounts Receivables Turnover Ratio (ART)

$$= \frac{\text{Net credit sales}}{\text{Average accounts receivable}}$$

The average accounts receivable is obtained by adding the beginning receivables of the period and the ending receivable, and dividing the sum by two. The sales figure in the numerator is only credit sales. Sometimes, the publicly available information on the firm may not give us the credit sales details; in that case, we have to assume that cash sales are insignificant and all sales are credit sales.

Higher the receivables turnover ratio, greater is the liquidity of the firm. However, care should be taken to see that to project higher receivables turnover ratio, the firm does follow a strict credit policy.

The accounts receivables position of the Lifeline Pharma for two years is as follows:

	2015	2014
Sundry debtors more than 6 months	8.38	2.62
Other debtors	91.32	71.99
Total debtors	99.70	74.60

$$\text{Average accounts receivables} = (99.70 + 74.60)/2$$
$$= 87.15$$
$$\text{Average receivables turnover} = 522/87.15$$
$$= 5.99 \cong 6 \, (\text{Approx.})$$

ART indicates how many times on an average the receivables are generated and collected during the year. In our case, the average receivables turnover ratio of 6 indicates that on an average receivables are rotated 6 times during the year. When we compare this with the industry ART of 5.16 times, we can say that the firm's liquidity of accounts receivables is on average 16.28% more than the industry. Higher the turnover ratio, lower is the credit period as indicated by ACP.

Average Collection Period (ACP)

ACP measures the speed of collections from receivables turnover ratio, but we cannot directly compare it with the terms of trade usually quoted by the firm. For example, the firm may be having a policy of giving certain percent of discount if the debtor pays in a certain period of time. Such comparison is best made by converting the turnover into days of sales tied up in receivables.

The ratio that gives the above comparison is ACP, which is defined as the number of days it takes to collect outstanding accounts receivables. It can be obtained by dividing 360 by the average receivables turnover ratio calculated above.

$$\text{Average collection period} = \frac{360}{\text{Average accounts receivables/turnover}}$$
$$= \frac{\text{Average accounts receivable}}{\text{Average daily sales}}$$

Higher the ACP, shorter is the collection period, and it is good for the organization.

For Lifeline Pharma, assuming that there is only one sundry debtor, the ACP is equal to 60 days (360/6). If the firm has a credit policy of giving substantial discounts, and if the receivables are collected within 30 days, the debtor will not be able to avail the discounts. If we compare the above with the industry figure (i.e., 360/5.16 = 69.76 days), the firm has an above-average collection period.

The ART ratio or collection periods can be compared to industry averages or to the credit terms granted by the firm to find out whether customers are paying on time. If the terms, for example, say the ACP is 30 days and the realized ACP is 60 days, it could reflect the following:

1. Collection department is lax in its working.
2. In spite of adequate collection efforts, there is some difficulty in obtaining prompt payments.
3. Customers are facing financial problems.

In such cases, suitable remedial action has to be taken by the finance manager.

Inventory Turnover Ratio (ITR)

The liquidity of a firm's inventory may be calculated by dividing the cost of goods sold by the firm's inventory. The inventory turnover, or stock turnover, measures how fast the inventory is moving through the firm and generating sales. Inventory turnover can be defined as

$$\text{Inventory turnover} = \frac{\text{Cost of goods sold}}{\text{Average inventory}}$$

Higher the ratio, greater is the efficiency of inventory management.
The presence of inventory involves two risks:

1. Running out of stock due to low inventory (high turnover).
2. Excessive carrying charges because of high inventory (low turnover).

A balance has to be struck between running out of goods to sell and investing in excessive inventory. While analyzing the ITR, the current turnover must be compared to previous periods or to some industry norms before it is designated as high, low, or normal. The nature of the business should also be considered in analyzing the appropriateness of the size and turnover of the inventory. For example, a manufacturing firm that has to import its key raw materials is justified in keeping high inventory of raw materials if it finds that its base currency has been depreciating against the exporting country's currency consistently and/or the lead time is significantly long.

In the case of Lifeline Pharma, the inventory turnover can be calculated as follows. First for getting the cost of goods sold, we have to add all the expenses in the income statement including depreciation charges and excluding interest expenses. Average inventory can be obtained by adding the closing inventory and the opening inventory and dividing them by two.

$$\text{Inventory turnover} = \frac{488.18}{92.60 + 80.96/2} = 5.63$$

The average industry inventory turnover is 4.3. Thus, the ITR of Lifeline Pharma is fairly high (Table 3.3).

TABLE 3.3
COMPARISON OF INVENTORY TURNOVER RATIO

Inventory Turnover Ratio	2015	2014	2013	2012
Lifeline Pharma Ltd	5.63	5.25	4.69	3.10
Pharma industry	4.31	4.40	4.28	3.87

Source: Author.

In Table 3.4, it can be noticed that the Lifeline Pharma's CR and QR are just below the average industry figures, and receivables turnover ratios are above the industry averages to an extent. Inventory turnover is in a better position compared to the industry which is concluded in the overall analysis of inventory turnover in the respective section.

TABLE 3.4
OVERALL LIQUIDITY POSITION

Ratios	Definition	Lifeline Pharma Ltd	Pharmaceutical Industry
Liquidity or CR	$\dfrac{\text{Current Assets}}{\text{Current Liabilities}}$	3.31	3.53
QR	$\dfrac{\text{Current Assets} - \text{Inventories}}{\text{Current Liabilities}}$	2.04	2.26
ART Ratio	$\dfrac{\text{Net credit sales}}{\text{Averager accounts receivable}}$	5.99	5.16
Average collection period	$\dfrac{360}{\text{Average accounts receivables/turnover}}$	60	70
Inventory turnover	$\dfrac{\text{Cost of goods sold}}{\text{Average Inventory}}$	5.63	4.31

Source: Author.

In conclusion, the liquidity position of the Lifeline Pharma Ltd can be said to be above-average.

Test Yourself

1. How can you correlate activity ratios with liquidity ratios to assess the short-term solvency position of a firm?
2. What is the cost of idle stock?
3. Very high stock turnover ratio represents slow moving stock. Comment.

Profitability Ratios

Profitability ratios measure the efficiency of the firm's activities and its ability to generate profits. Profitability is the ability to make profit. It depends on capacity and activity. Capacity is determined by investment in fixed assets, whereas activity measures the efficiency with which these assets are being used. Profitability ratios are of the following types:

Profits to Sales Ratio

These ratios determine whether the firm is able to generate adequate profit on each unit of sales. If sales lack a sufficient margin of profit, it is difficult for the firm to cover its fixed-charges on debt and to earn a profit for the shareholders. Two popular ratios in this category are gross profit margin (GPM) and net profit margin (NPM).

Profits to Assets Ratio

These ratios compare the profit generated by the firm to the capital invested by the shareholders and creditors. If the firm cannot produce a satisfactory profit on its asset base, it might be an indication of misuse of assets. They are also referred to as rate of return ratios, and the popular ratios in this category are asset turnover ratio (ATR), earning power, and return on equity (ROE).

Return Ratio

Return ratios help the shareholders to analyze their present and future investment in a firm. Shareholders are interested in knowing how the value of their holdings is affected by certain variables. These ratios compare the investment value with factors such as debt, earnings, dividends, and the stock's market price.

Profit to Sales Ratios

Gross Profit Margin (GPM)

The GPM ratio is defined as

$$= \frac{\text{Gross Profit}}{\text{Net Sales}}$$

where Net sales = Sales − Excise duty + Goods sent as sample.

This ratio shows the profits to sales after the direct costs are deducted. It may be used as an indicator of the efficiency of operation. GPM for Lifeline Pharma for the year 2015 is calculated as

$$= \frac{33.82}{460.52} = 7.34\%$$

GPM for industry is 10.60%, which is more than GPM of Lifeline Pharma.

Net Profit Margin (NPM)

The NPM ratio is defined as

$$= \frac{\text{Net Profit}}{\text{Net Sales}}$$

This ratio shows the earnings left for shareholders (both equity and preference) as a percentage of net sales. It measures the overall efficiency of production, administration, selling, financing, pricing, and tax management. Jointly considered, the GPM and NPM ratios provide information about the sources of business efficiency or inefficiency.

$$\text{NPM for Lifeline Pharma} = \frac{31.88}{460.54}$$
$$= 6.92\%$$
$$\text{NPM for Pharma Industry} = 6.39\%$$

In comparison with the industry NPM, Lifeline's NPM is just above the average percentage figure. Had this been below the industry average, it would have indicated some mismanagement in the post-production areas such as sales and distribution.

Profit to Assets Ratios

Asset Turnover Ratio (ATR)

The ability to generate a large volume of sales on a small asset base is an important part of the firm's profit picture. Idle or improperly used assets increase the firm's need for costly finances and the expenses for maintenance and upkeep. By achieving a high asset turnover, a firm reduces costs and increases the profit.

ATR is defined as

$$= \frac{\text{Sales}}{\text{Average assets}}$$

Average assets are calculated by adding the opening stock of assets and closing stock of assets of the present year.

Asset turnover for Lifeline Pharma

$$= \frac{522}{(314.66\ 263.48)/2} = 1.81$$

Industry asset turnover is 1.15. An ATR of 1.81 indicates that the firm with an asset base of 1 unit could produce 1.81 units of sales. This is healthy both in absolute terms and in comparison with the industry as the turnover of the industry is only 1.15.

Earning Power

Earning power is a measure of operating profitability on the deployment of assets. It is defined as

$$\frac{\text{Earnings before interest and taxes}}{\text{Average total assets}}$$

The earning power is a measure of the operating business performance which is not affected by interest charges and tax payments. As it does not consider the effects of financial structure and tax rate, it is well-suited for interfirm comparisons.

$$\text{Lifeline Pharma's earning power} = \frac{61.64}{289.07}$$
$$= 0.2132$$
$$= 21.32\%$$

Interfirm comparisons earning power percentages

Company	2015 Earning Power (%)
Lifeline Pharma	21.32
Argus Pharma	18.76
Marcus Pharma	19.20
Zodiac Pharma	15.17
Sudershan Pharma	18.23
Industry Pharma	18.54

From the above table, we can conclude that Lifeline Pharma tops the industry with a percentage of 21.32%, whereas the average is only 18.54%. Lifeline Pharma is operationally very efficient in comparison to all the players in the industry.

Return on Equity

ROE is an important profit indicator to shareholders of the firm. It is calculated as

$$\text{ROE} = \frac{\text{PAT}}{\text{Average Shareholders Fund}}$$

ROE measures the profitability of equity funds invested in the firm. It is regarded as a very important measure because it reflects the productivity of capital employed in the firm. It is influenced by several factors such as earning power, debt-equity ratio, average cost of debt funds, and tax rate.

$$\text{ROE for Lifeline Pharma} = \frac{31.88}{154.86} = 20.68\%$$

ROE for the industry is 13.18%. The firm's healthiness in this respect can also be easily seen from the differences in returns of equity. Lifeline Pharma is giving 20.68% return to the equity holders, whereas the industry is giving only 13.18%. Thus, we can conclude that Lifeline Pharma has employed its resources productively.

Overall Profitability Analysis

Lifeline Pharma's profitability ratios are summarized in the following table against the industry.

Ratios	Lifeline Pharma Ltd	Pharmaceutical Industry
Gross profit margin	7.34%	10.60%
Net profit margin	6.92%	6.39%
Asset turnover	1.81	1.75
Return on equity	20.68%	13.80%
Earning power	21.32%	14.12%

From the above table, it is clear that Lifeline Pharma is able to generate profits in relation to sales on an average scale, but in respect of efficient application of assets, it performs well above the average. This indicates that some remedial measures have to be taken from the sales' point of view.

Return Ratios

Earnings Ratios

Earnings Per Share (EPS)

Shareholders are concerned about the earnings of the firm. These earnings are expressed on a per share basis, which is in short called EPS. EPS is calculated by dividing the net income by the number of shares outstanding. Mathematically, it is calculated as follows:
EPS

$$\frac{\text{Net income (PAT)}}{\text{Number of outstanding shares}}$$

EPS of Lifeline Pharma for the year 2011 can be calculated as follows:

$$\text{EPS} = \frac{31.88}{2.88} = 13.68$$

Price–Earnings Ratio

The price–earnings ratio (also P/E multiple) is calculated by taking the market price of the stock and dividing it by EPS.

$$\text{Price-earnings multiple} = \frac{\text{Market price of the share}}{\text{Earnings per share}}$$

This ratio gives the relationship between the market price of the stock and its earnings by revealing how earnings affect the market price of the firm's stock. If a stock has a low P/E multiple, for example 3, it may be considered as an undervalued stock. If the ratio is 20, it may be viewed as overvalued. It is the most popular financial ratio in the stock market for secondary market investors. The P/E ratio method is useful as long as the firm is a viable business entity, and its real value is reflected in its profits (Table 3.5).

TABLE 3.5
DEPICTION OF P/E MULTIPLES

	2015	2014	2013	2012	2011
Share price	425	450	130	240	80
EPS	13.68	12.81	8.98	6.70	5.24
P/E	31.06	35.12	14.47	35.82	15.26

Source: Author.

The P/E multiples for Lifeline Pharma are calculated as follows:

The P/E ratio helps to determine the expected market value of a stock. For example, one firm A may be having a P/E of 6 and another firm B of 10. If we assume the average industry P/E and EPS as ₹8 and ₹4, respectively, and earning per shares of both the firms as ₹3, we will get the following results:

$$\text{Market value of industry} = 8 \times 4 = 32$$

$$\text{Market value of firm A} = 6 \times 3 = 18$$

$$\text{Market value of firm B} = 10 \times 3 = 30$$

The Capitalization Rate

$$\text{Capitalization rate} = \frac{\text{Earning per share}}{\text{Market price of the share}}$$

The P/E ratio also may be used to calculate the rate of return that investors expect before they purchase a stock. The reciprocal of the P/E ratio (i.e., market price/EPS) gives this return. For example, if a stock has ₹15 EPS and sells for ₹100, the marketplace expects a return of 15/100, that is, 15%. This is called the stock's **capitalization rate**. A 15% capitalization implies that the firm is required to earn 15% on the common stock value. If the investors require less than 15% return, they will pay more for the stock and the capitalization rate would drop.

	2015	2014	2013	2012	2011
Capitalization rate	0.032	0.028	0.069	0.0279	0.0655

For Lifeline Pharma, rates are very low because of very high prices in comparison to EPS.

Dividend Ratios

The common stockholder is very much concerned about the firm's policy regarding the payment of cash dividends. If the firm is not paying enough dividends, the stock may not be attractive to those who are interested in the current income from their investment in the company. If the firm is paying excessive dividends, it may not be retaining adequate funds to finance future growth. So depending on the shareholder's aspirations, a firm must formulate its dividend policy in a balanced way.

The firm must be liquid and profitable to pay consistent and adequate dividends. Without profits, the firm will not have sufficient resources to give dividends; without liquidity, the firm cannot get cash to pay the dividends. In the above respects, two dividend ratios are important. They are dividend payout ratio and dividend yield ratio.

Dividend Payout Ratio

This is the ratio of dividend per share (DPS) to EPS. It indicates what percentage of total earnings is paid to the shareholders. The percentage of the earnings that is not paid out (1 – dividend payout) is retained for the firm's future needs. There are well-laid-out rules in Indian Companies Act 1956 regarding dividend declaration and payment. If the firm is in need of funds, then it may cut the dividends in relation to earnings, and however, if the firm finds that it lacks opportunities to use the funds generated, it might increase the dividends. But in both the cases, consistency of dividend payment is important to the shareholders.

Dividend Yield

This is the ratio of DPS to market price of the share.

$$\text{Dividend yield} = \frac{\text{Market price of the share}}{\text{Dividend per share}}$$

This ratio gives the current ROI. This is mainly of interest to the investors who are desirous of getting income from dividends. No dividend yield exists for firms that do not declare dividends.

Dividend payout and yield for Lifeline Pharma are summarized in Table 3.6.

TABLE 3.6
DIVIDEND PAY OUT AND YIELD RATIO

Ratio	2015	2014	2013	2012	2011
DPS	3.50	2.84	2.18	2.40	2.20
EPS	13.68	12.81	8.98	6.70	5.24
Market price	425	450	130	240	80
Dividend payout	0.26	0.22	0.24	0.36	0.42
Dividend yield	0.008	0.006	0.017	0.010	0.0275
P/E	31.06	35.12	14.47	35.82	15.26

Source: Author.

Test Yourself

1. What are the implications of high GPM ratio?
2. Collect the EPS and P/E ratio data of select companies from *The Economic Times.* Give your comments on the same.

Leverage Ratios

When we extend the analysis to the long-term solvency of a firm, we have two types of leverage ratios. They are structural ratios and coverage ratios. Structural ratios are based on the proportions of debt and equity on the capital structure of the firm, whereas coverage ratios are derived from the relationship between debts servicing commitments and sources of funds for meeting these obligations.

Capital Structure Ratios

Important capital structure ratios are

- debt-equity ratio and
- debt-assets ratio.

Debt–Equity Ratio

The debt-equity ratio, which indicates the relative contributions of creditors and owners, can be defined as

$$\frac{\text{Debt}}{\text{Asset}}$$

The components in debt to equity ratio will vary depending on the nature of the business and the patterns of cash flows. Normally, the debt component includes all liabilities including current liabilities and the equity component consists of net worth and preference capital. It includes only the preference shares not redeemable in one year. Sometimes, it is calculated as the ratio of long-term debt (total debt–current liabilities) to equity. There is nothing wrong in doing so, but what is important is that consistency is followed when comparisons are made.

For Lifeline Pharma, the debt-equity ratio is

$$= 221.84/166.02 = 1.33$$

The debt-equity ratio of 1.33 implies that the debt portion is more than equity. The debt-equity ratio of the pharma industry on average is 1.42. In the manufacturing and other industries, a debt-equity ratio of 1.5:1 is considered to be healthy. By normal standards and also the industry's, the debt-equity ratio is within limits. In the heavy engineering industry, petroleum industry, and infrastructure industry, the ratio may even go more than 4:1 as the capital outlays required are very high.

In general, the lower the debt-equity ratio, the higher the degree of protection felt by the creditors. One of the limitations of the above ratio is that the computation of the ratios is based on book value, as it is sometimes useful to calculate these ratios using market values.

The debt-equity ratio indicates the relative proportions of capital contribution by creditors and shareholders. It is used as a screening device in the financial analysis.

The contemporary financial practices stress on zero debt or unlevered structure because of continuous fall in the interest rate structure. Corporates are busy in restructuring capital structure to make it appropriate.

Debt–Asset Ratio

The above ratio measures the extent to which borrowed funds support the firm's assets. It is defined as

$$\frac{\text{Debt}}{\text{Asset}}$$

The composition of debt portion is same as in the debt-equity ratio.

The denominator in the ratio is total of all assets as indicated in the balance sheet. The type of assets an organization employs in its operations should determine to some extent the sources of funds used to finance them. It is usually held that fixed and other long-term assets should not be financed by means of short-term loans. In fact, the most appropriate source of funds for investment in such kind of assets is equity capital, though financially sound organizations may go for debt finance.

Lifeline Pharma's debt-asset ratio for the 2015 is

$$= 221.84/314.66 = 0.70$$

A debt-asset ratio of 0.70 implies that 70% of the total assets are financed from debt sources. When we compare this with the industry average debt-asset ratio of (0.69), we find that the firm has leverage comparable to the industry.

Coverage Ratios

Coverage ratios give the relationship between the financial charges of a firm and its ability to service them. Important coverage ratios are interest coverage ratio, fixed-charges coverage ratio, and debt service coverage ratio (DSCR).

Interest Coverage Ratio

One measure of a firm's ability to handle financial burdens is the interest coverage ratio. This ratio tells us how many times the firm can cover or meet the interest payments associated with debt.

$$\text{Interest coverage ratio} = \frac{\text{EBIT}}{\text{Interest expense}}$$

For Lifeline Pharma, for the year 2015, it is equal to

$$61.64/19.16 = 3.22$$

The greater the interest coverage ratio, the higher is the ability of the firm to pay its interest expense.

Fixed Charges Coverage Ratio

Interest coverage ratio considers the coverage of interest of pure debt only. Fixed charges coverage ratio measures debt servicing ability comprehensively because it considers all the interest, principal repayment obligations, lease payments, and preference dividends. This ratio shows how many times the pretax operating income covers all fixed financing charges.

It is defined as

$$\frac{\text{Earnings before depreciation, debt interest and lease rentals and taxes}}{\text{Debt interest Lease rentals} + \dfrac{\text{Loan repayment installment}}{(1 - \text{tax rate})} + \dfrac{\text{Preference dividends}}{(1 - \text{tax rate})}}$$

While calculating this ratio, fixed charges that are not tax deductible must be tax adjusted. This is done by increasing them by an amount equivalent to the sum that would be required to obtain an after-tax income sufficient to cover such fixed charges. In the above ratio, preference-stock dividend requirement is one example of such nontax-deductible fixed charges. To get the gross amount of preference dividends, it has to be divided by the factor $(1 - \text{tax rate})$. For Lifeline Pharma, the fixed charges coverage ratio is calculated for the year 2015 as follows:

$$24.62/(19.16 + 14.74/0.75) = 1.92$$

For Lifeline Pharma, there are no lease rental payments and preference dividend payments. The loan repayment has been assumed to be ₹14.74 crore. The fixed charges coverage ratio of 1.92 indicates that its pretax operating income is 1.92 times of all fixed financial obligations.

Debt Service Coverage Ratio (DSCR)

Normally used by term-lending financial institutions in India, the DSCR, which is a posttax coverage ratio, is defined as

$$DSCR = \frac{\text{Interest on term loan Repayment of the term loan}}{\text{PAT Depreciation Other non cashvcharges} + \text{Interest on term loan}}$$

For Lifeline Pharma, the DSCR for the year 2015 is

$$(31.88 + 12.98 + 19.16) / (19.16 + 14.74) = 1.89$$

A DSCR of 1.89 indicates that the firm has posttax earnings that are 1.89 times the total obligations (interest and loan repayment) in the particular year to the financial institution.

Test Yourself

1. What is the ideal debt–equity ratio for manufacturing sector concern?

Comparative Analysis

We have seen that to find out whether ratios are within the limits or not, they were compared across the industry or against predetermined standards. To get a more meaningful picture of the position of the firm, sometimes it is useful to compare its financial information across many players in the industry (cross-sectional analysis) or to compare over a period of time (time-series analysis).

The comparison of financial statements is accomplished by taking the individual items of different financial statements and reviewing the changes that have occurred from year-to-year and over the years.

Different types of comparative analysis are

1. cross-sectional analysis,
2. time-series analysis, and

    i. year-to-year change
    ii. index analysis

3. common-size analysis.

Cross-sectional Analysis

To assess whether the financial ratios are within the limits, they are compared with the industry averages or with the ratios of an equivalent competitor under normal business conditions if an organized industry is absent. This is called cross-sectional analysis in which industry averages or standard player's averages are used as benchmarks.

In Table 3.7 is given the cross-sectional analysis of Lifeline Pharma against the industry and Argus Pharma, a good competitor of Lifeline Pharma in the pharmaceutical industry.

TABLE 3.7

COMPARISON OF VARIOUS RATIOS OF LIFELINE PHARMA AND ARGUS PHARMA

Ratios	Definition	Lifeline Pharma Ltd	Argus Pharma	Pharmaceutical Industry
Liquidity				
Current ratio	$\dfrac{\text{Currents Assets-Inventories}}{\text{Current Liabilities}}$	3.31	3.63	3.53
Quick ratio	$\dfrac{\text{Current Assets-Inventories}}{\text{Current Liabilities}}$	2.04	2.18	2.26
Inventory turnover	$\dfrac{\text{Cost of goods sold}}{\text{Average Inventory}}$	5.63	3.95	4.61
Leverage				
Debt-equity ratio	$\dfrac{\text{Total Debt}}{\text{Net Worth}}$	1.33	0.71	1.424
Debt-asset ratio	$\dfrac{\text{Total Debt}}{\text{Net Assets}}$	0.70	0.42	0.69
Interest coverage ratio	$\dfrac{\text{EBIT}}{\text{Interest}}$	3.22	1.81	2.00
Profitability gross margin (%)	$\dfrac{\text{Gross Profit}}{\text{Total Sales}}$	7.34	10.15	10.60
Net profit margin (%)	$\dfrac{\text{Net Profit}}{\text{Total Sales}}$	6.92	6.14	6.39
Return on equity (%)	$\dfrac{\text{Net Income}}{\text{Average Equity}}$	20.68	10.21	13.18
Earning power (%)	$\dfrac{\text{EBIT}}{\text{Average Total Assets}}$	21.32	18.76	18.54
Assets turnover	$\dfrac{\text{Sales}}{\text{Average Assets}}$	1.81	0.71	1.25

Source: Author.

We have seen in our earlier analysis that Lifeline Pharma Ltd is a top player in the industry. On comparison with Argus Pharma, it can be seen that Argus Pharma has better liquidity as per CR and QR. Although Argus has low debt–equity and debt–asset ratios, it has low coverage because of low earning before interest and tax (EBIT). In profitability ratios, there is not much difference in GPM and NPM ratios, but in returns ratios, Lifeline Pharma is far ahead of Argus Pharma.

Time-series Analysis

Year-to-Year Change

A comparison of financial statements over two to three years can be undertaken by computing the year-to-year change in absolute amounts and in terms of percentage changes.

Trends of liquidity and leverage ratios of Lifeline Pharma can be illustrated in Table 3.8.

TABLE 3.8

COMPARISON OF LIQUIDITY AND LEVERAGE RATIOS (AGRUS PHARMA)

Year	2015	2014	2013	2012	2011
Current ratio	3.31	3.78	3.98	2.93	1.94
Quick ratio	2.04	2.16	2.34	1.60	0.96
Debt to equity ratio	1.33	1.20	1.98	3.26	3.50
Interest coverage ratio	3.22	2.86	1.90	1.73	1.90

Source: Author.

Analysis of Table 3.8 reveals the following facts:

1. CR increased over a period of time. QR also increased steadily up to 2013 but slightly decreased in the next two years. That is because of initial decrease in the inventory levels up to 2013, and again increase in the inventory levels up to 2015 (can be observed from the balance sheet given in the beginning). One has to look into the causes of increase in the inventory levels that made the QR decrease. Apart from that, the overall liquidity has improved.
2. Debt–equity ratio has declined over a period of time and the interest coverage ratio increased, which are positive signs.

Index Number Trend Series

When a comparison of financial statements covering more than two to three years is undertaken, the year-to-year method of comparison may become too cumbersome. In such situations, the best method is the index number time-series method. The computation of a series of index numbers requires the choice of a base year that will, for all items, have an index amount of 100. As such a base year represents a frame of reference for all comparisons, we should choose a year that is as normal as possible from the point of view of business conditions.

This method is particularly useful when we want to see how all the variables of a particular statement are changing over a longer period of time.

Common-size Analysis

In common-size analysis, we find out the proportion that a single item represents a total group or subgroup. In a balance sheet, the assets as well as the liabilities and capital are each expressed as 100%, and each item in these categories is expressed as a percentage of the respective totals. Similarly, in the income statement, net sales are set at 100% and every other item in the statement is expressed as a percentage of net sales.

Common-size statements are very well suited to intercompany comparison because the financial statements of a variety of companies can be recast into the uniform common-size format regardless of the size of individual accounts. Comparison of the common-size statements of companies within an industry can help the finance manager in focusing his attention to variations in account structure or distribution.

The common-size balance sheets of Lifeline Pharma and Argus Pharma for the year 2011 are given in Table 3.9.

TABLE 3.9

COMMON SIZE BALANCE SHEET OF LIFELINE AND ARGUS PHARMA

	2015 Lifeline Pharma	2014 Atul Products
Liabilities		
Equity capital	7.40	9.69
Preference capital	0.00	0.00
Reserves (excl. revaluation reserves)	45.36	49.90
Revaluation reserves	0.00	0.00
Shareholders' funds	52.76	59.59
Secured loans	30.90	35.18
Unsecured loans	16.34	523
Loan funds	47.24	40.41
Total funds Used	100.00	100.00
Assets		
Gross block	69.95	83.03
Accumulated depreciation	33.06	34.53
Net block	36.88	48.50
CWIP	4.37	3.27
Investments	4.21	3.89
Inventory (total)	29.43	23.85
Sundry debtors	31.68	17.96
Cash & bank balances	1.18	0.77
Loans, advances & deposits	14.68	17.44

	2015 Lifeline Pharma	2014 Atul Products
Total current assets	76.97	59.92
Sundry creditors	20.57	13.68
Other current liabilities & provisions	2.69	2.87
Total current liabilities	23.26	16.55
Net current assets (current assets-liabilities)	53.71	43.37
Misc. Exp. not w/o	0.82	0.88
Total Assets	**100**	**100**

Source: Author.

- An analysis of Table 3.9 reveals the following:

1. Lifeline Pharma has used more loan funds than Argus Pharma, which implies higher debt-equity ratio. Keeping all the other factors constant, in a tight credit market, Argus Pharma will be able to get more loans than Lifeline Pharma's because of lower debt-equity ratio.
2. Lifeline pharma also has higher proportion of working capital compared to Argus Pharma. In busy periods, this may be useful, but in slack period, it works against the company. Similarly, each and every variable may be compared depending on the information requirements.

Du Pont Analysis

The Du Pont Company of the USA developed a system of financial analysis, which has got good recognition and acceptance. In the Du Pont System, return ratios are analyzed in terms of profit margin and turnover ratios.

Figure 3.1 shows the Du Pont chart as applied to Lifeline Pharma Limited for the year 2011.

The left-hand side of the Du Pont chart gives the details of the NPM ratio. This side is examined to find out whether cost reduction may improve the NPM. In addition, comparative common-size analysis is used to understand where cost control efforts should be directed. From the right-hand side of the Du Pont chart, we get the details of total assets turnover ratio. Further, if we study the turnover ratios (inventory turnover, fixed assets turnover, etc.), an insight can be gained into asset utilization efficiencies.

We can extend the basic Du Pont analysis to analyze the determinants of ROE. But the ROE ratios require an adjustment.

We can get the basic Du Pont equation for ROE as

$$\frac{\text{Net Profit}}{\text{Sales}} \times \frac{\text{Sales}}{\text{Average Assets}} \times \frac{\text{Average Assets}}{\text{Average Equity}}$$

The third component of the equation is called equity multiplier. The equity multiplier can be restated in terms of the total debt to assets ratio as follows:

FIGURE 3.1
DU PONT CHART

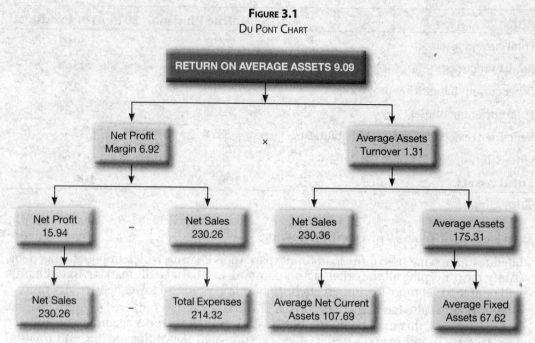

Source: Author.

$$\text{Equity multiplier} = \frac{\text{Average Assets}}{\text{Average Equity}}$$

$$= \frac{\text{Average Assets}}{\text{Average Assets} - \text{Average Debt}}$$

$$= \frac{1}{1 - (\text{Average Debt} / \text{Average Assets})}$$

$$= \frac{1}{\text{Debt to Assets Ratio}}$$

This way, we can break down each return ratio into its margin and turnover components.

Test Yourself

1. Explain the need of comparative analysis.
2. What is Du Pont analysis?
3. Which ratios will you consider the most important while assessing the interest payment capacity of a firm?

Limitations of Ratios

Analysis of financial statements using ratios can be very helpful in understanding a company's financial performance and condition. Yet, there are certain limitations.

Multiple Ratios

Many ratios are available for evaluating the financial performance, and financial analysts may use different methods for calculating the same ratios. This calls for judiciously selecting the ratios that are most appropriate and revealing for the purposes of the analysis.

Development of Benchmarks

Many companies have operations spread across a number of industries. As no other company may have a presence in the same industries, that too in the same proportion, development of a benchmark becomes a problem. Even when the company is not a diversified one, figures for the various firms are needed in addition to the industry average to draw a meaningful conclusion.

Window Dressing

Firms may window-dress the financial statements to show a rosy picture. In such a case, the whole exercise of analyzing the statements becomes useless. To draw some meaningful results out of the analysis, the average figures over a period of time should be looked into.

Price-level Changes

Financial statements do not take into account changes in price levels. Analysis of such statements may not give a true picture of the state of affairs.

Differences in Accounting Policies

Different companies may follow different accounting policies in respect of depreciation, stock valuation, and so on. Comparison between the ratios of two firms following different policies may not give the true result.

Interpretation of Results

A problem may arise on two accounts: interpretation of ratio on its own and interpretation of all the ratios taken together. It is difficult to decide the optimum level of a ratio, in spite of the presence of industry averages. For example, it is difficult to say whether a high CR shows a good liquidity position or an unnecessarily high level of inventories. Second, some ratios may be in favor of a company, while some others may be against it. In such a case, it may be difficult to form an overall opinion about the company.

Correlation among Ratios

There may be a high degree of correlation among the various ratios calculated, due to the presence of some common factor. This may make interpretation of all the ratios confusing. Hence, it becomes essential to choose a few ratios that can convey the required information.

Test Yourself

1. Industry ratios are the best way to judge the performance of a company. Comment.

Funds Flow Analysis

A balance sheet is a "snap shot" view of the financial condition of a business, whereas an income statement is a "motion picture" view of the changes in the owners' equity. However, "retained earnings" is only one of the many balance sheet items. Over a period of time, practically every item in the balance sheet undergoes a change. For instance, additional capital may be brought in, loans may be raised or retired, fixed assets acquired or disposed off, inventories built up or consumed, and so on. Also, although a business may show considerable profits in a particular year, there may be practically no cash in the business to meet the operational requirements. Or else, despite borrowing a considerable amount of working capital, the management may still find it difficult to support their inventory. Why does this happen? How does this happen? These are the questions, which are not answered by either the balance sheet or the income statement. The financial statement, which attempts to answer these questions, is the Statement of Changes in Financial Position (SCFP), which is also popularly known as the funds flow statement (FFS). **Although FFS has become insignificant and irrelevant, it may be read to understand cash flows statement better.**

Funds Flow Statement (FFS)

An FFS is a statement that tells us about the various sources from which funds were raised and the application of these funds. An FFS is different from a balance sheet, in that the former captures the movements in funds, whereas the latter merely presents a static picture of the sources and uses of funds. An FFS enables us to see how the business financed its fixed assets, built up the inventory and discharged its liabilities, paid its dividends and taxes, and so on. Similarly, it enables us to see how the business managed to meet the required capital or revenue expenditure. Was it financed by raising additional capital or through loans from the public?

Preparation of a Funds Flow Statement (FFS)

A simple FFS for a period may be prepared merely by finding out the difference between the corresponding balance sheet items at the beginning and the end of the period. In such a statement, all increases in liabilities and decreases in assets are shown as sources of funds and all decreases in liabilities and increases in assets are shown as applications of funds. Thus, for such an FFS, one needs the opening and closing balance sheets of the period for which the statement is to be prepared. However, a more sophisticated FFS can be prepared with the help of the two balance sheets (opening and closing) and the profit and loss statement of the intervening period. Such an FFS defines funds as "total resources."

An FFS may also be prepared so as to explain only the changes in the working capital (current assets – current liabilities) during a particular time period. Alternatively, it may be prepared to explain the changes in the cash position during the period.

Thus, an FFS can be prepared in three ways, namely

1. total resources basis,
2. working capital basis, and
3. cash basis.

Total Resources Basis

The sources and uses of funds can be summarized as follows:

Sources	Uses
1. Operations	1. Dividends
– Profit after tax	
– Depreciation and other non-cash charges	
2. Issue of equity capital	2. Decrease in liabilities
3. Increase in liabilities	3. Increase in assets
4. Decrease in assets	4. Payment and purchase of assets

To prepare FFS for a company on total resources basis, we find out the increases and decreases in various assets and liabilities and also see whether the company had any inflow of funds through the issue of equity or preference share capital. The income statements for the years are also analyzed to calculate the funds from operations (profit after taxes to which all noncash charges such as depreciation are added back) and dividend payments.

Let us consider the financial statements of Cure Well Pharma to understand the preparation of an FFS on total resources basis.

Income Statement

	2014	2015
	₹ in million	
Sales	1,030.00	1,115.00
Cost of goods sold	670.00	710.00
Materials	335.00	355.00
Labor	155.00	160.00
Overhead	180.00	195.00
Gross profit	360.00	405.00
Depreciation	15.00	10.00
Selling, general, and administrative expenses	298.80	362.20
Operating profit before interest and taxes	46.20	32.80
Interest	16.20	7.80
Profit before tax	30.00	25.00
Tax @ 50%	15.00	12.50
Profit after tax	15.00	12.50

Balance Sheet

	2014	2015
Assets	**₹ in million**	
Cash	2.00	2.00
Accounts receivable	250.00	180.00
Inventory	375.00	360.00
Total current assets	627.00	542.00
Fixed assets net of depreciation	110.00	100.00
Other assets	35.00	30.00
Total assets	772.00	672.00
Liabilities and net worth		
Bills payable	132.40	32.80
Accounts payable	105.00	85.00
Provisions	7.00	13.10
Accruals	30.00	35.00
Total current liabilities	274.40	165.90
Term loan	72.00	68.00
Total liabilities	**346.40**	**233.90**
Share capital	310.00	310.00
Reserves+Surplus	115.60	128.10
Total liabilities and net worth	**772.00**	**672.00**

Let us prepare the FFS on total resources basis. Table 3.10 is the statement of balance sheet changes for the company from 2014 to 2015. Table 3.11 classifies these changes into sources and uses of funds. Table 3.12 uses the information provided by the income statements for a more detailed analysis of the flow of funds.

It is to be noted that the gross fixed assets will not change usually unless there is a purchase or sale of a fixed asset, or the company changes its method of depreciation.

Interpreting the FFS

What information do we get from the FFS prepared above? Let us take a look at Table 3.11. We see that all the assets of the company have decreased over the period, leading to a source of funds. Why is decrease in assets treated as a source? When an asset account increases, it uses funds as funds are required for their purchase. Correspondingly, when an asset account decreases, it releases or provides funds and hence becomes a source. Similarly, when a liability

TABLE 3.10
STATEMENT OF BALANCE SHEET CHANGES

	2014	2015		Change ₹ in million
Assets				
Cash	2.00	2.00	(–)	–
Accounts receivable	250.00	180	(–)	70.00
Inventory	375.00	360.00	(–)	15.00
Total current assets	627.00	542.00	(–)	85.00
Fixed assets net of depreciation	110.00	100.00	(–)	10.00
Other assets	35.00	30.00	(–)	5.00
Total assets	**772.00**	**672.00**	**(–)**	**100.00**
Liabilities and net worth				
Bills payable	132.40	32.80	(–)	99.60
Accounts payable	105.00	85.00	(–)	20.00
Provisions	7.00	13.10	(+)	6.10
Accruals	30.00	35.00	(+)	5.00
Total current liabilities	**274.40**	**165.90**	**(–)**	**108.50**
Term loan	72.00	68.00	(–)	4.00
Total liabilities	346.40	233.90	(–)	112.50
Share capital	310.00	310.00		–
Reserves and surplus	115.60	128.10	(+)	12.50
Total liabilities and net worth	**772.00**	**672.00**	**(–)**	**100.00**

Source: Author.

account increases, it provides funds (acts as a source), and when it decreases, funds are required to make the reduction (the account uses up funds). Cure Well Pharma has increased its provisions, accruals, and reserves, which generated funds to the extent of ₹23.60 million, and additional funds to the extent of ₹100 million were generated by a decrease in assets. The amounts so released have been used up by the company in paying off its creditors (bills payable ₹99.60 million and accounts payable ₹20 million) and also in repaying ₹4 million toward term loan.

Further analysis of the FFS reveals that the largest source of funds was from accounts receivable by ₹70 million. A major use of funds has been in paying off short-term creditors for supplies. In spite of apparently efficient working capital management, we note that there has been no increase in cash. Is this because the management is following an aggressive working capital policy? Or is it an indicator of liquidity problems in the years to come? We cannot come to any valid conclusions with the data given, but we can definitely get an insight into those areas that require further investigation.

TABLE 3.11
STATEMENT OF SOURCES AND USES OF FUNDS FOR THE YEAR 2015

Sources	₹ in million
Reduction in accounts receivable	70.00
Reduction in inventory	15.00
Reduction in net fixed assets	10.00
Reduction in other assets	5.00
Increase in provisions	6.10
Increase in accruals	5.00
Increase in reserves and surplus	12.50
Total sources	123.60
Uses	
Reduction in bills payable	99.60
Reduction in accounts payable	20.00
Reduction in term loan	4.00
Total uses	123.60

Source: Author.

FFS on a Cash Basis

An FFS on cash basis is prepared by

1. selecting the net balance sheet changes that have resulted into an increase or decrease in cash,
2. selecting the income statement items that have resulted into an increase or decrease in cash, and
3. combining this information to generate an FFS.

The steps are similar to those followed while preparing an FFS on total resources basis, but here, instead of classifying increase or decrease in cash as use or source, all the other increases and decreases are classified into sources and uses, and if sources exceed uses, it indicates an increase in cash to that extent, and however, if uses exceed sources, it is an indication of a decrease in cash to that extent. In the earlier illustration of Cure Well Pharma, we can see that there has been no increase in cash.

The sources of funds that increase cash and the uses of funds that decrease cash are as follows:
Sources of funds that increase cash are

1. a net decrease in any asset other than cash or fixed assets,
2. a gross decrease in fixed assets,
3. a net increase in any liability,
4. proceeds from the sale of equity or preference stock, and
5. funds from operations.

TABLE 3.12
FFS FOR THE YEAR 2015

Sources		₹ in million
Profit before tax		25.00
Depreciation		10.00
Increase in liabilities:		
Provisions	6.10	
Accruals	5.00	11.10
Decrease in assets		
Accounts receivable	70.00	
Inventory	15.00	
Gross fixed assets	0.00	
Other assets	5.00	90.00
Total		**136.10**
Uses		
Taxes		12.50
Dividends	—	—
Decrease in liabilities:		
Bills payable	99.60	
Accounts payable	20.00	
Term loan	4.00	123.60
Increase in assets		
—		
—		
Total		136.10

Source: Author.

Note: When depreciation is shown as a source of funds, the changes in gross fixed assets must be analyzed to see whether funds have been generated or used. For this purpose, from the given data, gross fixed assets can be calculated as

$$\text{Gross fixed assets} = \text{Net fixed assets} + \text{Accumulated depreciation}$$

	2014	2015
Gross fixed assets	125.00	125.00
Accumulated depreciation	15.00	25.00
Net fixed assets	110.00	100.00

Funds from operations are not expressed directly in the income statement. To get funds from operations, depreciation has to be added back to profit after taxes. If, however, depreciation is added back to profit before taxes, taxes have to be shown separately as a use of funds.

Uses of funds which decrease cash include

1. a net increase in any asset other than cash or fixed assets,
2. a gross increase in fixed assets,
3. a net decrease in any liability,
4. a retirement or purchase of stock, and
5. cash dividends.

To illustrate the preparation of the FFS on a cash basis, we shall use the balance sheet and income statements of Phlox Pharma Ltd, as shown below:

PHLOX PHARMA BALANCE SHEET AS ON 31 MARCH

	2014	2015
Assets	₹ in million	
Fixed assets at cost	153.85	159.69
Less: accumulated depreciation	79.12	85.68
Net fixed assets	74.73	74.01
Long-term investments	—	6.54
Other assets	20.56	20.51
Current assets		
Inventories	123.47	132.90
Accounts receivable	74.07	67.83
Prepaid expenses	1.72	2.08
Other current assets	2.92	3.52
Cash & marketable securities	17.50	17.76
Total current assets	219.68	224.10
Total assets	314.97	325.15
Liabilities & net worth		
Share capital	78.19	78.20
Reserves & surplus	95.63	101.45
Total owner's equity	173.82	179.66
Long-term loans	62.65	63.08
Current liabilities		
Bills payable	35.65	44.85
Accounts payable	13.68	14.86
Accrued taxes	12.74	3.62
Outstanding	16.43	19.09
Total current liabilities	78.50	82.42
Total liabilities & net worth	314.97	325.15

PHLOX PHARMA LTD'S INCOME STATEMENTS FOR THE YEARS ENDED 31 MARCH

	2014	2015
	₹ in million	
Net sales	372.12	394.69
Cost of goods sold	250.00	268.03
Selling, general, or administrative expenses	72.70	80.14
Depreciation	11.40	6.56
Interest	6.98	8.53
Profit before tax	31.04	31.43
Income tax	17.24	16.37
Profit after tax	13.80	15.06
Cash dividends	8.86	9.23
Retained earnings	4.94	5.83

The funds from operations and the gross change in fixed assets may be calculated as follows:

Funds from Operations

	₹ in million
Net income after taxes	15.06
Add: Depreciation and other non-cash expenses	6.56
Funds from operations	21.62

Gross Change in Fixed Assets

As depreciation has been already shown as a source of funds, to avoid double counting, we compute gross changes in fixed assets by adding depreciation for the period to net fixed assets at the end of the financial statement date. From this figure, the net fixed assets at the beginning of the financial statement date is deducted.

The residual represents the gross change in fixed assets, which, if positive (as is usually the case), represents a use of funds; if negative, a source.

In this illustration, gross change in fixed assets can be calculated as follows:

Gross change in fixed assets = ₹74.01 + 6.56 − 74.73 million = ₹5.84 million

As this is a positive figure, it indicates a use of funds or, in other words, additions to fixed assets.

The FFS of Phlox Pharma Ltd on cash basis may be presented as follows:

FUNDS FLOW STATEMENT OF PHLOX PHARMA LTD

		₹ in million
Sources of cash		
Funds from operations		21.62
Net decrease in assets:		
Other than fixed assets and cash	0.05	
Other assets	6.24	
Accounts receivable		6.29
Increase in liabilities:	0.43	
Long-term loans	9.20	
Bills payable	1.18	
Accounts payable	2.66	
Outstanding		13.47
Increase in share capital		0.01
Total		41.38
Uses of cash		
Additions to fixed assets		5.84
Dividends paid		9.23
Net increase in assets:		
Other than fixed assets and cash	9.43	
Inventories	0.36	
Prepaid expenses		
Other current assets	0.60	10.39
Increase in investments		6.54
Decrease in liabilities		
Accrued taxes		9.12
Increase in cash		0.26

We find that when we subtract the total sources of cash from the total uses of cash, the difference (increase of ₹0.26 million) is equal to the actual change in cash between the two balance sheet dates. This tallying is a must. If there is a discrepancy in the figure of change in cash as indicated by the FFS and the financial statements, we should search for the cause of discrepancy. Frequently, discrepancies will occur due to surplus adjustments and the analyst should be alert to this possibility.

From the FFS of Phlox Pharma Ltd, the principal uses of funds for 2011 were additions to fixed assets, increase in inventories and investments, and a sizeable decrease in taxes payable. These uses were financed primarily by funds provided by operations after payment of dividends, by a decrease in accounts receivable, and by increases in bank loans, payable and outstanding.

FFS: Working Capital Basis

The preparation of a statement showing the source and use of working capital is very similar to the preparation of an FFS on a cash basis. The only difference is that in the former, changes in various components of current assets and current liabilities are omitted and greater attention is given to changes in fixed assets and long-term liabilities.

This statement is frequently used by bankers to determine whether borrowers are maintaining the minimum working capital requirement.

The following points are worth noting in relation to FFS on working capital basis:

- An increase in a current asset results in an increase in working capital.
- A decrease in a current asset results in a decrease in working capital.
- An increase in a current liability results in a decrease in working capital.
- A decrease in a current liability results in an increase in working capital.

The FFS of Phlox Pharma on working capital basis can be prepared as:

SOURCES AND USES OF WORKING CAPITAL 2014–2015

	₹ in million
Source of working capital	
Funds from operations	21.62
Decrease in other assets	0.05
Increase in share capital	0.01
Increase in long-term loans	0.43
Total	22.11
Uses of working capital	
Dividends	9.23
Additions to fixed assets	5.84
Increase in investments	6.54
Total ·	21.61
Net increase in working capital	0.50

To check the accuracy of the net change whether positive or negative, as disclosed by the FFS, students may prepare a schedule of changes in working capital as shown below.

SCHEDULE OF CHANGES IN WORKING CAPITAL

	Increase (+)	Decrease (−)
	₹ in million	
Current assets		
Inventories	9.43	
Prepaid expenses	0.36	
Other current assets	0.60	
Cash	0.26	
Accounts receivable		6.24
Current liabilities		
Bills payable		9.20
Accounts payable		1.18
Outstanding		2.66
Accrued taxes	9.12	
	19.77	19.28
Increase in working capital	**Increase (+)**	0.50
Total		**Decrease (−)**

Significance of an FFS

An analysis of the sources and uses of funds provide valuable insights into the operations of a firm. These can be summarized as follows.

Detection of Imbalances and Appropriate Action

For example, an analysis spanning several years might reveal a growth in inventories which is out of proportion with the growth of other assets and sales. This overstocking of inventories would have gradually led to a decline in profitability as the funds locked up in inventories could have been put to more profitable uses. This inefficiency in inventory management can be corrected before it leads to further losses.

Divisional Performance Appraisal

When a company has a number of divisions, individual funds statements will enable top management to appraise the performance of divisions in relation to the funds committed to each division.

Evaluation of the Firm's Financing

An analysis of the major sources of funds in the past reveals what portion of the firm's growth was financed internally and what portion externally. A funds flow analysis will also tell us whether short-term liabilities have been used to finance fixed assets and permanent portion of working capital, in which case, at least in the future, the mix of short- and long-term finance has to be strictly watched over.

Planning of Future Financing

An analysis of an FFS for the future (projected FFS) will reveal the firm's total prospective need for funds when these needs will arise and how these are to be financed depending on whether the need is for fixed assets, fluctuating component of working capital, and so on.

Thus, funds flow analysis is a very important analytical tool in the hands of the finance manager in developing information to be used in financial decision-making.

Cash Flow Statement

Although FFS is not mandatory, but the general understanding of the same is necessary for the students to know the concept of change in working capital and the factors contributing to the change in working capital.

Therefore, the concept of cash flow statement has been discussed.

Cash flow statement is used to illustrate the movement of cash into and out of a company for a specified period of time. Cash flow can be further categorized into operational cash flows, investment cash flows, and financing cash flows.

Operational cash flows—Cash flows relating to the operation of the company's business. For example, the cash flows relating to the selling of goods and services.

Investment cash flows—Cash flows relating to the sale or purchase of long-term assets.

Financing cash flows—Cash flows relating to the issuance of debt or equity, payment of dividends, and payment of debt. The relevant guidelines for cash flow (AS3) have been appended.

	A	B	C	D	E	G	H	I	J	
1				Cash Flow Statement						
2								January 1 - December 31, 2011		
3	Cash flows from Operations									
4			Income from continuing operations					5000.00		
5		Adjustments to reconcile net income to net cash provided by operating activities								
6			Depreciation and amortization					1000.00		
7			Deferred income taxes					(200.00)		
8			Other operating activities					300.00		
9			Changes in assets and liabilities							
10				Decrease (increase) in Accounts Receivable				(300.00)		
11				Decrease (increase) in Inventories				(300.00)		
12				Increase (decrease) in Accounts Payable				(300.00)		
13				Decrease (increase) in accrued Liabilities				(200.00)		
14	Net cash from operating activities of continuing operations							5000.00		
15	Net cash from operating activities of discontinued operations									
16	Net cash from operations							5000.00		
17	Cash flows from Investing									
18			Payments for property and equipment					(1000.00)		
19			Other investment					(500.00)		
20			Proceeds from the sale of fixed assets					1000.00		
21	Net cash from investing activities of continuing operations							(500.00)		
22	Net cash from investing activities of discontinued operations									
23	Net cash from investing							(500.00)		
24	Cash flows from Financing									
25			Increase (decrease) in commercial paper					1000.00		
26			Increase (decrease) in long term debt					1000.00		
27			Purchase of Company Stock					1000.00		
28			Dividends paid					(1000.00)		
29	Net cash from financing							2000.00		
30	Net increase in cash and cash equivalents							6500.00		
31	Cash and cash equivalents at beginning of year							5000.00		
32	Cash and cash equivalents at end of year							11500.00		

SUMMARY

1. A financial statement is a compilation of financial and accounting data, which is logically and consistently organized according to some generally accepted accounting principles.

2. Financial analysis can be used as a preliminary screening tool in the selection of stocks in the secondary market and as a forecasting tool of future financial performance.

3. There are several sources of financial information. Care should be taken while choosing them.

4. The widely used tools for financial analysis are ratio analysis, comparative analysis, Du Pont analysis, and funds flow analysis.

5. A ratio gives the mathematical relationship between two variables. In financial analysis, a particular ratio represents the relationship between two financial variables. One variable is dependent and the other variable is independent. The relationship is user defined.

6. Financial ratios can be broadly classified into four groups: liquidity ratios, activity ratios, profitability ratios, and leverage ratios.

7. Liquidity implies a firm's ability to pay obligation debts in the short run.

8. Liquidity ratios suffer from two main limitations:

   – Measuring and predicting the future fund flows
   – Measuring the adequacy of future fund inflows in relation to outflows

9. Activity ratios tell us about the utilization of assets to generate sales. Efficient utilization of assets depends on various managerial decisions relating to current as well as fixed assets.

10. Most frequently used turnover ratios are receivables, payables, and stock turnover ratios.

11. Profitability ratios measure the efficiency of the firm's activities and its ability to generate profits. Profitability is the ability to make profit. It depends on capacity and activity.

12. Coverage ratios give the relationship between the financial charges of a firm and its ability to service them. Important coverage ratios are interest coverage ratio, fixed charges coverage ratio, and DSCR.

13. The Du Pont Company of the USA developed a system of financial analysis, which has got good recognition and acceptance. In the Du Pont System, return ratios are analyzed in terms of profit margin and turnover ratios.

14. An FFS is a statement that tells us about the various sources from which funds were raised and the uses these funds were put to. An FFS is different from a balance sheet, in that the former captures the movements in funds, whereas the latter merely presents a static picture of the sources and uses of funds.

15. Cash flow statement is used to illustrate the movement of cash into and out of a company for a specified period of time. Cash flow can be further categorized into operational cash flows, investment cash flows, and financing cash flows.

KEY TERMS

- Liquidity ratios
- Current ratio
- Quick ratio
- Activity ratios
- Receivables turnover
- Average collection period
- Payables turnover
- Average payment period
- Stock turnover
- Stock holding period
- Net profit margin
- Gross profit margin
- Asset turnover
- Earning power
- Return on equity
- Earnings per share
- Price earnings ratio
- Capitalization rate
- Dividend payout
- Dividend yield
- Leverage ratio
- Capital structure ratios
- Coverage ratios
- Cross-sectional analysis
- Time-series analysis
- Common-size analysis
- Du Pont analysis
- Benchmarking
- Window dressing
- Fund flow analysis

Learning Outcomes

This chapter will make students to learn ratio analysis funds flow analysis, and cash flow analysis as key tools for financing statement analysis.

ASSESS YOURSELF

Concept Review and Critical Thinking Questions

1. What do you mean by financial analysis? Who are the interested parties in financial analysis? Discuss.
2. Discuss how financial analysis can be carried out for

   (a) service organizations
   (b) not-for-profit organizations

3. What do you mean by funds flow analysis? How is it prepared?
4. What is cash flow statement? How is it prepared?

STUDENT ACTIVITIES

Select two companies from the cement sector. Collect their last 3 years' financial information. Perform both the time-series and cross-sectional analysis on the data collected.

SUGGESTED READINGS

Brealey, R.A., & Myres, S.C. (2002). *Principles of corporate finance* (7th ed.). New York: McGraw-Hill.
Horne, J.C.V. (2002). *Financial management & policy* (12th ed.). Singapore: Pearson Education.
Ross, S.A., Westerfield, R.W., & Jordan, B.D. (2002). *Fundamentals of corporate finance* (6th ed.). New Delhi: Tata McGraw-Hill.

CASE STUDY I: FINANCIAL PLANNING

Welcure Pharma Ltd manufactures a range of bulk drugs that are used by itself and other pharma companies for various life-saving drugs and formulations including antibiotics. The company currently has five directors and an issued share capital of 50 lakh shares. All the directors also hold shares.

At a recent meeting of the board of directors, the following points emerged:

1. It is expected that the sales of the company would increase by 30% per year in the next two years and by 10% in the third year. The directors are also confident that the current gross profit as a percentage of sales ratios can be maintained.
2. Operating expenses are 25% of sales and depreciation is 10% of the operating expenses.
3. Interest charges relate to Long Term Loan of which repayment of principal will be over the planning period. The company currently has no borrowings.

4. The company currently distributes 50% of its after-tax profits as dividends. The directors wish to at least maintain this level of dividend payout over the planning period. Approximately, 25% of the shares are owned by a financial institution. The tax rate is 30% and is expected to remain constant.

5. The current ROI is expected to grow by 10% per year and reach a target level of 25% by the end of the planning period. The EPS should also double up by the end of the third year.

6. During the last two years, no capital expenditure has been made. However, for the expected sales growth and other objectives, the company has now to invest in new assets. The planned expenditure is ₹15 lakhs in year 1, ₹18 lakhs in year 2, and ₹20 lakhs in year 3.

The financial director of the company has prepared the projected financial statements for the current year (given below).

As an assistant to the financial director and based on the available information, you are **required** to

1. prepare proforma income statement for Welcure Pharma for the next three years,
2. calculate the relevant ratios for each year using the proforma income statement,
3. prepare statements showing the expected free cash flow for the current year and for each year for the planning period. You may assume that tax, interest, and dividends are all paid in the year in which they are incurred, and
4. comment on the company's plans and objectives based on your results.

SUMMARIZED INCOME STATEMENT FOR THE CURRENT YEAR

(₹ in lakhs)	
Sales	106.0
Cost of sales	61.00
Gross profit	45.00
Operating expenses	26.50
Depreciation	2.70
Operating profit	15.80
Interest	1.00
PBT	14.80
Tax	4.40
PAT	10.40
Dividends	5.20
Retained earnings	5.20

Balance sheet extracts as on 31 March

Fixed assets	53.0
Net current assets	26.5
Total assets less current liabilities	79.5
Long-term loan	10.0
Net assets	69.5

Source: Author.

PART II
Foundation of Financial Management

CHAPTER 4

Concept of Time

Learning Objectives

- To understand the concept and factors of the time value of money.
- To explain the future value (FV) and the present value (PV).
- To explain the application of the time value of money in financial decisions.
- To explain how timings of cash flow affect assets' value and rate of return.

PRELUDE

The value of money changes with time. Therefore, ₹1 today may or may not be more valuable tomorrow than today. It depends on what changes have taken place. If in the year 2015, the purchasing power of money is less than that of the year 2014, it may not be a good sign. It is erosion in value of money during the same period. If the value of money is more, it is a good sign as it enhances the purchasing power. The factors responsible for this may be inflation rate, fluctuation in the interest rate, flow of money in capital and money market, and risk and uncertainty involved with time. So, every prudent investor asks before investing money about his own required rate of return, which will compensate him for the sacrifice of current consumption and reduced purchasing power. If the investment option offers him the return more than the required return, he goes for investment, not otherwise. There comes the role of the time value of money. Any lender must be interested in knowing how to calculate the equated monthly install-ment (EMI) over loan horizon at some interest rate. What would happen to the duration of loan and amount of loan due to change in general interest rate in the economy? While preparing for retirement, how much a person should deposit every month to have desired amount at the time of retirement? These entire perplexed questions can be understood through navigating the time value of money.

Introduction

Suppose "A" promises to pay ₹10 lakhs in 2016, would you ask him to pay ₹9 lakhs in 2012? If yes, it is so because the value of ₹10 lakhs of 2015 is equal to ₹9 lakhs of 2012. Suppose you are going to retire in 2020, what would you like to do, to earn the same amount of earnings after retirement as you earn now, or would you like to maintain the same standard of life? If you opt for the latter one, then the question is, how much then must be saved now?

A rupee received now has more worth than a rupee expected to be received in future. It gives instant pleasure through consumption; however, a rational person may postpone his consumption, provided it is believed that future inflow will give more pleasure because of increased units of money than the present one. Thus, the issue is either to forego current consumption and have future benefit or to forego future benefits and have present comfort. So, it is very imperative for a manager to understand the time value of money.

The time value of money and its associated variables such as risk, money supply, expected return, and options for investment are vital parameters for considering any financial decision. All pertinent financial decisions have to be evaluated on these grounds to optimize net PV of cash inflow. The time can be past, present, and/or future. The past cannot be retrieved, but investment value of today will reflect the change in value. Hence, present and future have more relevance. As the future is coupled with risk and uncertainty, an individual is not sure about future cash inflows and prefers current consumption over future consumption unless there is enough motivation such as better rate of return for forgoing present consumption. That is why, people are more concerned about the future and present. For example, if a person is offered ₹200 now or ₹200 from 1 year from now. Definitely, he would prefer ₹200 now if there is inflation, which he could put in a bank account to earn an interest to protect the purchasing power. Therefore, three factors affecting individual preference for money are:

- risk,
- preference for consumption, and
- investment opportunities.

In this simplified financial model, Mr Avinash Mathur will receive ₹1,000 "now" and ₹1,540 "later." Mr Mathur can consume ₹1,000 now or wait for one time period and consume ₹1,540 also. This is what he will be forced to do in the absence of financial markets. However, given that financial markets exist (howsoever simple they are) and Mr Mathur is not satisfied with this consumption pattern, he can shift resources across time to suit the desired consumption pattern. For example, if he wants to consume ₹1,200 at present, he can borrow ₹200 now and return it with interest later. If the interest rate is 10% every year, he has to return ₹220 (200 + 20) at $t1$. As a result of this transaction, his present consumption increases to ₹1,200 and future consumption is reduced to ₹1,320 (1,540 – 220). Similarly, if he wants to consume less than ₹1,000 now, he can lend some of the resources till $t1$ and have an increased consumption in the future.

The line that we get by joining all the possible combinations of the present and future consumption is called the financial exchange line (Figure 4.1).

FIGURE 4.1

FINANCIAL EXCHANGE LINE DEPICTING COMBINATION OF PRESENT AND FUTURE CONSUMPTION

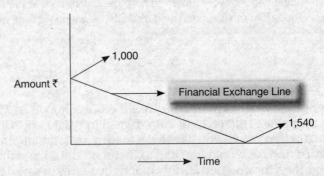

Source: Author.

The financial exchange line suggests the basic principles discussed in the following sections.

Equilibrium Interest Rate or the Opportunity Cost of Capital

When some participants wish to shift future resources to the present by borrowing and other participants wish to shift present resources to the future by lending there is a possibility of beneficial transaction between these two parties. However, the two parties must agree on the amount of future resources to be exchanged for present resources. This means that the lenders and borrowers must agree how many rupees worth of future resources will be necessary to expect in exchange for each rupee worth of current resources provided.

The forces of demand and supply make this decision. The interplay of demand for resources and supply of resources sets the "equilibrium interest rate" or the "required rate of return" or the "opportunity cost of capital." The "equilibrium interest rate" is the rate at which the exchange between the present and future resources takes place. For example, if the equilibrium interest rate is 10% per annum, a lender can expect to receive ₹110 at the end of the year for each ₹100 lent at the beginning of the year. The ₹110 consists of ₹100 originally lent plus ₹10 as interest.

The Principle of Financial Equivalence

Time preference for money is generally expressed in percentage in the form of interest rate. This interest rate is risk free rate of return. Suppose the FV of ₹1,200 at the end of 1 year, at 5% annual interest, is ₹1,260. What does this mean?

It means, there are two choices for you:

1. Either you can receive ₹1,200 now, or
2. You can receive ₹1,260 one year from now.

Which one would you prefer—₹1,200 now or ₹1,260 one year from now? The correct answer is that you would be indifferent. If you take ₹1,200 now, you could lend it for 1 year and have ₹1,260 in the bank at the end of this period. Of course, this is the same as the second choice offered to you.

So, if the interest rate is 5%, ₹1,200 today is the same as ₹1,260 one year from today. That is, ₹1,200 today is financially equivalent to ₹1,260 one year from today (at 5% interest rate.) Thus, the principle of financial equivalence may be stated as "A given cash flow receivable at some point of time in the future is equal to some amount of money in the present at a given rate of interest." This principle of financial equivalence is very important and applies in time value of money, as you will see later.

Principle of Asset Valuation

The value of an asset is what it is worth today in the market place. How do you determine the value of an asset? The Principle of Asset Valuation states that:

The value of an asset today is the value of all the cash flows expected from the asset at some point of time in future and expressed in terms of money of the current purchasing power.

This principle applies to the valuation of both financial assets (such as stocks and bonds) and real assets (such as machinery, real estate, etc.)

Thus, to value an asset, one needs to know

1. all future cash flows from this asset and
2. the interest rate.

Forecasting future cash flows is relatively easy in the case of bonds and difficult in the case of equity shares. The interest rate used to discount the cash flows needs to be forecasted. The relevant interest rate is the opportunity cost, for example, assume you wanted to value asset **A**. Suppose you were to forego the investment in asset **A** and you would invest your money elsewhere. What rate of return would you expect to earn from this alternative asset? By investing in asset **A**, you are giving up the opportunity to invest your money elsewhere. This is your opportunity cost.

Take another example, suppose you were considering investing in the common stock of a company. Instead, you could also invest your money in the general stock market. If you expect to earn say 18% from the stock market, then this is the opportunity cost for the stock investment. You would then discount the cash flows from the stock at this rate.

Test Yourself

1. What do you understand by the time value of money?
2. What are the factors affecting the time value of money?
3. What is opportunity cost of capital?
4. What is principal of equivalence?

Hence, it is clear that money has a time value because of the following reasons:

- Higher preference for present consumption than future consumption.
- Purchasing power of the currency declines with time due to inflation. Inflation is better than deflation.
- Money received today can be invested elsewhere to earn suitable returns.

To appreciate the concept of time value of money, it is desirable to go through the following terms:

1. **Required rate of return:** The time preference for money is generally expressed by an interest rate. In the absence of any risk, it is equivalent to risk-free rate of return. However, an investor is exposed to risk and uncertainty. And gradually with time, the purchasing power of money decreases. That is why, required rate of return will be:

$$\text{Required rate of return} = \text{risk free rate} + \text{expected rate of inflation} + \text{risk premium to compensate risk and uncertainty}$$

Risk-free rate is reward for sacrificing current compensation. Inflation rate compensates for reduction in purchasing power and risk premium provides protection against risk and uncertainty. Like an individual, a firm also needs required rate of return for evaluating the desirability of alternative financial decisions. In a firm's case, cost of capital is considered as required rate of return. The required rate of return helps the individual or firms to convert future cash flows into present. Let us assume an individual has been offered ₹230 after one year from now in exchange of ₹200 that he is giving now. His required rate of return is 10%. It means that he is indifferent between ₹200 now and ₹220 one year from now. So, he must accept ₹230 after one year as it is more than ₹220.

2. **PV:** PV of a cash flow due n years in the future is the amount which, if it were in hand today, would grow to equal the future amount.

3. **FV:** FV may be defined as an amount that will be received by an investor in future if the amount is invested today carrying a rate of interest, that is, how much will you receive tomorrow if you invest today at a given rate of interest?

4. **Discount rate:** The required rate of return (r) is used to discount the cash flows and it is known as discount rate (k).

5. **Compounding:** The process of calculating FVs of cash flows is known as compounding.

6. **Discounting:** The process of calculating PVs of cash flows is called as discounting.

7. **Cash flow:** Cash flow is different from profit. Net profit after tax+depreciation+other noncash expenses–non-operating income. Cash is of two types: single period and multi-period.

8. **Annuity:** An ordinary annuity involves a fixed number of equal cash flows which occur at the end of the respective time periods. For example, consider the EMIs. EMIs are payable to a housing finance company for repaying a loan that you have taken for purchasing a house.

9. **Annuity due:** An annuity due is like an ordinary annuity, but with one important distinction: Its cash flows occur at the beginning of the year instead of at the end.

10. **Perpetuity:** Perpetuity is a special kind of annuity. It has an infinite number of cash flows, all of the same amount.

11. **Time line conventions:** As all time value of money calculations involve cash flows occurring at different points in time, it is important to understand the graphical representation of these cash flows.

We will measure time along a line, from left to right (Figure 4.2).

FIGURE 4.2
TIME LINE CONVENTION

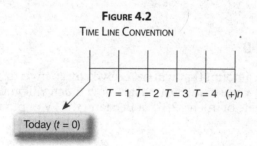

Source: Author.

The leftmost point on this line is today ("Now"), and is indicated as "0." It is the start of the first year from today. We will often refer to this point in time as "$t = 0$."

The next hash mark represents a point in time 1 year from today, and is indicated by "1," and can be referred to as "$t = 1$."

The interval between the "0" and the "1" is the next 1-year time period. Note that as "1" represents the end of the first year, it also represents the start of the second year.

The next hash mark represents the end of the second year, denoted by "2," and it also marks the start of the third year. We will often refer to this point in time as "$t = 2$."

We can continue to represent years in this fashion. The line so obtained is called a **time line** as it depicts the different points of time in the present and future.

To represent cash flows also on the time line, we will use the convention shown in Figure 4.3. Upward pointing arrows represent cash inflows. Downward pointing arrows represent cash outflows

FIGURE 4.3
TIME LINE CONVENTION

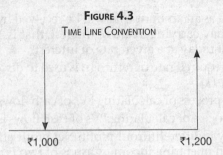

₹1,000   ₹1,200

Source: Author.

In Figure 4.3, there is a cash outflow of ₹1,000 occurring 1 year from today (the first arrow at $t=1$), and there is a cash inflow of ₹1,200 occurring 3 years from today (the second arrow at $t=3$).

Note that the cash inflow of ₹1,200 occurs at the end of 3 years from today (i.e., at $t=3$). But as $t=3$ also represents the start of the fourth year, the ₹1,200 cash flow can also be thought of as occurring at the beginning of the fourth year from today.

There are two ways by which cash flows can be adjusted according to the time value of money. The process of calculating FVs of cash flows is known as compounding and the process of calculating PVs of cash flows is called as discounting.

Application of Time Value of Money

1. FV
2. PV

FV and Compounding

FV may be defined as an amount that will be received by an investor in future if the amount is invested today carrying a rate of interest, that is, how much will you receive tomorrow if you invest today at a given rate of interest? To understand the FV of money, we will go through:

1. FV of single cash flow
2. FV of multi-period cash flow
3. FV of annuity
4. FV of annuity due

FV of a Single Cash Flow

Suppose you deposit ₹1,200 in a savings account that pays you 10% interest per year. How much amount will you receive in one year's time? As you are depositing ₹1,200, it is a cash outflow. This cash flow can be represented as shown in Figure 4.4.

We will call this amount the PV as the cash outflow is occurring today (i.e., at the present time), and denote it as PV. You want to find out how much this cash flow will be worth at a future point in time (1 year from now). So, you want to find its FV, or FV_1. Note that the arrow representing this FV is upward pointing—which represents a cash inflow. The interest rate is 10% per year. We will denote this rate as "k," and express the interest rate as a decimal. Thus, $k = 0.10$.

Now let's find the FV 1 year from today, given that the PV is ₹1,200 and the interest rate is 10% per year. At the end of the first year, you will not only have the original ₹1,200, but also

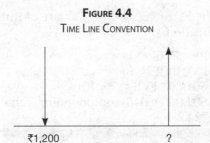

FIGURE 4.4
TIME LINE CONVENTION

₹1,200   ?

Source: Author.

the interest earned on this amount. Interest earned in the first year = Beginning amount × Interest rate × Time = ₹1,200 × 0.10 × 1 = ₹120. Thus, you will have ₹1,200 + ₹120 = ₹1,320 at the end of 1-year time. So the FV of ₹1,200 one year from today, at an interest rate of 10% per year, is ₹1,320. Symbolically, the FV at the end of n years:

$$FV_n = P_v(1+k)^n$$

where $\mathbf{FV}_n$ is the FV after n time periods, $\mathbf{P}_v$ is the value of cash flow today, k is the nominal interest rate or discount rate, and N is the number of time periods.

The FV of a cash flow can also be expressed as follows:

$$FV_n = P_v \times FVIF\,(k, n)$$

where FVIF (k, n) is the Future value interest factor (FVIF).

For the same reason, the process of finding the FV of a present sum is called compounding. FV of cash flows is calculated on the basis of compounding technique. Interest is compounded when interest earned on initial principal amount becomes the part of the principal at the end of the first compounding period. In the above formula, the expression $(1 + k)n$ represents the FV of an initial investment of ₹1 (₹1 invested today) at the end of the factor (FVIF, hereafter). To simplify calculations, this expression has been evaluated for various combinations of k and n, and these values are presented in Table A.1 in the appendix. This is called the FV Table. To calculate the FV of any investment for a given value of "k" and "n," the corresponding value of $(1 + k)n$ from the table has to be multiplied with the initial investment.

Illustration 1. The fixed deposit scheme of Andhra Bank offers the following interest rates:

Period of Deposit	**Rate Per Annum (%)**
48–179 days	10.0
180–<1 year	10.5
1 year and above	11.0

Find out the FV of ₹20,000 invested today, for the next 3 years.

$$\begin{aligned} FV &= PV * FVIF\,(k, n) \\ &= 20{,}000 * FVIF\,(11\%, 3) \\ &= 20{,}000 * 1.368 \\ &= ₹27{,}360 \end{aligned}$$

Illustration 2. Calculate the FV of ₹60,000 at 15% rate of interest for 10 years with traditional method and excel application.

$$FV = PV * FVIF$$
$$= PV * FVIF\ (k, n)$$
$$= 60{,}000 * FVIF\ (15\%, 10)$$
$$= 60{,}000 * 4.046\ \text{(compounding Table 1.1)}$$
$$= ₹24{,}276$$

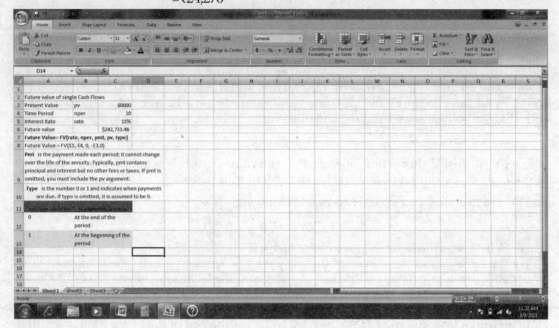

Rule of 72/69

A frequent question posed by the investor is, "How long will it take for the amount invested to be doubled for a given rate of interest?" This question can be answered by a rule known as "rule of 72." Although it is a crude way of calculation. This rule says that the period within which the amount will be doubled is obtained by dividing 72 by the rate of interest.

For instance, if the given rate of interest is 6%, then doubling period is 72/6 = 12 years.

However, an accurate way of calculating doubling period is the "rule of 69," according to which, doubling period.

$$= 0.35 + \frac{69}{\text{Interest rate}}$$

Simple Interest Versus Compound Interest

Interest paid (earned) on the original amount, or on principal borrowed (lent) is called the simple interest (SI).

Symbolically,

$$SI = P_0 * k * n$$

where SI is the simple interest, P_0 is the deposit today ($t=0$), k is the interest rate per period, and n is the number of time periods

Assume that you deposit ₹1,000 in an account earning 7% simple interest for 2 years. What is the accumulated interest at the end of the second year?

$$SI = P_0 * k * n = ₹1,000(0.07)(2) = ₹140$$

However, Compound Interest (CI) is the interest paid (earned) on any previous interest earned, as well as on the principal borrowed (lent).

Symbolically,

$$CI = P_0 (1+k)n - P_0$$

where CI is the compound interest, P_0 is the deposit today ($t=0$), k is the interest rate per period, and n is the number of time periods.

In business, CI is more relevant as it captures the overall compensation (return) for lending (borrowing). Hence, whenever we make a reference to the interest rate, it is to be taken as the compounded rate of interest only unless otherwise stated.

Figure 4.5 shows the FV of ₹1 for different interest rates.

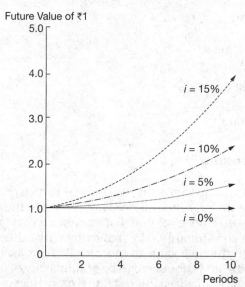

FIGURE 4.5

FUTURE VALUE OF RUPEE ONE FOR DIFFERENT INTEREST RATE

Source: Author.

The Power of Compound Interest

You are 21 years old and have just graduated from college. After reading the introduction to this chapter, you decide to start investing in the stock market for your retirement. Your goal is to have ₹1 million when you retire at the age of 65. Assuming you earn a 10% annual rate on your stock investments, how much must you invest at the end of each year to reach your goal? The answer is ₹1,532.24, but this amount depends critically on the returns earned on your investments. If returns drop to 8%, your required annual contributions would rise to ₹2,801.52, whereas if returns rise to 12%, you would only need to put away ₹825.21 per year.

What if you are like most of us and wait until later to worry about retirement? If you wait until the age of 40, you will need to save ₹10,168 per year to reach your ₹1 million goal, assuming you earn 10%, and ₹13,679 per year if you earn only 8%. If you wait until the age of 50 and then earn 8%, the required amount will be ₹36,830 per year. Although ₹1 million may seem like a lot of money, it will not be when you get ready to retire. If inflation averages 5% a year over the next 44 years, your ₹1 million nest egg will be worth only ₹116,861 in terms of today's dollars. At an 8% rate of return, and assuming you live for 20 years after retirement, your annual retirement income in terms of today's dollars would be only ₹11,903 before taxes. So, after celebrating graduation and your new job, start saving.

Test Yourself

1. What is time line?
2. What do you mean by compounding?
3. How can we calculate the FV of single cash flow?
4. What is the difference between simple interest and compound interest?

Types of Compounding

1. Multi-period compounding
2. Quarterly compounding
3. Monthly compounding
4. Daily compounding
5. Continuous compounding

Multi-period Compounding

When the interest is compounded annually, the interest earned on any deposit is credited to your account at the end of the year. But this need not always be the case. Interest may be compounded more frequently than once per year. For example, it may be compounded quarterly, monthly, daily, and even continuously. The frequency with which interest is compounded has an important effect on the time value of money calculations. The interest rate is usually specified on per annum basis and considered to be nominal rate of interest. If compounding is done more than once, actual annualized interest rate is more than nominal rate of interest rate and known as the effective rate of interest.

Quarterly Compounding

Suppose Bank A states that the interest rate is 12% per year (compounded annually), and you deposit ₹100 into this account. Then, your first year's interest is ₹12 = 12% (₹100), and this is credited to your account at the end of the first year. So, only the initial deposit of ₹100 earns interest for the entire year, and you will have ₹112 at the end of 1 year.

Now consider Bank B that states that the interest rate is 12% per year, compounded quarterly, and you deposit ₹100 in Bank B. With four quarters in a year, you will earn 12%/4 or 3% interest per quarter.

Particulars	1st Quarter	2nd Quarter	3rd Quarter	4th Quarter
Initial deposit	100	103	106.09	109.2727
Interest rate (%)	3	3	3	3
Interest amount	3	3.09	3.18	3.28
Ending amount	103	106.09	109.27	112.55

So with Bank A (which offers an interest rate of 12% per year compounded annually) you will have ₹112 at the end of the year, whereas with Bank B (which offers an interest rate of 12% per year compounded quarterly) you would have ₹112.55 at the end of the year. Of course this difference of ₹0.55 between the two Banks seems small because of the small amount you deposited in each Bank at the beginning of the year. But it is an important difference nevertheless. If you had deposited ₹10 lakhs in each Bank, at the end of the year you would have ₹5,508.81 more in Bank B.

Alternatively, as interest is compounded quarterly, the quarterly interest rate is 12%/4 = 3%. And there are four quarters in a year. So $n = 4$.

Now we can use the FV formula, with $k = 0.03$ and $n = 4$.

$$FV_{4\ quarters} = ₹100\ (1 + 0.03)^4 = ₹112.55$$

The only difference is that we are now redefining what we mean by n. With annual compounding, n is the number of years, but with quarterly compounding, n is the number of quarters.

Effective Interest Rates with Quarterly Compounding

You have seen that with Bank A, you will have ₹112 at the end of the year, and with Bank B, you will have ₹112.55. Recall that Bank A uses annual compounding, whereas Bank Q uses quarterly compounding. And both Banks have a stated rate of 12% per year.

What annually compounded rate must Bank A offer so that you will have the same amount in this Bank as you would in Bank B?

As a deposit of ₹100 grows to ₹112.55 in 1 year at Bank B, you can solve for the unknown annually compounded interest rate. Let us denote this interest rate as i'.

Now, PV = ₹100, FV_1 = ₹112.55, and $n = 1$. Using the FV equation, we obtain

$$₹112.55 = 100\ (1 + k')1$$
$$₹112.55/100 = 1 + k$$
$$₹1.1255 = 1 + k$$
$$₹1.1255 - 1 = k$$
$$0.1255 = k$$
$$k = 12.55\%$$

So Bank B must offer 12% compounded annually, whereas Bank B's effective interest rate is 12.55%, although its stated rate is 12% (compounded quarterly).

Monthly Compounding

Interest may also be compounded monthly. This means that interest on your deposit is credited every month. So, your money works harder for earning more interest. Suppose you deposit ₹100 in Bank C, which pays you 12% per year, compounded monthly. How much will you have at the end of one year?

The monthly interest rate is 12%/12 = 1% per month. And $n = 12$. As $FV_n = PV (1 + k)n$
So, FV12 months = ₹100 $(1 + 0.01)12$ = ₹112.68.

You can see that this amount is greater than ₹112.55 which you can get with Bank B, which uses quarterly compounding. It is also greater than ₹112 you can get with Bank A, which uses annual compounding.

Effective Interest Rates with Monthly Compounding

You can compute the effective interest rate when the interest is compounded monthly using the same equation as before. In the case of Bank C, $k = 0.12$ and $n = 12$. So, the effective interest rate is 12.68%.

Daily Compounding

Interest may also be compounded daily. This means that the interest on your deposit is credited every day. Suppose you deposit ₹100 in Bank D, which pays you 12% per year, compounded daily. How much will you have at the end of 1 year?

The daily interest rate is 12%/365 = 0.03288% per day. So, $k = 0.0003288$ and $n = 365$.
So FV365 days = ₹100 $(1 + 0.0003288)365$ = ₹112.75.

Note that this amount is higher than what you would get at Banks A, B, or C.

Effective Interest Rates with Daily Compounding

You can compute the effective interest rate when interest is compounded daily using the same equation as before.

In the case of Bank D, $k = 0.12$ and $n = 365$.
So the effective interest rate is 12.747%.

Continuous Compounding

As we move from quarterly to monthly to daily compounding, the compounding frequency increases. But you can go one step further, and consider continuous compounding.

When interest is continuously compounded, it is as if interest were computed and credited continuously to your account. In other words, a year is divided into an infinitely large number of time periods, with each period being infinitesimally small—an instant of time, as it were. So how do you use continuously compounded interest rates in time value of money computations?

$$FV = PV \times e^{k \, * \, n}$$
$$= PV \times e^{x}$$

X is the interest rate (k) multiplied by number of year's (n)

$$\text{Value of } e = 2.7183$$

Illustration 3. Find out the FV of ₹100 for 2 years at 12% rate of interest. Compounding is done continuously.

$$FV = 100 \times e^{.12*2}$$
$$= 100 \times 1.2713$$
$$= 127.13$$
$$PV = FV/e^{k*n}$$
$$PV = FV \times e^{-k*n}$$
$$PV = 127.13/1.2713 = ₹1,000$$

Effective Annual Rate (EAR)

The EAR is the rate of interest per annum under annual compounding that produces the same effect as that produced by an interest rate of 12% under quarterly compounding.

The general relationship between the effective and nominal rates of interest is as follows:

$$r = (1 + k/m)^m - 1$$

where r is the effective annual rate, k is the nominal interest rate, and m is the frequency of compounding per year.

For example, if the annual percentage rate is 12% and is quarterly compounded, then the EAR can be computed as follows:

$$r = (1 + k/m)^m - 1$$
$$r = \left(1 + \frac{0.12}{4}\right)^4 - 1$$
$$= (1 + 0.03)^4 - 1 = 1.126 - 1$$
$$= 0.126 = 12.6\% \text{ p.a}$$

Effective Annual Rate

EAR for different compounding periods at 10% can be understood with the following example. The formula used for EAR is ₹M ₹2 * (1 + ₹M ₹3/M6) ^ M6

Half-yearly Compounding	Quarterly Compounding	Monthly Compounding	Daily Compounding
$(1+k/2)^{n*2}-1$	$(1+k/4)^{n*4}-1$	$(1+k/12)^{n*12}-1$	$(1+k/365)^{n*365}-1$

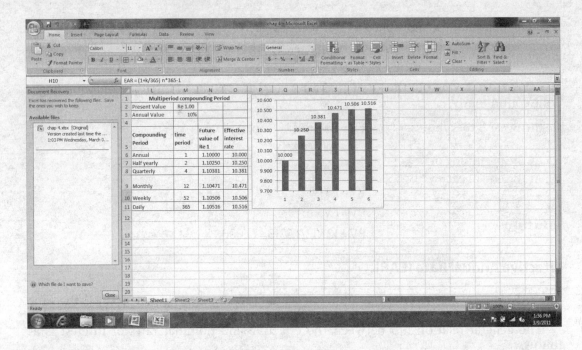

Test Yourself

1. What is continuous compounding?
2. What is effective rate of interest?
3. Why effective rate of interest is always more than nominal rate of interest?

Future Value of Multiple Cash Flows

The basic method used to calculate the FV of a single cash flow can be extended to find the FV of multiple cash flows. Suppose you deposit ₹1,200 today in an account that pays 8% interest annually. Two years later, you deposit an additional ₹1,400 into this account. How much will you have in the account 4 years from today?

This problem involves computing the FV at the end of year 4 of two deposits. When faced with multiple cash flows, you can break down the problem into simpler parts and solve each part separately.

Part 1

First, calculate the FV of the first deposit of ₹1,200. Using the formula for FV_n, note that

$$PV = 1,200, \ k = 0.08, \text{ and } n = 4. \text{ So you can calculate } FV_4 \text{ as } 1,200(1 + 0.08)_4 = ₹1,632.58$$

Part 2

Now the second deposit is made at time 2. As you want to calculate its FV at $t = 4$, this deposit of ₹1,400 will earn interest for only 2 years. Thus, PV = 1,400, k = 0.08, and n = 2. So using the formula for FV_n, we get $FV_4 = 1,400(1 + 0.08)^2 = 1,632.96$.

Finally, you should add the answers to these two parts. You can add them as both FVs are at the same point in time ($t=4$). The final answer is ₹1,632.58+1,632.96=₹3,265.54. This is the amount you would have in 4 years from today.

Illustration 4. Mr X has deposited each year ₹500, ₹1,000, ₹1,500, ₹2,000, and ₹2,500 in his bank account for 5 years. The interest rate is 5%. Find out the FV of his deposits at the end of the fifth year if the amount is deposited:

1. At the beginning of each year
2. At the end of each year

Solution:

$$FV = PV \times (1+k)n$$

1. Calculation of FV when the deposit is made at the beginning of each year.

Beginning of the Year	Amount Deposited	No. of Years Compounded	FVF	FV
1	500	5	1.276	638
2	1,000	4	1.216	1,216
3	1,500	3	1.158	1,737
4	2,000	2	1.103	2,206
5	2,500	1	1.05	2,625

2. Calculation of FV at the end of the year

Beginning of the Year	Amount Deposited	No. of Years Compounded	FVIF	FV
1	500	4	1.216	608
2	1,000	3	1.158	1,158
3	1,500	2	1.103	1,654
4	2,000	1	1.050	2,100
5	2,500	0	1	2,500

Future Value of Equal Cash Flows: Annuities and Perpetuties

Many financial applications involve a series of equal annual cash flows. For example, you may have to repay a loan in seven equal annual installments. Or a corporate bond may pay you a fixed annual interest of say ₹150 per year for 10 years. These periodic cash flows of equal amounts are called annuities.

There are two types of annuities:

- Ordinary or Regular annuity
- Annuity Due

Ordinary Annuity

An ordinary annuity involves a fixed number of equal cash flows which occur at the end of the respective time periods. For example, consider the EMIs payable to a housing finance company for repaying a loan that you have taken for purchasing a house. The number of such payments is fixed depending on the tenure of the loan. The amount payable in each EMI is also fixed. The EMIs are payable at the end of each month. These EMIs, thus, represent an ordinary annuity. However, the power bill or the telephone bill that you pay does not constitute an annuity as the amount payable varies depending on usage, as well as the time is also not fixed, as you may discontinue the services at your choice.

Future Value of an Ordinary Annuity

Suppose you deposit ₹10,000 at the end of each of the next 3 years. If the bank pays 8% interest annually, how much would you have in 3 years from today?

There are three deposits being made as shown in the time line below.

And you want to find how much you will have in the bank immediately after the last deposit is made. This can be done by adding up the FVs, at $t = 3$, of each cash flow.

Note that the first deposit earns interest for 2 years (from $t = 1$ to $t = 3$), the second deposit earns interest for 1 year (from $t = 2$ to $t = 3$), and the third deposit does not earn any interest at all. So here is how you would compute their FVs:

FV of first deposit	10,000(1.08)2=11,664
FV of second deposit	10,000(1.08)1=10,800
FV of third deposit	10,000(1.08)0=10,000
Sum of FVs	32,464

So, you would have ₹32,464 in the bank account in 3 years from today, and this is the FV of the annuity.

The FV of a regular annuity for a period of n years at a rate of interest "k":

$$FV_{An} = A\left[\frac{(1+k)^n - 1}{k}\right]$$

where A is the amount deposited/invested at the end of every year for n years, k is the rate of interest (expressed in decimals), n is the time horizon, and FV_{An} is the accumulation at the end of n years.

The expression $A\left[\frac{(1+k)^n - 1}{k}\right]$ is called the Future Value Interest Factor for Annuity (FVIFA). It represents the accumulation of ₹1 invested or paid at the end of every year for a period of n years at the rate of interest "k."

Illustration 5. Compute FV of ₹5,000 annuity occurring at the end of every year for 5 years at 5% rate of interest through excel application.

Excel function for FV of annuity is the same as FV of single cash flow except that value of PMT is required to be filled in. We will consider PV as zero and pmt would be taken with negative sign.

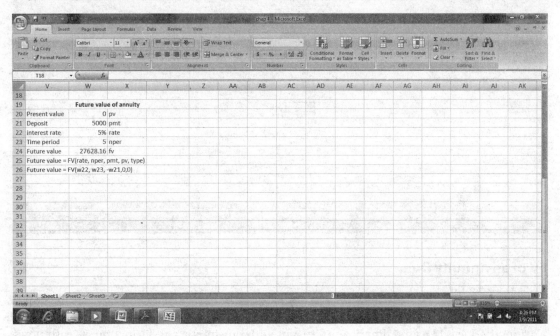

Sinking Fund Factor

We have the equation

$$FV_A = A\left[\frac{(1+k)^n - 1}{k}\right]$$

We can rewrite it as

$$A = FV_A\left[\frac{k}{(1+k)^n - 1}\right]$$

The expression $\left[\dfrac{k}{(1+k)^n - 1}\right]$ is called the sinking fund factor. It represents the amount that has to be invested at the end of every year for a period of "n" years at the rate of interest "k," to accumulate ₹1 at the end of the period.

By taking the previous illustration into consideration, amount of annuity could be computed through Excel application in the following way:

FV of an Annuity Due

Annuity Due

An annuity due is like an ordinary annuity, but with one important distinction: Its cash flows occur at the beginning of the year instead of at the end. For example, consider the insurance premium payable on a life insurance policy. Such premiums are to be paid for a fixed period of time depending on the maturity period of the policy. The amount of each premium is also fixed. The premium is payable at the beginning of each time period for which risk is to be covered. Thus, it represents an annuity due. Similarly, rent payable for accommodation and hire-purchase installments for an automobile are also examples of annuity due. Annuity due is a series of fixed receipts or payments starting at the beginning of each period for a specified number of periods.

Suppose you are depositing ₹100 in a bank account at the beginning of each year for 5 years to earn 10% interest. How much will be the compound value at the end of each year? In this case, the amount that is deposited in the beginning of the first year is entitled for a 5-year interest and last year deposit in the beginning is entitled for a 1-year interest.

$$FV = 100(1+.10)^5 + 100(1+.10)^4 + 100(1+.10)^3 + 100(1+.10)^2 + 100(1+.10)^1$$
$$= 100 \times 1.10 + 100 \times 1.210 + 100 \times 1.331 + 100 \times 1.464 + 100 \times 1.611$$
$$= 110 + 121 + 133.1 + 146.4 + 161.10$$
$$= 671.60$$

Or

$$\text{Future value of Annuity} = \text{Future value of annuity} \times (1+k)$$
$$= A \times FVIFA(k,n) \times (1+k)$$
$$= A \times \frac{(1+k)^n - 1}{k} \times (1+k)$$
$$= 100 \times 6.105 \times 1.10$$
$$= 671.6$$

Each cash flow in the annuity due is compounded for one more year than it would be if the annuity were an ordinary annuity.

So, to compute the FV of an annuity due, first find the FV as if it were an ordinary annuity. Then, multiply the answer by $(1 + k)$.

Suppose you deposit ₹5,000 at the beginning of each of the next 4 years (with the first deposit being made today). If the bank pays you 6% interest annually, how much would you have in the bank 4 years from today?

As the cash flows are at the beginning of each year, this is an annuity due.

First, let us find the FV as if it were an ordinary annuity.

$$FVA_{ordinary} = 5,000 \left[\frac{1.06^4 - 1}{0.06} \right] = ₹21,873.08$$

Next, multiply this by (1.06):

$$FV_{Due} = 21,873.08(1.06) = ₹23,185.46$$

The FV of a four-year annuity due of ₹5,000 per year, at an interest rate of 6% per year, is ₹23,185.46.

Test Yourself

1. What is annuity and annuity due?
2. What is sinking fund factor? How it is computed?
3. Calculate FV for multiple cash flow.

FV depends on compounding interest to measure the value of future amounts. When interest is compounded, the initial principal in one period, along with the interest earned on it, becomes the beginning principal of the following period and so on. Interest can be compounded annually, semi-annually quarterly, monthly, and so on. The more frequently interest is compounded, the larger is the future amount that would accumulate.

PV and Discounting

PV *of a cash flow due n years in the future is the amount which, if it were in hand today, would grow to equal the future amount.* X says that he will pay ₹100 at the end of year. You say that pay ₹99 now instead of ₹100 at the end, that is, the PV is the discounted value of the future inflow. The CI rate is used for discounting cash flows and is known as the discount rate. To understand the PV of money, we will go through:

1. PV of single cash flow
2. PV of multi-period cash flow
3. PV of annuity
4. PV of annuity due
5. PV of growing annuity
6. PV of perpetuity

PV of a Single Cash Flow

PV equation for a single cash flow can be readily obtained by manipulating the compounding equation as under.

$$FV_n = PV(1+k)^n$$

By dividing both sides of this equation by $(1+k)n$, we obtain

$$PV = \frac{FV_n}{(1+k)^n}$$

$$Present\ Value = Future\ Value \times \frac{1}{(1+k)^n}$$

$$= Future\ Value \times Present\ value\ interest\ factor_{(k,n)}$$

$$= Future\ Value \times PVIF_{(k,n)}$$

where PV is the value of cash flow today, FV is the FV of cash flow, k is the interest rate per period, n is the number of compounding periods, and $[(1+k)_n]$ is the compound factor.

where $PVIF_{(k,n)}$ is the present value interest factor, or the discount factor.

The process of finding the PV of a future sum is called discounting. If ₹100 are borrowed with a promise to pay it back with an interest (10%) after one time period, the amount paid, ₹110, represents the FV of ₹100. In other words, given the rate of interest, ₹100 is the PV of ₹110. PV is defined as the amount of money you must invest or lend at the present time so as to end up with a particular amount of money in the future (FV).

Suppose you need to have ₹15,000 two years from today. How much should you deposit today if the bank pays you 8% interest annually?

Now you are given the FV at $t = 2$. That is, $FV_2 = ₹15,000$. And $k = 0.08$. The time line is as follows:

Using the formula, $PV = 15,000(1+0.08)_{-2} = 15,000(0.8573) = ₹12,859.50$

So you need to deposit ₹12,859.50 today, earning 8% per year, so that you can have ₹15,000 two years from today (Figure 4.6).

FIGURE 4.6

RELATIONSHIP AMONG PV, INTEREST RATES, AND TIME FOR ₹1

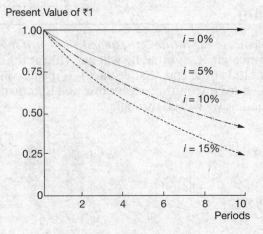

Source: Author.

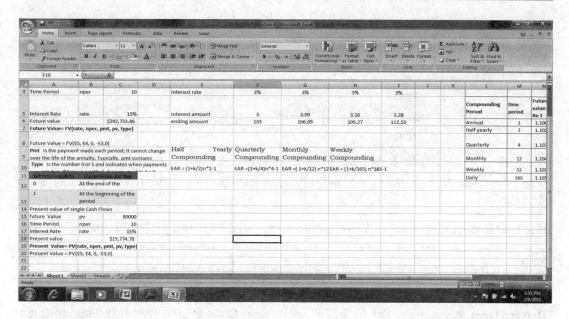

Illustration 6. What is the PV of ₹1,000 receivable after 6 years if the rate of discount is 10% per annum?

$$PV = FV \times PVIF_{(10\%,\,6)}$$
$$= ₹1,000 \times 0.565$$
$$= ₹565$$

PV of Multiple Cash Flows

The basic method of calculating the PV of a single cash flow can be extended suitably to find PV of multiple cash flows. This needs some additional steps:

- Calculate the PV of cash flow individually.
- Aggregation of PVs obtained previously.

Suppose you want to withdraw ₹3,000 in 2 years and an additional ₹5,000 four years from today. How much should you deposit in your bank today, if the bank pays you 7% interest?

You should first find the PV of the first cash flow (at $t = 2$) using the formula. Here, $FV_2 = ₹3,000$, $k = 0.07$, and $n = 2$.

This yields $PV = ₹3,000 (1 + 0.07) - 2 = ₹2,620.32$.

Next, you can find the PV of the second cash flow (at $t = 4$) using the same formula. But now, $FV_4 = ₹5,000$, $k = 0.07$, and $n = 4$. This yields $PV = ₹5,000(1 + 0.07)^{-4} = ₹3,814.48$. The total PV is thus ₹2,620.32 + ₹3,814.48 = ₹6,434.80.

Alternative Approach

First discount the second cash flow to time 2. This can be done using the PV formula and setting $FV = ₹5,000$, $k = 0.07$, and $n = 2$. The discounted value at $t = 2$ is ₹4,367.20.

As this amount is at the same point in time as the first cash flow, you can add this to the first cash flow of ₹3,000 to get a total of ₹4,367.20 + ₹3,000 = ₹7,367.20 at $t = 2$. You can now find the PV of this total amount by discounting it by 2 years (as the total amount of ₹7,367.20 is at $t = 2$).

CALCULATION OF PV

Year	Cash Flow (₹)	PVIF (14%, n)	PV (₹)
0	5,000	1.000	5,000
1	6,000	0.877	5,262
2	8,000	0.769	6,152
3	7,000	0.675	4,725
4	10,000	0.592	5,920

So $FV_2 = ₹7,367.20$, $k = 0.07$, and $n = 2$ in the PV formula. This yields a final PV of $₹7,367.20(1.07)_{-2}$ = ₹6,434.80.

Illustration 7. Calculate the PV of the following cash flow stream if the discount rate is 14%.

Year	0	1	2	3	4
Cash flow	5,000	6,000	8,000	7,000	10,000

Illustration 8. Calculate the PV of following cash flows at 10% rate of interest through excel application.

Year	Cash Flow (₹)
1	10,000
2	2,000
3	800
4	10,000
5	4,000

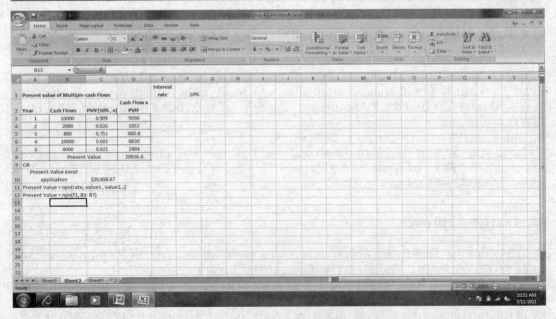

Test Yourself

1. What is the PV and how is it calculated?
2. What is difference between the PV and FV?

PV of an Ordinary Annuity

If the payment comes at the end of each year, then the annuity is considered to be **ordinary annuity**. Suppose that you wish to make annual withdrawals of a fixed amount every year for a given number of years. To fund these withdrawals, you will make a single deposit today in a bank account. How much amount should you deposit so that you will have just enough money in the bank to be able to make the withdrawals?

As any deposit you make will earn interest, you would need to deposit an amount less than the sum of the planned future withdrawals. In other words, you will need to calculate the PV of the planned withdrawals, that is, the PV of the annuity.

Suppose you want to withdraw ₹1,000 per year at the end of each of the next 5 years from a bank account that pays 8% interest annually. How much should you deposit today to meet your needs?

As there are five withdrawals to be made, you can think of depositing five different amounts today, each one being just sufficient to fund one withdrawal.

In other words, you can find the PV of each one of the five withdrawals using the formula $PV = FV_n(1 + k)^{-n}$, and add them up to get the answer. Let us do it.

PV of first withdrawal	₹1,000(1.08)−1=₹925.93
PV of second withdrawal	₹1,000(1.08)−2=₹857.34
PV of third withdrawal	₹1,000(1.08)−3=₹793.83
PV of fourth withdrawal	₹1,000(1.08)−4=₹735.03
PV of fifth withdrawal	₹1,000(1.08)−5=₹680.58
Sum of PVs	₹3,992.71

So you would need to deposit ₹3,992.71 today.

The PV of an annuity "A" receivable at the end of every year for a period of *n* years at a rate of interest *k* is equal to

$$PVA_n = \frac{A}{(1+k)} + \frac{A}{(1+k)^2} + \frac{A}{(1+k)^3} + \cdots + \frac{A}{(1+k)^n}$$

which reduces to

$$PVA_n = A\left[\frac{(1+k)^n - 1}{k(1+k)^n}\right]$$

The expression $\left[\dfrac{(1+k)^n - 1}{k(1+k)^n}\right]$ is called the Present Value Interest Factor Annuity (PVIFA) and it represents the PV of a regular annuity of ₹1 for the given values of k and n. It must also be noted that PVIFA (k, n) is not the inverse of FVIFA (k, n) although PVIF (k, n) is the inverse of FVIF (k, n).

Illustration 9. A person is going to receive ₹100 at the end of each year for the next 3 years. The discount rate is 5%. How much should be the PV of such receipts.

Solution:

$$\text{Present value} = \text{Annuity} \times \text{Present value interest Factor Annuity}_{(k,n)}$$

$$\text{Present Value} = 100 * \frac{(1+.05)^3 - 1}{.05(1+.05)^3}$$

$$= 100 * 2.723 = ₹272.3$$

Or

$$PV = 100 \times (1+0.05)^{-1} + 100 \times (1+0.05)^{-2} + 100 \times (1+0.05)^{-3}$$

$$= 100 \times 0.952 + 100 \times 0.907 + 100 \times 0.864$$

$$= 95.2 + 90.7 + 86.4$$

$$= ₹272.3$$

Time Line

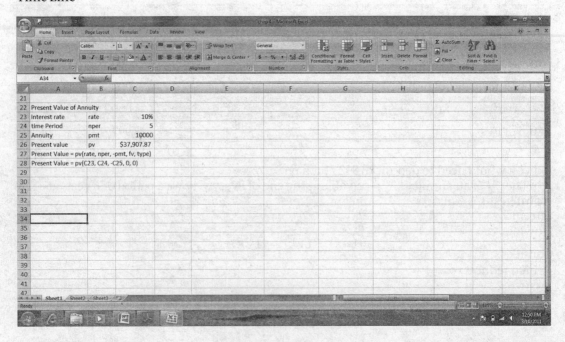

Illustration 10. Calculate the PV of annuity through Excel application for the problem given below.

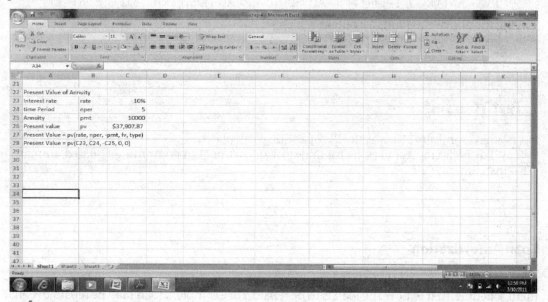

Capital Recovery Factor

Manipulating the relationship among PVA_n, A, k, and n, we get the following equation:

$$A = PVA_n \left[\frac{k(1+k)^n}{(1+k)^n - 1} \right]$$

$\left[\frac{k(1+k)^n}{(1+k)^n - 1} \right]$ is known as the capital recovery factor. Capital recovery factor helps in preparing loan amortization schedule.

PV of a Growing Annuity

In business or otherwise, there are a number of situations where the cash flows are expected to grow at a compound rate. If the annuity increases each year at a given rate of growth, it is called a growing annuity. For instance, in case of rental premises the owner may put a clause in the rental agreement that the annual rent shall increase by a given percentage each year. The valuation of growing ordinary annuity can be done in a manner similar to that of a simple ordinary annuity.

Consider the following growing annuity:

Year	Cash Inflow
1	A
2	A(1+g)
3	A(1+g)^2
N	A(1+g)$^{n-1}$

If the interest rate is k, the PV of the above stream of cash flows can be found as follows:

$$PVA = A/(1+k) + A(1+g)/(1+k)^2 + A(1+g)^2/(1+k)^3 + A(1+g)^3/(1+k)^4 \ldots A(1+g)^{n-1}/(1+k)^n$$

Solving the above equation, we obtain

$$PVA = A\{1 - [(1+g)/(1+k)]^n/(k-g)\}$$

Test Yourself

1. What is annuity? How is the PV of annuity calculated?
2. What is capital recovery factor and how does it help in computing equated annual installment?

Loan Amortization

Whenever a loan is extended, the lender in consultation with the borrower draws up a repayment schedule, that is, how the loan is to be repaid. For example, a loan may be repaid in equal annual installments or it might be repaid in a single lump sum. The installments may be increased gradually (step-up repayment) or there might be a "balloon" repayment (entire repayment at the end of loan duration by single payment) at the end of the term of the loan. There are a number of possibilities. We have considered three basic types of loan repayment schedules, which are as follows:

1. Discounted loans
2. Interest-only loans
3. Amortized loans

Discounted Loan Repayment

In this type of loan repayment schedule, the borrower receives loan money today and repays a single lump sum at some point of time (mutually agreed on between the lender and the borrower) in future. For example, if Mr A borrows ₹1,000 at the rate of 10% per annum, he has to repay $1,000 (1.10)^2 = ₹1,210$ after 2 years.

The T-bills issued by the RBI on behalf of GOI are an example of discounted loan repayment. The T-bills are issued at a discount to their face value and redeemed at the face value. The difference represents the interest for the period of the loan. Similarly, loan repayment for loans taken from pawn brokers against the security of gold are also discounted loan repayment schedule.

Interest-only Repayment

In this type of loan repayment plan, the borrower has to repay interest for each sub-period during the life of the loan and to repay the entire principal at some time (mutually agreed on) in future. Suppose if time period says 5 years and principal borrowed is ₹1,000 at 8%, the borrower has to pay ₹80 every year for five years and return ₹1,000 at the end of 5 years. The corporate bonds represent interest-only loan repayment plan, as during the life of the bond the company has to pay only interest to the bond holder and return the principal at the end of the life of the bond.

Amortized Loan Repayment

In this type of loan repayment schedule, the borrower has to repay both the interest and the principal periodically for an agreed-upon time period till the loan is fully paid. This process of paying a loan by making periodic repayment of interest as well as well as principal is called *loan amortization.* In this type of loan repayment, the borrower may be asked to repay equal installments inclusive of both the interest and principal components or may be asked to repay the principal in equal installments plus some interest. Again, the variant may depend on the negotiations between the borrower and the lender.

Let us consider an example. A has borrowed ₹50,000 at the rate of 9% per annum for 5 years. The terms and conditions of the loan agreement require A to repay the principal in five equal installments plus interest on the outstanding balance.

The repayment schedule will be as follows:

Year	Principal Outstanding at the Beginning of the Year (₹)	Interest @ 9% p.a.	Principal Repayment (₹)	Total Installment (₹)	Principal Outstanding at the End of the Year (₹)
1	50,000	4,500	10,000	14,500	40,000
2	40,000	3,600	10,000	13,600	30,000
3	30,000	2,700	10,000	12,700	20,000
4	20,000	1,800	10,000	11,800	10,000
5	10,000	900	10,000	10,900	0
	Total	**13,500**	**50,000**	**63,500**	

Suppose, for the same loan, the lender may insist on five equal installments. That is the amount of equated annual installment is required to be calculated here. EMI must be inclusive of both interest and principal components. EMI can be calculated through capital recovery factor.

$$₹50,000 = A \times PVIFA_{(9\%, 5)}$$

$$₹50,000 = A \times 3.890$$

$$A = 50,000/3.890$$

$$A = ₹12,853$$

In that case, the repayment schedule would look like as given in the following table:

Year	Principal Outstanding at the Beginning of the Year (₹)	Interest @ 9% p.a.	Principal Repayment (₹)	Total Installment (₹)	Principal Outstanding at the End of the Year (₹)
1	50,000	4,500	8,353	12,853	41,647
2	41,647	3,748	9,105	12,853	32,542
3	32,542	2,929	9,924	12,853	22,618
4	22,618	2,035	10,818	12,853	11,800
5	11,800	1,062	11,792	12,853	—

PV of Annuity Due

The calculation of the PV of an annuity due is similar to computing the FV of the annuity due. Each cash flow in the annuity due is required to be discounted for 1 year less than it would be if the annuity were an ordinary annuity. Hence, the PV of the annuity due is given by the following formula:

$$PV = Annuity \times PVIFA_{(k,n)} \times (1+k)$$

Illustration What is the PV of ₹10, 4-year annuity? The payment is made in the beginning of the year.

Solution:

$$PV = 10 \times (1+0.10)^{-3} + 10 \times (1+0.10)^{-2} + 10 \times (1+0.10)^{-1} + 10 \times (1+0.10) 0$$
$$= 10 \times 0.751 + 10 \times .826 + 10 \times 0.909 + 10 \times 1$$
$$= 7.51 + 8.26 + 9.09 + 10$$
$$= ₹34.86$$

or

$$PV = A \times PVIFA_{(k,n)} \times (1+k)$$
$$= PVA_n \left[\frac{k(1+k)^n}{(1+k)^n - 1} \right] \times (1+k)$$
$$= 10 \times 3.170 \times 1.10$$
$$= ₹34.87$$

PV of Perpetuity

Perpetuity is a special kind of annuity. It has an infinite number of cash flows, all of the same amount. Thus, it is an annuity that never ends! There are three kinds of perpetuities:

Ordinary Perpetuity

Like ordinary annuities, an ordinary perpetuity has cash flows at the end of each year. Here is how you would represent it on a time line, assuming the annual cash flows are all equal to ₹A.

Perpetuity Due

Like an annuity due, perpetuity due has cash flows at the beginning of the year, as shown below.

Deferred Perpetuity

And like a deferred annuity, a deferred perpetuity has an infinite number of cash flows, but its first cash flow occurs beyond year 1. Here is an example of a deferred perpetuity of ₹A per year, whose cash flows begin 4 years from today.

As all these perpetuities have an infinite number of cash flows, you cannot compute their FVs. After all, with an infinite number of cash flows, the FV would be infinitely large!

But you can compute their PVs.

An annuity of an infinite duration is known as perpetuity. The PV of such a perpetuity can be expressed as follows:

$$P_\infty = A \times PVIFA_{k, \infty}$$

where P_∞ is the PV of a perpetuity, A is the constant annual payment, and $PVIFA_{i, \infty}$ is the PV interest factor for a perpetuity.

We can say that PV interest factor of a perpetuity is simply one divided by interest rate expressed in decimal form. Hence, PV of a perpetuity is simply equal to the constant annual payment divided by the interest rate.

Test Yourself

1. What are perpetuities?
2. How is annuity due different from ordinary annuity?

SUMMARY

1. Individuals always prefer current possession of money. The reason being that value of money varies with time. The time preference for money changes due to uncertainty, risk, and preference for current consumption.
2. Required rate of return = Risk free rate + expected rate of inflation + risk premium to compensate risk and uncertainty.
3. Risk-free rate compensates the individual for time and expected rate of inflation compensates for reducing purchasing power, whereas risk premium compensates for risk.
4. The compounding is the process of finding out FV of cash flow at a given interest rate at the end of a given time period.
5. The process of discounting computes the PV of cash flow at a required rate of return at the beginning of a given time period.

6. When the interest is compounded for more than once in a period, effective rate of interest is always greater than the nominal rate of interest.

7. Capital recovery factors help the banks in designing loan amortization tale, and it is the reciprocal of FV interest factor annuity.

KEY TERMS

- Annuity
- Annuity due
- Capital recovery factor
- Cash flow
- Compounding
- Discounting
- FV

- Loan amortization
- Perpetuity
- PV
- Required rate of return
- Risk Free return
- Sinking fund
- Time value of money

Learning Outcomes

Students will be able to address the magic of the PV and FV in the calculation of time and rate for compounding, discounting, and multiplying.

READY RECKONER—FORMULAE

1. FV of a single cash flow: $FV_n = P(1+k)^n$

2. FV of annuity $= FV_A = A \times \dfrac{(1+k)^n - 1}{K}$

3. Sinking fund factor, $A = FV_A \times \dfrac{k}{(1+k)^n - 1}$

4. Present value of single cash flow $= FV_n \times \dfrac{FV_n}{(1+k)^n}$

5. Present value of annuity $= PV_A = A \times \left[\dfrac{(1+k)^n - 1}{k(1+k)^n} \right]$

6. Capital recovery factor $= A = PV_A \times \left[\dfrac{k(1+k)^n}{(1+k)^n - 1} \right]$

7. Effective rate of interest $= r = (1 + k/m)^m - 1$

8. Present value of annuity due $= A \times \left[\dfrac{(1+k)^n - 1}{k(1+k)^n} \right] \times (1+k)$

9. FV of annuity due $= A \times \dfrac{(1+k)^n - 1}{k} \times (1+k)$

10. Present value of perpetuity $= \dfrac{A}{k}$

Formula Used for Time Values of Money through Excel in-Built Functions

Future Value

11. FV of single cash Flow=FV (rate, nper, pmt, pv, type)
12. FV of annuity=FV (rate, nper, pmt, pv, type); the only difference is the PV column zero is supposed to be taken.
13. Sinking fund factor=PMT (rate, nper, pv, fv, type)

Present Value

14. PV of single cash flow=PV (rate, nper, -pmt, pv, type)
15. PV of multiple cash flow=nPV (rate, value1, value2, value3,…)
16. PV of annuity=pv (rate, nper, -pmt, pv, type); the only difference is in the PV column zero is supposed to take.

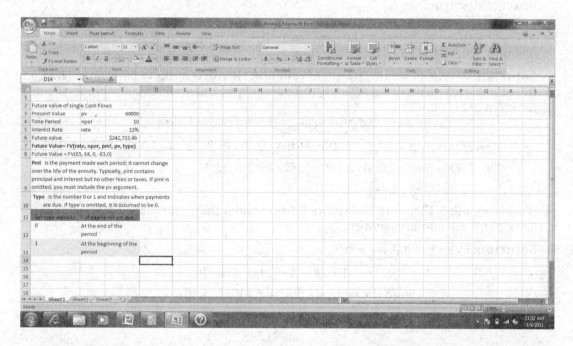

SOLVED PROBLEMS

1. Suppose you invested ₹1,000 in shares of Colgate Palmolive India Ltd 10 years ago. If these shares are now worth ₹2,839.42, what rate of return did your stocks earn?

   Solution: In this case, the initial investment of ₹1,000 has become ₹2,839.42 in a period of 10 years. According to the FV formula, $FV_n = PV(1+k)^n$. Substituting, the given values, we get

   $$2839.42 = 1{,}000\,(1+k)^{10}$$
   $$2.83942 = (1+k)^{10}$$
   $$(2.83942)^{1/10} - 1 = k$$
   $$0.1099 = k \text{ or } k = 10.99\%$$

In other words, an investor who invested ₹1,000 in the shares of Colgate Palmolive Ltd has earned a compounded annual return of 10.99%.

2. You are currently investing your money in a bank account which has a nominal annual rate of 9%, compounded annually. If you invest ₹6,500 today, how many years will it take for your account to grow to ₹10,000?

   Solution: In this case, PV = ₹6,500, FV = ₹10,000, $k = 9\%$, $n = ?$

   Again using the FV formula $FV_n = PV \times FVIF (k, n)$ and substituting the values, we get

   $$₹10000 = ₹6500 \times FVIF (9, n)$$

   $$1.538 = FVIF (9, n)$$

   By referring to the FVIF table for $k = 9\%$, we see that the corresponding value is equal to 1.539 for $n = 5$. In other words, if the interest rate is 9% compounded annually, ₹6,500 would become ₹10,000 in 5 years.

3. Assume that you will receive ₹2,000 a year in years 1–5, ₹3,000 a year in years 6–8, and ₹4,000 in year 9, with all cash flows to be received at the end of the year. If you require a 12% rate of return, what is the PV of these cash flows?

   Solution: As we can see this stream of cash flows involves annuity payments. There are five annuity payments of ₹2,000 each, three annuity payments of ₹3,000 each, and a single payment of ₹4,000.

   The PV of this stream of cash flows can be determined as follows:

   $$PV = 2,000 \times PVIFA (12, 5) + 3,000 \times PVIFA (12, 3) \times PVIF (12, 5) + 4,000 \times PVIF (12, 9)$$

   $$PV = 2,000 \times 3.605 + 3,000 \times 2.402 \times 0.567 + 4,000 \times 0.361$$

   $$= 7,210 + 4,086 + 1,444 = ₹12,740$$

4. If a 5-year ordinary annuity has a PV of ₹10,000, and if the interest rate is 10%, what is the amount of each annuity payment?

   Solution: PVA = ₹10,000, $k = 10\%$

   $$10,000 = A \times PVIFA (5, 10)$$

   From the table, we find that PVIFA $(5, 10) = 7.722$

   $$10,000 = A \times 7.722$$

   $$A = ₹1,295$$

5. You recently received a letter from a reputed commercial bank that offers you a new credit card that has no annual fee. It states that the annual percentage rate (APR) is 18% on outstanding balances. What is the effective annual interest rate? (Hint: Remember these companies bill you monthly.)

   Solution: The annual percentage rate is 18%, but the compounding will be done monthly. The relationship between APR and effective interest rate is given by

   $$r = \left(1 + \frac{k}{m}\right)^m - 1$$

   where r is the effective annual rate, i is the annual percentage rate, and m is the frequency of compounding.

   In the given case, compounding is done monthly, that is, $m = 12$.

Annual percentage rate is 18%.
Substituting the given values, we obtain

$$r = \left(1 + \frac{0.18}{12}\right)^{12} - 1$$
$$= (1 + 0.015)^{12} = 0.1956 = 19.56\%$$

Thus, the effective rate of interest charged by the bank is 19.56%.

6. You deposit ₹2,000 in a savings account that pays 10% interest, compounded annually. How much will your account be worth in 15 years?

Solution:

$$FV = PV * FVIF$$
$$= PV * FVIF_{(k, n)}$$
$$= ₹2,000 * FVIF_{(10\%, 15)}$$
$$= ₹2,000 *$$
$$4.177 = ₹8,354$$

7. Ram bought a share 15 years ago for ₹100. It is now selling at ₹276. What is the growth rate of share price?

Solution:

$$\text{Future Value} = \text{Present Value} * FVIF_{(k,n)}$$
$$276 = 100 * FVIF_{(k, 15)}$$
$$FVIF_{(k, 15)} = \frac{276}{100} = 2.760$$
From the table k = 7%

8. A company has issued debentures of ₹5 lakhs to be repaid after 7 years. How much should the company invest in a sinking fund earning 12% to be able to repay debentures?

Solution:

$$\text{Future value} = \text{present Value} * FVIF_{(k,n)}$$
$$50 = PV * FVIF(12\%, 7)$$
$$50 = PV * 10.089$$
$$\text{Present value} = \frac{50}{10,000} = ₹4.96 \text{ lakh}$$

9. ABC bank pays 12% interest and interest is compounded quarterly. If ₹2,000 is deposited, how much would it grow at the end of 2 years?

Solution:

$$\text{Effective rate of Interest} = r = (1 + k/m)^m - 1$$
$$= (1 + 0.12/4)^4 - 1$$
$$= 0.1255 = 12.55\%$$
$$FV = 2,000 * FVIF_{(0.1255, 2)}$$
$$= 2,000 * 1.2667$$
$$= ₹2,533.4$$

10. You can earn 8% interest, compounded annually. How much should you deposit today to withdraw ₹10,000 in 6 years?

Solution:

$$FV = ₹10,000$$
$$Number\ of\ years = 6$$
$$Interest\ rate = 8\%$$
$$PV\ to\ be\ deposited = FV * PVIF_{(k,\ n)}$$
$$PV = ₹10,000 * PVIF_{(8\%,\ 6)}$$
$$= ₹10,000 * 0.630 = ₹6,300$$

CASELET

1. Mr X wants to start one project for which he has approached the Bank of Baroda for a loan of ₹10,000. He wants to repay the loan in five equal annual installments. The interest rate prevailing in the market is 10% per annum. (a) How much do you need to repay per year to the nearest if payments are due (i) at the beginning of each year, (ii) at the end of each year? (b) Which loan in part (a) is preferable, (i) or (ii)? Explain your answer.

Solution: Suppose you take out a loan of ₹10,000, repayable by five equal annual installments. The interest rate is 10% per year.

(a) How much do you need to repay per year to the nearest center, if payments are due?
Amount of loan $10,000
Interest rate 10%

$$Capital\ Recovery\ Factor = Amount\ of\ Loan \times \frac{k(1+k)^n}{(1+k)^n - 1}$$

$$Or, Present\ Value\ of\ Annuity = Annuity \times \frac{(1+k)^n - 1}{k(1+k)^n}$$

At the end of the year

$$10,000 = Annuity * PVIFA_{(k,\ n)}$$
$$= Annuity * PVIFA_{(10\%,\ 5)}$$
$$= Annuity * 3.791\ (from\ the\ table)$$
$$Annuity = 10,000/3.791 = \$2637.82$$

At the beginning of the year

$$10,000 = Annuity * (1+k) * PVIFA_{(k,\ n)}$$
$$= Annuity * (1+.10) * 3.791$$
$$Annuity = 10,000/4.1701$$
$$= \$2,398$$

According to the problem statement, equated monthly installment is less in case of beginning of the year; therefore, loan payment at the beginning of each year is preferable.

ASSESS YOURSELF

Concepts Review and Critical Thinking Questions

1. Why is time such an important factor in financial decision-making? How can time be adjusted? Illustrate your answer.

2. What happens if the frequency of compounding increases? Illustrate your answer.

3. What is an annuity due? How can you calculate the present and FVs of annuity due? Illustrate.

4. Refer to the opening example of IDBI at the beginning of the chapter. Why do you think would IDBI be willing to accept such a small amount today in exchange for a promise to repay 40 times that amount in the future?

5. Refer to the opening example of IDBI at the beginning of the chapter. What would be the key consideration in deciding whether to invest in IDBI bond or not? Discuss.

STUDENT ACTIVITY

Students should collect data of those mutual fund schemes which have beaten the erosion in the value of money during 2010–2015.

SUGGESTED READINGS

Brealey, R.A., & Myers, S.C. (2002). *Principles of corporate finance* (7th ed.). New York: McGraw-Hill.

Hore, J.C.V. (2002). *Financial management & policy* (12th ed.). Singapore: Pearson Education.

Ross, S.A., Westerfield, R.W., & Jordan, B.D. (2002). *Fundamentals of corporate finance* (6th ed.). New Delhi: Tata McGraw-Hill.

Concept of Risk and Return

- To understand the meaning and importance of risk and return.
- To quantify and establish the relationship between risk and return.
- To know portfolio theory and diversification.
- To understand capital asset pricing model (CAPM).
- To examine portfolio risk, return, and beta.

PRELUDE

Risk (uncertainty) and return are two sides of a coin. "No risk, no return," "higher risk, higher return," and so on are some terms which you may come across along with "risk free," "risk class" assets, and so on. Risk is present in all investment, financial, and operating decisions. Risk may increase or decrease return. Thus, one has to understand the concept of risk and return to have fail-safe financial planning.

Introduction

The basic parameters that affect investment decisions are risk and return. Risk and returns are the two sides of the same coin and go side by side. Investment options may be categorized into financial and physical assets. Financial assets are stocks, debt, derivative, mutual funds, and insurance products, whereas physical assets are tangible investments such as real estate and vehicles. The fact is that no investment (financial or physical) is free from risk and return.

The Concept of Risk

The dictionary meaning of Risk is "a hazard, a peril, exposure to loss or injury." The term "risk" usually refers to the variability in returns due to uncertainty. If the outcome says that the dividend or expected market price is certain, then there is no uncertainty. For example, if we invest our money in the stock market, then what is the chance that we will lose our money? We can refer to this "risk of loss" as (R–). But "risk" is also about gain (R+). Why do we "gamble" on the possibilities of a boom in the stock market? We do that to gain possible positive outcomes. R– and R+ are intertwined, in a holistic fashion. One cannot have R– without R+, and vice versa. And as one changes, the other will also follow.

In other words, risk can also be defined as the chance that the actual outcome from an investment will vary from the expected outcome. The variability of return may be defined as the extent of the deviations of individual return from the average return.

We can therefore say that there are two elements that are crucial when defining risk. These are

- **Indeterminacy:** As there are two possible outcomes (R+ and R–) and it is not known with certainty that which outcome will happen.
- **Adversity:** One of the outcomes (R–) is undesirable but cannot be avoided altogether.

To further appreciate the concept of risk, let us consider the equity shares of two companies: A and B.

The shares of company A have a price that appears to be virtually fixed in place. It is a utility company (e.g., power supply company) issuing dividends regularly such as a fixed income security. Naturally, the price of the utility stock will vary somewhat over time but it does not appear to deviate too much from its central level because of lesser uncertainty associated with returns.

On the contrary, the price of the shares of the second company B only moves in double digit percentage. There have been some frightening moves to the downside as well as healthy appreciations in the price of company B shares in the recent past.

The question arises, which one of these two shares is riskier? A or B.

The answer depends on how you define risk. If you think of using the simple concept of risk, then the potential for price change would be more for B as being the riskier of the two assets, logically. Its daily price movement constitutes a greater percentage of its underlying price.

The above discussion of risk leads to the following conclusions:

- First, the concept of **risk is not subjective but a real world concept**. When we want to invest in the stock market, we are interested in knowing the risk associated with that investment. All investments carry risk. Whether will we gain or lose money? Risk is always an inherent part of investment.
- Second, **risk exists whether it is perceived or not**. Although investment in a firm such as Infosys or Reliance can be considered an excellent investment, but we cannot say that it is not risky. Remember the decline in the share price of, say Infosys in April 2003 by ₹2,000 in just two days.
- Finally, **risk can be imagined** even where the possibility of loss is not there. Consider investing in GOI paper. It is virtually risk free, but we can imagine a possibility of civil war and government defaulting on payment.

Types of Risk

There are various types of risks that a financial manager usually comes across in financial decision-making:

1. **Business Risk:** This refers to the risk of doing business in a particular industry or economic system. Once a firm is in a particular economic system (e.g., India or China or USA) or a particular industry (e.g., Steel, Cement, and Pharma), it is controlled by certain economy-wide or industry-wide factors which lead to variability of returns. For example, frequent fluctuation of cash reserve ratio, repo rate, and reverse repo rate by RBI affects spread of other commercial banks.

2. **Financial Risk:** Financial risk arises when companies resort to financial leverage using debt financing. The more the company resorts to debt financing, the greater is the financial risk. When Tata acquired Land Rover and Jaguar, it thought of paying $2.3 million through debt loan due to which, the debt equity ratio were likely to go up. That is why Tata dropped this idea. Financing of these two brands were done through equity finance.

3. **Liquidity Risk:** Liquidity risk arises when an asset cannot be liquidated easily in the secondary market.

4. **Interest Rate Risk:** Interest rate risk is the variability in a security's return resulting from changes in the level of interest rates. Other things being same, security prices move inversely to interest rates. This risk affects bondholders more directly than equity investors.

5. **Market Risk:** Market risk refers to the variability of returns due to fluctuations in the securities market. All securities are exposed to market risk but equity shares get the most affected. This risk includes a wide range of factors exogenous to securities themselves such as depressions, wars, and politics.

6. **Inflation Risk:** With rise in inflation there is reduction of purchasing power, hence, this is also referred to as purchasing power risk and affects all securities. This risk is also directly related to interest rate risk, as interest rates generally go up with inflation.

Total risk of scrip is the variance of its return. It consists of

1. Systematic risk
2. Unsystematic risk

Systematic risk arises due to macroeconomic variable and cannot be diversified. It is related to the macro economy and hence cannot be eliminated by diversification, and therefore, is called **nondiversifiable risk**. Nondiversifiable risk is also referred to as market risk or systematic risk.

Some of the factors that may give rise to nondiversifiable risk are as follows:

- Change in tax rates
- War and other calamities
- Change in inflation rates
- Change in economic policy
- Industrial recession
- Change in international oil prices, and so on

Unsystematic risk: It is the risk specific to the company or industry and hence can be eliminated by diversification and is called **diversifiable risk**.

Diversifiable risk is also called unsystematic risk or specific risk.

Some of the factors that may give rise to diversifiable risk are

- Strikes in the company
- Bankruptcy of a major supplier
- Exit/Death of a key company officer
- Unexpected entry of the new competitor into the market, and so on

Unsystematic risk is firm specific. An investor wants compensation for bearing systematic risk. He is more concerned about that risk which he cannot diversify.

The Concept of Return

In simple terms, return means the reward that one gets by investing in an investment options. The Oxford English Dictionary defines return as "Profit or income from investment of money or the expenditure of effort or skill." The term "return" itself has different connotations. Is it the periodic cash flow that is generated by the asset? For example, when a company declares a dividend of 30%, does that mean the investors have generated a return of 30%? Or is it the difference between the purchase price and selling price? For instance, if we purchase an equity share for ₹100 and sell it for ₹120, can we say that the profit or return is ₹20, *or is* it periodical withdrawal?

In fact, the return is made up of two components:

1. **Periodic cash flows from the asset:** These are the cash flows that you receive in the intervening time periods between when the investment is made and when the investment matures. For example, when we purchase the bonds issued by a company and we receive interest on these bonds periodically say after every six months when we purchase some equity shares of a company and we receive dividends every year, or when an investment is made by a company in a capital project which generates a cash flow every year for the life of the project.

   So, when a company declares a dividend of 30%, it is only one part of the return that is earned by the investors, that is, dividend yield. The dividends are always paid on the paid-up value of share.

2. **Capital appreciation:** This represents an increase in the market price of the asset during the life of the investment. For example, the market price of the bonds purchased by you at ₹100 per bond increases to ₹120 per bond after one year, or the market price of shares purchased by you at ₹100 per share increases to ₹150 per share after six months, or the market value of the project having an initial investment of ₹50 lakhs increases to ₹75 lakhs after 3 years. In all these cases, there is an appreciation in the price of the asset. If the market price is more than investment or acquisition price, it means capital appreciation. If the market price is less than the investment or acquisition price, it means a negative return or loss (capital depreciation).

Measuring the Rate of Return

The measurement of return depends on investment horizon. It can be classified as follows:

1. Single period return
2. Multiple period return

Similarly, return also depends on time. It matters whether an investor wants to measure historical returns generated on an asset or the future expected return. Therefore, the return can be classified as follows:

1. Ex-post return: historical return
2. Ex-ante return: expected return

It can be a combination of single-period ex post return, multiple-period ex post return, single-period ex ante return, or multiple-period ex ante return.

Single-period Ex Post Return

$$r_{it} = \frac{P_t - P_{t-1} + D_t}{P_{t-1}}$$

where r_{it} is the return on the ith asset at time t. P_t is the price of the ith asset at time t. P_{t-1} is the price of the ith asset at time $t-1$. D_t is the cash flow generated by the asset during the period. Return is the dividend yield and capital gain

The return that we calculate using the above formula is known as the realized or historical or holding period return or ex post return. Let us use the above formula for calculating the ex post return on equity shares and bonds.

Illustration 1. An investor Mr X has purchased the shares of ITC Ltd at ₹250 per share on 1 April, 2015. The company paid a dividend of ₹5 per share during the financial year 2014-2015 and the price of ITC Ltd as on 31st March, 2015 is ₹375. If Mr X decides to sell the shares of ITC, the rate of return earned by him is

$$r = \frac{(375 - 250) + 5}{250} = \frac{125 + 5}{250} = 0.52 \text{ or } 52\%$$

Illustration 2. Suppose another investor Mr Y who has purchased the bonds issued by Premium Steel Ltd at ₹1,000 per bond. The bond has a coupon rate of 10% payable annually. At the end of one year, the bonds are trading at ₹1,200. If Mr Y decides to sell the bonds, the return earned by him is

$$r = \frac{(1,200 - 1,000) + 100}{1,000} = 30 \text{ or } 30\%$$

Multi-period Ex Post Return

Suppose we want to calculate that over a period of ten years, what has been the annual return on a security. How do we calculate this return? To understand this, let us consider a security whose market prices for the last two years are as follows:

Time Period	Market Price (₹)
2015	195
2014	250
2013	160

The single-period return over the 2-year period can be calculated as

$$\text{Return} = \frac{P_2 - P_0}{P_0} = \frac{195 - 160}{160} = 0.21875 \Rightarrow 21.875\%$$

What is the annual return on this security over the two-year period?

Recall the compounding formula, where we relate the present value and future value.

$$FV_n = PV (1+r)^n$$

Going two years back in time, the market price of the security was ₹160. After 2 years, it is ₹195. Therefore

$$195 = 160(1 + r)^2$$
$$\Rightarrow \quad r = 0.10397 \Rightarrow 10.40\%$$

Alternatively, if we know the single-period return, we can calculate the multi-period annual return using the following relationship:

$$(1+r)^n = 1 + r_{0,n'}$$

where r is the annual return over the period and $r_{0,n}$ is the single-period return over the period.

Let us use this formula to determine the annual return using the single-period return.

The single-period return over the 2-year period is 21.875%.

$$(1+r)^2 = 1.21875$$
$$r = \sqrt{1.21875} - 1 = 0.10397 \Rightarrow 10.40\%$$

As you can see, the value is same as calculated above.

Single-period Ex Ante Return: Expected Return

While calculating the historical return on a single asset, we faced no problem, as precise data were available about the returns generated.

However, in reality, an investor frequently has to decide whether to make an investment in a given asset on the basis of "expected returns." The returns as the name suggests are "expected," hence will be generated in future. As future cannot be predicted with accuracy, there is uncertainty associated with these returns. In other words, if it is assumed that there is an asset "A" and the expected return on that asset in future time period is 12%. It is very difficult to say with certainty that a return of 12% will be generated on the same asset. So, how can the investors find out the return on this asset that they expect to earn with some degree of certainty? To overcome this problem, we have to specify the "chance" of generating 12% return and the other possible returns on the asset "A." This "chance" is referred to as probability and when we specify all the possible returns with their respective probabilities, that distribution is called as "probability distribution."

Probability

The chance of an event taking place is called its probability. Probability can never be greater than 1 or less than 0. The sum total of all the probabilities of all mutually exclusive and collectively exhaustive events is always equal to 1.

Probability distribution is a listing of all the possible outcomes with a probability assigned to each. A discrete probability distribution is one in which the number of possible outcomes is limited, or finite. However, a continuous probability distribution, the number of possible outcomes is unlimited, or infinite.

Normal Probability Distribution

Normal distributions are a family of distributions that have the same general shape, that is, bell shape. They are symmetric with scores more concentrated in the middle than in the tails. The graph never touches the X-axis. Examples of normal distributions are shown below. Note that they differ in how spread out they are. The area under each curve is the same, that is, 1. The height of a normal distribution can be specified mathematically in terms of two parameters: the mean (μ) and the standard deviation (σ).

The standard normal curve is a member of the family of normal curves with $m=0.0$ and $d=1.0$. The value of 0.0 was selected because the normal curve is symmetrical around m and the number system is symmetrical around 0.0. The value of 1.0 for d is simply a unit value. The X-axis on a standard normal curve is often relabeled and called Z scores.

There are three areas on a standard normal curve in all the introductory statistics that the students should know. The first is that the total area below 0.0 is 0.50, as the standard normal curve is symmetrical like all normal curves. This result generalizes to all normal curves, in that the total area below the value of mu (mean $= \mu$) is 0.50 on any member of the family of normal curves.

For a normal distribution, the larger the value of σ, the greater the probability that the actual outcome will vary widely from, and hence perhaps be far below, the expected, or most likely, outcome.

This bell-shaped curve tells us that 99% of the values lie within ±3 standard deviations from the mean, 95% of the values lie within ±2 standard deviations from the mean and 68% of the values lie within ±1 standard deviation from the mean.

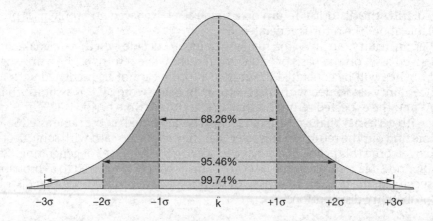

So we have to specify what are the other possible returns expected from investing in asset "A" and what are the respective "chances" (i.e., probabilities). Suppose, an investor is told that the possible returns on asset "A" are 10%, 12%, and 14% with 20%, 50%, and 30% chances of occurrence. Probabilities for likely outcomes are calculated on the basis of past experience, future expectation, and other relevant information pertaining to the event. The probability distribution will look like this:

Possible Returns (%)	Probability
10	0.20
12	0.50
14	0.30

What is the expected return on the asset "A" now?

The expected return on asset A can be calculated as the weighted average of all possible returns, the weights being the respective probabilities. It is the sum of the product of each possible outcomes and its associated probability (Figure 5.1).

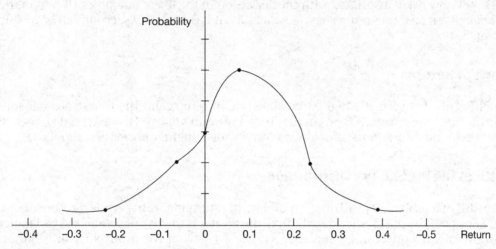

FIGURE 5.1
PROBABILITY DISTRIBUTION OF A'S RATE OF RETURN

Source: Author.

$$\text{Symbolically, } E(r_i) = \sum_{t=1}^{n} r_i p_i,$$

where r_i is the ith expected return on the asset and P_i is the probability of ith return$= 0.10 \times 0.20 + 0.12 \times 0.50 + 0.14 \times 0.30 = 12.2\%$

Illustration 3. Calculate the expected return from the following information.

Scenario	Rate of Return	Probability	Expected Rate of Return
Bullish	8.5	0.5	4.25
Stagnation	1.5	0.3	0.45
Bearish	−6	0.2	−1.2
			3.5

Test Yourself

1. What is return and how is it calculated?
2. Distinguish ex post and ex ante return?
3. What is normal probability distribution? Explain.

Measuring Risk

It is stated that risk is the chance where actual outcome differs from expected outcome. But the question is how do we measure this "chance?" Is it possible to measure risk? Are there any tools available for measuring risk?

Let us have a look at the most commonly used risk measurement tools.

As we know risk is associated with the dispersion in the likely outcomes. Dispersion refers to variability. If an asset's return has no variability, it has no risk. Dispersion can be measured in many ways.

Range of Returns

The difference between the highest possible rate of return and the lowest possible rate of return is called the **range**. It is one of the crudest measures of risk. However, as it is based only on two extreme values, it may not always convey meaningful information about risk.

Width of the Probability Distribution

The width of a probability distribution of rates of return is another crude measure of dispersion. The wider the probability distribution, the greater is the risk or greater the variability of return. This variability can be appraised visually. A look at the probability distribution of company X in comparison with that of company Y indicates that firm X which has a narrower probability distribution is less risky when compared with firm Y which has a wider probability distribution (Figure 5.2).

FIGURE 5.2

COMPARATIVE PROBABILITY DISTRIBUTION OF RATES OF RETURN IN FIRMS X AND Y

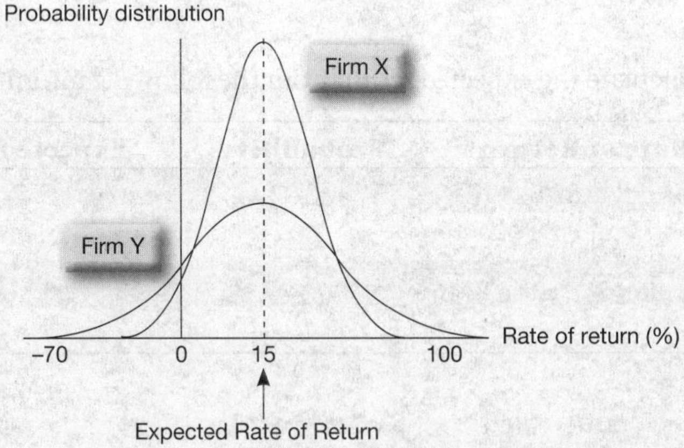

Source: Author.

Variance of Returns

This is the quantitative measure of dispersion and is also the most reliable measure of risk. It measures the variability in the rates of returns. The variance of an asset's rate of return can be found as the sum of the squared deviation of each possible rate of return from the expected rate of return multiplied by the probability that the rate of return occurs.

$$VAR(k) = \sum_{i=1}^{n} P_i(k_i - \bar{k})^2$$

where VAR(k) is the variance of returns, P_i is the probability associated with the ith possible outcome, k_i is the rate of return from the ith possible outcome, k is the expected rate of return, and n is the number of years.

Standard Deviation of Returns

The most popular way of measuring variability of returns is standard deviation. The standard deviation denoted by sigma (σ) is simply the square root of the variance of the rates of return explained above. Or it is the square root of average squared deviation of individual return from the expected return. It is the dispersion of return around mean/expected value.

Standard Deviation for Historical or Ex post Returns

$$\sigma = \sqrt{\sum_{i=1}^{n} \frac{(r_i - r')}{n-1}}$$

where σ is the standard deviation, r_i is the ith return on the asset, and n is the number of observations.

Standard Deviation for Expected or Ex ante Returns

$$\sigma = \sqrt{\sum_{i=1}^{n} [r_i - E(r)] P_i}$$

where σ is the standard deviation, r_i is the ith return on the asset, and p_i is the probability of the ith outcome.

The standard deviation and variance are conceptually equivalent quantitative measures of total risk.

Standard deviation is preferred to range because of the following advantages:

- Unlike the range, standard deviation considers every possible event and assigns each event a weight equal to its probability.
- Standard deviation is a very familiar concept and many calculators and computers are programmed to calculate it.
- Standard deviation is a measure of dispersion around the expected (or average) value. This is in absolute consensus with the definition of risk as "variability of returns."
- Standard deviation is obtained as the square root of variance. It can be calculated by taking the square root of sum of squares of deviations taken from mean. This is why standard deviation is preferred to variance as a measure of risk.

Coefficient of Variation

Coefficient of variation is the standardized relative measure of dispersion. It indicates the variability per unit of average return. It is calculated by dividing standard deviation of asset with its expected mean value. The larger the CV, the larger the risk of the asset (Figure 5.3).

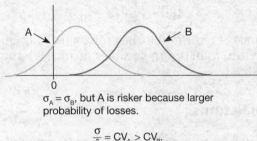

Figure 5.3
COEFFICIENT OF VARIATIONS

$\sigma_A = \sigma_B$, but A is risker because larger probability of losses.

$$\frac{\sigma}{k} = CV_A > CV_B.$$

Source: Author.

Symbolically

$$CV = \frac{\sigma}{r'}$$

Semi-deviation

This is a new approach of risk measurement. The proponents of this approach argue that as an investor will be more concerned about the risk of loss or the chance of market price going below the purchase price while calculating risk, we should consider only the negative deviations or downside deviations. As we ignore the positive deviations (which are favorable) and consider only the negative deviations, hence the name semi-deviation.

Illustration 4. The quarterly returns for the MG Mutual Fund are as follows:

Year	Quarter	Return
2013	I	–1.08
	II	–27.35
	III	–13.81
	IV	–1.87
2014	I	–19.67
	II	1.65
	III	–13.97
	IV	16.18
2015	I	22.08

Determine the variability in the fund's returns using downside deviations (semi-deviation) as a measure of risk.

Solution:

The variability in the funds return using semi-deviation as a measure of risk can be calculated as follows:

Year	Quarter	Return	$(x_4 - \bar{x}_4)$	$(x_4 - \bar{x}_4)^2$
2013	I	−1.08	0.03	0.00
	II	−27.35	−26.23	688.10
	III	−13.81	−12.69	161.07
	IV	−1.87	0.75	0.56
2014	I	−19.67	−18.55	344.16
	II	1.65	−	0
	III	−13.97	−12.85	165.16
	IV	16.18	−	0
2015		22.08	−	0
		25.92	−	0
		−9.75	−8.63	74.50
		8.25	−	0
		−13.42		1,433.58

$$x_4 = -1.11833 \text{ Semi-deviation} = \sqrt{\frac{(x_4 - \bar{x}_4)^2}{11}} \, 1,433.58 = 11.416\%$$

Test Yourself

1. What is risk and how is it calculated?
2. Explain how standard deviation and variance is calculated?

Excel Exercise of Calculation of Risk and Return

For Excel exercise, the following steps are required:

1. Take daily values of share price.
2. Calculate daily return in the next column by this formula, $\text{Return} = \dfrac{P_1 - P_0}{P_0}$
3. For the calculation of average, standard deviation, and variance, Column C is required.
4. Formula for average, standard deviation, and variance is shown in the exhibit.

EXHIBIT 1

	A	B	C	D
	C27		fx	
1	Days	Punjlloyt (share price)	Return	
2	5/21/2010	62.53		
3	5/20/2010	59.1	-5.49%	
4	5/19/2010	63.02	6.63%	
5	5/18/2010	64.03	1.60%	
6	5/17/2010	65.57	2.41%	
7	5/14/2010	66.39	1.25%	
8	5/13/2010	68.71	3.49%	
9	5/12/2010	68.62	-0.13%	
10	5/11/2010	68.18	-0.64%	
11	5/10/2010	70.27	3.07%	
12	5/7/2010	65.98	-6.11%	
13	5/6/2010	64.75	-1.86%	
14	5/5/2010	69.22	6.90%	
15	5/4/2010	68.5	-1.04%	
16	5/3/2010	71.44	4.29%	
17		Average	1.03%	average(C3:C16)
18		Standard Deviation	3.91%	stdev(C3:C16)
19		Variance	0.15%	Var(C3:C16)
20				
21				

Concept of Diversification

Generally, investing in a single security is riskier than investing in a "diversified group" of assets, because in case of a single asset the returns to the investor are based on the future of a single asset. Hence, it is often suggested that to reduce risk, investors should hold a "diversified group" of assets which might contain equity capital, bonds, real estate, savings accounts, bullion, collectibles, and various other assets. In other words, the investors are advised not to put all his eggs into one basket. This "diversified group" of assets is called as **portfolio**. For example, if we have invested in equity shares, bonds, bullion, and real estate, we have created a portfolio of different assets class. However, we may create a portfolio within the same asset class also. For instance, we are holding the equity shares of 10 companies; we have created an all-equity portfolio. If we are holding the bonds/debentures of 5 companies we have created a fixed income portfolio.

It is possible to construct a portfolio in such a way that the total risk of the portfolio is less than the sum of the risk of the individual assets taken together.

How does diversification helps in risk reduction? Let us understand the concept of diversification through a very simple illustration.

Let us assume that "A" put his money equally into the stocks of two companies Sunflame Ltd, a manufacturer of room heating systems and Duracool Ltd, a manufacturer of air conditioners. If the temperatures soar high during summers in a particular year, the earnings of Duracool Ltd would go up leading to an increase in its share price and returns to shareholders. However, the earnings of Sunflame would be on the decline, leading to a corresponding decline in the share prices and investor's returns. But, if there is a prolonged and severe winter, the situation would be just the opposite.

Whereas the return on each individual stock might vary, the return on A's portfolio (50% Sunflame and 50% Duracool stocks) could be quite stable because the decline in one will be offset by the increase in the other. In fact, at least in theory, the offsetting could eliminate this risk entirely.

Assuming that low, moderate, and high temperatures are equally likely events (1/3 probability each), the expected return and standard deviation of the two stocks individually and of the portfolio of 50% SunFlame and 50% Duracool stocks can be calculated as follows:

Temperature	Return on Sunflame Stock (%)	Return on Duracool Stock (%)	Return on Portfolio (50% SunFlame + 50% Duracool) (%)
Low	0	20	10
Moderate	10	10	10
High	20	0	10

Possible Outcomes	Probabilities	Return on Sunflame Stock (%)	Return on Duracool Stock (%)	Rp
Low	1/3	0	20	10
Moderate	1/3	10	10	10
High	1/3	20	0	10
Expected rate of return (k)		10%	10%	10%
σ (sigma denotes standard deviation and measure risk)		$\sqrt{66.67} = 8.16\%$	$\sqrt{66.67} = 8.16\%$	$\sqrt{0} = 0\%$

From the above table, it can be noted that the portfolio earns 10%, no matter what the weather is. Hence, through diversification, two risky stocks have been combined to make a riskless portfolio.

The returns on SunFlame and Duracool are said to be **perfectly negatively correlated** as they always move in opposite directions exactly. However, two stocks which go up or down together in the same manner are said to be **perfectly positively correlated**. Both these situations rarely happen in practice. In general, all stocks have some degree of positive correlation because certain variables such as economic factors and political climate tend to affect all stocks.

However, we do not need stocks which are perfectly negatively correlated in a portfolio to achieve the benefit of risk reduction through diversification. As long as the assets in a portfolio are not perfectly positively correlated, diversification does result in risk reduction.

Diversifiable and Nondiversifiable Risk

The fact that returns on stocks do not move in perfect tandem means that risk can be reduced by diversification. But the fact that there is some positive correlation means that in practice risk can never be reduced to zero. So, there is a limit on the amount of risk that can be reduced through diversification.

This is due to two major reasons:

1. **Degree of correlation:** The extent of risk reduction through diversification depends on the degree of positive correlation between stocks. The lower the correlation, the greater is the amount of risk reduction that is possible.

2. **Number of stocks in the portfolio:** Risk reduction achieved by diversification also depends on the number of stocks in the portfolio. As the number of stocks increases (up to a certain extent), the diversifying effect of each additional stock diminishes as shown in Figure 5.4.

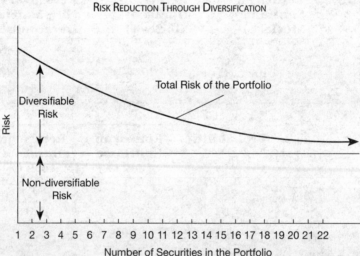

FIGURE 5.4
RISK REDUCTION THROUGH DIVERSIFICATION

Source: Author.

As Figure 5.4 indicates, the major benefits of diversification are obtained with the first 10 to 12 stocks, provided they belong to industries that are not closely related. Additions to the portfolio beyond this point continue to reduce total risk but at a decreasing rate. From Figure 5.4, it is also apparent that only one component of the total risk is being reduced and the other component remains constant whatever the number of stocks in your portfolio is.

The fixed component is that part of the total risk (from various sources such as interest rate risk, inflation risk, and financial risk), which is related to the macro economy or the stock market as a whole and hence cannot be eliminated by diversification is called **nondiversifiable risk**. Nondiversifiable risk is also referred to as market risk or systematic risk.

That part of the total risk that reduces due to diversification is the risk specific to the company or industry and hence can be eliminated by diversification is called **diversifiable risk**. Diversifiable risk is also called unsystematic risk or specific risk.

Return on a Portfolio of Assets

The return on a portfolio of assets is the weighted average of the returns on individual assets, the weights being the proportion in which funds have been invested in various assets in the portfolio.

Symbolically

$$E_{(rP1)} = \sum_{i=1}^{4} p_i r_i^{P1} = \sum_{i=1}^{4} p_i (w_1 r_i^A + w_2 r_i^B)$$

Risk on a Portfolio

The risk on a portfolio of two assets A and B is given by

$$\sigma_P^2 = w_A^2 \sigma_A^2 + w_B^2 \sigma_B^2 + 2 cov(r_A, r_B)$$

where σ_P^2 is the variance of the portfolio, w_A is the proportion of funds invested in asset A, w_B is the proportion of funds invested in asset B, σ_A^2 is the variance of returns on asset A, σ_B^2 is the variance of returns on asset B, $cov(r_A, r_B)$ is the co-variance of returns on assets A and B, measures the amount by which the returns on the assets "'move together" under the different events.

$$cov(r_A, r_B) = \sum_{i=1}^{4} p_i (r_A - E(r_A))(r_B - E(r_B))$$

From the above equation, it is clear that the co-variance between the two stocks must be counted twice. One more point that has to be noted is that as long as the correlation coefficient between two securities is less than 1.00, the standard deviation of the portfolio will be less than the weighted average of the two individual standard deviations. In other words, benefits of diversification will be realized when the coefficient of correlation is less than one.

Minimum Variance Portfolio

The objective of diversification is to reduce risk. A portfolio that has the lowest level of risk is the optimal portfolio or the minimum variance portfolio.

The proportion of investment in an asset A of a two-asset portfolio (A and B) that will result into a minimum variance portfolio can be found using the following formula:

$$W_A^* = \frac{\sigma_B^2 - Cov_{A,B}}{\sigma_A^2 + \sigma_B^2 - 2Cov_{A,B}}$$

where symbols are in standard notation.

The proportion to be invested in asset B $= 1 - W_A^*$.

Test Yourself

1. What is diversification?
2. How does it help in reducing risk?
3. How to measure return and risk of a portfolio?

EXHIBIT 2: EXCEL EXERCISE FOR PORTFOLIO RETURN AND RISK

	A	B	C	D	E	F
1		A	B	AB		
2	Expected return(%)	7.5	10			
3	Standard Deviation(%)	10	15			
4	Correlation			0.5		
5						
6			Weight		Portfolio	
7		A	B	return	Stdev	
8		1.00	0.00	7.50	10.00	
9	RETURN	0.90	0.10	7.75	9.84	
10		0.80	0.20	8.00	9.85	
11		0.70	0.30	8.25	10.04	
12		0.60	0.40	8.50	10.39	
13		0.50	0.50	8.75	10.90	
14	return fx =$B$2*B8+$C$2*C8	0.40	0.60	9.00	11.53	
15		0.30	0.70	9.25	12.28	
16		0.20	0.80	9.50	13.11	
17	RISK	0.10	0.90	9.75	14.03	
18		0.00	1.00	10.00	15.00	
19						
20	Stdev fx =($B$3^2*B8^2+$C$3^2*C8^2+2*B8*C8*$B$3*$C$3*$D$4)^0.5					
21						
22						
23	Minimum Variance Portfolio	0.86	0.14	7.86	9.82	
24	fx =(C3^2-B3*C3*D4)/(B3^2+C3^2-2*B3*C3*D4)					
25						

Expected return and standard deviation of stocks A and B are given. The correlation between stocks A and B is 0.5. Stocks A and B can be combined in different proportions to make portfolio. The likely weights of stocks A and B are taken. Return and standard deviation of different portfolios, according to different weights have been calculated. Formula for return and standard deviation is shown in the exhibit. Weight for minimum variance portfolio can be calculated with the formula mentioned here.

Capital Asset Pricing Model

William F. Sharpe, John Lintner, and Jan Mossin developed the *CAPM*. It is one of the major developments in financial theory. The CAPM establishes a linear relationship between the required rate of return on a security and its systematic or *undiversifiable* risk or beta.

The CAPM is represented mathematically by

$$R_i = R_f + \beta_i (R_m - R_f)$$

where R_j is the expected or required rate of return on security j, R_f is the risk-free rate of return, β_j is the beta coefficient of security j, and R_m is the return on market portfolio.

Assumptions

The CAPM is based on some critical assumptions as follows:

- Investors are risk-averse and use the expected rate of return and standard deviation of return as appropriate measures of risk and return for their portfolio. In other words, the greater the perceived risk of a portfolio, the higher return a risk-averse investor expects to compensate the risk.
- Investors make their investment decisions based on a single-period horizon, that is, the next immediate time period.
- Transaction costs in financial markets are low enough to ignore and assets can be bought and sold in any unit desired. The investor is limited only by his wealth and the price of the asset.
- Taxes do not affect the choice of buying assets.
- All individuals assume that they can buy assets at the going market price and they all agree on the nature of the return and risk associated with each investment.

The assumptions listed above are somewhat limiting, but the CAPM enables us to be much more precise about how trade-offs between risk and return are determined in financial markets.

In the CAPM, the expected rate of return can also be thought of as a required rate of return because the market is assumed to be in equilibrium. The expected return as we have explained earlier is the return from an asset that investors anticipate or expect to earn over some future period. The required rate of return for a security is defined as the minimum expected rate of return needed to induce an investor to purchase it.

What do investors require (expect) when they invest? First of all, investors can earn a risk-free rate of return by investing in risk-free assets such as T-bills. This risk-free rate of return is designated as R_f and the minimum return expected by the investors. In addition to this, because investors are risk-averse, they will expect a risk premium to compensate them for the additional risk assumed in investing in a risky asset.

$$\text{Required Rate of Return} = \text{Risk-free rate} + \text{Risk premium}.$$

The CAPM provides an explicit measure of the risk premium. It is the product of Beta for a particular security j and the market risk premium $R_m - R_f$

$$\text{Risk premium} = \beta_j (k_m - R_f)$$

This beta coefficient "β_j" is the nondiversifiable risk of the asset relative to the risk of the market. If the risk of the asset is greater than the market risk, that is, β exceeds 1.0, the investor assigns a higher risk premium to asset j than to the market. For example, suppose a fertilizer company had a β_j of 1.5, that its required rate of return on the market (km) was 15% per year and that its risk-free interest rate (R_f) was 6% per annum. Using the CAPM, the required rate of return can be calculated as follows:

$$R_j = R_f + \beta_j (k_m - R_f)$$
$$= 0.06 + 1.5(0.15 - 0.06)$$
$$= 0.195 \text{ or } 19.5\%$$

The above calculation shows that the required rate of return on this stock would be 19.5% – the sum of 6% risk-free return, and a 13.5% risk premium. This 19.5% is larger than the 15% required return on the market because the fertilizer stock is riskier than the market.

The Characteristic Line

Suppose we compare the expected return on a particular stock with the expected return on the market portfolio. As both would contain a premium for risk, it would be better to compare the excess returns. Excess return is the return on the security/portfolio over and above the market portfolio. These excess returns can be determined either from the historical data (ex post) or estimates about the future returns.

After calculating the excess returns on the security and the market portfolio, we can either plot the results on a graph paper or run a regression using MS Excel.

By doing so, we get a line of "best fit." This line describes the historical relationship between the excess returns for the stock and excess returns for the market portfolio. This line is known as the characteristic line and is used as a proxy for the expected relationship between the stock returns and the market returns.

In Figure 5.5, alpha (α) is the intercept of the characteristic line on the Y-axis. It denotes the expected excess return on the security if the expected excess return on the market portfolio is zero. Theoretically, α should be zero. This is so because if it is negative investors would avoid the stock because they can earn better returns by investing in some other asset or a combination of assets. If it is positive, the demand for such a security would increase resulting into an increase in its market price and consequently a decline in its expected return.

FIGURE 5.5
CHARACTERISTIC LINE

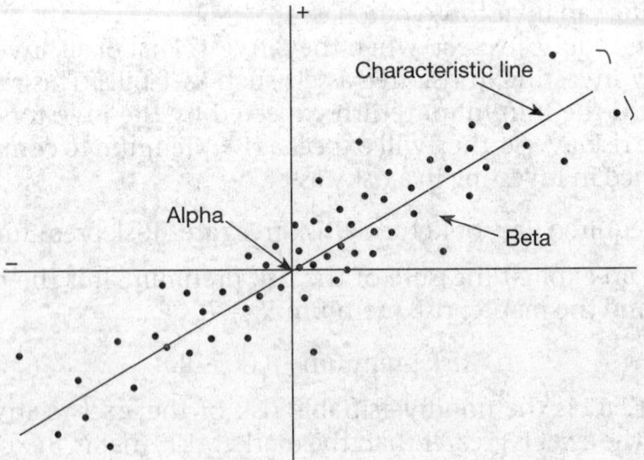

Source: Author.

The Security Market Line

The line that we get by plotting the relationship between the required rate of return (R_i) and nondiversifiable risk (beta) is called *the Security Market Line (SML). This line* describes the relationship between systematic risk and expected return in financial markets (Figure 5.6).

FIGURE 5.6
SECURITY MARKET LINE (SML)

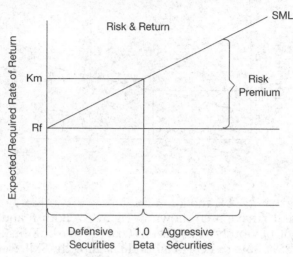

Source: Author.

As per the CAPM assumptions, any individual security's expected return and beta statistics should lie on the SML. The SML intersects the vertical axis at the risk-free rate of return R_f and $R_m - R_f$ is the slope of the SML.

As all securities are expected to plot along the SML, the line provides a direct and convenient way of determining the expected or required return of a security if we know the beta of the security. The SML can also be used to classify securities. Those with betas greater than 1.00 and plotting on the upper part of the SML are classified as aggressive securities, whereas those with betas less than 1.00 and plotting on the lower part of the SML can be classified as defensive securities, which earn below-average returns.

From the data given in the following table, chart the SML and classify the securities.

	Expected Return	Risk-free Return	Beta	Market-risk Premium
Market	12.0	5	1.00	7
Security A	?	5	1.20	?
Security B	?	5	0.80	?

One of the major assumptions of the CAPM is that the market is in equilibrium and that the expected rate of return is equal to the required rate of return for a given level of market risk or beta. In other words, the SML provides a framework for evaluating whether high-risk stocks are offering returns more or less in proportion to their risk and vice versa. Let us see how we can appraise the value securities using CAPM and the SML.

Once a security's expected rate of return and beta has been computed, they may be plotted with reference to the SML. If the security's expected rate of return differs from the required rate of return, the security may be over or under priced and may fall below or above the SML. Let us clarify with the help of Figure 5.7.

FIGURE 5.7

OVERPRICED AND UNDERPRICED SECURITIES

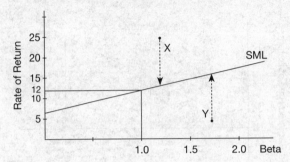

Source: Author.

From Figure 5.7, we see that $R_f = 6\%$ and $R_m = 12\%$.

Two securities X and Y have been shown in Figure 5.7. Both X and Y should have been on the SML, but are not, obviously. Why? Let us take the case of X first. The expected rate of return of X is around 25%. But at a beta of around 1.2, using the SML we see that the required rate of return need be only around 13%. This tells us that security X is undervalued or priced too low because its average rate of return is inappropriately high for the level of risk it bears. However, security Y with a beta of around 1.7 requires a rate of return of around 16%, but its expected return is only about 7%. This tells us that the asset is overvalued or overpriced and hence unattractive because it is expected to produce a return lower than stocks with similar betas. These two assets should move toward their equilibrium—required return positions on the SML (i.e., expected rate of return should be equal to required rate of return and correspond to their respective betas). The actual return as we know is computed as below:

$$\text{Actual return } \bar{k} = \frac{D_t + (P_t - P_t - 1)}{P_{t-1}}$$

Hence, while estimating the expected return in a year and in the absence of historic data on returns and probabilities, the following formula, which is derived from the basic formula, may be used:

$$\text{Expected Return} = \frac{D_0(1+g)}{P_0} + g\ D(1g)$$

where D_0 is the last paid dividend, P_0 is the current purchase/market price, and g is the growth rate.

To reach equilibrium and their required rate of return positions on the SML, both stocks have to go through a temporary price adjustment. To reach equilibrium, assuming betas remain the same, the expected return of X has to be brought down to be equal to the required rate of return and be plotted on the SML. To accomplish this, the denominator of the above formula namely, the purchase price has to be sufficiently increased. Similarly, for security Y, the purchase price has to be sufficiently reduced so that the expected return rises to be the same as the required rate of return.

Security X

$$R_f = 6\%,\ \beta_x = 1.5,\ R_m = 12\%$$

$$\text{Required rate of return} = R_f + \beta_x(R_m - R_f)$$
$$= 6 + 1.5\,(12 - 6)$$
$$= 15\%$$

Expected rate of return in a year, hence, is

$$\text{Last paid dividend } (D_0) = ₹2.50$$
$$\text{Current purchase price } (P_0) = ₹10$$
$$\text{Growth rate} = 5\%$$

$$\text{Expected rate of Return} = \frac{D_0(1+g)}{P_0} + g$$

$$= \frac{2.5(1.05)}{10} + 0.05$$

$$= 31.25$$

By how much should the purchase price of X be increased so that it is at equilibrium? As at equilibrium, the required rate is equal to the expected rate, this can be solved as follows:

$$0.15 = \frac{2.5(1.05)}{P_0} + 0.05$$
$$P_0 = ₹31.25$$

In practice, how does the price of security X get pushed up to its equilibrium price? Investors will be interested in purchasing security X because it offers more than proportionate returns in comparison to the risk. This demand will push up the price of X as more of it is purchased and correspondingly bring down the returns. This process will continue till it reaches the equilibrium price and expected returns are the same as required returns.

Security Y

$$R_f = 6\%,\ \beta_y = 1.25,\ R_m = 12\%$$
$$\text{Required rate of return} = R_f + \beta_y\,(R_m - R_f)$$
$$= 6 + 1.25\,(12 - 6)$$
$$= 13.5\%$$

Expected rate of return in a year, hence, is

$$\text{Last paid dividend} = ₹2.00$$
$$\text{Current purchase price} = ₹25$$
$$\text{Growth rate} = 3\%$$
$$\text{Expected rate of Return} = \frac{2(1.03)}{25} + 0.03 = 11.24\%$$

$$\text{Equilibrium price} = 0.135 = \frac{2(1.03)}{P_0} + 0.04$$

$$= 21.68$$

Investors will be tempted to sell security Y because it offers less than the required rate of return. This increase in the supply of Y will drive down its price and correspondingly increase the return until the expected return *rises* enough to reach the SML and the security is once again in equilibrium.

Thus, the CAPM provides many useful insights to the finance manager to maximize the value of the firm. It shows the type of risk for which shareholders require compensation in the form of a higher risk premium, and hence, a higher return. Because finance managers also perform the investment function on behalf of the shareholders, they must keep sight of the returns shareholders expect for taking risks.

Test Yourself

1. What is CAPM?
2. How does CAPM help in identifying overvalued and undervalued stocks?
3. What is SML?
4. What is beta and how does it measure systematic risk?

Shifts in SML

The slope of the SML is given by the term $(R_m - R_f)$, and this is the risk premium that the investors demand for investing in a risky asset. As the capital markets are dynamic and constantly in flux in response to the new information, the risk-return parameters change and consequently the SML shifts in the risk-return space over a period of time.

Two important factors that affect the SML are

1. Inflation
2. Risk aversion

Shift Due to Inflation

The risk-free interest rate is comprised of three components, namely, the real interest rate, expected inflation rate, and a liquidity premium.

Symbolically

$$rf = r' + i^* + lp$$

In other words, we can say that the risk-free interest rate is composed of the real interest rate and the expected inflation rate. It implies that whenever the expectation of the financial markets about the expected inflation will change, the nominal rate will also change accordingly. Any change in the risk-free interest rate will correspondingly affect the SML also. If the inflation is expected to increase, the risk-free interest rate will increase accordingly and, as it is the base rate for all the required rates of returns in the financial markets, the required rates of return will also change.

For example, suppose the risk-free rate is 5%, the real component is 3%, and inflation component is 2%. Now, if the expected inflation rate increases to 4% with no change in the real interest rate, the risk-free rate increases to 7% and consequently SML moves up indicating an increase in the required rate of return. A decline in expected inflation rate would shift the SML downwards (Figure 5.8).

FIGURE 5.8
SHIFT IN SML DUE TO INFLATION

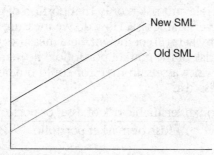

Source: Author.

Shift Due to Risk Aversion

In the SML equation, the term $(R_m - R_f)$ represents the risk premium. The risk premium would depend on the degree of risk aversion in the investors. If the investors perceive too much uncertainty, they would demand a high risk premium for undertaking any risky investment, otherwise they would demand a risk premium commensurate with return. If the investors demand higher risk premium, the slope of SML would increase and it would shift upwards, whereas if the investors demand lesser risk premium, the slope of SML would decrease and it would shift downwards (Figure 5.9).

FIGURE 5.9
SHIFT IN SML DUE TO RISK AVERSION

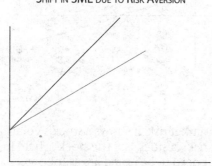

Source: Author.

SML and Cost of Capital

The SML tells us about the return expected on a security in the financial market for a given level of risk. The cost of capital however is the rate of return required by the investors for supplying the capital to the firm. The investors will benefit by supplying capital to the firm only if the firm promises to provide them a return which is higher than what they can earn directly by investing in the financial markets. Thus, while deciding whether a given project would lead to an increment in the shareholders wealth, we need to compare the expected return on that project with what the financial markets offer on an investment with the same degree of risk, that is, same beta.

Thus, SML helps in finding out the "opportunity cost of the capital."

Measuring Nondiversifiable Risk

For a diversified investor, the relevant risk is only that portion of the total risk that cannot be diversified away or its nondiversifiable risk. How do we measure nondiversifiable or market risk? It is generally measured by Beta (β) coefficient. Beta measures the relative risk of any individual portfolio vis-à-vis the risk of the market portfolio. The market portfolio represents the most diversified portfolio of risky assets an investor could buy as it includes all risky assets. This relative risk can be expressed as

$$\beta = \frac{\text{Non diversifiable risk of asset or portfolio j}}{\text{Risk of market portfolio}}$$

Thus, the beta coefficient is a measure of the nondiversifiable or systematic risk of an asset relative to that of the market portfolio. A beta of 1.0 indicates the risk associated with market portfolio. A beta coefficient greater than 1.0 indicates risk greater than that of the market portfolio. Beta coefficient less than 1.0 signifies assets less riskier than the market portfolio. Beta can be less than zero also, though a negative beta is highly unlikely (Figure 5.10).

FIGURE 5.10
BETA MEASURE

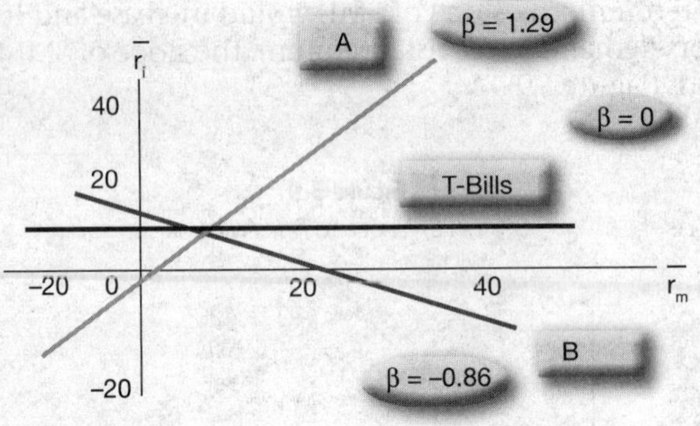

Source: Author.

Thus, beta measures a stock's market risk. It shows a stock's volatility relative to the market. In other words, beta shows how risky a stock is if the stock is held in a well-diversified portfolio.
Two important points that need to be noted are as follows:

- The risk of the market portfolio is nondiversifiable, which an investor cannot avoid because all the possible diversification has already been done.
- As long as the asset's returns are not perfectly positively correlated with returns from other assets, there will be some way to diversify its unsystematic risk. As a result, beta depends only on those factors which lead to nondiversifiable risk.

Measuring Beta

To calculate beta, we run a regression of past returns of Stock i on returns from the market. The slope of the regression line so obtained is nothing but the beta coefficient (Figure 5.11).

FIGURE 5.11
ILLUSTRATION OF BETA CALCULATIONS

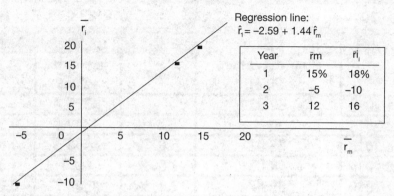

Regression line:
$\hat{r}_i = -2.59 + 1.44\,\hat{r}_m$

Year	r̄m	r̄i
1	15%	18%
2	–5	–10
3	12	16

Source: Author.

The systematic relationship between the return on the security or a portfolio and the return on the market can be described using a simple linear regression, identifying the return on a security or portfolio as the dependent variable k_j and the return on market portfolio as the independent variable k_m, in the single-index model or market model developed by William Sharpe. This can be expressed as

$$k_j = \alpha_j + \beta_j\,k_m + e_j.$$

The beta parameter in the model represents the slope of the above regression relationship and as explained earlier, measures the responsiveness of the security or portfolio to the general market and indicates how extensively the return of the portfolio or security will vary with changes in the market return. The beta coefficient of a security is defined as the ratio of the security's covariance of return with the market to the variance of the market. This can be calculated as follows:

$$\beta_j = \frac{\text{Cov}(k_j k_m)}{\text{Var}(k_m)} = \frac{\sum P(k_j - \bar{k}_j)(k_m - \bar{k}_m)}{\sum P(k_m - \bar{k}_m)}$$

$$\alpha = \bar{k}_j - \beta \bar{k}_m.$$

The alpha parameter α is the intercept of the fitted line and indicates what the return of the security or portfolio will be when the market return is zero. For example, a security with an α of +2% would earn 2% even when the market *return* was zero and would earn an additional 2% at all levels of market return. The converse is true if a security has α of –2%. The positive α thus represents a sort of bonus return and would be a highly desirable aspect of a portfolio or security whereas a negative α represents a penalty to the investor.

The third term is the unexpected return resulting from influences not identified by the model. Frequently referred to as random or residual return, it may take on any value but is generally found to average out to zero.

Excel Sheet for Calculating Beta through Excel

E20			f_x	=COVAR(C3:C16, E3:E16)

	A	B	C	D	E
1	Days	Punjlloyt (share price)	Return	Nifty(index value)	return
2	5/21/2010	62.53		4325.8	
3	5/20/2010	59.1	-5.49%	4342.4	0.38%
4	5/19/2010	63.02	6.63%	4414.3	1.66%
5	5/18/2010	64.03	1.60%	4500	1.94%
6	5/17/2010	65.57	2.41%	4500.7	0.02%
7	5/14/2010	66.39	1.25%	4643	3.16%
8	5/13/2010	68.71	3.49%	4679.5	0.79%
9	5/12/2010	68.62	-0.13%	4599.7	-1.71%
10	5/11/2010	68.18	-0.64%	4573.2	-0.58%
11	5/10/2010	70.27	3.07%	4622.2	1.07%
12	5/7/2010	65.98	-6.11%	4507.4	-2.48%
13	5/6/2010	64.75	-1.86%	4598.6	2.02%
14	5/5/2010	69.22	6.90%	4692	2.03%
15	5/4/2010	68.5	-1.04%	4753.3	1.31%
16	5/3/2010	71.44	4.29%	4807.1	1.13%
17		Average	1.03%		0.77%
18		Standard Deviation	3.91%		1.54%
19		Varaiance of Market			0.02%
20	Covariance between company and Index				0.03%
21		Beta			1.5
22					

Steps for Calculation of Beta

1. Calculate daily return of Punjlloyd share and Nifty.
2. From daily return column find out average, standard deviation, and variance of the company and Nifty.
3. Covariance between company and Nifty can be calculated with the help of this formula (C3:C16, E3:E16).
4. Beta=Covariance/variance of market which is C20/C19.

Beta (β) of a Portfolio

Beta of a portfolio is the weighted average of the betas of the individual assets in the portfolio, the weights being the proportion in which funds are invested in various assets in the portfolio.
   Symbolically

$$\beta_p = \Sigma\, w_i \beta_i$$

For example, if the beta of a security A is 1.5 and that of security B is 0.8 with 40% y of the funds being invested in security A and 60% in security B, the beta of our portfolio will be 1.08 $(1.5 \times 0.4 + 0.8 \times 0.6)$.

Test Yourself

1. What factors cause shift in SML?
2. How do nondiversifiable risks measured?
3. How can beta of a portfolio calculated?

How to Calculate Beta through Regression Line with Excel In-built Functions

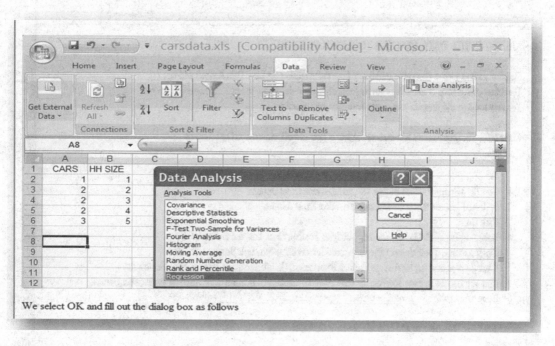

We select OK and fill out the dialog box as follows

We select OK and fill out the dialog box as follows

We obtain

| 8 | SUMMARY OUTPUT |

ADDING-IN THE DATA ANALYSIS TOOLPACK TO EXCEL

Statistical analysis such as descriptive statistics and regression requires the Excel Data Analysis add-in.
The default configuration of Excel **does not** automatically support descriptive statistics and regression analysis.
You may need to add these to your computer (a once-only operation).

Excel 2007: The Data Analysis add-in should appear at right-end of Data menu as Data Analysis.
If not then

1. Click the **Microsoft Office Button** , and then click **Excel Options**.
2. Click **Add-Ins**, and then in the **Manage** box, select **Excel Add-ins**.
3. Click **Go**.
4. In the **Add-Ins available** box, select the **Analysis ToolPak** check box, and then click **OK**.
   Tip If **Analysis ToolPak** is not listed in the **Add-Ins available** box, click **Browse** to locate it.
   If you get prompted that the Analysis ToolPak is not currently installed on your computer, click **Yes** to install it.
5. After you load the Analysis ToolPak, the **Data Analysis** command is available in the **Analysis** group on the **Data** tab.
6. If you have trouble see: http://office.microsoft.com/en-us/excel/HP100215691033.aspx:

Excel 2003: The Data Analysis add-in should appear in the Toools menu.
If not then

1. On the **Tools** menu, click **Add-Ins**.
2. In the **Add-Ins available** box, select the check box next to **Analysis Toolpak**, and then click **OK**.
   Tip If **Analysis Toolpak** is not listed, click **Browse** to locate it.
3. If you see a message that tells you the Analysis Toolpak is not currently installed on your computer, click **Yes** to install it.
4. Click **Tools** on the menu bar. When you load the Analysis Toolpak, the **Data Analysis** command is added to the **Tools** menu.
5. If you have trouble see http://office.microsoft.com/en-us/excel/HP011277241033.aspx

SUMMARY

1. For valuation of any asset/securities, risk, and return are the two main concepts.
2. Return of any share consists of capital appreciation and dividend yield

$$r_{it} = \frac{P_t - P_{t-1} + D_t}{P_{t-1}}$$

3. Risk is the variability in return. It is the chance that the actual outcome differs from expected outcome.
4. Return and risk can be measured through ex ante and ex post.
5. Expected return is

$$E(ri) = \sum_{i=1}^{n} r_i p_i$$

6. Risk is measured through variance and standard deviation of returns of a security. Standard deviation is the square root of variance.
7. Standard Deviation for Historical or Ex post returns

$$\sigma = \sqrt{\sum_{i=1}^{n} \frac{(r_i - r')}{n-1}}$$

8. Standard deviation for expected or ex ante returns

$$\sigma = \sqrt{\sum_{i=1}^{n} [r_i - E(r)] P_i}$$

9. Investors are generally of three types. On the basis of risk preferences, they can be categorized as risk averse, risk seeker, and risk neutral.
10. Return on shares is generally normally distributed.
11. Difference between average return and T-bill yield is risk-free return.
12. Collection of various securities is known as portfolio.
13. Portfolio return is equal to

$$E_{(rP1)} = \sum_{i=1}^{4} p_i r_i^{P1} = \sum_{i=1}^{4} p_i (w_i r_i^A + w_2 r_i^B)$$

14. Portfolio risk is equal to

$$\sigma_P^2 = w_A^2 \sigma_A^2 + w_B^2 \sigma_B^2 + 2 \text{cov}(r_A, r_B)$$

15. $\text{cov}(r_A, r_B)$ = Covariance of returns on Assets A and B, measures the amount by which the returns on the assets "move together" under different events.

$$\text{cov}(r_A, r_B) = \sum_{i=1}^{4} p_i (r_A - E(r_A))(r_B - E(r_B))$$

16. Portfolio risk includes individual security risk and covariance between securities. The covariance further depends on the standard deviation of individual securities and correlation between them.

17. Magnitude of risk depends on the correlation between securities. Portfolio risk is the weighted average risk of individual securities if correlation coefficient is +1.0. For a correlation coefficient less than 1, portfolio risk is less than the weighted average risk. For perfectly negative correlated security, portfolio risk is zero.

18. Investor will prefer a portfolio with higher expected return and when the expected returns are the same, investor would prefer portfolio with minimum risk. Choice between higher return or low risk would depend on investor's risk preference. This is referred to as mean variance criteria.

19. The total risk of security is equal to variance. Risk can be further categorized as systematic and unsystematic risk.

20. Unsystematic risk can be eliminated through diversification. Efficient Portfolio consists of zero unsystematic risk.

21. Systematic risk cannot be eliminated and is related to market risk. It is measured through beta.

22. Beta is ratio of covariance of security and market to the variance of market portfolio.

$$\beta = \frac{\text{Non} = \text{diversifiable risk of asset or portfolio j}}{\text{Risk of market portfolio}}$$

23. CAPM helps in establishing the relationship between risk and return. It emphasizes is that risk premium is directly proportional to market risk.

$$R_i = R_f + \beta_j(k_m - R_f)$$

24. CAPM also helps in evaluating overvalued and undervalued stocks.

KEY TERMS

- Beta
- Risk
- Market risk
- Capital asset
- Security market line
- Risk-free return
- Correlation
- Probability return
- Risk-Free rate of return

- Covariance
- Standard deviation
- Variance
- Pricing model
- Characteristic line
- Risk premium
- Expected rate of return
- Normal distribution

Learning Outcomes

The students would have learnt the origin of risk, return, and factors affecting them.

SOLVED EXAMPLES

1. Risk and return of two securities X and Y are given below:

Portfolio	Expected Return	Standard Deviation	Weight
X	12	16	0.5
Y	20	24	0.5

If the desired portfolio standard deviation is 20%, determine correlation coefficient that would yield the desired level of risk.

Solution:

$$\sigma^2_p = (W_x)^2 (\sigma_x)^2 + (W_y)^2 (\sigma_y)^2 + 2 W_x W_Y \sigma_x \sigma_Y \rho_{xy};$$

$$(20)^2 = (0.5 \times 16)^2 + (0.5 \times 24)^2 + 2 \times 0.5 \times 0.5 \times 16 \times 24 \times \rho_{xy};$$

$$400 = 64 + 144 + 192 \rho_{xy};$$

$$192 \rho_{xy} = 400 - 128;$$

$$\rho_{xy} = 192/192 = 1.$$

Hence, there is a positive perfect correlation between X and Y.

2. Y company limited share has the following expected return with probabilities. Calculate the expected return and risk.

Return	Probability
−20	0.05
−10	0.10
10	0.20
15	0.25
20	0.20
25	0.15
30	0.05

Solution:

Expected Return $= E(ri) = \sum_{i=1}^{n} r_i p_i = -20 \times 0.05 + -10 \times 0.10 + 10 \times 0.20 + 15 \times 0.25 + 20 \times 0.20$

$+ 25 \times 0.15 + 30 \times 0.05 = 13\% \ \sigma^2 = (-20 - 13)^2 \times 0.05 + (-10 - 13)^2 \times 0.10 + (10 - 13)^2 \times 0.20$

$+ (15 - 13)^2 \times 0.25 + (20 - 13)^2 \times 0.20 + (25 - 13)^2 \times 0.15 + (30 - 13)^2 \times 0.05 \ \sigma^2 = \sqrt{156} = 12.49\%$

3. A portfolio consists of three securities X, Y, and Z with following parameters:

Particulars	X	Y	Z	Correlation
Coefficient				
Expected return	25	22	20	
Standard deviation	30	26	24	
Correlation				
XY				−0.5
YZ				+0.4
XZ				+0.6

If each security has equal weight, how much is the risk and return of the portfolio.

Solution:

$$\text{Portfolio return} = E(r_x) \times W_x + E(r_y) \times W_y + E(r_z) \times W_z$$
$$= 25 \times (1/3) + 22 \times (1/3) + 20 \times (1/3) = 22.32\%$$
$$\sigma^2_p = (W_x)^2 (\sigma_x)^2 + (W_y)^2 (\sigma_y)^2 + 2\,W_x\,W_y\sigma_x\sigma_y\rho_{xy}$$
$$\sigma^2 = (30 \times 1/3)^2 + (26 \times 1/3)^2 + (24 \times 1/3)^2 + 2 \times 1/3 \times 1/3 \times 30 \times 26 \times -0.5 + 2 \times 1/3$$
$$\times 1/3 \times 26 \times 24 \times 0.4 + 2 \times 1/3 \times 1/3 \times 30 \times 24 \times 0.6 = 303.91$$
$$\sigma = \sqrt{303.91} = 17.43\%$$

4. From the following data, compute, beta of a security, and expected return from securities.

$$\sigma_x = 10\%, \ \sigma_m = 8\%, \ \rho_{xm} = 0.72, \ R_f = 8\%, \ R_m = 15\%$$

Solution:

$$\beta = \frac{\sigma_x \sigma_m \rho_{xm}}{\sigma^2_m} = \frac{10 \times 8 \times 0.72}{8 \times 8} = 0.9$$
$$R_i = R_f = \beta(k_m - R_f) = 8 + 0.9(15 - 8) = 14.3\%$$

5. Mr Vijay Sharma owns two securities: Reliance and Infosys. Reliance has an expected return of 15% with a standard deviation of those returns being 11%. Infosys has an expected return of 12%, and a standard deviation of 7%. The correlation of returns between Reliance and Infosys is 0.81. If the portfolio consists of ₹60,000 in Infosys and ₹40,000 in Reliance, what is the expected standard deviation of the portfolio returns?

Solution:
Expected return on Reliance $E(r_1) = 15\%$
Expected return on the Infosys Stock $E(r_2) = 12\%$
Standard deviation of returns on Reliance $(\sigma_1) = 11\%$
Standard deviation of returns on Infosys $(\sigma_2) = 7\%$
Coefficient of Correlation $(\sigma_{12}) = 0.81$
Proportion of investment in Reliance stock $(W_1) = 0.40$
Proportion of investment in Infosys stock $(W_2) = 0.60$
Variance of a portfolio of two assets is given by the following formula:

$$\sigma^2 = W_1^2\,\sigma_1^2 + W_2^2\,\sigma_2^2 + 2W_1W_2\sigma_1\sigma_2\sigma_{12}$$

Substituting the given values, we obtain

$$\sigma^2 = (0.40)^2\,(11)^2 + (0.60)^2\,(7)^2 + 2\cdot 0.40\cdot 0.60\cdot 11\cdot 7\cdot 0.81$$

$$= 19.36 + 17.64 + 29.94$$

$$= 66.94$$

$$\sigma = \sqrt{66.94} = 8.18\%$$

6. Security A offers an expected return of 14% with a standard deviation of 8%. Security B offers an expected return of 11% with a standard deviation of 6%. If you wish to construct a portfolio with a 12.8% expected return, what percentage of the portfolio will consist of security A?

    Solution: Let the proportion of investment in Security A = W
      Then, investment in security B = (1 − W)
      Expected return on a portfolio $(E\,[r_p]) = W_1\,E\,(r_1) + W_2\,E\,(r_2)$

$$12.8 = W\cdot 14 + (1-W)\cdot 11$$

$$12.8 = 14W + 11 - 11W$$

$$1.8 = 3W$$

$$W = 0.6$$

    Thus, investment in security A = 60% and investment in security B = 40%.

7. Deepak has a portfolio of eight securities, each with a market value of ₹5,000. The current beta of the portfolio is 1.28 and the beta of the riskiest security is 1.75. Deepak wishes to reduce his portfolio beta to 1.15 by selling the riskiest security and replacing it with another security with a lower beta. What must be the beta of the replacement security?

    Solution: Beta of a portfolio = Weighted average beta of the constituent securities = $\sigma w_i \beta_i$
      The current beta of Deepak's portfolio = 1.28
      Market value of the portfolio = ₹40,000

$$\text{Weight of each security in the portfolio} = \frac{5,000}{40,000} = \frac{1}{8}$$

$$\text{Sum of the betas of eight securities} = 1.28 \times 8 = 10.24$$

$$\text{The beta of the portfolio after replacement} = 1.15$$

$$\text{Sum of the betas of eight securities} = 1.15 \times 8 = 9.20$$

    As the riskiest security with a beta of 1.75 is replaced, it means

$$10.24 - 1.75 + x = 9.20$$

$$x = 9.20 - 8.49 = 0.71$$

    Thus, the beta of the replacement security = 0.71.

8. Mikkelson Corporation's stock had a required return of 13.50% last year, when the risk-free rate was 5.50% and the market risk premium was 4.75%. Then, an increase in investor risk aversion caused the market risk premium to rise by 2%. The risk-free rate and the firm's beta remain unchanged. What is the company's new required rate of return?

Solution:

$$R_i = R_f + \beta_j(k_m - R_f)$$
$$13.50 = 5.50 + \beta_j \times 4.75$$
$$\beta_j = 8/4.75 = 1.68$$

Investor risk aversion has caused risk premium to risk by 2%.

$$R_i = R_f + \beta_j(k_m - R_f)$$
$$= 5.50 + 1.68 \times 6.75 = 16.84\%$$

9. The risk-free rate of return is 8% and market rate of return is 16%. Betas of four shares A, B, C, and D are 0.60, 1.00, 1.50, and –0.20. What are the required rates of return for these shares?

Solution:

$$R_i = R_f + \beta_j(k_m - R_f)$$
$$R_A = 8 + 0.60(16 - 8) = 12.8\%$$
$$R_B = 8 + 1.00(16 - 8) = 16\%$$
$$R_C = 8 + 1.50(16 - 8) = 20\%$$
$$R_D = 8 + -0.20(16 - 8) = 6.4\%$$

10. The monthly returns for TISCO and BSE Sensex for the last 12 months are given below:

Month	TISCO Closing Price (₹)	BSE Sensex
August	252.10	4,244.73
September	271.70	4,453.24
October	358.45	4,906.87
November	361.05	5,044.82
December	444.05	5,838.96
January	404.45	5,695.67
February	429.70	5,667.51
March	383.50	5,590.60
April	357.80	5,655.09
May	296.25	4,759.62
June	300.80	4,795.46
July	392.00	5,170.32

(a) Determine the TISCO's beta coefficient.
(b) Calculate the unsystematic risk of TISCO.

Solution:

Month	BSE Sensex	TISCO Closing Price (?)	Return on TISCO Stock (y)	Return on the SENSEX (x)	y−y'	x−x'	(y−y')²	(x−x')²	(x−x')(y−y')
August 2003	4,244.73	252.1							
September 2003	4,453.24	271.7	7.77	4.91	2.50	5.66	6.27	32.09	14.19
October 2003	4,906.87	358.45	31.93	10.19	26.66	29.82	710.68	889.15	794.92
November 2003	5,044.82	361.05	0.73	2.81	−4.54	−1.38	20.65	1.92	6.29
December 2003	5,838.96	444.05	22.99	15.74	17.72	20.88	313.95	435.91	369.94
January 2004	5,695.67	404.45	−8.92	−2.45	−14.19	−11.03	201.30	121.61	156.46
February 2004	5,667.51	429.7	6.24	−0.49	0.97	4.13	0.95	17.08	4.02
March 2004	5,590.60	383.5	−10.75	−1.36	−16.02	−12.86	256.69	165.42	206.07
April 2004	5,655.09	357.8	−6.70	1.15	−11.97	−8.81	143.32	77.64	105.49
May 2004	4,759.62	296.25	−17.20	−15.83	−22.47	−19.31	505.01	372.97	433.99
June 2004	4,795.46	300.8	1.54	0.75	−3.73	−0.57	13.94	0.33	2.14
July 2004	5,170.32	392	30.32	7.82	25.05	28.21	627.46	795.76	706.62
		Totals	57.94	23.24			2,800.22	2,909.88	2,800.13
		Average	5.27	2.11					

Variance of Returns on SENSEX $= \dfrac{1}{n-1}\Sigma(x-x')^2 = \dfrac{1}{10} = \times 2,909.88 = 290.99$

Covariance of Returns between SENSEX and TISCO $= \dfrac{1}{10} = \times 2,800.13 = 280.01$

Beta of Stock $= \dfrac{\text{Covariance between returns on Stock and on market Inde}}{\text{Variance of returns on market Index}}$

Beta of TISCO $= \dfrac{280.10}{290.99} = 0.962$

Total Risk on a Stock = Systematic Risk + Unsystematic Risk = Variance of Returns on the Stock

Variance of Returns on TISCO Stock $= \dfrac{1}{n-1}\Sigma(y-y')^2 = \dfrac{1}{10} = \times 2,800.22 = 280.02$

Systematic Risk on TISCO Stock $= \beta^2\sigma_m^2 = (0.962)^2 \times 290.99 = 269.29$

Unsystematic Risk $= 280.02 - 269.29 = 10.73$

CASE STUDY

ConocoPhillips started in 1875 with a vision of providing kerosene oil to the townspeople. It is the third largest energy solution company in USA and the fifth largest refinery in the world. The main objective of ConocoPhillips is to provide energy solution to the world. The company explores, produces, supplies, and markets energy resources to the individual and businesses, and also produces plastic and chemicals. It also deals in natural gas gathering and operations. The emerging business of ConocoPhillips is e-gas, power generation, and water sustainable center. The main competitors of ConocoPhillips are BP PLC, Chevron Corp., and ExxonMobil Corporation. The sector of the company is basic material and industry is integrated oil and Gas, and is headquartered at Houston, Texas. As of December 31, 2009, the company had 8.36 billion barrels of oil equivalent of proven reserves. It focuses on the power generation, and technologies related to conventional and nonconventional hydrocarbon recovery, refining, alternative energy, biofuels, and the environment. The company shares are traded on New York Stock Exchange (NYSE). Taking Standard & Poor's (S&P) as a benchmark, they analyze company's return and beta correlation with the market.

CALCULATION OF MONTHLY RETURN OF S&P AND CONOCOPHILLIPS

Date	SPY Closing Value	SPY Dividend	COP Closing Price	COP Dividend	Return SPY (%)	Return COP (%)
Tuesday, March 01, 2011	132.59	0.553	79.86	0.66	−0.01	3.40
Tuesday, February 01, 2011	133.15		77.87		3.47	8.97
Monday, January 03, 2011	128.68		71.46		2.33	4.93
Wednesday, December 01, 2010	125.75	0.653	68.1		6.68	13.18
Monday, November 01, 2010	118.49		60.17	0.55	0.00	2.24
Friday, October 01, 2010	118.49		59.39		3.82	3.41
Wednesday, September 01, 2010	114.13	0.602	57.43		8.95	9.54
Monday, August 02, 2010	105.31		52.43	0.55	−4.50	−4.06
Thursday, July 01, 2010	110.27		55.22		6.83	12.49
Tuesday, June 01, 2010	103.22	0.531	49.09	0.55	−5.14	−4.28
Monday, May 03, 2010	109.37		51.86		−7.95	−12.38
Thursday, April 01, 2010	118.81		59.19		1.55	15.67

Date	SPY Closing Value	SPY Dividend	COP Closing Price	COP Dividend	Return SPY (%)	Return COP (%)
Monday, March 01, 2010	117		51.17	0.5	5.65	7.65
Monday, February 01, 2010	110.74		48		3.12	0.00
Monday, January 04, 2010	107.39		48		−3.63	−6.01
Tuesday, December 01, 2009	111.44	0.59	51.07		1.90	−1.35
Monday, November 02, 2009	109.94		51.77	0.5	6.16	4.17
Thursday, October 01, 2009	103.56		50.18		−1.92	11.12
Tuesday, September 01, 2009	105.59	0.508	45.16		3.55	0.29
Monday, August 03, 2009	102.46		45.03	0.47	3.69	4.10
Wednesday, July 01, 2009	98.81		43.71		7.46	3.92
Monday, June 01, 2009	91.95	0.518	42.06	0.47	−0.07	−7.22
Friday, May 01, 2009	92.53		45.84		5.85	11.80
Wednesday, April 01, 2009	87.42		41		9.93	4.70
Monday, March 02, 2009	79.52	0.561	39.16	0.47	8.32	6.10
Monday, February 02, 2009	73.93		37.35		−10.74	−21.42
Friday, January 02, 2009	82.83		47.53		−8.21	−8.24
Monday, December 01, 2008	90.24	0.719	51.8		0.96	−1.37
Monday, November 03, 2008	90.09		52.52	0.47	−6.96	1.88
Wednesday, October 01, 2008	96.83		52.01		−16.52	−29.00
Tuesday, September 02, 2008	115.99	0.691	73.25		−9.40	−11.22
Friday, August 01, 2008	128.79		82.51	0.47	1.55	1.67

Date	SPY Closing Value	SPY Dividend	COP Closing Price	COP Dividend	Return SPY (%)	Return COP (%)
Tuesday, July 01, 2008	126.83		81.62		−0.90	−13.53
Monday, June 02, 2008	127.98	0.669	94.39	0.47	−8.34	1.89
Thursday, May 01, 2008	140.35		93.1		1.51	8.07
Tuesday, April 01, 2008	138.26		86.15		4.77	13.04
Monday, March 03, 2008	131.97	0.642	76.21	0.47	−0.90	−7.29
Friday, February 01, 2008	133.82		82.71		−2.58	3.25
Wednesday, January 02, 2008	137.37		80.11		−6.05	−9.28
Monday, December 03, 2007	146.21	0.775	88.3		−1.13	10.32
Thursday, November 01, 2007	148.66		80.04	0.41	−3.87	−5.31
Monday, October 01, 2007	154.65		84.96		1.36	−3.20
Tuesday, September 04, 2007	152.58	0.719	87.77		3.87	7.18
Wednesday, August 01, 2007	147.59		81.89	0.41	1.28	1.81
Monday, July 02, 2007	145.72		80.84		−3.13	2.98
Friday, June 01, 2007	150.43	0.656	78.5	0.41	−1.46	1.91
Tuesday, May 01, 2007	153.32		77.43		3.39	11.65
Monday, April 02, 2007	148.29		69.35		4.43	1.46
Thursday, March 01, 2007	142	0.551	68.35	0.41	1.15	5.27
Thursday, February 01, 2007	140.93		65.32		−1.96	−1.64
Wednesday, January 03, 2007	143.75		66.41		1.50	−7.70

Date	SPY Closing Value	SPY Dividend	COP Closing Price	COP Dividend	Return SPY (%)	Return COP (%)
Friday, December 01, 2006	141.62		71.95		0.78	6.91
Wednesday, November 01, 2006	140.53		67.3	0.36	1.99	12.32
Monday, October 02, 2006	137.79		60.24		3.15	1.19
Friday, September 01, 2006	133.58	0.579	59.53		2.69	−6.15
Tuesday, August 01, 2006	130.64		63.43	0.36	2.18	−7.07
Monday, July 03, 2006	127.85		68.64		0.45	4.75
Thursday, June 01, 2006	127.28	0.555	65.53	0.36	0.25	4.11
Monday, May 01, 2006	127.51		63.29		−3.01	−5.40
Monday, April 03, 2006	131.47		66.9			

Particulars	S&P	COP
Average monthly return	0.31%	0.95%
Standard deviation	5.17%	8.63%
Correlation	0.70	
Regression equation	$Y = 0.00591 + 1.17X$	

Graphical Presentation of Return

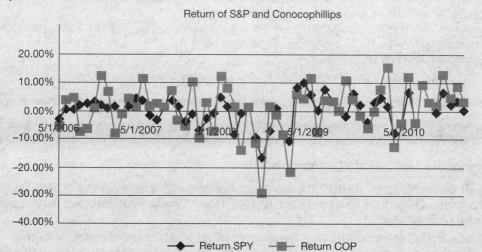

Return of S&P and Conocophillips

RESULTS FOR BETA THROUGH IN-BUILT EXCEL APPLICATION FOR REGRESSION ANALYSIS

Regression Statistics

Multiple R	0.704	SS	MS	F	Significance F
R^2	0.495	0.214	0.214	55.881	0.00000000051
Adjusted R^2	0.486	0.218	0.004		
Standard error	0.062	0.432			
Observations	59				

	Coefficients	Standard Error	t-stat	p-value	Lower 95%	Upper 95%
Intercept	0.00591	0.0081	0.7324	0.46693	–0.01025	0.02208
X Variable 1	1.17505	0.1572	7.4753	5.13E-10	0.86029	1.48982

Regression equation $Y = 0.00591 + 1.17X$

Beta signifies systematic risk. It can be calculated through regression equation. Regression equation is generally $\alpha + \beta_x$. β is the slope of line and measures systematic risk. Beta of the company is 1.17. It is an aggressive stock as beta is more than 1.17.

Mean and Standard Deviation: The average return of S&P and ConocoPhillips are 0.31% and 0.95%, respectively. The standard deviation of S&P and ConocoPhillips are 5.17% and 8.63%, respectively. The risk and return goes side by side. The benchmark has less risk and return. COP is more risky with 8.63% return.

Symbols

β: beta. it is the slope of SML and identifies systematic risk.
ρ: rho. It expresses the correlation between return of two stocks.
σ: sigma. It denotes standard deviation and is used to find out risk of investment option
μ: mu; mean of Population. It is used to calculate the mean return of stocks.
α: alpha. It is the intercept of the characteristic line on the Y-axis. It denotes the expected excess return on the security if the expected excess return on the market portfolio is zero.
K or r. These symbols are used to denote return from stocks.
R_f: risk-free return. It denotes return on government securities, fixed deposit, T-bills, post office investment options are considered to be risk-free return.
α_p: Standard deviation of a portfolio

Source: Author (compiled from http://concophillips.comand modified there on).

ASSESS YOURSELF

Concept Review and Critical Thinking Questions

1. What do we mean by return? If a company declares a dividend payout of 50% on shares (face value ₹10) issued at a premium of ₹140, does it mean that investors have earned a return of 50%? Discuss.

2. What is risk? Is more volatility in the stock markets good for the investors? Discuss.

3. Earnings announcements by companies are followed by changes in the market price of the stock. Given the historical nature of these earnings and the fact that these are accounting figures and not cash flows, why are they so important? Discuss.

4. What is efficient frontier? Why the efficient frontier is not a straight line? Discuss.
5. CAPM attempts to explain the returns generated on a security. To what extent one can depend on CAPM? Discuss in the light of shortcomings of the model.
6. What is SML? How is it different from the characteristic line? Discuss.
7. What is beta? How can a portfolio manager change the beta of his portfolio? Discuss.

STUDENT ACTIVITIES

Students should make a study of value of return, beta and risk of select scripts in S&P CNX Nifty in 2014–2015 and establish a relationship between risk and return.

SUGGESTED READINGS

Brealey, R.A., & Myers, S.C. (2002). *Principles of corporate finance* (7th ed.). New York: McGraw-Hill.

Elton, E.J., & Gruber, M.J. (1991). *Modern portfolio theory and investment management.* New York: John Wiley & Sons.

Horne, J.C.V. (2002). *Financial management & policy* (12th ed.). Singapore: Pearson Education.

Markowitz, H.A. (1992, March). Portfolio selection. *Journal of Finance.*

Ross, S.A., Westerfield, R.W., & Jordan, B.D. (2002). *Fundamentals of corporate finance* (6th ed.). New Delhi: Tata McGraw-Hill.

Concept of Value

- To learn about valuation of bonds and shares.
- To understand the relationship between the interest rate and value of bond.
- To focus on establishing linkage between earnings, dividend yield, P/E ratio, and value of bond.
- To understand equity share valuation in constant dividend, constant growth, and variable growth.

PRELUDE

The Indian economy has emerged as one of the fastest-growing economies in the world. It is rated as the third largest economy in the world. The recent crisis in China and the recessionary mode over Euro Zone and other countries have made India's prospects brighter. About 7% growth rate in the GDP, impressive saving rates, current account deficit under control, and continuous falling prices have built up pressure on the RBI to reduce the rate of interest to further stimulate growth in the economy. If this happens, then what will be the relationship between interest rate, yield, and return? It is believed that there is an inverse relationship between the interest rate and price of bond. Similarly, how is the value created with changing market price and dividend in the case of equity shares? The present chapter is an attempt to understand the concept of value, different dimensions, and risk and return to investors with varying maturity and investments. Read on.

Valuation establishes the relationship between the risk and return to determine the value of an asset. The concept of risk and return is fundamental to valuation of security. The prerequisites for valuation of assets are expected cash flow along with timings and the required rate of return based on risk profile. How are bonds and shares valued? Does value have a different concept? In financial management, there are various concepts of value such as book value, market value (MV), intrinsic value, liquidation value, replacement value, and going-concern value.

Book Value

Book value is the value at which an asset is shown in a balance sheet, generally at its historic cost less accumulated depreciation. The book value of debt is stated as the outstanding amount. The difference between the book value of assets and liabilities is equal to paid-up equity capital plus reserves and surplus, which is also known as shareholders' funds. Book value per share is calculated by dividing shareholders' fund (also known as equity, net worth, etc.) by number of outstanding shares (issued shares). Book value reveals historical value.

Market Value

Market value of an asset is the current price at which the asset is being currently sold or bought in the market. This value is determined by the interaction of supply and demand for the asset. It is sometimes difficult to determine the MV of an asset if there is no secondary market in existence for that asset. MV of asset by and large is generally higher than the book value of the growing companies. In efficient capital market, MV of asset is equal to intrinsic value of share.

Intrinsic Value

This represents what the asset is worth based on the expected present and future cash flows from the asset. It is determined by discounting the PV of all the expected future cash flows from the asset at an appropriate risk-adjusted required rate of return.

Replacement Value

Replacement value of an asset is the amount that is required to replace the existing asset in the current condition. It is very difficult to find out the worth of existing assets. Replacement value does not take into consideration intangibles.

Liquidation Value

Liquidation value is the amount that is realized if the company sells its assets after having terminated its business. It does not include value of intangibles. It is the minimum amount that company could accept if it sold its business.

Going-concern Value

Going-concern value is the amount that is realized if a business is sold in operating condition. This value would always be higher than the liquidation value. Going-concern value is generally higher than liquidation value as it takes into consideration future value of the asset and intangibles.

Basic Valuation Model (BVM)

To construct a valuation model, the following components are required:

1. Estimate of size and timing of expected cash flows from the prospective investment
2. Estimate of the investor's required rate of return from the prospective investment

The BVM defines the value of an asset is the present value of all its expected future cash flows discounted at an appropriate rate of return. This is nothing but the intrinsic value of the asset.

Any asset can be regarded simply as a series of cash flows receivable over a period of time. Therefore, value of any asset can be defined as the PV of these future cash flows, that is, the intrinsic value of an asset is equal to the PV of the benefits associated with it. Symbolically, it can be represented as

$$V_0 = \frac{CF_1}{(1+k)^1} + \frac{CF_2}{(1+k)^2} + \ldots + \frac{CF_n}{(1+k)^n}$$

$$= \sum_{t=1}^{n} \frac{CF_t}{(1+k)^t},$$

where V_0 is the PV of the asset, CF_t is the expected cash flow at the end of period t, k is the discount rate or the required rate of return on the cash flows, and n is the expected life of an asset.

$\sum_{t=1}^{n}$ denotes summation of cash flows from year 1, 2, 3…till n

This is the BVM, which applies to all types of assets with some modifications depending on the individual cash flow and the risk characteristics of the asset (Figure 6.1).

FIGURE 6.1

VALUATION OF ASSETS THROUGH DISCOUNTED CASH FLOW

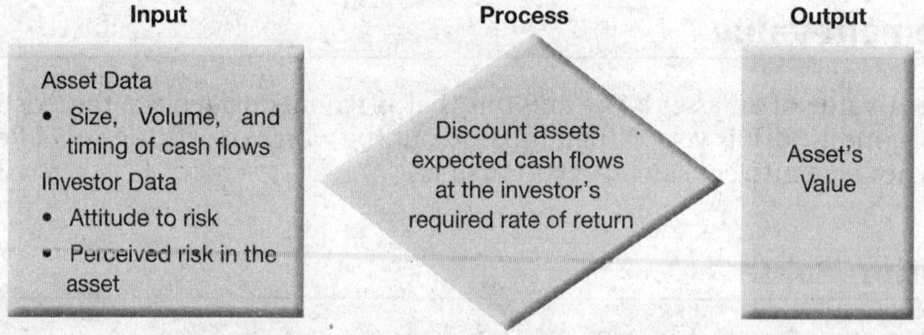

Source: Author.

Illustration 1. Calculate the intrinsic value of an asset if the expected annual cash inflow is ₹2,000 per year for the next 7 years and the required rate of return is 18%.

Solution: The value of an asset can be calculated as

$$V_0 = \sum_{t=1}^{n} \frac{CF_t}{(1+k)^t} = \sum_{t=1}^{7} \frac{2,000}{(1+0.18)^t}$$

$$= \sum_{t=1}^{7} \frac{2,000}{(1+0.18)^t} = 2,000(\text{PVIFA*})$$

$$= 2,000 \times 3.812 = ₹7,624$$

The MV of a Firm

A firm can raise the capital required either in the form of share capital (equity or preference) or through loans. In order that investors may provide the required capital, the firm must offer them the rate of return on their capital commensurate with the risk that they undertake. If the firm is not able to give the investors the rate of return on their investment that they expect, they would not supply any capital to the firm in future and in the present. They would simply move out as shareholders or bondholders by offloading their holdings in the secondary market. As a result, the firm may get starved of necessary funds in the future. However, if the firm is able to generate a return equal to or greater than the rate of return required by the capital suppliers or creditors (investors), the firm not only experiences an enhancement in its value, but also can have easy access to required funds. Thus, if the finance manager wishes to enhance the MV of the firm, he needs to enhance the MV of equity and the MV of debt. In fact, all the financial decisions need to be directed toward this ultimate objective. This also implies that the finance manager needs to know how the financial markets value the firm's equity and debt.

Therefore, the MV of a firm (MV_0) is the sum of the MV of its equity (MV_E) and the MV of its debt (MV_D).

$$MV_0 = MV_E + MV_D$$

The BVM discussed earlier helps in determining the intrinsic value of an asset. At any point of time, the MV of an asset and the intrinsic value need not be equal. However, it is expected that in the long run the market will recognize the intrinsic worth of the asset and the market price will move toward its intrinsic value. This necessitates the need to understand how we can determine the intrinsic value of equity and debt (the value can be sustained from the PV table given in the appendix).

Test Yourself

1. What is value? Compare book value with MV.
2. What is intrinsic value?
3. What is BVM?

In the following sections, we discuss the valuation of debt and equity.

Valuation of Bonds/Debentures

A bond is a long-term debt instrument issued to finance firm's activities. Bonds and debentures are interchangeable. Bonds are normally floated by public sector undertakings, government bodies, and municipal corporations, and they are generally secured by creating a fixed charge against certain specific assets of the firm. The private sector company issues bonds that are called as debentures. Bonds issued by the Government are secured. Debentures can be secured or unsecured. The rate of interest on bonds/debentures is generally fixed and known to the investor. Bonds can be redeemable, which is repayable after a specific period. The main features of bonds/debentures are as discussed in the following subsections.

Face Value

The value stated on the face of the bond is called its face value. It is also known as the par value. It represents the amount borrowed by the firm, which a company specifies to repay after a specified period of time, that is, at the time of maturity. Face value or par value is usually ₹100 and may sometimes be ₹1,000.

Coupon Rate

The specified rate of interest payable on a bond is called the coupon rate. The interest is payable on the face value of the bond irrespective of its MV. For example, if a bond of face value ₹100 and coupon rate 9% is currently selling in the market at ₹125, the interest will still be calculated on the face value. The interest payable is simply the par value of the bond × coupon rate, and so in this case it will be ₹9. Interest payable is tax deductible.

Maturity

A bond/denture is issued for a specific period of time. The principal is repaid at the time of maturity. Typically, corporate bonds have a maturity period of 7 to 10 years, whereas government bonds have a maturity period ranging from 1 to 30 years.

Redemption Value

The value which a bondholder gets on maturity is called the redemption value. A bond may be redeemed at par, at premium (more than par), or at discount (less than par value).

Credit ratings: To reduce default risk, a company before issuing bonds and debentures, obtain rating from credit rating agencies such as Credit rating Information Services of India Limited (CRISIL). Bonds with highest ratings as AAA and BBB are treated as investment grade debentures. Investors prefer investing in highly rated bonds and debentures (see Exhibit 1 for CRISIL Ratings).

EXHIBIT 1: RATING SCALE FOR LONG-TERM INSTRUMENTS

Aaa (Triple A) Highest safety	Bonds rated "**aaa**" are judged to offer the highest degree of safety, with regard to timely payment of financial obligations. Any adverse changes in circumstances are most unlikely to affect the payments on the instrument.
Aa (Double A) High safety	Bonds rated "**aa**" are judged to offer a high degree of safety, with regard to timely payment of financial obligations. They differ only marginally in safety from "**aaa**" issues.
A Adequate safety	Bonds rated "**a**" are judged to offer an adequate degree of safety, with regard to timely payment of financial obligations. However, changes in circumstances can adversely affect such issues more than those in the higher rating categories.
Bbb (Triple B) Moderate safety	Bonds rated "**bbb**" are judged to offer moderate safety, with regard to timely payment of financial obligations for the present; however, changing circumstances are more likely to lead to a weakened capacity to pay interest and repay the principal than for instruments in higher rating categories.
Bb (Double B) Inadequate safety	Bonds rated "**bb**" are judged to carry inadequate safety, with regard to timely payment of financial obligations; they are less likely to default in the immediate future than instruments in lower rating categories, but an adverse change in circumstances could lead to inadequate capacity to make payment on financial obligations.

B High risk	Bonds rated "**b**" are judged to have high likelihood of default; while currently financial obligations are met, adverse business or economic conditions would lead to lack of ability or willingness to pay the interest or principal.
C Substantial risk	Bonds rated "**C**" are judged to have factors present that make them vulnerable to default; timely payment of financial obligations is possible only if favorable circumstances continue.
D Default	Bonds rated "**D**" are in default or are expected to default on scheduled payment dates.
NM Not meaningful	Bonds rated "**NM**" have factors present in them, which render the outstanding rating meaningless. These include reorganization or liquidation of the issuer, the obligation being under dispute in a court of law or before a statutory authority.
Note:	CRISIL may apply "+" (plus) or "−" (minus) signs for ratings from "AA" to "C" to reflect comparative standing within the category.

Source: http://www.crisil.com/ratings/credit-ratings.html.

MV

MV is the price at which the bond is currently traded in the market. MV may be different from par value or redemption value.

Bond Valuation

The intrinsic value of an asset represents what the asset is worth, based on the expected present and future cash flows from the asset. It is determined by calculating the PV of all the expected future cash flows from the asset at an appropriate risk-adjusted required rate of return. The expected cash flow consists of annual interest payment and repayment of the principal. The required rate of return depends on the risk of debenture. The cash flow of government bond has to be discounted at a lower rate and cash flow of debenture has to be discounted at a higher rate.

Redeemable Bond

The holder of a redeemable bond receives a fixed annual interest payment for a certain number of years and a fixed principal repayment (less than, equal to, or greater than the par value) at the time of maturity. The PV of a bond is the discounted value of annual interest stream and the maturity value. The discount rate is that interest rate which an investor could earn on bonds with similar characteristics. By comparing PV with the current MV, it can be analyzed whether bond is undervalued or overvalued. Therefore, using the BVM, the intrinsic value of a redeemable bond can be found out as follows:

$$V_0 = \sum_{t=1}^{n} \frac{C_t}{(1+k_d)^t} = \frac{F}{(1+k_d)^n}$$
$$V_0 = C \times (\text{PVIFA } k_d, n) + F \times (\text{PVIFA } k_d, n)$$

where V_0 is the intrinsic value of the bond, C is the annual interest payable on the bond, F is the principal amount (par value) repayable at the maturity time, n is the maturity period of the bond, and k_d is the required rate of return.

$$\sum_{t=1}^{n} = \text{denotes summation of cash flows from year } 1, 2, 3 \ldots \text{till } n_t = 1$$

So, PVIFA is the present value interest factor of annuity.

Annuity is a series of equal cash flow over a period of time.

PVIF = Present value interest factor.

Illustration 2. A bond having a par value of ₹1,000 and a coupon rate of 12% matures in 3 years. The rate of return required by the investors on the bond is 10%. What is the value of this bond?

Solution:

Annual interest payable = 1,000 × 12% = ₹120

Principal repayment at the end of 3 years = ₹1,000

The value of the bond

$$V_0 = ₹120 \times \text{PVIFA} (10, 3) + 1,000 \times \text{PVIF}(10, 3)$$

$$= ₹120 \times (2.487)^* + 1,000 \times (0.751)$$

$$= ₹298.44 + 751$$

$$= ₹1,049.44^*$$

This value can also be taken from the PV annuity table. Students are advised to refer 10% (horizontal line) for 3 years (vertical line) and the value is 2.487.

Irredeemable Bond

Irredeemable bonds are like perpetuities paying a regular cash flow in the form of interest payments. As the bond is never redeemed, no terminal cash flow is involved. Therefore, we can use the PV of a perpetuity equation to determine the PV of the perpetual interest payments.

$$V_0 = \frac{I}{k}$$

where V_0 is the PV of the irredeemable bond, I is the interest payable on the bond, and k is the required rate of return.

Accrued Interest

In the above examples, we have assumed that bond values are determined at the beginning of the time period when interest becomes payable and hence there is no accrued interest. But in practice, bonds pay interest periodically in arrears and as they trade continuously in the markets, their prices often include accrued interest. The accrued interest is simply the interest that has become due as the last payment date. For example, if a bond pays annual interest on March 31 each year, by June 30, it would have accumulated an accrued interest for three months.

The concept of accrued interest is important because the price at which bonds are traded in the market includes the interest accrued on the bond from its last payment date.

Bonds with Semiannual Interest

Bonds usually pay interest semiannually. As these half-yearly interest receipts can be reinvested, the value of such bonds would be more than the value of the bonds with annual interest payments. The bond valuation equation gets modified as follows:

$$V_0 = \sum_{t=1}^{2n} \frac{I/2}{\left(1 + k_d/2\right)^t} = \frac{F}{\left(1 + k_d/2\right)^{2n}}$$

where V_0 is the value of the bond, $I/2$ is the semiannual interest payment, F is the par value of the bond payable at maturity, $k_d/2$ is the required rate of return for the half-year period, and $2n$ is the maturity period expressed in half-yearly periods.

In other words, while calculating the value of a bond with semiannual interest payments, the interest receivable and the required rate of return for each period get reduced to half and the number of time periods doubles. Similarly, if the interest is paid quarterly, the interest receivable and the required rate of return gets reduced to one-fourth and the number of time periods quadruples.

Illustration 3. A bond of ₹1,000 value carries a coupon rate of 12% and a maturity period of 5 years. Interest is payable semiannually. If the required rate of return is 14%, calculate the value of the bond.

Solution:

$$V_0 = \sum_{t=1}^{10} \frac{120/2}{\left(1 + 0.14/2\right)^t} = \frac{1,000}{\left(1 + 0.14/2\right)^{10}}$$

$$= ₹60 \times \text{PVIFA}\,(7, 10) + 1,000 \times \text{PVIF}\,(7, 10)$$

$$= ₹60 \times 7.024 + 1,000 \times 0508$$

$$= ₹421.44 + 508$$

$$= ₹929.44$$

Bond-yield Measures

Current Yield or Interest Yield

Interest yield (IY) measures the rate of return earned on a bond if it is purchased at its current market price and if the coupon interest is received.

$$\text{Interest Yield} = \frac{\text{Coupon Interest}}{\text{Current Market Price}}$$

In the example cited above, if the current market price of the bond is ₹1,200, then IY $= \frac{120}{1,200} = 10\%$.

Coupon rate and current yield are two different measures. Coupon rate and IY will be equal if the bond's market price equals its face value.

Yield to Maturity (YTM)

The YTM is the discount rate, which equals the PV of expected cash flows from the bond to the current market price or purchase price. It is the rate of return earned by an investor when he purchases a bond and holds it till maturity. The YTM of a bond consists of two elements, an IY and the capital yield (CY), that is, YTM=CY+IY. The YTM is the relevant yardstick for comparing expected returns from bonds as it includes both the IY and the CY.

Illustration 4. Consider ₹1,000 par value bond whose current market price is ₹965. The bond carries a coupon rate of 9% and has a maturity period of 6 years. What would be the rate of return that an investor earns if he purchases the bond and holds it till maturity?

Solution: The rate of return earned also referred to as YTM is the value of k_d in the following equation:

$$P_0 = \sum_{t=1}^{n} \frac{I}{(1+k_d)^t} = \frac{F}{(1+k_d)^n}$$

$$₹965 = \sum_{t=1}^{6} \frac{90}{(1+k_d)^t} = \frac{1,000}{(1+k_d)^6}$$

$$= ₹90 \times PVIFA(k_d,6) + 1,000 \times PVIFA(k_d,6)$$

By trial and error, we can find the YTM as follows: At k_d=10.

Right-hand side=$90 \times$ PVIFA $(10, 6)+1,000\times$PVIF $(10, 6)=90\times 4.355+1,000\times 0.564=955.95$

At k_d=9%

Right-hand side=$90\times$PVIFA $(9, 6)+1,000\times$PVIF $(9, 6)=90\times 4.486+1,000\times 0.596=999.74$

From the above, it is clear that k_d lies between 9% and 10%. Using linear interpolation, we can find the value of k_d as follows:

$$= 9\% + (10\% - 9\%) \times \frac{999.74 - 965}{999.74 - 955.95}$$

$$= 9\% + (1\%) \times \frac{34.74}{43.79}$$

$$= 9\% + (1\%) \times 0.793$$

$$= 9.793\%$$

The YTM is 9.793%.

Shortcut Formula for YTM: As trial-and-error method calculations are too tedious, the following approximation formula can be used to find out the approximate YTM on a bond.

$$YTM = \frac{I+(F-P)/n}{0.4F+0.6P} \text{ or } \frac{I+(F+P)/n}{(F+P)/2}$$

where YTM is the yield to maturity, *I* is the annual interest payment, *F* is the par value or redemption value of the bond, *P* is the current market price of the bond, and *N* is the number of years to maturity.

Illustration 5. The bond of Balaji Telefilms Ltd with a par value of ₹1,000 is currently traded at ₹935. The coupon rate is 9% and it has a maturity period of 5 years. What is the YTM?

Solution:

$$YTM \approx \frac{I+(F-P)/n}{0.4F+0.6P}$$
$$= \frac{90+(1,000-935)/5}{0.4 \times 1,000 + 0.6 \times 935}$$
$$= \frac{90+13}{400+561} = \frac{103}{961} = .1072$$
$$= 10.72\%$$

Example of Some Recent Bonds in India

Zero coupon bonds: These bonds involve no coupon interest payment, that is, there is no explicit rate of interest. These bonds are issued at a substantial discount to their par or redeemable value and the YTM can therefore be very attractive. Firms may find it beneficial as it does not involve any intermediate cash outflows.

Deep discount bonds: These bonds are similar to zero coupon bonds, in that they are also issued at a substantial discount to their par value. However, unlike zero coupon bonds these bonds do pay an annual interest, but the rate is at a substantial discount to the prevailing interest rates.

Junk bonds: A junk bond is a bond that pays a high coupon, usually 3 to 5 percentage points above the high-grade bonds but correspondingly has a high risk of default.

Test Yourself

1. What is a bond/debenture? Explain the features of bonds.
2. How is the value of bond calculated?
3. What is YTM and IY?

Why Does Bond Price Fluctuate?

Based on the bond valuation model, it is apparent that the following factors affect the intrinsic value of bond:

- The relationship between required rate of return and the coupon rate
- Number of years to maturity
- YTM

If there is any change in any or all the above factors, the bond values tend to change. Let us examine how a change in the abovementioned parameters affects the bond values.

I. Relationship between the required rate of return and the coupon rate and its effect on the bond values.

Case I. The required rate of return (k_d) is equal to the coupon rate or interest rate (I) that is, $K_d = I$

Let us consider a bond of Dinshaw Ltd having a face value of ₹100, coupon rate of 12% and 5 years to maturity. If the rate of return required by the investors is also 12%, the value of the bonds of Dinshaw Ltd can be calculated as follows:

$$V = I \times PVIFA\,(k_d, n) + F \times PVIF\,(k_d, n)$$
$$= 12 \times PVIFA\,(12, 5) + 100 \times PVIF(12, 5)$$
$$= 12 \times 3.605 + 100 \times 0.567$$
$$= 43.26 + 56.7 = 99.96 = ₹100$$

Thus, the intrinsic value of the bond is same as its face value. This result can be generalized as follows:

If the required rate of return on a bond is equal to the coupon rate, the intrinsic value of the bond is equal to its face value or par value.

Case II. The required rate of return (k_d) is greater than the coupon rate (I), that is, $k_d > I$

Let us once again consider the same bond of Dinshaw Ltd as above, except that its required rate of return is 14%. The value of the bond can be found out as follows:

$$V_0 = I \times PVIFA\,(k_d, n) + F \times PVIF\,(k_d, n)$$
$$= 12 \times 3.433 + 100 \times 0.519$$
$$= 41.196 + 51.9$$
$$= 93.1$$

Thus, if the required rate of return is more than the coupon rate of interest, the value of the bond is less than its face value or par value.

Case III. The required rate of return is less than the coupon rate, that is, $k_d < I$

Let us consider the same bond as above but the required rate of return is 10%, then the value of the above bond is

$$V_0 = I \times PVIFA\,(k_d, n) + F \times PVIF(k_d, n)$$
$$= 12 \times PVIFA\,(10, 5) + 100 \times PVIF\,(10, 5)$$
$$= 12 \times 3.791 + 100 \times 0.621$$
$$= 45.492 + 62.1$$
$$= 107.59$$

This implies that if the required rate of return is less than the coupon rate, the value of the bond is greater than its face value or par value.

The above results can be summarized as follows:

Relationship between k_d and Coupon Rate	Bond Value
$k_d <$ Coupon rate	Bond value > Face value
$k_d =$ Coupon rate	Bond value = Face value
$k_d >$ Coupon rate	Bond value < Face value

II. Number of years to maturity and its effect on bond values.

As the number of years to maturity decline, the premium or the discount on the bond also declines and the intrinsic value approaches the par value.

Case I. The required rate of return (k_d) is greater than the coupon rate I, that is, $k_d > I$

To illustrate the above, consider a bond of par value ₹1,000, Coupon rate 10% and 5 years to maturity.

If the required rate of return is 12%, then the value of the bond for 5 years is

$$V = I \times PVIFA\ (k_d, n) + F \times PVIF\ (k_d, n)$$
$$= 100 \times PVIFA\ (12,5) + 1{,}000 \times PVIF\ (12, 5)$$
$$= 100 \times 3.605 + 1{,}000 \times 0.567$$
$$= 360.5 + 567 = 927.50$$

After 1 year, when the maturity period will be 4 years, the value of the bond will be

$$V = 100 \times PVIFA\ (12, 4) + 1{,}000 \times PVIF\ (12, 4)$$
$$= ₹100 \times 3.037 + ₹1{,}000 \times 0.636$$
$$= 303.7 + 636 = 939.70$$

After 3 years, when the maturity period will be 2 years, the value of the bond will be

$$V = 100 \times PVIFA\ (12, 2) + 1{,}000 \times PVIF\ (12, 2)$$
$$= ₹100 \times 1.690 + 1{,}000 \times 0.797$$
$$= 169 + 797 = ₹966$$

This implies that the discount on the bond declines as maturity approaches if the required rate of return on the bond is greater than the coupon rate.

Years to Maturity	Bond Value
5	927.50
4	939.70
3	952.20
2	966
1	982.3
0	1,000

Case II. The required rate of return (k_d) is less than the coupon rate.

If the required rate of return on the above bond is 9%, it will have a value of

$$V = ₹100 \times PVIFA\,(9, 5) + 1,000 \times PVIF\,(9, 5)$$
$$= ₹100 \times 3.891 + 1,000 \times 0.650$$
$$= ₹389.10 + .650 = 1,039.10$$

One year hence, when the maturity period will be 4 years, the value of the bond will be

$$V = ₹100 \times PVIFA\,(9, 4) + 1,000 \times PVIF\,(9, 4)$$
$$= ₹100 \times 3.240 + 1,000 \times 0.708$$
$$= ₹324 + 708 = 1,032$$

This implies that the premium on the bond declines as maturity approaches if the required rate of return on the bond is less than the coupon rate.

Years to Maturity	Bond Value
5	1,039.10
4	1,032.00
3	1,025.10
2	1,017.90
1	1,008.70
0	1,000

III. YTM and its effect on bond values

Case I. Bond price is inversely related to YTM.

A bond's price is inversely proportional to its YTM as is evident from theBVM. The PV principle states that the PV of a cash flow varies in inverse proportion to the interest rate used as a discount rate. As such if the YTM of the bond rises, the bond's market price drops and if the YTM falls, the bond's market price rises.

Consider a bond having par value of ₹1,000, a coupon rate of 10%, and maturing in 10 years. Its YTM is 12%

The MV of the bond is

$$100 \times PVIFA\,(12, 10) + 100 \times PVIF\,(12, 10)$$
$$= 100 \times 5.650 + 100 \times 0.322$$
$$= ₹887$$

Now, if the YTM of this bond increases to 14%, the MV of the bond will be

$$100 \times PVIFA\,(14, 10) + 1,000 \times PVIF\,(14, 10)$$
$$= 100 \times 5.216 + 1,000 \times 0.270$$
$$= ₹791.60$$

YTM (%)	Bond Prices (₹)
12	887
14	791.60

This shows that YTM has negative relationship between YTM and Bond's value.

Case II. For a given difference between YTM and the coupon rate, the longer the term to maturity, the greater will be the change in price for a given change in YTM.

It is so because, in case of long maturity bonds, a change in YTM is cumulatively applied to the entire series of the coupon payments and the principal payment is discounted at the new rate for the entire number of YTM; whereas in case of short-term maturity bonds, the new YTM is applied to comparatively few coupon payments; and also, principal payment is discounted for only a short period of time. Thus, long-term bonds are more variable to changes in interest rates than short-term bonds.

Particulars	Bond A	Bond B
Face value	₹100	₹100
Interest rate (%)	10	10
YTM (%)	12	12
YTM	4	6
Value of bond at 10%	10 × PVIFA (10%, 4) + 100 × PVIF (10%, 4) = 100	10 × PVIFA (10%, 6) + 100 × PVIF (10%, 6) = 100
Value of bond at 12%	10 × PVIFA (12%, 4) + 100 × PVIF (12%, 4)	10 × PVIFA (12%, 6) + 100 × PVIF (12%, 6)
	93.97	91.81
Price change (%)	6.03	8.19

Case III. Given the maturity, the change in bond price will be greater with a decrease in the bond's YTM than the change in bond price with an equal increase in the bond's YTM.

Particulars	Bond A
Face value	₹100
Interest rate	10%
YTM	10%
YTM	5
Value of bond at 10%	10 × PVIFA (10%, 5) + 100 × PVIF (10%, 5) = 100
Value of bond at 9%	10 × PVIFA (9%, 5) + 100 × PVIF (9%, 5) = 103.90
Price change	3.90%
Change in YTM	1%

The increase in bonds yield caused a price decrease that is smaller than the price increase caused by an equal size decrease in the yield.

Case IV. For any given change in YTM, the percentage price change in case of bonds of high coupon rate will be smaller than that in the case of bonds of low coupon rate, other things remaining the same.

Particulars	Bond A	Bond B
Face value	₹100	₹100
Interest rate (%)	10	12
YTM	4	4
Value of bond at 10%	10 × PVIFA (10%, 4) + 100 × PVIF (10%, 4)	12 × PVIFA (10%, 4) + 100 × PVIF (10%, 4)
	100	106.34
Value of bond at 12%	10 × PVIFA (12%, 4) + 100 × PVIF (12%, 4)	12 × PVIFA (12%, 4) + 100 × PVIF (12%, 4)
	93.97	100.044
Price change (%)	6.03	5.96

Case V. A change in the YTM affects the bonds with a higher YTM more than it does bonds with a lower YTM.

Particulars	Bond A	Bond B
Face value	₹100	₹100
Interest rate (%)	12	12
YTM	6	6
YTM (%)	20	10
Change in YTM (%)	By 20	By 20
New YTM (%)	24 (20 × 1.2)	12 (10 × 1.2)
Value of bond at 10%	12 × PVIFA (20%, 6) + 100 × PVIF (20%, 6)	12 × PVIFA (10%, 6) + 100 × PVIF (10%, 6)
	73.41	108.67
Value of bond at 12%	12 × PVIFA (24%, 6) + 100 × PVIF (24%, 6)	12 × PVIFA (12%, 6) + 100 × PVIF (12%, 6)
	63.74	100.032
Price change (%)	13.17	7.94

Valuation of Warrants and Convertibles

Warrants

Warrants are distributed to stockholders in lieu of a stock or cash dividend or sold directly as a new security issue. Sometimes, the companies issue preference shares or debentures with less favorable terms (than those investors would get otherwise). Hence, to compensate, it issues warrants to "sweeten" the offering.

Warrants enable the holder to buy a fixed number of shares at a predetermined price during some specified period of time. The term specifies the number of shares that can be purchased for each warrant, based on the exercise price per share, and the expiry date of a warrant. When a warrant is issued, the exercise price is always greater than the current market price. The existence of the positive premium on a warrant means that it will be more beneficial for the warrant holder to sell his warrant, thus realizing its theoretical value plus premium, when he exercises it. The premium associated with a warrant will shrink as the expiry date approaches. The actual value of the warrant will be equal to the theoretical value on the expiry date. Most warrants are detachable from the bond or preferred stock to which they were attached at the time of issue. Detachable warrants can be traded as independent securities.

Convertible Debentures

A convertible debenture is a debenture that is convertible partly or fully into equity shares. If it is partially converted, it is referred to as "partly convertible debenture," and if the debentures are converted fully into equity shares at the end of maturity, it is referred to as "fully convertible debentures." Conversion may be discretionary or compulsory. Convertible bond or a preferred stock is converted into specified number of shares. Usually, in this conversion, no cash is involved; simply, the old security is traded and appropriate number of new securities are issued in exchange.

Conversion Ratio and Conversion Value

The conversion ratio gives the number of shares of stock received for each convertible security. If only the conversion ratio is given, the par conversion price can be obtained by dividing the conversion ratio multiplied by the face or par value of the convertible security.

The conversion value represents the MV of the convertible, if it were converted into stock; this is the minimum value of the convertible based on the current price of the issuer's stock.

Conversion value is obtained by multiplying the conversion ratio by the stock's current market price. For example, consider a convertible bond with ₹1,000 (par value) converted into 20 equity shares. If the market price of the share is, say, ₹55, then the conversion value of the bond is ₹1,100 (20 × 55). If the conversion price of the bond is, say, ₹1,200, then conversion premium of the bond is ₹1,200 − 1,100, that is, 100.

To understand how the valuation of convertibles is done, let us consider an illustration. KGK Ltd has issued fully convertible debentures at a face value of ₹1000 with coupon rate of 9% p.a., which is converted into four equity shares (at a price of ₹250 each) at the end of 3 years.

An investor wanted to buy debentures in the secondary market after a year of issue. Let us find out the value of the convertible, if his required rate of return is 12% and price of share is expected to be ₹260 at the end of 3 years.

The value of convertible is determined as

$$\sum_{t-1}^{n} \frac{C}{(1+r)t} = \frac{P_n \times \text{Conversion Ratio}}{(1+r)n}$$

where C is the coupon rate, r is the required rate of return, P_n is the expected price of equity share on conversion, and n is the number of years to maturity.

$$= \frac{90}{(1.12)^1} + \frac{90}{(1.12)^2} + \frac{260 \times 4}{(1.12)^2}$$

$$= 80.36 + 71.75 + \frac{1,040}{(1.12)^2}$$

$$= 80.36 + 71.75 + 829.08$$

$$= 981.19$$

Thus, value of the convertible is approximately ₹981.

Test Yourself

1. What is the relationship between bond prices and YTM?
2. How does the relationship between discount rate and coupon rate affect the value of bonds?
3. How can we find out the value of convertible debentures?

Valuation of Preference Shares

Preference shares are hybrid securities, as they possess certain characteristics of debt as well as equity. They resemble equity shares in that the preference shareholder is entitled to dividends. It resembles debt in that the preference dividend is fixed and paid in preference to the equity shareholders. Theoretically, preference shares can be irredeemable as well as redeemable. Redeemable preference shares are issued with maturity, whereas irredeemable preference shares are issued without any maturity. In case of cumulative preference shares, unpaid dividend gets accumulated and payable in the near future. Dividend payments do not accumulate in case of non-cumulative preference shares.

Features of preference shares:

- **Claims:** Preference shareholders have preference on assets and incomes over equity shareholders.
- **Dividend:** Preference share dividend is fixed and it is generally cumulative. Dividend keeps on accumulating till it is not finally paid to the preference shareholders. Dividend payments are not tax deductible.
- **Redemption:** Preference shares are both redeemable and irredeemable. However, now in India as per the changes in Companies Act, now only redeemable preference shares with a maximum maturity of 20 years can be issued.

- **Conversion:** Company can issue convertible preference share. Convertible preference shares can be converted into equity shares after the stipulated time period.

As the expected cash flows on preference shares are fixed, the valuation of preference shares is similar to bond valuation. The value of preference share is sum of the PV of dividend and redemption value.

Redeemable Preference Shares

$$V_0 = \sum_{t=1}^{n} \frac{Dt}{(1+k_d)^t} = \frac{RV}{(1+k_d)^n}$$

where Dt is the preference share dividend, RV is the redemption value, and k_p is the discount factor for preference share.

Irredeemable Preference Shares

$$V_0 = \frac{Dt}{K_p}$$

where Dt is the preference share dividend and K_p is the discount factor for preference shares.

Equity Valuation

The equity share capital is the core capital in any business. It is a permanent capital as the equity share capital is never redeemed. The only cash flows expected by the owners are the dividends receivable on these shares. In addition, the investors also expect a capital apprecia-tion, that is, an increase in the price of the shares. The payment of dividend is not mandatory. Even if the company earns profits, dividend payment depends on the discretion of the direc-tors. The rate of dividend is not known on equity shares. It is very difficult to estimate timings and amount of cash flow. It is easy to predict cash flows associated with bonds and preference shares. Earnings and dividends on equity shares are expected to grow in future. Due to these factors, the valuation of equity shares is difficult.

There are various approaches for valuation of equity shares. Some of them are as follows:

- Dividend capitalization approach
- Asset-based approach
- Earnings-based approach
- Free cash flow (FCF)-based approach

Dividend Capitalization Approach

The value of share depends on cash inflows expected by investor and risk associated with those cash inflows. In case of equity shares, the expected cash flows consist of an infinite stream of dividends. As there is no maturity period for equity share, value of equity share is calculated by capitalizing the future dividend series at the required rate of return. The required rate of return is the return that investor could earn from an investment of equivalent risk in the capital market. The value of share is the PV of its future dividend. So the model has been called dividend capitalization approach or dividend discount model (DDM).

According to the dividend capitalization approach or DDM, the value of an equity share is the PV of dividends received plus the PV of the price expected to be realized if the equity share is sold. The price which investor is expected to fetch when he sells share, will include original investment amount plus or minus a capital gain or loss.

This approach rests on the following assumptions:

- Dividends are paid annually.
- The first payment of dividend is made one year after the equity share is bought. However, prorate dividend can also be paid.

Thus

$$P_0 = \frac{D_1}{(1+k_e)^t} + \frac{D_2}{(1+k_e)^2} + ... + \frac{D_\infty}{(1+k_e)^\infty}$$

$$= \sum_{t=1}^{\infty} \frac{D_t}{(1+k_e)^t},$$

where P_0 is the current market price of the equity share, D_1 is the expected dividend a year hence, D_2 is the expected dividend 2 years hence, $D\infty$ is the expected dividend at infinite duration, and k_e is the expected rate of return or required rate of return.

The above equation is the valuation for an equity share of infinite duration. The same can be applied to the valuation of an equity share with a finite duration, provided the investor holds the same for n years and then sells it at a price P_n. The value of an equity share of finite duration would thus be

$$P_0 = \frac{D_1}{(1+k_e)^t} + \frac{D_2}{(1+k_e)^2} + ... + \frac{D_n}{(1+k_e)^n} + \frac{P_n}{(1+k_e)^n}$$

$$= \sum_{t=1}^{n} \frac{D_t}{(1+k_e)^t} + \frac{P_n}{(1+k_e)^n}$$

Using the dividend capitalization principle, the value of P_n in the above equation would be the PV of the stream of dividend beyond the nth period which is evaluated at the end of nth year. Therefore

$$P_n = \frac{D_{n+1}}{(1+k_e)} + \frac{D_{n+2}}{(1+k_e)^2} + ... + \frac{D_\infty}{(1+k_e)^{\infty-n}}.$$

Substituting the value of P_n in the above equation and simplifying it, we get

$$P_0 = \sum_{t=1}^{n} \frac{D_t}{(1+k_e)^t}$$

If the holding period is 1 year, the intrinsic value of shares can be expressed as

$$P_0 = \frac{D_1}{(1+k_e)} + \frac{P_1}{(1+k_e)}$$

where P_0 is the current market price of the share, D_1 is the expected dividend a year hence, P_1 is the expected price of the share a year hence, and k_e is the required rate of return on the equity share.

Depending up on the dividend policy followed by the firm, the dividends may be

1. constant dividends,
2. constant growth of dividends, and
3. changing growth rates of dividends.

As a result, the valuation model as per dividend capitalization approach will also be different. We discuss below the three cases separately.

1. **Valuation with Constant Dividends:** Assume that the dividend per share is constant year after year, whose value is D, then

$$P_0 = \frac{D_1}{(1+k_e)^t} + \frac{D_2}{(1+k_e)^2} + \cdots + \frac{D_\infty}{(1+k_e)^\infty}$$

Simplifying, we obtain

$$P = \frac{D}{k_e}$$

2. **Valuation with Constant Growth in Dividends:** Dividends per share increase at a constant rate year after year.

$$D_t = D_0 (1+g)^t$$

where D_t is the dividend for year t, D_0 is the dividend for year 0, and g is the constant compound growth rate.

The valuation of the share where dividend increases at a constant, compound rate is given as

$$P_0 = \frac{D_1}{(1+k_e)} + \frac{D_2(1+g)}{(1+k_e)^2} + \frac{D_1(1+g)^2}{(1+k_e)^3} + \cdots$$

Simplifying, we obtain

$$P_0 = \frac{D_1}{k_e - g}$$

Illustration 6. Industrial Gadgets Ltd is expected to grow at the rate of 7% per annum and dividend expected a year hence is ₹5.00. If the rate of return is 12%, what is the price of the share today?

Solution:
The price would be

$$P_0 = \frac{5.00}{0.12 - 0.07} = \frac{5.00}{0.05} = ₹100$$

3. **Valuation with Variable Growth in Dividends:** Dividends tend to grow at supernormal growth rates followed by normal growth rates

$$P_0 = \frac{D_1}{(1+k_e)} + \frac{D_2(1+g_a)}{(1+k_e)^2} + \cdots + \frac{D_1(1+g_e)^{n-1}}{(1+k_e)^n}$$

$$+ \frac{D_1(1+g_n)}{(1+k_e)^{n+1}} + \frac{D_n(1+g_n)^2}{(1+k_e)^{n+2}} + \cdots$$

where P_0 is the price of the equity share, $D_n = D_1(1+g_e)n-1$, D_1 is the expected dividend a year hence, g_a is the supernormal growth rate of dividends, and g_n is the normal growth rate of dividends.

Illustration 7. Consider the equity share of Lifeline Pharma Ltd.

Solution:

D_0 is the current dividend per share $=$ ₹2.50, n is the duration of the period of supernormal growth $= 5$ years, g_a is the growth rate for the period of supernormal growth $= 20\%$, g_n is the normal growth rate after supernormal growth period is 5%, and k_e is investor's required rate of return $= 12\%$.

Supernormal Growth Period

Dividend stream during supernormal growth period:

$$D_1 = ₹2.50\,(1.20)$$
$$D_2 = ₹2.50\,(1.20)^2$$
$$D_3 = ₹2.50\,(1.20)^3$$
$$D_4 = ₹2.50\,(1.20)^4$$
$$D_5 = ₹2.50\,(1.20)^5$$

The PV of the above stream of dividends is

$$= \frac{2.50(1.20)}{(1.12)} + \frac{2.50(1.20)^2}{(1.12)^2} + \frac{2.50(1.20)^3}{(1.12)^3} + \frac{2.50(1.20)^4}{(1.12)^4} + \frac{2.50(1.20)^5}{(1.12)^5}$$
$$= 2.67 + 2.86 + 3.07 + 3.29 + 3.53 = 15.42$$

Normal Growth Period

The price of the share at the end of 5 years, applying the constant growth model at that point of time will be

$$P_5 = \frac{D_6}{k_e - g_n} + \frac{D_5(1+g_n)}{k_e - g_n}$$
$$= \frac{2.50(1.20)^5(1.05)}{0.12 - 0.05} = 93.31$$

The discounted value of this price is

$$P_0 = \frac{93.31}{(1.14)^2} = ₹\,48.46$$

The value of the share $P_0 = ₹48.46 + 15.42 = 63.87$.

Impact of Dividend Growth Rate on Price, Returns, and Price–Earning (P/E) Ratio

Different companies have different expected growth rates. Some companies remain stagnant, others show normal growth, and still others grow at a supernormal growth rate. If the required rate of return remains constant, difference in growth rates translates into a difference in prices, dividend yields, CY, and P/E ratio.

To illustrate the above, let us consider three firms A, B, and C. Firm A has a zero growth rate, firm B grows at a normal rate of 5%, and firm C has a supernormal growth rate of 15%.

The expected earning per share and dividend per share of each of the above firms are ₹3.00 and ₹2.00, respectively. The required rate of return from equity investments is 16%.

We can calculate the stock price, dividend yield, CY, and P/E ratio for all the above cases with the given information as follows:

Price	Dividend Yield (%)	Capital Yield (%)	P/E Ratio (P/E) (%)
Firm A: No growth firm $P_0 = \dfrac{D_1}{K}$	16	0	2.5
$\dfrac{2.00}{0.16} = ₹12.5$			
Firm B: Normal growth firm $P_0 = \dfrac{D_1}{K-g}$	11	5	6.06
$\dfrac{2.00}{0.16-0.05} = ₹12.5$			
Firm C: Super growth firm $P_0 = \dfrac{D_1}{K-g}$	1	15	66.67
$\dfrac{2.00}{0.16-0.05} = ₹12.5$			

Following observations can be made from the analysis of the above table:

- As the expected growth rate in dividend increases, the expected return (i.e., the total return = dividend yield + capital gain yield) depends more on the CY and less on the dividend yield other things remaining constant.
- The P/E ratio increases as the expected growth rate in dividend increases.
- High dividend yield and low P/E ratio imply limited growth prospects.
- Low dividend yield and high P/E ratio imply considerable growth prospects.

Test Yourself

1. What are preference shares? Discuss cumulative convertible preference share?
2. What is dividend capitalization method?
3. How is share valued when dividends grow in two stages first with supernormal growth rate and later at normal growth rate? Calculate.
4. Explain the relationship among dividend yield, P/E ratio, and value of shares.

Asset-based Approach

Asset-based approach values the company's equity in terms of the value of the company's net assets rather than in terms of its expected future dividends or earnings. The equity valuation based on book value, MV, and liquidation value is described below.

Book Value

This is the most basic approach to valuation. It considers the net value of company's assets at their balance sheet values and divides by the number of equity shares outstanding to find the net asset value per equity share.

$$\text{Book Value Per Share} = \frac{\text{Total book value of assets} - \text{Total book value of liabilities}}{\text{Number of equity shares outstanding}}$$

As the approach is asset-based, the relevant information is obtained from the balance sheet. As the balance sheet gives a static and historical view of the assets and liabilities of the firm and also the values are dependent on the accounting policies being followed by the firm, the valuation model may not give the true and fair value of equity. Further, using this approach, the intangible assets such as brand equity, highly skilled work force, and expert management cannot be valued. This approach being historic in nature also ignores the future earnings potential of the assets. As a result, this approach may not always provide a realistic valuation of the firm.

Market Value (MV)

The MV approach is better than the book value approach as it values the assets at their current MVs. This approach does not consider the future earnings potential of the assets. This is a serious drawback as the assets are acquired with the objective of maximizing the wealth; they are not an end in themselves, but a means to an end. Besides, it may not always be easy to determine the MVs of the company's assets. If the company uses highly specialized assets, there may be no secondary market for the company's assets and there may be no other comparison available.

$$\text{Market Value Per Share} = \frac{\text{Market value of assets} - \text{Total Market value of liabilities}}{\text{Number of equity shares outstanding}}$$

Liquidation Value

Liquidation per share is the net asset value per share if the company is liquidated. It is the value which an ordinary shareholder is expected to realize after paying to the creditors and for the liquidation expenses also. Liquidation value per share is calculated as follows:

$$\text{Liquidation Value Per Share} = \frac{(\text{Market value of assets} - \text{Liquidation Costs}) - \text{Total liabilities}}{\text{Number of equity shares outstanding}}$$

Liquidation value is the "floor value" per share as it represents what a share would be worth in the event of the worst possible situation, that is, liquidation. However, MV per share is the "ceiling value" as it represents what the company's asset would be worth if it is sold as a going concern.

Earnings-based Approach

One of the key weaknesses of the asset-based valuation methods is that they ignore all the future earnings or cash flow-generating potential of a company. The earnings-based approach focuses on expected future earnings.

Price–Earnings ratio

P/E ratio, more popularly known as the earnings multiple, is the most popular valuation model used by investment bankers, financial analysts, and investors.

$$\text{Intrinsic Value of Equity Share} = \text{EPS} \times \text{P/E Ratio}$$

$$\text{Earning Per Share} = \frac{\text{PAT} - \text{Preference Dividend}}{\text{Number of outstanding equity shares}}$$

The market price of equity shares of a company at any point of time reflects the expectations of the market about the future earnings of the company. A high P/E ratio therefore indicates that the market is very much confident about the future prospects of the company. But a word of caution is very much required here. A high P/E ratio also indicates that the company is a risky bet. This is so because when the risk is high, the expected return is also high. So, a high risk share is likely to have a high P/E ratio. A low P/E ratio may reflect that the future prospects are not very bright, but it may also indicate the low risk inherent in that share and hence may be a "safer bet."

One more point that needs to be understood is that P/E ratio can be historic or prospective depending on whether past earnings are used to determine the EPS or expected earnings are used. For valuation purposes, historic P/E ratios are of no use as the past earnings may not always be indicative of future earnings. For valuation, we should always consider the prospective P/E ratio.

Free Cash Flow-based Approach

One of the drawbacks of using P/E ratio approach is that it is essentially an accounting-based valuation model. It may be recalled that in Chapter 1, we discussed the drawbacks of accounting profits and how cash flows are a better measure of performance. We also defined cash flow as follows:

$$\text{Cash Flow} = \text{Operating Profit} + \text{Depreciation} + \text{Other Non-Cash Items}$$

We also noted in Chapter 1 that many financiers and analysts prefer an estimate of FCF:

$$\text{FCF} = \text{Cash Flow} - (\text{Investment Expenditures} + \text{Dividends} + \text{Taxes})$$

FCF represents the amount of cash available for discretionary purposes such as purchasing new machinery, repaying a loan or paying dividends. FCF-based approach to valuation aims at calculating the FCF per equity share.

According to this approach, the intrinsic value of equity shares is obtained as follows:

$$P_0 = \frac{\text{PV(Expected Free Cash Flow)} - \text{Total liabilities}}{\text{Number of equity shares outstanding}}$$

However, one may come across various practical problems in using the FCF approach such as estimating the expected FCFs, specifying the time horizon for estimation, and estimating the cash flow growth rate.

Modern Valuation Models

Shareholder Value Analysis

According to this approach, the firm's value is dependent on some value drivers and it is possible to create value for shareholders by focusing on these value drivers. These value drivers are

- Sales growth rate
- Operating profit margin
- Cash tax rate
- Investment in long-term assets
- Investment in short-term assets
- Cost of capital
- Planning horizon

The first five drivers are used to determine the future cash flow estimates. The Shareholder Value Analysis (SVA) approach focuses on these value drivers to maximize the cash flow-generating potential of a company's operations.

Market Value Added

The fundamental objective of financial management is to maximize shareholders wealth. It was also noted that for all practical purposes, it means maximizing the market price of the equity shares of the company. However, the advocates of the concept of Market Value Added (MVA) argue that it is possible to increase the market price of equity shares without really increasing the shareholder's wealth. So they argue what should be focused on is not the market price of the shares, but the difference between the MV of firm's equity and the equity capital invested (including retained profits). This is what they call the MVA. This reflects the real value added to the MV of a firm's equity. It reflects the value added over the entire life of the company.

$$MVA = MV \text{ of Firm's Equity} - Equity \text{ Capital Invested}$$

In other words, MVA is the difference between the equity market valuation of a listed/quoted company and the sum of the adjusted book value of debt and equity invested in the company, that is, it is the sum of all capital claims held against the company; the MV of debt and the MV of equity. The higher the MVA, the better. A high MVA indicates that the company has created substantial wealth for the shareholders. Negative MVA means that the value of the actions and investments of management is less than the value of the capital contributed to the company by the capital markets. This means that wealth or value has been destroyed. MVA cannot be calculated at divisional (Strategic Business Unit) level.

Economic Value Added

This technique was originally developed by a New York based management consultancy firm, Stern Stewart. Economic Value Added (EVA) measures the real economic profit earned by a firm. It considers not only the operating costs but also the capital coasts for this purpose. The traditional accounting profit measures such as PBT and PAT do consider the cost of debt in the form of interest paid and opportunity cost of equity capital.

EVA can be calculated as follows:

$$\text{EVA} = \text{Operating Profit} - \text{Cost of Capital}$$

$$\text{Operating Profit} = \text{Total Revenue} - \text{Operating Costs} - \text{Taxes}$$

Cost of capital is the weighted average cost of all the sources of capital employed by the business. According to the EVA approach, shareholder value increases only if a company generates a return, which covers not only the operating costs but also the capital costs. Unlike MVA, which is a forward-looking measure, EVA is a historic measure as it is based on financial statements.

Test Yourself

1. Why is the FCF approach better than the P/E approach?
2. What is SVA?
3. How is EVA calculated?
4. What is the difference between liquidation value and MV approach?

SUMMARY

1. PV of a bond and a share is equal to the discounted value of future cash flow stream.
2. Discounted rate is the required rate of return which an investor expects from securities of comparable risk.
3. Bonds are debt instruments. Value of bond is equal to the PV of annual interest payments and repayment of the principal amount.

$$V_0 = \sum_{t=1}^{n} \frac{C_t}{\left(1+k_d\right)^t} = \frac{F}{\left(1+k_d\right)^n}$$

4. YTM is the discount rate, which equals the PV of expected cash flows from the bond to the current market price/purchase price. YTM is inversely related to bond prices.

$$\text{YTM} = \frac{I+(F-P)/n}{0.4F+0.6P} \text{ or } \frac{I+(F+P)/n}{(F+P)/2}$$

5. Warrants enable the holder to buy a fixed number of shares at a predetermined price during some specified period of time. The terms specify the number of shares that can be purchased for each warrant, based on the exercise price per share, and the expiry date of warrant.

6. Preference shares are hybrid securities, as they possess certain characteristics of debt as well as equity. They resemble equity shares in that the preference shareholder is entitled to dividends. It resembles debt because preference dividend is fixed and paid in preference to the equity shareholders.

7. In case of redeemable preference shares

$$V_0 = \sum_{t=1}^{n} \frac{Dt}{(1+k_d)^t} = \frac{RV}{(1+k_d)^n}$$

8. In case of irredeemable preference shares

$$V_0 = \frac{Dt}{K_p}$$

9. **Dividend capitalization model:** The value of an equity share is the PV of dividends received plus the PV of the price expected to be realized if the equity share is sold. The price which investor is expected to fetch when he sells share will include original investment amount plus or minus a capital gain or loss. The formula for share valuation is

$$P_0 = \frac{D_1}{(1+k_e)^t} + \frac{D_2}{(1+k_e)^2} + \cdots + \frac{D_\infty}{(1+k_e)^\infty} = \sum_{t=1}^{\infty} \frac{D_t}{(1+k_e)^t}$$

$$P_0 = \frac{D_1}{(1+k_e)^t} + \frac{D_2}{(1+k_e)^2} + \cdots + \frac{D_n}{(1+k_e)^n} + \frac{P_n}{(1+k_e)^n} = \sum_{t=1}^{n} \frac{D_t}{(1+k_e)^t} + \frac{P_n}{(1+k_e)^n}$$

10. **Valuation with constant dividends:** Assume that the dividend per share is constant year after year, whose value is D, then

$$P_0 = \frac{D_1}{(1+k_e)^t} + \frac{D_2}{(1+k_e)^2} + \cdots + \frac{D_\infty}{(1+k_e)^\infty} = \frac{D}{k_e}$$

11. **Valuation with constant growth in dividends:** Dividends increase at a constant rate year after year.

$$D_t = D_0(1+g)^t$$

$$P_0 = \frac{D_1}{k_e - g}$$

12. **Valuation with variable growth in dividends:** Dividends tend to grow at supernormal growth rates followed by normal growth rates.

$$P_0 = \frac{D_1}{(1+k_e)} + \frac{D_2(1+g_a)}{(1+k_e)^2} + \cdots + \frac{D_1(1+g_e)^{n-1}}{(1+k_e)^n}$$

$$+ \frac{D_1(1+g_n)}{(1+k_e)^{n+1}} + \frac{D_n(1+g_n)^2}{(1+k_e)^{n+2}} + \cdots$$

13. EVA = Operating Profit − Cost of Capital

KEY TERMS

- Bond
- Book value
- Constant growth
- Convertible debenture
- Debenture
- Discount rate
- Dividend yield
- Earnings ratio
- Economic value added

- Free cash flow
- Opportunity cost
- Intrinsic value
- Liquidation value
- Market value
- Market value added
- Preference share
- Price/earnings
- Yield to maturity

Learning Outcomes

Student would have learnt the basic relationship between the rate of interest, holding period, and return along with the basic valuation model (BVM).

SOLVED EXAMPLES

1. Consider the following information regarding the bond issued by M/s Biotin Ltd:

Face value of the bond	₹1,000
Coupon (payable annually)	9% p.a.
Maturity period	5 years

The above bonds are issued at a discount of 5% and are redeemed at a premium of 10%. Calculate the intrinsic value of the bond.

Solution: The value of the bond is computed as

$$V_0 = I\,(PVIFA_{k\%,\,n}) + F\,(PVIF_{k\%,\,n}),$$

where I is the annual interest payment and F is the redemption value.

$$V_0 = 90 \times PVIFA(9\%, 5\ years) + 1,100\ PVIF(9\%, 5\ years)$$

$$= 90 \times 3,890 + 1,100 \times 0.650 = ₹1,065.10.$$

2. The face value of 5 years, 10% bond is ₹100. The interest is payable semiannually. Assuming 12% required rate of return, compute the value of the bond.

Solution:

$$V_0 = I \times PVIFA\,(k\%,\ n) + F \times PVIF(k\%,\ n)$$

where I is the annual interest payment and F is the redemption value.

$$V_0 = 5 * \text{PVIFA } (6\%, 10) + 100 * \text{PVIF } (6\%, 10)$$
$$V_0 = 5 * 7.360 + 100 * 0.558$$
$$= 36.8 + 55.8 = ₹92.60$$

3. The required rate of return is 14%. Expected dividend is ₹2.50. Compute price at which the shares will sell if the investor expects the earnings or dividends to grow at 12%.

Solution:

$$P_0 = \frac{D_1}{k_e - g}$$

$$= \frac{250}{0.14 - 0.12} = \text{Rs } 125$$

4. M/s Veena Granites Ltd issued fully convertible debentures of face value ₹100 each with a coupon rate of 10% p.a. The debentures will be converted into two equity shares of ₹50 each at the end of 1 year. The expected share price at the end of 1 year is ₹60 and the required rate of return is 12%. What is the value of the convertible?

Solution: Value of convertible = PV of interest + PV of MP of received shares

$$= \frac{10}{1.12} + \frac{2 \times 60}{1.12} = 8.93 + 107.14 = ₹ 116.07$$

5. Morgan International's balance sheet shows a debt of ₹222.60 million. The firm has 49 million outstanding shares, and the market price of each share is ₹85 (face value ₹100). It is considering issuing ₹850 million more debt and using the cash to repurchase its equity. Management estimates that as a result of this restructuring, the market price per share will jump to ₹100. Should it undertake the restructuring exercise?

Solution:

$$\text{Current MV of the firm} = ₹(49 \times 85 + 222.60) \text{ million}$$
$$= ₹4,387.60 \text{ million}$$
$$\text{MV after restructuring} = ₹(39 \times 100 + 1,222.60) \text{ million}$$
$$= ₹5,122.60 \text{ million}$$

As the value is declining after restructuring, Morton should not take up the restructuring exercise.

6. Zubina Ltd recently paid a dividend of ₹2.50 per share that is expected to grow by a constant rate of 8% in each year. If the investor needs a return of 16%, what is the intrinsic value of the equity share?

Solution: According to the dividend discount model, the intrinsic value of the equity share is given by the formula

$$P_0 = \frac{D_1}{k - g}$$

Here, $D_1 = ₹2.50 \times 1.08 = ₹2.70$, $k = 16\%$, and $g = 8\%$.

Substituting the given values, the required intrinsic value is

$$P_0 = \frac{2.70}{0.16 - 0.08} = ₹33.75$$

7. A company is currently paying a dividend of ₹3 per share. The dividend is expected to grow at a 15% annual rate for 3 years, then at 10% for the next 3 years, after which it is expected to grow at 5% rate for forever. What is the PV of the share if the discount rate is 10%?

Solution:

The PV during supernormal growth rate

Year	Dividend	PVIF at 10%	PV
1	3.00(1.15)=3.45	0.909	3.14
2	3.45(1.15)=3.96	0.826	3.27
3	3.96(1.15)=4.56	0.751	3.42
4	4.56(1.10)=5.02	0.683	3.43
5	5.02(1.10)=5.52	0.621	3.43
6	5.52(1.10)=6.07	0.564	3.43
		Total	20.12

$$\text{Present value at the end of 6 year} = P_0 = \frac{D_1}{k - g}$$

$$= \frac{6.07(1 + 0.05)}{0.10 - 0.05}$$

$$= \frac{6.07}{0.05} = ₹\,127.47$$

PV of ₹127.47 now at 10%=127.47 * 0564=₹71.89
PV of share=71.89+20.12=₹92.01.

8. A company current share price is ₹50 and dividend per share is 5. If its required rate of return is 11%. What is the dividend growth rate?

Solution:

$$P_0 = \frac{D_1}{k - g}$$

$$P_0 = \frac{D(1 + g)}{k - g}$$

$$50 = \frac{5(1 + g)}{0.11 - g}$$

$$5.5 - 50g = 5 + 5g$$

$$+55g = -0.5$$

$$g = -0.5/-55 = 9.09\%$$

9. A bond has 3 more years to mature. It has par value of ₹100. The interest rate is 10% and paid annually. Compute YTM at a market price of ₹110.

Solution:

$$YTM = \frac{I + (F - P)/n}{0.4F + 0.6P} \quad \text{or} \quad \frac{I + (F + P)/n}{(F + P)/2}$$

$$= \frac{10 + \dfrac{100 - 110}{3}}{\dfrac{100 + 110}{2}} = \frac{6.67}{105} = 6.35\%$$

10. Sun India Ltd is expected to declare a dividend of ₹2.50 and reach a price of ₹35.00 a year hence. What is the price at which the share would be sold to the investor now, if the required return is 12%?

Solution:

$$P_0 = \frac{D_1}{(1 + k_e)} + \frac{P_1}{(1 + k_e)}$$

$$= \frac{2.50}{(1 + 0.12)} + \frac{35.00}{(1 + 0.12)}$$

$$= 2.23 + 31.25 = ₹\, 33.48$$

11. Consider the case where an investor purchases a bond whose face value is ₹1,000, maturity period is 4 years and coupon rate is 8%. The required rate of return is 10%. What should be he willing to pay now to purchase the bond if it matures at par?

Solution:

Annual interest payable = ₹80

Redemption value after 4 years = ₹1,000

Value of share = $V_0 = I \times PVIFA\,(k\%, n) + F \times PVIF(k\%, n)$

where I is the annual interest payment and F is the redemption value.

$= ₹80 \times PVIFA\,(10\%, 4) + ₹1,000 \times PVIF\,(10\%, 4)$

$= ₹80 \times 3.170 + ₹1,000 \times 0.683$

$= 253.6 + 683$

$= ₹936.60$

The investor would not be able to pay more than ₹936.60 for the bond today.

12. Copeland Ltd recently paid ₹4.00 per share as dividend for the last year. Its dividend is expected to grow by 15% every year for the next 3 years; thereafter, it will continue a normal growth rate of 6% per annum. If the required rate of return is 16%, what is the intrinsic value of the equity share of Copeland Ltd?

Solution: Dividends for the next 3 years are as follows:

Year	1	2	3
Dividend (₹)	4 × 1.15 = 4.60	4 × 1.15 × 1.15 = 5.29	4 × (1.15)3 = 6.084

So, the required intrinsic value of the share is

$$= \frac{4.60}{1.16} + \frac{5.29}{(1.16)^2} + \frac{6.084}{(1.16)^3} + \frac{6.084 \times 1.06}{0.16 - 0.06} \times \frac{1}{(1.16)^3}$$
$$= 3.97 + 3.93 + 3.90 + 41.32 = 53.12 \approx ₹\ 53\ \text{(approx.)}$$

ASSESS YOURSELF

Concept Review and Critical Thinking Questions

1. Why do you think that a financial manager should be concerned about the valuation process? Discuss.
2. Determining bond prices and yields is an application of the BVM. Discuss.
3. Bond values move in the direction opposite to that of interest rate leading to potential gains or losses for the bond investors. Discuss.
4. "The only risk associated with owning a bond is that the issuer will not make all the payments." Discuss.
5. Does the value of a share depend on how long you expect to keep it? Discuss.
6. "Managers should not focus on the current market price of the share because doing so will lead to an overemphasis on short-term profits at the expense of long-term profits." Discuss.
7. "Valuation models are theoretical in nature with little practical utility." Discuss.
8. Discuss the modern techniques of valuing a firm. How the MVA differs from EVA? Discuss.

STUDENT ACTIVITY

Student should undertake a project on "Study of EVA by select Indian Companies" and its social implications.

SUGGESTED READINGS

Arzac, E.R. (1986). Do your business units create shareholder value? *Harvard Business Review*, (January–February), 121-126.

Brealey, R.A., & Myers, S.C. (2002). *Principles of corporate finance* (7th ed.). New York: McGraw-Hill.

Damodaran, A. (2001). *The dark side of valuation.* Prentice Hall.

Damodaran, A. (2002). *Investment valuation: Tools and techniques for determining the value of any asset.* New York: John Wiley & Sons.

Hawawini, G., & Viallet, C. (2002). *Finance for executives: Managing for value creation* (2nd ed.). South-Western Educational Publishing.

Hitchner, J.R. (2003). *Financial valuation: Applications and models.* New York: John Wiley & Sons.

Horne, J.C.V. (2002). *Financial management & policy* (12th ed.). Singapore: Pearson Education.

King, A.M. (2001). *Valuation: What assets are really worth.* New York: John Wiley & Sons.

McKinsey & Company Inc., Copeland, T., Koller, T., & Murrin, J. (2000). *Valuation: Measuring and managing the value of companies* (3rd ed.). John Wiley & Sons.

Rappaport, Alfred. (1986). *Creating shareholder value: The new standard for business performance.* New York, NY: The Free Press, A Division of Macmillan Publishers.

Ross, S.A., Westerfield, R.W., & Jordan, B.D. (2002). *Fundamentals of corporate finance* (6th ed.). New Delhi: Tata McGraw-Hill.
To understand how the valuation of convertibles is done, let us consider an illustration. KGK Ltd has issued fully convertible debentures at a face value of ₹1000 with coupon rate of 9% p.a., which is converted into four equity shares (at a price of ₹250 each) at the end of 3 years.

PART III
Strategic Financial Decision

CHAPTER 7

Capital Structure Decisions

Learning Objectives

- To understand the concept and theories of capital structure.
- To establish the relationship between capital structure and value of firm.

PRELUDE

Capital structure is one of the key decisions for management as it defines the basic relationship between risk and returns, value of the firm while having different components of capital. Here, **capital** is denoted as all the long-term sources—equity and debentures. Equity has a different mandate so are debentures. Capital structure decision therefore tries to strike an equilibrium between equity and debentures in case the company is a levered company. It is clear that the growth of a levered firm is faster than the growth of an unlevered firm as long as the cost of debt is lower than the cost of equity. Capital structure decision is valid for all the industries. Consider the following (*Source*: www.ibef.org):

"India's pharmaceutical sector will touch US$ billion by 2020, according to a major study by global management and consulting firm, McKinsey & Company. The reasons for this optimism are well founded. In the period 2002–2012, the country's health care sector grew three times in size, touching US$70 billion from US$23 billion. India's pharmaceutical market experienced a similar boom, reaching US$18 billion in 2012 from US$6 billion in 2005. The report further states that the Indian pharmaceutical market will be the sixth largest in the world by 2020.

The rise of pharmaceutical outsourcing and investments by MNCs, allied with the country's growing economy, committed health insurance segment and improved healthcare facilities, is expected to drive the market growth.

India is today one of the top emerging markets in the global pharmaceutical scene. The sector is highly knowledge based and its steady growth is positively affecting the Indian economy. The organized nature of the Indian pharmaceutical industry is attracting several companies that are finding it viable to increase their operations in the country."

In view of the above, it is expected that pharma companies will revisit their capital structure to take advantages of emerging opportunities.

Capital structure denotes the long-term source of funds primarily equity and loan. Equity includes paid-up capital, share premium, reserves, and retained earnings. Whenever there is the need of a long-term fund, a capital structure decision is involved. Loan includes term loan or institutional support including debentures.

It is a fact that the capital structure decision is a significant strategic managerial decision, which influences companies' risk and return, cost of funds, and market value of the firm. **The total sources of funds (short-term and long-term) used by the firm are known as its financial structure and the mix or proportion of the long-term sources of funds along with equity used by the firm is known as its capital structure**. The company will have to plan its capital structure initially when it starts operating and also subsequently whenever it has to raise additional funds for new projects and expansion. Capital structure process describes various elements of capital structure and their impact on EPS, return and value, and the form. A company having both debt and equity in its capital structure is known as a levered company (Figure 7.1).

FIGURE 7.1
CAPITAL STRUCTURE PROCESS

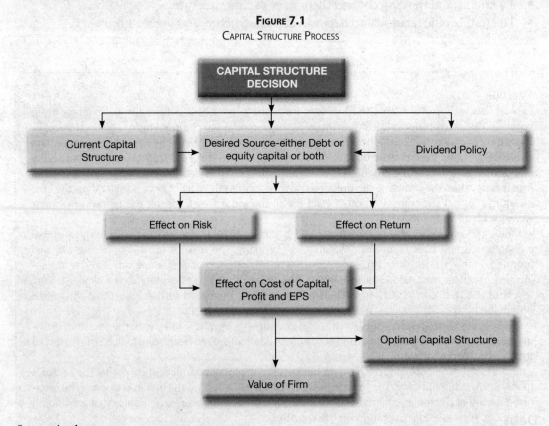

Source: Author.

Capital Structure Theories

Is there any relationship between the capital structure, the cost of capital, and the value of the firm? Capital structure theories address this issue while highlighting optimum capital structures.

It is known that under favorable conditions the earnings per share increases with leverage where debt and share capital form the capital of the company. Leverage, at the same time, also increases the financial risk of the shareholders. As a result, it cannot be stated definitely whether or not the value of the firm will increase with leverage. If leverage affects the cost of capital and the value of the firm, an optimum capital structure would be obtained at that combination of debt and equity that optimizes if not maximizes the total value of the firm (value of shares plus value of debt) or minimizes the weighted average cost capital.

Various theories have, therefore, been propounded to explain this relationship between the capital structure and the value of the firm. To understand these theories, let us go through the following assumptions.

Assumptions

- A firm employs only two types of capital: debt and equity.
- The degree of leverage can be changed by issuing debt or shares.
- Investors have the same subjective probability distributions of expected future operating earnings for a given firm.
- The firm has a policy of distributing 100% of its earnings as dividends, that is, it follows 100% dividend payout.
- The operating earnings of the firm are not expected to grow or to decline over a period of time.
- The business risk is assumed to be constant and independent of capital structure and financial risk.
- A firm can instantaneously change its capital structure without incurring any transaction costs.
- The corporate and personal income taxes do not exist. (This assumption is relaxed later.)

In understanding of capital structure theories, the following legends are used:

E = Market value of ordinary or equity shares
D = Amount of debt
V = Total market value of the firm (E+D)
NOI = $\bar{X}$ = Expected net operating income, that is, EBIT
INT = Interest charges = Cost of debt × Amount of debt
NI = Net income or shareholders' earnings = EBIT – INT (when corporate taxes do not exist) and (EBIT – INT) (1– T) when corporate taxes are considered.

The costs associated with the different sources of finance are defined as follows:

Debt

$$\text{Cost of Debt } (k_d) = \frac{\text{INT}}{D}$$

Equity

$$\text{Cost of Equity } (k_e) = \frac{D_1}{P_0} + g$$

As all the earnings are distributed as dividends, the equation can also be written as follows:

$$\text{Cost of Equity } k_e = \frac{E_1}{P_0} + g$$

where D_1 is the expected dividend per share, E_1 is the earnings per share next year, P_0 is the current market price per share, and g is the growth rate.

Cost of equity can also be expressed as follows:

$$k_e = \frac{NOI - INT}{V - D} = \frac{NI}{E}$$

Weighted average cost of capital of the firm

$$k_0 = k_2[E/V] + k_d[D/V] \quad \text{or} \quad k_0 = \frac{EBIT}{V}$$

Total value of the firm

$$V = (E + D) = NOI/k_0$$

Test Yourself

1. Define capital structure.
2. Discuss any two assumptions of capital structure theory.

The theories of capital structure explains the relationship between k_o (overall cost of capital or weighted average cost of capital WACC) and k_d (cost of debt), k_e (cost of equity), and V (value of firm). The theories of capital structure can be grouped into two categories:

1. Relevance theories
2. Irrelevance theories

Relevance Theories

These theories endorse that debt plays a significant role in affecting the value of the firm and overall cost of capital. Under relevance theory, there are

- Net income approach
- Traditional theory

Net income (NI) Approach

According to the NI approach, **a firm can increase its value or lower the overall cost of capital by increasing the proportion of debt in the capital structure.**

This implies that the capital structure is relevant in determining the value of the firm. The financial manager can reduce the cost of capital and consequently increase the value of the firm by increasing the proportion of debt in the capital structure. The NI approach clearly underlines the importance of debt as it is the determinant of value of the firm (V).

This approach is based on the following assumptions:

- The use of debt does not change the risk perception of investors; as a result, the equity capitalization rate, k_e, and the debt capitalization rate, k_d, remain constant with changes in leverage.
- The risk arising out of change in capital structure mix is presumed to be assent. This is so because if the risk perception changes, then the rate of return required by investors would increase. As we would see later, this is an unrealistic assumption.
- The debt capitalization rate is less than the equity capitalization rate (i.e., $k_d < k_e$). In other words, the rate of return required by the debt provider is less than the rate of return required by equity capital holders, that is, debt is cheaper than equity.
- The corporate income taxes do not exist.

Given these assumptions, when a firm increases its financial leverage, that is, it uses more of a cheaper source of finance (debt), the overall cost of capital declines.

We know, weighted average cost of capital is given by

$$k_o = k_e [E/V] + k_d [D/V] \text{ or } k_o = V/EBIT$$

As k_d is less than k_e, an increase in the proportion of debt in the capital structure would mean higher value of D/V resulting into lower value of k_o, that is, overall cost of capital.

Given that value of the firm is $V = NOI/k_o$, a decline in k_o for a given value of NOI would mean an increase in V (the value of the firm) (Figure 7.2).

FIGURE 7.2
INVERSE RELATIONSHIP BETWEEN K_o AND V

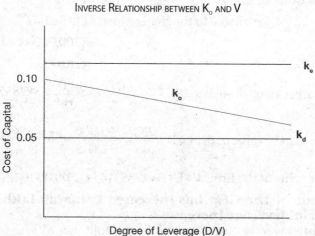

Source: Author.

To sum up, there is an inverse relationship between k_o and V. If k_o goes down because of change in leverage, V is bound to increase.

Illustration 1. Assume that a firm expects an annual net operating income (NOI) of ₹200,000, an equity capitalization rate, k_e, of 14% and ₹1,000,000 debt of 6%. What is the value of the firm as per the NI approach?

Solution: The value of the firm according to the NI approach can be calculated as follows:

$$NOI = ₹200,000$$

$$\text{Total cost of debt, INT} = (₹1,000,000 \times 0.06) = ₹60,000$$

$$\text{Net income (NI) available to the shareholders} = EBIT - INT$$

$$= 200,000 - 60,000$$

$$= ₹140,000$$

$$\text{Market value of equity} = E = \frac{EBIT - INT}{K_e} = \frac{140,000}{0.14} = ₹1,000,000$$

$$\text{Market value of debt} = D = \frac{INT}{K_d} = \frac{60,000}{0.06} = ₹1,000,000$$

Market value of the firm, $V = E + D = ₹1,000,000 + ₹1,000,000 = ₹2,000,000$.

The costs of equity and debt are, respectively, 10% and 6% and are assumed to be constant under the NI approach. The overall cost of capital, k_0, is

$$k_0 = \frac{NOI}{V} = \frac{200,000}{2,000,000} = 0.10 = 10\%$$

Illustration 2. If the firm is assumed to have used a debt of ₹1,500,000 instead of ₹1,000,000, what would be the value of the firm under NI approach?

Solution: $NOI = EBIT - ₹200,000$

$$\text{Total Cost of Debt, INT} = ₹1,500,000 \times 0.06) = ₹90,000$$

$$\text{NI available to the shareholders} = EBIT - INT$$

$$= ₹200,000 - ₹90,000$$

$$= ₹110,000$$

$$\text{Market value of equity} = E = \frac{EBIT - INT}{k_e} = \frac{110,000}{0.14} = ₹785,714$$

$$\text{Market value of debt} = D = \frac{INT}{k_d} = \frac{90,000}{0.06} = ₹1,500,000$$

Market value of the firm, $V = E + D = ₹785,714 + ₹1,500,000 = ₹2,285,714$.

Thus, the value of the firm has increased from ₹20 lakhs to ₹22.85 lakhs when the financial leverage increases.

Overall or weighted average cost of capital (k_0) is as follows:

$$k_0 = \frac{NOI}{V} = \frac{200,000}{2,285,714} = 0.0875 = 8.75\%$$

The optimum capital structure would occur at the point where the value of the firm is maximum and overall cost of capital is minimum. However, there is no quantified parameter for maximum or minimum as both are imaginary; thus, we strive for optimum. Under the NI approach, the firm will have the maximum value and the lowest cost of capital when it is fully debt-financed. But in real life, can there be a company without equity? No, the company would definitely have equity in all respects.

Effect of Leverage on Value and Cost of Capital under NI

Leverage (%)	0	10	20	25	50	75	90
Capital required	200	200	200	200	200	200	200
Debt	0	20	40	50	100	150	180
Equity	200	180	160	150	100	50	20
(EBIT)	100	100	100	100	100	100	100
Interest	0	1	2	2.5	5	7.5	9
k_d (%)	5	5	5	5	5	5	5
k_e (%)	10	10	10	10	10	10	10
Value of debt (INT/k_d)	0	20	40	50	100	150	180
Value of equity (EBIT−INT)/k_e	1,000	990	980	975	950	925	910
Value of firm ($D+e$)	1,000	1,010	1,020	1,025	1,050	1,075	1,090
k_o=NOI/V (%)	20	18	16	15	10	5	2

Traditional Approach

According to the traditional approach, there exists an optimal capital structure for every firm. In this capital structure, the overall cost of capital (WACC) of the firm is minimum and the value of the firm is maximized. **The traditional viewpoint states that the value of the firm increases with increase in financial leverage but up to a certain limit only. Beyond this limit, the increase in financial leverage will increase its WACC also and hence the value of the firm will decline.**

Under the traditional approach, the cost of debt (k_d) is assumed to be less than the cost of equity (k_e). In case of 100% equity firm, the overall cost of capital of the firm (k_o) is equal to the cost of equity (k_e), but when debt is introduced in the capital structure and the financial leverage increases, the cost of equity (k_e) remains constant as the equity investors expect a minimum leverage in every firm. k_e does not increase even with increase in leverage. The argument for k_e remaining unchanged may be that up to a particular degree of leverage, the interest charge may not be large enough to pose a real threat to the dividend payable to the shareholders. This constant k_e and lower k_d make k_o to fall initially. Thus, it shows that the benefits of cheaper debts are available to the firm. But this position does not continue when leverage is further increased. The increase in leverage beyond a limit increases the risk of the equity investors also and as a result k_e also starts increasing. However, the benefits of using a debt may be so large that even after offsetting the effects of increase in k_e, k_o may still go down or may become constant for some degree of leverages. However, if the firm increases the leverage even further, increase in financial risk of the company causes k_d to increase. The already increasing k_e and the now increasing k_d will result in an increase in k_o. Therefore, the use of leverage beyond a point will result in an increase in the overall cost of capital of the firm and a decrease in the value of the firm.

Thus, there is a level of financial leverage in any firm up to which it favorably affects the value of the firm but thereafter if the leverage is increased further, then the effect may be adverse and the value of the firm may decrease. In other words, a firm can be benefited from a moderate level of leverage when the advantages of using debt (having lower cost) outweigh the disadvantages of increasing k_e (as a result of higher financial risk).

Figure 7.3 shows the graphical representation of the traditional approach.

FIGURE 7.3
GRAPHICAL REPRESENTATION OF TRADITIONAL APPROACH

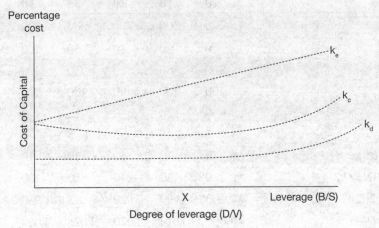

Source: Author.

Illustration 3. ABC Ltd having an EBIT of ₹150,000 is contemplating to redeem a part of the capital by introducing debt financing. Presently, it is a 100% equity firm with equity capitalization rate, k_e of 16%. The firm is to redeem the capital by introducing debt financing up to ₹300,000, that is, 30% of total funds or up to ₹500,000, that is, 50% of the total funds. It is expected that for the debt financing up to 30%, the rate of interest will be 10% and k_e will increase to 17%. However, if the firm opts for 50% debt financing, then interest will be payable at the rate of 12% and k_e will be 20%. Find out the value of the firm and its WACC under different levels of debt financing.

Solution: On the basis of the information given, the total funds of the firm seem to be of ₹1,000,000 (whole of which is provided by the equity capital), of which 30% or 50%, that is, ₹300,000 or ₹500,000 may be replaced by the issue of debt bearing interest at 10% or 12%, respectively. The value of the firm and its WACC may be ascertained as follows:

	0% Debt	30% Debt	50% Debt
Total debt (in ₹)	–	300,000	500,000
Rate of interest (%)	–	10	12
EBIT (in ₹)	150,000	150,000	150,000
Interest (in ₹)	0	30,000	60,000
PBT (in ₹)	150,000	120,000	90,000
Equity capitalization rate (%)	16	17	20
Value of equity (E) (PBT/k_e)	937,500	705,882	450,000
Value of debt (D)(INT/k_d) (in ₹)	–	300,000	500,000
Total value (V) ($D+E$) (in ₹)	937,500	105,882	950,000
Overall cost of capital (k_o) (EBIT/V) (%)	16	14.90	15.80

It is clear from the above that with the increase in leverage from 0% to 30%, the firm is able to reduce its WACC from 16% to 14.9%, and the value of the firm increases from ₹937,500 to ₹1,005,882. This happens as the benefits of employing a cheaper debt are available and k_e does not rise too much. However, thereafter, when the leverage is increased further to 50%, both the cost of debt and the cost of equity rise to 12% and 20%, respectively. The equity investors have increased the equity capitalization rate to 20% as they find the firm now to be more risky (as a result of 50% leverage). The increase in cost of debt and the equity capitalization rate has increased k_0 and hence as a result the value of the firm has reduced from ₹1,005,882 to ₹950,000 and k_0 has increased from 14.9% to 15.8%.

Thus, Illustration 3 shows that the value of the firm increases up to an optimum level of leverage only and any further increase in leverage would reduce the value of the firm. So, by a judicious use of the financial leverage, the firm can optimize its value.

Test Yourself

1. What is relevance theory of capital structure?
2. Explain the net income approach.
3. Discuss the traditional theory of capital structure.

Irrelevance Theories

Under these theories, capital structure decisions do not affect the value of the firm, and value of the firm is independent of the method of financing of the capital structure. It is categorized into:

- Net operating income approach
- Miller and Modigiliani (M&M) approach

Net Operating Income Approach

According to the NOI approach, the market value of the firm is not affected by the capital structure changes. The market value of the firm is ascertained by capitalizing the NOI at the overall or the weighted average cost of capital, k_0, which is a constant.

Symbolically

$$V = D + E = \frac{NOI}{k_0} = \frac{\overline{X}}{k_0}$$

where k_0 is the overall capitalization rate and depends on the business risk of the firm. It does not depend on the financial mix. If NOI and k_0 are independent of financial mix, and V will be a constant and independent of capital structure changes.

The critical assumptions of the NOI approach are as follows:

- The market capitalizes the value of the firm as a whole. Thus, the proportion in which debt and equity have been used in the capital structure is not relevant in determining the value of the firm.

- The market uses an overall capitalization rate, k_0 to capitalize the net operating income. k_0 depends on the business risk. If the business risk is assumed to remain unchanged, k_0 is a constant.
- The use of debt funds increases the risk of shareholders. This causes the equity capitalization rate to increase. Thus, the advantage of debt is offset exactly by the increase in the equity capitalization rate, k_e.
- The debt capitalization rate k_d is a constant.
- The corporate income taxes do not exist.

As stated above, under the NOI approach, the total value of the firm is found out by dividing the NOI by the overall cost of capital, k_0. The market value of equity, E, can be determined by subtracting the value of debt, D, from the total market value of the firm V (i.e., $E = V - D$). The cost of equity, k_e will be measured as follows:

$$k_e = \frac{NOI - INT}{V - D} = \frac{\overline{EBIT} - kdD}{E}$$

Alternatively, the cost of equity can be defined as follows:

$$k_e = k_e + \frac{D}{E}(k_o - k_d)$$

From the above equation, it is clear that if k_0 and k_d are constants, k_e would increase linearly, with financial leverage (denoted by debt–equity ratio, D/E).

Illustration 4. A firm has an annual operating income of ₹200,000, an average cost of capital k_0 of 10% and an initial debt of ₹200,000 at 6% rate of interest. What is the value of the firm as per the NOI approach?

Solution: Under the NOI approach, the total value of the firm can be calculated as follows:

$$NOI = EBIT = ₹200,000$$

Market value of the firm, $V = E + D = ₹200,000/0.10 = ₹2,000,000$

Market value of debt, $D = ₹200,000$

Market value of the equity, $E = V - D = ₹2,000,000 - ₹200,000 = ₹1,800,000$

The cost of equity will be

$$k_e = \frac{NOI - INT}{V - D} = \frac{\overline{EBIT} - INT}{E} = \frac{₹200,000 - ₹12,000}{₹1,800,000}$$

$$= 0.1044 = 10.44\%$$

If debt is increased from ₹200,000 to ₹400,000, the value of the firm would still remain at ₹2,000,000. The value of equity will drop to ₹1,600,000. The equity capitalization rate will be

$$k_e = \frac{NOI - INT}{V - D} = \frac{\overline{EBIT} - kdD}{E} = \frac{₹200,000 - ₹24,000}{₹1,600,000}$$

$$k_e = 0.11 = 11\%$$

Thus, we find that the overall cost of capital is constant and the cost of equity increases as debt is substituted for equity capital.

This approach implies that there is not any unique optimum capital structure. In other words, as the cost of capital is the same at all capital structures, every capital structure is optimum (Figure 7.4).

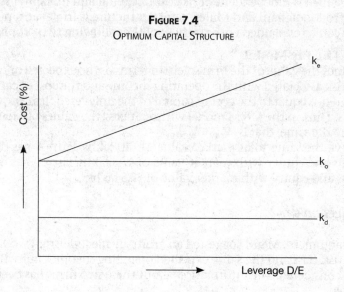

FIGURE 7.4

OPTIMUM CAPITAL STRUCTURE

Source: Author.

Miller and Modigliani (M&M) Approach

Franco Modigliani and Merton Miller (generally referred to as M&M), both Nobel Prize winners in financial economics, have had a profound influence on capital structure theory ever since their seminal paper on capital structure was published in 1958. M&M approach does not agree with the traditional theory. It emphasizes that in perfect market situation without taxes and additional transaction cost, a value of firm and cost of capital remain unchanged. Rather, it depends on earnings and business risk.

Assumptions of the M&M Model

- Capital markets are perfect. Information is costless and readily available to all investors. There are no transaction costs, and all securities are infinitely divisible. The implication of this assumption is that investors can borrow and lend funds at the same rate and can move quickly from one security to another without incurring any transaction cost.
- Investors are assumed to be rational and behave accordingly, that is, they would like to maximize the return for a given level of risk.
- The probability distribution of the expected future operating earnings values is the same for all the investors.
- Firms can be grouped into "equivalent return" classes on the basis of their business risks. All firms falling into one class have the same degree of business risk.
- There is no corporate or personal income tax. (Later on we shall drop the assumptions about the absence of taxes to study the effect of taxes.)

M&M Model without Taxes

Modigliani and Miller in their paper argued against the traditional approach and proposed that the value of a firm is independent of its cost of capital and its capital structure. In other words, according to Modigliani and Miller, capital structure is irrelevant in determining the value of a firm. It can be explained with the help of the following two propositions:

Proposition I: The Pie Model

Proposition I defines the value of the firm solely in terms of the expected operating income of the firm and the risk associated with the operating income and the cost of capital for any firm, levered or unlevered, is equal to the cost of capital of the unlevered firm, provided both are in the same risk class. Thus, in the M&M model without taxes, the values of a levered firm and an unlevered firm are the same, that is, $V_{LEV} = V_{UNLEV}$.

Two firms have the same total market value of ₹10 lakhs. Firm A has debt with market value of ₹2.5 lakhs and equity with market value of ₹7.5 lakhs. Firm B has debt with market value of ₹7.5 lakhs and equity with market value of ₹2.5 lakhs.

The Arbitrage Mechanism

To support their argument, M&M suggested an arbitrage mechanism. Two firms UNLEV and LEV in the same risk class and the same expected operating incomes but with varying financial leverages are considered. The information about these two firms has been summarized in the following table:

	UNLeV & Co	LeV & Co
Expected operating income	X	X
Market value of equity	E_{UNLEV}	E_{LEV}
Market value of debt	–	D_{LEV}
Market value on the firm	V_{UNLEV}	V_{LEV}
Cost of debt	–	k_d
Interest burden	–	$k_d D_{LEV}$

Case I: $V_{UNLEV} < V_{LEV}$

The market value of the unlevered firm is less than the market value of the levered firm. Consider an investor who holds E'_{LEV} rupees worth of equity shares of firm LEV & Co, representing a fraction of the total outstanding market value of equity shares of firm LEV & Co ($E'_{LEV} = áE_{LEV}$). The return earned by the investor will be

$$P_{LEV} = \alpha (EBIT - k_d D_{LEV})$$

If the investor sells his shares, that is, αE_{LEV} worth of shares of firm LEV & Co and borrows αD_{LEV} at an interest rate of k_d percent on his personal account, then he can purchase $\alpha (E_{LEV} + D_{LEV})/E_{UNLEV}$ of the equity shares of firm UNLEV. (For firm UNLEV & Co, $V_{UNLEV} = E_{UNLEV}$ as it is an all-equity firm.)

The return obtained by the investor as a result of these transactions would be

$$P_{UNLEV} = \alpha \frac{(E_{LEV} + D_{LEV})}{E_{UNLEV}} \overline{EBIT} - k_d \alpha D_{LEV}$$

$$= \alpha \frac{V_{LEV}}{V_{UNLEV}} \overline{EBIT} - k_d D_{LEV}$$

As long as $V_{LEV} > V_{UNLEV}$, we have $P_{UNLEV} > P_{LEV}$, which means that the equity shareholders of the levered firm LEV & Co will sell their shareholding and acquire shares of the unlevered firm UNLEV & Co by borrowing on personal account (homemade leverage), as it is profitable to do so. In this process, E_{LEV} (and hence V_{LEV}) will decline and E_{UNLEV} (and hence V_{UNLEV}) will increase till the equality between V_{LEV} and V_{UNLEV} is established. Hence, the difference in the values of the levered firm and the unlevered firm would be abolished by the personal leverage of the investors.

Case II: $V_{UNLEV} > V_{LEV}$

Let us denote the ratio of the values of the unlevered and the levered firms as $V_{UNLEV}/V_{LEV} = \beta > 1$.

Now consider an investor who holds equity shares worth E'_{UNLEV} of the firm UNLEV & Co, representing a fraction α_{UNLEV} of the total market value of the outstanding shares, E_{UNLEV}. The return earned by the investor will be

$$P_{UNLEV} = \frac{E'_{UNLEV}}{E_{UNLEV}} \overline{X} = \alpha \overline{X}$$

If he sells his shareholding worth αV_{UNLEV} ($V_{UNLEV} = E_{UNLEV}$), he can buy a fraction $\alpha\beta$ of the equity shares and bonds of firm LEV & Co because the market value of the firm UNLEV & Co is β times the market value of the firm LEV & Co

The return earned by the investor as a result of this transaction would be

$$P_{LEV} = \alpha\beta(\overline{X} - k_d D_{LEV}) + \alpha\beta(k_d D_{LEV}) = \alpha\beta\overline{X}$$

As long as $V_{UNLEV} > V_{LEV}$, that is, $\beta > 1$, we have $P_{LEV} > P_{UNLEV}$, which means that equity shareholders of firm UNLEV & Co will sell their shareholding and buy a portfolio consisting of shares and bonds of firm LEV & Co as it is profitable to do so. In the process, V_{UNLEV} will decline and V_{LEV} will rise till both become equal.

Illustration 5. Suppose there are two firms, LEV & Co and ULE & Co. These firms are identical in all respects except that the LEV & Co is a levered firm and has 10% debt of ₹3,000,000 in its capital structure. However, the ULE & Co is an unlevered firm and has raised funds only by the issue of equity share capital. Both these firms have an EBIT of ₹1,000,000 and the equity capitalization rate k of 20%.

The other information about the two companies is as follows:

	LeV & Co	UNLeV & Co
EBIT	₹1,000,000	1,000,000
Interest	300,000	–
PBT	700,000	1,000,000
Equity capitalization rate (k_e) (%)	20	20
Value of equity (E) (in ₹)	3,500,000	5,000,000
Value of debt (D) (in ₹)	3,000,000	–
Total value (V) (in ₹)	6,500,000	5,000,000
WACC (k_0) (%)	15.38	20

Suppose an investor holds 10% equity share capital of LEV & Co. The value of his ownership right is ₹350,000, that is, 10% of ₹3,500,000. Further, out of the total net profit of ₹700,000 of LEV & Co, he is entitled to 10%, that is, ₹70,000 per annum and getting a return of 20%, on his worth. To avail the opportunity of making a profit, he now decides to convert his holdings from LEV & Co to ULEV & Co. He disposes off his holding in LEV & Co for ₹350,000, but to buy 10% holding of ULEV & Co, he requires total funds of ₹500,000, whereas his proceeds are only ₹350,000. Therefore, he takes a loan @10% of an amount equal to ₹300,000 (i.e., 10% of the debt of the LEV & Co). Now he has total funds of ₹650,000 (i.e., the proceeds of ₹350,000 and the loan of ₹300,000). Of the total funds of ₹650,000, he invests ₹500,000 to buy 10% shares of ULEV & Co. Still he has funds of ₹150,000 available with him. Assuming that the ULEV & Co continues to earn the same EBIT of ₹1,000,000, the net returns available to the investor from the ULEV & Co are as follows:

Profit available from ULEV & Co=₹100,000

(being 10% of the net profit)

Interest payable @10% on ₹300,000 loan=₹30,000

Net return=₹70,000

Therefore, the investor is able to get the same return of ₹70,000 from ULE & Co, which he was receiving also as an investor of LEV & Co, but he is left with funds of ₹150,000 for investment elsewhere. Thus, his total income may now be more than ₹70,000 (inclusive of some income on the investment of ₹150,000). Moreover, his risk is the same as before. Although his new outlet, that is, ULEV Co, is an unlevered firm (hence no risk), the position of the investor is levered because he has created a homemade leverage by borrowing ₹300,000 from the market. In fact, he has replaced the corporate leverage of LEV & Co, by his personal leverage.

The above example shows that the investor who originally owns a part of the levered firm and enter into the arbitrage process as above will be better off selling the holding in levered firm and buying the holding in unlevered firm using his homemade leverage.

The arbitrage process described above involves a transfer of investment from a levered firm to unlevered firm. This arbitrage process will work in the reverse direction also when the value of the levered firm is less than the value of the unlevered firm. Consider the total value of LEV & Co is ₹4,500,000 (consisting of ₹3,000,000 debt capital and ₹1,500,000, equity share capital), and the value of the ULEV & Co is the same as before, that is, ₹5,000,000. Now, the investor holding 10% share capital of ULEV & Co sells his ownership right for ₹500,000. Of these proceeds, he buys 10% of the share capital of LEV & Co for ₹150,000 and invests ₹300,000 (i.e., 10% of ₹3,000,000) in 10% government bonds. Still he will be left with funds of ₹50,000 with him and his position in respect of incomes from two firms would be as under:

	UNLeV & Co	LeV & Co
10% of profits (in ₹)	100,000	70,000
Interest on bonds (10%) (in ₹)	0	30,000
Total income (in ₹)	100,000	100,000

Thus, by performing the arbitrage process, the investor will not only be able to maintain his income level, but also be having additional cash flows of ₹50,000 at his disposal. The prices of the shares of ULEV & Co and LEV & Co must adjust until the values of both the firms are equal.

Hence, by performing the arbitrage process, the investor will not only be able to maintain his income level, but also be having additional cash flows of ₹50,000 at his disposal. The prices of the share of ULEV & Co and LEV & Co must adjust until the values of both the firms are equal.

Proposition II. The expected yield on equity, k_e, is equal to the appropriate capitalization rate, k_a, for a pure equity stream in the same risk class plus a premium related to the financial risk equal to the debt–equity ratio times. The difference between k_a and the yield on debt k_d and value of the firm depends on the operating income and the opportunity cost of capital, k_a which is the same for both levered and unlevered firms.

Symbolically,

$$k_e = k_a + (k_a - k_d) \times (D/E)$$

The term $(k_a - k_d) \times (D/E)$ in the preceding equation represents the financial risk premium, that is, the premium related to the use of debt.

In other words, Proposition II of the M&M model says that the cost of capital of a firm is a linear function of its capital structure.

From Figure 7.5, it is clear that as the financial leverage measured by the debt–equity ratio increases, it simultaneously increases the risk of the equity capital and hence the required rate of return on equity or the cost of equity, k_e. The WACC or k_o remains constant, as there is a change in capital structure. This implies that a trade-off takes place between debt and equity: The advantages of using cheaper debt are neutralized by the increasing costs of equity.

FIGURE 7.5
TRADE-OFF BETWEEN DEBT AND EQUITY

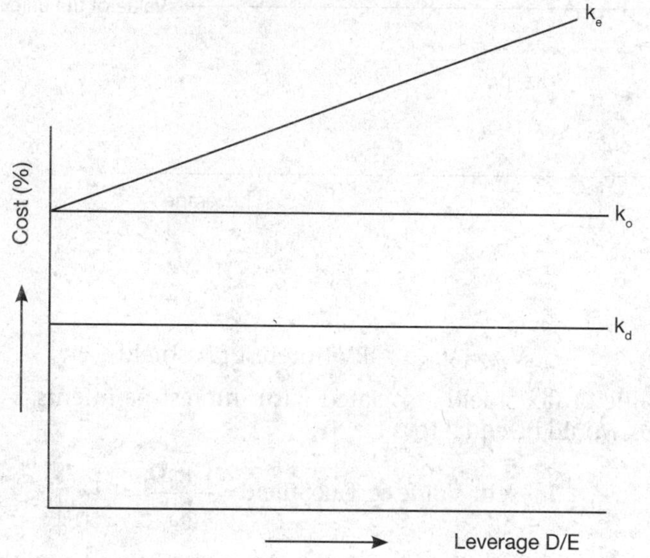

Source: Author.

M&M's Model with Taxes

In response to criticism of their original no-tax propositions, M&M (1963) subsequently modified their no-tax case to include corporate taxes.

Proposition I (with taxes)

Case I. Only Corporate Taxes

According to M&M, when corporate taxes are considered, the value of an unlevered firm becomes

$$V_{UNLEV} = \frac{EBIT(I-T)}{k_{eu}}$$

As the firm can retain only the after tax earnings, it is these earnings which the markets use to value the firm. Clearly, an unlevered firm does not have the benefits of the interest tax shield.

The value of a levered firm V_{LEV} in a tax environment is equal to the value of an unlevered firm plus the present value of the interest tax shield (Figure 7.6).

FIGURE 7.6

VALUE OF LEVERED FIRM EQUAL TO VALUE OF UNLEVERED FIRM IN TAX ENVIRONMENT

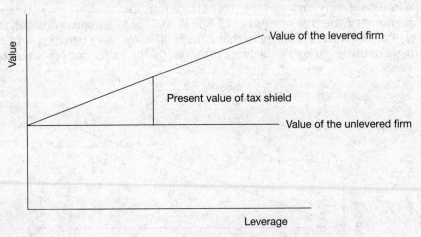

Source: Author.

Symbolically,

$$V_{LEV} = V_{UNLEV} + PV \text{ (interest tax shield)}$$

The present value of tax shield associated with interest payments, assuming debt to be perpetual in nature, would be equal to

$$\text{Present Value of Tax Shield} = \frac{t_c k_d D}{k_d} = t_c D$$

where t_c is the corporate tax rate, D is the market value of debt, and k_d is the cost of debt.

$$\text{Value of the unlevered firm } V_{UNLEV} = \frac{EBIT(I-T)}{k_{eu}}$$

Therefore, the value of the levered firm $V_{LEV} = V_{UNLEV} + PV \text{ (IT)}$

$$= \frac{EBIT(I-T)}{k_{eu}} + t_c D$$

From the above equation, it is quite clear that other things being equal, the greater the leverage, the greater the value of the firm. This implies that the optimal strategy of a firm should be to maximize the degree of leverage in its capital structure.

Case II. Both Corporate and Personal Taxes

If personal taxes are also there in addition to corporate taxes and the investors pay the taxes on debt as well as stock returns at the same rate, the above advantage of corporate tax resulting from leverage remains intact.

If the personal tax rate is t_p and the corporate tax rate is t_c, the tax advantage of debt is given by

$$\text{Present Value of Tax Shields} = t_c D(1-t_p)$$

The above formula is valid when the same personal tax rate is applicable to stock as well as debt income. However, it is not the same in many countries including India. Stock income, which includes dividend income and capital gains, is taxed at a lower rate when compared with that of debt income.

When the tax rate on stock income (t_{ps}) differs from the tax rate on debt income (t_{pd}), the tax advantage of debt capital may be expressed as follows:

$$\text{Tax Shield} = \left[1 - \frac{(1-t_c)(1-t_{ps})}{(1-t_{pd})}\right] \times D$$

where t_c is the corporate tax rate, t_{pd} is the personal tax rate on debt income, and t_{ps} is the personal tax rate on equity income.

Proposition II (with taxes)

The cost of equity for a levered firm in a tax environment is given by

$$k_e = k_a + (k_a - k_d)(I-T) \times (D/E)$$

The second term in the above equation still represents the financial risk premium related to the firm's debt, only this time it is modified by including $(1-T)$ to reflect the effect of corporate taxes. As the debt-equity ratio increases, this increases the firm's financial risk and pushes up the cost of equity k_e. However, as the impact of corporate taxes is to subsidize the cost of debt k_d, the weighted average cost of capital k_a declines (Figure 7.7).

FIGURE 7.7

FLUCTUATIONS IN THE VALUE OF THE FIRM

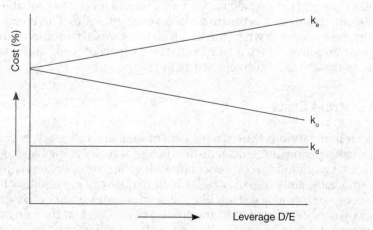

Source: Author.

The basic conclusion of M&M is that in a corporate tax environment, capital structure is relevant in determining the value of a firm. Given that the goal of a firm is to maximize its value, it can do so by substituting debt for equity in its capital structure. As the ratio of debt to equity is increased, the value of the firm rises and the overall cost of capital reduces.

Test Yourself

1. What is the irrelevance theory of capital structure?
2. What is arbitrage process? Explain.
3. What is net operating income approach? Explain.

Imperfections Affecting the Value of the Firm

In addition to taxes, there are several other imperfections in the market, which affect the value of the firm. The effect of taxes on the value of the firm has already been considered in detail. Let us now see how other imperfections affect the value of the firm.

The three important imperfections that adversely affect the value of the firm are:

1. Bankruptcy costs
2. Financial distress costs
3. Agency costs

Bankruptcy Costs

In a perfect capital market, there are no costs associated with bankruptcy. Assets of a bankrupt firm can be sold at their economic values and legal and administrative expenses are not present. However, in the real world, there are costs associated with bankruptcy. Under distress conditions, assets are sold at a significant discount to their economic values. Moreover, costs, such as legal and administrative costs, associated with bankruptcy proceedings are high. Finally, an impending bankruptcy entails significant costs in the form of sharply impaired operational efficiency.

The probability of bankruptcy for a levered firm is higher than for an unlevered firm, with the other things being equal. Beyond a threshold level, the probability of bankruptcy increases at an increasing rate as the financial leverage increases. This means that the expected cost of bankruptcy increases when the financial leverage increases. Investors expect a higher rate of return from a firm, which is faced with the prospect of bankruptcy, as bankruptcy costs represent a loss that cannot be diversified away (Figure 7.8).

Financial Distress Costs

Bankruptcy or liquidation is the extreme case of financial distress. It is possible for a firm to struggle through a period of financial distress before actually going bankrupt. During a period of financial distress, additional costs associated with the state of distress will be incurred. These costs are considerable and often may be difficult to quantify in monetary terms. For example, many of the costs of financial distress like the possible unpleasant behavior on the part of the managers or owners, deterioration in the employee morale, and the potential loss of supplier and customer goodwill will be difficult to quantify. Suppliers may insist on prompt payment

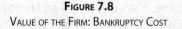

FIGURE 7.8
VALUE OF THE FIRM: BANKRUPTCY COST

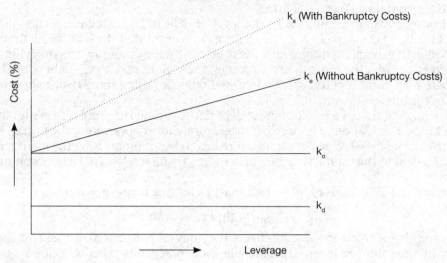

Source: Author.

and may even reduce or eliminate the credit period. This may adversely affect the cash flow of the firm. Similarly, if the customers doubt the firm's ability to provide future supplies and honor its warranties, product guarantees, and so on, they may shift to alternative suppliers thus further reducing the cash flow.

Agency Costs

Agency costs are defined as those costs which are incurred in attempting to minimize the agency problem. The agency problem is the potential for conflict in objectives, which exists in principal–agent relationship. In the corporate world, the principals are the shareholders who own the firm and managers act as their agents. For shareholders of the firm, the agency problem is that the managers who control the day-to-day affairs of the firm may tend to act in their own personal interest rather than in the interest of the shareholders. Owners of a firm will incur agency costs whenever they introduce procedures and mechanisms aimed at reducing the potential for conflict between the personal objectives of the manager and the objectives of the owners. Incurring agency costs has the potential effect of reducing the shareholders.

In the context of capital structure, when debt is introduced, the agency problem is extended to the relationship between the shareholders and lenders. When a lender is considering whether to advance credit to the firm or not, the decision will be based on an assessment of the risk of the firm and the expected cash flows of the firm. Once funds have been borrowed, the managers can take advantage of the lenders by using the funds for a more risky investment than that disclosed to the lenders. This is referred to as the asset substitution problem.

To minimize this type of managerial behavior, lenders impose certain restrictions on the firm in the form of some restrictive covenants and provisions incorporated in the loan contract. They could be in the form of obtaining prior approval of the creditors for matters relating to key managerial appointments, maintenance of current ratio above a certain level, restriction on the rate of dividend during the currency of the loan, constraints on the additional issue of capital, limitation on further investments, and so on.

The above-said restrictions generally entail legal and enforcement costs, which also impair the operating efficiency of the firm. All these costs, referred to as monitoring costs or agency costs, detract from the value of the firm.

Monitoring costs are a function of the level of debt in the capital structure. When the amount of debt is considerably less, the creditors may limit their monitoring activity. But if the level of debt is high, then they may insist on continuous monitoring which entails substantial costs. Clearly, the more debt a firm uses, the greater will be the debt-related agency costs. There may come a point when additional costs of raising more debt may exceed the benefits of the interest tax shield.

It is also argued that as a result of using debt in the capital structure, a firm's total agency costs may in fact be reduced. This is so because raising more debt exposes the firm to external scrutiny by the lenders. For owners, it means reduced cost of monitoring the managers. Thus, introducing debt in the capital structure may indirectly have a beneficial effect on the firm's market value.

According to Modigliani & Miller, the value of a levered firm is given by

$$V_{LEV} = V_{UNLEV} + PV \text{ (Interest tax shields)}$$

However, given the value-reducing effects of agency costs, financial distress cost, and bankruptcy costs, the value of a levered firm may be more practically stated as follows:

$$V_{LEV} = V_{UNLEV} + PV \text{ (Interest Tax Shields)} - PV \text{ (Bankruptcy Costs)} - PV$$

$$\text{(Financial Distress Costs)} - PV \text{ (Agency Costs)}$$

Other Models of Capital Structure

Two other models of capital structure which have emerged in the recent years are as follows:

1. Information asymmetry and signaling model
2. Pecking order model

Information Asymmetry and Signaling Model

This model attempts to explain capital structure in terms of the ways in which the financial manager uses issues of debt and equity to signal information about the future prospects of the firm to less well-informed investors.

Modigliani & Miller assumed perfect markets where information is free-flowing and all the investors have access to the same information. However, you will recall that one of the causes of agency cost is information asymmetry. In reality, managers have greater access to inside information about the present performance and future expectations about the company. They may share this information with shareholders and other stakeholders or withhold the information. This unequal access to and distribution of information between managers and shareholders is known as information asymmetry and is an agency cost borne by the shareholders.

How information asymmetry is important in capital structure decisions? To understand this, consider an example. A firm has come up with a new product and wants to raise funds for manufacturing, marketing, and distributing the same. The project has a very high positive NPV. Should it raise the funds through issue of equity or debt?

If the financial manager decides to issue equity, the share price will start rising when the new project is implemented and cash inflows from the project start. Both the existing and the new shareholders will benefit from this. However, the existing shareholders will have to share their wealth with the new shareholders. If the company had decided to raise funds by issuing debt, the existing shareholders would have been better off as in that case, they would not share their wealth with anyone. From the point of view of the shareholders, issuing debt is a better option for financing the new project.

If the financial manager decides to issue debt, he would be signaling to the investors and existing shareholders that the future prospects of the company are bright. However, if the company decides to issue equity, it would be considered as a negative signal indicating that company's future prospects are not so good and that its equity is presently overvalued.

However, if the managers believe that the equity shares of the firm are presently undervalued in light of the good future prospects of the firm, why should they issue fresh equity at an undervalued price?

This implies that a firm should maintain some reserve borrowing capacity which it should use to take advantage of good investment opportunities as and when they arise.

Pecking Order Model

Stewart Myers proposed the Pecking Order Model in 1984. According to this model, firms will follow a distinct order while raising finances from different sources. As a result, they need not maintain an optimal or target capital structure. First of all, the financial manager would like to use the retained earnings. Only if the retained earnings are not sufficient to finance the new investment, they would turn to external financing. In external financing also, they would first prefer to issue debt or fixed charges securities such as preference shares. If the funds were still not sufficient then only the firm would resort to equity financing. Thus, at any point of time, the capital structure is only a reflection of its past pecking order preferences.

Test Yourself

1. How do personal and corporate taxes affect the implication of MM approach?
2. What are financial distress costs?
3. Discuss the Pecking Order Model.

Designing the Capital Structure

We have seen that the main benefit of debt financing is the treatment of interest as a tax-deductible expense, which results in relatively higher profits for the shareholders. However, we have also seen that there are certain costs attached with debt financing such as bankruptcy costs, financial distress costs, and agency costs. Thus, the financial manager has to strike a balance between debt financing and equity financing. There is no mathematical technique or method available to determine the optimal debt–equity mix; the financial manager has to weigh the costs and benefits of debt financing and accordingly take a decision.

Two guiding principles in this regard are as follows:

1. The capital structure should be designed in such a way so as to lead to the objective of maximization of shareholders wealth.
2. It may be impossible to determine the exact optimal capital structure and therefore, efforts should be made to achieve the best approximation to the optimal capital structure.

In practice, firms differ from one another in respect of size, nature, earnings, cost of funds, competitive conditions, market expectations, risk, and so on. Therefore, the theories of capital structure may provide only a broad theoretical framework analyzing the relationship between leverage and cost of capital and value of the firm. A financial manager, however, should go beyond these considerations as no theoretical model can incorporate all these subjective features. There is, in fact, a whole lot of factors, qualitative and quantitative, which should be considered and factored in the process of planning and designing a capital structure for a firm. Besides these considerations, care should be taken that the capital structure should be evaluated in its totality and a finance manager should find out as to which capital structure is most advantageous to the firm. The interest of the shareholders, debt holders, and also that of the management is to be suitably taken care of. Above all, the legal provisions if any regarding the capital structure should also be considered.

Factors Determining the Capital Structure

The capital structure of a new firm is designed in the initial stages of the firm and the financial manager has to take care of many considerations. He is required to assess and evaluate not only the present requirement of capital funds but also the future requirements. The present capital structure should be designed in light of a future target capital structure. Future expansion plans, growth, and diversification strategies should be considered and factored in the analysis.

An existing firm may require additional capital funds for meeting the requirements of growth, expansion, diversification, or even sometimes for working capital requirements. Every time additional funds are required, the firm has to evaluate various available sources of funds vis-à-vis the existing capital structure. The decision for a particular source of funds is to be taken in the totality of capital structure, that is, in light of the resultant capital structure after the proposed issue of capital or debt.

A financial manager has to critically evaluate various costs and benefits, implications, and the after-effects of a capital structure before deciding the capital mix. Moreover, the prevailing market conditions are also to be analyzed. For example, the present capital structure may provide a scope for debt financing, but either the capital market conditions may not be conducive or the investors may not be willing to take up the debt instrument. Thus, a capital structure before being finally decided must be considered in light of the firms' internal factors as well as the investor's perceptions.

Thus, there are many factors that affect the capital structure of a firm. What follows is an indicative list of factors that should be considered while designing the capital structure of a firm. These are discussed in the following sections.

Optimization of Risk

We have already discussed in the previous chapter what business risk is and how financial leverage affects the business and financial risk. We know that business risk varies among firms and is not affected by capital structure decisions. Once the firm has decided to operate in a particular economic system and a particular industry, its business risk is given. However, the firm can definitely control its financial risk by deciding on its capital structure. The higher a firm's business risk, the more cautious the firm must be in establishing its capital structure. Firms with high business risk therefore tend toward less levered capital structure, and vice versa. A capital structure may be called an efficient capital structure if it keeps the total risk of the firm to the minimum level. The long-term solvency and financial risk of a firm should be assessed for a given capital structure. As increase in debt financing affects the solvency as well as the financial risk of the firm, excessive use of debt financing should be avoided. It may be noted that the balancing of both financial and business risks is needed so that the total risk of the firm is kept within desirable limits. A firm having higher business risk should keep the financial risk to the minimum level; otherwise, the firm will become a high-risk proposition resulting in higher cost of capital.

Control

Although retail equity shareholders have a very little say in the day-to-day affairs of the firm, the big equity shareholders enjoy the ultimate decision-making power of the firm. To have no dilution of control, the management may prefer to issue debt rather than equity shares to raise funds. The capital structure of a firm should reflect the management's philosophy of control over the firm. Various instruments are available for raising finances, which do not confer any voting rights to the holders and hence do not result in dilution of control like redeemable debentures and preference shares.

Flexibility

The flexibility of a capital structure refers to the ability of the firm to raise additional capital funds whenever needed to finance profitable and viable investment opportunities. The capital structure should be one which enables the firm to meet the requirements of the changing situations. More precisely, flexibility means that a capital structure should always have an untapped borrowing power which can be used in conditions which may arise any time in future due to uncertainty of capital market, Government policies, and so on. If the capital market conditions are conducive to the issue of capital, then the preference may be given to the issue of capital, rather than to the issue of debt. Further, if there is still untapped borrowing capacity, then debt instruments may be issued, subject to conditions prevailing in the capital market.

Profitability

A capital structure should be the most profitable from the point of view of equity shareholders. Therefore, within the given constraints, the capital structure which will increase the returns available to the equity shareholders should be selected. In addition, an analysis of the rate of return on total assets and the cost of debt may be made. We have already seen that if the return on investment is more than the cost of debt, then the financial leverage enhances the returns for the equity shareholders.

Approaches for Determining Optimal Capital Structure

The three most common approaches to decide about a firm's capital structure are as follows:

1. EBIT–EPS approach
2. Cash flow approach
3. Valuation approach

EBIT–EPS Approach

It has been mentioned that the financial leverage increases the variability of the EPS of the firm. Therefore, in search for an appropriate capital structure for a firm, the financial manager must, inter alia, analyze the effects of various alternative financial leverages on the EPS. For this, he must understand as to how sensitive is the EPS to a change in EBIT under different financial plans. The EBIT-EPS analysis is of significant importance and if undertaken properly can be an effective tool in the hands of a financial manager to get an insight into the planning and designing of the capital structure of the firm.

If maximization of the EPS is the only criterion for selecting the particular debt-equity mix, then that capital structure that is expected to result in the highest EPS will be selected always by all the firms. However, achieving the highest EPS need not be the only goal of the firm. The main shortcomings of the EBIT-EPS analysis are as follows:

1. **The EPS criterion ignores the risk dimension:** The EBIT–EPS analysis ignores as to what is the effect of leverage on the overall risk of the firm. With every increase in financial leverage, the risk of the firm and therefore that of investors also increase. The EBIT-EPS analysis fails to deal with the variability of EPS and the risk return trade-off.
2. **EPS is more of a performance measure:** The EPS basically depends on the operating profit, which in turn depends on the operating efficiency of the firm. It is a resultant figure and it is more a measure of performance rather than a measure of decision-making. These shortcomings of the EBIT-EPS analysis do not, in any way, affect its value in capital structure decisions. The following aspects may be considered in the EBIT-EPS analysis to make it more meaningful.

Cash Flow Approach

The cash flow approach can be used to judge the propriety or otherwise of capital structure also. A firm is said to be prudently financed if it can pay for all the obligations with any problem and under any circumstances. However, if it faces problems in servicing its debt then there may be a problem. That indicates the excessive borrowing by the firm.

While designing the capital structure of the firm, the financial manager may look at the DSCR. DSCR indicates the number of times the fixed financial obligations are covered by the net cash inflows generated by the firm. The higher the ratio, the greater the extent to which the firm can use debt in its capital structure.

Valuation Approach

According to this approach, the firm should use the cost of different sources of finance as a guiding principle to decide whether to use that source or not in its capital structure. As debt is a cheaper source of finance than equity capital, the firm will prefer to use debt than equity. Using the cost of capital of the source of finance as a criterion for financing decisions while ignoring the risk, a firm would always prefer to use debt as it is the cheapest source of finance. It can be noticed that this approach is similar to the Pecking Order Model discussed earlier.

Deleveraging

In the context of Indian corporate sector, the concept of deleveraging is emerging fast. It has been established that financial cost (the cost of interest) is one of the main reasons for failure of big companies on account of non-payment of interest and installment in time. Moreover, there has been a continuous decline in interest rate for the last couple of years due to increased inflow of funds from abroad. This created supply plus situation which along with poor offtake of credit caused a sharp decrease in the interest rate. Thus, companies are trying to reduce their financial cost by prepaying loan by selling of zero debt company till the investment rate is stabilized.

Test Yourself

1. What are the factors affecting capital structure?
2. What is EBIT-EPS analysis? What is its limitation?
3. Explain valuation approach of capital structure.

SUMMARY

1. Capital structure of the firm can be defined as the blend of debt and equity which help in maximizing the value of the firm.
2. The firm can change its capital structure with proportionate change leverage/in mixture of debt and equity.
3. Capital structure theory can be classified as relevance and irrelevance theories.
4. Under relevance theories, it is stated that capital structure decisions are relevant to the extent that debts affect the value of the firm and cost of capital.
5. According to the NI approach, a firm can increase its value or lower the overall cost of capital by increasing the proportion of debt in the capital structure. This implies that the capital structure is relevant in determining the value of the firm. The financial manager can reduce the cost of capital and consequently increase the value of the firm by increasing the proportion of debt in the capital structure.
6. Traditional viewpoint states that the value of the firm increases with increase in financial leverage, but up to a certain limit only. Beyond this limit, the increase in financial leverage will also increase its WACC and, hence, the value of the firm will decline.
7. Irrelevance theories assume that the capital structure decisions do not affect the value of the firm.
8. As per the NOI approach, the market value of the firm is not affected by the capital structure changes. The market value of the firm is calculated by capitalizing the NOI at the overall, or the weighted average cost of capital, k_0 which is a constant.
9. M&M approach does not agree with the traditional theory. It emphasizes that in perfect market situation without taxes and additional transaction cost, the value of the firm and cost of capital remain unchanged. Rather, it depends on earnings and business risk.
10. Agency costs are defined as those costs, which are incurred in attempting to minimize the agency problem. The agency problem is the potential for conflict in objectives, which exists in the principal-agent relationship. In the corporate world, the principals are the shareholders who own the firm and managers act as their agents.
11. As per the Pecking Order Model, the financial manager would like to use the retained earnings. Only if the retained earnings are not sufficient to finance the new investment, they would turn to external financing.

Student would learn the basic relationship between cost of debt, cost of equity, and value of the firm under different theories.

KEY TERMS

- Agency costs
- Arbitrage process
- Bankruptcy cost
- Capitalization rate
- Corporate tax
- Cost of debt
- Cost of equity
- Dividend
- EBIT

- Financial distress
- Leverage
- Net income approach
- Pecking order theory
- Personal tax
- Tax shield
- Value of the firm
- Weighted average cost of capital
- Weighted average of firm

FORMULAS

Debt

$$\text{Cost of Debt } (k_d) = \frac{\text{INT}}{\text{D}}$$

Equity

$$\text{Cost of Equity} = \frac{\text{D}_1}{\text{P}_0} + g$$

or

$$\text{Cost of Equity} = \frac{\text{E}_1}{\text{P}_0} + g$$

$$\text{Cost of Equity} = \frac{\text{NOI} - \text{INT}}{\text{V} - \text{D}} = \frac{\text{NI}}{\text{E}}$$

Weighted average cost of capital of the firm

$$k_0 = k_2[\text{E/V}] + k_d[\text{D/V}] \quad \text{or} \quad k_0 = \frac{\text{EBIT}}{\text{V}}$$

Total value of the firm

$$V = (E + D) = NOI/k_0.$$

1. Anil Automobiles operates in the auto spares industry. The income statement of the company is as follows:

	(₹ in lakhs)
Sales	500
Cost of sales	300
Net operating income	200
Interest	60
Earnings to equity shareholders	140

The capitalization rate for debt is 10% and the capitalization rate for the entire firm is 12.5%. Assume that the NOI approach to capital structure is applicable. Then,

1. What is the market value of the debt of the firm?
2. What is the total market value of the firm?
3. What is the market value of the equity of the firm?
4. What is the equity capitalization rate?
5. If other things remain the same, then what is the maximum amount of funds that the firm can borrow in terms of market value so that its equity capitalization rate does not exceed 16%?

Solution:

a)   Market Value of Debt $= \dfrac{\text{Internet expense}}{\text{Debt capitalization rate}} = \dfrac{60}{0.10} = ₹600 \text{ lakhs}$.

b)   Total Market Value of the Firm $= \dfrac{\text{Net operating income}}{\text{Overall capitalization rate for the firm}}$

$\qquad = \dfrac{200}{0.125} = ₹1,600 \text{ lakhs}$

c)   Market value of equity = Total market value of the firm – Market value of debt = 1,600 – 600 = ₹1,000 lakhs.

d)   Equity Capitalization Rate $= \dfrac{\text{Equity earning}}{\text{Market value of equity}} = \dfrac{140}{1,000} = 0.14,$ i.e., 14%

e)   According to the NOI approach

$$k_e = k_0 + (k_0 - k_d)\, B/S.$$

Let the market value of debt after increase be B. Market value of equity = Total market value of the firm – Market value of debt = 1,600 – B.

$$k_e \leq 16\%$$

$$\therefore 0.16 \geq 0.125 + (0.125 - 0.10)\frac{B}{1,600 - B} \quad \text{or} \quad 0.035 \geq \frac{0.025B}{1,600 - B}$$

$$\text{or } 56 - 0.035B \geq 0.025B \text{ or } 56 \geq 0.06B \text{ or } B \leq \frac{56}{0.06} \quad \text{or} \quad B \leq 933.33 \text{ lakhs}$$

$$\therefore \text{Increase in Market Value of Debt} = 933.33 - 600 = ₹333.33 \text{ lakhs}$$

Hence, the firm can increase debt by a maximum amount of ₹333.33 lakhs in terms of market value.

2. Regal Sports Equipment Ltd is trying to determine its optimal capital structure. The company's capital structure consists of debt and common stock. To estimate the cost of debt, the company has produced the following table:

Percentage Financed with Debt (%)	Before Tax Cost of Debt (%)
10	7.0
20	7.2
30	8.0
40	8.8
50	9.6

The company's tax rate is 40%.

The company uses the CAPM to estimate its cost of common equity, r_s. The risk-free rate is 5% and the market risk premium is 6%. Regal estimates that if it had no debt its beta would be 1.0. (Its "unlevered beta," β_{UNLEV} equals 1.0.)

Based on this information, what is the company's optimal capital structure, and what is the firm's cost of capital at this optimal capital structure?

Solution:

$$r_{RF} = 5\%; \ r_M - r_{RF} = 6\%$$

$$r_s = r_{RF} + (r_M - r_{RF})\beta$$

$$WACC = r_d \times w_d \times (1 - T) + r_s \times w_c$$

We need to use the D/E ratio given for each capital structure to find the levered beta using the Hamada equation. Then, use each of these betas with the CAPM to find r_s for that capital structure. Use this r_s and r_d for each capital structure to find the WACC. The optimal capital structure is the one that minimizes the WACC.

$$(D/E)\beta = \beta_U[1 + (1 - T)(D/E)]$$

$$r_s = r_{RF} + (r_M - r_{RF})\beta$$

w_c	b	r_e	w_e	r_d	w_d	WACC
0.11	1.0667	11.4005%	0.9	7.0%	0.1	10.68%
0.25	1.1500	11.9000	0.8	7.2	0.2	10.38
0.43	1.2571	12.5429	0.7	8.0	0.3	10.22
0.67	1.4000	13.4000	0.6	8.8	0.4	10.15
1.00	1.6000	14.6000	0.5	9.6	0.5	10.18

For example, if the D/E ratio is 0.11:

$$\beta = 1.0[1 + (1 - T)(D/E)] = 1.0[1 + (1 - 0.4)(0.1111)] = 1.0667$$

$$r_s = r_{RF} + (r_M - r_{RF})b = 5\% + 6\%(1.0667) = 11.40\%$$

The weights are given at 0.9 and 0.1 for equity and debt, respectively, and r_d for that capital structure is given as 7%.

$$\text{WACC} = r_d \times w_d \times (1 - T) + r_s \times w_c$$
$$= 7\% \times 0.1 \times (1 - 0.4) + 11.40\% \times 0.9 = 10.68\%$$

We can do the same calculation for each of the capital structures and find out each WACC. The optimal capital structure is the one that minimizes the WACC, which is 10.15%. Therefore, the optimal capital structure is 40% debt and 60% equity.

3. Venus Electronics currently has no debt. Its operating income is ₹20 million and its tax rate is 40%. It pays out all its NI as dividends and has a zero growth rate. The current stock price is ₹40 per share, and it has 2.5 million shares of stock outstanding. If it moves to a capital structure that has 40% debt and 60% equity (based on market values), its investment bankers believe its weighted average cost of capital would be 10%. What would its stock price be if it changes to the new capital structure?

Solution:
Step 1: Find the new value of the firm after the recapitalization. Because growth is zero, free cash flow is equal to NOPAT

$$V = \text{FCF}/\text{WACC} = \text{NOPAT}/\text{WACC} = \text{EBIT}(1 - t)/\text{WACC} = ₹20(1 - 0.4)/0.1 = ₹120 \text{ million}$$

Step 2: Find the new value of equity and debt after the recapitalization

$$E = w_e V = 0.6(₹120) = ₹72 \text{ million}$$

$$D = w_d V = 0.4(₹120) = ₹48 \text{ million}$$

Step 3: Find the new price per share after the recapitalization

$$P = [E + (D - D_0)]/n_0 = [₹72 + (₹48 - 0)]/2.5 = ₹48$$

4. OXY Manufacturing Co has a total capitalization of ₹100,000 and EBIT worth ₹10,000. The Chief Financial Officer of the company wants to take decision regarding capital structure of the company. What should be the amount of debt used as per the traditional theory?

Amount of Debt	Interest Rate (%)	Cost of Equity (%)
0	–	9
10,000	5	9.5
20,000	5	9.5
30,000	5.5	10.00
40,000	6.0	11.00
50,000	6.5	11.50
60,000	8.0	12.00
70,000	8.0	20.00

Solution: As per traditional theory, optimal capital structure exists at a point where weighted average cost of capital is minimum. As per the following table, the overall weighted average cost of capital is minimum at 20,000 amount of debt.

Capital Required			**100,000**					
Amount of Debt	Interest Rate % or k_d	Cost of Equity % or k_e	Amount of Equity	w_e	w_d	$w_e * k_e$	$w_d * k_d$	Overall Cost of Capital = $w_e * k_e + w_d * k_d$
0	–	9	100,000	1	0	9	9.00	
10,000	5	9.5	90,000	0.9	0.1	8.55	0.5	9.05
20,000	5	9.5	80,000	0.8	0.2	7.6	1	8.60
30,000	5.5	10	70,000	0.7	0.3	7	1.65	8.65
40,000	6	11	60,000	0.6	0.4	6.6	2.4	9.00
50,000	6.5	11.5	50,000	0.5	0.5	5.75	3.25	9.00
60,000	8	12	40,000	0.4	0.6	4.8	4.8	9.60
70,000	8	20	30,000	0.3	0.7	6	5.6	11.60

5. Shyam Ltd has overall cost of capital at 15%. It has 8% debt capital amounting to ₹1,000,000. The expected earnings before interest and tax is ₹300,000. Calculate value of the firm and cost of equity capital as per net operating approach.

Solution:

$$\text{Earnings before interest and tax} = ₹300,000$$

$$\text{Value of the firm} = \frac{\text{EBIT}}{k_o} = \frac{300,000}{0.15} = 20,00,000$$

$$\text{Value of debt} = ₹1,000,000$$

$$\text{Value of equity} = 2,000,000 - 1,000,000 = 1,000,000$$

$$\text{Interest charges} = 10,00,000 \times \left(\frac{8}{100}\right) = ₹80,000$$

$$\text{Cost of Equity} = \frac{\text{NOI} - \text{INT}}{V - D} = \frac{\text{NI}}{E} = \frac{(3,00,000 - 80,000)}{10,00,000} = 22\%$$

6. X and Y companies are identical in all respect except that Y does not use any debt capital in its capital structure whereas X has a debt of ₹500,000 with 10% interest rate. The expected NOI is ₹300,000 and the overall cost of capital is 12%. What would be the value of the firm according to Modigliani Miller approach? Verify it.

Solution:

Particulars	X	Y
EBIT	₹300,000	₹300,000
Value of the firm	₹2,500,000	₹2,500,000
Less value of debt	₹500,000	
Value of equity	₹2,000,000	₹2,500,000
Cost of equity	=0.125 or 12.5%	=0.12 or 12%

Verification:

$$k_o = k_e[E/V] + k_d[D/V] \quad \text{or} \quad k_o \frac{EBIT}{V}$$

$$= 0.125 \times \frac{20,00,000}{25,00,000} + 0.10 \times \frac{5,00,000}{25,00,000}$$

$$= 0.12 = 12\%$$

CASE STUDY: CAPITAL STRUCTURE OF TATA MOTORS

Tata Motors Ltd (Tata Motors) is an automobile company. The Company is engaged mainly in the business of automobile products consisting of all types of commercial and passenger vehicles, including financing of the vehicles sold by the Company. The Company has two segments: automotive and others. The other segments include construction equipment, engineering solutions, and software operations.

Initiated in the year 1945, Tata Motors has a wide network of retailers and suppliers across India. It was in 1954 that the company launched its first vehicle. Today, more than 3 million Tata cars and heavy vehicles glide through the Indian roads. The company gained the prestige of being the first from engineering industry of India to be listed under the New York Stock Exchange in September 2004.

Besides being the second biggest in the passenger car division, Tata Motors is also ranked as the fifth highest in the category of medium and heavy commercial vehicles at international level. With the help of its associates, Tata Motors offer high-end manufacturing and automotive solutions to its customers. Its foremost indigenously made car was Tata Indica, followed by a mini-truck Tata Ace in 2005. In the year 2009, the firm marked its name in the pages of automotive history by introducing the world's fuel efficient and cheapest car—Tata Nano.

Tata Motors required fresh equity to reduce its debt–equity ratio by deleveraging its balance sheet. Due to excess borrowings, Tata Motors debt–equity ratio has increased to 1.06 in the year 2008–2009 from 0.8. Debt burden of US$ 3.2 billion was the root cause of higher debt–equity ratio. The debt proceedings were used to acquire Jaguar & Land Rover and keep these brands running successfully. To reduce the debt–equity ratio, two right issues are carried out to mobilize US$ 850 million. Due to these right issues, promoter's shareholding went down up to 41.4% so that the debt–equity ratio can be reduced back to industry norms. To reduce the debt–equity ratio, the company has to either reduce debt or dilute equity ownership. Dilution of equity seems to be a more easy solution. So the right issue is done in the year 2009. Tata Motors debt/equity ratio was 1.11 in the year 2009–2010. That is why it has been reduced to 0.79 in 2010–2011. The consolidated debt was reduced to 20.70% due to funds generation on account from institutional buyers and conversion of foreign securities. Reduction in debt was due to better improvement quality, qualified institutional placements, and conversion of foreign currency convertibles. The above discussion vividly reflects that the capital structure of the company keeps on changing. Look at certain data of Tata Motors.

	2011	2010	2009	2008	2007
Equity share capital	634.65	570.6	514.05	385.54	385.41
Reserves	19,375.59	14,394.87	11,855.15	7,428.45	6,458.39
Revaluation reserves	0	0	25.07	25.51	25.95
Net worth	20,013.30	14,965.47	12,394.27	7,839.50	6,869.75
Secured loans	7,766.05	7,742.60	5,251.65	2,461.99	2,022.04
Unsecured loans	8,132.70	8,883.31	7,913.91	3,818.53	1,987.10
Total debt	15,898.75	16,625.91	13,165.56	6,280.52	4,009.14
Debt equity ratio	0.79	1.11	1.06	0.8	0.59
Long-term debt equity ratio	0.79	1.11	0.49	0.5	0.31
Debt coverage ratios					
Interest cover	3.05	2.77	2.43	6.28	7.19
Total debt to owners fund	0.79	1.12	1.06	0.8	0.59
Financial charges coverage ratio	4.33	3.56	3.64	7.19	7.62

Source: Author (taken from published financial statement of Tata Motors and modified thereafter).

ANALYZE

Which capital structure and debt-equity ratio is the optimum is a major area of concern. How with time, capital structure undergoes change?

ASSESS YOURSELF

Concept Review and Critical Thinking Questions

1. Is capital structure relevant in determining the value of the firm? Discuss the issue in light of the various theories of capital structure.
2. What is NI approach? How is it different from NOI approach? Illustrate.
3. How the consideration of control affects the composition of capital structure?
4. Explain the feature of EBIT–EPS analysis, cash flow analysis, and valuation models approach to determinations of capital structure.
5. Explain the capital structure decision from the point of view of minimization of risk.

STUDENT ACTIVITY

Student should correlate with capital structure, EPS, and MPS of selected Indian companies vs. MNCs for last 5 years and establish relationship among leverage, EPS, and value of the first.

SUGGESTED READINGS

Brealey, R.A., & Myers, S.C. (2002). *Principles of corporate finance* (7th ed.). New York: McGraw-Hill.

Horne, J.C.V. (2002). *Financial management & policy* (12th ed.). Singapore: Pearson Education.

Price Water House Coopers. (1999). *Cost of capital: Survey of issues and trends in India.* Retrieved from www.pwcylobal.com (accessed on June 9, 2016).

Ross, S.A., Westerfield, R.W., & Jordan, B.D. (2002). *Fundamentals of corporate finance* (6th ed.). New Delhi: Tata McGraw-Hill.

CHAPTER 8

Leverage

Learning Objectives

- To understand the concept of leverage.
- To learn the measurement of leverage.
- To learn the application of operating leverage and financial leverage.

PRELUDE

Read this "No Discount Fireworks this Diwali as E-tailers play safe on margins. Clothes, shoes, electronics, and mobile devices won't be cheaper this festive season. Hoping for big online discounts this Diwali? The wait may be fruitless. Shoppers may not get cheaper rates on clothes, shoes, electronics, and mobile devices this festive season as e-commerce companies look to protect margins after having pursued an aggressive discounting policy in previous years to gain market share and traffic, suggesting a watershed moment in online retail could be around the corner … Last year's discounts were needed to build awareness. This season, lesser discounts and offers are expected to be floated as compared to last year as there needs to be more focus on tightening delivery systems and processes" along with.[1] Fall of Lehman Brothers: Lehman Brothers borrowed substantial amount of debt which resulted into its insolvency in 2008. This is known as ill effect of leverage. The US Economy was facing slum which resulted in loss of employment opportunity. Gradually, income levels of people started falling down. A significant proportion of borrowed fund of the public was invested in housing-related assets, which made it vulnerable during economic downturn. Lehman and other financial institutions were finding difficulty in recovering money from up country investors. That is why leverage ratio, a ratio of external debt to equity of Lehman increased to 31:1 in the year 2007. This vulnerable position caused decline in the value of assets which had eroded the entire book value of equity (negative equity). In August 2007, Lehman closed its subprime lending. In year 2008, Lehman suffered unprecedented loss due to exposure in subprime mortgage crisis. This incident emphasizes the role of finance manager that how he should use leverage to generate positive value for the stakeholders.

---

[1] *The Economic Times*, Wednesday, September 23, 2015.

The Concept of Leverage

The concept of leverage can be traced to the use of "lever" to lift heavy objects. That is possible because the force applied on the lever gets magnified in proportion to the length of the lever. The lever thus exerts influence on the heavy object. The longer the lever, the easier it is to move the object. Aristotle said, "Give me a lever long enough and I can move the earth."

In financial analysis, though essentially the meaning of leverage remains the same, we use the term to indicate the responsiveness of one financial variable (the independent variable) to the other financial variable (the dependent variable). When leverage is measured between two financial variables, it explains how the dependent variable responds to a particular change in the independent variable. Let us suppose that there are two financial variables X and Y. X is an independent financial variable and Y its dependent variable. The leverage, which Y has with respect to X, can be measured by the percentage change in Y to a given percentage change in X.

Symbolically

$$L\left(\frac{Y}{X}\right) = \frac{\Delta Y/Y}{\Delta X/X}$$

Types of Leverage

To understand the concept of leverage, it is essential to know the following types of leverages:

1. Operating leverage
2. Financial leverage
3. Combined leverage

Operating Leverage

Operating leverage of a firm exists due to fixed operating expenses. There are three categories of operating cost: (i) fixed cost which does not vary with sales volume and such cost exists due to time element; (ii) variable cost which is directly proportionate to sales volume and it varies with sales volume; and (iii) semi-variable costs are partly fixed and partly variable. Such a cost is fixed up to a certain range of sales volume and thereafter it increases in proportion with sales. Factory rent is a fixed cost and material is a variable cost. Electricity expenses are semi-variable cost. *Operating leverage is the firm's capability to use fixed operating cost to amplify the effects of change in sales on its earnings before tax and interest.*

The higher the proportion of fixed costs in the total cost structure, the higher is the operating leverage. Fixed operating costs do not include debt interest, which is a fixed financial cost. However, it includes costs such as administrative costs, depreciation, selling, and advertisement expenses, and so on. If there are no fixed costs, the firm has no operating leverage.

Operating leverage is to measure the operating risk. The risk arising out of variability in earnings due to change in the quantity produced and sold. Operating leverage measures, in simple language, the change in EBIT because of change in Q (Quantity produced and sold).

Measures of Operating Leverage

1. Fixed costs/total cost ratio: As we define operating leverage as the proportion of fixed costs in the total cost structure, the ratio of fixed costs to total costs can be used as a measure of operating leverage.

$$\text{Operating Leverage} = \frac{\text{Fixed Costs}}{\text{Total Costs}}$$

or

$$\text{Operating leverage} = \text{Contribution/EBIT}$$

Impact of operating leverage on operating profit

Operating leverage is a double-edged sword. Operating profit of a highly levered firm would increase at a faster rate for any given increase in sales. However, if the sales decline, a firm with higher operating leverage would suffer more loss than a firm with low operating leverage. This is so because fixed costs have to be met irrespective of the level of revenues generated. When sales are increasing, the fixed costs can be easily provided for and the remaining sales revenue goes toward increasing the operation of the firm (assuming the variable cost to sales ratio of the firm is less than 1). But when the sales decline, the fixed costs are still to be paid for from this reduced level of revenues. As a result, the operating profit declines.

Illustration 1. There are two firms A and B manufacturing the same product. The selling price is ₹8 per unit. The variable costs of A and B are ₹6 and ₹4, respectively. The fixed costs are ₹20,000 and ₹80,000, respectively. What is the effect on profit if the sales change from 20,000 to 40,000 units? What happens if the sales decline to 10,000 units?

Solution:

(amount in ₹)

	Firm A			Firm B		
Sales (in units) (in ₹)	10,000	20,000	40,000	10,000	20,000	40,000
Sales Revenue (in ₹)	80,000	160,000	320,000	80,000	160,000	320,000
Variable cost (in ₹)	60,000	120,000	240,000	40,000	80,000	160,000
Contribution (in ₹)	20,000	40,000	80,000	40,000	80,000	160,000
Fixed costs (in ₹)	20,000	20,000	20,000	80,000	80,000	80,000
Profit (in ₹)	0	20,000	60,000	−40,000	0	80,000

It is clear that an increase in sales if the operating leverage is high, leads to a greater increase in profits than that of a firm with lower operating leverage. However, if the sales decline, then a firm with higher operating leverage loses more than a firm with lower degree of operating leverage (DOL).

2. DOL: We have seen that the operating profit of a firm with higher operating leverage would increase at a faster rate for any given increase in sales. However, if the sales decline, the firm with a higher operating leverage would suffer more than a firm with lower operating leverage. The responsiveness of operating profit to change in sales is measured by the DOL.

DOL is defined as the percentage change in operating profit for a given percentage change in sales.

DOL = Percentage change in EBIT/Percentage change in sales

$$= \frac{\Delta \text{EBIT/EBIT}}{\Delta S/S}$$

or

$$=\text{Contribution/EBIT}$$

where EBIT is the earnings before interest and tax, ΔEBIT is the change in EBIT, S is the net sales of the firm, ΔS is the change in sales contribution = sales – variable cost

Illustration 2. The long-term capital of a firm consists of the following:

(₹ in crore)

Equity share capital (20 lakh shares at par value of ₹10)	2
Reserves and surplus	1
Preference share capital (10 lakh shares at par value of ₹10)	1
Nonconvertible debentures (4 lakh debentures at par value of ₹100)	4
Term loan	4

The rate of dividend on the preference shares is 12%. The debentures carry a coupon rate of 9%. The rate of interest on the term loan is 11%. The tax rate applicable to EIL is 35%. It is expected that by the end of the current financial year, EIL will achieve sales of ₹30 crore. The total cost for the current financial year is expected to be ₹22 crore, which includes variable costs of ₹18 crore and fixed costs of ₹4 crore.

What is the DOL for the firm?

Solution:

Sales	30
Less: Variable costs	18
Contribution	12
Less: Fixed cost (F)	4
Profit before interest and tax (PBIT)	8
Less: Interest (I)	0.80
Profit before tax (PBT)	7.20
Tax (7.20×0.35)	2.52
Profit after tax (PAT)	4.68
Less: preference dividend (D_p) (1×0.12)	0.12
Earnings available to equity shareholders	4.56
I Interest on term loan: 4×0.11	0.44
I Interest on debentures: 4×0.09	0.36
Total	0.80
$\text{DOL} = \dfrac{\text{Contribution}}{\text{PBIT}} = \dfrac{12}{8}$	1.50

Salient Characteristics of DOL

1. For each level of sales, there is a distinct DOL.
2. If quantity sold is less than the operating break-even point, then DOL will be negative (which does not imply that an increase in quantity sold leads to a decrease in EBIT). Similarly, if quantity sold is greater than the operating break-even point, then the DOL will be positive. However, the DOL will start to decline as the level of sales quantity increases and will reach a limit of 1.

Test Yourself

1. Define leverage.
2. Define operating leverage. How is it measured?

Applications of DOL

Measurement of Business Risk

We know that the greater the DOL, the more sensitive is EBIT to a given change in unit sales, that is, the greater is the risk of exceptional losses if sales become depressed. **DOL is therefore a measure of business risk of the firms.** Business risk refers to the uncertainty or variability of the firm's revenue (EBIT). It is an unavoidable risk. Revenue is affected by factors like economic conditions, business cycle, competitor's strategy, change in technology, change in consumer preference, market strategy, and so on. Expenses will vary with sales. Higher the proportion of fixed expense to total expenses, higher would be the DOL. Higher operating leverage leads to increase in EBIT with increase in sales.

Production Planning

DOL is also important in production planning. For instance, the firm may have the opportunity to change its cost structure by introducing labor saving machinery, thereby reducing variable labor overhead while increasing the fixed costs. Such a situation will increase the DOL. Any method of production, which increases DOL, is justified only if there is a very high probability that sales will be higher so that the earnings will also correspondingly increase with an increase in the DOL.

Break-even Analysis

Break-even analysis, sometimes called cost–volume–profit analysis, is used by the firm to

1. Determine the level of operations necessary to cover all operating costs, and
2. Evaluate the profitability associated with various levels of sales.

The firm's operating break-even point is the level of sales necessary to cover all operating costs. At that point, earnings before interest and taxes are

equal to zero. The first step in finding the operating break-even point is to divide the cost of goods sold and operating expenses into fixed and variable operating costs. Fixed costs are a function of time, not sales volume, and are typically contractual. For example, rent payable for the factory premises is a fixed cost. Variable costs vary directly with sales and are a function of volume, not time. For example, shipping costs are variable.

Determining the Operating Break-even Point

The operating break-even point can be determined algebraically or graphically. Let us discuss the two approaches one by one.

The Algebraic Approach

$$EBIT = (P \times Q) - FC - (VC \times Q)$$

where EBIT is the earnings before interest and taxes, P is the sale price per unit, Q is the sales quantity in units, FC is the fixed operating cost per period, and VC is the variable operating cost per unit.

Simplifying the equation

$$EBIT = Q \times (P - VC) - FC$$

As noted above, the operating break-even point is the level of sales at which all fixed and variable operating costs are covered—the level at which EBIT is equal to zero. Setting EBIT equal to 0 and solving the equation for Q yields

$$Q^* = FC/P - VC$$

where Q^* is the firm's operating break-even point.

Illustration 3. A gifts and novelties retailer has fixed operating costs of ₹25,000, its sale price per unit is ₹100, and its variable operating cost per unit is ₹50. What is the operating break-even point for the firm?

Solution: Using the above equation, the operating break-even point for the firm can be determined as follows:

$$Q = ₹25,000/₹100 - ₹50 = ₹25,000/50 = 500 \text{ units}$$

At sales of 500 units, the firm's EBIT should just be equal to 0. The firm will have positive EBIT for sales greater than 500 units and negative EBIT, or a loss for sales less than 500 units, along with the other values given.

The Graphic Approach

The break-even point can be determined graphically. A break-even chart depicts the relationship between costs, volume, and profit. For constructing the break-even chart, we have to draw the fixed cost line, the total cost line, and the sales line. The break-even point is obtained where the total cost line and total sales line intersect (Figure 8.1).

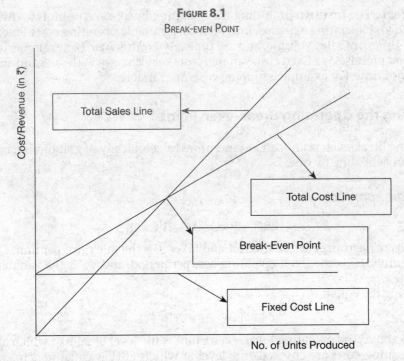

FIGURE 8.1

BREAK-EVEN POINT

Source: Author.

Factors Affecting the Operating Break-even point

A firm's operating break-even point is sensitive to a number of variables: fixed operating cost (FC), the sale price per unit (*P*), and the variable operating cost per unit (VC). As might be expected, an increase in cost (FC or VC) tends to increase the operating break-even point, whereas an increase in the sale price per unit (*P*) will decrease the operating break-even point.

Illustration 4. In case of the gifts and novelties retailer in Figure 8.1, evaluate the impact of: (i) increasing fixed operating costs to ₹30,000, (ii) increasing the sale price per unit to ₹125, (iii) increasing the variable operating cost per unit to ₹75, and (iv) simultaneously implementing all three of these changes.

Solution: Using the formula for operating break-even point, we can determine the operating break-even point in each of the above case as follows:

1. Operating break-even point = 30,000/100 – 50 = 600 units
2. Operating break-even point = 25,000/125 – 50 = 333 1/3 units
3. Operating break-even point = 25,000/100 – 75 = 1,000 units
4. Operating break-even point = 30,000/125 – 75 = 600 units

Comparing the resulting operating break-even points to the initial value of 500 units, we can see that the cost increases (actions 1 and 3) raise the break-even point, whereas the revenue increase (action 2) lowers the break-even point. The combined effect of increasing all three variables (action 4) also results in an increased operating break-even point.

Fixed Costs and Operating Leverage

Changes in fixed operating costs affect operating leverage significantly. Firms can sometimes incur fixed operating costs rather than variable operating costs and at other times may be able to substitute one type of cost for the other. For example, a firm could make fixed-rupee lease payments rather than payments equal to a specified percentage of sales or it could compensate sales representatives with a fixed salary and bonus rather than a percent of sales on commission basis.

Illustration 5. A firm forecasts that it will produce 1,500 units and generate EBIT of ₹300,000. The DOL for a quantity level of ₹15,000 units is 2.5. There is a possibility that the actual output could range from 10% below to 5% above the general forecast value. Calculate the range of possible forecast errors for EBIT in percentage term and also the corresponding EBIT values.

Solution: Given actual output Q will vary between 10% below and 6% above the forecast value.

If Q is less than the forecast value by 10%

$$\text{Change in EBIT} = -(0.1) * 2.5 = -0.25 = -25\%$$

If Q is more than the forecast value by 5%

$$\text{Change in EBIT} = 0.05 * 2.5 = 12.5\%$$

Range of possible forecast errors for EBIT is between −25% and 12.5% and corresponding EBIT values are ₹225,000 and ₹337,500.

Test Yourself

1. Discuss the application of operating leverage.
2. Define operating break-even point.

Financial Leverage

The use of fixed-charge source of funds in the capital structure like debt and preference capital is referred to as the financial leverage. It is also sometimes called capital gearing. A gear is a toothed wheel that works with other similar and smaller wheels to alter the relation between the speed of an engine and the speed of the driven parts. The use of debt in the capital structure acts as adding a gear to the capital which will affect the relation between EBIT and EPS.

In simple words, financial leverage stands for measuring financial risk. The financial risk is due to inclusion of debts in capital structure. **Change in EPS because of change in EBIT is financial leverage.** Financial leverage is also sometimes referred to as "trading on equity" because it is the equity capital base which is traded on, that is, equity capital is used as the basis to raise debt. The larger the equity base, the easier it is to raise more debt.

Financial leverage is used with the objective of increasing the returns to the shareholders. This is so because the payment to fixed-charge sources of funds will be a given amount (i.e., fixed) and if the firm is able to generate returns which are higher than the return payable to these sources, the additional returns would belong to the shareholders. For example, a firm invests ₹100 crore of equity in a project which has an expected return of 15%. The firm can also raise another ₹50 crore as debt at a post-tax cost of 12%. If the firm uses only equity, the return to the shareholders will be 15% of 100 crore, that is, ₹15 crore. However, if the firm decides to borrow and invest the additional funds also in the project, the return on the funds invested will be 15% of ₹150 crore, that is, ₹22.5 crore. After paying to the debt suppliers an amount equal to 12% of 50 crore, that is, ₹6 crore, the return to the shareholders is 22.5 – 6 crore, that is, ₹16.5 crore. We can observe that use of debt has increased the return to the shareholders from ₹15 crore to ₹16.5 crore.

However, if the interest rate on debt is 18%, in that case the interest payable to the debt suppliers will be 18% of ₹50 crore, that is, ₹9 crore. So, the return to the shareholders will be ₹22.5 – 9 crore, that is, ₹13.5 crore. That means, in this case the returns to the shareholders decline as a result of the usage of debt in the capital structure. Thus, financial leverage or capital gearing is a double-edged sword.

Measures of Financial Leverage

Whereas operating leverage measures the change in the EBIT of a company to a particular change in the output, the financial leverage measures the effect of the change in EPS on change in EBIT of the company.

The commonly used measures of financial leverage are as follows:

1. **Debt Ratio:** This is the proportion of long-term debt in the total capital used in the business.

$$DR = \frac{D}{D+E}$$

where D is the book value of debt. E is the book value of equity (i.e., shareholders' funds). Instead of the book values, we may also use the market values. This ratio indicates the extent to which the firm relies on debt as a source of long-term finance.

2. **Debt-Equity Ratio:** This is the ratio of long-term debt to the shareholders funds in the capital structure of the firm.

$$D - E\ Ratio = \frac{D}{E}$$

where D is the book value of debt and E is the book value of equity (i.e., shareholders' funds).

3. **Interest Coverage Ratio:** This ratio measures the ability of the firm to meet out its interest payment obligations. In other words, the ability to pay the fixed financial charges. It indicates the firm's capacity to meet fixed financial charges. The reciprocal of interest coverage ratio is income gearing.

$$ICR = \frac{EBIT}{Interest}$$

However, this ratio suffers from some limitations as a measure of risk. First, for determining the company's ability to meet its interest payment obligations, the relevant information is cash inflows and not the accounting profit. This ratio uses earnings before interest and taxes, which is an accounting figure, to find out whether adequate funds are available to meet the interest payment obligations. During recession, there can be huge difference between cash inflows and accounting profit. Second, as the ratio is based on historical figures (from the income statement), its ability to determine financial risk in the future time period is questionable. Furthermore, financial leverage refers to the use of debt in the capital structure. So, we should be concerned with long-term effect of the use of debt.

Impact of Financial Leverage on Investor's Return and Risk

The equity shareholders are the residual claimants on the earnings of the firm. Two measures of return that are important from the point of view of shareholders are EPS and ROE.

$$\text{Earnings per share (EPS)} = \frac{\text{Profit After Tax}}{\text{Number of Share}}$$

$$\text{EPS} = \frac{(\text{EBIT} - \text{I})(1 - \text{T})}{N}$$

$$\text{ROE} = \frac{\text{Profit After Tax}}{\text{Shareholders Funds}}$$

Is the return to the shareholders affected by the usage of debt in the capital structure? What is the effect of financial leverage on EPS and ROE of the firm?

To understand the impact of financial leverage on shareholders return let us consider two situations:

1. Alternative financing plans with EBIT held constant, and
2. Alternative financing plans with varying EBIT.

Case I. Alternative Financial Plans: Constant EBIT
Apex Ltd is considering investment in an expansion project which requires an investment of ₹25 lakhs. The management of the firm is expecting a before tax rate of return of 20%. To finance the expansion, the firm is considering two alternative plans:

Plan A: Raise the entire amount by issuing 250,000 equity shares at ₹10 per share.

Plan B: Raise 1,250,000 by issuing 125,000 equity shares at ₹10 per share and raise the remaining amount through debt at 15%.

The tax rate applicable to the firm is 40%. What is the effect of the two plans on EPS? Which plan is better?

This is an example of constant EBIT because whether the firm chooses plan A or plan B, the EBIT will be 20% of ₹2,500,000 or ₹500,000.

Let us see what happens to the EPS under the two plans:

(amount in ₹)

	Plan A	Plan B
EBIT	500,000	500,000
Less: Interest @15%	0	187,500
PBT	500,000	312,500
Less: Tax @40%	200,000	125,000
PAT	300,000	187,500
No. of Equity shares (N)	250,000	125,000
EPS=PAT/N	1.20	1.50
ROE	12%	15%

It is clear that financial leverage has a positive effect on EPS and ROE in this case. When the firm uses 50% debt in its capital structure, the EPS and ROE increase by 25%. But there is no magic in this. If we look at the figures once again, we will find the reason for this positive effect. The firm expects to earn 20% return on the expansion project. It can raise debt at 15%. It means that if it borrows partly to finance the project, it will generate returns on these funds also at 20%, whereas it has to pay only 15% to the creditors. The excess return thus generated belongs to the shareholders. To understand this, consider that the rate of interest on debt is 24%. In that case, the EPS and ROE under the two financing plans would appear as follows:

	Plan A	Plan B
EBIT (in ₹)	500,000	500,000
Less: Interest @24%	0	300,000
PBT	500,000	200,000
Less: Tax @40%	200,000	80,000
PAT	300,000	120,000
No. of Equity shares (N)	250,000	125,000
EPS=PAT/N	1.20	0.96
ROE	12%	9.6%

Thus, if the interest rate on debt is more than the return expected from the project, financial leverage acts to the disadvantage of the shareholders.

Tax Shield

Further, when it partly finances the project through borrowing, the number of shareholders and the shareholder's funds are relatively lower than what they are when the entire financing is done through equity. This has a positive effect on the EPS and ROE. In addition, when the firm goes for plan B, the tax payable by the firm is ₹75,000 less than the tax payable under the financing plan A. This implies that the firm is saving on taxes. This happens because the interest on debt is a tax-deductible expense. The tax saving that results due to usage of debt in the capital structure is called as Interest tax shield. The interest tax shield can be calculated as follows:

Interest tax shield = Tax rate × Interest payable

In the above example, the amount of interest payable under the financing plan B is ₹187,500 and the tax rate is 40%, the interest tax shield as per the above formula will be 0.40 × ₹187,500 = ₹75,000.

As you can see, this is equal to the difference between the taxes payable under the two financing plans (i.e., ₹200,000 − ₹187,500 = ₹75,000).

Thus, we reach to a conclusion that if the EBIT is expected to be constant, financial leverage is going to be beneficial if the rate of interest payable on the debt is less than the return on investment expected from the project. If the interest payable is more than the return expected from the project, then financial leverage will result into a decline in value for the shareholders.

Case II. Alternative financial plans—Variable EBIT
Let us extend the above example. Consider that the return on investment expected from the new project is variable. Suppose, it varies with the expected economic conditions in the economy as follows:

	Recession	Normal	Boom
ROI (%)	5	20	25

In such a situation, the EBIT will also become variable and for the three expected economic scenarios discussed hereinbefore, it will be as follows:

	Recession	Normal	Boom
ROI (%)	5	20	25
EBIT (in ₹)	125,000	500,000	625,000

Given these expected values of EBIT, let us see what happens to EPS and ROE under the two financing plans.

(amount in ₹)

	Plan A			Plan B		
	Recession	Normal	Boom	Recession	Normal	Boom
EBIT (in ₹)	125,000	500,000	625,000	125,000	500,000	625,000
Less: Interest @15%	0	0	0	187,500	187,500	187,500
PBT	125,000	500,000	625,000	–62,500	312,500	437,500
Less: Tax @40%	50,000	200,000	250,000	–25,000	125,000	175,000
PAT	75,000	300,000	375,000	–37,500	187,500	262,500
No. of equity shares (N)	250,000	250,000	250,000	125,000	125,000	125,000
EPS=PAT/N	0.30	1.20	1.50	–0.3	1.50	2.10
ROE (%)	3	12	15	–30	15	21

Thus, we see that if the EBIT is variable, the range over EPS and ROE can vary. In other words, the variability of EPS and ROE denotes the increased risk to the shareholders. This does not mean that when there is no financial leverage there is no variability in EPS or ROE. EPS and ROE are both dependent on EBIT and hence given that operating (business) risk, EPS and ROE will be variable. The variability of EPS and ROE due to financial leverage is referred to as financial risk. We can measure this risk by developing a probability distribution of the EPS and calculating the standard deviation for the same.

Test Yourself

1. What do you understand by financial leverage? What are the measures available for financial leverage?
2. Analyze the impact of financial leverage on return and earnings of the firm.
3. What is tax shield?

Indifference Point

It is the level of EBIT for which the finance manager is indifferent between the two financing plans.

Two approaches are available for this:

1. Algebraic approach
2. Graphical approach

Algebraic Approach

We know that the formula for calculating EPS is

$$EPS = \frac{(EBIT - I)(1 - T)}{N}$$

Under the two financing plans, the difference will be on account of interest payable and the number of shares. If we denote the number of shares under the two financing plans as N_1 and N_2 and the interest payable as I_1 and I_2, the finance manager will be indifferent between the two financing plans if the EPS under the two financing plans is equal.

Symbolically,

$$EPS_1 = \frac{(EBIT - I_1)(1 - T)}{N_1}$$

$$EPS_2 = \frac{(EBIT - I_2)(1 - T)}{N_2}$$

The finance manager will be indifferent between the two financing plans when EPS 1 = EPS2

$$\frac{(EBIT - I_1)(1 - T)}{N_1} = \frac{(EBIT - I_2)(1 - T)}{N_2}$$

Solving this equation, we can determine the indifference level of EBIT.

Graphical Approach

The EBIT-EPS analysis with variable EBIT can be represented graphically to see the impact of alternative financing plans. We take EPS on the Y-axis and EBIT on the X-axis; then the point at which the lines representing the two financing plans intersect is called the indifference point. At this point, the EPS from the two financing plans is equal (Figure 8.2).

Degree of Financial Leverage

Financial leverage affects the EPS of the firm. Financial leverage acts as a double-edged sword. If the economic conditions are favorable and EBIT is increasing, a higher financial leverage has a positive impact on the EPS. The degree of financial leverage (DFL) captures this relationship between EBIT and EPS. DFL is defined as the percentage change in EPS for a given percentage change in EBIT. That is,

DFL = (percentage change in EPS)/(percentage change in EBIT)

Symbolically,

$$DFL = (\Delta EPS/EPS)/(\Delta EBIT/EBIT)$$

FIGURE 8.2

EBIT–EPS ANALYSIS—GRAPHICAL APPROACH

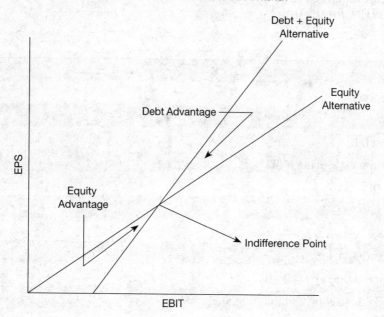

Source: Author.

Substituting Equation (ii) for EPS, we obtain

$$DEL = \frac{EBIT}{EBIT - I - \dfrac{Dp}{(1-T)}}$$

If there is no preference capital in the capital structure of the firm

$$DEL = \frac{EBIT}{EBIT - I} = \frac{EBIT}{PET} = 1 + \frac{Interest}{PBT}$$

Illustration 6.

The long-term capital of a firm consists of the following:

(₹ in crore)	
Equity share capital (20 lakhs shares at par value of ₹10)	2
Reserves and surplus	1
Preference share capital (10 lakhs shares at par value of ₹10)	1
Non-convertible debentures (4 lakhs debentures at par value of ₹100)	4
Term loan	4

The rate of dividend on the preference shares is 12%. The debentures carry a coupon rate of 9%. The rate of interest on the term loan is 11%. The tax rate applicable to EIL is 35%. It is expected that by the end of the current financial year EIL will achieve sales of ₹30 crore. The total cost for the current financial year is expected to be ₹22 crore, which includes variable costs of ₹18 crore and fixed costs of ₹4 crore.

What is the DFL for the firm?

Solution:

Sales	30
Less: Variable costs	18
Contribution	12
Less: Fixed cost (F)	4
Profit before interest and tax (PBIT)	8
Less: Interest (I)	0.80
Profit before tax (PBT)	7.20
Tax (7.20×0.35)	2.52
Profit after tax (PAT)	4.68
Less: Preference dividend (D_p) (1×0.12)	0.12
Earnings available to equity shareholders	4.56
Interest on term loan: 4×0.11	0.44
Interest on debentures: 4×0.09	0.36
Total	0.80

$$DEL = \frac{PBIT}{PBIT - I - \dfrac{D_p}{(1-t)}} = \frac{8}{8 - 0.80 - \dfrac{0.12}{1 - 0.35}} = 1.14$$

Salient Characteristics of the DFL

1. Each level of EBIT has a distinct DFL.
2. DFL will be negative when the EBIT level goes below the financial break-even point. DFL will be positive for all values of EBIT that are above the financial break-even point. This will however start to decline as EBIT increases and will reach a limit of 1.

By assessing the DFL, one can understand the impact of a change in EBIT on the EPS of the company. In addition to this, it also helps in assessing the financial risk of the firm.

Test Yourself

1. Define financial indifference point.
2. Discuss the degree of financial leverage.

Identify the issue. Suggest possible solution.

EXHIBIT 1: HIGH LEVERAGE

India Inc. did some deft debt management in 2010–2011. BW's analysis of 578 firms shows interest payouts rose by 12.5% to ₹28,243 crore even as total debt went up by 13.7% to ₹4,37,370 crore. These companies clocked a growth of more than 20% in revenues. And this percolated to the bottom line, which grew by 24% on the back of higher non-operational, other income, and a check on interest expenses.

"Funding costs for the Indian corporate universe have risen considerably given the tight and uncertain interest rate environment. But interest payouts fell due to Refinancing of existing loans at cheaper rates," says Tirthankar Patnaik, Director-strategist (institutional research) at Religare Capital Markets. There is also a technical reason. For 2010–2011, the funding environment was fairly benign. This helped corporate India keep its interest costs under control. "The charge of interest costs in a company's profit-and-loss statement will be a function of the purpose of debt—for a company that is implementing projects, the interest on project debt is capitalized, and will not be reflected in the income statement," adds Pawan Agarwal, Director, CRISIL ratings.

JSW Energy and Bharti Airtel were the loan guzzlers, and reported a staggering 159.8% and 136.1% rise in their total debt. JSW Energy spent its money on expanding capacity at its power projects, while Bharti Airtel leveraged its books to chase growth through acquisition (snapped Zain Group of Africa for US$10.7 billion) and paid ₹12,285.46 crore for 3G spectrum in 13 circles. In terms of absolute numbers, Reliance Industries, Tata Steel, and Adani Power were the top three debtors—more than 25% of corporate India's total borrowings were on the trio's books. Tata Steel, JSW Steel, and telecom–construction player Unitech together managed to reduce interest costs—interest payouts were slashed by 8.76%, 5.48%, and 5.04%, respectively—even in a rising interest rate scenario.

With many of the large corporations raising more debt in the fiscal year (FY) 2010, the debt-to-equity (DE) ratio became a matter of concern. Among large debtors, Jet Airways was the most leveraged with a DE ratio of 16.11. It was followed by Adani Power (2.74) and Essar Oil (2.23). As many as 34 of the 578 companies had a DE ratio of more than 2. However, other large companies kept it under control—for instance, Reliance Industries (0.46), Tata Steel (0.66), Tata Motors (0.80), and JSW Steel (0.72).

Loans and advances for FY 2011 jumped to 40.39%, an indicator that many gave advanced loans to other companies including group companies. Larsen & Toubro, Sterlite Industries, Reliance Industries, Tata Steel, and Bharti Airtel were the top five on this list. Incidentally, these companies were also among the top debtors for the year. Of course, this does not mean they took loans to give it to group companies. "Loans and advances in many cases are given to group entities out of internal accruals, without affecting overall leverage," notes Patnaik.

While interest payouts were managed well, a tightening of liquidity was clearly evident in the first quarter of the current fiscal. Interest payments spiked 18.88% for 376 companies (from the universe of 578), which reported their first quarter results. Net profits grew 12.77% on revenue rise of 28.3%. In effect, the quality of earnings has declined. "For 2011–2012, we expect the average interest costs for corporates to increase by nearly 175–200 basis points. The overall profitability will reduce driven by higher input, wage, and fuel costs. Together, this will imply that the growth in after-tax profits will be lower than the revenue growth," adds Agarwal. Ominous words.

Source: http://www.businessworld.in/businessworld/businessworld/content/Clever-Footwork.html,
Business world, August 15, 2011, pp. 40–42.

Combined Leverage

Combined leverage indicates that change in EPS is because of change in Q (Quantity produced and sold).

Degree of Total Leverage

A combination of the operating and financial leverages is the total or combined leverage. Thus, the degree of total leverage (DTL) is the measure of the output and EPS of the company. Operating leverage and financial leverage cause fluctuation in EPS for a given change in sales. If operating and financial leverage is very high, it implies that small change in sales causes a magnificent change in EPS. DTL is the product of DOL and DFL and can be calculated as follows:

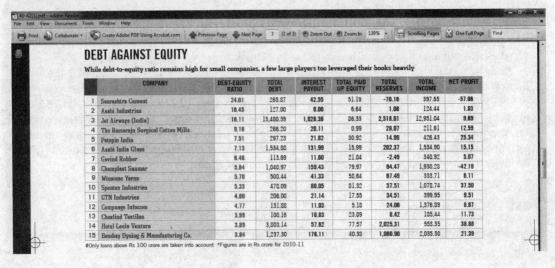

DTL = Percent change in EPS/Percent change in output

$$= (\Delta EPS/EPS)/(\Delta Q/Q)$$

DTL = DOL × DFL

$$= \{[Q(S-V)]/[Q(S-V)-F]\} \; X$$

$$\{[Q(S-V)-F]/Q(S-V)-F-I-[D_p/1-T)]\}$$

$$= \frac{Q(S-V)}{Q(S-V)-F-I-\dfrac{D_p}{(1-T)}}$$

Salient Characteristics of DTL

1. There is a unique DTL for every level of output.
2. At the overall break-even point of output, the DTL is undefined. The overall break-even point is that level of output at which the DTL will be undefined and EPS is equal to zero. This level of output can be calculated as follows:

$$i.\; Q = \frac{F + I + \dfrac{D_p}{(1+T)}}{(S-V)}$$

3. If the level of output is less than the overall break-even point, then the DTL will be negative. If the level of output is greater than the overall break-even point, then the DTL will be positive. DTL decreases as Q increases and reaches a limit of 1.

Applications of DTL

The DTL has the following applications in analyzing the financial performance of a company:

1. **Measures Changes in EPS:** DTL measures the changes in EPS to a percentage change in Q. Thus, the percentage change in EPS can be easily assessed as the product of DTL and the percentage change in Q. For example, if DTL for Q of 3,000 units is 6 and there is a 10% increase in Q, the affect on EPS is 60%.

$$\text{Percentage change in EPS} = \text{DTL (Q=3,000)} \times \text{Percent Change in Q}$$

$$= 6 \times 10\%$$

$$= 60\%$$

2. **Measures Total Risk:** DTL measures the total risk of the company as it is a measure of both operating risk and financial risk. Thus, by measuring total risk, it measures the variability of EPS for a given error in forecasting Q.

Test Yourself

1. Define combined leverage. How is it measured?
2. Elaborate the application of combined leverage.

SUMMARY

1. Leverage is measured between two financial variables. It explains how the dependent variable responds to a particular change in the independent variable.

$$L\left(\frac{Y}{X}\right) = \frac{\Delta Y/Y}{\Delta X/X}$$

2. Employment of an asset or source of funds for which firm has to pay fixed cost or fixed return may be termed as leverage.

3. Operating leverage is the firm's capability to employ fixed operating cost to amplify the effects of change in sales on its earnings before tax and interest.

4. Operating leverage of the firm exists due to fixed operating expenses. There are three categories of operating cost (i) fixed cost which do not vary with sales volume and such cost exists due to time element; (ii) variable cost which is directly proportional to sales volume and it varies with sales volume; and (3) semi-variable costs are partly fixed and partly variable.

5. The responsiveness of operating profit to change in sales is measured by the DOL. DOL is defined as the percentage change in operating profit for a given percentage change in sales.

6. DOL = Percentage change in EBIT/Percentage change in sales.

$$= \frac{\Delta EBIT/EBIT}{\Delta S/S}$$

or

$$Contribution/EBIT$$

where EBIT is the earnings before interest and tax, $\Delta EBIT$ is the change in EBIT, S is the net sales of the firm, and ΔS is the change in sales.

7. Operating leverage helps in measuring business risk, production planning, and operating break-even point.

8. The use of fixed-charge source of funds in the capital structure line debt and preference capital in addition to equity capital is referred to as the financial leverage. It is also sometimes called capital gearing.

9. Financial leverage is used with the objective of increasing the returns to the shareholders. This is so because the payment to fixed-charge sources of funds will be a given amount (i.e., fixed) and if the firm is able to generate returns which are higher than the return payable to these sources, the additional returns would belong to the shareholders.

10. The DFL captures this relationship between EBIT and EPS. DFL is defined as the percentage change in EPS for a given percentage change in EBIT.

DFL = (percentage change in EPS)/(percentage change in EBIT)

DFL = ($\Delta EPS/EPS$)/($\Delta EBIT/EBIT$)

$$DEL = \frac{EBIT}{EBIT - I - \dfrac{D_p}{(1-T)}}$$

11. The tax saving that results due to usage of debt in the capital structure is called as interest tax shield. The interest tax shield can be calculated as follows:

Interest Tax Shield = Tax Rate × Interest Payable

12. The finance manager will be indifferent between the two financing plans when EPS 1 = EPS 2.

13. The DTL is the measure of the output and EPS of the company. Operating leverage and financial leverage cause fluctuation in EPS for a given change in sales. If operating and financial leverage is very high, it implies that small change in sales causes magnificent change in EPS. DTL is the product of DOL and DFL and can be calculated as follows:

$$DTL = \text{Percent change in EPS} / \text{Percent change in output}$$
$$= (\Delta EPS / EPS) / (\Delta Q / Q)$$
$$DTL = DOL \times DFL$$
$$\frac{(EBIT - I_1)(1 - T)}{N_1} = \frac{(EBIT - I_2)(1 - T)}{N_2}$$

14. It measures change in EPS due to change in sales. It also helps in measuring the total risk of the firm.

KEY TERMS

- Break-even point
- Capital gearing
- Contribution
- Earnings before interest and tax
- Leverage
- Financial risk
- Income gearing
- Operating leverage
- Tax Shield
- Indifferent level of EBIT

- Business risk
- Combined leverage
- Coverage ratio
- Earnings per share
- Financial leverage
- Gearing
- Indifference point
- Risk
- Trading on equity
- Business risk

Learning Outcomes

The students would have been exposed to how operating and financial risk affect the organization and how they are handled.

SOLVED EXAMPLES

1. The installed capacity of a machine is 8,000 units per annum. Actual used capacity is 5,000 units per annum. Selling price per unit is ₹10 and variable expenses are ₹5 per unit. Calculate the operating leverage in the following cases.

- When fixed cost is ₹6,000 p.a.
- When fixed cost is ₹8,000 p.a.

Solution:

Particulars	Option I	Option II
Sales 5,000 × 10	50,000	50,000
Less: Variable cost 5,000 × 5	25,000	25,000
Contribution $S - V$	25,000	25,000
Less: Fixed cost	6,000	8,000
EBIT	19,000	17,000
Operating leverage contribution/EBIT	$\dfrac{25,000}{19,000} = 1.13$	$\dfrac{25,000}{19,000} = 1.13$

Due to increase in the proportion of fixed cost in the total cost, the operating leverage of the firm has increased from 1.13 to 1.47.

2. From the following information, calculate the operating leverage.

Particulars	Current Situation	New Situation
No. of units sold	3,000	4,000
Selling price per unit	100	100
Variable cost	60	60
Fixed cost	50,000	50,000

Solution: Calculation of Operating Leverage

Particulars	Current Situation	New Situation
Sales	300,000	400,000
Less variables expenses	180,000	240,000
Contribution	120,000	160,000
Fixed cost	50,000	50,000
EBIT	70,000	110,000
Percentage change in sales	$= \dfrac{400,000 - 300,000}{300,000} = 33\dfrac{1}{3}\%$	
Percentage change in EBIT	$= \dfrac{110,000 - 300,000}{70,000} = 57.14\%$	
Degree of operating leverage	$= \dfrac{\text{Percentage Change in EBIT}}{\text{Percentage Change in Sales}}$ $= 57.14/33.33 = 1.71$	

3. A company has an operating leverage of 1.2 as against 1.25 during the previous year. If the current fixed cost is 20% more than the previous year, then to what extent has the contribution earned by the firm changed over the previous year?

Solution: Previous year's contribution is supposed to be ₹100.

$$\text{Operating Leverage} = \frac{\text{Contribution}}{\text{EBIT}}$$

$$1.25 = \frac{₹100}{\text{EBIT}}$$

$$\text{EBIT} = 100/1.25 = ₹80$$

$$\text{Fixed Cost} = ₹100 - ₹80 = ₹20$$

$$\text{Current year fixed cost} = 20 + 20\% \text{ of } 20$$

$$= ₹24$$

Operating leverage = Contribution/EBIT

= Contribution/Contribution – Fixed cost

2.2 = Contribution/Contribution – 24

1.2 Contribution – 28.8 = Contribution

0.2 Contribution = 28.8

Contribution = 28.8/0.2 = 144

Change in contribution from the previous year is 44%.

4. Following are the details of A Ltd for the year ended March 31, 2015:

Operating leverage = 1.5:1

Financial leverage = 2.5:1

Interest charges per annum = ₹12 lakhs

Tax rate = 40%

Variable cost of sales = 50%

Calculate financial and operating leverage.

Solution:

Financial leverage = EBIT/ EBIT – Interest

2.5 = EBIT/EBIT – 12

2.5EBIT – 30 = EBIT

2.5EBIT – EBIT = 30

1.5EBIT = 30

EBIT = 30/1.5

EBIT = 20 lakhs

Operating leverage = Contribution/EBIT

1.5 = contribution/20

$$\text{Contribution} = 1.5 \times 20 = 30 \text{ lakhs}$$

$$\text{Variable cost of sales} = 50\%$$

$$\text{Let us assume sales} = ₹100$$

$$\text{Variable cost} = ₹50$$

$$\text{Contribution} = ₹50$$

$$\text{Sales} = \frac{100}{50} \times 30 = 60 \text{ lakhs}$$

INCOME STATEMENT

Particulars	Amount in Lakhs (₹)
Sales	60
Variable cost	30
Contribution	30
Less fixed cost	10
EBIT	20
Less interest	12
PBT	8
Less tax	3.2
PAT	4.8

5. A firm's sales, variable cost, and fixed cost amount to ₹7,500,000, ₹4,000,000, and ₹500,000, respectively. It has borrowed ₹5,000,000 at 9% and its equity capital of ₹5,000,000. What is the firm's ROI? Calculate all the three leverages? Industry asset turnover ratio is 2. Does it have high or low asset leverage?

Solution:

$$\text{ROI} = \frac{\text{EBIT}}{\text{Investment}}$$

$$\text{EBIIT} = \text{Sales} - \text{Variable Cost} - \text{Fixed Cost}$$

$$= 75,00,000 - 40,00,000 - 5,00,000 = 30,00,000$$

$$\text{Investment} = 50,00,000 + 50,00,000 = 100,00,000$$

$$\text{ROI} = \frac{30,00,000}{100,00,000} = 0.30 = 30\%$$

$$\text{Operating Leverage} = \frac{\text{Contribution}}{\text{EBIT}} = \frac{75,00,000 - 40,00,000}{30,00,000} = 1.167$$

$$\text{EBT} = \text{EBIT} - \text{Int} = 30,00,000 - 450,000 = 2,550,000$$

$$\text{Financial Leverage} = \frac{\text{EBIT}}{\text{EBT}} = \frac{30,00,000}{25,50,000} = 1.17$$

$$\text{Combined Leverage} = \text{OL} \times \text{FL} = 1.167 \times 1.17 = 1.36$$

$$\text{Industry Asset Turnover Ratio} = \frac{\text{Sales}}{\text{Total Assets}} = 2$$

$$\text{Company Asset Turnover Ratio} = \frac{75,00,000}{100,00,000} = 0.75 \text{ it is lower than industry average.}$$

6. The Well-skilled Company's Balance Sheet is as follows:

Liabilities	Amount	Assets	Amount
Equity capital (₹10=per share)	60,000	Net fixed assets	150,000
10% long-term debt	100,000	Current asset	50,000
Current liabilities	40,000		
Total	200,000		200,000

The company asset turnover ratio is 3. Its fixed operating cost is ₹200,000 and the variable cost ratio is 50%. The tax rate is 40%. Calculate all the three leverages. Determine the likely EBIT if EPS is ₹1.

Solution:

(a) Total asset turnover ratio:=Sales/Total asset=3

$$3 = \frac{\text{Sales}}{200,000}$$
$$3 \times 200,000 = \text{Sales}$$
$$\text{Sales} = ₹600,000$$

INCOME STATEMENT

Sales	600,000
Less variable expenses (50%)	300,000
Contribution	300,000
Less fixed cost	200,000
EBIT	100,000
Less interest	10,000
EBT	90,000
Less tax (40%)	36,000
Earnings	54,000

$$\text{Operating Leverage} = \frac{\text{Contribution}}{\text{EBIT}} = \frac{300,000}{100,000} = 3$$

$$\text{Financial Leverage} = \frac{\text{EBIT}}{\text{Earning before Tax}} = \frac{100,000}{90,000} = 1.1$$

Combined Leverage = OL × FL = 3 × 1.1 = 3.3

Financial leverage=Earnings before tax=90,000

Combined leverage=OL×FL=3×1.1=3.3

$$EPS = \frac{(EBIT - INT)(1-t)}{N}$$

(b)
$$₹1 = \frac{(EBIT - 10,000)(1 - 0.40)}{6,000}$$

$$₹6,000 = 0.60\,EBIT - 6,000$$

$$EBIT = \frac{6,000 + 6,000}{0.60} = 20,000$$

CASE STUDY

The income statement of Convergys Ltd is given below:

	(₹ in lakhs)
Net sales	2,070
Cost of goods sold	1,100
Selling expenses	550
Administrative expenses	65
Interest	75
Taxes	84
Net profit	196

About 25% of the cost of goods sold and 20% of the selling expenses are fixed costs. Administrative expenses are entirely fixed in nature. The paid-up equity share capital of the company consists of 1 lakh equity shares of ₹10 each. Further, the company has employed preference share capital which has a book value of ₹1.5 crore and the dividend rate on the same is 12%. It is expected that there will be no change in its capital structure in the near future.

1. Calculate the DOL.
2. Calculate the DFL.
3. Calculate the DTL.
4. If the company plans to increase its EPS by 25%, then by what percentage should it increase its net sales? It is assumed that the unit selling price, the unit variable cost, the fixed costs, the interest, and the preference dividend will remain constant in the forthcoming year.
5. If the company cannot increase its sales revenues due to competition, then what should the company do to increase its EPS by 25%? Show relevant calculations. It is assumed that the unit selling price, the interest, and the preference dividend will remain constant in the forthcoming year.

Solution

(a) Degree of operating leverage (DOL)

$$= \frac{Q(P-V)}{Q(P-V)-F} = \frac{QP-QV}{QP-QV-F}$$

$$= \frac{Sales - Variable\ cost}{Sales - Variable\ cost - Fixed\ cost}$$

Particulars	(₹ in lakhs)
Variable costs:	
Cost of goods sold (75%)	825
Selling expenses (80%)	440
Total variable cost	1,265
Fixed costs:	
Cost of goods sold (25%)	275
Selling expenses (20%)	110
Administrative expenses	65
Total fixed cost	450

$$\text{Sales} = ₹2,070 \text{ lakhs (given)}$$

$$\therefore \text{DOL} = \frac{2,070 - 1,265}{2,070 - 1,265 - 450} = 2.268$$

(b) Degree of Financial Leverage (DFL) $= \dfrac{\text{EBIT}}{\text{EBIT} - I - \dfrac{Dp}{(1-T)}}$

$$\text{EBIT} = \text{Net profit} + \text{Taxes} + \text{Interest}$$

$$= 196 + 84 + 75 = ₹355 \text{ lakhs}$$

$$\text{Interest} = ₹75 \text{ lakhs (given)}$$

$$\text{Dividend on preference shares adjusted for tax} = \frac{Dp}{(1-T)}$$

$$\text{Tax rate, t} = \frac{\text{Taxes}}{\text{Profit before tax}} = \frac{\text{Taxes}}{\text{Net profit} + \text{Taxes}} = \frac{84}{196 + 84} = 0.30, \text{ i.e. } 30\%$$

$$\text{Preference Dividend } (D_p) = 150 \times 0.12 = ₹18 \text{ lakhs.}$$

$$\therefore \quad \frac{D_p}{(1-T)} = \frac{18}{1 - 0.30} = ₹25.71 \text{ lakhs}$$

$$\therefore \quad \text{DFL} = \frac{355}{355 - 75 - 25.71} = 1.396$$

(c) Degree of total leverage (DTL)

$$= \text{DOL} \times \text{DFL} = 2.268 \times 1.396 = 3.166$$

(d) $\text{DTL} = \dfrac{\text{Percentage change in EPS}}{\text{Percentage change in sales revenue}}$

$$\therefore \quad \text{Percentage change in sales revenue} = \frac{\text{Percentage change in EPS}}{\text{DTL}}$$

Given: Desired Increase in EPS = 25%.

$$\therefore \text{ Required Increase in Net Sales} = \frac{25}{3.166} = 7.9\% \text{ (approximately)}$$

$$\therefore \text{ Net sales should increase by 7.9\% to increase EPS by 25\%}$$

(e) The EPS can be increased if the EBIT can be increased. Given the fact that there is no change in the financing expenses and the capital structure, this can be done either by increasing sales or by decreasing costs (both variable and fixed) or by doing both.

$$\text{DFL} = \frac{\text{Percentage change in EPS}}{\text{Percentage change in EBIT}}$$

$$\therefore \text{ Percentage change in EBIT (required)} = \frac{\text{Desired percentage increase in EPS}}{\text{DFL}}$$

$$= \frac{25}{1.396} = 17.91\% \text{ increase}$$

$\therefore$ So, EBIT should increase by 17.91% to increase EPS by 25%.

As sales cannot be increased due to competition, the company must try to reduce the cost of sales (total of variable and fixed costs).

$$\text{EBIT} = Q(P-V) - F = QP - QV - F.$$

$$= \text{Sales} - (\text{Variable cost} + \text{Fixed cost}) = \text{Sales} - \text{Cost of sales}$$

Since EBIT has to be increased by 17.91%, targeted EBIT.

$$= 1.1791 \text{ (Existing EBIT)} = 1.1791 \times 355 = ₹418.58 \text{ lakhs}$$

$$\therefore \text{ Sales} - \text{Cost of sales} = 418.58$$

or

$$2070 - \text{Cost of sales} = 418.58$$

or

$$\text{Cost of sales} = 2,070 - 418.58 = ₹1,651.42 \text{ lakhs}$$

$$\therefore \text{ Required cost of sales} = ₹1,651.42 \text{ lakhs}$$

$$\text{Existing cost of sales} = ₹1,715 \text{ lakhs}$$

$$\therefore \text{ Cost of sales must be reduced by } \frac{1,715 - 1651.42}{1,715} \times 100$$

$$= 3.71\% \text{ in order to increase EPS by 25\%}$$

(f) The capital structure of Magnus Computer Ltd (MCL) consists of equity shares, debentures, preference shares, and retained earnings. The equity share capital consists of 100,000 equity shares. The amount of debenture capital is ₹50 lakhs and the coupon rate on it is 10%. The preference share capital amounts to ₹50 lakhs and the rate of dividend payable on it is 12%. As per the forecast of operations for the current financial year, the EPS is expected to be ₹7. The DOL on the basis of the forecast for the current financial year is 1.5.

The debentures are to be redeemed on March 31, 2005. MCL has planned to redeem the debentures by selling off one of its old machines which is expected to fetch an amount sufficient to repay the debentures on the due date. It is assumed that there will be no gain or loss on the sale of the machine. As a result of the disposal of the machine, the next financial year's sales and variable expenses are expected to decrease by ₹20 lakhs and ₹14 lakhs, respectively. Moreover, the fixed costs are expected to decrease by ₹2.50 lakhs. It is assumed that selling price per unit and variable costs per unit will remain constant. The tax rate applicable to the company is 35%.

Calculate

1. The DTL for the current financial year.
2. Percentage change in earnings per share that will occur if the sales revenues of the current financial year decrease by 10%.
3. The degree of the total leverage for the next financial year.

Solution

1. **Current Financial Year**

$$EPS = ₹7.00$$

$$\text{No. of equity shares} = 100,000$$

$$\text{Earnings available for equity shareholders} = 7.00 \times 100,000 = ₹700,000$$

$$PAT = \text{Earnings available for equity shareholders} + \text{Preference dividend}$$

$$= 700,000 + (5,000,000 \times 0.12)$$

$$= ₹1,300,000$$

$$PBT = PAT/(1-t)$$

$$= 1,300,000/(1-0.35)$$

$$= ₹2,000,000$$

$$EBIT = PAT + \text{Interest}$$

$$= ₹2,000,000 + (₹5,000,000 \times 0.10)$$

$$= ₹2,500,000$$

Computation of DFL for the Current Year

$$DFL = EBIT/[(EBIT - I - \text{Preference Dividend}/(1-t)].$$

$$= \frac{25,00,000}{25,00,000 - 5,00,000 - \dfrac{6,00,000}{(1-0.35)}} = 2.32$$

$$\therefore DTL = DOL \times DFL = 1.50 \times 2.32 = 3.48$$

2. Percentage change in EPS that will occur if sales revenues of the current financial year decrease by 10%

$$= DTL \times \text{Percentage change in sales revenues}$$

$$= 3.48 \times -10\%$$

$$= -34.8\%$$

∴ EPS will decrease by 35% (approximately) if the sales and revenues decrease by 10%.

Finding the Value of Contribution for the Current Financial Year

$$DOL = [Q \, (S-V)] \div [Q \, (S-V) - F]$$

$$= \text{Contribution} \div \text{EBIT}$$

Or,

$$\text{Contribution} = DOL \times EBIT$$

$$= 1.5 \times ₹2,500,000$$

(EBIT $= ₹2,500,000$ as shown in [a] above)

Or,

$$\text{Contribution} = ₹3,750,000$$

Finding the Fixed Cost (F) for the Current Year

$$EBIT = Q \, (S-V) - F$$

$$= \text{Contribution} - F$$

$$F = \text{Contribution} - EBIT$$

$$= 3,750,000 - 2,500,000$$

$$= ₹1,250,000$$

Computing the DOL for the Next Financial Year

Contribution for the next year

$= $ Contribution for the current year $-$ Decrease in contribution in the next year

$= 3,750,000 - ($ Decrease in sales $-$ Decrease in variable cost $)$

$= 3,750,000 - (2,000,000 - 1,400,000)$

$= ₹3,150,000$

EBIT for the Next Year

Contribution for the next year $-$ Fixed costs for the next year

$= 3,150,000 - ($ Fixed cost for the current year $-$ Decrease in fixed cost for the next year $)$

$= 3,150,000 - (1,250,000 - 250,000)$

$= ₹2,150,000$

$$DOL \text{ for the next year} = \frac{\text{Contribution for the next year}}{\text{EBIT for the next year}}$$

$$= \frac{31,50,000}{21,50,000} = 1.465 \text{ (approximately)}$$

Computation of DFL for the Next Year

$$DFL = EBIT/[EBIT - I - \text{Preference dividend}/(1-t)]$$

$$= \frac{21,50,000}{21,50,000 - 0 - \dfrac{6,00,000}{(1-0.35)}} = 1.752 \text{ (approximately)}$$

$\therefore$ DTL for the next year $= DOL \times DFL = 1.465 \times 1.752 = 2.57$ (approximately).

Source: Author (compiled from various sources).

ASSESS YOURSELF

Concept Review and Critical Thinking Questions

1. What do you mean by leverage? How the concept of leverage is relevant in financial analysis?

2. What do you mean by operating leverage? How do we measure operating leverage? What is the DOL?

3. What do you mean by operating break-even point? Given that firms rarely operate at their operating break-even points, do you think there is any practical utility of the concept? Discuss.

4. What do you mean by financial leverage? How financial leverage leads to financial risk? Discuss.

5. What do you understand by EBIT–EPS Analysis? Explain with the help of an illustration.

6. If financial leverage magnifies the EPS, why firms do not use more debt in the capital structure? Discuss.

7. What is total leverage? Is there any optimal combination of operating and financial leverage?

STUDENT ACTIVITY

Student should take relevant data from Sun Pharma and Lupin Ltd balance sheet. Calculate operating and financial risk for last 3 years.

SUGGESTED READINGS

Brealey, R.A., & Myers, S.C. (2002). *Principles of corporate finance* (7th ed.). New York: McGraw-Hill.

Horne, J.C.V. (2002). *Financial management & policy* (12th ed.). Singapore: Pearson Education.

Ross, S.A., Westerfield, R.W., & Jordan, B.D. (2002). *Fundamentals of corporate finance* (6th ed.). New Delhi: Tata McGraw-Hill.

CHAPTER 9

Cost of Capital

- To learn concept of cost of capital.
- To determine the cost of debt, equity, and preference share.
- To understand weighted average and weighted marginal cost of capital.

PRELUDE

The cost of capital has become a very crucial issue. On the one hand, it is cost of long-term resources to the company, and on the other hand it is the rate of return to investors. So, there is always a tug of war. Read the following also—Indian banks will have to tap global markets to face the challenge of rising capital requirements, besides managing liquidity effectively to meet the long-term funding requirements.

When a firm accepts an investment proposal, it also needs funds for financing. These funds are supplied by different types of investors, that is, equity shareholders, preference shareholders, debenture holders, depositors, and so on. These investors will provide the funds to the firm in expectation of receiving a minimum return from the firm. The minimum return expected by the investors depends on the risk perception of the investor as well as on the risk-return characteristics of the firm. This rate of return is the return required by investors of capital/debt to the firm. From the point of view of the company, it is the cost of procuring this capital/debt. In other words, the cost of capital is the minimum required rate of return a project must earn to cover the cost of financing the project. If the firm wants an easy access to capital/debt, it must provide the required rate of return to its capital suppliers. If the firm fails to satisfy its capital/debt suppliers, it may not find any capital supplier in future on normal rate.

Significance of Cost of Capital

The concept of cost of capital is very much significant in the financial theory because of its relationship with the most fundamental goal of financial management of wealth maximization. **The value of the firm is inversely related to the cost of all the inputs, including capital, being used by the firm.** Given this relationship, if we want to maximize the value of the firm we must "optimize or reduce" the cost of capital of the firm. This means that when we use various sources of funds to finance the investment decisions of the firm, the aim should be to use these various sources in such a proportion that the overall cost of capital is minimized. The objective of cost minimization is in support of the objective of wealth maximization.

Utility of Cost of Capital

The cost of capital can be used for the following:

Investment Evaluation

The cost of the capital is also used to evaluate the investment projects. Thus, when the firm is selecting investment projects, it needs to do so in such a manner that the return earned on these projects is greater than or equal to the rate of return required by capital/debt suppliers, that is, greater than the cost of capital. Or the cost of capital is used as a discount rate to find out the PV of future cash flows and judge the desirability of the project. The project that provides positive NPV when its cash flows are discounted by the cost of capital makes a contribution to the wealth of shareholders. The cost of capital represents a standard for allocating a firm's fund, supplied by various investors, to different investment projects in the foremost efficient manner.

Designing Debt Policy

Debt policy of the firm very much depends on cost. Debt helps the firm in reducing the overall cost of capital as interest on debt is tax deductible. Employment of debt in capital structure would increase the financial risk but cost will definitely be reduced. The cost of capital would help in designing the capital structure of the firm. Thus, the cost of capital is important while taking investment as well as financing decisions.

Types of Cost of Capital

Explicit Cost and Implicit Cost

The explicit cost of capital of a particular source may be defined in terms of the interest or dividend that the firm has to pay to the suppliers of funds. For example, the firm has to pay interest on debentures, dividend at fixed rate on preference share capital and also some expected dividend on equity shares. These payments refer to the **explicit cost** of capital, that is, the rate of interest or dividend is clearly known to the investors.

However, when the profits earned by the firm are not distributed to the equity shareholders but are reinvested within the firm, there is an implicit cost involved. Had these profits been distributed to the equity shareholders, they could have invested these funds elsewhere and would have earned some return. The investors forego this return when the profits are ploughed back. Therefore, these funds have an implicit cost and this implicit cost is nothing but the opportunity cost of investors. **The implicit cost of retained earning is the**

return which could have been earned by the investor, had the profit been distributed to them. This is also called opportunity cost of capital. Opportunity cost of capital is the rate of return forgone on the next best alternative investment opportunity of comparable risk. Except the retained earnings, all other sources of funds have explicit cost of capital.

Specific Cost and Overall Cost

A company obtains capital/debt from various sources. The cost of capital of each source differs because of the difference in the risk-return profile of these sources. The cost of capital of each source of capital is known as **specific cost of capital**. And when we take combined costs of all the components, it is called **overall cost of capital**. The components are assigned certain weights and then the weighted average cost of capital is determined. The advantage of using the overall cost of capital is its simplicity. Once it is computed, projects can be evaluated using a single rate that does not change unless underlying business and financial market conditions change.

FIGURE 9.1
THE COST OF CAPITAL

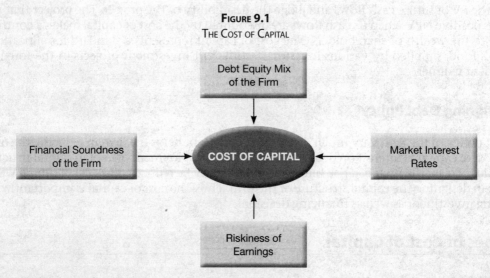

Source: Author.

Test Yourself

1. Define cost of capital.
2. Explain the significance of cost of capital.
3. Define explicit cost.
4. What is the opportunity cost of capital?

Costs of Different Sources of Finance

Cost of Debt

The main sources of Funds are equity capital and debt. Debts are funds borrowed from financial institutions or public, either in the form of public deposit or debentures for a specific period of time at a certain rate of interest. Debt may be in the form of secured/unsecured loans, debentures, bonds, and so on. Debt carries a fixed rate of interest and the payment of interest is mandatory irrespective of the profit earned or loss by the firm. By taking debt, the firm increases the total capital employed in the business and if it is able to generate a high rate of return on capital employed, the return to shareholders increases as debt carries a fixed rate of interest and the additional return earned belongs to the shareholders. However, the usage of debt is like using a double-edged sword because if the firm is not able to generate adequate returns on capital employed, the return to shareholders would decline as interest is to be paid compulsorily. Another point about using debt in the capital structure is that the interest payable on debt is tax deductible. As a result, the reported profits decline when interest is paid and consequently the tax liability of the firm also reduces. In other words, usage of debt provides a tax shield to the company. There are various types of debts. We shall examine their costs as follows.

Cost of Perpetual Debt

The cost of perpetual debt can be calculated using the following formula:

Without Tax Rate

$$K_d = \frac{I}{D}$$

With Tax Rate

$$k_d = \frac{I(1-r)}{D}$$

where k_d is the post-tax cost of debt, I is the annual interest payment, T is the company's effective corporate tax rate, D is the net proceeds of issue of debentures, bonds, terms loans, etc.

Cost of Redeemable Debt

The cost of redeemable debt is defined as **the discount rate which equates the net proceeds from the debt to the expected cash outflows in the form of interest and principal repayments,** that is

$$P = \sum_{t-1}^{n} \frac{I(1-t)}{(1+k_d)} + \frac{F}{(1+k_d)^n}$$

where k_d is the post-tax cost of debt, I is the annual interest payment, t is the corporate tax rate, F is the redemption value of debt, P is the net amount realized, and n is the maturity period.

The interest payment (I) is multiplied by the factor (1−t) because as discussed above, interest on debt is a tax-deductible expense. However, it should be noted that the tax-shield is available only when the firm is profitable. A firm incurring losses is not required to pay any taxes and hence its actual cost of debt is the before-tax cost, not the post-tax cost.

An approximation formula as given below can also be used.

$$k_d = \frac{I(1-t) + \dfrac{F-P}{n}}{\dfrac{F+P}{2}}$$

Let us understand through an example, how the cost of debt can be calculated.

Illustration 1. Mohan limited issues 1,500 debenture (10%) of ₹100 each at 5% premium redeemable at par after five years. The company tax rate is 50%. Determine the cost of debt before and after tax.

Cost of debt (before tax

$$k_d = \frac{I + \dfrac{F-P}{n}}{\dfrac{F+P}{2}}$$

$$= \frac{15,000 + \dfrac{1,50,000 - 1,57,500}{5}}{\dfrac{1,50,000 + 1,57,500}{2}} = 8.78\%$$

Cost of debt after Tax = $K_d(1-\text{tax}) = 8.78\% \times (1-0.5) = 4.39\%$.

Illustration 2. Simco Ltd has recently made an issue of non-convertible debentures for ₹5 crore. The terms of the issue are as follows: Each debenture has a face value of ₹100 and carries a rate of interest of 10%. The interest is payable annually and the debenture is redeemable at a premium of 5% after 5 years.

If Simco Ltd realizes ₹97 per debenture and the corporate tax rate is 40%, what is the cost of the debenture to the company?

Solution
Given I = ₹10, t = 0.4, P = ₹97, and n = 5 years,
F = ₹105, the cost per debenture (k_d) will be

$$k_d = \frac{10(1-0.4) + \dfrac{105-97}{5}}{\dfrac{105+97}{2}} = 7.52\%$$

Cost of Term Loans

The cost of the term loans will be simply equal to the interest rate multiplied by (1−tax rate). While calculating the cost of term loans, we have to use the interest cost of new term loans and not the existing term loans. The interest is multiplied by (1−tax rate) as interest on term loans is also tax deductible.

Symbolically,

$$k_t = I(1-t)$$

where k_t is the cost of term loan, I is the interest rate, and t is the tax rate.

Illustration 3. A company decides to issue 7 year 16% debentures of ₹100 each at a premium of ₹10. Calculate the cost of debt.

$$D = \text{Net proceed} = ₹100 + 10 = ₹110$$
$$\text{Interest} = 16\% \text{ of } ₹00 = ₹16$$
$$k_d = \left(\frac{16}{110}\right) \times 100 = 14.54\%$$

Test Yourself

1. What is the cost of debt and how is it calculated?
2. Why is the cost of debt adjusted for taxes?

Cost of Preference Share Capital

Preference shares are less risky as compared to equity shares as they get preferences over equity shares at the time of payment of dividend and payment of capital in case of liquidation of the company. However, preference shares are more risky as compared to debt because dividend payment even on preference shares is not mandatory, whereas interest is a mandatory payment. As a result of this risk profile, the rate of return required on preference shares is less than that on equity shares but more than that on debt. Thus, the cost of preference capital is more than the cost of debt but less than the cost of equity capital.

Cost of irredeemable preference share is

$$k_d = \frac{PD}{NP}$$

where PD is the preference share dividend

NP = Net Proceed

The cost of a redeemable preference share (k_p) is defined as the discount rate which equates the proceeds from preference capital issue to the dividend payment and principal payments.

Symbolically,

$$P = \sum_{t=1}^{n} \frac{D}{(1+k_p)^t} + \frac{F}{(1+k_p)^n}$$

where k_p is the cost of preference capital, D is the preference dividend per share payable annually, F is the redemption price, P is the net amount realized per share, and n is the maturity period.

As in the case of debt, an approximation formula as given below can also be used

$$k_p = \frac{D + \dfrac{F - P}{n}}{\dfrac{F + P}{2}}$$

Illustration 4. Life Color Ltd, a photographic film manufacturing company, has recently issued preference share with a face value of ₹100 and a dividend rate of 12% payable annually. The share is redeemable after 10 years at par. If the net amount realized per share is ₹96, what is the cost of the preference capital?

Solution:

Given that D=12, F=100, P=96, and n=10

$$k_p = \frac{12 + \dfrac{100 - 96}{10}}{\dfrac{100 + 96}{2}} = 0.1265 \text{ or } 12.65\%$$

Illustration 5. A company issues 10% irredeemable preference shares. The face value of share is ₹100 and issued at ₹97. What is the cost of preference share?

Solution:

Net Proceed = ₹97

Dividend = 10% of ₹100 = ₹10

Cost of preference share

$$k_p = \left(\frac{10}{97}\right) \times 100 = 10.31\%$$

Illustration 6. A company wishes to issue 2,000, 9% preference shares of ₹100 each. The expenses of the capital issues are underwriting commission 2.50%, brokerage 0.50%, and printing ₹2,000. Calculate the cost of preference share if a share is issued at 5% discount.

Solution:

Cost of preference share capital if shares are issued at discount.

Net proceed = Face value − Discount-issue expenses = 100 − 5 − (2.50 + 0.50 + 1.00) = ₹91

Preference share dividend = 9% of ₹100 = ₹9

$$k_d = \frac{PD}{NP},$$

$$k_p = \left(\frac{9}{91}\right) \times 100 = 9.89\%$$

Note: It should be known that irredeemable preference shares cannot be issued now in India. Only preference shares which are redeemable up to a maximum time period of 20 years can be issued.

Test Yourself

1. What is the cost of preference share and how is it calculated?
2. What is redeemable preference share and how is it calculated?

Cost of Equity Share Capital

The cost of equity capital is the most difficult to measure because of the nature of equity share capital. We know that the dividend payment on equity capital is not compulsory and the capital is practically irredeemable. Hence, in the case of equity share capital, the cost has to be viewed in the opportunity cost framework. The investor has supplied funds to the firm in the expectation of some suitable return. The investment was made, presumably on a logical basis, because the type of risk embodied in the firm reasonably matched with the investor's risk preference and because the expectations about earnings, dividends, and market appreciation were satisfactory. But at the same time, the investor has foregone other investment opportunities when he selected this investment. So, we need to measure the opportunity cost of equity capital, that is, the benefit foregone by the investor when he chose to invest in a particular firm. The question is how do we do that? There are various approaches for determining the cost of equity. Let us discuss these approaches one by one.

Dividend Discount Model Approach

Dividend discount model is designed to compute the intrinsic value of an equity share. According to the dividend discount approach, the intrinsic value of an equity stock is equal to the sum of the PVs of the expected dividends associated with it, that is,

$$k_e = \frac{D_1}{P_e} + g$$

where P_e is the price per equity share, D_t is the expected dividend per share at the end of year one, and k_e is the rate of return required by the equity shareholders.

If we know the current market price (P_e) and forecasted the future stream of dividends, we can determine the rate of return required by the equity shareholders (k_e) using the above equation, which is nothing but the cost of equity capital. In practice, the model suggested by the above equation cannot be used in the given form because it is not possible to forecast the dividend stream accurately over the life of the firm. Therefore, the growth in dividends can be categorized as nil or constant growth or super normal growth, and the above equation can be modified accordingly.

Illustration 7. The market price per share of Hodder Headline Ltd is ₹525. The dividend expected per share a year hence is ₹50 and the DPS is expected to grow at a constant rate of 10% per annum. What is the cost of the equity capital to the company?

Solution:
The cost of equity capital (k_e) is calculated as follows:

$$k_e = \frac{D_1}{P_e} + g = \frac{50}{525} = 19.5\%$$

Realized Yield Approach

According to this approach, the returns earned on a security in the past are taken as a proxy for the return required in the future by the investors. This approach rests on the following assumptions:

1. Actual returns have been as per the expected returns.
2. Investors' expectations from the security will not change in future.

The above given assumptions generally do not hold good in real life. Hence, in practice, we can use this approach to arrive at a starting point for the estimation of the required return.

The realized return over an n-year period is calculated as

$$r = (W_1 \times W_2 \times \ldots W_n)^{1/n} - 1$$

where W_t is referred to as the wealth ratio.

$$W_t = \frac{D_t + P_t}{P_{t-1}} \text{ and } t = 1, 2, \ldots n$$

= Dividend per share for year t payable at the end of year

P_t = Price per share at the end of year t

Illustration 8.

Year	1	2	3
DPS (₹)	2.00	2.50	3.50
Price per share at the end of the year	12.00	12.50	16.50

Solution:

If the price per share at the beginning of the year 1 is ₹10, the wealth ratios can be calculated as follows:

Year	1	2	3
Wealth ratio	1.40	1.50	2.00

Realized yield = (1.40 × 1.50 × 2.00)1/3 – 1 = 0. 6134 or 61.34%

Capital Asset Pricing Model

Capital Asset Pricing Model (CAPM) method provides an alternative approach to calculate the cost of equity capital. According to this approach, the rate of return required on a security is given by the following equation:

$$k_i = R_f + \beta_i (R_m - R_f)$$

where k_i is the rate of return required on security I, R_f is the risk-free rate of return, β_i is the beta of security I, and R_m is the rate of return on market portfolio.

As per CAPM assumptions, any individual security's expected return and beta statistics should lie on the SML. The SML intersects the vertical axis at the risk-free rate of return R_f and $R_m - R_f$ is the slope of the SML. Security market line is the line that we get when we plot the relationship between the required rate of return (R_i) and non-diversifiable risk (beta). This line describes the relationship between systematic risk and expected return in financial markets.

Bond Yield Plus Risk Premium Approach

The logic behind this approach is that the return required by the investors is directly based on the risk profile of the security. The risk borne by the equity investors is higher than that borne by the bondholders or preference shareholders, Therefore, the rate of return required by them should also be higher. Hence, the required rate of return on equity capital can be calculated as

Required rate of return = Yield on the long-term bonds of the company + Risk premium.

This risk premium is arrived at after considering the various operating and financial risks faced by the firm.

Earnings Price Ratio Approach

According to this approach, the cost of equity can be calculated as the ratio of expected earnings (E1) to the current market price (P). If we can estimate the growth rate at which earnings are expected to grow, the expected earnings per share can be easily determined. This ratio assumes that the EPS will remain constant from the next year onwards.

$$k_e = \frac{E_1}{P_0}$$

That this approach may provide some meaningful result, we need to analyze the dividend pay-out ratio and the rate of return the firm is capable of earning on the retained earnings. This ratio provides meaningful results in the following two cases:

1. The dividend payout ratio is 100%.
2. The dividend payout ratio is less than 100% and retained earnings are expected to earn a rate of return equal to the cost of equity.

In practice, the abovementioned cases may also be difficult to come across, hence this approach need to be used cautiously.

Illustration 9. The market price of ₹10 equity share of X Ltd is ₹18 per share. The average rate of dividend paid during last 6 year is 30%. The growth rate is 5%. Calculate the cost of equity.

Solution:

$$\text{Market price of share} = ₹18$$
$$\text{Dividend} = 30\% \text{ of } ₹10 = ₹3$$

Cost of equity share is

$$k_e = \frac{D_1}{P_e} + g$$

$$k_e = \frac{3}{18} \times 100 + 5\% = 21.67\%$$

Cost of Retained Earnings and Cost of External Equity

The payment of dividend depends on the discretion of the directors of the firm. They are expected to keep the wealth maximization objective in mind while exercising their discretion. If they think that they do not have any profitable projects in hand where the available earnings can be invested, then it is better to distribute more dividends to the shareholders. But if they have some profitable investments in the near future, which are expected to generate a rate of return, which the shareholders cannot earn in the market, it would be in the interest of the shareholders to retain the earnings.

There is a common misconception, that these earnings, which are retained by the firm, are cost-free as no new claims arise when earnings are retained. However, this is not correct because these funds ultimately belong to the shareholders and they have given their consent for retention of earnings and have forgone some current dividends in the expectation of higher returns. Hence, the retained earnings are not cost-free. The cost of retained earnings is the return, which shareholders could have earned elsewhere in the market by investing the dividends. However, the cost of retained earnings is always less than the cost of new issue of common stock due to the absence of floating costs when retained earnings are used instead of raising fresh capital.

There are certain flotation costs involved in the process of raising equity from the market. The cost of external equity is the rate of return that the company must earn on the net funds raised, to satisfy the equity holders' demand for return. **Under the dividend capitalization model, the following formula can be used for calculating the cost of external equity:**

$$k'_e = \frac{D_1}{P_0(1-f)} + g$$

where k'_e is the cost of external equity, D_1 is the dividend expected at the end of year 1, P_0 is the current market price per share, g is the constant growth rate applicable to dividends, and f is the floatation costs as a percentage of the current market price.

Illustration 10. Jaideep Realtors Ltd is coming up with a township project costing around ₹2 crore in the outskirts of Hyderabad. It is planning to finance the project by ₹100 lakhs of retained earnings and ₹100 lakh of external equity through a fresh issue. The equity investors expect a rate of return of 18%. The cost of issuing external equity is 5%. What is the cost of equity capital for Jaideep Realtors?

Solution:
The cost of retained earnings and the cost of external equity can be determined as follows:
Cost of retained earnings: $k_r = k_e$, that is, 18% cost of external equity raised by the company

Now $k'_e = \frac{k_e}{(1-f)} = \frac{0.18}{1-0.05} = 18.95\%$

Test Yourself

1. What is external equity? How is its cost calculated?
2. What is realized yield approach of cost of equity?
3. What is a flotation cost?

Weighted Average Cost of Capital

Weighted average cost of capital (WACC) is defined as the weighted average of the cost of various sources of finance, weights being the market values of each source of finance outstanding. According to CIMA, London, the WACC "is the average cost of company's finance (equity, debentures, bank loans) weighted according to the proportion each elements bears to the total pool of capital, weighting is usually based on market valuation current yields and costs after tax."

Overall cost of capital is of utmost importance as this rate is to be considered while deciding the optimal financing mix for the firm and is to be used as the discount rate or the cut-off rate while evaluating the capital budgeting proposals. This overall cost of capital should take care of the relative proportion of different sources of financing used by the firm. Therefore, this overall cost of capital should be calculated as the weighted average rather than simple average of different specific cost of capital.

Thus, WACC is important in both financing as well as investment decisions.

Assuming that there are only two sources of finance used by the firm, the WACC can be calculated as follows:

WACC = Cost of Equity × Proportion of Equity in the Financing Mix + Cost of debt

× Proportion of Debt in the Financing Mix.

$$WACC = k_e \times w_e + k_d \times w_d$$

$$= k_e \times \left(\frac{E}{D+E} \right) + k_d(1-t) \times \left(\frac{D}{D+E} \right)$$

Which Weights Are of Use?

As we can see above, in the calculation of WACC, we need to use the proportion of each source of finance used. The question is which weights we should use? Should we use the values as given in the balance sheet, which reflects the historical values of the amounts of funds raised from various sources, or should we use the market values of the various claims? Should we take the total funds into consideration while calculating WACC for a new project or use the proportion of new funds raised?

In other words, the weights used for calculating WACC can be

1. Historical or existing weights

   a. Book value
   b. Market value

2. Marginal weights

Historical or Existing Weights

Historical or existing weights are the weights based on the actual or existing proportions of different sources of finance in the overall financing mix. Such weighing system is based on the actual proportions at the time when the WACC is being calculated. In other words, the weights are the proportions in which the funds have already been raised by the firm.

The use of historical weights is based on the following assumptions:

1. That the firm would raise the additional resources required for financing the investment proposals, in the same proportions in which they have been used in the existing financing mix.

2. The present financing mix is optimal, and therefore, the firm wants to continue with the same pattern in future also.

However, these assumptions may not always be correct. The firm may not be able to raise additional finance in the same proportion as existing one because of prevailing economic and capital market conditions, legal constraints, or other factors. Furthermore, the existing financing mix may not be the optimal one and the firm has a target financing mix that is optimal.

Book Value Weights

The weights are said to be book value weights if the proportions of different sources of finance are determined on the basis of the accounting values. The book value weights can be easily calculated by taking the relevant information from the balance sheet of the firm.

Book value weights are easy to determine as they are based on the accounting information. They appear to be logical also as the firm may design its future financing mix as per the existing one. But the concept of book value weights is not consistent with the objective of the firm, which is to maximize the market value of the firm. As book value weights are based on accounting values, they simply ignore the market values.

To illustrate the calculation of the WACC using book value weights, let us consider the following illustration.

Illustration 11. Priti Sewing Company Ltd has the following financing mix:

(₹ in lakh)

Equity capital (10 lakh shares at par value)	100
12% preference capital (10,000 shares at par value)	10
Retained earnings	120
14% non-convertible debentures (70,000 debentures at par value)	70
14% term loan from RFC (Rajasthan Finance Corporation)	100
Total	400

The equity shares of the company are trading at ₹25. The next expected dividend per share (DPS) is ₹2.00 and the DPS is expected to grow at a constant rate of 8%. The preference shares are redeemable after 7 years at par and are currently quoted at ₹75 per share on the stock exchange. The debentures are redeemable after 6 years at par and their current market price is ₹90 per share. The tax rate applicable to the firm is 50%. What is the WACC of the company?

Solution:

First, let us determine the costs of the various sources of finance.

Cost of Equity

$$k_e = \frac{D_1}{P_0} + g = \frac{2.00}{25} + 0.08 = 0.16$$

Cost of Retained Earnings

$$k_r = k_e = 0.16$$

Cost of Preference Capital

$$k_p = \frac{D + \dfrac{F-P}{n}}{\dfrac{F+P}{2}}$$

$$= \frac{12 + \dfrac{100-75}{7}}{\dfrac{10+75}{2}} = 0.1780$$

Cost of Debentures

$$k_p = \frac{I(1+t) + \dfrac{F-P}{n}}{\dfrac{F+P}{2}}$$

$$= \frac{14(1-0.5) + \dfrac{100-90}{6}}{\dfrac{100+90}{6}} = 0.0912$$

Cost of Term Loans

$$k_t = 0.14(1-0.5) = 0.07.$$

Next step would be to determine the weights associated with the various sources of finance.

Source	Book Value Weight
Equity capital	$W_e = \dfrac{100}{400} = 0.25$
Retained earnings	$W_r = \dfrac{120}{140} = 0.30$
Preference capital	$W_p = \dfrac{10}{400} = 0.025$
Debentures	$W_d = \dfrac{70}{400} = 0.175$
Term loans	$W_i = \dfrac{100}{400} = 0.25$

Now that we know the costs of specific sources of capital and the book value weights, we can determine the WACC based on book value weights as follows:

$$WACC = W_e k_e + W_r k_r + W_p k_p + W_d k_d + W_i k_i$$
$$= (0.25 \times 0.16) + (0.30 \times 0.16) + (0.025 \times 0.1780) + (0.175 \times 0.0912) + (0.25 \times 0.07)$$
$$= 0.1259 \text{ or } 12.59\%$$

Market Value Weights

The weights may also be calculated on the basis of the market values of different sources, that is, the proportion of each source at its market value. To calculate the market value weights, the current market price of the securities need to be determined. This may not always be possible. Still market value weights are better than historical value weights for a number of reasons:

- Consistent with the concept of wealth maximization, i.e. maximizing the market value of the firm.
- Provide current estimate of the investor's required rate of return.
- Yield good estimate of the cost of capital that would be incurred, should the firm require additional funds from the market.

However, the market values weights suffer from some limitations, as follows:

- The market values of all types of securities issued have to be obtained which may not always be possible,
- The market values are subject to change from time to time and so the concept of optimal financing mix in terms of market values no longer remains relevant,
- External factors, which affect the market values, will affect the cost of capital also and therefore, the investment decision process will be influenced by the external factors.

The weights to be assigned to different sources of finance are clearly going to be different if one chooses to apply current market value weights as against the book values as stated in the balance sheet. One must be guided by the purpose of the analysis in deciding which value is relevant. For example, if the purpose is to derive criterion against which to judge the expected return from future investment, we should use the current market values of different sources. The investors, certainly, do not invest in the book values of the equity shares, which may differ significantly from the market values. The book values are static and not responsive to changing performance.

With respect to the choice between the book value and market value weights, the following points are to be noted.

- It is argued that the book value is more reliable than market value because it is less volatile. Although it is true that book value does not change as often as market value, this is more a reflection of the weakness than of strength, as the true value of the firm changes over time as both the firm-specific and the market-related information is revealed.
- The WACC based on the market value will generally be greater than the WACC based on book values. The reason being that the equity capital having higher specific cost of capital usually has market value above the book value.

Illustration 12. Using the information given in the above illustration of Priti Sewing Company, let us use the market value weights to determine the WACC.

Solution:

The balance sheet of the company using the market values would appear as follows:

Equity capital (10 lakh shares at market value)	250
12% preference capital (10,000 shares at market value)	7.5
Retained earnings	120
14% non-convertible debentures (70,000 debentures at market value)	63
14% term loan from RFC	100
Total	540.50

The market value weights can be determined as follows:

Source	Market Value Weight
Equity capital	$W_e = \dfrac{240}{540.5} = 0.462$
Retained earnings	$W_r = \dfrac{120}{540.5} = 0.222$
Preference capital	$W_p = \dfrac{7.5}{540.5} = 0.014$
Debentures	$W_d = \dfrac{63}{540.5} = 0.117$
Term loans	$W_i = \dfrac{100}{540.5} = 0.185$

WACC based on market value weights $= W_e k_e + W_r k_r + W_p k_p + W_d k_d + W_i k_i = 0.462 \times 0.16 + (0.222 \times 0.16) + (0.014 \times 0.1780) + (0.117 \times 0.0912) + (0.185 \times 0.07) = 0.1355$ or 13.55%.

Marginal Weights

Does the WACC remain constant irrespective of the extent of financing? In other words, once the WACC has been determined using book value or market value weights, does it remain the same forever? It does not. Normally, the WACC increases with the level of financing required. The suppliers of capital generally require a higher return if they supply more capital.

If WACC is going to change when more funds are raised for financing a new project, what is the sanctity in using it for determining the worth of that project?

To overcome this problem, it is suggested that instead of using the historical or existing weights, we should use marginal weights. The marginal weights refer to the proportions in which the firm wants or intends to raise funds from different sources. In other words, the proportions in which "additional funds" are to be raised to finance the investment proposals are known as marginal weights. Using marginal weights to calculate the weighted average cost-effectively means calculating the actual WACC of the incremental funds. The weighted average cost using the marginal weights is also referred to as the Weighted Marginal Cost of Capital (WMCC).

Theoretically, the concept of WMCC seems to be good enough as the return from investment will be compared with the actual cost of funds. Moreover, if a particular source which has been used in the past but is not being used now to raise additional funds, or cannot be used now for one or the other reason, then why should it be allowed to enter the decision-making process even through the weighing system?

However, there are some shortcomings of the WMCC. A particular project may be financed by equity or debt depending on their relative costs and the access to that source at a particular point of time. However, in the long run, the firm would like to move toward its target financing mix. If it chooses to finance the current projects with only equity, in future it would be forced to use more of debt to maintain the target financing mix. Hence, it is always better to use the "target financing mix" weights and not the actual financing mix weights.

Illustration 13. D.E. Shaw Ltd is planning to raise equity, preference, and debt capital in the following proportions:

Equity: 0.50
Preference: 0.20
Debt: 0.30

The cost of the three sources of finance for different levels of usage has been estimated as below:

Source of Finance	Range of New Financing from the Source (₹ in lakh)	Cost %
Equity	0–15	16.00
	15–25	17.00
	≥25	18.00
Preference	0–3	14.00
	≥3	15.00
Debt	0–20	8.00
	≥20	10.00

Solution:
To calculate WMCC, first of all we need to determine the "cut-off point" when the cost of capital is going to change as new finance is being raised. This is so because the suppliers of capital, as indicated above, would require higher rates of return when they supply more capital. Once these cut-off points have been determined, we can determine how much funds can be raised from that source at the new or marginal cost of capital. In other words, we can determine the range of total new financing at a given cost before the cost changes again. Using this information, we can calculate the weighted marginal cost of capital for different ranges of total new financing or the weighted marginal cost of capital schedule.

Calculation of Cut-off Points

Source of Finance	Cost %	Range of New Financing (₹ in lakh)	Cut-Off Point (₹ in lakh)	Range of Total New Financing (₹ in lakh)
Equity	16.00	0–15	15/0.5=30	0–30
	17.00	15–25	25/0.5=50	30–50
	18.00	≥25	–	≥50
Preference	14.00	0–3	3/0.2=15	0–15
	15.00	≥3	–	≥15
Debt	8.00	0–20	20/0.3=66.67	0–66.67
	10.00	≥20	–	≥66.67

WACC for Different Ranges of Total New Financing

Range of Total New Financing (₹ in lakh)	Source of Finance	Proportion	Cost (%)	Weighted Cost (%)
0–15	Equity	0.5	16	8.00
	Preference	0.2	14	2.80
	Debt	0.3	8	2.40
	WACC			**13.20**
15–30	Equity	0.5	16	8.00
	Preference	0.2	15	3.00
	Debt	0.3	8	2.40
	WACC			**13.40**
30–50	Equity	0.5	17	8.50
	Preference	0.2	15	3.00
	Debt	0.3	8	2.40
	WACC			**13.90**
50–66.67	Equity	0.5	18	9.00
	Preference	0.2	15	3.00
	Debt	0.3	8	2.40
	WACC			**14.40**
≥66.67	Equity	0.5	18	9.00
	Preference	0.2	15	3.00
	Debt	0.3	10	3.00
	WACC			**15.00**

Weighted Marginal Cost of Capital Schedule

Range of Total New Financing (₹ in lakhs)	Weighted Marginal Cost of Capital (%)
0–15	13.2
15–30	13.4
30–50	13.9
50–66.67	14.4
≥66.67	15.0

Test Yourself

1. What is WACC?
2. What is marginal cost of capital?
3. How is it different from WACC?

Project and Divisional Costs of Capital

A firm can be looked on as a portfolio of projects and divisions. Given the "assets" this portfolio (i.e., the firm) will have a particular risk-return profile. When a new asset is to be added to this portfolio, we need to consider the risk-return profile of the new investment. If the asset (i.e., the project) has the same risk profile as the portfolio (i.e., the firm), we can use the WACC to evaluate the asset. For example, if a restaurant is thinking of coming up with a new outlet at another location, WACC is the appropriate rate to use to evaluate the proposal. But what if the project's risk profile is different? Can a firm use its WACC for evaluating a project, which has a different risk profile than that of the firm?

In fact, use of WACC in such cases may lead to incorrect decisions. Let us understand how?

Consider an all-equity firm with a beta (β) of 1. The risk-free rate of return is 5% and the market risk premium is 7%. Given this information, the required rate of return or the cost of equity capital as per the SML approach will be

$$k_e = R_f + \beta (R_m - R_f) = 5 + 1 \times 7 = 12\%.$$

Suppose this firm uses WACC to evaluate all investments. This means that all the investment proposals with an expected return of greater than 12% will be accepted and others would be rejected.

The SML can be plotted as shown in the following figure:

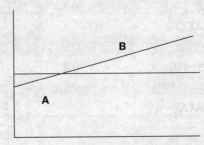

Let us first consider project A, which has a beta of 0.7 as compared with the firm's beta of 1. It has an expected return of 11%. Shall we select the project? The answer is yes, as its required rate of return is only 9.9%

$$\text{Required rate of return is } 5+0.7\times7=9.9\ \%.$$

However, if we use WACC as the selection criterion, this project would be rejected. Thus, using WACC may result into rejection of profitable projects, which are less risky than the overall firm.

Consider Project B. It has a beta of 1.2 and an expected return of 13%. If we use WACC as the selection criterion, project B would be accepted as its expected return is greater than the WACC. But the required rate of return of project B as per SML is

Required Rate of Return $= 5+1.2\times7=13.4\%$ which is greater than the expected return. It may be so that using WACC may lead to selection of unprofitable projects which are more risky than the firm.

Thus, if a firm uses WACC to evaluate all the projects, over a period of time the portfolio (i.e., the firm) would accumulate unprofitable and risky assets (i.e., projects) and the portfolio itself would become more risky.

Similar problem may arise if the firm has multiple divisions. Some divisions may be more risky than others. The firm's overall cost of capital would be the mix of the divisional costs of capital.

If these divisions are competing for the limited resources of the firm and the firm uses WACC as the criterion, the riskier divisions would emerge as winners. This is so because given the high risk, the expected rate of return would tend to be higher. But this higher expected return may not be equal to or greater than the required rate of return commensurate with high risk. Less risky divisions even though may be promising would be ignored.

How should the firm determine the cost of capital in such cases? There are two approaches. The firm can estimate the relevant project cost of capital by finding out the cost of capital of the firms, which are already in the line of business in which the firm wants to enter. For example, if Reliance Industries wants to enter into fast food business, it can refer to the cost of capital of firms like Mc Donald's. However, this approach has its own problems. First, it is possible that there are no existing benchmarks available and the firm is pioneering the project idea. Even if there are benchmarks available, the cost of capital applicable to big and established firms in the industry will be different from that of the new entrants. In such cases, the reference cost of capital can at the most be used as the starting point for estimating the actual cost of capital.

Another approach can be to subjectively assign some risk premiums to different types of projects like replacement, expansion, diversification, and so on. As diversifying into a new line of business will be riskier as compared with expansion, the risk premium would be higher and consequently the cost of capital to be used for evaluating the project would be higher. The problem with this approach is that it is very subjective.

Reducing the Cost of Capital

1. **Attract International Shareholders:** International shareholders would regard Indian companies as less risky because the turbulence in their domestic economies is not going to affect the Indian companies significantly. Hence, they would require a lower rate of return than they would expect from their domestic companies. So Indian companies can attract international shareholders to reduce their cost of capital.

2. **Achieve Transparency in Information Disclosure:** The more transparent the firm is in information disclosure, the less the uncertainty about its performance and less the perceived risk.

3. **Ensure Liquidity of Securities:** The more widespread the holding, the greater is the liquidity, and hence less the risk. Lesser risk would translate into lower cost of capital.

Test Yourself

1. How does the cost of capital help in appraising of projects? Explain.

SUMMARY

1. Cost of capital is the minimum required rate of return, which a firm must earn to compensate the supplier of capital for time and risk. It is the price of procuring capital.

2. Cost of capital is a decision-making tool and helps the firm in evaluating various financial decisions like debt–equity mix and appraising projects.

3. Equity share capital has no explicit cost. In case of equity, payment of dividend is not compulsory. It has opportunity cost. It is the price which company must pay to its shareholders. It is the minimum return required by equity shareholders on securities of comparable risk.

4. According to the Dividend Discount Model, the intrinsic value of an equity share is equal to the sum of the PVs of expected dividends associated with it

$$k_e = \frac{D_1}{P_e} + g$$

5. CAPM method provides an alternative approach to calculate cost of equity capital. According to this approach, the rate of return required on a security is given by the following equation

$$k_i = R_f + \beta_i (R_m - R_f)$$

6. *Realized Yield Approach:* According to this approach, the returns earned on a security in the past are taken as a proxy for the return required in the future by the investors. The realized return over an n-year period is calculated as $r = (W_1 \times W_2 \times \ldots W_n)^{1/n} - 1$, where W_t is referred to as the wealth ratio

$$W_t = \frac{D_t + P_t}{P_{t-1}(1-f)} \text{ and } t = 1, 2 \ldots n$$

7. Debt is an interest bearing instrument. Interest is the return which lender expects from the amount lent to the borrower. Interest is the cost of debt for borrower.
   Without tax rate:

$$k_d = \frac{I}{D}$$

With tax rate:

$$k_d = \frac{I(1-r)}{D}$$

9. **Cost of Preference Share Capital:** Preference shares are less risky as compared with equity shares as they get preferences over equity shares at the time of payment of dividend and payment of capital in case of liquidation of the company. Thus, the cost of preference capital is more than the cost of debt but less than the cost of equity capital.

10. Cost of irredeemable preference share is

$$k_p = \frac{PD}{\text{Net proceed}}$$

11. The cost of a redeemable preference share (k_p) is defined as the discount rate which equates the proceeds from preference capital issue to the dividend payment and principal payments.

Symbolically

$$P = \sum_{t=1}^{n} \frac{D}{(1+k_p)^t} + \frac{F}{(1+k_p)^n}$$

or

$$k_p = \frac{D + \dfrac{F-P}{n}}{\dfrac{F+P}{2}}$$

12. The WACC is the average cost of company's finance (equity, debentures, and bank loans) weighted according to the proportion each element bears to the total pool of capital; weighting is usually based on market value/book value and costs after tax.

13. WACC is calculated by multiplying each component's cost of capital to respective weights.

$$WACC = k_e \times w_e + k_d \times w_d$$

$$= k_e \times \left(\frac{E}{D+E}\right) + k_d(1-t) \times \left(\frac{D}{D+E}\right)$$

14. The proportions in which "additional funds" are to be raised to finance the investment proposals are known as marginal weights. Using marginal weights to calculate the weighted average cost-effectively means calculating the actual WACC of the incremental funds. The weighted average cost using the marginal weights is also referred to as the Weighted Marginal Cost of Capital (WMCC).

KEY TERMS

- Cost of capital
- Cost of debt
- Cost of preferred share

- Irredeemable debenture
- Super normal growth
- Irredeemable debenture

- Cost of retained earnings
- Cost of equity
- Weighted average cost of capital
- Tax shield
- Opportunity cost

- Flotation cost
- Realized yield
- Beta
- Earnings per share
- Weighted marginal cost of capital

Learning Outcomes

Students would have fairly understood different aspects of the cost of capital.

SOLVED EXAMPLES

1. The shares of Isabella Ltd are selling at ₹240 per share. The firm has paid dividend @ ₹24 per share. The estimated growth of the company is approximately 5% per year. Determine the cost of equity capital of the company.

   Solution:
   According to the dividend capitalization model,

   $$k_e = D_1/P_0 + g$$
   $$D_0 = ₹24$$
   $$D_1 = D_0(1+g) = 24 \times 1.05 = 25.2$$
   $$P_0 = ₹240$$
   $$k_e = 240 = 0.105 + 0.05 = 0.155 = 15.5\%$$

2. Celeron Ltd has a beta of 0.80. If the current risk-free rate is 6.5% and the expected return on the stock market as a whole is 16%, using SML approach determine the cost of equity capital for the firm.

   Solution:
   According to SML approach, the cost of equity capital of the company is given by the following formula:

   $$R_i = R_f + \beta_i (R_m - R_f)$$

   In the above question, $R_f = 6.5\%$, $R_m = 16\%$, $\beta_i = 0.80$.
   Substituting the given values, we get

   $$R_i = 6.5 + 0.80 (16 - 6.5)$$
   $$= 6.5 + 7.6 = 14.1\%$$

3. Phoenix Shoes (PS) is considering as expansion project. PS has no long-term debt. The current risk-free rate of return is 7% and the current market risk premium is 8.3%. If CB's beta is 20% greater than the overall market, what is the firm's cost of capital?

Solution:

$$R_i = R_f + \beta_i (R_m - R_f)$$

In the above question, $R_f = 7\%$, $R_m - R_f = 8.3\%$, $\beta_i = 1.20$.
Substituting the given values, we get

$$R_i = 7 + 1.20 (8.3)$$

$$= 16.96\%$$

4. The following information is given about the debentures issued by M/s Xetra Ltd

Face value	= ₹100
Rate of interest	= 10% p.a.
Amount realized per debenture	= ₹96
Corporate tax rate	= 40%

Debenture is redeemable at a premium of 2% after 6 years. The difference between the redemption price and the net amount realized can be written off over the life of the debenture and the amount so written off is tax-deductible. What is the cost of debt?

Solution:

Cost of debt capital when the difference between the redemption price and the net amount realized can be written off over the life of the debenture and the amount so written off is tax-deductible, is given by the following formula:

$$k_d = \frac{I(1-t) + \dfrac{F-P}{n}}{\dfrac{F+P}{2}}$$

Substituting the given values, we get

$$\frac{10(1-0.40) + \dfrac{102-96}{6}}{\dfrac{102+96}{2}} = 7.07\%$$

5. The following information is given about M/s Su Kumar Ltd

(₹)	Year 1	Year 2	Year 3
DPS (Dividend per share)	2.50	3.00	3.00
Price per share at the beginning of the year	13	15	16.00

If the price per share at the beginning of the fourth year is ₹14, what is the realized yield over the period of 3 years?

Solution:

The realized yield over a period of three years can be computed as $(W_1 \times W_2 \times W_3)1/3 - 1$, where W_1, W_2, and W_3 are the wealth ratios in the years 1, 2, and 3, respectively.

Wealth ratio in the year t can be computed as $\dfrac{D_t + P_t}{P_{t-1}}$, where D_t is the dividend paid in the year t, P_t is the price at the end of year t and P_{t-1} is the price at the beginning of the year t

$$\text{Hence, wealth ratio for year } 1 = \frac{2.5 + 15}{13} = 1.346$$

$$\text{Wealth ratio for year } 2 = \frac{3.0 + 16}{15} = 1.267$$

$$\text{Wealth ratio for year } 3 = \frac{3.0 + 14}{16} = 1.0625$$

Hence, realized yield over a period of three years

$$= (1.346 \times 1.267 \times 1.0625)1/3 - 1 = 0.2191 \text{ or } 21.91\%$$

6. The following details are available regarding the long-term sources of finance of M/s. Asthetic Garments Ltd

Source of Finance	Range of New Financing from the Source (₹ crore)	Cost %
Equity	0–10	14
	10–20	15
	≥20	16
Preference	0–2	13
	≥2	14
	0–12	8
Debt	12–18	9
	≥18	10

The company is considering to expand its operations and requires ₹50 crore for the same. It is planning to raise in the following proportions:

Equity shares	0.4
Debt	0.4
Preference shares	0.2

Determine the weighted marginal cost of capital of new financing in the range of ₹25 crore–30 crore for Aesthetics Ltd.

Solution:
Calculation of cut-off points

Source of Finance	Cost (%)	Range of New Financing (₹ in crore)	Breaking Point (₹ in crore)	Range of Total New Financing (₹ in crore)
Equity	14	0-10	10/0.4=25	0-25
	15	10-20	20/0.4=50	25-50
	16	≥20	–	≥50
Preference	13	0-2	2/0.2=10	0-10
	14	≥2	–	≥10
	8	0-12	12/0.4=30	0-30
Debt	9	12-18	18/0.4=45	30-45
	10	≥18	–	≥45

If the new financing is in the range of ₹25–30 crore

$$\text{Cost of equity} = 15\%$$
$$\text{Cost of preference} = 14\%$$
$$\text{Cost of debt} = 8\%$$

Weighted marginal cost of capital in the above range

$$= 0.15 \times 0.4 + 0.14 \times 0.2 + 0.08 \times 0.4 = 12\%$$

7. The Vishnu Electrical Company has the following capital structure:

Equity shares (200,000)	₹4,000,000
10% preference shares	₹1,000,000
14% debentures	₹3,000,000

The current market price of the share is ₹20. The expected dividend next year is ₹2 per share, which will grow at 7% forever. If the company raises an additional ₹200,000 debt by issuing 15% debentures, the expected dividend increases to ₹3 and the price of share falls to ₹15. The growth rate remains the same. What is the WACC for the firm (assuming a tax rate of 50%)?

Solution:

The capital structure of Vishnu Electrical after the issue of 15% debentures will be

	Source	Amount (in ₹)
	Ordinary shares	4,000,000
10%	Preference shares	1,000,000
14%	Debentures	3,000,000
15%	Debentures	2,000,000

Cost of equity prior to this change can be calculated as follows:

$$k_e = \frac{D_1}{P_0} + g = \frac{2}{20} + 0.07 = 17\%.$$

Cost of equity after the change in capital structure

$$k_e = \frac{3}{15} + 0.07 = 27\%,$$
$$WACC = w_e k_e + w_p k_p + w_d k_d (1 - T)$$

Substituting the given values, we get

$$WACC = 0.40 \times 0.27 + 0.10 \times 0.10 + 0.30 \times 0.07 + 0.20 \times 0.075 = 0.154 = 15.40\%.$$

8. The X Ltd is considering a debt issue on the following terms:

Face Value	₹100 per debenture
Term of maturity	7 years

Yearly Coupon rate

Years	1-2	9%
Years	3-4	10%
Years	5-7	11%

The current market rate on similar debenture is 12% per annum. The company proposes to price the issue so as to yield a return of 10% per annum. Determine the issue price. Redemption is done at premium of 5% on face value.

Solution:
Present value of debenture of cash flow at 10%

Years	Cash Flow	PVIF at 10%	Total PV
1	₹9	0.909	8.181
2	9	0.826	7.434
3	10	0.751	7.51
4	10	0.683	6.83
5	11	0.621	6.83
6	11	0.564	6.20
7	11	0.513	5.64
7	105	0.513	53.86
		Total	**102.484**

9. A company has its following book values and specific cost of capital. Calculate WACC as book value as weight.

Type of Capital	Book Value	Cost
Debt	₹400,000	5
Preference capital	₹100,000	8
Equity	₹600,000	15
Retained earnings	₹200, 000	13

Solution:
Calculation of WACC

Type of Capital	Book Value	Cost	Total Cost
Debt	₹400,000	5	20,000
Preference capital	₹100,000	8	8,000
Equity	₹600,000	15	90,000
Retained earnings	₹200,000	12	24,000
Total	**₹1,300,000**		**142,000**

$$\text{WACC} = \left(\frac{142,000}{1,00,0000}\right) \times 100 = 10.92\% = d1,000,000$$

10. An investor has invested in a company which is growing at an above-average rate. The company is expected to provide annual increase in dividend of 20% for the next 15 years. Thereafter, growth rate of dividend is expected to be 6%. The capitalization rate is 10%. Current dividend per share is ₹1 per equity share. Determine the value of the share.

Solution:

D_0	1.00	Growth Rate in Dividend	20%
Years	Dividend	PVIF (10%)	Total PV
1	1.20	0.909	1.091
2	1.44	0.826	1.190
3	1.73	0.751	1.298
4	2.07	0.683	1.416
5	2.49	0.621	1.545
6	2.99	0.564	1.686
7	3.58	0.513	1.839
8	4.30	0.467	2.006

D_0	1.00	Growth Rate in Dividend	20%
Years	Dividend	PVIF (10%)	Total PV
9	5.16	0.424	2.188
10	6.19	0.386	2.387
11	7.43	0.350	2.604
12	8.92	.0.319	2.841
13	10.70	0.290	3.099
14	12.84	0.263	3.381
15	15.41	0.239	3.688
		Total	32.260

Value of share at the 15th year $= \#\#\# = ₹816.73$

PV of share at $t=0 = 816.73 \times 0.239 = ₹195.19$

Value of equity share $= 195.19 + 32.260$

11. A company is considering raising an additional loan of ₹100 lakhs either by 13 conventional term loan or 12% non-convertible debenture. The term loan attracts no incidental cost. The debenture would have been issued at a discount of 2% and involve ₹2 lakhs cost of issue. Tax rate applicable is 40%.

Solution:

Cost of term loan $= k_t = I(1-t) = 12\% \times (1-0.40) = 7.20\%$

Amount mobilized through debenture

$= ₹100 - 2 - (100 * 2/100) = ₹96$ lakhs

Amount of interest $= 13\% \times 100$ lakhs $= ₹13$ lakhs

Cost of debt $= \#\#\# = 0.08125 = 8.125\%$

Cost of loan is economical and should be considered.

12. Explain the cost of debt when debentures are sold at premium of 10% and flotation costs are 5% of the issue price. Face value of debenture is ₹100. Coupon rate is 10%. Maturity period is 10 years and tax rate is 40%.

Solution:

$$k_d = \frac{I(1-t) + \frac{(F-P)}{n}(1-t)}{\frac{(F+P)}{2}}$$

$$k_d = \#\#\#\# = 5.42\%$$

CASELET

Your company is planning an expansion and needs to develop an estimate of the firm's **cost of capital**. You have gathered the following data: Tax rate is 40%, the price of the company's 12% coupon, semiannual payment, non-callable ₹1,000 face value bonds with 15 years to maturity is ₹1,153.72. The company does not use short-term debt on a permanent basis. New bonds would be privately placed with no flotation cost. The price of Company's 10%, ₹100 par value, quarterly dividend preferred stock is ₹111.10. The Company's common stock is selling for ₹50 per share. Its last dividend was ₹4.19, and dividends are expected to grow at a constant 5% rate. If Company issues new common stock, it will incur a 15% flotation cost. The Company's target capital structure is 30% long-term debt, 10% preferred stock, and 60% cent equity.

   Determine

1. The cost of debt.
2. The cost of retained earnings.
3. The cost of new equity.
4. The WACC using retained earnings.

Solution:

Equity

Dividend	4.19
Growth rate	0.05
Expected dividend	=4.19+.05 * 4.19=₹4.40
Floatation charges	15%

$$\text{Cost of equity } k_e = \frac{D_1}{P_0} + g.$$
$$= 4.40 / 50 + 0.05 = 0.138 = 13.8\%$$

Cost of Preference Share	
Price	₹100
Dividend rate	10%
Market price	₹111.10
Dividend amount	₹10

Cost of preference share

$$K_p = \frac{PD}{Not} = 10/111.10 = 0.090009\%$$

Cost of debt

Coupon rate	12%
Face value	₹1,000
Years to maturity	15
Value of bond	₹1,153.72
Payment	Semi-annually
Interest payment	60
No. of payments	30
Half-yearly interest rate	6%
K_d has to be lesser than 6% only then the value of bond comes out to be greater than ₹1000	
We try 5% first	
K_d	60* PVIFA(k, n) + ₹1000 * PVIF(k, n)
	1,153.38
Roughly it comes out to be closer to the value given	
Cost of debt half-yearly	5%
Cost of debt annually	10%
Cost of debt after tax	6%

$$WACC = k_e \times w_e + k_d \times w_d.$$

$$= k_e \times \left(\frac{E}{D+E} \right) + k_d (1-t) \times \left(\frac{D}{D+E} \right)$$

Calculation of Weighted Average Capital Structure

Particulars	Weight	Cost	Weight * Cost
Debt	0.3	6%	1.8%
Preferred stock	0.1	9.00%	0.90%
Equity	0.6	13.80%	8.28%
Weight average cost of capital			10.98%
WACC			11.0%

ASSESS YOURSELF

Concept Review and Critical Thinking Questions

1. What is the relationship between the required rate of return and the cost of capital? Discuss.
2. What do you mean when we say that the cost of equity capital is 15%? What are the various approaches for determining the cost of equity capital?
3. Are retained earnings cost-free, If not then calculate the cost of retained earnings.
4. What is WACC? Why is it important? Which weights are the most appropriate to use for determining WACC?
5. Why is it not appropriate to use the firm's WACC when evaluating a project or division which differs from the firm in its risk profile? How can we determine the relevant cost of capital in such cases?

STUDENT ACTIVITY

Student should collect empirical data of few select companies in FMCG and find out the relationship between interest rate, ROI, and cost of capital since 2012.

SUGGESTED READINGS

Brealey, R.A., & Myers, S.C. (2002). *Principles of corporate finance* (7th ed.). New York: McGraw-Hill.

Horne, J.C.V. (2002). *Financial management & policy* (12th ed.). Singapore: Pearson Education.

Price Water House Coopers. (1999). *Cost of capital: Survey of issues and trends in India.* Retrieved from www.pwcylobal.com (accessed on June 9, 2016).

Ross, S.A., Westerfield, R.W., & Jordan, B.D. (2002). *Fundamentals of corporate finance* (6th ed.). New Delhi: Tata McGraw-Hill.

Capital Budgeting Decision

- To learn the nature of capital budgeting decisions.
- To understand discounted and non-discounted evaluation criteria of the project appraisal.
- To understand the NPV and IRR.

PRELUDE

Capital budgeting decision is a long-term strategic investment decision which provides the basic structure and foundation to an organization. Capital budgeting means planning and execution of financial aspect of acquiring long-term preferably tangible assets—plant, machinery, etc. It includes various dimensions like application of time value of money, risk pattern, net present value (NPV), internal rate of return (IRR), discount rate, capitalization rate, and so on. Before we start going through the chapter, read the following empirical evidence: In the year 2007, Ford sold both Jaguar and land Rover to Tata Motors at the price of $2.3 billion. Ford will continue to supply power trains, stamping, and unnamed vehicle components to Tata for "differing periods," as well as Research and Development (R&D), environmental, and platform technologies, and even accounting services, among others. In the meantime, Tata launched "Nano." Year 2008 brought Tata into international limelight with troubled launch of "Nano" and leveraged buyout of Jaguar and Land Rover from Ford. Tata invested nearly US$400 million in "Nano" and US$2.3 billion in Jaguar and Land Rover acquisition. March 2009 the company bled money, losing a record US$517 million on US$14.7 billion in revenues, just on its India operations. Jaguar and Land Rover lost an additional US$510 million in the 10 months, and Tata owned it until March 2009. The above examples are of strategic investment decisions and it is observed that a huge amount has been invested in such decisions and with strong bearing on growth and profitability of firms (www.moneycontrol.com).

This chapter introduces the concept and practice of capital budgeting which is a part of investment decisions. Investment decisions are long-term strategic decisions to create value for stakeholders.

A finance manager has to make various strategic investment decisions for enhancing shareholder's value in terms of growth and profitability. Investment decision deals with efficient allocation of the capital and deployment of a firm's funds to the long-term assets. Strategic investment decision relates to long-term horizon and is known as capital budgeting decision. Capital budgeting decision may be defined as the firm's decision to invest in long-term assets in anticipation of expected cash flow benefits over a period of time. Investment decisions are long-term strategic decisions in nature. This is so because a finance manager needs to "plan" or "budget" the long-term sources of funds while making such decisions. Investment decisions like acquisition, replacement, expansion, and modernization of assets fall under this category. When a pharmaceutical firm decides to invest in R&D, a car manufacturer considers investment in a new plant, an airliner plans to buy a fleet of jet aircraft, a commercial bank plans an ambitious computerization program, or a firm plans to launch a new product line, and so on, they are all capital budgeting decisions.

Capital investment decisions have following features:

- Substantial capital expenditure
- Deployment of funds in long-term assets
- Irreversible projects
- Long-term consequences
- Benefits over for a period of time
- Growth and profitability of the company mainly depends on the type and quality of capital expenditure decision

Test Yourself

1. What is investment decision? Explain.
2. What are the features of investment decision?

Types of Investment Decisions

1. **Replacement Projects:** These are the routine investment decisions. The assets owned by a firm become less efficient due to wear and tear resulting from usage and sometimes even become obsolete with the passage of time or change in technology. Hence, the firm has to replace such assets in order to reduce costs (of labor, raw material, and power), increase return, and improve the quality of end products. Replacement decisions aim at introducing efficient and economical assets and are known as cost reduction investments. Replacement decisions also involve substantial modernization and technology improvements.
2. **Expansion Projects:** These investments are meant to increase the capacity and widen the distribution network. As this can be risky and complex, expansion projects normally warrant more careful analysis than replacement projects.
3. **Diversification Projects:** These investments are aimed at producing new products or services or entering into new markets. Often diversification projects entail substantial risks, large outlays, and require considerable managerial efforts and attention. Given their strategic importance, such projects call for thorough evaluation, both quantitative and qualitative. Diversification can be of two types: related and unrelated. Tata Motor's launch of

Nano is an example of related diversification. Ranbaxy has started Religare share broking firm, which is an unrelated diversification.

4. **R&D Projects:** R&D projects are characterized by uncertainties and involve sequential decision-making. Such projects are evaluated on the basis of new R&D. Expiring intellectual property rights (IPRs) and generic competition have forced pharmaceutical firms to spend huge amounts on R&D. Consumer durable industry, aviation industry, and telecommunication industry need to spend on technology upgradation to win the market.

5. **Mandatory Investments:** These are expenditures required to comply with statutory requirements, for example, pollution control equipments, medical dispensary, firefighting equipment, and so on. These are often non-revenue producing investments. In analyzing such investments, the focus is mainly on finding the most cost-effective way of fulfilling a given statutory need.

All the investment decisions can be further categorized as mutually exclusive investments and independent investments. Mutually exclusive investments are those projects which are meant for the same purpose and compete for same resources. Independent projects are meant for different purposes and do not compete for the same reasons.

Capital Budgeting Process

The capital budgeting process involves a number of steps depending on the size of the firm, nature of projects, and so on. The various stages involved in the capital budgeting process can be outlined as follows:

1. Identification of investment proposals
2. Preliminary screening
3. Evaluation
4. Establishing priorities
5. Final approval
6. Implementation
7. Review

Identification of Investment Proposals

The first step in the capital budgeting process is the identification of investment proposals. Some investment projects are mandatory in nature, whereas others are replacement decisions. In such cases, the identification is not difficult because the investment has to be made out of compulsion. If the law requires an effluent treatment plant to be installed, there is no way out but to install it; similarly, if a machine has worn out or become obsolete, it has to be replaced. But investment decisions like R&D, expansion, and diversification involve discretion, hence the need to identify profitable and strategically coherent investment projects that get well with the existing risk profile of the firm. In such cases, the management has to keep a vigil on the developments taking place in the market and keep scouting for ideas. The project ideas may come from different sources like industrial magazines, journals, industrial trade fairs, exhibitions, or from the competitors. For example, if a new product has been launched by a foreign manufacturer in some foreign market and is being displayed in some industrial exhibition, the production manager may seek information about the product and its expected acceptance in the domestic markets, and take a decision accordingly.

An analysis of the following parameters can help in generating potentially viable project ideas:

1. Demand and supply conditions in the industry
2. Product profiles of various industries
3. Import-export potential
4. Commercial viability of emerging technologies
5. Social and economic trends
6. Consumption patterns
7. Possibility of backward/forward integration

Preliminary Screening

Once the investment proposals have been identified, the next step is a preliminary screening. This is important because it is quite possible that some projects may appear to be very attractive but still may not be desirable because of so many reasons like their integration with the firm's existing portfolio of projects may be difficult. At the same time if a less risky but profitable project is rejected, it would mean loss of an opportunity. So, every care has to be exercised before accepting or rejecting a project.

Preliminary screening helps to assess the technical feasibility of the project, availability of resources, and judge the adequacy of expected returns to compensate for the risk involved.

Evaluation

All the proposals, which pass through the preliminary screening process, are then analyzed in more detail. A detailed market analysis, technical analysis, and financial analysis is then undertaken to judge the profitability of the project. Projects are classified according to their nature, for example, expansion projects, diversification projects, and so on, and ranked within each classification in terms of profitability, risk, and degree of urgency. There are many methods which may be used for financial analysis such as payback period method, rate of return method, NPV method, and so on.

Establishing Priorities

Once the projects have been selected, the next step would be prioritizing these projects. This is required because it may not be possible for the firm to invest immediately in all the acceptable proposals. Thus, it is essential to rank the various proposals and to establish priorities on the basis of urgency and expected returns.

Final Approval

Proposals finally recommended by the committee are sent to the top management along with a detailed report, both of capital expenditures and of sources of capital for final approval. The top management then calls a meeting where these proposals are examined and the financial manager is asked to present several alternative capital expenditure budgets for the recommended proposals. The top management then finally selects some of the important proposals.

Once capital expenditure proposals have been finally selected, funds are allocated for them. Projects are then sent to the committee for incorporating them in the capital budget.

Implementation

Once a capital expenditure budget has been prepared and a proposal has been included in the budget, the next step is to request the authority to go ahead with the project. Before such an authorization, the capital expenditure committee may like to review the profitability of the project in the changed circumstances. If it is satisfied, it gives a green signal and work on the project can be started without any delay. The project manager usually assigns responsibilities for completing the project within the given time frame and cost limit so as to avoid unnecessary delays and cost over runs. Network techniques, such as PERT and CPM can also be applied to monitor the implementation of the projects.

Review

Last but not the least is the review of the project, after it has been fully implemented. The objective of this review is to evaluate the performance of the project. It is the duty of the top management or executive committee to ensure that funds are being spent in accordance with the allocation made in the capital budget. A control over such capital expenditure is very much essential and for that purpose a monthly report showing the amount allocated, amount spent, and approved but not spent should be prepared and submitted to the controller. The evaluation involves comparison of actual expenditure on project with the budgeted ones, and the comparison of the actual return from the investment with the anticipated return. The unfavorable variances, if any, should be looked into and the causes of the same be identified so that corrective action may be taken in future.

Test Yourself

1. How is replacement project different from diversification project?
2. Why is capital budgeting process important?

Financial Appraisal Criteria

Any investment will be justified if it is able to generate sufficient future economic returns. In other words, the cash inflows, which are expected from the project, to justify the initial cash outflow. While evaluating the capital projects, the adopted methods should take into account this basic trade-off of current cash outflows against the future cash inflows, that is, the financial manager must consider the following components:

1. Net initial investment
2. Operating cash inflows
3. Economic life of the project

The essential criterion is that the project undertaken must enhance the shareholder's wealth. An objective investment analysis must relate these three components and then provide an indication about investment worthiness of the project. The criteria should also help in ranking the project on the basis of their profitability. It is also helpful in selecting among mutually exclusive project.

There are different techniques available for evaluation and selection of a proposal.

These techniques can be grouped into two categories (Figure 10.1).

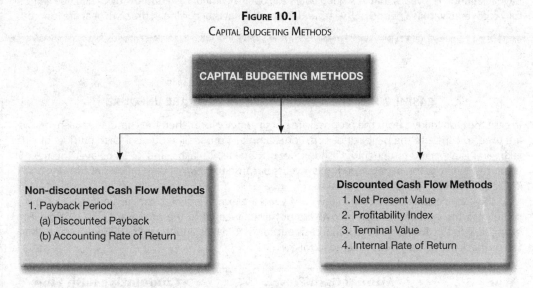

FIGURE 10.1
CAPITAL BUDGETING METHODS

Source: Kothari and Dutta (2005). *Contemporary Financial Management.* McMillian.

Non-discounted Cash Flow Methods

These methods do not take into account the time value of money concept as such value of money would remain the same over a period of time, which is not true while evaluating the projects.

The two most commonly used methods under this category are

1. The payback period method, and
2. The accounting rate of return (ARR).

These are essentially rules of thumb that intuitively grapple with the trade-off between net initial investments and operating cash inflows.

Payback Period

The payback period finds out **in how much time the initial investment will be "paid back" by the project**. In other words, it measures the length of time required to recover the initial outlay of the project.

Methods: The payback period can be calculated in two different situations as follows:

CASE I: WHEN CASH INFLOWS ARE IN THE FORM OF ANNUITY

When the cash inflows are in the form of an annuity, the payback period can be computed by dividing the cash outflow by the amount of annuity. For example, if a proposal requires a net investment of ₹10 lakhs and is expected to generate cash inflows of ₹2 lakhs p.a. for 6 years. In this case, the payback period is 5 years, that is, ₹1,000,000/₹200,000. The initial cash outflow of ₹1,000,000 will be fully recovered within a period of 5 years and the cash inflows occurring in the sixth year are ignored.

CASE II: WHEN THE ANNUAL CASH INFLOWS ARE UNEQUAL

In case the cash inflows from the proposal are not in annuity form, then the cumulative cash inflows are used to compute the payback period. For example, a proposal requires a cash outflow of ₹10 lakhs and is expected to generate cash inflows of ₹2 lakhs, ₹3 lakhs, and ₹4 lakhs over the next 5 years, respectively. The payback period is 4 years because the sum of cash inflows of first 4 years is ₹10 lakhs (i.e., ₹2+₹3+₹3+₹2=₹10 lakhs)

In the above example, the cash inflows of 4 years are exactly equal to the cash outflow. However, sometimes the cumulative cash inflows are not exactly equal to the proposal's cash outflow. For example, if in the above case the initial cash outflow is ₹9 lakhs and the inflows are the same, then the payback period may be calculated as follows:

Year	Annual Cash Flow (₹ in lakhs)	Cumulative Cash Flow (₹ in lakhs)
1	2	2
2	3	5
3	3	8
4	2	10
5	4	14

Now, the required cumulative cash outflow is ₹9 lakhs. At the end of third year, the cumulative cash inflow is ₹8 lakhs. For the fourth year, the annual cash inflow is ₹2 lakhs. Therefore, cash inflow of ₹1 lakh only during the fourth year will be sufficient to make the total cumulative cash inflows to be ₹9 lakhs. The precise period required to earn cash inflow of ₹1 lakh during fourth year can be calculated by linear interpolation assuming that the cash inflows occur evenly throughout the year. The payback period is 3 years + (1/2)=3.5 years or 3 years and 6 months.

Acceptance Rule

Payback period is used as an investment evaluation criterion. A project the payback period of which is less than the standard payback period would be chosen. As per the ranking method, the project with a shorter payback period is given the highest ranking and the lowest ranking is allotted to the project with the highest payback period. The shorter the payback period, the better it is because the firms using the payback period as a decision criterion for accepting or rejecting projects usually specify an appropriate cut-off period depending on the risk profile of the firm. Projects with payback periods less than or equal to the cut-off period will be accepted and others will be rejected.

Merits

Though the payback period method does not take into account the time value of money concept and is a crude method of evaluation, its merits are:

1. It is simple to understand and calculate.
2. It facilitates the selection of less risky projects. The project with a shorter payback period will be less risky as compared to a project with a longer payback period, as the cash inflows which arise further in the future will be less certain and hence more risky.
3. The payback period requires less effort in comparison with other sophisticated techniques.

Demerits

The payback period criterion suffers from the following serious shortcomings:

1. It ignores the time value of money, which is fundamentally valid for actual assessment of gain or loss.
2. It does not consider the cash inflows occurring after the payback period. As a result, the application of the payback criterion leads to discrimination against projects that generate substantial cash inflows in later years.
3. A firm may face difficulty in establishing the maximum acceptable payback period. Moreover, payback fails to consider the pattern, magnitude, and timings of cash inflows.
4. The cut-off period is chosen arbitrarily and applied uniformly for evaluating projects regardless of their life spans. Consequently, the firm may accept too many short-lived projects and too few long-lived ones.
5. The payback period also ignores the salvage value and the economic life of the project. A project, which has substantial salvage value, may be ignored (though it may be more profitable) in favor of a project with higher cash inflows in earlier years. It is also insensitive to the economic life and thus not truly a meaningful criterion for determining the economic viability of a proposal. The speed with which the initial investment is recovered is not sufficient to appraise the profitability.
6. The payback period is more a method of capital recovery than a method of evaluating profitability. Capital recovery though essential is not the objective of investment.
7. The payback method can be used to evaluate conventional projects, which involve substantial initial cash outflow followed by cash inflows in later years. However, it cannot be used to evaluate projects which have other cash flow patterns like zero cash outflow, a mix of cash outflow and inflow in later years, and so on.

Consider the cash flows from the following two projects A and B.

Year	Project A (₹ in lakhs)	Project B (₹ in lakhs)
0	–10	–10
1	5	2
2	3	2
3	2	2
4	2	4
5	–	6
6	–	8

The payback period of project A is 3 years, whereas that of B is 4 years. So the payback period will recommend the selection of project A over project B even though project B generates substantial cash inflows in years 5 and 6.

Discounted Payback Period

To overcome the limitation of not using time value of money concept, an improved version of the payback period method is sometimes used, which is known as the "discounted payback period." While calculating the discounted payback period, the discounted value of the cash flows using an appropriate rate is considered before the payback period is computed. Discounted payback period is the number of years taken for recovering the investment outlay on the PVs. Discounted value does not take into consideration the cash flows occurring after the payback period. For example, consider Project A and Project B where both are involved in as outlay of ₹40,000. Both the projects have the same payback period, that is, 2 years. NPV of project B is higher than that of project A, which is further supported by discounted payback period of 2.8 years. On the basis of the payback period method, both the projects seem to be equally desirable.

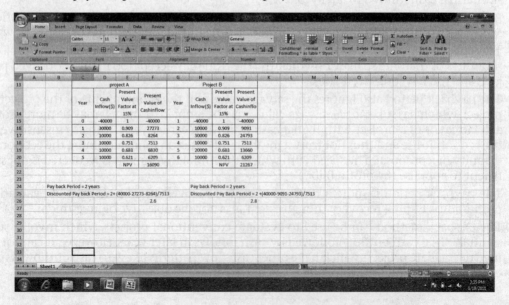

For instance, if a project involves an initial outlay of ₹10 lakhs, and is expected to generate a net annual inflow of ₹4 lakhs for the next 4 years, the discounted payback will be that value of '*n*' for which

$$4 \times \text{PVIFA}(12, n) = 10$$
$$\Rightarrow \quad \text{PVIFA}(12, n) = 2.5$$

From PVIFA Tables, we find that

$$\text{PVIFA}(12, 3) = 2.402$$
$$\text{PVIFA}(12, 4) = 3.037$$

Interpolating we obtain

$$n = 3 + \frac{3.037 - 2.5}{3.037 - 2.402} = 3.84$$

Thus, the discounted payback period as an appraisal criterion is relatively better than the undiscounted payback period. It considers the time value of money and thereby does not give an equal weight to all flows before the cut-off date. But it still suffers from the other shortcomings of the payback period. This criterion also depends on the choice of an arbitrary cut-off date and ignores all subsequent cash flows. In practice, companies do not give much importance to the payback period as an appraisal criterion.

Accounting Rate of Return (ARR)

The ARR is based on the accounting-concept of return on investment or rate of return. It may be **defined as the annualized net income earned on the average funds invested in a project**. In other words, the annual returns of a project are expressed as a percentage of the net investment in the project.

Symbolically

$$\text{ARR} = \frac{\text{Average annual post-tax profit}}{\text{Average investment in the project}} \times 100$$

Thus, ARR is a measure based on the accounting profit rather than the cash flows and is very similar to the measure of rate of return on the capital employed, which is generally used to measure the overall profitability of the firm.

Average Investment

The average investment refers to the average amount of funds that remains invested or blocked in the proposal over its economic life. The average investment of a proposal is affected by the method of depreciation, salvage value, and the additional working capital required by the proposal. The following two approaches can be used to calculate the level of average investment in a project.

Initial Cash Outflow as Average Investment

In this case, the initial investment in the project is taken as the amount invested in the project. For example, a project costing ₹100,000 is expected to generate after-tax profit of ₹15,000 every year. The ARR for the proposal would be 15% (i.e., ₹15,000/₹100,000×100). Theoretically, this approach of average investment seems to be good but considering the initial investment as the average investment is definitely not correct on logical and technical grounds.

Average Annual Book Value after Depreciation as Average Investment

In this case, the average annual book value (after depreciation) of the proposal is taken as the average investment of the proposal. The average annual book value after depreciation may be calculated as follows:

1. Determine the opening book values and the closing book values of the project for all the years of its economic life.
2. Find out the average book values for all the years by taking the simple arithmetic mean of the opening and closing book values.
3. Determine the average of all the annual averages. This average will be the average investment of the proposal.

The Additional Working Capital

Sometimes, the project may also require additional working capital for its smooth operation. Although this additional working capital will be released back, when the project comes to an end yet this amount of additional working capital is blocked throughout the life of the project. So, this additional working capital entails the investment of funds of the firm and should also be added to the average investment calculated as above.

Average investment=1/2 (Initial cost+Installation expenses–Salvage value)+Salvage

value+Additional working capital.

Acceptance Rule

The ARR calculated as above is compared with the prespecified rate of return. If the ARR is more than the prespecified rate of return, then the project is likely to be accepted, otherwise not. The ARR can also be used to rank various mutually exclusive proposals. The project with the highest ARR will have the top priority, whereas the project with the lowest ARR will be assigned the lowest priority.

Merits

1. It is very simple to understand and calculate.
2. It can be calculated from accounting information. There is no need to make any adjustments to compute cash inflows.

Demerits

This criterion, however, suffers from following several drawbacks:

1. It is based on accounting profit and not cash flows.
2. It does not take into consideration the changing value of money due to time.

3. As it is based on accounting profit, the standard against which it is compared is also based on accounting profit. Usually, the benchmark is the book rate of return. This rate of return is based on historical book values. This rate of return may not reflect the actual rate of return and hence may result in acceptance of bad projects and rejection of good projects.

4. The ARR also ignores the life of the proposal. A proposal with a longer life may have the same ARR as another proposal with a shorter life. On the basis of ARR, both the proposals may be placed at par, but the proposal with a longer life should be preferred over the proposal with a shorter life (as the former proposal will generate the returns for a longer period). However, the ARR method fails to distinguish between the two.

Test Yourself

1. What is payback method? Discuss its merits and demerits.
2. How is ARR calculated?

Illustration 1. Hyderabad Chemicals is considering investment in a project which requires an investment of ₹12,000,000. The project has a life of 5 years. The project is expected to have a salvage value of ₹2,000,000 after 5 years. During its life, the project will require an additional working capital of ₹2,000,000 and it is expected to generate an after-tax profit of ₹1,800,000 per annum for the entire life of the project. What is the ARR of the project?

Solution:

$$ARR = \frac{\text{Average Annual Post-Tax Profit}}{\text{Average Investment in the Project}} \times 100$$

Average Annual Post-tax Profit = ₹1,800,000.

Average investment = 1/2 (Initial cost + Installation expenses − Salvage value)

$$+ \text{Salvage value} + \text{Additional working capital.}$$

Average investment = 1/2 (12,000,000 − 2,000,000) + 2,000,000 + 2,000,000 = ₹9,000,000

$$ARR = \frac{₹18,00,000}{₹90,00,000} \times 100 = 20\%$$

Discounted Cash Flow Methods

These methods also explicitly consider the time value of money by properly discounting the cash flows occurring at different points of time. These methods argue that value of money keeps changing with time.

Net Present Value (NPV)

NPV method considers the time value of money concept and hence discounts all the future expected cash flows to the present time in order to calculate the net benefit from the project. In other words, in order to calculate the NPV of a project, we discount the future expected cash flows using a suitable discount rate and also adjust the cash flow taking place in the present. Suitable discount rate is the opportunity cost of capital, which is the minimum required rate of return expected by investors on projects of equivalent risk. If the cash flow is a typical project involving cash outflow in the ($t=0$) and cash inflows in the future time periods ($t=1, 2, 3,...,$ n), computing NPV means finding out the PV of all the future cash inflows and deducting the cash outflow from it. The project with positive NPV should be accepted.

Symbolically

$$NPV = -CF_0 + \sum_{t=1}^{n} \frac{CF_t}{(1+k)^t}$$

where CF_0 is the cash outflow at time period$_0$, CF_t is the cash inflow at time periods 1, 2, 3, 4,..., n, t is the time period, and k is the required rate of return or the cost of capital for the project.

Illustration 2. BR Ltd is considering investment in a project, which has a life of 5 years and has the following expected cash flows:

Year	Cash Flow (₹ in Lakhs)
1	–10
2	2
3	3
4	5
5	6

If the cost of capital relevant for the project is 14%, whether the project should be expected?

Solution:

Year	Cash Flow (₹ in lakhs)	PVIF Factor for 14%	PV of Cash Flows
1	–10	1.000	–10
2	2	0.877	1.754
3	3	0.769	2.307
4	5	0.675	3.375
5	6	0.592	3.552

$$NPV = -10 + 1.754 + 2.307 + 3.375 + 3.552 = ₹0.988 \text{ lakhs}$$

What Does NPV Imply?

In Illustration 2, the NPV of the project is ₹0.988 lakhs. What does it mean? Whether the project should be selected or not?

While calculating the NPV we are considering all the expected cash flows from the project and appropriately discounting them to find out the "net benefit" from the project. Remember that we are considering the cash flows from the project and not the accounting profits. Also, even when debt is used to finance a project, it entails some fixed payment to the creditors. This means that the cash flows resulting from the project after paying to the debt suppliers belong to the common shareholders. Thus, NPV would reflect the change in the wealth of the share-holders as a result of the project. It implies that if the NPV is positive, it means an increase in the wealth of the shareholders, and if the NPV is negative, a decline in the wealth of the share-holders. In Illustration 2, an NPV of ₹0.988 lakhs implies that the wealth of the shareholders is expected to increase by ₹0.988 lakhs if the project is undertaken.

As the fundamental objective of a finance manager is to ensure an increase in the wealth of the shareholders, in case of mutually exclusive projects, the project with the highest posi-tive NPV is given the top priority and the project with the lowest positive NPV is assigned the lowest priority. The projects with negative NPV should outrightly be rejected as these entail decrease in the wealth of the shareholders. However, if the NPV of the project is 0, then the firm may be indifferent between acceptance and rejection of the project. The only difficulty which would arise is the calculation of NPV at a discount rate. Funds which are available in the company can be distributed to the shareholders or reinvested in projects. Therefore, dis-count rate is the opportunity cost of investing in projects rather than capital market.

Test Yourself

1. What do you mean by NPV? How is NPV calculated?
2. Under what circumstances should we accept the projects under NPV?
3. Explain the merits and demerits of NPV.

NPVs Are Additive

The NPVs of different projects can be added to arrive at a cumulative NPV.

$$\text{NPV (Cumulative)} = \text{NPV (project A)} + \text{NPV (project B)} + \cdots + \text{NPV (project Z)}$$

This makes comparison between the projects easier. Sometimes it may be beneficial to invest in two to three small projects with a higher cumulative NPV than a single large project. For example, consider a situation of capital rationing where the firm cannot invest more than ₹5 lakhs. There are three projects A, B, and C. Project A involves an investment of ₹5 lakhs and has an NPV of ₹2 lakhs; project B involves an investment of ₹2 lakhs and has an NPV of ₹1.0 lakhs; project C involves an investment of ₹3 lakhs and an NPV of ₹1.5 lakhs. Considered individually, of the three projects, project A is the best. However, if we look at the combination of projects B and C, we find that for the same investment of ₹5 lakhs, it offers a higher NPV of ₹2.5 lakhs.

Spreadsheet Exercise No. 2

Manco PLC invests in a new machine which cost ₹15,000. It is hoped that the net cash flows over the next 5 years will correspond to those given in the table below:

Year 1 net cash flow	₹1,500
Year 2 net cash flow	₹2,750
Year 3 net cash flow	₹4,000
Year 4 net cash flow	₹5,700
Year 5 net cash flow	₹7,500

Calculate the NPV of the investment, using a discount rate of 15%.

The formula used in B8 gets reflected in the functional tool bar.

Merits and Demerits of NPV

The merits of the NPV technique can be enumerated as follows:

1. It takes into account the concept of time value of money. It helps in evaluation of projects involving cash flows over a period of time. The cash flows occurring at different points of time are not directly comparable but they can be made comparable by the application of the discounting procedure.

2. The NPV technique considers the entire cash flow stream associated with a project. All the cash inflows and outflows, irrespective of the timing of their occurrence, are incorporated in the calculation of the NPV.

3. The NPV technique is based on the cash flows rather than the accounting profit. By considering the cash flows, NPV method helps in analyzing the effect of the proposal on the wealth of the shareholders in a better way.

4. The discount rate, k, applied for discounting the future cash flows is the cost of capital of the project. The weighted average cost of capital for the firm may not be the relevant cost of capital because the project may have a different risk profile than that of the firm. NPV method permits this flexibility and hence allows objective analysis.

5. As discussed above, NPV represents the net contribution of a proposal toward the wealth of the shareholder and is therefore, in full conformity with the objective of wealth maximization.

The above merits of the NPV technique make it a popular technique of evaluation of capital budgeting proposals. The NPV technique correctly reflects the trade-off of equivalent cash outflows and inflows, while allowing for additional returns at a required rate as well as the recovery of the initial investment. The very fact that this technique is capable of evaluating the proposals that are profit seeking and involve cash flows over a period of several years make it a preferred technique of evaluation of capital budgeting proposals. But this does not mean that it is free from shortcomings.

The NPV technique has the following shortcomings:

1. It may not be able to overcome the uncertainty involved with cash flows emerging at a different point of time in future.
2. The NPV technique requires the predetermination of the required rate of return or the cost of capital, k. If cost of capital is not correctly estimated, then the NPV method may give misleading signals.
3. NPV method ignores the differences in initial outflows, size of different proposals, differences in life of projects, and so on, while evaluating mutually exclusive proposals.

Profitability Index (PI)

One of the shortcomings of the NPV technique as discussed earlier is that it ignores the differences in initial investments required for the projects and also the differences in the life spans. However, quite often the finance manager may be faced with a choice involving several alternative investments of different sizes. In such a case, he cannot be indifferent to the fact that even though the NPV of different alternatives may be close or even equal, these involve commitments of different amounts. In other words, it does make a difference whether an investment proposal promises an NPV of ₹100,000 for an outlay of ₹1,000,000; or whether an outlay of ₹2,500,000 is required to get the same NPV of ₹100,000, even if the life of the projects are assumed to be the same. In the first case, the NPV is a much larger fraction (₹100,000/1,000,000) than what it is in the second case (i.e., ₹100,000/2,500,000), which makes the first proposal clearly more attractive.

Profitability Index (PI) is a formal way of expressing this cost–benefit relationship. In other words, **PI indicates the net benefits expected from the project per rupee of investment. This technique, which is a variant of the NPV technique, is also known as benefit-cost ratio, or PV Index.**

Symbolically

$$PI = \frac{PV}{CF_0}$$

where PI is the profitability index, PV is the present value of future cash flows, and CF_0 is the initial investment.

Alternatively, the above formula may be expressed as follows:

$$PI = \sum_{t=1}^{n} \frac{CF_t}{(1+k)^t} \div CF_0$$

Illustration 3. Consider the illustration that we used for NPV

Year	Cash Flow (₹ in Lakhs)
1	–10
2	2
3	3
4	5
5	6

As we calculated above, the PV of the cash inflows=₹10.988 lakhs. The cash outflow is ₹10 lakhs. Using the formula for PI

$$PI = \frac{PV}{CF_0}, \text{ we get}$$

$$PI = \frac{10.988}{10} = 1.0988$$

This implies that for every ₹1 invested, the project is expected to return ₹1.0988.
Thus, we can generalize that

- If the PI is greater than 1: Accept the project.
- If the PI is less than 1: Reject the project.
- If the PI is equal to 1, then the firm may be indifferent because the PV of inflows is expected to be just equal to the PV of the outflows.

While ranking of mutually exclusive projects, the project with the highest positive PI will be given top priority, whereas the project with the lowest PI will be assigned the lowest priority. The projects with a PI of less than 1 are likely to be out rightly rejected. Thus, we can see that the PI is an extension of the NPV method. In case of NPV, we calculate the difference between the PV of cash inflows and the cash outflows, whereas in case of PI we calculate the ratio of the PV of cash inflows and the cash outflows.

A variant of the PI is the Net Profitability Index (NPI) or the net benefit-cost ratio (NBCR) which is defined as

$$NPI = NBCR = \frac{NPV}{I}$$

$$= \frac{PV - I}{I} = \frac{PV}{I} - 1$$

$$= PI - 1$$

Evaluation of Profitability Index

It recognizes the time value of money.

- This method is consistent with shareholders, wealth maximization principle. The project the PI of which is greater than 1, would definitely create shareholders wealth.
- It is a relative measure of projects profitability.
- First, it provides no means for aggregating several smaller projects into a package that can be compared with a large project.
- Second, when the investment outlay is spread over more than one period, this criterion cannot be used.

NPV Versus PI

As far as the accept-reject decision is concerned, both the NPV and the PI will give the same decision. The reasons for this are obvious. The PI will be greater than one only for projects which have a positive NPV. However, if the PI is equal to one then the NPV would also be 0. Similarly, projects with a PI of less than one will also have the negative NPV. However, a conflict between the NPV and the PI may arise in case of evaluation of mutually exclusive projects.

As PI criterion calculates net benefits per rupee of cash outflow, it can discriminate between the projects with large outlays and projects with smaller outlays. For example, consider a firm which is evaluating two proposals, A and B, with costs of ₹1,000,000 and ₹800,000, respectively. The PVs of the cash inflows expected from these projects are ₹1,200,000 and ₹1,000,000. Consequently, both the proposals have NPV of ₹200,000 and therefore, a financial manager using NPV as the decision criterion will be indifferent between the two projects. In this case, the PI technique seems to give a better result. The PI of both the projects can be calculated as follows:

$$PI(A) = \frac{1,200,000}{1,000,000} = 1.20$$

$$PI(B) = \frac{1,000,000}{800,000} = 1.25$$

In terms of the NPV technique, both projects are alike, but in terms of the PI technique, Project B is better. The reason being that the Project B entails lesser cash outflow of ₹800,000 and still generates net benefits of ₹200,000, against the project A which is also generating net benefits of ₹200,000 but requires a larger outlay of ₹1,000,000.

In the above case, we considered that the net monetary benefits from the two projects were same. However, NPV and the PI may give contradictory decisions even if the net monetary benefits and the initial cost are different for different projects. For example, two projects, A and B with initial cash outflows of ₹1,500,000 and ₹1,100,000 are being evaluated. The PVs of cash inflows of these projects are ₹2,100,000 and ₹1,650,000, respectively. In such a case, the NPV of the proposals are ₹600,000 and ₹550,000, respectively, and therefore Project A is to be preferred over project B. But the PIs of these two projects are 1.4 and 1.5, respectively, and therefore as per PI technique project B is to be preferred.

Which of the two projects is to be accepted? In such a situation, the NPV decision should be preferred unless there is a capital constraint. If there is no capital constraint, then project A (as per the NPV technique) should be adopted. This will result in increase in shareholders wealth to the extent of ₹600,000 against Project B that will increase the wealth only by ₹550,000. The better project, obviously, is one, which adds more to the wealth of the shareholders.

Terminal Value

Terminal Value (TV) technique is another variant of the NPV criterion. To calculate the NPV of a project, the future cash flows are discounted to make them comparable. **In the TV technique, the future cash flows are first compounded at an expected rate of interest for the period from their occurrence till the end of the economic life of the project. The compounded values are then discounted at an appropriate discount rate to find out the PV.** This PV is compared with the initial outflow to find out the suitability of the proposal.

The TV technique is based on the assumption that all future cash inflows are reinvested elsewhere at the then prevailing rate of interest until the end of the economic life of the project.

Illustration 4. A project costing ₹120,000 has a useful economic life of 4 years over which it is expected to generate cash inflows of ₹40,000 at the end of each of the next 4 years. Given the rate of return as 10% and that the firm can reinvest the cash inflows for the remaining period at the rate of 8%.

What is the NPV as per the TV technique?

Solution: The TV profile of the project can be calculated as follows:

Year	Cash Inflows (₹)	Remaining Years	FVIF (8%, *n*)	Future Values
1	40,000	3	1.260	50,400
2	40,000	2	1.166	46,640
3	40,000	1	1.080	43,200
4	40,000	0	1.000	40,000
			Total	**180,240**

The amount of ₹180,240 is to be discounted at 10% (i.e., rate of discount) for four years to find out its PVs. The PVF (10%, 4) is 0.683. So, the PV of ₹180,240 is ₹180,240 × 0.683 = ₹123,104. This PV can now be compared with the initial investment of ₹120,000 to find out the NPV of ₹23,104. So, the project has a NPV of ₹23,104 as per the TV technique.

Thus, using the TV technique a project is to be accepted if the PV of the total compounded value of all the cash inflows is greater than the PV of the cash outflows.

Both the NPV and the TV techniques would give the same result and the same decision if the rate of discount and the rate of interest are the same. As TV technique is a variant of the NPV technique, the merits and shortcomings of the NPV techniques are applicable to the TV technique also. However, the TV technique has a specific drawback, which is not applicable to the NPV technique. The shortcoming is that the TV technique requires the estimation of future rate of interest at which the future cash inflows are to be compounded.

Test yourself

1. What do you mean by PI method?
2. How will you evaluate PI method?
3. Explain terminal value.

IRR

The IRR is the discount rate at which the PV of cash inflows will equate with the PV of the cash outflow. This is the rate of return, which is internal to the project. In other words, this rate depends only on the cash flows associated with the project and is not determined externally unlike the discount rate.

Suppose Mr A is depositing ₹10,000 with a bank and is expected to get ₹10,600 after one year. The rate of return after one year would be

$$\text{Rate of Return} = \frac{₹10,600 - ₹10,000}{₹1,00,000} = 6\%$$

Future cash inflow (₹10,600) that we are expected to earn would have initial investment (₹10,000) and return on your investment (₹600). It means that if we discount ₹10,600 with 6% discount rate, you will get ₹10,000. Here, we can develop the formula for calculating the PV of cash flows. For example, r is the rate of return on initial investment (I_0) and expected to generate a cash flow of I_1.

$$r = \frac{I_1 - I_0}{I_0}$$

$$r = \frac{I_1}{I_0} - 1$$

$$r + 1 = \frac{I_1}{I_0}$$

$$I_0 = \frac{I_1}{(1+r)}$$

That is why, IRR is an internal factor and depends on investment's cash flow. IRR is the discount rate which makes NPV = 0.

Symbolically, the IRR is equal to the value of "*r*" in the equation

$$CF_0 = \sum_{t=1}^{n} \frac{CF_i}{(1+r)^t} + \frac{SV + WC}{(1+r)^t}$$

where CF_0 is the cash outflow at time 0, CF_i is the cash inflow at different points of time, n is the life of the project, r is the rate of discount (yet to be calculated), SV is the salvage value at the end of project life, and WC is the working capital released at the end of project life.

Like NPV, IRR is also based on a critical assumption. The assumption underlying IRR is that the intermediate cash flows are reinvested at a rate of return equal to IRR. Thus, IRR method differs from the NPV method which assumes that the intermediate cash flows are reinvested at a rate of return equal to the discount rate.

The detailed procedure for the calculation of IRR can be explained in two different situations:

1. when future cash flows are equal, and
2. when future cash flows are unequal.

CASE I. WHEN FUTURE CASH FLOWS ARE EQUAL

A project with a life of 6 years costs ₹100,000. It will generate ₹25,000 at the end of each year for the next 6 years. There is no salvage value. The IRR of the project may be calculated as follows:

Step 1
Make an approximation of the IRR on the basis of cash flows data. A rough approximation may be made with reference to the payback period. The payback period in the given case is 4(100,000/25,000) years. Now, search for a value nearest to 4 in the 6th year row of the PVIFA table. The closest figures are given in rate 12% (4.111) and the rate 13% (3.998). This means that the IRR of the proposal is expected to lie between 12% and 13%.

Step 2

To make a precise estimate of the IRR, find out the NPV of the project for both these rates as follows:

$$\text{At } 12\%, \text{NPV} = (₹25,000 \times \text{PVAF} (12\%, 6y) - ₹100,000$$

$$= (₹25,000 \times 4.111) - ₹100,000$$

$$= ₹2,775.$$

$$\text{At } 13\%, \text{NPV} = (25,000 \times \text{PVAF} (13\%, 6y) - ₹100,000$$

$$= (₹25,000 \times 3.998) - ₹100,000$$

$$= ₹ -50$$

Step 3

Find out the exact IRR by interpolating between 12% and 13%. It may be noted that IRR is the rate of discount at which the NPV is zero. At 12%, the NPV is ₹2,775 and at 13% the NPV is −50. Therefore, the rate at which the NPV is zero will be higher than 12% but less than 13%.

Interpolating, we obtain

$$r = 12\% + \frac{2,775}{2,775 + 50} = 12.98\%$$

So, the IRR of the project is 12.98%.

CASE II. WHEN FUTURE FLOWS ARE NOT EQUAL

In case when the project is expected to generate an uneven stream of cash flows, the calculation of the IRR is complicated. In such a case, we can follow the trial and error approach. Suppose a firm is evaluating a proposal costing ₹160,000 and expected to generate cash inflows of ₹40,000, ₹60,000, ₹50,000, ₹50,000, and ₹40,000 at the end of each of the next 5 years, respectively. Salvage value is nil. In this case, there is an uneven stream of cash inflows and the IRR can be approximated as follows.

Step 1

Find out the average annual cash inflow to get a "Notional Annuity."

Year	Cash inflows (₹)
1.	40,000
2.	60,000
3.	50,000
4.	50,000
5.	40,000
Total	240,000

Notional annuity = ₹240,000/5 = ₹48,000

Step 2

Divide the initial outlay with the average cash inflows of ₹160,000/₹48,000 = 3.33 years.

Step 3

Now, search for a value nearest to the value obtained in step 2 hereinbefore in the PVIFA table for the corresponding value of *n*. In this case, it is 3.33 in 5 years row of the PVIFA table. The closest figures given in the table are at 15% (3.352) and at 16% (3.274). This means that the IRR of the proposal is expected to lie between 15% and 16%.

Step 4

Find out the NPV of the proposal for both of these approximate rates.

In the given case, at 15%, the NPV=₹1,540 and at 16% the NPV=₹–2,250

Step 5

Find out the exact IRR by interpolating between 15% and 16%. At 15%, the NPV is ₹1,540 and at 16% the NPY is ₹–2,250. Therefore, the rate at which NPV is zero will be more than 15%, but less than 16%.
   By interpolating

$$r = 15\% + \frac{1,540}{1,540 + 2,250} = 15.4$$

Interpretation of IRR

What does IRR indicate? For example, if you are told that the IRR of a project is 20%, what do you understand from this? Two interpretations are possible:

1. IRR is the rate of return earned on the initial investment in the project. For example, if the initial investment is ₹100,000 and the life of the project is 3 years, an IRR of 20% according to this approach would mean that the project would be worth ₹100,000 (1.20)3=₹172,800.
2. IRR is the rate of return earned on the unrecovered investment balance in the project. In other words, IRR represents the return earned on the amount of funds still invested in the project. For example, consider a project which involves an investment of ₹100,000 and has the following cash inflows over its life:

Year	Cash Inflow (₹)
1	24,000
2	50,000
3	84,000

In this case, the investment balance in the project would appear as follows:

Year	Investment Outstanding at the Beginning of the Year	Interest Cost @20%	Cash Inflow	Investment Outstanding at the End of the Year
0	100,000	20,000	0	120,000
1	120,000	24,000	24,000	100,000
2	100,000	20,000	50,000	70,000
3	70,000	14,000	84,000	0

Test Yourself

1. What is IRR technique?
2. Discuss its advantage and disadvantage.

Using IRR for Accepting/Rejecting Projects

To make a decision on the basis of the IRR technique; the firm has to determine, in the first instance, its own required rate of return or the opportunity cost of capital. This rate is also known as the *cut-off rate* or the *hurdle rate*. A particular proposal may be accepted if its IRR, *r*, is greater than the minimum rate. However, if the IRR is just equal to the minimum rate, then the firm may be indifferent. In case of ranking of mutually exclusive proposals, the proposal with the highest IRR is given the top priority, whereas the project with the lowest IRR is given the lowest priority. Projects the IRR of which is less than the minimum required rate may altogether be rejected. This decision rule is based on the fact that the NPV of the project is zero if its cash flows are discounted at the minimum required rate. If the project can give a return higher than this minimum required rate, then it is expected to contribute to the wealth of the shareholders.

Merits and Demerits of IRR

The merits of the IRR technique are

1. The IRR technique takes into account the time value of money and the cash flows occurring at different points of time are adjusted for change value of money.
2. Like the NPV technique, the IRR technique is also based on the consideration of all the cash flows occurring at any time. The salvage value and the working capital used and released are also considered.

   IRR has some drawbacks as follows:

1. As far as the calculation of IRR is concerned, it involves a tedious and complicated trial and error procedure.
2. An important drawback of the IRR technique is that it makes an implied assumption that the future cash inflows of a proposal are reinvested at a rate equal to the IRR. Say, in case of mutually exclusive proposals, say A and B with an IRR of 18% and 16%, the IRR technique makes an implied assumption that the future cash inflows of project A will be reinvested at 18%, whereas the cash inflows of project B will be reinvested at 16%. It is imaginary to think like that.

Spreadsheet Exercise No. 3: Calculation of IRR with Excel Sheets

It is very easy to compute IRR through spreadsheets. Cash outlay is given in B2. Cash inflows are given from B3:B6. For the calculation of IRR, the formula used is IRR (B2:B6, guess rate). But it is not necessary to use the guess rate. This formula has been used in B7 cell.

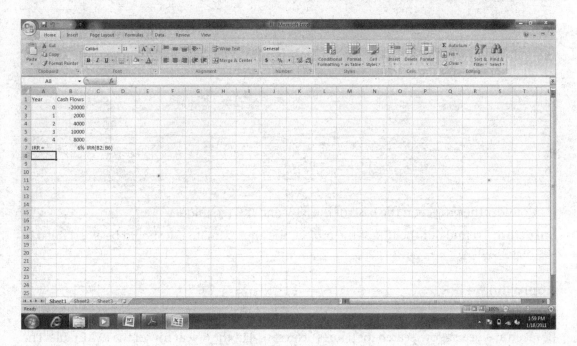

NPV Versus IRR

Let us compare NPV and IRR as appraisal criteria for different types of investment decisions that we come across in capital budgeting. The investment projects can be classified into the following three categories:

1. Accept-reject decisions
2. Replacement decisions
3. Mutually exclusive decisions

Accept–Reject Decisions

The accept-reject decision is the simplest of all the capital budgeting decisions. Such a decision occurs when:

1. Different projects are economically independent, that is, the cash inflows and outflows of one project do not affect the cash flows of other projects.
2. Accepting or rejecting a project has no impact on the desirability of other projects.
3. There are no two projects, at the same time, which are competing with each other.

Illustration 5. Zen Fibre-Optics Ltd is considering an expansion of the installed capacity of one of its plant at a cost of ₹35 lakhs. The firm has a minimum required rate of return of 12%. The following are the expected cash inflows over the next 6 years after which the plant will be scrapped away for nil value.

Year	Cash Inflows (₹ in lakhs)
1	10
2	10
3	10
4	10
5	5
6	5

Consider the project on the basis of the NPV and IRR techniques.

Solution: To find out the IRR of the project, the approximate IRR should be ascertained in the first instance.

Approximate IRR

As the stream of cash inflows are more or less an annuity of ₹1,000,000, the payback period can be taken at 4 years. Now, search for figures nearest to 4 in the 6-year row of the PVAF table. The respective figures are 4.111 (12%) and 3.998 (13%). Thus, the IRR is expected to lie between 12% and 13%. Now the calculation of NPV (at 12%) and the IRR of the project can be taken up as follows:

Year	Cash Inflows (₹)	PVF (12%, 6')	PVF (13%, 6)	PV (12%) (₹)	PV (13%) (₹)
1	1,000,000	0.893	0.885	893,000	885,000
2	1,000,000	0.797	0.783	797,000	783,000
3	1,000,000	0.712	0.693	712,000	693,000
4	1,000,000	0.636	0.613	636,000	613,000
5	500,000	0.567	0.543	283,500	271,500
6	500,000	0.507	0.480	253,500	240,000
	Total			3,575,000	3,485,500

NPV of the project (required rate of return 12%)

$$NPV = ₹3,575,000 - ₹3,500,000$$
$$= ₹75,000$$

IRR of the project

$$NPV \text{ at } 12\% = ₹75,000$$
$$NPV \text{ at } 13\% = ₹3,485,500 - ₹3,500,000$$
$$= ₹-14,500$$

Interpolating between 12% and 13%

$$IIR = 12\% + \frac{35,75,000 - 35,00,000}{35,75,000 - 34,85,500}$$

$$= 12.84\%.$$

So, the IRR of the project is 12.84% and the NPV of the project is ₹75,000. Therefore, the project is acceptable on the basis of both the NPV and the IRR techniques.

In most of the accept-reject decisions, both the NPV and the IRR produce identical results. This fact can further be testified in terms of conventional cash flows and unconventional cash flow as follows.

Conventional Cash Flows in Accept–Reject Decision Situation

A conventional cash flow stream is one in which the initial cash outflow is followed by a series of cash inflows. A conventional cash flow series has only one change in the signs of the cash flows, that is, a conventional cash flow series may be described as "– + + +."

The reason for identical results can be explained by computing the NPV values at different discount rates. The linkage between the NPV and the IRR is most visible when the NPV is graphed as a function of discount rate in a NPV profile. The NPV profile measures the sensitivity of the NPV to change in the discount rate.

Figure 10.2 given shows the relationship between the NPV and the IRR. In this figure, the highest NPV is OA, which is achieved if the rate of discount is O. At this point, the NPV is simply the difference between the cash inflows and the outflows. As the rate increases from O toward R, the NPV decreases. When the rate of discount is R, the NPV is 0. By definition, R is the IRR of the project. If the rate of discount is increased further, then the NPV becomes negative.

FIGURE 10.2
NPV–IRR (CONVENTIONAL CASH FLOWS)

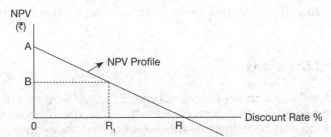

Source: Kothari and Dutta (2005). *Contemporary Financial Management.* McMillian.

NPV–IRR (conventional cash flows)

Thus, if the required rate of return is any rate less than R, the project is acceptable under both the NPV and the IRR techniques, as the NPV will be positive and the IRR will be higher than the cut-off rate. For illustration, at the required rate of return, R_i, the NPV is Oa, a positive value and the IRR of the project, that is, R is more than the cut-off rate, that is, R_i. Similarly, both the technique will reject the project if the required rate of return (or the cut-off rate) is more than R as in this situation and the NPV will also be negative.

Unconventional Cash Flows in Accept–Reject Decision Situation

An unconventional cash flow stream is one in which there is regular cash inflows and out-flows. There may be more than one change in signs of the cash flows, for example, "—+ +— +" is an unconventional cash flows series. In case of accept–reject decision situation involves an unconventional cash flows series, then a dilemma may arise. The NPV of the project can no doubt be calculated in the usual way. But when the IRR is calculated for such a series, they may appear more than IRR. This has already been explained in detail as a drawback of the IRR. In such a case, the number if IRR depends on the number of times the signs of the cash flows change. If there are two changes in the signs of the cash flows, then the NPV–IRR profile may appear as presented in Figure 10.3.

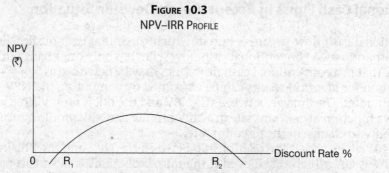

FIGURE 10.3
NPV–IRR PROFILE

Source: Kothari and Dutta (2005). *Contemporary Financial Management.* McMillian.

NPV–IRR (unconventional cash flows)

In such a case, the project will have zero NPV at two different rates, R_1 and R_2. The NPV of the project is positive for all the rates ranging between R_1 and R_2. But what about the decision based on the IRR technique?

It may be noted that the IRR technique fails to resolve such a situation if the cut-off rate is in between R_1 and R_2.

The Replacement Decisions

The replacement decision is another common type of capital budgeting decisions. A replacement decision occurs when one asset is proposed to be replaced with another. The objective of a replacement decision may be to increase the output or to decrease the cost. For illustration, an existing machine has become worn out and hence needs to be replaced to enhance the production or it has become obsolete hence needs to be replaced to stay competitive. To discuss the replacement decision, an important assumption is that the economic life of the new asset is equal to the remaining economic life of the existing asset being replaced. For illustration, if an asset, which can still be used in a normal way for a period of 6 years, is to be replaced, then the assumption is that the new asset also has an economic life of 6 years only.

The replacement decisions are not very different from other capital budgeting decisions. These decisions also require measurement of cost and benefits of the projects. However, as a replacement decision involves disposal of some existing asset currently owned by the firm, which is expecting to realize increased benefit as a result of replacement, these decisions often pose the problem of measurement of cost and benefits.

To evaluate a replacement decision, the incremental net investment (cash outflows) and the incremental cash inflows that result from the replacement action are to be ascertained. For this purpose, incremental cash inflows may be defined as the cash inflows of the new asset less than the cash inflows of the existing asset.

Illustration 6. Xtra Ltd. whose required rate of return is 10% is considering replacing one of its existing weaving loom by a new and more sophisticated loom. The relevant data for the existing plantas well as the proposed plant are as follows:

	Existing Loom	New Loom
Present book value/cost	₹24,000	₹54,000
Remaining life	6 years	6 years
Depreciation (per annum)	₹4,000	₹9,000
Salvage value (current)	₹20,000	–
Profit before depreciation and tax (annual)	8,000	15,000

Evaluate the project as per both the NPV and the IRR techniques given that

1. The tax rate applicable to the firm is 40%.
2. The loss on disposal of an asset is not tax deductible.

Solution:
Incremental Net Investment or Net Initial Outflow

Cost of the proposed plant	₹54,000
(-)Current scrap value of the existing plant	₹54,000
Net cash outflow	₹54,000

Incremental Annual Cash Inflows	Existing Plant (₹)	Proposed Plant (₹)
Profit before depreciation	8,000	15,000
- Depreciation	4,000	9,000
Profit before tax,	4,000	6,000
- Tax @40%	1,600	2,400
Profit after tax	2,400	3,600
+ Depreciation (added back)	4,000	9,000
Cash inflow	6,400	12,600
∴ Incremental annual cash inflow		6,200

NPV of the Project at 10%

$$NPV = (₹6,200 \times PVAF[10\%,6Y]) ₹34,000$$
$$= (₹6,200 \times 4.355) - ₹34,000$$
$$= ₹-6,999$$

IRR of the Project

As the incremental cash inflows are an annuity of ₹6,200, the IRR may be approximated on the basis of the payback period, which is 5.5 years. Now, on the basis of the PVAF table, the values nearest to 5.5 in 6-year row are 5.601 (2%) and 5.242 (3%). Thus, the IRR of the project will lie between 2% and 3%. As the cut-off rate is 10%, which is much more than 3%, there is no purpose of calculation of the exact IRR.

The project for replacing the old plant by a new one should be rejected. Both the NPV (i.e., ₹6,999) and the IRR (i.e., between 2% and 3%) reject the project. Thus, the firm may continue with the existing plant only.

In case of replacement decision, both the NPV and the IRR techniques produce identical decisions.

In such a case, either

1. The NPV will be positive and the IRR will be more than the cut-off rate, or
2. NPV will be negative and the IRR will be less than the cut-off rate.

Mutually Exclusive Decisions

Two or more capital budgeting projects are said to be mutually exclusive when the acceptance of one of them results in implied and automatic rejection of all others. The mutually exclusive decision situation arises when a choice is to be made between two or more competing projects and usually the projects require to be ranked in the order of priority. For instance, a construction firm is considering a project to construct a residential apartment or an office building on a piece of land. Now the selection of one of these courses of actions will reject the other.

It may be noted at this stage that the ranking of mutually exclusive projects, as given by the NPV and the IRR, may either be identical or different. Let us discuss these two situations one by one.

Identical NPV and IRR Ranking

In most of the cases, the mutually exclusive projects are ranked in the same order by both the NPV and the IRR techniques. For example, two mutually exclusive investment projects, A and B, with 5-year economic life are being considered. Project A requires a net investment of ₹30,000 and produces a cash inflow of ₹10,000 per annum. Project B requires a net investment of ₹20,000 and produces a cash inflow of ₹6,000 p.a. Which project is preferable, given that the minimum required rate of the firm is 10%?

The NPV and IRR of these two projects are as given in the table below

Project	NPV at10%	IRR (%)
A	₹7910	19.87
B	₹2,746	15.24

Thus, according to both the NPV and the IRR criteria, project A is better because its NPV is positive and more than that of B; and the IRR is greater than the cut-off rate and is also more than the IRR of project B.

Conflicting NPV and IRR Ranking

The ranking of alternative project and the decision regarding selection of a project based on NPV and IRR may not always be the same.

Why one project is acceptable as per the NPV technique and some other project is acceptable as per the IRR technique?

Such conflicts in ranking may arise under the following situations:

Size Disparity

The cost or scale of one project may be different from that of others. A conflict in ranking can arise because of the size difference of different projects. The ranking as per the NPV technique, which deals with absolute net benefits, will be affected by the size of the projects. Higher the cash outflow, larger would be the expected returns in absolute terms, and hence higher ranking would be required to accept the project. However, the IRR deals with relative returns (i.e., in percentage form) and hence ignores the size of the project. For instance, if all the cash flows of a project are doubled, then the NPV will also double but its IRR would remain unchanged. The effect of the size of the project on the ranking as per NPV and IRR techniques can be explained with the help of the Illustration 7.

Illustration 7. The following is the relevant information for two mutually exclusive projects, X and Y, year being evaluated by a firm.

Year	Cash Flows (X)	Cash Flows (Y)
0	–10,000	–30,000
1	5,000	14,000
2	6,000	19,000
3	4,000	10,000

Evaluate and rank these projects as per the NPV and the IRR techniques given that the minimum required rate of return is 10%.

Solution: The NPV and the IRR of both the projects have been calculated and presented in the following table.

Project	NPV @10%	IRR (%)
X	₹2,509	24.30
Y	₹5,942	21.50

As you can see, the NPV and IRR techniques have given contradictory ranking. Project X should be selected as per the IRR technique, whereas project Y is better as per the NPV technique. The conflict between the two is arising because project Y is 3 times the size of project

X. This gives higher net absolute benefits from project Y, that is, the NPV of project Y is higher than that of project X. But in relative terms, the project Y is less profitable with a lower percentage return of 21.5%. In view of the objective of maximization of shareholders wealth, the project Y is definitely preferable and should be selected.

However, it may be noted that the above decisions is based on the implied assumption that the firm has adequate funds of ₹30,000 to take up the project Y. Otherwise, the decision may be reversed.

If the firms use only the NPV technique to rank the mutually exclusive projects, then the above problem may not arise. But firms prefer the percentage rate of return criterion (i.e., IRR) to evaluate capital budgeting projects. Thus, a wrong decision may be taken if only the IRR technique is used. However, the following procedure may be used to check the ranking given by the IRR technique.

Whether the additional investment of ₹20,000 in project Y is really worthwhile?

The incremental yield approach may suggest a way out. The incremental yield may be defined as the IRR of the incremental cash flows between the two projects.

Year	Cash Flows (X)	Cash Flows (Y)	Incremental Cash Flows
0	–10,000	–30,000	–20,000
1	5,000	14,000	9,000
2	6,000	19,000	13,000
3	4,000	10,000	6,000

The IRR of these incremental cash flows comes out to be 20%. Now, the required rate of return of the firm is 10% and the project Y is giving 20% return on incremental cash outflows. Therefore, project Y should be selected. This is the same decision as given by the NPV technique also.

Time Disparity

The ranking of mutually exclusive projects as per the NPV and the IRR technique may be different even when they involve the same or almost the same outlay. The different ranking may then occur as a result of different timings of the cash inflows of different projects. The situation may arise when larger cash inflows from one project may occur during early period of its lifetime whereas larger cash inflows from some other competitive project may occur toward the end of the economic life. For example, the cash inflows from one project may increase over time, whereas those of others may decrease or remains constant over time.

Illustration 8. Polaris Ltd, with a required rate of return of 8%, is evaluating two mutually exclusive projects A and B for which the relevant data is as follows:

Year	Cash Flows (a) (₹)	Cash Flows (b) (₹)
0	–2,500	–3,000
1	2,000	500
2	1,000	1,000
3	500	3,000

Evaluate and rank these projects.

Solution. The NPV and the IRR of both the projects have been calculated and presented in the following table:

Project	NPV @8%	IRR (%)
A	₹606	24.80
B	₹702	17.50

In this case, the NPV and IRR techniques are giving contradictory results.

As per the NPV technique Project B is better, whereas as per the IRR technique, Project A is preferable. The difference in ranking is because of a difference in the timing of cash inflows of the two projects. Project A is producing higher inflows in early years, whereas Project B is producing higher cash inflows in later years.

The reason for this is the difference in the reinvestment assumption of the NPV and the IRR techniques. You will recall that we discussed that NPV method implicitly assumes that the intermediate cash inflows are invested at a rate of return equal to the discount rate, whereas IRR techniques assume that the intermediate cash flows are invested at a rate equal to the IRR of the project.

The conflict in the ranking of mutually exclusive projects as per the NPV and the IRR techniques arises as a result of different reinvestment rate assumptions of the two techniques acting in different ways on the projects with time disparity of cash inflows.

To continue with the Illustration, the NPV technique assumes that the cash inflows of both the projects A and B are being reinvested at 8% for the rest of the economic life of the project. However, the IRR technique assumes that the cash inflows of project A will be reinvested at 24.8%, whereas the cash inflows of project B will be reinvested at 17.5%.

In practice, however, it may not be realistic to assume that the reinvestment rate of the firm will depend on the project being accepted. The reinvestment rate is fixed and being an external variable it has nothing to do with the project being accepted or rejected.

Life Disparity

The mutually exclusive projects may have different economic lives and this very fact should not affect the choice between them, even if the ranking as per the NPV and the IRR may be different.

Illustration 9. Lee Garments Ltd with a minimum required rate of return of 12% is considering two mutually exclusive projects X and Y. The relevant data for the projects are given below:

Year	Cash Flows (X) (₹)	Cash Flow (Y) (₹)
0	–50,000	–50,000
1	75,000	20,000
2	20,000	–
3	70,000	–

Evaluate the project on the basis of the NPV and the IRR techniques.

Solution: The NPV and the IRR of the two projects have been calculated and placed in the following table:

Project	NPV @12%	IRR (%)
A	₹16,975	50.00
B	₹33,640	36.45

Thus, the two techniques are suggesting for contradictory decisions. The NPV technique proposes that project Y is preferable and should be selected, whereas the IRR technique suggests that project X is with a higher IRR and should be selected. This contradiction in ranking appears in spite of the fact that both the projects are of the same size (i.e., initial outlay of ₹50,000). The reason for difference in ranking is the difference in economic lives of the projects. Project X has an economic life of only 1 year, whereas project Y has an economic life of 3 years.

Test Yourself

1. How do replacement decisions vary on the basis of NPV and IRR?

How Do We Resolve Conflict Due to Life Disparity?

In this case, we can calculate the equivalent annual cost (EAC) or equivalent annual benefit (EAB) to select the appropriate project.

On the basis of the earlier discussion, it can be stated that when a firm is evaluating mutually exclusive projects, it may come across conflicting ranking suggested by the NPV and the IRR techniques. The most important reason for such conflict lies in the difference in the implied reinvestment. When the conflict occurs, the decisions as per the NPV technique may be preferred for the following reasons:

1. The reinvestment rate assumption of NPV is consistent for all the competing projects, which is not so in case of the IRR.
2. The NPV technique assumes that a firm will accept those projects the rate of return of which is more than or is equal to the minimum required rate of return, whereas the IRR presupposes that the firm will accept only those projects whose rate of return is more than or is equal to the implied reinvestment rate.
3. Furthermore, the NPV technique will always give the correct ranking of the mutually exclusive projects in view of the wealth maximization objective. The IRR technique may not do so but can always be modified to give the correct ranking by using the incremental yield technique.

Capital Budgeting under Capital Rationing

It is a situation where the firm has limited funds available but cannot be undertaken in view of the limited funds. This situation may occur when a firm is either unable or unwilling to obtain additional funds in order to undertake financially viable capital budgeting projects. Thus, a firm by choice or under compulsions sets absolute ceiling on its capital spending in a period at a level that will cause it to reject or avoid some of the profitable projects.

For example, if a firm has different projects with positive NPV but the initial funds required for the implementation of all these projects are not available or cannot be procured from the capital market for one reason or the other, the firm is said to be operating under the condition of capital rationing. In other words, a firm faces capital rationing when it finds itself unable to take on projects that earn returns more than the cut-off rate because it does not have (i) the funds on hand or (ii) the capacity to raise the funds needed to finance these projects. In the context of the NPV rule, this implies that the firm does not have and cannot raise the funds to take all the positive NPV projects. Capital rationing is a situation where a firm is not in a position to obtain sufficient funds to undertake all investment projects which have positive NPV. Under capital rationing, the management has to decide combination of profitable projects which earns highest NPV within available funds.

Capital rationing may be

1. Internal
2. External

Internal Capital Rationing

It is a situation where the firm has imposed a limit on the funds allocated for fresh investment though (i) the funds might otherwise be available within the firm, or (ii) additional funds can be procured by the firm from the capital market. It is self-imposed restrictions by the management. Sometimes, management may resort to capital rationing by requiring minimum rate of return higher than the cost of capital. Whatever may be the restrictions, the ultimate result is that firm would have to forgo the projects because of the lack of funds. Some firms may follow a policy of using only internally generated funds (by plough back of profits) for new investments. Some firms avoid debt capital because of the associated financial risk and avoid external equity because of a desire not to lose control. This type of capital rationing implies that the firm is not willing to grow further. It is very difficult to justify internal rationing because it is used as a mean to control financial resources. Obviously, the internal capital rationing is not in the best interest of the shareholders in the long run, as it results in foregoing the profitable projects.

External Capital Rationing

External rationing occurs due to imperfections in the capital market. Imperfection occurs due to lack of information in the market that restricts the free flow of capital. It is a situation when the firm is willing to undertake the financially viable projects, but is unable to do so because either it does not have sufficient funds available at its disposal or the capital market conditions are not conclusive enough to let the firm raise the required funds from the market. For example, a wholly owned company does not want to issue shares to start a new project because of fear of losing control of the business or a small and medium enterprise are not in a position to fulfill listing norms of Security Exchange Board of India. Hence, it is not allowed to conduct initial public offerings.

A firm with no capital rationing would like to take all the capital budgeting projects which have positive NPV and reject those which have negative NPV. In case of mutually exclusive projects, the firm would like to take that project which has the highest positive

NPV irrespective of the fund requirements. But the problem is that if the firm is facing capital rationing, then how to distribute the available scarce and limited capital funds among competitive projects.

At this stage, it is also necessary to classify different projects into two classes, that is, divisible projects and indivisible projects.

Divisible Projects

There are certain projects, which can either be taken in full or can be taken in parts. For illustration, a building (with five floors) can be constructed at a cost of ₹5 crore. However, if the funds are not sufficiently available, then only a part of the building, say only two floors, can be constructed for the time being. But all the projects may not be divisible.

Indivisible Projects

There are certain projects, which are indivisible. These projects have a feature that either the project as a whole be taken in its totality or not taken at all. For Illustration, a project to buy a helicopter cannot be taken in parts. Similarly, a multi-stage plant can only be installed fully but not in parts. There can be many instances of indivisible projects.

Decision Process in Capital Rationing

We know that limited capital funds can finance fewer feasible projects. This necessitates to restructure the decision process to a certain extent. The simple way is to rank the various projects in a descending order of attractiveness and, then go on accepting the projects top down until the available funds are exhausted.

It is already seen in the previous session that different methods may not give the same ranking. Following are some of the methods and procedures to deal with capital rationing.

Aggregation of Projects or Feasible Set approach

Under this approach, the NPV of various projects are put in different possible combinations and then that combination is selected which has the maximum total NPV. The followings two points are worth considering:

1. The total outlay of the combination is within the limits of capital rationing.
2. The total NPV of the combination is the highest among all the combinations.

Illustration 10. A firm has a capital budget of ₹10,00,000 and it has under consideration the following four independent projects.

Project	Capital Outlay (₹)	NPV (₹)
A	450,000	150,000
B	400,000	100,000
C	300,000	80,000
D	200,000	40,000

Solution

These projects can be combined in different groups as follows:

Combination	Total Outlay (₹)	Total NPV (₹)
A, C, D	950,000	270,000
A, B	850,000	250,000
B, C, D	900,000	220,000

It may be noted that other combinations of these projects, are either not feasible (because the total outlay is more than ₹1,000,000) or are not good enough (because do not utilize the total funds of ₹1,000,000). For Illustration, a combination of A, B, and C is not feasible because the total outlay is ₹1,150,000, which is more than the available funds of ₹1,000,000; a combination of A and C is not good enough because the outlay is ₹750,000 which leaves a sum of ₹250,000.

Of the three feasible combinations as given above, the combination of A, C, and D has the maximum NPV of ₹270,000. It may be noted that the other project B (although with an NPV of ₹100,000) has been left out because the combined NPV of C and D is more than the NPV of B. Therefore, the firm should adopt the combination of A, C, and D.

However, if the firm is dealing with mutually exclusive projects, then it should be noted that in no combination there should be any two mutually exclusive projects. For instance, in the above case, if projects B and C are mutually exclusive, then combination B, C, and D (outlay ₹900,000 and NPV ₹220,000) also becomes not feasible and the firm will have to select only out of two combinations, that is, A, C, and D and A and B.

The feasible set approach thus can be summarized as follows:

1. Find out all the feasible combinations of different projects in the light of the capital funds constraints and project's independence.
2. Find out the total NPV of each of these combinations and arrange these combinations in order of decreasing NPVs.
3. Select the combinations with the highest NPV.

The above process of feasibility set approach can be easily applied if the number of available projects is limited to, say, five or six only. However, if the number of available projects is more, then help of mathematical techniques may be taken. Thus, the above feasibility set approach (based on the NPV technique) helps selecting those projects, which will result in maximum contribution to the wealth of the shareholders. However, in capital rationing, it may not always be so. The firm will select the projects with higher NPVs but higher NPVs also involve higher outlay, and hence using up most of the scarce capital. What is needed in such a situation is, therefore, some sort of relative measure of profitability.

Incremental Outlay Analysis

In case, the firm wants to select the projects on the basis of their profitability, then the above feasibility set approach may not be of much relevance. In such a situation, the incremental outlay analysis based on the IRR technique may be adopted.

In this approach, the following steps are required.

Step 1

Find out the IRR of the individual projects and arrange them in descending order of their IRR.

Step 2

Then proceed to select all projects from the highest IRR down, until the funds are exhausted or the IRR of the project is less than the cut-off rate.

Illustration 11. A firm is considering the following six projects for implementation and it has a total capital outlay of ₹2,000,000 only.

Project	Capital Outlay (₹)	IRR (%)	Cumulative Outlay
1	700,000	20	700,000
2	500,000	19	1,200,000
3	600,000	18	1,800,000
4	350,000	17	2,150,000
5	200,000	16	2,350,000
6	750,000	12	3,100,000

Suppose the firm has a cut-off rate of 15%, then projects 1, 3, 5, 2, and 4 are eligible. Project 6, which is giving an IRR of 12%, is not eligible as the cut-off rate is higher. Further, if the firm has unlimited funds, then it may undertake all these five projects (with an IRR > 15%). However, as the capital budget of the firm is restricted to ₹2,000,000 only, the firm should start from the top and should select projects 1, 2, and 3 requiring total capital outlay of ₹1,800,000. The firm still has a balance of ₹200,000 for investment purposes, but the next project in the order, that is, project 4 requires a capital outlay of ₹350,000. So, the firm cannot undertake the project 4.

At this stage, the firm has two options:

1. To keep ₹200,000 for investment during next year, or
2. To go down the list and find out a project, which requires an outlay of ₹200,000 or less and also with the IRR of 15% or more. In the list given above, the next project is number 4, which requires a capital outlay of ₹200,000 and is also eligible as the IRR is 16%. Thus, the projects to be selected by the firm are projects 1, 3, 5, and 4. The total outlay for these projects is ₹2,000,000.

Test Yourself

1. What is capital rationing? Also classify capital rationing.
2. How does decision process get affected due to capital rationing?

The main shortcoming of this incremental outlay analysis is that it may not give the best solution to the capital budgeting situation. The reason being that a firm strives for maximization of shareholders' wealth, but the above procedure ignores it. A firm should select the projects in such a way so as to maximize the NPV rather than in order of IRR.

Profitability Index

The PI is yet another way of ranking different projects on the basis of the return per rupee invested in the project. In the previous section, the PI has been defined as the ratio of PV of cash inflows to PV of cash outflows of a project. Under this method, the PI of different projects may be calculated and placed in order.

The firm may start from the top and go on accepting the projects subject to that:

1. Funds are available.
2. The PI is more than 1. In a true sense, the PI is not a measure of yield in itself, but it can definitely be used to give the appropriate ranking for projects, which will then be selected to maximize the NPV.

Illustration 12 will explain the use and suitability of all these three techniques of dealing with the capital rationing.

Illustration 12. ABC Ltd has a capital budget of ₹2,000,000 for the year 1999. It has the following six projects for which the necessary information is provided here.

Project	Outlay (₹)	NPV (₹)	IRR (%)
A	700,000	300,000	20.0
B	250,000	160,000	17.0
C	500,000	200,000	19.0
D	200,000	100,000	17.5
E	550,000	450,000	18.0
F	750,000	−250,000	12.0

Find out the ranking of the projects, given that

(i) the projects are indivisible, and
(ii) the projects are divisible.

Also evaluate the ranking and make a final selection.

Solution

Project	Outlay (₹) (1)	NPV (₹) (2)	Inflow (1+2)	PI = Inflow/outlay	IRR
A	700,000	300,000(2)	1,000,000	1.428(4)	20%(1)
B	250,000	160,000(4)	410,000	1.640(2)	17%(5)
C	500,000	200,000(3)	700,000	1.400(5)	19%(2)
D	200,000	100,000(5)	300,000	1.500(3)	17.5%(4)
E	550,000	450,000(1)	1,000,000	1.818(1)	18%(3)
F	750,000	−250,000(0)	500,000	0.667(0)	12%(0)

Note: The integers in the brackets denote the ranking of different projects as per different methods.

It may be noted from the above that different techniques have been given different ranking in different projects. The project F has not been assigned any ranking because it has a negative NPV and its PI is also less than 1. Now, the firm has to select out of these projects so that the total capital outlay is within the budget constraint of ₹2,000,000.

When the Projects Are Indivisible

As already explained, the indivisible projects are those, which can be taken up in totality, and the part acceptance is not possible. Further after selecting a few projects in a particular order, if the firm does not have sufficient funds to take up the next project then in such a situation, the firm can move on to the next project if it can be taken up within the remaining available funds. The selection of different projects subject to capital rationing of ₹2,000,000 has been presented as follows:

	Feasibility Set (based on NPV)	Incremental Outlay (based on IRR)	PI
Project selected	E, A, C, B	A, C, E, D	E, B, D, A
Total outlay	₹2,000,000	₹1,950,000	₹1,700,000
Total NPV	1,110,000	1,050,000	1,010,000

The firm should select the projects on the basis of feasibility set approach because it results in the selection of those projects which are expected to bring maximum contribution to the wealth, that is, ₹1,110,000.

When the Projects Are Divisible

In this case, the firm should invest full budgeted amount of ₹2,000,000 and should take up the projects even in parts.

It is however implied that

1. a fraction of a part can be undertaken, and
2. the relationship between the capital outlay and the NPV is linear.

Illustration 13. If 30% of a project is undertaken, then the NPV generated by part implementation will be 30% of the total NPV of that project.

Feasibility Set Approach

Project	Outlay (₹)	Cumulative Outlay	NPV (₹)
E	550,000	550,000	450,000
A	700,000	1,250,000	300,000
C	500,000	1,750,000	200,000
B	250,000	2,000,000	160,000
Total			**1,110,000**

Incremental Outlay Approach

Project	Outlay (₹)	Cumulative Outlay	NPV (₹)
E	700,000	700,000	300,000
A	500,000	1,200,000	200,000
C	550,000	1,750,000	450,000
B	200,000	1,950,000	100,000
		2,000,000	32,000
Total			**1,082,000**

PI Approach

Project	Outlay (₹)	Cumulative Outlay	NPV (₹)
E	550,000	550,000	450,000
B	250,000	800,000	160,000
D	200,000	1,010,000	100,000
A	700,000	1,700,000	30,000
C (300/500)	300,000	2,000,000	120,000
Total		550,000	**1,130,000**

Thus, if the projects are divisible, then the firm can achieve the highest NPV of ₹1,130,000 by selecting projects as per the PI approach.

To conclude the discussion on capital budgeting, we can say that, if the projects before the firm exceed the limits of the funds available, which is fairly a common condition, the issue of capital rationing arises. This forces choosing among projects that might all be acceptable, if the funds were unlimited. The capital budgeting criteria have to rank these projects in terms of relative desirability. If the firm faces capital rationing in the current period only, then the use of ranking technique depends on whether the projects are divisible or not.

In case of divisible projects, the best results are given by the PI technique. But in case of indivisible projects, the PI may not be used. In such a case, the optimum solution can only be obtained by considering the projects as per the feasibility set approach.

Essentially, the firms should choose that group of projects within the budget limit which will generate the highest aggregate NPV. The projects can be ranked in declining order of their PI until the budgeted amount has been exhausted. The firm should maximize the PV benefits expected per rupee of investment.

SUMMARY

1. Every investment/project involves cash flows. Each project has to be evaluated by cash flow.
2. NPV, IRR, and PI are the discounted cash flow criteria for evaluating the value of an investment.

3. NPV is a process of calculating the PV of the project's cash flow, using the cost of capital as the discount rate and finding out the NPV by subtracting the initial investment from the PV of cash flows.

4. The project which has positive NPV is accepted. This is believed that the market value of share is expected to be increased by the project's positive NPV.

5. IRR is that discount rate at which project has NPV equal to zero. As per this approach, the project whose IRR is greater than the cost of capital is accepted.

6. PI is the ratio of the PV of cash inflows to initial outlay. The project should be accepted when it has PI greater than one.

7. In case of mutually exclusive projects, NPV method should be preferred over PI as it is consistent with wealth maximization.

8. Payback period is the number of years required to recover the initial cash outlay of a project. This approach does not take into consideration the time value of money and cash flows after the payback period. To overcome this problem, discounted payback period is considered.

9. ARR is calculated by dividing average net profit after tax by average amount of investment. The project has to be selected if ARR is greater than the cost of capital.

KEY TERMS

- Accounting rate of return
- Capital budgeting
- Cost of capital
- Incremental approach
- Mutually exclusive events
- Payback period
- Replacement decision

- Benefit-cost ratio
- Capital rationing
- Discounted payback
- Internal rate of return
- Net present value
- Profitability index
- Time value of money

Learning Outcomes

The student would have been exposed to NPV and IRR and the calculation of various inputs required for capital budgeting.

SOLVED PROBLEMS

1. The initial investment required for a project is ₹20 lakhs. The project manager projected the following annual cash flows that is expected to be generated uniformly over the years:

Year	0	1	2	3	4	5	6
Cash Flow (₹ in lakhs)	(20)	4	5	5	5	4	7

What is the payback period of the project?

Solution: Here, the amount of cash generated for the first 4 years is ₹19 lakhs against an investment of ₹20 lakhs. This amount can be recovered by the first quarter of the fifth year assuming that the cash flows occur uniformly.

$$\text{Hence, the payback period} = 4 + 0.25 = 4.25 \text{ years.}$$

2. A project has a life of 3 years and requires an initial investment of ₹210,000. It is expected to generate profit after taxes of ₹30,000 in the first year, ₹45,000 in the second year, and ₹75,000 in the third year. What is the ARR of the project?

Solution: Average annual income = (30,000 + 45,000 + 75,000)/3 = ₹50,000

$$\text{Average net book value of investment} = (210,000 + 0)/2 = ₹105,000$$

$$\text{ARR} = (50,000/105,000) \times 100 = 47.62\%$$

3. Hindustan Ferro Alloys (HFA) is planning to set up a new plant in West Bengal with an initial investment of ₹45 lakhs. The project has a life of 5 years and the cash flows associated with the project are as follows:

(₹ in lakhs)

Year	1	2	3	4	5
Cash Inflows	11.00	13.50	15.50	13.00	16.50

If the cost of capital relevant for the project is 14%, what is the NPV of this project?

Solution:

$$\text{NPV} = -45 + \frac{11.10}{1.14} + \frac{13.50}{(1.14)^2} + \frac{15.15}{(1.14)^3} + \frac{13.00}{(1.14)^4} + \frac{16.50}{(1.14)^4}$$
$$= -45 + 9.65 + 10.39 + 10.46 + 7.70 + 8.57$$
$$= ₹1.77 \text{ lacs.}$$

4. Shyam Pharma is planning to start a formulations unit. The initial investment required for the project is ₹70 crore. The project has a life of 5 years. The expected cash inflows from the project is

Year	1	2	3	4	5
Cash Inflows (₹ in crore)	18.0	20.0	28.0	23.0	26.0

What is the IRR of the project?

Solution: Let the IRR be r

$$70 = \frac{18}{(1+r)} + \frac{20}{(1+r)^2} + \frac{28}{(1+r)^3} + \frac{23}{(1+r)^4} + \frac{26}{(1+r)^6}$$

Using PVIF tables, at $r = 18\%$, the RHS = 69.89;
At $r = 17\%$, the RHS = 71.61.
The value (70) lies in between these two values

By interpolation, we obtain

$$\frac{r-17}{70-71.61} = \frac{18-17}{69.89-71.61}$$

$$\Rightarrow \quad r-17 = \frac{-1.61}{-1.72} = 0.936$$

$$\Rightarrow \quad r = 17.936\% \approx 17.94\%.$$

5. Mayur Synthetic Leathers Ltd (MSL) is considering investment in a machine. There are three machines offered by three different manufacturers. The information about the three machines is given below:

Manufacturers	A	B	C
Cost of machine (₹)	800,000	1,200,000	1,800,000
Annual cost of operations (₹)	160,000	120,000	100,000
Useful life (years)	5	8	10

If the cost of capital for the company is 15%, from which of these three suppliers should MSL purchase the machine?

Solution

Supplier A:

$$\text{Cost of the machine} = ₹800,000$$

$$\text{Annual cost of operation} = ₹160,000$$

The PV of the annual cost of operation $= ₹160,000 \times \text{PVIFA}\,(15\%, 5)$

$$= ₹160,000 \times 3.352 = ₹536,320$$

Hence, the PV of costs $= ₹800,000 + 536,320 = ₹1,336,320$

The annual capital change will be $= ₹\dfrac{13,36,320}{\text{PVIFA}(15\%,\ 5)} = \dfrac{13,36,320}{3.352} = ₹3,98,663$ (approx.)

Supplier B:

$$\text{Cost of the machine} = ₹1,200,000$$

$$\text{Annual cost of operation} = ₹120,000$$

The PV of the annual cost of operation $= ₹120,000 \times \text{PVIFA}\,(15\%, 8\ \text{years})$

$$= ₹120,000 \times 4.487 = ₹538,440$$

Hence, the PV of the cost $= ₹1,200,000 + ₹538,440 = ₹1,738,440$

The annual capital change will be $= \dfrac{17,38,440}{\text{PVIFA}(15\%,\ 8)} = \dfrac{17,38,440}{4,487} = ₹3,87,439$ (approx.)

Supplier C:

$$\text{Cost of the machine} = ₹1,800,000$$

$$\text{Annual cost of operation} = ₹100,000$$

$$\text{The PV of the annual cost of operations} = 100,000 \times \text{PVIFA (15\%, 10)}$$

$$= 100,000 \times 5.019 = ₹501,900$$

$$\text{Hence, the present value of costs} = 1,800,000 + 501,900 = 2,301,900$$

$$\text{The annual capital change} = \frac{23,01,900}{\text{PVIFA}(15\%, 10)} = \frac{23,01,900}{5,019} = ₹4,58,637 \text{ (approx.)}$$

The annual capital charge is least for the machine manufactured by supplier B. Hence, machine should be purchased from B.

ASSESS YOURSELF

1. What is capital budgeting decision? How is it significant for a firm?
2. Explain various approaches to capital budgeting technique.
3. What is discounted payback period? Why is it better than the payback method?
4. What are mutually exclusive projects? Explain the conditions when conflicting ranking would be given by the NPV and IRR.
5. Why is NPV a better technique than payback method?
6. What is PI? Discuss its limitation.

STUDENT ACTIVITY

Student should undertake a project of finding out NPV and IRR in case of select startups.

CASE STUDY I

Following advice from an agent in Vietnam TNA have an opportunity to purchase a majority interest in a small local firm that manufactures equipment for the food processing and packaging industry. This firm has a factory in a convenient location close to the ports and transport routes and a loyal and hardworking workforce. Unfortunately, the factory has outdated equipment and a relatively high cost structure and the firm is increasingly falling behind its competitors. However, the Agent's advice may provide an opportunity for TNA to establish a production facility in the heart of Asia without the problems and lead time involved in developing a Greenfield facility.

Following further enquiries, TNA management determines that they could complete the takeover of the Vietnamese company that owns the factory for an investment of A$10 million, A$6 million of which would be to purchase 100% of the Vietnamese company and A$4 million in the form of capital equipment to replace some of the aging factory infrastructure.

If TNA proceeds with the takeover, they estimate that they can be operational by mid-2011. They further consider that the existing contracts from the Vietnamese company will provide underpinning revenue equivalent to A$200,000 per month at current exchange rates. They are also confident of rapidly gaining additional food processing and packaging business because of the superiority of their new equipment. Their estimates of the value of sales growth per annum in the Vietnamese market are shown in the following table.

Year

Year 1	Year 2	Year 3	Year 4	Year 5	Year 6
20%	30%	30%	20%	10%	5%

Total costs are assumed to be 60% of revenue in the first year and 50% of revenue for subsequent years. The exchange rate as on September 20, 2010 is 18,419 Vietnamese Dong per Australian dollar, and it is assumed that the inflation rate will be 4% higher in Vietnam than Australia for the first year, 3% p.a. higher for the next 2 years and 2% higher in each of the following 3 years. Based on the information provided and further research, answer the following questions:

Carry out a capital budget evaluation of the proposed takeover assuming a 5-years time frame and a residual value of A$200,000 for the capital equipment at the end of the 5 years. Assume that TNA uses a weighted average cost of capital of 10% in their financial evaluations. Does the takeover represent a good investment for TNA based on your evaluation? What would be the situation if the investment required was A$12 million?

Solution:

Amount in A$

Year	0	1	2	3	4	5	6
Investment outlay	1,000,000						
Revenue		2,400,000.0	2,880,000.0	3,744,000.0	4,867,200.0	5,840,640.0	6,424,704.0 6,745,939.2
Cost		1,440,000	1,728,000.0	1,872,000.0	2,433,600.0	2,920,320.0	3,212,352.0 3,372,969.6
Depreciation		Nil	Nil	Nil	Nil	Nil	Nil
Profit before tax		1,152,000	1,872,000	2,433,600	2,920,320	3,212,352	3,372,970
Tax		Nil	Nil	Nil	Nil	Nil	Nil
Profit after tax		1,152,000	1,872,000	2,433,600	2,920,320	3,212,352	3,372,970
Residual value of capital equipment							200,000
Cash flows		1,152,000	1,872,000	2,433,600	2,920,320	3,212,352	3,372,970

Note: As tax rate and depreciation rate are not given in the question, both are ignored in the question.

Cost of capital = 10%
As inflation rate is given, we are required to adjust the discount rate.

Year	Cash Flows	Inflation Adjusted Cash Flow	Discount Rate (10%) PVIF	PV of Cash Flows
0	(10,000,000)		1	
1	1,152,000	1,198,080	0.909	1,089,163.64
2	1,872,000	1,986,005	0.826	1,641,326.28
3	2,433,600	2,659,260	0.751	1,997,941.72
4	2,920,320	3,161,048	0.683	2,159,038.51
5	3,212,352	3,546,696	0.621	2,202,219.28
6	3,572,969.6	4,023,744	0.564	2,271,298.64

Total PV			**11,360,988.07**
Less initial investment			**10,000,000.00**
NPV			**1,360,988.07**
NPV at A$12, 000,000	**11,360,988.07**		
Total PV	**12,000,000**		
Less initial investment	**NPV**	**–639,011.931**	

CASE STUDY II

Sabyasachi PLC provides engineering and consultancy services to the oil and gas industry. Over the past few years, they have incurred an expenditure of ₹1 million researching and developing a new product, the "Techno sensor" for which they have registered a patent.

Techno sensor is a system which provides innovative wireless technology (as opposed to conventional cabling) to measure the pressure and temperature of oil and gas wells.

Sabyasachi has conducted market research which has indicated that the new product has an expected life of 5 years. Predicted sales are as follows:

	Year 1	Year 2	Year 3	Year 4	Year 5
No. of units	20	35	40	30	15

The company's Board of Directors wish to progress to the manufacture and sale of the Techno sensor system and are considering the following proposals:

Operations Director's Proposal—"In-House"

Sabyasachi will manufacture the Techno sensor system themselves. Sabyasachi has so far concentrated on providing engineering and consultancy services. Manufacturing would be a departure from the current activity.

The selling price per unit will be ₹200,000. Variable production costs are expected to be ₹125,000 per unit and product-specific fixed production costs (including depreciation) will be ₹800,000 per annum. Marketing costs are estimated to be ₹200,000 per annum.

Under this proposal, they will have to purchase plant and equipments costing ₹4 million. Sabyasachi intends to depreciate the plant and equipments using the straight-line method and based on an estimated residual value of ₹500,000 at the end of 5 years.

Financial Director's Proposal "Outsource"

Under this proposal, Sabyasachi will "outsource" the manufacturing and marketing of the Techno sensor system under license, but will retain the patent.

XY Technologies PLC is a multinational business which already provides similar, more conventional products to the global market, and they have offered to undertake the manufacture and marketing of the Techno sensor system.

With XY's presence, reputation, and existing customer base, annual sales volumes are estimated to be 25% higher than if Sabyasachi were to manufacture and market the system themselves. All costs would be borne by XY and they would retain any profits.

In return, XY Technologies PLC will make a royalty payment to Sabyasachi of ₹15,000 per unit sold.

Marketing Director's Proposal—"Sell Patent Rights"

Under this proposal, Sabyasachi will sell the patent rights to XY Technologies. This option would give XY the exclusive right to manufacture and market the Techno sensor system. XY have offered ₹2 million for the patent, and payment would be made in three installments; ₹1 million payable immediately and £500,000 payable at the end of year 1 and year 2.

Additional Information

The company has a current capitalization of ₹20 million equity (annual dividend=12%) and long-term corporate debenture debt of £10 million (annual post-tax interest cost=6%). The company does not anticipate any further finance requirement to progress the Techno sensor project.

Required

1. Prepare for the 5 years of the project, calculations for the annual earnings before interest, taxation, depreciation, and amortization (EBITDA) and a breakeven analysis, assuming that the operations director's proposal is progressed.
2. Prepare a capital investment appraisal analysis, which includes a consideration of the NPV of each of the three proposals.
3. Using the calculations and analysis in parts 1 and 2 together with any other information you consider relevant, prepare a short report for the senior management of Sabyasachi PLC, recommending one of the three proposals to progress with.

Solution: Capital budgeting decision is defined as a firm's decision to invest its current resources most efficiently in the fixed asset in anticipation of an expected flow of benefits over a series of years.

Capital Expenditure decisions are very crucial as they are irreversible in nature. Such decisions include expansion, diversification, modernization, replacement, and other decision. Under the given case, the company wants to manufacture Techno sensor system. Such investment decisions are very crucial because they influence the firm's growth in the long run. It will affect the risk profile of the firm. The company has already spent £1 million on research and other development expenditure. The company has three options available: manufacture, outsource, and sell patent. The company wants to evaluate which option is the best and the most deserving.

Break-even Point: The company also wants to know its break-even point in case if it goes for manufacturing of Techno sensor system. A break-even is that level of sales where company has recovered all its fixed cost. At this level, the company is at no profit or no loss situation. After this level, company starts enjoying the profit. Before BEP, company's total cost is greater than the total revenue. That is why the company is in the loss zone. After BEP, the company's total revenue is greater than the total cost and the profit is enjoyed by the company. For manufacturing decision, BEP analysis is very important. Outsourcing and selling patent option could require break-even analysis.

Break-even point = Fixed cost/contribution per unit

Selling Price Per Unit	200,000
Variable cost	125,000
Fixed cost with depreciation	800,000
Marketing expenses	200,000
Cost of plant & machinery	4,000,000
Residual value	500,000
Method of depreciation	Straight
No. of useful life	5
Equity capital	20,000,000
Debt	10,000,000
Total investment	30,000,000
Amount of depreciation	700,000
Weighted average cost of capital is taken as a discount factor	
WACC (calculated)	10%
Total investment	5,000,000
Fixed cost excluding depreciation	100,000

Break-even analysis

Contribution per unit	75,000
Fixed cost	4,000,000
BEP = Fixed cost/Contribution per unit	53
BEP point	53 units

It means after selling 53 units at £20,000 per unit, the company could easily recover £4,000,000. At 53 units level of sales, the company would be at no profit, no loss situation. BEP point is 53 units.

EBITDA analysis and NPV calculations

Particulars	Year 0	Year 1	Year 2	Year 3	Year 4	Year 5	Year 6
No. of units		20	35	40	30	15	
Selling price		4,000,000	7,000,000	8,000,000	6,000,000	3,000,000	
Less variable cost		2,500,000	4,375,000	5,000,000	3,750,000	1,875,000	
Contribution		1,500,000	2,625,000	3,000,000	2,250,000	1,125,000	
Less fixed expenses		100,000	100,000	100,000	100,000	100,000	
EBIT DA		1,400,000	2,525,000	2,900,000	2,150,000	1,025,000	
Depreciation		700,000	700,000	700,000	700,000	700,000	
Interest		600,000	600,000	600,000	600,000	600,000	
EBT		100,000	1,225,000	1,600,000	850,000	−275,000	
Tax not given		0	0	0	0	0	
PAT		100,000	1,225,000	1,600,000	850,000	−275,000	
Cash flows		800,000	1,925,000	2,300,000	1,550,000	425,000	
Salvage						500,000	
Total cash flow	−5,000,000	800,000	1,925,000	2,300,000	1,550,000	925,000	
Discount rate	10%	0.909	0.826	0.751	0.683	0.621	Total
NPV		727,272.7	1,590,909.1	1,728,024.0	1,058,670.9	574,352.2	5,679,228.9
						less	−5,000,000
						NPV	10,679,228.9

NPV Method: NPV is a technique to evaluate projects. The NPV is calculated after deducting initial investment from the total PV of future cash flow. The project with positive cash flow has to be accepted. The project with negative cash flow needs to be rejected. To calculate the NPV, we need to discount the future cash inflow at the required rate of return to find out the PV. In this case, discount rate is not given, and that is why weighted average cost of capital is taken as the required rate of return. Sabyasachi has equity capital and debt as a source of capital. Appropriate discount rate should be identified to discount the forecasted cash flows. The suitable discount rate is the project's opportunity cost of capital, which is equal to the required rate of return expected by the investment of equivalent risk. the PV of cash flow can be calculated using the required rate of return. NPV takes into consideration the time value of money. It is the true estimate of profitability. NPV method is consistent with shareholders' value maximization. The only one difficulty which could be faced is the estimation of cash flow with accuracy. The cost of equity is 12% and the cost of debt is 6%. WACC turns out to be 10%. After discounting cash flow at 10%, it is observed that the company enjoys positive NPV with £617,480.85.

Prepare a capital investment appraisal analysis which includes a consideration of the NPV of each of the three proposals.

Outsourcing

Particulars	Year 0	Year 1	Year 2	Year 3	Year 4	Year 5
No. of units		20	35	40	30	15
Increment 25%		5	8.75	10	7.5	3.75
New units		25	44	50	38	19
Royalty		375,000	656,250	750,000	562,500	281,250
Present value of cash flow	–1,000,000	375,000	656,250	750,000	562,500	281,250
NPV	914,163.41					

Selling out patent

Particulars	0	0	1	2	
Payments	–1,000,000	1,000,000	500,000	500,000	
PVIF	1	1	0.909	0.829	NPV
PV	–1,000,000	1,000,000	454,500	414,500	869,000

On comparison, it is evaluated that outsourcing is the most deserving proposal. Manufacturing has an NPV of 617,480.85. Outsourcing option has 914,163.41 NPV. Selling out patent gave only 869,000 as NPV. Therefore, on the basis of the NPV analysis, outsourcing is better. That is why the company Sabyasachi should outsource the manufacturing and marketing of the Techno sensor system a under license, but should retain the patent.

SUGGESTED READINGS

Brealey, R.A., & Myers, S.C. (2002). *Principles of corporate finance* (7th ed.). New York: McGraw-Hill.
Horne, J.C.V. (2002). *Financial management & policy* (12th ed.). Singapore: Pearson Education.
Ross, S.A., Westerfield, R.W., & Jordan, B.D. (2002). *Fundamentals of corporate finance* (6th ed.). New Delhi: Tata McGraw-Hill.

CHAPTER 11

Estimating Cash Flows

Learning Objectives

- To understand the difference between cash flow and profit.
- To explain the principle of incremental cash analysis.
- To show the effect of inflation in capital budgeting.

PRELUDE

Estimation of cash flow is a crucial component in capital budgeting decision. The cash flow may be defined as Net Profit + Depreciation. So, in determining cash flow there are various components to be considered. Read the following: Balrampur Chini Mills Ltd (BCML) has decided to set up a fully automated integrated sugar complex in Uttar Pradesh with an investment of ₹120 crores. Funding will be through debt and internal accruals in the ratio of 1:1. To be set up in Barabunki, the complex will have a capacity of 4,000 TCD, a 60 kl per day ethanol plan, a 16 MW cogeneration plant, and a bio compost manufacturing plant. In addition to the integrated complex, the company has plans to set up a distillery to produce ethanol at its Bhabnan unit. By the production of a variety of sugar-derived products, the company will be able to cushion flat sugar realization with surpluses from its ancillary business. The company is aiming at integration and product value addition. Balrampur Chini's byproduct, bagasse will be consumed by its two power plants, and molasses will be consumed by the ethanol plant. The BCML plans strategic investment or capital budgeting decisions as they are called. It has to estimate expected future cash inflows and outflows to take decision for accepting or rejecting the project.

In capital budgeting, the cost and benefits of a project are measured in terms of cash flows. The costs are denoted as cash *outflows*, whereas the benefits are denoted as cash inflows. Uncertainty and accounting ambiguities make estimation of cash flows little difficult. Events affecting capital investment decisions are changing very rapidly. It is difficult to anticipate those events and related changes. Cash flows are based on accounting assumptions, estimations, and allocations which make estimation of data little difficult. Wrong estimation of cash flow would produce wrong result for decision-making.

Cash Flow Versus Profit

Both discounted and non-discounted techniques of project appraisal depend on estimated cash flows. Cash flow is the difference between cash inflow and cash outflow. Cash flows gets interchangeable with profit. There is, however, difference between cash and profit. *First,* profit is measured on the basis of accrual concept. It means revenue is recognized when it is earned. It does not matter whether equivalent cash has been received or not. Similarly, expenses are recognized when it is incurred, whether actually paid. *Second,* for computation of profit only revenue expenditure is taken into account. Revenue expenditures are transferred to profit and loss account, whereas capital expenditure is capitalized as an asset. They are shown in the balance sheet at depreciated value. Calculation of profit excludes capital expenditure. *Third,* profit is calculated after taking into consideration non-cash expenses like depreciation, loss on sale of assets, and so on, whereas calculation of cash flows ignores non-cash expenses. *Fourth,* profit gets changed due to change in accounting policy. Change in inventory valuation method would cause change in profit. It is clear that profit does not focus on cash basis. The objective of finance manager is not to maximize profit, but to maximize the wealth of the shareholders which depends on the PV of future cash flow.

Relevant Cash Flows

Relevant cash flows mean those cash flows that will undergo a change if a project is undertaken. This implies that in capital budgeting decisions, the cash flows are measured in incremental terms, that is, only those cash flows are considered, that differ or occur as a result of undertaking or accepting the particular project. These refer to those cash flows, which can be associated and attributed to adoption of a particular project. Every investment involves a comparison of alternatives. The problem of choice will arise only if there are at least two possibilities. The minimum investment opportunity, which a company has, will be either to invest or not to invest in a project. Assume that the question before a company is to introduce a new product. The incremental cash flows in this case will be determined by comparing cash flows resulting with and without the introduction of the new product. If, for example, the company has to spend ₹50,000 initially to introduce the product, we are implicitly comparing cash outlay for introducing the product with a zero cash outlay of not introducing the product. **When the incremental cash flows for an investment are calculated by comparing with a hypothetical zero-cash-flow project, we call them *absolute cash flows*.** Assume that the question before a company is to invest either in project A or in project B. One way of analyzing can be to compute the absolute cash flows for each project and determine their respective NPVs. Then, by comparing their NPVs, a choice can be made. Alternatively, two projects can be compared directly. For example, we can subtract (algebraically) cash flows of project B from that of project A (or vice versa) to find out incremental cash flows (of project A *minus* project B). The positive difference in a particular period will tell how much more cash flow is generated by project A relative to project B. **The incremental cash flows found out by such comparison between two *real* alternatives can be called *relative cash flows*. NPV of this series of relative cash flows will be equal to NPV of the absolute cash flows from project A minus NPV of the absolute cash flows from project B.** Thus, NPV (A−B)=NPV (A) − NPV (B).

Principles of Incremental Cash Flow Analysis

The principle of relevant cash flows or incremental cash flows in capital budgeting analysis is critical. Any cash inflow or outflow that can be directly or indirectly traced to a project must be considered. First, we measure the cash flows as and when they occur and not when they accrue in an accounting sense. In other words, we measure actual cash flows and not accounting profits. Second, we always measure cash flows in post-tax terms. On the basis of this basic principle of relevance, the following principles emerge:

Incremental Overheads Versus Allocated Overheads

Generally, the budgeted overheads are allocated to projects including new projects under consideration. However, this approach is not correct. This is so because the general overheads will be incurred whether or not the project is undertaken. In other words, these overheads are not going to change as a result of the project. Such overheads should be ignored in computing the net cash flows of an investment. Only those overheads that change as result of the project are to be considered. Incremental cash flow rule suggests that only incremental overheads are relevant. Hence, incremental and not the allocated overheads are relevant in capital budgeting.

Opportunity Costs

Sometimes the firm may use some existing assets in a project that it already owns, and hence when the project is taken up there are no explicit and adequate cash outflows. However, as the principle of opportunity cost tells us that though there may not be any explicit cost for using these resources, the firm foregoes some potential benefits from these resources by allowing the usage of these resources in a particular project. These benefits foregone represent the opportunity cost of these resources and are relevant in decision-making. They have to be considered in incremental analysis.

Incidental Effects

All the incidental effects of the proposal should be considered for determining the relevant cash flows. For example, if a firm is considering setting up a project in a remote area, it has to provide for approach roads, housing facilities for the employees, medical facilities, schools, colleges, transportation, and so on. All the relevant expenses need to be considered as relevant cash outflows. The estimation of cash outflows for creating basic facilities for workforce is known as **contingent costs**. Similarly, if a firm is launching a new product, it should consider the effect of the new product on the demand for its existing products. For example, When TATA MOTORS launched a new version of Indigo, it had to take into account the effect of the new model on the demand for other models. It means launching of a new product in the same segmentation would erode the company's market share of its existing product. The cash flow estimation of the new product would have **cannibalization** effect with a loss of contribution of its existing product.

Sunk Costs

Sunk costs are the costs that have already been incurred in the past, whether we take up the project or not, they are not going to change. As they do not influence future decisions, they are considered to be irrelevant. They are unavoidable and irrecoverable historical costs. They should be ignored in investment analysis. As you would appreciate, these costs are irrelevant from the point of view of economic analysis of the project. For example, a construction firm had purchased a piece of land 2 years ago at ₹50 lakhs. Now the firm is considering two options—to construct a shopping mall on that land or to construct residential apartment. While conducting the financial analysis of the proposal, the cost of ₹50 lakhs that was incurred is irrelevant. As this cost has already been incurred and is not going to change whether the firm constructs a shopping mall or residential apartments, or nothing at all.

Financing Costs

In analyzing capital budgeting decisions, we do not consider the financing costs like interest, dividends, and so on. This is so because we are interested in the cash flows generated by the project. Financing cost paid to the capital/loan suppliers are a component of cash flow to the creditors and not a cash flow from the project. The objective of the project appraisal is to compare the cash flows from the project to the cost of acquiring that project. This does not mean that financing decisions are not important. Moreover, we do consider the rate of return required from a project in terms of the relevant cost of capital for that project.

Tax Incentive

There are tax and non-tax benefits available to a firm when it undergoes a project. For promoting projects in backward area, government provides interest-free non-refundable subsidy. In some specified backward areas, tax exemption and sales tax referral are also available. To encourage capital investment, the Income Tax Act provides three to rebate and investment allowance under section 80HH and 80I. The main objective of investment allowance is to encourage investment in fixed assets by companies.

Test Yourself

1. What is the difference between cash flow and profit?
2. Define the concept of incremental cash flow.
3. What is sunk cost? How is it treated for incremental cash analysis?

Components of Cash Flows

The cash flows associated with a project may be classified as

1. initial cash outflow (initial investment),
2. operating cash flows (annual cash inflows), and
3. terminal cash flow.

Computation of cash flows will depend on the nature of the project. Projects can be categorized into

1. single/new project,
2. replacement projects, and
3. mutually exclusive projects.

We will discuss components of cash flow for categories of capital projects given above.

Initial Cash Flow

All the capital projects require a substantial initial cash outflow before any future inflow is realized. In most of the capital budgeting projects, the initial cost of the project reflects the cash spent to acquire the asset. It comprises its cost and freight and installation expenses.

CASE I: SINGLE PROJECT/NEW PROJECT

In case of a new project, the calculation of outflow is quite easy. The cash outflow consists of the purchase price of the various assets used, plus the installation cost, plus the working capital. Thus, the initial cash outflow includes the cost of plant, transportation cost, installation cost, and any other incidental cost to bring the project in workable condition.

Another item that needs consideration to ascertain the initial cash outflow is the working capital required for the project, as the change in working capital affects the cash flows, it is important that the working capital requirement of every alternative project be analyzed and considered for the capital budgeting decision.

Almost every investment project requires an additional investment in all or any of the three main components of working capital. Although, every firm tries to keep its investment in working capital to the minimum level, yet the new project, if undertaken, would require the firm (i) to extend additional credit to its customers, (ii) to carry additional inventory to serve customer orders, and (iii) to enlarge its cash balance to meet its enlarged transactions. Generally speaking, the working capital requirement of a project will be a function of the expected growth in revenues and expenses from that project, although the exact linkage will vary from business to business. Thus, if the firm undertakes the projects, it requires additional working capital to support the operations of the project and therefore, this additional working capital required is the additional investment to be made in the project, and is thus included in the initial cash outflows of the project. However, it may be noted that the additional working capital is required only for the period equal to the life of the project. At the end of the project, this additional working capital being invested will be released and recaptured by the firm. Thus, the cash inflow for the last year of the life of the project would also include the working capital released by the project. Failure to consider the working capital needs in the capital budgeting decision may have two consequences, that is, (i) the cash flows will be overestimated, and (ii) even if the working capital is salvaged fully at the end of the project life, the NPV of the cash flows created by change of working capital will be negative and hence the capital budgeting decision may be taken wrongly.

CASE II: REPLACEMENT SITUATIONS

In case of replacement, an old machinery is replaced with the new one. As usually the old machine has a salvage value (SV), our outflows in the form of purchase price will be reduced. Cash outflow in a replacement situation consists of the cost of new project, installation cost, and working capital. The sales proceeds of existing machine are inflows hence deducted while calculating the cash outflows. The taxes/tax savings due to the sale of existing assets are adjusted accordingly.

CASE III: MUTUALLY EXCLUSIVE PROJECTS

Cash outflow in a mutually exclusive project is the same as that in case of replacement situation. Mutually exclusive means the selection of one project precludes the choice of the other project.

Calculation of Initial Cash Flow

- Land and side development
- Building
- Plant and machinery
- Duty and transportation
- Preliminary expenses
- Contingency
- Net working capital
- Misc. capital expenditure
- Total initial expenditure

Miscellaneous capital expenditure includes amount spent on water supply, electricity, fire fighting arrangements, and transportation facility. Preliminary expenses are those expenses that are incurred before the commencement of company and include commission, legal charges, and promotional expenses. Contingency are provided for delay in projects. Delay causes cost overrun in projects. Contingencies should not be associated with uncertainties in the estimation of cash flow.

Operating Cash Flows

The original investment cost or the initial cash outflow of the project is expected to generate a series of cash inflows in the form of cash profits contributed by the project. Cash flows should be estimated on after-tax basis. These cash inflows may be the same every year throughout the life of the project or may vary from one year to another. The timings of the inflows may also be different. The cash inflows mostly occur annually, but in some cases may occur half-yearly or biannually also. These cash inflows generated during the life of the project may also be called *operating cash flows. Net operating cash flows are computed. It is the difference between cash receipts and cash payments inclusive of taxes.* These are positive cash flows for most of the conventional revenue generating projects; however, in case of cost reduction projects these cash flows may be negative.

Sometimes, the project may require some subsequent cash outflows also in the form of periodic intensive repair, periodic shutting cost, and so on. All these cash inflows and outflows are to be considered for the capital budgeting decision. Similarly, if additional working capital is required by the project in any of the subsequent years, then it should be considered as outflow for that year. However, if the working capital is released in any of the subsequent years, then it should be considered as cash inflow for that year. It is important to recognize the timing of these subsequent cash inflows and outflows, as these are to be adjusted for the time value of money. The more quickly and earlier they occur, the more valuable these are.

CASE I: SINGLE PROJECT/NEW PROJECT

In case of a new project, the calculation of inflow is quite easy. We will take into consideration only the cash flows and compute the operating cash inflow as follows:

Cash Sales Revenue

- Less cash operating cost
- Cash inflows before depreciation and tax
- Less depreciation
- Taxable income
- Less tax
- Earnings after tax
- Plus depreciation
- Cash inflows after tax
- Plus SV in the nth year
- Plus recovery of working capital

CASE II: REPLACEMENT SITUATION AND MUTUALLY EXCLUSIVE PROJECTS

Cash inflow in mutually exclusive projects is same as that in case of replacement situation. Operating cash flows are adjusted for the following:

1. Depreciation and Taxes,
2. Net Working Capital, and
3. Additional Capital Expenditure (ACE).

Depreciation and Taxes

In computing the post-tax cash flows, we have seen depreciation (and other non-cash items are added back). Depreciation is an allocation of the cost of the asset. The assets were acquired at some cost and when that asset is used to generate revenues, correct matching of expenses and revenues requires that the cost of using the asset should also be considered. **The cost of asset usage is called depreciation. Depreciation does not require any cash outflow, however depreciation is a tax deductible expense. As a result, it helps in saving some taxes. The tax saving that result due to depreciation is called depreciation tax shield.**

$$\text{Depreciation tax shield} = \text{Tax rate} \times \text{Depreciation}$$

$$\text{Tax payable} = T\,(\text{Revenue} - \text{Expenses} - \text{Depreciation})$$

$$\text{Cash flow CF} = \text{Revenues (R)} - \text{Expense (E)} - \text{Tax payable (D)}$$

$$= R - E - T\,(R - E - D)$$

$$= R - E - T\,(R - E) + T * D$$

$$= (R - E)\,(1 - T) + T * D$$

$$= EBDIT\,(1 - T) + T * D$$

Consider an example

Particulars	Amount (₹)
Cash revenue	50,000
Less cash expenses	30,000
EBIDT	20,000
Less depreciation	5,000
EBIT	15,000
Less tax 40%	6,000
PAT	9,000
Add depreciation	14,000

Operating cash flow can be calculated in the following way:

$$CF = Revenues - Expense - Tax\ payable$$

$$= R - E - T(R - E - D)$$

$$= 50,000 - 30,000 - 0.40(50,000 - 30,000 - 5,000)$$

$$= 50,000 - 30,000 - 0.40(50,000 - 30,000) + 0.40 \times 5,000$$

$$= (50,000 - 30,000)(1 - 0.40) + 0.40 \times 5,000$$

$$= 12,000 + 2,000$$

$$= ₹14,000$$

Depreciation tax shield $= Tax \times Amount\ of\ depreciation = 0.40 \times 5,000 = ₹2,500$.

Net Working Capital

In addition to cash inflows that occur periodically, there may be cash outflows on account of requirements of the net working capital during the life of the project. Such changes in net working capital should be considered in computing the net cash inflows. Any increase in net working capital from one period to the next implies a cash outflow, whereas a decline in net working capital from one period to the next implies a cash inflow. Change in working capital could be because of following three situations.

Change in Accounts Receivables: Credit sales would overstate the cash inflow. To nullify the effect, increase in receivables should be subtracted from revenues for calculating actual cash payments.

Change in Inventory: Purchase of raw material on credit would increase the level of inventory in store. Payment has not been yet paid. Therefore, expenses understate the actual cash payment. That is why, increase in inventory should be added to expenses for calculating cash payments.

Change in Accounts Payable: The firm will delay the payment of material. This would cause increase in accounts payable. The value of inventory equivalent to increase in accounts payable has already been added to expenses. Thus, increase in accounts payable should be subtracted from expenses for computation of cash flows.

Change in working capital components should be taken during computation of working capital. Instead of taking them individually, we can adjust change in net working capital. Increase in net working capital should be subtracted, and the decrease added to after-tax operating profit.

Operating cash flow = EBDIT (1 − tax) + Depreciation − Net working capital

Additional Capital Expenditure (ACE)

In addition to the initial cash outflow in long-term assets at the start of the project, the project may need additional capital investment. Such ACEs are cash outflows taking place in later years and have to be taken into account while computing the net cash flow during the life of the project.

Operating cash flow = EBDIT (1 − T) + Depreciation − NWC − ACE,

where EBDIT is the earnings before depreciation and tax. NWC is the net working capital, ACE is the additional capital expenditure, and *T* is the tax rate.

Terminal Cash Inflows

The cash inflows in the last year, which are in addition to annual cash inflows, are called terminal cash flows. Two common terminal cash inflows may occur in the last year. First, as already noted, the estimated salvage or scrap value of the project realizable at the end of the economic life of the project or at the time of its termination is the cash inflow for the last year. Second, as already noted, the working capital that was invested in the beginning will no longer be required as the project is being terminated. This working capital released will be available back to the firm and is considered as a terminal cash inflow. Terminal value of a new product depends on cash flow which could be generated beyond the assumed horizon. The firm makes an assumption about the growth rate after the horizon period. The following formula is used:

$$\text{Terminal Value} = \frac{\text{Operating cash flow}_n (1+g)}{k-g}$$

SV

SV may be defined as the residual price of an asset realized at the time of its termination. These cash proceeds are treated as cash inflows in the last year. In case of replacement decisions, in addition to the SV of the new investment, the SV of the existing investment now and at the end of its economic life are also to be considered. This is so because if the existing asset is sold now it would result in increased cash inflow in the present, thereby reducing the net investment in the new investment. However, this would also mean reduced cash inflow in future, as the existing asset will no longer be there to realize its SV.

Tax Effect of SV

SV is the residual market price of an asset at the time of its sale. A company will incur a loss if an asset is sold for a price less than the asset's depreciated book value. Similarly, the company will make a profit if the asset's SV is more than its book value. The profit on the sale of an asset may be divided into ordinary income and capital gain. **Capital gain is equal to SV minus the original value of the asset, and ordinary income is equal to the original value minus the book value of the asset. Capital gains are generally taxed at a rate lower than the ordinary income.** Assuming tax implications of the sale of an asset, the net proceeds can be calculated as follows:

1. SV < BV: LOSS

$$\text{Net proceeds} = \text{Salvage value} + \text{Tax credit on loss}$$

$$\text{Net proceeds} = SV + T(SV - BV)$$

2. SV > BV, but SV < OV: Ordinary profit

$$\text{Net proceeds} = \text{Salvage value} - \text{Tax on profit}$$

$$\text{Net proceeds} = SV - T(SV - BV)$$

3. SV > OV: Ordinary profit and capital gain

$$\text{Net proceeds} = \text{Salvage value} - \text{Tax on ordinary profit} - \text{Tax on capital gain}$$

$$\text{Net proceeds} = SV - T(OV - BV) - Tc(SV - OV)$$

where SV is the salvage value; BV is the book value; OV is the original value; T is the ordinary income tax rate; and Tc is the capital gain tax rate.

Test Yourself

1. How is depreciation treated for the calculation of working capital?
2. What is terminal value? How is it treated for estimation of cash flow?
3. What is the effect of change in working capital on the calculation of cash flow? Explain.

Release of Net Working Capital

The changes in net working capital taking place during the life of the project are considered while computing the net operating cash flows during the life of the project. When the project comes to an end, the working capital that was tied up in the project is assumed to be fully released at its face value.

Investment Decision under Inflation

Capital budgeting decision would not depict the real purchasing power picture if inflation is not properly incorporated in cash flow estimation and analysis. Cash should be adjusted for the inflation rate. Inflation is rise in prices of commodities. Discount rate used in capital budgeting decision is nominal rate. Nominal rate under inflation is calculated as per the following formula:

$$\text{Nominal discount rate} = (1 + \text{Real discount rate})(1 + \text{Inflation rate}) - 1.$$

SUMMARY

1. Estimation of cash flow is a crucial step in capital budgeting decisions.
2. For the estimation of cash flow, profit is not taken into consideration. Rather cash flow is preferred. Profit is the difference between income earned and expenses incurred. Profit calculation also makes a difference between the capital and revenue expenditure. Cash flow is the difference between cash received and cash paid.
3. Cash flow is estimated on the basis of incremental cash basis, which could be calculated by comparing alternative investment projects.

4. The three components of cash flow are initial investment, annual operating cash flow, and terminal value.

5. Initial investment includes original cost of investment and any increase in the working capital. In case of replacement decisions, after-tax SV of old assets is required to be subtracted from the initial investment.

6. Annual operating cash flows is the difference between cash inflow and cash outflow. The difference is duly adjusted for tax and tax shield on depreciation.

7. Net operation cash flow = $EBIT(1 - t) + t$ Depreciation

8. Cash flows are duly adjusted for change in the working capital and ACE.

9. Terminal cash flows occur in projects last year. It consists of after-tax SV of a project and release of the working capital.

10. Terminal value of a new product depends on cash flow that could be generated beyond the assumed horizon. The firm makes an assumption about the growth rate after the horizon period. The following formula is used:

$$\text{Terminal Value} = \frac{\text{Operating cash flow}_n(1+g)}{k-g}$$

11. Inflation: Capital budgeting decision would not depict the real purchasing power picture, if inflation is not properly incorporated in cash flow estimation and analysis.

12. Nominal rate under inflation is calculated as per the following formula: Nominal discount rate = $(1 + \text{Real discount rate})(1 + \text{Inflation rate}) - 1$

KEY TERMS

- Accrual
- Cannibalization
- Capital expenditure
- Contingency cost
- Incremental cash flow
- Mutually exclusive events
- Operating cash flow
- Profit
- Replacement decision
- Salvage value
- Tax shield on depreciation
- Allocated overhead
- Capital allowance
- Cash
- Depreciation
- Inflation
- Nominal discount rate
- Opportunity cost
- Relevant cash flow
- Revenue expenditure
- Sunk cost
- Terminal value

Learning Outcomes

Students would have got exposed to the concept of how cash flow is estimated for capital budgeting decision.

SOLVED EXAMPLES

1. Jaipur Golden Ltd is presently using a truck that has a book value of ₹6.50 lakhs. It is being depreciated on a straight line basis, and will be written-off over the next 6 years. Presently,

the SV of the truck is ₹300,000, and that after 6 years will be ₹50,000. The company is planning to replace the old truck with a new one that is improvised and more efficient. The new truck costs ₹14 lakhs. It will be depreciated on a straight line basis over the period of next 6 years and will be fully written-off at the end of the 6-year period. The new truck will have a SV of ₹350,000 at the end of the 6-year period. The savings in annual operating and maintenance costs will be ₹150,000. The income from the operations will increase by ₹250,000 per year. The cost of capital for the company is 12% and the tax rate applicable to it is 30%. Determine the cash flows related with the replacement decision, and advise whether the project should be accepted or not.

Solution: Cash flows associated with the replacement project:

Year	0	1	2	3	4	5	6
Net investment in a new truck[1]	(1,100,000)						
Savings in costs		150,000	150,000	150,000	150,000	150,000	150,000
Incremental income		250,000	250,000	250,000	250,000	250,000	250,000
Incremental depreciation[2]		75,000	75,000	75,000	75,000	75,000	75,000
Pre-tax profit (E: B+C−D)		325,000	325,000	325,000	325,000	325,000	325,000
Taxes		97,500	97,500	97,500	97,500	97,500	97,500
Post-tax profit		227,500	227,500	227,500	227,500	227,500	227,500
Initial flow	(1,100,000)						
Operating flow: G+D		302,500	302,500	302,500	302,500	302,500	302,500
Terminal flow[3]							300,000
Net cash flow: H+I+J	(1,100,000)	302,500	302,500	302,500	302,500	302,500	602,500

Working Notes

1. Net investment in a new truck = 14 − 3 = ₹11 lakhs
2. Existing depreciation (on the old truck) per year over the next 6 years

$$\frac{650,000-50,000}{6}=₹1,75,000$$

Depreciation on the new truck for each year over the next 6 years

$$\frac{14,00,000-3,50,000}{6}=₹1,75,000$$

∴ Incremental depreciation in each year = 175,000 − 100,000 = ₹75,000.

3. Terminal flow = Incremental SV

$$NPV=\sum\frac{CF_t}{(1+k)^t}-I$$

The NPV is positive. So, the investment in the new truck is justified.

2. JKJ Enterprises is considering a project which will entail the following revenues and expenses:

(₹ in crores)

Year	1	2	3	4	5
Sales	50	50	60	60	60
Operating cost	30	30	35	35	35
Depreciation	4	4	4	4	4
Interest on short-term bank loan	5	5	5	5	5
Interest on term loan	1.30	1.04	0.78	0.52	0.26

The tax rate applicable to the company is 30%. The project involves the following outlays:

(₹ in crores)

Plant and machinery	25.00
Working capital	46.25
Total outlay	71.25

The proposed scheme of financing is given below:

(₹ in crores)

Equity capital	30.00
Term loan	10.00
Short-term bank loan	31.25
Total financing	71.25

At the end of 5 years, the net SV of the current assets will be equal to their book value and the net SV of the fixed assets will be equal to ₹5 lakhs. The short-term bank loan will be repaid at the end of 5 years and the term loan will be repaid over the life of the project in equal installments. The cost of capital for the project is 19%.

(a) Derive the net cash flows relating to the long-term funds invested in the project.

(b) Appraise the project using the NPV criterion.

Solution: (a)

Year	0	1	2	3	4	5
Investment[1]	(40)					
Profit before tax[2]		11	11	16	16	16
Tax (30%)		(3.3)	(3.3)	(4.8)	(4.8)	(4.8)
Profit after tax		7.7	7.7	11.2	11.2	11.2
Net SV of fixed assets						5
Net SV of current assets						46.25
Repayment of short-term bank loan						(31.25)
Initial flow	(40)					
Operating flow (D+4)[3]		11.7	11.7	15.2	15.2	15.2
Terminal flow (E+F–G)						20
Net cash flow (H+I+J)	(40)	11.7	11.7	15.2	15.2	35.2

Working Notes

1. Investment = Total long-term funds invested in the project

   $$= \text{Equity capital} + \text{Term loan} = 30 + 10 = ₹40 \text{ lakhs}$$

2. Profit before tax (PBT) = Sales – Operating cost – Depreciation – Interest on short-term bank loan. Interest on term loan has been excluded from the calculation of PBT and profit after tax (PAT) because the post-tax cost of long-term funds that is used for discounting the net cash flows relating to long-term funds, includes the post-tax cost of term loan.

3. Operating Flow = PAT + Depreciation

   Depreciation = 4
   ∴ Operating flow = PAT + 4

   (b) Net Present Value (NPV) $= \sum_{t=0}^{t=5} \dfrac{CF_t}{(1+k)^t} - I$

   $$= \frac{11.7}{1.19} + \frac{11.7}{(1.19)} + \frac{15.2}{(1.19)^3} + \frac{15.2}{(1.19)^4} + \frac{35.2}{(1.19)^2} - 40 = ₹9.44 \text{ lakhs}$$

3. Your company is considering a machine that will cost ₹1,000 at Time 0, and which can be sold after 3 years for ₹100. To operate the machine, ₹200 must be invested at Time 0 in inventories; these funds will be recovered when the machine is retired at the end of Year 3. The machine will produce sales revenues of ₹900/year for 3 years; variable operating costs (excluding depreciation) will be 50% of sales. Operating cash inflows will begin 1 year from today (at Time 1). The machine will have depreciation expenses of ₹500, ₹300, and ₹200 in years 1, 2, and 3, respectively. The company has a 40% tax rate, enough taxable income from other assets to enable it to get a tax refund from this project if the project's income is negative, and a 10% cost of capital. Inflation is zero. What is the project's NPV?

Solution:

Particulars	0	1	2	3
Sales		900	900	900
Less costs (50%)		450	450	450
Less depreciation		500	300	200
EBIT		(50)	150	250
Less tax (40%)		20	60	100
PAT		(30)	90	150
Cash flow PAT+Depreciation		470	390	350
Cost	1,000			
Inventory	200			
SV				100
Tax on SV (40%)				(40)
Working capital recovered				200
Cash flow	(1,200)	470	390	610

$$\text{Total Present Value of Cash Inflow} = \frac{470}{1+10} + \frac{390}{(1.10)^2} + \frac{610}{(1+10)^3}$$
$$= 427.23 + 322.14 + 458.11 = 1,207.48$$

$$NPV = 1,207.48 - 1200 = ₹7.48$$

4. College Coffee and Pastry (CCP) is considering a proposal to electronically monitor and limit the time that customers use their wireless hotspot. It has been realized that stores are full with customers, but revenues are not growing due to students spending long periods of time using their computers while making minimal purchases. Other customers are complaining about not finding tables. New technology routers could be purchased and installed in each store at a cost of ₹25,000 each of the 200 stores. These routers are planned not only to monitor customer usage, but enable advertising to be displayed on computer screens. In addition, for the development of the routers, the vendor in year 0 will incur a depreciable cost of ₹8,000,000. The routers presently in place cost ₹300 each. The investment would be depreciated straight line over 5 years and this includes the development costs. The expected life is also 5 years with no SV. Service and support of the routers will be centralized in the corporate offices and is budgeted at ₹1,000,000 in year 0 with a 15% annual increase over the life of the project. Sales at present stores average ₹0.5 million per store with labor and materials averaging 40% of the revenues. Overhead including rent, management, and general maintenance is ₹250,000 per store and this is not expected to change with the new routers. It is expected that the use of the routers would increase revenues by 10% per year starting in year 1, especially as advertising will eventually be sold to be displayed on customer computers via the routers. Inventory, accounts receivable, and accounts payable should be ignored in this proposal. If the rate used for CCP investment proposals is 10% and the tax rate is 30%, should the 5-year router proposal be funded? State assumptions, if any.

Solution:

Each New Router Cost	₹25,000	Per Store
Present router cost	₹300	
No. of stores	200	
Router purchase cost	5,000,000	(25,000 200)
Design and testing	8,000,000	
Project length	5	Years
Depreciation	5	Years straight line
Amount of depreciation	8,000,000/5=1,600,000	
Service expense	1,000,000	Starting in year 0
Service expense growth	15%	Annually
Present sales	500,000	Annually per store
COGS	40%	Revenues
Overhead	250,000	Store
Sales increase	10%	
Tax rate	30%	
Discount rate	10%	

Cash Flow Estimation

Year	0	1	2	3	4	5
Sales	100,000,000	110,000,000	121,000,000	133,100,000	146,410,000	161,051,000
COGS	40,000,000	44,000,000	48,400,000	53,240,000	58,564,000	64,420,400
Gross profit	60,000,000	56,000,000	61,600,000	67,760,000	74,536,000	81,989,600
Service expenses	1,000,000	1,150,000	1,322,500	1,520,875	1,749,006.25	2,011,357.188
Overhead	50,000,000	50,000,000	50,000,000	50,000,000	50,000,000	50,000,000
Depreciation		1,600,000	1,600,000	1,600,000	1,600,000	1,600,000
Net profit before tax	9,000,000	3,250,000	8,677,500	14,639,125	21,186,993.75	28,378,242.81
Tax at 30%	2,700,000	975,000	2,603,250	4,391,737.5	6,356,098.125	8,513,472.844
PAT	6,300,000	2,275,000	6,074,250	10,247,387.5	14,830,895.63	19,864,769.97
Add depreciation		1,600,000	1,600,000	1,600,000	1,600,000	1,600,000
Cash flows	6,300,000	3,875,000	7,674,250	11,847,387.5	16,430,895.63	21,464,769.97
PV interest factor at 10%	1	0.909	0.826	0.751	0.683	0.620
PV of cash flow	6,300,000	3,522,727.273	6,342,355.372	8,901,117.581	11,222,522.8	13,327,933.37

Initial Investment

Cost of routers	5,000,000
Development cost	8,000,000
Total	**13,000,000**
Discounted value of cash flow	49,616,656.39
NPV	(36,616,656.39)

5. Acme R&D, LLC is considering a new product line, which will require an investment of ₹250,000 in the current year. Shown below is a worksheet that is to be used to evaluate the proposal where the interest rate used in proposals is 12%. The quantity sold is to be constant for all years and equal to the sales in year 1. Determine the present worth. Explain or show how you arrived at your answer. COGS are 66.67% of sales. General, sales, and administration expenses per year is ₹1,000,000. Depreciation up to seventh year is ₹36,000. Tax rate is 35%.

Particulars	Year 0	Year 1	Year 2	Year 3	Year 4	Year 5	Year 6	Year 7	Year 8	Year 9	Year 10
Quantity sold		100,000	100,000	100,000	100,000	100,000	100,000	100,000	100,000	100,000	100,000
Price per unit (₹)		50	47.5	45	43	41	39	37	35	33	32

Solution:

Earnings Forecast (? 000s)	0	1	2	3	4	5	6	7	8	9	10
Sales revenue		5,000	4,750	4,513	4,287	4,073	3,869	3,675	3,492	3,317	3,151
Cost of goods sold		(3,335)	(3,168)	(3,010)	(2,859)	(2,716)	(2,581)	(2,452)	(2,329)	(2,213)	(2,102)
Gross profit		1,665	1,582	1,503	1,428	1,356	1,288	1,224	1,163	1,105	1,049
General, sales, and admin.		(1,000)	(1,000)	(1,000)	(1,000)	(1,000)	(1,000)	(1,000)	(1,000)	(1,000)	(1,000)
Depreciation		(36)	(36)	(36)	(36)	(36)	(36)	(36)	0	0	0
Net operating income		629	546	467	392	320	253	188	163	105	49
Income tax @35%		(220)	(191)	(163)	(137)	(112)	(88)	(66)	(57)	(37)	(17)
Net income		409	355	304	255	208	164	122	106	68	32
Add depreciation		36	36	36	36	36	36	36	0	0	0
Cost of machine	(250)										
Cash flow	–250	445	391	339	290	244	200	158	106	68	32

Calculation of NPV

Year	Cash Inflow	PV at 12%	PV of Cash Inflow
1	445	0.893	397.10
2	391	0.797	311.41
3	339	0.712	241.46
4	290	0.636	184.55
5	244	0.567	138.45
6	200	0.507	101.29
7	158	0.452	71.50
8	106	0.404	42.72
9	68	0.361	24.52
10	32	0.322	10.33
Total PV			1,523.32
Initial investment			250
NPV			1,273.32
NPV			1,273,324

6. Project Z requires initial investment of ₹250,000 with no SV. The method of depreciation is the straight line method. Life of the project is 5 years. The tax rate is 40%. The cash flows are required to discount at 10%. Advise the company whether the project should be accepted: (a) when there is no inflation, (b) when there is inflation of 15%. The earnings are also expected to grow at 12%. The earnings before depreciation, interest, and tax are:

Year	1	2	3	4	5
EBDT	70,000	76,000	82,000	62,000	52,000

Solution:

(a) Determination of NPV when there is no inflation

Year	EBDT	Depreciation = 250,000/5	PBT	Tax	PAT	Cash Flow PAT + Dep	PVIF @10%	PV of CF
1	70,000	50,000	20,000	8,000	12,000	62,000	0.909	56,358
2	76,000	50,000	26,000	10,400	15,600	65,600	0.826	54,186
3	82,000	50,000	32,000	12,800	19,200	69,200	0.751	51,969
4	62,000	50,000	12,000	4,800	7,200	57,200	0.683	39,068
5	52,000	50,000	2,000	800	1,200	53,200	0.621	33,037
Total PV							234,618	
Less initial investment							250,000	
NPV								-15,382

(b) Determination of NPV when there is inflation @

Year	EBDT	Revised EBDT=EBDT $(1+r)^n$	Depre-ciation	PBT	Tax 40%	PAT	Cash Flow	Deflated Factor @15%	Real Cash Flow=Cash Flow * Deflated Factor
1	70,000	$70,000(1+0.15)=80,500$	50,000	30,500	12,200	18,300	68,300	$1/1.15=0.869$	59,352
2	76,000	$76,000(1+0.15)^2=100,510$	50,000	50,510	20,204	30,306	80,306	$1/(1.15)^2=0.756$	60,711
3	82,000	$82,000(1+0.15)^3=124,712$	50,000	74,712	29,885	44,827	94,827	$1/(1.15)^3=0.658$	62,396
4	62,000	$62,000(1+0.15)^4=108,438$	50,000	58,438	23,375	35,063	85,063	$1/(1.15)^4=0.572$	48,656
5	52,000	$52,000(1+0.15)^5=104,590$	50,000	54,590	21,836	32,754	82,754	$1/(1.15)^5=0.497$	41,129

Year	Real Cash Flow	PVIF @10%	PV of Real Cash Flow
1	59,352	0.909	53,952
2	60,711	0.826	50,147
3	62,396	0.751	46,860
4	48,656	0.683	33,232
5	41,129	0.621	25,540
Total PV			209,731
Less initial investment			250,000
NPV			–40,269

ASSESS YOURSELF

Concept Review and Critical Thinking Questions

1. What are different cash flows associated with a typical capital budgeting project? Discuss.
2. What is SV? How do we adjust the tax effect of tax value in capital budgeting situations?
3. Why depreciation is important in capital budgeting decisions? What is the tax effect of depreciation?
4. Discuss how the cash flow computations under a replacement decision are different from those for a single/new project.
5. What do you mean by the incremental cash flow analysis? Discuss the various principles of incremental cash flow analysis.

STUDENT ACTIVITY

Student should take a project in which approval, contingency cost, in a mutually exclusive events are incorporated with the help of instructor.

SUGGESTED READINGS

Brealey, R.A., & Myers, S.C. (2002). *Principles of corporate finance* (7th ed.). New York: McGraw-Hill.

Horne, J.C.V. (2002). *Financial management & policy* (12th ed.). Singapore: Pearson Education.

Mao, James C.T. (1969). *Quantitative analysis of financial decisions.* Macmillan.

Ross, S.A., Westerfield, R.W., & Jordan, B.D. (2002). *Fundamentals of corporate finance* (6th ed.). New Delhi: Tata McGraw-Hill.

CHAPTER 12

Risk Analysis in Capital Budgeting

Learning Objectives

- To discuss the concept of risk in capital budgeting decision.
- To learn sensitivity analysis (SA) and decision tree approach.

PRELUDE

Risk is omnipresent in all financial, investment, and operating decision. Capital budgeting is no exception to this. There are various sources of risk. These sources have to be tracked and ensured that they may be favorable to the organization. Not only are the sources important, but their treatments are equally important. Read on…

Paying a Price: TATA Nano[1]

If Tata Motors pulls out of Singur, it could cause the project cost to increase and therefore affect the company's ability to produce a low-cost car. But other factors have also changed in the external environment, points out John Paul MacDuffie, Wharton Management Professor and Co-director of its International Motor Vehicle Program. "A lot of things have happened to threaten the $2,500 price point," he says. "Commodity prices have been going through the roof and there are other cost increases that are going to affect everybody. The real question is: What cost increases are idiosyncratic and distinctive only to Tata that might erode any kind of advantage they have?" The current crisis will eventually show up in the cost of the car. But he says he wouldn't be surprised if Tata pulls out. "Of course, it will cost them to do that, but better to do it now than to be open to blackmail in the future. There will be a onetime relocation cost, but I'm sure he will find another state willing to take the project."

MacDuffie believes the new costs brought on by the Singur standoff could compel Tata to take a second look at its competitive edge in the domestic Indian market. "There may be some Maruti products at the low end of the market that will continue to be very strong price competitors because they have such high volume and they have long established facilities, which are probably all paid for in India," he says. These inputs highlight that all capital investment

---

[1] http://knowledge.wharton.upenn.edu/india/article.cfm?articleid=4318 (accessed on June 9, 2016).

decision has been affected by various extraneous and related variables. It is, therefore, to analyze their impact and incorporate risk factors into investment decision.

In the previous chapter, we discussed how the cash flows associated with a capital budgeting project are estimated. The cash flows from an investment are estimated when the project is evaluated; however, **the returns from the project are not known with certainty until the cash flows actually occur. This uncertainty is a primary determinant of a project's risk**. The suppliers of capital to a firm are ordinarily concerned with the riskiness of their capital, and management must therefore take risk into account in evaluation of capital budgeting projects.

In case the cash flows associated with a project are known with certainty, then the techniques such as NPV, IRR, or any other may be used to evaluate the desirability of the project. However, when the cash flows are not known with certainty, the risk associated with the project need to be ascertained.

For example, an investment requiring an initial outlay of ₹5 lakhs is expected to result in a cash inflow of ₹6 lakhs at the end of 1 year. In this case, there is no risk involved, as both the inflow and outflow are known with certainty. However, if the inflow at the end of 1 year may be ₹6 lakhs, or ₹7 lakhs, or ₹8 lakhs, or any other amount, then the project contains a risk element. Further, in the same case, if the project is expected to have the expected cash inflows of ₹2 lakhs at the end of year 1; ₹3 lakhs or ₹3.5 lakhs at the end of year 2; ₹1 lakh or ₹2.5 lakhs at the end of year 3, and ₹2.5 lakhs or ₹3 lakhs at the end of year 4. In this case, the cash flow of year 1 is known with certainty but of year 2, year 3, and year 4 are uncertain and any one cash flow may occur out of the two values available for that year.

Risk occurs because of uncertainty in predicting the right cash flow. Forecasting cannot be done with certainty, as future events on which they depend are uncertain. The problem arises because we cannot estimate probability of occurrence of future event with certainty. That is why, correct prediction of cash flow is vague. There are large numbers of events which can influence predictions. They are economic factors, industry-specific factors, and company-specific factors. "Risk is defined as variability that is likely to occur in future returns from investment. If a person invests in 9% fixed deposit of bank, such an investment is considered to be risk-free investment, whereas if the same investor goes for equity market, it is very difficult for him to predict the future returns. The greater the variability of expected returns, the riskier the capital investment.

Types and Sources of Risk

The various sources of risk in capital budgeting have been described in the following sections.

Project-specific Risk

This type of risk is project-specific, that is an individual project may have higher or lower cash flows than expected, either because of the wrong estimation or because of factors specific to that project. For example, BPL's investment in power projects that had long gestation periods, was riskier than its core line of business, that is, color televisions.

Competition Risk

Although a good project analysis might consider the reactions of the competitors, the actual actions taken by the competitors may be different from those expected.

Industry-specific Risk

The third type of risk is the industry-specific risk, that is, the risk that primarily affects the earnings and cash flows of a specific industry only. This risk may arise because of three factors. The first is **technology risk**, which reflects the effects of change in technologies, the second is **legal risk**, which reflects the effect of changing laws and regulation affecting a particular industry only and the third is the **commodity risk**, which reflects the effects of price changes in goods and services that are used or produced.

International Risk

This type of risk is faced when it takes on projects outside its domestic market. In such cases, the earnings and cash flows might be different from that expected owing to exchange rate movements or political changes. Some of this risk may be diversified by taking on projects in different countries, not all the currencies of which may move in the same direction. Multinational firms which hold projects in number of countries are able to diversify away this risk.

Market Risk

If risk arises by the factors that affect essentially all companies and all projects, of course in varying degrees. For example, changes in interest rate structure will affect the projects already taken as well as those yet to be taken, both directly through the discount rate and indirectly through cash flows. Other factors that affect all the projects may be inflation, economic conditions, and so on. Although the expected values of these entire variables may be considered in the capital budgeting analysis, changes in these variables will affect their values. Firms cannot diversify away this risk in the normal course of business, although may be considered to some extent only.

Assumptions

The discussion on capital budgeting under risky situations is based on the following assumptions:

1. There is no capital rationing.
2. The project's net investment is known with certainty.
3. The required rate of return of the firm is given and is indicative of the risk-return characteristics of the project.
4. The firm is basically risk-averse. This assumption is important, as it implies that the finance manager will not accept a risky project unless its expected profits are sufficient to compensate for the risk. The risk aversion also means that the additional risk will be accepted only if it results in disproportionately larger increase in expected returns.

Incorporating Risk in the Capital Budgeting Analysis

There are several techniques available to handle the risk perception of capital budgeting projects. These techniques can be grouped into two categories:

1. Conventional techniques.
2. Statistical techniques.

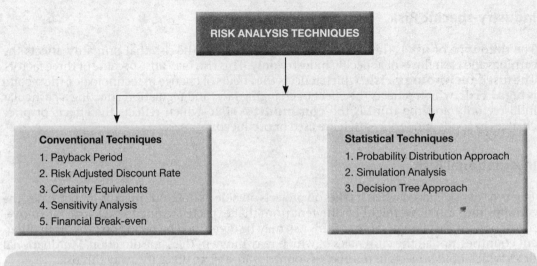

Conventional Techniques
1. Payback Period
2. Risk Adjusted Discount Rate
3. Certainty Equivalents
4. Sensitivity Analysis
5. Financial Break-even

Statistical Techniques
1. Probability Distribution Approach
2. Simulation Analysis
3. Decision Tree Approach

Test Yourself

1. What is risk? What are various sources of risk?

Conventional Techniques of Risk Analysis

These techniques are also known as traditional or non-mathematical techniques to evaluate risk. These approaches are simple and based on theoretical assumptions. Some of the conventional techniques are as follows:

Payback Period

The payback period is the time period in which the original investment in the project will be recovered by the firm from the cash inflows of the project. The payback period is then compared with the target payback period. If the project's payback period is less than or equal to the target payback period, it may be accepted, otherwise rejected.

The payback period approach to handle risk is simple and straightforward. But it fails to measure the risk, which may be of different degrees in different alternative projects. Moreover, it considers only that risk which arises due to time and provides no hedging against other types of risks. The payback period also ignores the time value of money as well as the cash flows arising after the payback period. At best, it can be considered as a crude measure of risk.

Risk-adjusted Discount Rate

The risk-adjusted rate in a capital budgeting decision process is a more direct method to take risk into consideration. It is based on the premise that riskiness of a project may be taken care of by adjusting the discount rate. The cash flows from a more risky project should be discounted at a relatively higher discount rate as compared to other projects the cash flows of which are less risky. The risk-adjusted discount rate may be expressed as follows:

$$k' = k_f + p$$

where k' is the risk-adjusted discount rate, k_f is the risk-free discount rate, and p is the risk premium.

Although in real world, there is no asset which may really be called totally risk free, however the free discount rate is the rate of return on the government securities which can be considered risk free for all practical purposes but for inflation-led erosion in value. As all the business projects have higher degree of risk as compared to zero degree of risk of government securities, the risk-adjusted discount rate is always greater than the risk-free rate. As the risk of a project increases, the risk adjustment premium also increases. The relationship between the risk-free rate, the risk premium, and the risk–return relationship has been explained in Figure 12.1.

FIGURE 12.1

RISK-FREE RATE, RISK PREMIUM, AND RISK–RETURN RELATIONSHIP

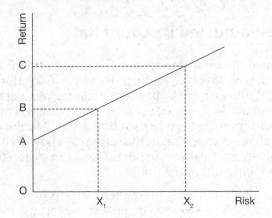

Source: Author.

Figure 12.1 reflects that if the risk of a project is zero, then the minimum required rate of return, that is, the discount rate will be just equal to the risk free rate, that is, OA. However, as the risk increases, say, up to X_1, then the required rate of return also increases from OA to OB. The component AB is known as the risk adjustment premium, Similarly, if the level of risk of a project is X, then the risk premium can be AC, and the discount rate for such project will be equal to OC. The risk premium being added to the risk-free rate reflects the greater risk attached to a project. As the risk increases, the risk premium also increases, therefore, the risk-adjusted discount rate also increases. If time preference for money is to be recognized by discounting estimated future cash flows at some risk-free rate to their PV, then, to allow for the riskiness of those future cash flows, a risk premium rate may be added to risk-free discount rate. Such composite discount rate is called as risk-adjusted discount rate.

This risk-adjusted discount rate can be used to find out the risk-adjusted NPV of the project as follows:

$$RANPV = \sum_{t=1}^{n} \frac{CFt}{(1+k')^t} - CF_0$$

RANPV = Risk Adjusted NPV

CF_t = Cash inflows Occurring at different point of time.

CF_0 = Initial Cash Outflow

k' = Risk Adjusted Discount Rate

It may be noted that the risk-adjusted discount rate approach for risk incorporation is the same as the NPV technique. The only difference is that the rate of discount used in this approach is higher. The risk-adjusted discount rate reflects the return that must be earned by a project to compensate the firm for undertaking the risk. The higher the risk of a project, the higher the risk adjusted discount rate would be and therefore the lower the NPV of a given set of cash flows.

The acceptance–rejection rule of the RANPV is the same as that of NPV, accept the project if the RANPV is positive or even zero, and reject the project if it is negative. In case of mutually exclusive projects, the project with the highest positive RANPV will be selected.

In case, the firm is applying the IRR technique for evaluation of capital budgeting projects, then the IRR of the project can be compared with the risk-adjusted discount rate to accept or reject the project.

Limitations of Risk-adjusted Discount Rate

Although the risk-adjusted discount rate approach considers the time value of money and explicitly incorporates the risk involved in the project by making the discount rate as a function of the project's risk, it suffers from the basic shortcoming relating to the determination of the risk adjustment premium. As discussed earlier, though CAPM is available to estimate the risk-adjusted discount rate, it suffers from its own limitations. Moreover, the risk-adjusted discount rate as explained above does not adjust the future cash flows, which are risky and uncertain. Assume that the investors are risk averse. But we have risk seekers too who do not demand additional premium for taking additional risk.

Illustration 1. A firm is considering investment in a project requiring investment of ₹500,000. The project has a life of 4 years. The project is expected to generate cash flows of ₹250,000, ₹200,000, ₹100,000, and ₹100,000 in respective 4 years. What is the risk-adjusted NPV of the project, if the project is considered to be risky and the firm considers a discount rate of 15% as appropriate to discount the cash flows?

Solution:

$$\text{RANPV} = \sum_{t=1}^{n} \frac{CFt}{(1+k')^t} - CF_0$$

$$\text{RANPV} = -500,000 + \frac{250,000}{(1.15)} + \frac{200,000}{(1.15)^2} + \frac{100,000}{(1.15)^3} + \frac{100,000}{(1.15)^4} = ₹-8,450$$

As the risk-adjusted NPV is negative, the project is unacceptable.

Certainty Equivalent Approach

In case of risk-adjusted discount rate approach as discussed hereinbefore, we incorporated the risk of the project by adjusting the rate used for discounting the future cash flows. An alternative approach to incorporate the risk is to adjust the cash flows of a project to reflect the riskiness. **The CE approach attempts at adjusting the future cash flows instead of adjusting the discount rates.** The expected future cash flows, which are taken as risky and uncertain, are converted into "equivalent certain cash flows" using some conversion factors. Intuitively, more risky cash flows will be adjusted lower than the less risky cash flows. These adjusted cash flows are then discounted at risk-free discount rate to find out the NPV of the project.

The conversion factors or "certainty equivalents," as they are called, reflect the proportion of the future cash flow a finance manager would be ready to accept now in exchange for the future cash flow. The conversion factors represent the level of present money at which the firm would be indifferent between accepting the present money or the future cash flow. For example, cash inflow of ₹10,000 is receivable after 2 years. However, if the inflow is available right now, the firm may be ready to accept even 75% of ₹10,000, that is, ₹7,500 only. This 75% or 0.75 is the certainty equivalent (CE) factor. For different years, the CE factors will be different to account for the timing as well as the varying degree of risk involved. It may be noted that higher the riskiness of a cash flow, the lower will be the CE factor. It may be noted that the value of the CE factors will vary between 0 and 1, and will vary inversely to risk. The greater the risk involved, the lower will be the value of CE factor.

Symbolically, the CE approach may be described as follows

$$RANPV = \sum_{t=1}^{n} \frac{\alpha_i CF_t}{(1+R_f)^t} - CF_0$$

where RANPV is the risk-adjusted NPV of the project, α_i is the CE factors for different years, CF_t is the expected cash flows for different years, and R_f is the risk-free discount rate.

Limitations

The CE approach explicitly recognizes the risk and incorporates it by deflating the cash flow to CE cash flows. This approach seems to be conceptually superior to the risk-adjusted discount rate and does not assume that risk increases over time at a constant rate. But the CE approach involves the determination of CE factors, which may turn out to be very subjective.

Illustration 2. Sultan Chand & Company is considering two mutually exclusive projects. The firm uses the CE approach to account for the riskiness of the projects. The expected cash flows and the associated CE factors for each project have been estimated as follows:

Year	Project A		Project B	
	Cash Flow (in ₹)	**CE Factor**	**Cash Flow (in ₹)**	**CE Factor**
0	−300,000	1.00	−400,000	1.00
1	150,000	0.95	250,000	0.90
2	150,000	0.85	200,000	0.80
3	100,000	0.70	150,000	0.70
4	100,000	0.65	100,000	0.60

Which project should the firm accept if the risk-free discount rate is 5%?

Solution:

The risk-adjusted NPV of the two projects using the CE approach can be calculated using the following formula:

$$RANPV = \sum_{t=1}^{n} \frac{\alpha_i CF_t}{(1+R_f)^t} - CF_0$$

RANPV of Project A

$$RANPV = 1.0(-300,000) + \frac{0.95(150,000)}{(1.05)} + \frac{0.85(150,000)}{(1.05)^2} + \frac{0.70(100,000)}{(1.05)^3} + \frac{0.65(100,000)}{(1.05)^4}$$

$$= -300,000 + 135,714.29 + 115,646.258 + 60,468.63 + 53,475.67$$

$$= ₹65,280$$

RANPV of Project B

$$RANPV = 1.0(-400,000) + \frac{0.90(2,500,000)}{(1.05)} + \frac{0.80(200,000)}{(1.05)^2} + \frac{0.70(150,000)}{(1.05)^3} + \frac{0.60(100,000)}{(1.05)^4}$$

$$= ₹99,420$$

As the risk-adjusted NPV of project B is greater than the risk-adjusted NPV of project A, project B should be selected.

Test Yourself

1. How does payback period incorporate the risk?
2. Discuss risk-adjusted discount rate.

Sensitivity Analysis (SA)

The NPV of a project depends upon the stream of cash flows and the discount rate used. Both these determinants in turn depend upon many variables such as sales revenue, input cost, competition, and so on. For a given level of all these variables, there will be a corresponding series of cash flows and some resulting NPV of the project. However, if any of these variables changes, then the NPV will also change. It means that the NPV is sensitive to all these variables. However, in most of the cases, the NPV will not change in the same proportion for a given change in any one of these variables. For some variables the NPV may be less sensitive, while for others the NPV may be more sensitive. **SA deals with the consideration of sensitivity of the NPV in relation to different variables contributing to the NPV.**

In general, the SA is a theoretical procedure whereby values of the input variables are changed to denote different situations or assumptions, and the effect of these changes is measured on the expected value of the outcome. When applied to the capital budgeting situations, the SA is a technique to evaluate the effect of changes in factors contributing to cash flows on the NPV of the project.

Till now we have used single point estimates of cash flows for evaluating capital budgeting proposals. **The "single point" estimates of cash flows or the expected results are based on the judgment of the analyst and the information available. In fact, these are the averages of the possible outcome, implicitly weighed by their respective probabilities.** However, in practice, it may not be possible to determine the point estimates for expected cash flows. So, instead of point estimates a range of expected levels of cash inflows and outflows can be used. By doing so, the consequences of expected fluctuations can be taken into consideration and thus the degree of risk can be estimated. The greater the fluctuations, the greater the risk. The following steps are required to apply the SA to capital budgeting projects:

1. Estimate the project cash flows.
2. Identify the variables, which have a bearing on the cash flows of a project. For example, some of these variables may be the selling price, cost of inputs, market share, market growth rate, and so on.
3. Establish the relationship, between these variables and the output value, that is, the effect of these variables on the value of NPV of the project.
4. Find out the range of variations and the most likely value of each of these variables.
5. Find out the effect of change in any of these variables on the value of NPV. This exercise should be performed for all the factors individually. For example, in case of a project involving the product sale, the effect of change in different variables such as number of units sold, selling price, discount rate, and so on, can be taken up on the NPV or IRR of the project. This information can be used in conjunction with the basic capital budgeting analysis to decide whether to take up the project.

Illustration 3. Quality Confectioners is evaluating an investment proposal. The proposal requires an investment of ₹12,000 and has a life of 4 years. It will generate cash inflows of ₹4,500. The required rate of return is 14%.

Analyze the sensitivity of different variables with respect to the NPV.

[Note: PVAF (14%, 4y)=2.9137 PVAF (14%, 3y)=2.3216]

Solution:
The NPV of the project is

$$NPV = -12,000 + 4,500 \times (2.9137)$$

$$= ₹1,112$$

Now, the sensitivity of different variables with respect to this value of NPV (₹1,112) may be analyzed as follows:

Sensitivity with Respect to Initial Outlay

As NPV is ₹1,112, the outlay can increase from ₹12,000 (present outlay) to ₹13,112 (i.e., ₹12,000+₹1,112) before the NPV becomes zero. Therefore, there is a margin of ₹1,112 or 9.4% of the initial outlay. Margin for Initial Outlay=(1,112/12,000)×100=9.4%.

Sensitivity with Respect to the Payback Period of the Project

Payback period when NPV is 0. The PVF at 14% is ₹12,000/4,500=2.667. From the PVF table, the values nearest to 2.667 in the 14% column are 2.322 (3 years) and 2.914 (4 years). Therefore, the payback period lies between 3 years and 4 years. The exact payback period by interpolating between 3 years and 4 years results in 3.58 years.

The life of the project is given as 4 years, whereas the payback period is 3.58 years. Therefore, the life of the project could fall by 42 months (4 – 3.58), before the project becomes unviable.

Sensitivity with Respect to Annual Cash Inflows

The PVAF (14%, 4Y)=2.9137

Therefore, 12,000=Annual inflows×2.9137

Annual inflows=4,118

Therefore, the annual cash inflows can decrease from the present level of ₹4,500 to ₹4,118 before the NPV becomes 0. So, the annual cash inflows have a margin of ₹382 (i.e., ₹4,500 – ₹4,118) or 8.5%, that is, 8.5% (382/4,500 × 100).

Sensitivity with Respect to Discount Rate

Say the discount rate, at which the NPV is 0, is x

$$\therefore ₹12,000 = 4,500x$$

$$\text{or } x = 2.667$$

The PVAF of 2.667 for 4 years period is approximately, found in 18% column in the PVAF table. Therefore, the discount rate can increase from the present level of 14% to 18% before the NPV becomes negative. Therefore, there is a margin of 4% (i.e., 18% – 14%) or 29% (i.e., 4/14 × 100).

It may be said that the project is most sensitive to the annual cash inflows and even a change of 8.5% in the cash inflows can make the project unviable.

Limitations of Sensitivity Analysis

1. It may be observed that the SA is neither a risk-measuring nor a risk-reducing technique. It does not provide any clear-cut decision rule.
2. Moreover, the study of effect of variations in one variable by keeping other variables constant may not be very effective as the variables may be interrelated. In practice, the variables are often related and move together, for example, the selling price and the expected sales volume are interrelated.
3. The analysis present results for a range of values, without providing any sense of the likelihood of these values occurring.
4. Another limitation of the SA is the subjective use of the analysis. The same SA which leads one decision maker to reject a project might lead some other to accept it and the preference may be traceable in the risk preferences of the decision-makers.

Nevertheless, SA helps in identifying the different variables having an effect on the NPV of a project. It helps in establishing the sensitivity or vulnerability of the project to a given variable and showing areas where additional analysis may be undertaken before a project is finally selected. The final decision on whether to take up the project will be based on the regular capital budgeting analysis and the information generated by the SA.

Break-even Analysis

In SA, we are trying to figure out the effect of changes in various variables on the NPV of the project. Instead, we can also find out when the project is profitable and when it becomes unprofitable if the inputs change. In other words, we can determine when the project breaks even. A capital budgeting project may be analyzed as to how much revenue will be needed for a project to break even in financial terms, that is, to make the net PV equal to zero.

The financial break even is computed by first estimating the annual cash flows needed to make the net PV zero, then ascertaining the revenues needed to generate this annual cash flow, and finally estimating the number of units that have to be sold to create this revenue (Figure 12.2).

FIGURE 12.2
FINANCIAL BREAK-EVEN

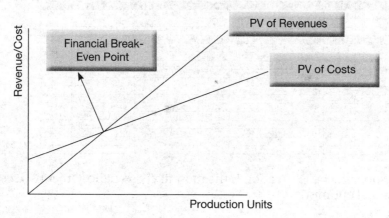

Source: Author.

Scenario Analysis

SA assumes that variables under study are independent of each other. But it is not true. Variables depend on each other and change in combination also. The other way to incorporate risk in the analysis of the project is **to analyze the combination of various alternatives. It is scenario analysis**. We can have pessimistic and optimistic kinds of situations where sales units, selling price per unit, cost of goods sold, and expenses could vary together. Let us understand this example.

Illustration 4. Mary field R&D, LLC is considering a new product line which will require an investment of ₹250,000 in the current year. Following is a worksheet that was created to evaluate the proposal. Forecasts for four critical estimates were collected for three scenarios, and are given in the table. Perform an analysis and make recommendations to the management concerning the new product line?

Scenario	Year 1 Quantity Sold	Annual % Increase in Quantity Sold	Starting Year 1 Price	COGS % of Revenue
Most likely	175,000	9	₹50	70
Pessimistic	100,000	1	₹38	72
Optimistic "Rosy"	300,000	14	₹70	65

Additional Information:

- Additional expenses are 1,000,000 each year.
- Depreciation is charged on the straight line method. It is required to be calculated for 7 years.
- Tax rate applicable is 35%.

Solution:
Steps for Scenario Analysis

- For scenario analysis, Excel is required to be used. According to the question, create an excel sheet as given below for basic situation. The main objective is to find out the basic NPV.
- Calculation of NPV for the most likely situation through Excel application.

	A	B	C	D	E	F	G	H	I	J	K	L	M	N	O	P
8		Quantity	% Increase	Price	COGS %											
9		175,000	9%	$50	70%											
10		Year Zero	Year One	Year Two	Year Three	Year Four	Year Five	Year Six	Year Seven	Year Eight	Year Nine	Year Ten				
11	Quantity Sold		175,000	190,750	207,918	226,630	247,027	269,259	293,493	319,907	348,698	380,081				
12	Price each		50.0	47.5	45.1	42.9	40.7	38.7	36.8	34.9	33.2	31.5				
13																
14	Earnings Forecast ($000s)	Year Zero	Year One	Year Two	Year Three	Year Four	Year Five	Year Six	Year Seven	Year Eight	Year Nine	Year Ten				
15	Sales revenue		8750.00	9060.63	9382.28	9715.35	10060.24	10417.38	10787.20	11170.14	11566.68	11977.30				
16	Cost of goods sold		-6125.00	-6342.44	-6567.59	-6800.74	-7042.17	-7292.17	-7551.04	-7819.10	-8096.68	-8384.11				
17	Gross profit		2625.00	2718.19	2814.68	2914.60	3018.07	3125.21	3236.16	3351.04	3470.01	3593.19				
18	General, sales and Admin.		-1000.00	-1000.00	-1000.00	-1000.00	-1000.00	-1000.00	-1000.00	-1000.00	-1000.00	-1000.00				
19	Depreciation		-35.71	-35.71	-35.71	-35.71	-36.71	-35.71	-35.71	0.00	0.00	0.00				
20	Net operating income		1589.29	1682.47	1778.97	1878.89	1982.36	2089.50	2200.45	2351.04	2470.01	2593.19				
21	Income tax @ 35%		-556.25	-588.87	-622.64	-657.61	-693.83	-731.33	-770.16	-822.87	-864.50	-907.62				
22	Net income		1033.04	1093.61	1156.33	1221.28	1288.53	1358.18	1430.29	1528.18	1605.50	1685.57				
23	Add depreciation		35.71	35.71	35.71	35.71	35.71	35.71	35.71	0.00	0.00	0.00				
24	Cost of Machine	-250														
25	Cash flow	-250	1068.75	1129.32	1192.04	1256.99	1324.25	1393.89	1466.00	1528.18	1605.50	1685.57				
26																
27	Present Worth	7814														

In the question, the basic situation is the most likely scenario. Other two scenarios given are pessimistic and optimistic.

- In excel, data option of the file helps in "what if analysis."

Go to what if analysis, click scenario manager

- In scenario manager, we have an add button.
- Click on it. A box will appear. Write down the scenario name and in changing cell, mention the cell address which would undergo change. As per the given problem, B9 to E9 are cells which would change as per the scenario. Click OK.

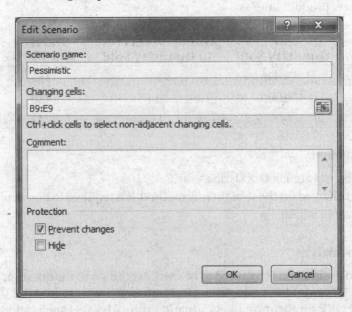

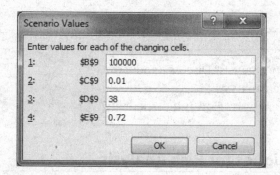

- Thereafter, scenario value box will appear, which will show the values of pessimistic assumptions. The first cell will show sales units, the second one will show percent increase in sales, and so on. Then click Ok. Thereafter, scenario manager dialogue book will appear again.
- Click on add, and repeat this whole procedure for entering optimistic scenario values.
- If you select the pessimistic option in the highlight box and then click on the show button, the basic calculation or worksheet will change according to the pessimistic solution, as shown in the following figure.

	Quantity	% Increase	Price	COGS %								
	100,000	1%	$38	72%								
	Year Zero	Year One	Year Two	Year Three	Year Four	Year Five	Year Six	Year Seven	Year Eight	Year Nine	Year Ten	
Quantity Sold		100,000	101,000	102,010	103,030	104,060	105,101	106,152	107,214	108,286	109,369	
Price each		38.0	36.1	34.3	32.6	31.0	29.4	27.9	26.5	25.2	23.9	
Earnings Forecast ($000s)	Year Zero	Year One	Year Two	Year Three	Year Four	Year Five	Year Six	Year Seven	Year Eight	Year Nine	Year Ten	
Sales revenue		3800.00	3646.10	3498.43	3356.75	3220.80	3090.36	2965.20	2845.11	2729.88	2619.32	
Cost of goods sold		-2736.00	-2625.19	-2518.87	-2416.86	-2318.97	-2225.06	-2134.94	-2048.48	-1965.51	-1885.91	
Gross profit		1064.00	1020.91	979.56	939.89	901.82	865.30	830.26	796.63	764.37	733.41	
General, sales and Admin.		-1000.00	-1000.00	-1000.00	-1000.00	-1000.00	-1000.00	-1000.00	-1000.00	-1000.00	-1000.00	
Depreciation		-35.71	-35.71	-35.71	-35.71	-35.71	-35.71	-35.71	0.00	0.00	0.00	
Net operating income		28.29	-14.81	-56.15	-95.83	-133.89	-170.41	-205.46	-203.37	-235.63	-266.59	
Income tax @ 35%		-9.90	5.18	19.65	33.54	46.86	59.65	71.91	71.18	82.47	93.31	
Net income		18.39	-9.62	-36.50	-62.29	-87.03	-110.77	-133.55	-132.19	-153.16	-173.28	
Add depreciation		35.71	35.71	35.71	35.71	35.71	35.71	35.71	0.00	0.00	0.00	
Cost of Machine	-250											
Cash flow	-250	54.10	26.09	-0.79	-26.57	-51.31	-75.06	-97.83	-132.19	-153.16	-173.28	
Present Worth	-516											

- In the worksheet shown above, cash flows and NPV has changed according to the pessimistic situation. You can also select the optimistic scenario, then click OK.
- Summary of the results can be created by clicking the summary option. Scenario summary report will look like in the following figure:

Scenario Summary				
	basic	Most likely	Pessimistic	OPtimistic
Changing Cells:				
sales Units	200,000	175,000	100,000	300,000
% cchange in Slaes	10%	9%	1%	14%
Sales Price	50	50	38	70
COGS	67%	70%	72%	65%
Result Cells:				
NPV	11466	7814	-516	36349

Notes: Current Values column represents values of changing cells at time Scenario Summary Report was created. Changing cells for each scenario are highlighted in gray.

Test Yourself

1. What is sensitivity analysis? Discuss its advantages.
2. Explain break-even analysis.
3. What is scenario analysis? How is it carried out?

Statistical Techniques for Risk Analysis

We have already discussed the various measures of risk using statistical techniques. The same statistical measures and some other can be used to measure risk in capital budgeting situations also. The most important concept used in these statistical techniques is that of probability. Let us recapitulate.

The Concept of Probability

The probability may be defined as the likelihood of happening or non-happening of an event. It may be described as a measure of chance of happening or non-happening of an event. For example, one may say that there are 20% chances that the sales will increase by 80% during the year, or that there are 75% chances that the firm will be able to achieve 50% market share over a period of next 5 years. These descriptions of 20% and 75% chances are the description of probability of the respective events. So, the probability may be taken as a measure of an opinion about the likelihood of happening of an event. If the event is certain to happen, then the probability is defined as one and if the event has no chance of occurrence, then the probability is described as 0. So, the probability always has a value between 0 and 1.

As said earlier, the cash inflows expected from a project are not known with certainty. So they have to be estimated. Instead of single-point estimate, we may specify a series of cash flow for each year and the respective probabilities. For example, the following is the series of estimated cash inflows together with their probabilities at the end of year 1.

Cash Flows (₹)	Probabilities
100,000	0.2
150,000	0.4
175,000	0.3
200,000	0.1

The series of expected cash inflows together with the associated probabilities for a particular year is also known as probability distribution.

Probability Distribution

The probability distribution may be defined as a set of possible cash flows that may occur at a point of time and their probabilities of occurrence. In the probability distribution given above for year 1, there are four possible cash inflows. The probabilities given for these cash inflows can be interpreted as follows: There is a 20% chance that the cash inflows will be ₹100,000; there is 40% chance that the cash inflow will be ₹150,000, and so on.

In some cases, the probabilities can be assigned on the basis of the past experience or historical data. But it may not always be possible in a capital budgeting decision. The reason for this is obvious. The capital budgeting decisions are, generally, not of repetitive nature. Moreover, data available from the experience of other firms may not be available or not at all relevant, because each capital budgeting situation is a specific situation. Therefore, in most of the capital budgeting situations, the decision-maker on the basis of some relevant facts and figures and his subjective considerations usually assigns the probabilities. These probabilities are called subjective probabilities and the resulting distribution is called subjective probability distribution.

Expected Value of a Probability Distribution

To find out the expected value of probability distribution for each year, each cash flow of the probability distribution is multiplied by the respective probability of the cash flow and then adding the resulting products. This final figure is then considered as the expected value of the cash inflow for that year for which the probability distribution has been considered.

Symbolically,

$$ECFi = \sum p_i.CF_i.$$

The expected value of the cash flow does not mean that the actual cash flow will be the same as the expected value of the cash flow. The cash flow in any year may be different from the expected value of the cash flow.

Illustration 5. ABC and Co is evaluating a project with an initial outlay of ₹140,000 and an economic life of 2 years. The cash inflows and the "respective probabilities" have been found to be as follows:

Year 1		Year 2	
Cash Inflows	**Probabilities**	**Cash Inflows**	**Probabilities**
₹100,000	0.3	₹140,000	0.5
80,000	0.5	70,000	0.3
10,000	0.2	60,000	0.2

What is the expected cash flows in year 1 and year 2?

Solution:

$$ECF \text{ in year } 1 = 100,000 \times 0.30 + 80,000 \times 0.50 + 10,000 \times 0.20$$
$$= 30,000 + 40,000 + 2,000 = ₹72,000$$
$$ECF \text{ in year } 2 = 140,000 \times 0.50 + 70,000 \times 0.30 + 60,000 \times 0.20$$
$$= 70,000 + 21,000 + 12,000 = ₹103,000$$

Measurement of Risk

The concepts of probability distribution and the expected value of the probability distribution help in incorporating the variability of cash flows, that is, the risk of cash flows into the capital budgeting decision process. However, it does not measure the variability of actual cash flows from the estimated ones. In other words, a measure of risk or variability of cash flows is still needed. For this purpose, the dispersion of the probability distribution, that is, the difference between the possible cash flows that may occur and the expected values may be analyzed. We already know that two measures of dispersion that may be considered to assess the variability of the cash flows are (i) the standard deviation, which is an absolute measure of variability, and (ii) the coefficient of variation (CV), which is a relative measure of variations. We have already discussed how to calculate standard deviation and coefficient of variation. Let us now see again how these measures can be used in capital budgeting situations.

Standard Deviation

The statistical tool of standard deviation provides a measure of spread of the distribution of expected cash flows. The standard deviation as a technique of measuring dispersion can be used to measure the deviations of each possible cash flow about the expected value of cash flow. These deviations refer to the difference between possible cash flow and the expected value of the cash flow.

Steps to Determine the Standard Deviation of Cash Flows

The following steps are needed to ascertain the standard deviation of the probability distribution of cash flows

1. Find out the probability distribution of the cash flows over different years and find out the expected value of cash flow for each year.
2. Subtract each cash flow (CF) from the expected value of the cash flow, that is, ECF and get the square of the differences, that is, $(CF - ECF)2$.
3. Multiply the squared deviations, that is, $(CF - ECF)2$ by the probabilities of the occurrence of its corresponding cash flow, that is, find out $P_i(CF1 - ECF)2$, where P_i is the probability of a particular cash flow.
4. Add these products, that is, find out the sum of $P_i (CF_i - ECF)2$ and get the square root of this figure.

Symbolically,

$$\sigma = \sqrt{P_i(CF_i - ECF)2}$$

This value σ is called the standard deviation. It may be noted that the standard deviation is calculated by taking all deviations, positive or negative. This implies that the risk aversion extends to all the deviations from the expected value even if the deviations are positive, that is, when the possible cash flow is more than the expected value of the cash flow. The larger dispersion will produce a larger standard deviation, and therefore, larger standard deviation indicates riskier capital budgeting projects.

Illustration 6. Zodiac Ltd is evaluating two equal-sized mutually exclusive proposals A and B for which the respective cash flows together with associated probabilities are as follows:

	Project A		Project B	
Cash Flow (in ₹)	**Probability**		**Cash Flow (in ₹)**	**Probability**
2,000	0.30		1,000	0.10
4,000	0.40		3,000	0.10
6,000	0.30		5,000	0.40
			7,000	0.30
			9,000	0.10

Which of the two projects is more risky?

Solution:

The expected value of cash flows of projects A and B may be calculated as follows:

Project A = 2,000 (0.3) + 4,000 (0.4) + 6,000 (0.3) = ₹4,000

Project B = 1,000(0.1) + 3,000 (0.1) + 5,000 (0.4) + 7,000 (0.3) + 9,000 (0.1) = ₹5,400

The standard deviation of cash flows of the two projects may be calculated as follows:

	Project A				Project B			
Cash Flow (in ₹)	**Probabilities**	**ECF**	**Pi (CF-ECF)²**	**Cash Flow (in ₹)**	**Probabilities**	**ECF**	**Pi (CF-ECF)²**
2,000	0.30	4,000	1,200,000	1,000	0.10	5,400	1,936,000
4,000	0.40	4,000	0	3,000	0.10	5,400	576,000
6,000	0.30	4,000	1,200,000	5,000	0.40	5,400	64,000
				7,000	0.30	5,400	768,000
							1,296,000
Total			2,400,000	9,000	0.10	5400	4,640,000

Standard deviation of cash flows of Project A = $\sqrt{2,400,000}$ = ₹1,549

Standard deviation of cash flows of Project B = $\sqrt{4,640,000}$ = ₹2,154

As the standard deviation of project B is more than that of A, it is riskier as compared to A.

Coefficient of Variation

CV is a relative measure of dispersion and can be applied in capital budgeting decision process to measure the risk of a project, particularly in case when the alternative projects are of different sizes. CV is defined as the standard deviation of the probability distribution divided by its expected value, that is, CV = σ/ECF.

It may be noted that CV is a pure number and is not affected by the measuring unit. The advantage of CV over standard deviation is that the former can be used to compare the riskiness of mutually exclusive projects even if their expected values are not equal. CV is also useful in evaluation of those projects the initial outlays of which differ substantially.

Illustration 7. Consider two Projects A and B which have the following information:

	Project A	**Project B**
Expected NPV (₹)	120,000	450,000
Standard deviation (₹)	80,000	270,000

Which of the two projects is better?

Solution:
If we use standard deviation as a measure of risk, we find that project A is less risky as it has a low standard deviation. However, in this case as the expected NPVs of the two projects differ significantly, it would be better to use a relative measure of risk rather than an absolute measure of risk.
 CV is a relative measure of risk. The CV of the two projects can be calculated as follows:

$$CV_A = \sqrt{2,400,000} = 0.67$$
$$CV_B = \sqrt{4,640,000} = 0.60$$

According to this measure, project B is better as it has a much higher expected NPV and lower CV.

Test Yourself

1. Define the concept of probability.
2. How is risk measured through standard deviation?
3. What is expected cash flows?

Probability Distribution Approach

The probability distribution approach attempts to determine the probability that the actual NPV occurrence is going to be less than 0, and that the project has therefore, been accepted wrongly. Thus, the probability distribution approach helps in determining the error of judgment in selecting a project, which at a later stage turns out to be a negative NPV project. To develop the probability distribution approach, an important assumption regarding the behavior of cash flows needs to be made. The required assumption is whether the cash flows associated with a project are independent cash flows or dependent cash flows. A project is said to be having independent cash flows when the cash flow of any period is not affected by the cash flow or flows of any of the preceding period. For example, the expected cash flow of year 2 is not affected by the cash inflow of year 1, and similarly the cash flow of year 5 is not affected by the cash inflow of the year preceding the period, that is, year 1 through year 4. However, a project is said to have dependent cash flows when the favorable or unfavorable cash flow in a particular period affects the cash flow of any period thereafter. In practice, most of the projects have dependent cash flows. The effect of the nature of cash flow on the calculation of the value of NPV may be analyzed as follows:

Independent Cash Flows

If the cash flows associated with a project are independent, then the cash flows for different years are not related to one another. Such a pattern of cash flows is also known as uncorrelated cash flows. In such a case, the expected NPV and the standard deviation of the NPV may be defined as follows:

$$NPV = \sum_{t=1}^{n} \frac{ECF_t}{(1+k_f)^t} - CF_0$$

$$\sigma_{NPV} = \sqrt{\sum_{t=1}^{n} \frac{\sigma_i^2}{(1+k_f)^{2t}}}$$

where NPV is the expected NPV of the project, ECF_t is the expected value of cash flow for different years, k_f is the risk-free discount rate, CF_0 is the initial cost of the proposal, σ_{NPV} is the standard deviation of the NPV, and σ_t is the standard deviation of cash flows for different years.

The discount factor R_f is the risk-free discount rate. The reason for taking risk-free discount rate is that the risk has already been incorporated when the probabilities are considered to find out the ECF. If the discount factor were not risk-free, then the risk of cash flows would be discounted twice; first, in the cash flows and then in the k.

Illustration 8. Consider a project that costs ₹80,000 and has an expected life of 3 years. The expected cash flows from the project are as follows:

Year 1		Year 2		Year 3	
Probability	Cash Inflow (₹)	Probability	Cash Inflow (₹)	Probability	Cash Inflow (₹)
0.10	60,000	0.15	30,000	0.25	60,000
0.40	50,000	0.50	40,000	0.20	50,000
0.30	40,000	0.25	50,000	0.35	40,000
0.20	30,000	0.10	60,000	0.20	30,000

The risk-free rate of discount is 10%. Calculate the expected NPV of the project and the standard deviation of NPV.

Solution:

Year 1			Year 2			Year 3		
Probability	Cash Inflow (₹)	$P_i\,CF_i$	Probability	Cash Inflow (₹)	$P_i\,CF_i$	Probability	Cash Inflow (₹)	$P_i\,CF_i$
0.1	60,000	6,000	0.15	30,000	4,500	0.25	60,000	15,000
0.4	50,000	20,000	0.5	40,000	20,000	0.2	50,000	10,000
0.3	40,000	12,000	0.25	50,000	12,500	0.35	40,000	14,000
0.2	30,000	6,000	0.1	60,000	6,000	0.2	30,000	6,000
	ECF	44,000		ECF	43,000		ECF	45,000

	Year 1				Year 2				Year 3			
	Probabilities	Cash Inflow (₹)	CF–ECF	P_i (CF–ECF)^2	Probabilities	Cash Inflow (₹)	CF–ECF	p_i (CF–ECF)^2	Probabilities	Cash Inflow (₹)	CF–ECF	P (CF–ECF)^2
	0.1	60,000	16,000	25,600,000	0.15	30,000	–13,000	25,350,000	0.25	60,000	15,000	56,250,000
	0.4	50,000	6,000	14,400,000	0.5	40,000	–3,000	4,500,000	0.2	50,000	5,000	5,000,000
	0.3	40,000	–4,000	4,800,000	0.25	50,000	7,000	12,250,000	0.35	40,000	–5,000	8,750,000
	0.2	30,000	–14,000	39,200,000	0.1	60,000	17,000	28,900,000	0.2	30,000	–15,000	45,000,000
				84,000,000				71,000,000				115,000,000

Standard Deviation of Cash Flows for Year $1 = \sqrt{84,000,000} = 9,170$

Standard Deviation of Cash Flows for Year $2 = \sqrt{17,000,000} = 8,430$

Standard Deviation of Cash Flows for Year $3 = \sqrt{115,000,000} = 10,720$

Present Value of the Expected Cash Flows $= \dfrac{44,000}{(1.10)} + \dfrac{43,000}{(1.10)^2} + \dfrac{43,000}{.(1.10)^3} = ₹109,320$

Expected NPV $= -80,000 + 109,320 = ₹29,320$

As the cash flows are independent, the standard deviation is given by

$$\sigma_{NPV} = \sqrt{\sum_{t=1}^{n} \dfrac{\sigma_t^2}{(1+k_f)^{2t}}} = \sqrt{\dfrac{9,170^2}{(1.10)^2} + \dfrac{8,430^2}{(1.10)^4} + \dfrac{10,720^2}{(1.10)^6}} = \sqrt{182,808,700} = ₹13,521$$

Standardizing the Cash Flow Distribution

Once the NPV and the standard deviation of the NPV of a project have been calculated, then normal distribution can be applied for further analysis of the risk features of the project. The normal distribution can be used to find out the probability of occurrence of different values of the NPV. In other words, the theory of normal distribution helps to find out the probability that the NPV of the project will be less than, equal to, or more than 0.

To use the theory of normal distribution, what is required is the standardization of the cash flow distribution, that is, the expected values of cash flows are converted into standard normal variate, z. A standard normal distribution is a normal distribution with mean equal to zero (i.e., $\mu = 0$) and standard deviation equal to one (i.e., $\sigma = 1$).

The standard normal vitiate z is defined as follows:

$$Z = \dfrac{X - \bar{X}}{\sigma}$$

Illustration 9. Consider the project in the above illustration. The expected NPV of the project is ₹29,320 and the standard deviation of the NPV is ₹13,521. What is the probability that the NPV will be less than zero?

Solution:
The value of z will be equal to $\dfrac{X - \bar{X}}{\sigma} = \dfrac{0 - 29,320}{13,521} = -2.17$.

This implies that the NPV of zero lies 2.17 standard deviations to the left of the expected value of the probability distribution of NPVs. The probability of a value being less than 2.17 standard deviations from the expected value according to the normal distribution table is 0.015.

This means that the NPV of the project will be less than zero is 0.015 or 1.5%.

Dependent Cash Flows

It is already stated that in most of the capital budgeting situations, the cash flows over a period of time are related and dependent. The cash flow for any period is affected by the cash flows of the preceding periods. If a project has favorable outcomes in the initial periods usually these are followed by favorable outcomes in the later periods also. When cash flows are dependent over time, the standard deviation would be greater than what it would be if the cash flows are independent. The greater the dependence, the greater would be the standard deviation.

CASE I: PERFECT DEPENDENCE

If the cash flows show perfect dependence from year to year; it means that the cash flows in different time periods would exhibit the same degree of deviation. In such a case, the standard deviation of the cash flows is given by:

$$\sigma = \sum_{t=1}^{n} \frac{\sigma_1}{(1+k_f)^t}.$$

CASE II: MODERATE DEPENDENCE

If the cash flows are neither independent nor show perfect dependence, it is a case of moderate dependence. In case of moderate dependence, the earlier discussion cannot be used. In such cases, we have to use the concept of conditional and joint probabilities. In the figure that follows, we have discussed the case of moderately dependent cash flows.

Illustration 10. XYZ Ltd is considering a proposal with an initial outlay of ₹150,000 and a life of 2 years. The firm's required rate of return is 10%. It is expected that the cash inflow for year 2 be affected by the cash flow of year 1. Other details of the cash inflows are as follows:

Year 1		Year 2	
Cash Flows (in ₹)	Probabilities	Cash Flows (in ₹)	Probabilities
100,000	0.40	140,000	0.5
60,000	0.60	70,000	0.3
		60,000	0.2
		200,000	0.6
		120,000	0.3
		80,000	0.1

Evaluate the proposal.

Solution:

The cash flows for year 2 are given to be dependent on the cash flow for year 1 and therefore, the probability as given for year 2 are conditional. This can be interpreted as follows: There is a 40% chance that the cash inflow of year 1 may be ₹100,000 and 60% chance that the cash inflow may be ₹60,000. Further, if the cash flow for year 1 happens to be ₹100,000, then there is a 50% chance that cash flow in year 2 will be ₹140,000; 30% chance that it will be ₹60,000; and 20% chance that it will be ₹70,000. Similarly, if the cash flow for year 1 happens to be ₹60,000 (60% chances); then the chance of year 2 cash flow are also given. The situation can also be interpreted by way of joint probability. The chance of a cash flow of ₹100,000 in year

1 and ₹140,000 in year 2 is 0.4×0.5=0.20. The chance of cash flow of ₹100,000 in year 1 and ₹60,000 in year 2 is 0.4×0.3=0.12, and so on. These values of 0.20 and 0.12, and so on, are known as *joint probabilities*.

The NPV of the proposal may be ascertained with the help of joint probabilities as follows:

Year 1		Year 2		Total PV
CF	**PV @ 10%**	**CF**	**PV @ 10%**	
100,000	90,900	140,000	1,156,400	206,540
100,000	90,900	60,000	49,560	140,460
100,000	90,900	70,000	57,820	148,720
60,000	54,540	200,000	165,200	219,740
60,000	54,540	120,000	99,120	153,660
60,000	54,540	80,000	66,080	120,620

Total PV (in ₹)	Probabilities Year 1	Probabilities Year 2	Joint Probabilities	Expected Value of PV (PV×joint Probability)
206,540	0.40	0.50	0.20	41,308
140,460	0.40	0.30	0.12	16,855
148,720	0.40	0.20	0.08	11,898
219,740	0.60	0.60	0.36	79,106
153,660	0.60	0.30	0.18	27,659
120,620	0.60	0.10	0.06	7,237
Total				184,063

$$NPV = \text{Expected value of cash inflows} - \text{Cash outflow}$$
$$= ₹184,063 - ₹150,000 = ₹34,063$$

Simulation Analysis

Simulation is yet another statistical technique to deal with uncertainty and is also based on the concept of probabilities. **Simulation refers to representation of a system that reacts to a change in any of the input variable in a similar way as to that variable which is being simulated.** There are several techniques of simulation, however, the Monte Carlo method is the most common. The Monte Carlo method is based on the concept of random numbers and is useful in the analysis of uncertainty.

When applied to capital budgeting, the simulation requires the generation of values of cash flows using predetermined-probability distribution and the random numbers. The cash flows are expressed in terms of a mathematical model. The process of generating the values of cash flows is repeated numerous times to result in a probability distribution of cash flows. The process of generating the random numbers and using the probability distribution of cash flows result in generating different values for various variables. These values are then put in a mathematical model to calculate the NPV. By repeating the same process for a number of times, say a thousand or ten thousand times, a probability distribution of NPV is created. The simulation allows considering the project under alternative scenarios. The decision-maker can consider the effect of a limited number of plausible combinations of variables affecting the outcome of a project.

Advantages and Disadvantages of Simulation

As a tool of capital budgeting, the simulation analysis offers the following advantages:

1. It can handle situations involving too many external variables and complex relationships among these variables.
2. It allows studying the interactive effect of each variable.
3. Simulation does not interact with the real world, but only with table models; therefore, it results in saving of cost.
4. The simulation techniques can be used even when the variables do not follow any standard type of probability distribution.

However, the simulation analysis suffers from the following disadvantages:

1. Simulation is not an optimizing technique.
2. Voluminous data is required for developing a real simulation model and hence may be expensive.
3. Complex mathematical workout, often with the help of a computer, is also required.
4. Results are possible only if the simulation is carried out for a very large number of times.

Decision Tree Approach

Quite often a firm may have to take a sequential decision, that is, the present decision is affected by the decisions taken in the past or it affects the future decisions of the same firm. In capital budgeting, the evaluation of a project frequently requires a sequential decision-making process, where the accept–reject decision is made in several stages. For example, consider a firm, which is planning to launch a new product and to install a plant manufacturing the same with the capacity of 10,000 units a month. It is estimated that the entire production shall be sold. However, if due to one or the other factor, the demand is not generated for even the break-even level of production, the firm will incur a loss. In this case, it will be better for the firm to first install a pilot project and go for test marketing of the product. If the market accepts the product, full-fledged plant may be installed in the next stage. Thus, it is a two-stage decision. The first stage occurs before the test market. At that point, the cash flows related to both the test and to the production must be considered. After the test, another decision must be made. At this point, the cash flows related to the market test are sunk costs and are irrelevant to the decision to be made. At this second point, the decision to be made cannot be affected by the cash outflows in connection with the market test.

An analytical technique used in sequential decisions is a decision tree. A decision tree is a branching diagram which represents a decision problem as a series of decisions to be taken under conditions of uncertainty. The decision tree approach gets its name because of its resemblance with a tree with a number of branches. In a typical decision tree, the project is broken down into clearly defined stages, and the possible outcomes at each stage are listed along with the probabilities and cash flows effect of each outcome.

Steps in Decision Tree Approach

A decision tree analysis typically consists of four steps

1. Structuring the problem as a tree in which the end nodes of the branches are the payoffs associated with a particular path (scenario) along the tree.
2. Assigning subjective probabilities to events represented on the tree.
3. Assigning payoffs for consequences (dollar or utility value associated with a particular scenario), and
4. Selecting course(s) of action based on analyses (e.g., rolling back of the tree, sensitivity analyses, Monte Carlo simulations).

Illustration 11. Abhishek Computers must decide whether to introduce a new product now. If it chooses to introduce it, sales will either be high or low. The firm is considering a market survey to collect information on expected sales. The market research firm contacted will report one of the three results: great, good, or poor, where great means high sales are likely. Marketing management feels that if the firm introduces the product now, its probability of high sales is 0.4. The company has had past experience with this market research firm and knows that 60% of high-sales products in the past had great survey results, 30% had good survey results, and 10% had poor survey results. Similarly, 10% of its low-sales products had great survey results, 30% had good survey results, and 60% had poor survey results. If sales are high, the firm expects net profits (excluding the cost of the survey) to be ₹100,000; if sales are low, it expects a net loss of ₹50,000 (excluding survey costs). What should the company do?

Solution:
This problem can be structured as a decision tree in the following exhibit. The chronology of events begins on the left and flows to the right. The first thing that happens is that marketing management must decide whether to run a market survey. If it does run a survey, it then learns the results and decides whether to introduce the product. Finally, it learns sales results.

A decision tree has two types of nodes: decision nodes (marked D), meaning management has control over the course of action, and chance nodes (marked C), where the decision-maker has no control.

At the end of each path of the decision tree, the consequences of the several courses of action are indicated. For instance, if the firm runs a market survey and that survey reports great results and the firm manufactures the product and sales are high, the result is a net gain of ₹84,000 which is ₹100,000 less the ₹16,000 survey cost. All consequences are measured against the do-nothing strategy of no survey, no manufacturing, and no sales.

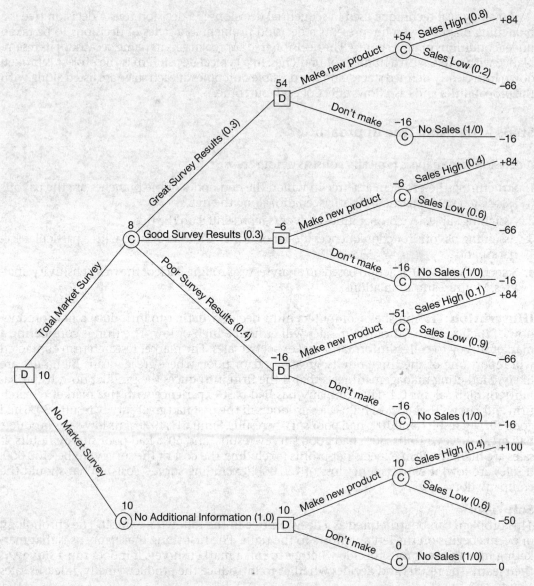

Beside those segments of the tree beginning at chance nodes are the conditional probabilities (the numbers in parentheses) that the event associated with that segment occurs, given that everything else up to that point in the tree *does* occur. Thus, for instance, the probability that the survey is *great*, given that the firm runs the survey, is 0.3, or 30%. The conditional probability is that the sales are high, given that survey results are great and the firm decides to manufacture 0.8, or 80%.

To summarize the given information, the firm knows from its past experience

$$p \,(\text{great survey} \mid \text{high sales}) = 0.6$$

$$p \,(\text{good survey} \mid \text{high sales}) = 0.3$$

$$p \,(\text{poor survey} \mid \text{high sales}) = 0.1$$

$$p \,(\text{great survey} \mid \text{low sales}) = 0.1$$

$$p \text{ (good survey | low sales)} = 0.3$$

$$p \text{ (poor survey | low sales)} = 0.6$$

$$p \text{ (high sales)} = 0.4$$

$$p \text{ (low sales)} = 0.6$$

To get the probability that the survey would be great, we use the theorem of total probabilities

$$p \text{ (great survey)} = p \text{ (great survey | high sales)} \, p \text{ (high sales)}$$

$$+ p \text{ (great survey| low sales)} \, p \text{ (low sales)}$$

$$= 0.6 \times 0.4 + 0.1 \times 0.6 = 0.3$$

Similarly

$$p \text{ (good survey)} = 0.3$$

$$p \text{ (poor survey)} = 0.4$$

To get p (great survey | high sales), we use Bayes' theorem

$$p \text{ (high sales | great survey)} = \frac{p(\text{great survey high sales}) | p \text{ (high sales)}}{p \text{ (great survey)}}$$

$$= \frac{0.6 \times 0.4}{0.3}$$

Similarly, we get

$$p \text{ (high sales | good survey)} = 0.4$$

$$p \text{ (high sales | poor survey)} = 0.1$$

$$p \text{ (low sales | great survey)} = 0.2$$

$$p \text{ (low sales | good survey)} = 0.6$$

$$p \text{ (low sales | poor survey)} = 0.9$$

We can now use these probabilities to average out and fold back. The numbers beside each node represent the expected profit associated with being at that node. If we conduct a market survey, have great results, and introduce the product now, then there is an 80% chance of high sales, implying a net profit of ₹84,000, and a 20% chance of low sales, with a net loss of ₹66,000. Thus, the expected profit (averaging out) of being at that chance node is

$$0.8 \, (₹84,000) - 0.2 \, (₹66,000) = ₹54,000$$

At the node immediately below, if we have the same great results on the survey and then choose not to manufacture, we will lose ₹16,000. Now backing up (folding back) to the decision node before these chance nodes, the firm can either introduce the product with an expected profit of ₹54,000 or not introduce the product now with an expected loss of ₹16,000. The best choice is to make the product; therefore, the expected profit of that decision node is ₹54,000. In addition, if we fold back to the start, we find the best choice is not to do the survey.

Evaluation of Decision Tree Approach

The decision tree approach allows a firm to deal with uncertainty by considering the project in stages, and the decision at any stage depends on the outcome of the previous stage. The decision tree approach is no doubt, a useful technique in case of sequential decision process. It gives a sequential outlook to the entire situation and deals with the present decision as they affect the future decisions. It helps in visualizing the different alternatives in more explicit form, that is, the graphic presentation. However, it has got some limitations also. In particular, the requirement that the project be broken down into several stages and that the outcomes be discrete at every stage, reduces the number of projects for which decision tree approach can be applied. Moreover, the approach becomes more and more complicated as the numbers of stages of the decision-making are incorporated. Sometimes, it may fail to incorporate too many interdependent variables.

Test Yourself

1. What is simulation analysis? Explain.
2. What is decision tree approach? How is it conducted?

SUMMARY

1. The returns from the project are not known with certainty until the cash flows actually occur. This uncertainty is a primary determinant of a project's risk. Risk is defined as variability that is likely to occur in future returns from investment.

2. The payback period is the time period in which the original investment in the project will be recovered by the firm from the cash inflows of the project. The payback period is then compared with the target payback period. But it fails to measure the risk, which may be of different degrees in different alternative projects.

3. The risk-adjusted rate in a capital budgeting decision process is a more direct method to take risk into consideration. It is based on the premise that riskiness of a project may be taken care of, by adjusting the discount rate. The cash flows from a more risky project should be discounted at a relatively higher discount rate as compared with other projects the cash flows of which are less risky.

$$k' = k_f + p$$

where k' is the risk-adjusted discount rate, k_f is the risk-free discount rate, and p is the risk premium.

4. **The CE approach attempts at adjusting the future cash flows instead of adjusting the discount rates.** The expected future cash flows, which are taken as risky and uncertain, are converted into "equivalent certain cash flows" using some conversion factors.

$$RANPV = \sum_{t=1}^{n} \frac{\alpha_i CFt}{(1 + R_f)^t} - CF_0,$$

where RANPV = Risk-adjusted NPV of the project, α_i is the CE factors for different years, CFt is the expected cash flows for different years, and R_f is the risk-free discount rate.

5. SA deals with the consideration of sensitivity of the NPV in relation to different variables contributing to the NPV. It cannot handle large number of interdependent variables.

6. Scenario analysis is further extension of SA. It is used to calculate NPV, IRR under normal, pessimistic, and optimistic cases.

7. The probability may be defined as the likelihood of happening or non-happening of an event. It may be described as a measure of chance of happening or non-happening of an event.

8. The standard deviation as a technique of measuring dispersion can be used to measure the deviations of each possible cash flow about the expected value of cash flow

$$\sigma = \sqrt{P_i(CF_i - ECF)2}$$

9. CV is a relative measure of dispersion and can be defined as the standard deviation of the probability distribution divided by its expected value, that is, $CV = \sigma/ECF$.

10. Simulation refers to representation of a system that reacts to a change to any of the input variable in a similar way as to that variable which is being simulated. There are several techniques of simulation, however, the Monte Carlo method is the most common. The Monte Carlo method is based on the concept of random numbers and is useful in the analysis of uncertainty.

11. The decision tree approach allows the firm to deal with uncertainty by considering the project in stages, and the decision at any stage depends on the outcome of the previous stage. The decision tree approach is no doubt, a useful technique in case of sequential decision process. It gives a sequential outlook to the entire situation and deals with the present decision as they affect the future decisions. It helps in visualizing the different alternatives in more explicit form, that is, the graphic presentation.

KEY TERMS

- Certainty
- Coefficient of variation
- Decision tree
- Scenario analysis
- Simulation
- Expected cash flow
- Risk-adjusted discount rate
- Probability distribution approach
- Certainty equivalents
- Break-even analysis
- Sensitivity analysis
- Standard deviation
- Monto Carlo simulation
- Risk seeker
- Probability
- Payback

Learning Outcomes

Student would have become familiar with the origin and technique of risk analysis and so on.

SOLVED EXAMPLES

1. Cure Well Pharmaceuticals is planning to invest ₹18 lakhs during October 2004 in a formulation project. It has been estimated that there is a 60% chance of the project being successfully completed by the end of first year. If the project is not completed by September 2005, the company may either choose to abandon the project for ₹5 lakhs or incur an additional

cost of ₹8 lakhs to complete the project by next year. The chance of successful completion in the second year is 30%. In case the project is not completed by the end of the second year, the project will be abandoned for ₹7 lakhs. On successful completion, annual cash inflows until the end of the life of project are expected to be as follows:

Cash Inflow (₹ in lakhs)	Probability
08	20%
10	40%
12	30%
14	10%

The life of the project, including the construction period, is 5 years. The opportunity cost of capital is 12%.

Using the decision tree analysis approach, advise what the company should do?

Solution

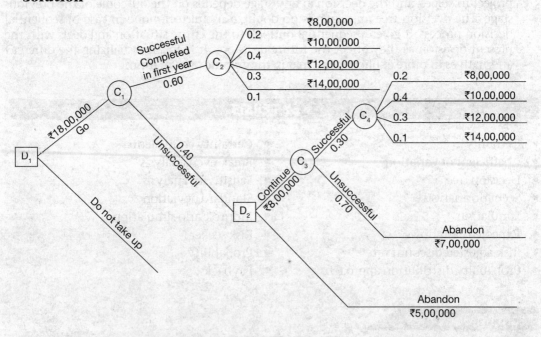

Value at C_4 = PV of annual cash inflows for 3 years as the end of the second year.

$$= [0.2 \times 8 + 0.4 \times 10 + 0.3 \times 12 + 0.1 \times 14] \times \text{PVIFA}(12, 3)$$

$$= 10.6 \times 2.402$$

$$= 25.46$$

Value at C_3 = $0.30 \times 25.46 + 0.70 \times 7.00$

$$= 12.54$$

Value at D_2 = Maximum of [(PV of 12.54 − 8), 5]

$$= \text{Maximum of } [3.19, 5]$$

Hence, optimum value at D_2 is ₹5 lakhs

Value at C_2 = PV of annual cash inflows for 4 years at the end of 4 years.

$$= 10.6 \times 3.037 = 32.19.$$

Value at C_1 = [Value at $C_2 \times 0.6$ + Value at $D_2 \times 0.4$]

$$= (32.19 \times 0.6 + 5 \times 0.4)$$

$$= 21.32.$$

Value at D_1 = Max [PV of 21.32 – 18.00), 0]

$$= 1.03$$

∴, optimal decision is to take up the project and abandon the project if it is not successfully completed by the end of the first year.

2. Lakshya Ceramics Limited is evaluating one of its dream projects which has an estimated life of 4 years. The initial outlay of this project is ₹80 lakhs. The possible cash flows are given as follows:

(₹ IN LAKHS)

	Year 1		Year 2		Year 3		Year 4	
Cash Flow	Probability	Cash Flow	Probability	Cash Flow	Probability	Cash Flow	Probability
20	0.2	30	0.4	40	0.3	35	0.2
30	0.5	40	0.3	45	0.5	30	0.4
35	0.3	45	0.3	50	0.2	20	0.4

Consider that the cash flows of various years are independent and the risk-free rate of return is 6%.

(a) Compute the expected NPV of the project and the standard deviation of NPV.

(b) Calculate the probability that the profitability index of the project is greater than 1.2 if the NPV is approximately normally distributed.

Solution

Expected annual cash-inflows and their corresponding standard deviations are as follows:

Year	Cash Flow ($\overline{A}_t$)	Standard Deviation (σ_t)
1.	$20 \times 0.2 + 30 \times 0.5 + 35 \times 0.3 = 29.5$	$= \sqrt{0.2 \times (20 - 29.5)^2 + 0.5 \times (30 - 29.5)^2 + 0.3 \times (35 - 29.5)^2}$
2.	$30 \times 0.4 + 40 \times 0.3 + 45 \times 0.3 = 37.5$	$= \sqrt{0.4 \times (30 - 37.5)^2 + 0.3 \times)(40 - 37.5)^2 + 0.3 \times (45 - 37.5)^2}$
3.	$40 \times 0.3 + 45 \times 0.5 + 50 \times 0.2 = 44.5$	$= \sqrt{0.3 \times (40 - 44.5)^2 + 0.5 \times (45 - 44.5)^2 + 0.2 \times (50 - 44.5)^2}$
4.	$35 \times 0.2 + 30 \times 0.4 + 20 \times 0.4 = 27$	$= \sqrt{6.075 + 0.125 + 6.05} = 3.5$

Now, expected NPV

$$= \sum_{t=1}^{n} \frac{\bar{A}_t}{(1+i)^t} - I$$

$$= \frac{29.5}{1.06} + \frac{37.5}{(1.06)} + \frac{44.5}{(1.06)} + \frac{27}{(1.06)^4} - 80$$

$$= 27.83 + 33.37 + 37.36 + 21.39 - 80 = 39.95$$

$$\sigma_{NPV} = \left[\sum_{t=1}^{n} \frac{\sigma_t^2}{(1+k_f)^{2t}} \right]^{1/2}$$

$$= \left[\frac{(5.22)^2}{(1.06)^2} + \frac{(6.42)^2}{(1.06)^4} + \frac{(3.5)^2}{(1.06)^6} + \frac{(6.0)^2}{(1.06)^8} \right]^{1/2}$$

$$= (24.25 + 32.64 + 8.64 + 22.59)^{1/2}$$

$$= (88.12)^{1/2} = 9.39$$

(b) Profitability Index $= \dfrac{\text{PV of cash in flow}}{\text{Initial outlay}} = 1.2$

or,

$$\frac{\text{PV of cash in flow} - \text{Initial outlay}}{\text{Initial outlay}} = 0.2$$

or,

$$NPV = IO \times 0.2$$

$$= 80 \times 0.20$$

$$= 16.$$

$$P(PI \geq 1.2) = P(NPV \geq 16) = P\left(Z \geq \frac{16 - 39.95}{9.39} \right)$$

$$= P(Z \geq -2.55)$$

$$= (1 - 0.0054)$$

$$= 99.46\%.$$

3. A project involving an initial investment of ₹16 crore has the following probability distribution of net cash flows during its life of 4 years

(₹ IN CRORE)

Year 1		Year 2		Year 3		Year 4	
Net Cash Flow	Probability	Net Cash Flow	Probability	Net Cash Flow	Probability	Net Cash Flow	Probability
4	0.30	5	0.30	4	0.10	3	0.10
5	0.60	6	0.50	5	0.60	4	0.50
6	0.10	8	0.20	7	0.30	5	0.40

The cash flows for the various years are independent of each other. The NPV of the project is expected to be approximately normally distributed. The risk-free rate is 6%. What is the probability that the internal rate of return of the project will exceed the risk-free rate?

Solution

The IRR will exceed a given hurdle rate if the NPV at the hurdle rate is positive. Hence, the probability that IRR will exceed the risk-free rate (hurdle rate) is equal to the probability that NPV will be positive at the risk-free rate.

Year 1	$\overline{A}_1 = (4 \times 0.30) + (5 \times 0.60) + (6 \times 0.10)$	₹4.8 crore
	$\sigma^2_1 = (4-4.8)^2\,0.30 + (5-4.8)^2 0.60 + (6-4.8)^2\,0.10$	0.36 (₹ crore)^2
Year 2	$\overline{A}_2 = (5 \times 0.30) + (6 \times 0.50) + (8 \times 0.20)$	₹6.10 crore
	$\sigma^2_2 = (5-6.1)^2\,0.30 + (6-6.10)^2\,0.50 + (8-6.10)^2\,0.20$	1.09 (₹ crore)^2
Year 3	$\overline{A}_3 = (4 \times 0.10) + (5 \times 0.60) + (7 \times 0.30)$	₹5.50 crore
	$\sigma^2_3 = (4-5.5)^2\,0.10 + (5-5.5)^2\,0.60 + (7-5.5)^2\,0.30$	1.05 (₹ crore)^2
Year 4	$\overline{A}_4 = (3 \times 0.10) + (4 \times 0.50) + (5 \times 0.40)$	₹4.30 crore
	$\sigma^2_4 = (3-4.3)^2\,0.10 + (4-4.3)^2\,0.50 + (5-4.3)^2\,0.40$	0.41 (₹ crore)^2

Expected NPV

$$NPV = \sum_{t=1}^{4} \frac{\overline{A}_t}{(1+i)^t} - I$$

$$= \frac{4.80}{1.06} + \frac{6.10}{1.06^2} + \frac{5.50}{1.06^4} + \frac{4.30}{1.06^4} - 16 = ₹1.98 \text{ lakhs}$$

$$\sigma_{NPV} = \left[\sum_{t=1}^{4} \frac{\sigma^2_t}{(1+i)^{2t}} \right]^{1/2}$$

$$= \left[\frac{0.36}{(1.06)^2} + \frac{1.09}{(1.06)^4} + \frac{1.05}{(1.06)^6} + \frac{0.41}{(1.06)^8} \right]^{1/2} = ₹1.477 \text{ crores}$$

$$= (24.25 + 32.64 + 8.64 + 22.59)^{1/2}$$

$$= (88.12)^{1/2} = 9.39$$

It is assumed that the NPV of the project will be approximately normally distributed.

$$P(NPV \text{ is positive}) = P(NPV > 0)$$

$$P(NPV > 0) = P(-1.34 < Z < 0) + 0.50$$

$$= 0.4099 + 0.50$$

$$0.9000 = 91\%$$

∴, the probability that the NPV will be positive is 91%. Hence, the probability that the IRR will exceed the risk-free rate is 91%.

4. RC company is considering two mutually exclusive projects. The initial cost of both the projects is ₹5,000 each. Both projects have an expected life of 5 years. Annual cash flows and associated probabilities are as follows:

Economic Condition	Probability	Cash Flow Project A	Cash Flow Project B
Good	0.3	60,000	50,000
Normal	0.4	40,000	40,000
Bad	0.3	20,000	30,000

If discount rate is 7%, which project should be accepted?

Solution
Project A

Expected cash flow $= 0.3 \times 60,000 + 0.4 \times 40,000 + 0.3 \times 20,000 = 40,000$

$$\sigma^2 = (60,000 - 40,000)^2 \times 0.3 + (40,000 - 40,000)^2 \times 0.4 + (20,000 - 40,000)^2 \times 0.3$$

$$= 120,000,000 + 0 + 120,000,000 = 240,000,000$$

$$\sigma = \sqrt{240,000,000} = 154,919.93$$

Expected NPV $= -50,000 + 40,000 \times \text{PVIFA}_{(0.07,5)}$

$$= -50,000 + 40,000 \times 4.100 = ₹114,000$$

Project B

Expected cash flow $= 0.3 \times 50,000 + 0.4 \times 40,000 + 0.3 \times 30,000 = 40,000$

$$\sigma^2 = (50,000 - 40,000)^2 \times 0.3 + (40,000 - 40,000)^2 \times 0.4 + (30,000 - 40,000)^2 \times 0.3$$

$$= 30,000,000 + 0 + 30,000,000 = 60,000,000$$

$$\sigma = \sqrt{30,000,000}$$

Expected NPV $= -50,000 + 40,000 \times \text{PVIFA}(0.07,5)$

$$= -50,000 + 40,000 \times 4.100 = ₹114,000$$

Project A and Project B have equal expected cash flow and NPV. But standard deviation of project A is higher than that of project B. So Project B must be undertaken.

ASSESS YOURSELF

Concept Review and Critical Thinking Questions

1. "The CE approach is a superior to the risk-adjusted discount rate method for risk analysis in capital budgeting". Comment.
2. What is SA? How is it useful as a tool of risk analysis?
3. Is financial break-even analysis better than accounting break-even analysis? Discuss.
4. How can probability theory be used for risk analysis in capital budgeting? Discuss.
5. What is simulation? How is this technique useful in investment decision-making?
6. Describe the decision tree approach with the help of an example.

STUDENT ACTIVITY

Student should select relevant data from the balance sheet and calculate cash flow. Apply probability on the selected cash flow and compare with actual outcome.

SUGGESTED READINGS

Brealey, R.A., & Myers, S.C. (2002). *Principles of corporate finance* (7th ed.). New York: McGraw-Hill.

Horne, J.C.V. (2002). *Financial management & policy* (12th ed.). Singapore: Pearson Education.

Magee, J.F. (1964). How to use decision trees in capital investment? *Harvard Business Review, 42*, September–October, 76–96.

Mao, James C.T. (1969). *Quantitative analysis of financial decisions.* Macmillan.

Ross, S.A., Westerfield, R.W., & Jordan, B.D. (2002). *Fundamentals of corporate finance* (6th ed.). New Delhi: Tata McGraw-Hill.

CHAPTER 13

Dividend Decisions

- To understand the objectives and factors affecting the dividend policy.
- To understand the theories of dividend payment.

PRELUDE

Dividend decision relates to rewarding the investors. An investor makes investment in equity shares primarily for earning dividend. Dividend is nothing but profit sharing in proportion to the paid-up capital. For a long time, there has been a debate whether dividend decision does influence market price with share or it is irrelevant for market price—especially when public issues are made at hefty premium. Read also—the uncertainty in the equity market over extremely negative global cues has offered long-term investors an opportunity to pick stocks selectively. Analysts say that many companies with good dividend payouts record have corrected significantly even though their earnings continue to remain stable. They advise risk-averse investors to focus on high-dividend-yield stocks as they offer a margin of safety in volatile market conditions. Dividend yield is the ratio of equity dividend per share divided by the stock price. Historically, dividend-paying companies offer the best resistance to downward price pressure. Generally, regular dividend paying companies are considered as blue chip companies where rewarding the investors is equally important as ploughing back the profit. In any case, the stock of such companies are set to be growth stocks to be preferred by investors who are keen to get a regular flow called dividend and capital appreciation on maturity.

Dividend decision is an integral part of the firm's strategic financial decisions. Dividend is defined as the amount of a firm's earning after interest and tax that is distributed among a number of outstanding equity shares. It essentially involves deciding how much of the firm's earnings after interest and taxes, as a proportion of the paid-up capital, should be distributed to the shareholders as return for their investment in the firm and how much should be retained to finance the future growth and development of the firm. The returns to the shareholders either by way of the dividend receipts or capital gains are affected by the dividend policies of the firms. The objective of the dividend decisions—such as, all strategic financial decisions—is to optimize, if not maximize, the shareholder's wealth. Interestingly, an investor makes investment in a firm for two reasons: (1) regular income (in the form of dividend) and (2) capital appreciation (in the form of higher market price). **Dividend is always paid on paid-up value of shares, not on face value or market price.** That is the reason why dividend does not attract investors in case of premium issue. Although, whether there is any effect of the dividend policy on the value of the firm is in itself a highly debatable issue. If dividend policy is considered relevant, then it follows that there must be an optimal policy by following which it is possible to maximize the value of the firm. If an optimal dividend policy exists, then finance mangers should determine the same and if there is no such thing as optimal policy, any dividend policy is as good as the other one.

There are three forms of dividend policies:

1. Constant dividend per share.
2. Constant dividend payout.
3. Stable and increasing dividends.

Constant Dividend per Share

In this dividend policy, the company pays a fixed amount per share or pays fixed rate on paid-up capital as dividend per year, irrespective of the fluctuations in the earnings. This does not mean that the company will never increase the dividend rate. When the company reaches to new levels of earnings, the annual dividend per share may be increased. It is easy to follow this policy when company has stable income. The companies with wide fluctuation in earnings will find it difficult to follow such a policy. This kind of policy is preferred by those shareholders who want dividend as regular source of income. Such dividend does not have a direct effect on the market price of the shares (Figure 13.1).

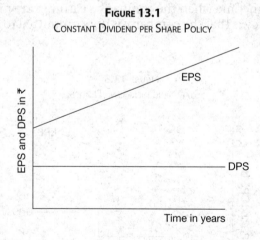

FIGURE 13.1
CONSTANT DIVIDEND PER SHARE POLICY

Source: Author.

Constant Payout Ratio

In this type of policy, the company pays a fixed percentage of earnings as dividend every year. The ratio of dividend to earnings is known as the payout ratio. With such a policy, the amount of dividend would fluctuate in direct proportion to earnings. This policy is related to the company's ability to pay dividend. If the company incurs losses, then the payment of dividend is not mandatory. Unlike constant dividend per share, this policy does not put pressure on the liquidity position of the company. The reason is that dividend is distributed only when profit is there. For example, the face value of share is ₹10 per share, the dividend payout ratio is 20%, and the earnings per share is ₹20. The amount of dividend payable is ₹4 per share (Figure 13.2).

FIGURE 13.2
CONSTANT PAYOUT DIVIDEND POLICY

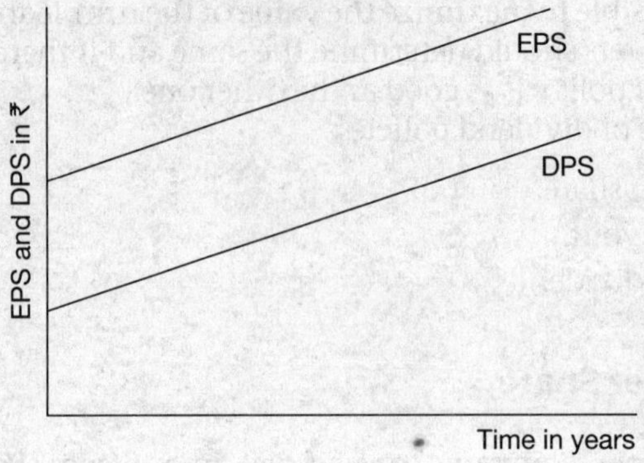

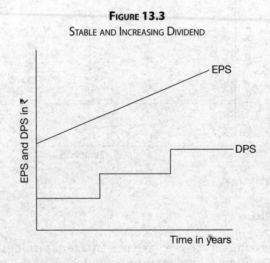

Stable and Increasing Dividends

In this type of policy, the company pays some minimum dividend each year and in addition pays some extra dividend. Companies with stable earnings usually follow this type of policy. For companies with fluctuating earnings, the policy to pay a minimum dividend per share with a step-up feature is desirable. This policy enables a company to pay a constant amount of dividend regularly without any default and allows the company to supplement the shareholders' income when the company's earnings are more than the usual. The advantage of such a policy is that the company is not committed to pay a large, future fixed dividend (Figure 13.3).

FIGURE 13.3
STABLE AND INCREASING DIVIDEND

Source: Author.

Forms of Dividend Payments

1. Cash dividend
2. Bonus share

Cash Dividend

Normally, companies pay cash dividend. The cash balance and reserve balance of the company gets reduced by the amount of dividend. Sufficient cash balance is required to distribute the dividend. If company follows a stable dividend policy, predicting upcoming cash requirement is not a difficult task. But unstable dividend policy has such problems. At the time of dividend payment, a special escrow account is opened with the bank. The amount of earning which is distributed is credited. Cash dividends are considered to be the income of the shareholders and it is taxed.

Bonus Share

Bonus shares means issuing additional shares in proportion of existing shares free of cost. Bonus shares are issued in addition to cash dividend. Issue of bonus shares would increase the number of outstanding shares. The market price of shares may increase due to the issue of bonus shares. Bonus shares are not taxable unless they are sold in less than 12 months. The issue of bonus shares has a psychological effect on the shareholders. Bonus share indicates the future growth in earnings. Cash dividends are definitely going to reduce the cash balance. Bonus shares will help the company in conserving the cash reserve. But bonus shares cannot be issued in lieu of cash dividend. In fact, the issue of bonus shares is also known as capitalization of profit, where undistributed profit and reserve and surplus are converted into capital by issuing shares.

Test Yourself

1. Define dividend. Why is it important to pay it?
2. Explain the forms of dividend.

Theories of Dividend Policy

Over time, many theories of dividend policy have emerged to address the key issue whether the dividend policy of a firm affects the market value of the firm or not. As we saw in the previous chapter, the question is whether the capital structure has any impact on the market value of the firm. Similarly, the question is whether dividend decisions have any effect on the market value of the firm. Here also, there are two schools of thought. According to one school, dividend is a relevant variable whereas according to the other, dividends are not relevant in determining the value of the firm. As such, dividends do not affect the market price and share. Thus, dividend policies can be broadly grouped into two categories:

1. Dividend relevance theories.
2. Dividend irrelevance theories.

Dividend Relevance Theory

Dividend is a relevant variable for affecting market price and the value of the firm. There are the following models under this approach:

1. Traditional model.
2. Walter's model.
3. Gordon's model.
4. Bird-in-hand theory.
5. Dividend signaling theory.
6. Agency cost theory.

Traditional Model

The traditional model of dividend policy, developed by B. Graham and D.L. Dodd, emphasizes the relationship between the **dividend and the stock market. According to this model, the stock price and, consequently, the market value of the firm are positively related to higher dividends. This means that the market price of the share would increase if there were higher dividends and would decline if the dividends were lower.** Not only this, the earnings per share is also an important variable in determining the market price.

The traditional model expresses the relationship between market price and dividends as follows: P=m (D+E/3) (It is presumed that dividend is equal to four times the weight retained earnings; weights provided by Graham and Dodd are based on their subjective judgments and not on empirical analysis), where P is the market price, m is the multiplier, D is the dividend per share, and E is the earnings per share

Walter's Model

Professor James E. Walter argues that the choice of dividend policies always affects the value of the firm. This model establishes the relationship between the rate of return, cost of capital, and the dividend policy. His model is based on the following assumptions:

1. The firm finances all investment through retained earnings, that is, debt or new equity is not issued.
2. The firm's rate of return, r, and its cost of capital, k, are constant.
3. All earnings are either distributed as dividends or reinvested internally immediately.
4. The firm has an infinite life.

Based on the above assumptions, Walter put forth the following model for valuation of shares

$$P_0 = \frac{D+(E-D)r/k}{k}$$

where P_0 is the market price per share, D is the dividend per share, E is the earnings per share, E−D is the retained earnings per share, r is the firm's average rate of return, and k is the firm's cost of capital.

From the model, it is clear that the market price per share is the sum of two components

1. The first component, D/k, is the present value of an infinite stream of cash flows in the form of dividends.
2. The second component $\frac{(E-D)r/k}{k}$ is the present value of an infinite stream of returns from the retained earnings.

CASE I: r > K GROWTH FIRMS

Growth firms are those firms which expand rapidly due to profitable investment opportunities yielding returns greater than the cost of capital. When the return on investment is more than the cost of equity capital, it would be in the interest of the shareholders that maximum earnings are retained by the firm since it has better and more profitable investment opportunities within organization. It implies that the returns the investor gets when the company reinvests the earnings will be greater than what they can earn by investing the dividend income elsewhere. **Firms which have their $r > k_e$ are the growth firms and the dividend policy that suits such firms is the one which has a zero payout ratio. This policy will enhance the value of the firm.**

CASE II: R < K DECLINING FIRMS

Declining firms do not have any profitable investment projects to invest their earnings. The returns of such firms are less than the minimum required rate of return of the investors. In this situation, investors will have better investment opportunities than the firm. Thus, it will be in the interests of the shareholders that maximum earnings are distributed to them. This suggests a dividend policy of 100% payout **to maximize the value of the firm.**

CASE III: R = K NORMAL FIRMS

Normal firms are those firms who have rate of return equals to cost of capital. In this case, **the firms' dividend policy will not affect the value of the firm.** The optimum dividend policy for such normal firms will range between 0% and 100% payout ratio, since the value of the firm will remain constant in all cases. There is no optimum dividend policy for such firms.

Illustration 1. Consider the following information about a firm:

Equity capitalization rate $(k_e) = 12\%$

Earnings per share $(E) = ₹4$

Assumed return on investments (r) are as follows:

1. $r = 15\%$
2. $r = 10\%$
3. $r = 12\%$

What will be the market price of the share if the dividend payout ratio is 0%, 25%, 50%, and 100% if the Walter model is used?

Solution

Case I: $r > k_e$ $(r = 15\%, k_e = 12\%)$
(a) D/P ratio = 0; dividend per share = 0

$$P = \frac{0 + 0.15/0.12(4-0)}{0.12}$$

$$= ₹41.67$$

(b) D/P ratio=25%; dividend per share=₹1

$$P = \frac{1 + 0.15/0.12(4-1)}{0.12}$$

$$= ₹39.58$$

(c) D/P ratio=50%; dividend per share=₹2

$$P = \frac{2 + 0.15/0.12(4-2)}{0.12}$$

$$= ₹37.50$$

(d) D/P ratio=100%; dividend per share=₹4

$$P = \frac{4 + 0.15/0.12(4-4)}{0.12}$$

$$= ₹33.33$$

From the above calculations, it is observed that when the return on investment is greater than the cost of capital, there is an inverse relation between the value of the share and the payout ratio. Thus, the value of the firm is the highest when the D/P ratio is zero (P=₹41.67) and this goes on declining as the D/P ratio increases. Hence, the optimum dividend policy for a growth firm is a zero dividend payout ratio.

Case II: $r < k_e$ (r=10%, k_e=12%)

(a) D/P ratio=0; dividend per share=0

$$P = \frac{0 + 0.10/0.12(4-0)}{0.12}$$

$$= ₹12.78$$

(b) D/P ratio=25%; dividend per share=₹1

$$P = \frac{1 + 0.10/0.12(4-1)}{0.12}$$

$$= ₹29.17$$

(c) D/P ratio=50%; dividend per share=₹2

$$P = \frac{2 + 0.10/0.12(4-2)}{0.12}$$

$$= ₹30.56$$

(d) D/P ratio=100%; dividend per share=₹8

$$P = \frac{4 + 0.10/0.12(4-4)}{0.12}$$

$$= ₹33.33$$

The above calculations reveal that the firm's value will increase as the D/P ratio increases. Therefore, firms which have their returns on investment less than the cost of equity capital should prefer a higher dividend payout ratio to maximize the share value.

Case III: $r = k_e$ ($r = 12\%$; $k_e = 12\%$)

(a) D/P ratio = 0; dividend per share = 0

$$P = \frac{0 + 0.12/0.12\,(4-0)}{0.12}$$

$$= ₹33.33$$

(b) D/P ratio = 25%; dividend per share = ₹1

$$P = \frac{1 + 0.12/0.12\,(4-1)}{0.12}$$

$$= ₹33.33$$

(c) D/P ratio = 50%; dividend per share = ₹2

$$P = \frac{2 + 0.12/0.12\,(4-2)}{0.12}$$

$$= ₹33.33$$

(d) D/P ratio = 100%; dividend per share = ₹4

$$P = \frac{4 + 0.12/0.12\,(4-4)}{0.12}$$

$$= ₹33.33$$

Thus, in this case the price remains the same irrespective of the dividend payout.

Limitations of the Walter Model

The assumptions on which Walter model is based limit its applicability in practice.

1. The assumption of exclusive financing by retained earnings makes the model suitable for all-equity firms. Some amount of financial leverage is always present.
2. Further, the return on investment cannot remain constant forever. The model also ignores the business risk by assuming that the required rate of return remains constant. When the firm takes up new investments its risk profile changes. In such a case, the rate of return required by the shareholders cannot remain constant.

Gordon's Dividend Capitalization Model

Gordon's dividend capitalization model says that the market price of a share is equal to the present value of the infinite streams of dividends received. His model is based on the following assumptions:

1. The firm is an all-equity firm, and it has no debt.
2. Retained earnings would be used to finance any expansion.
3. The internal rate of return, r, of the firm's investment is constant.
4. The appropriate discount rate, k, for the firm remains constant and is greater than the growth rate.
5. Corporate taxes do not exist.
6. The retention ratio, b, once decided upon, is constant.
7. Cost of capital is greater than growth rate.
8. The firm's stream of cash flow is perpetual.

Based on the above assumptions, Gordon put forward the following valuation model:

$$P_0 = \frac{E_1(1-b)}{k-b_r}$$

where P_0 is the price per share at the end of year is 0, E_1 is the earnings per share at the end of year is 1, $(1-b)$ is the fraction of earnings the firm distributes by way of earnings, b is the fraction of earnings the firms ploughed back, k is the rate of return required by the shareholders, r is the rate of return earned on investments made by the firm, and b_r is the growth rate of earnings and dividends.

Illustration 2. Consider the following information about a firm:

Equity capitalization rate (k_e)=11%

Earnings per share (E)=₹15

Assumed return on investments (r) are as follows:

1. r=12%
2. r=11%
3. r=10%

What will be the market price of the share if the dividend payout ratio is 10%, 20%, 30%, and 50% if Gordon model is used?

Solution

(i) Case I: $r > k_e$
(a) D/P ratio=10%

$$b = 90\%$$
$$g = br = 0.90 \times 0.12 = 0.108$$
$$P = \frac{E(1-b)}{k_e - b_r}$$
$$= \frac{15(1-0.9)}{0.11-0.108}$$
$$= ₹750$$

(b) D/P ratio=20%

$$= 80\%$$
$$b = b_r = 0.80 \times 0.12 = 0.096$$
$$P = \frac{15(1-0.8)}{0.11-0.096}$$
$$= ₹214.28$$

(c) D/P ratio=30%

$$b = 70\%$$
$$g = b_r = 0.70 \times 0.12 = 0.084$$
$$P = \frac{15(1-0.7)}{0.11-0.084}$$
$$= ₹173.08$$

(d) D/P ratio = 50%

$$b = 50\%$$
$$g = b_r = 0.50 \times 0.12 = 0.006$$
$$P = \frac{15(1-0.5)}{0.11 - 0.006}$$
$$= ₹150$$

Case II: r = k_e
(a) D/P ratio = 10%

$$b = 90\%$$
$$g = b_r = 0.90 \times 0.11 = 0.099$$
$$P = \frac{15(1-0.9)}{0.11 - 0.099}$$
$$= ₹136.36$$

(b) D/P ratio = 20%

$$b = 80\%$$
$$g = b_r = 0.80 \times 0.11 = 0.088$$
$$P = \frac{15(1-0.8)}{0.11 - 0.088}$$
$$= ₹136.36$$

(c) D/P ratio = 30%

$$b = 70\%$$
$$g = b_r = 0.70 \times 0.11 = 0.077$$
$$P = \frac{15(1-0.7)}{0.11 - 0.077}$$
$$= ₹136.36$$

(d) D/P ratio = 50%

$$b = 50\%$$
$$g = b_r = 0.50 \times 0.11 = 0.055$$
$$P = \frac{15(1-0.5)}{0.11 - 0.055}$$
$$= ₹136.36$$

Case III: r < k_e
(a) D/P ratio = 10%

$$b = 90\%$$
$$g = b_r = 0.90 \times 0.10 = 0.09$$
$$P = \frac{15(1-0.9)}{0.11 - 0.09}$$
$$= ₹75$$

(b) D/P ratio = 20%

$$b = 80\%$$
$$g = b_r = 0.80 \times 0.10 = 0.08$$
$$P = \frac{15(1 - 0.8)}{0.11 - 0.08}$$
$$= ₹100$$

(c) D/P ratio = 30%

$$b = 70\%$$
$$g = b_r = 0.70 \times 0.10 = 0.07$$
$$P = \frac{15(1 - 0.7)}{0.11 - 0.07}$$
$$= ₹112.5$$

(d) D/P ratio = 50%

$$b = 50\%$$
$$g = b_r = 0.50 \times 0.10 = 0.05$$
$$P = \frac{15(1 - 0.5)}{0.11 - 0.05}$$
$$= ₹125$$

The above illustration shows the relevance of dividends as given by the Gordon's model. In the given three situations, the firm's share value is positively correlated with the payout ratio when $r_e < k_e$ and decreases with an increase in the payout ratio when $r > k_e$. Thus, firms with a rate of return greater than the cost of capital should have a higher retention ratio and those firms, which have a rate of return less than the cost of capital, should have a lower retention ratio. The dividend policy of firms, which have a rate of return equal to the cost of capital, will, however, not have any impact on its share value.

Bird-in-Hand Theory

John Lintner and Myron Gordon propounded this theory. Accordingly, the shareholders are not entitled to any fixed return. The return to the shareholders is in the form of dividends and capital gains. Current dividends are relatively certain than the future capital gains. Shareholders are risk averse and prefer to receive dividends in the present time period to future capital gains. They consider dividends to be more certain than the expected future capital gains. Hence, they have a preference for a certain level of dividends now rather than the prospect for a higher but uncertain income in the form of capital gains. The payment of dividends in the present time period resolves the uncertainty associated with the income. This goes in line with the adage "A bird in hand is worth more than two in the bush." Hence, the name bird-in-hand theory.

Lintner and Gordon argued that since shareholders consider dividends to be less risky than the future capital gains, they will discount these inflows at a lower rate of return and thus the value of firm's shares increases. (Recall that the market value of a share as per the dividend discount model is given by $\frac{D_1}{k - g}$, where k is the investors required rate of return and g is the expected growth rate of the firm's earnings and dividends.

Dividend Signaling Theory

It is perceived that managers have greater access to inside information about the company. They may share this information with the shareholders through an appropriate dividend policy. Constant or increasing dividends convey positive signals about the future prospects of the company resulting in an increase in the share price. Similarly, the absence of dividends or decreasing dividends convey negative signal resulting in decline in the share price.

Agency Cost Theory

Agency costs are defined as those costs, which are incurred in attempting to minimize the agency problem. The agency problem is the potential for conflict in objectives, which exists in principal–agent relationship. In the corporate world, the principals are the shareholders and managers act as their agents. For shareholders of the firm, the agency problem is that the managers who control the day-to-day affairs of the firm may tend to act in their own personal interest rather than the interest of the shareholders. A firm's owners will incur agency costs whenever they introduce procedures and mechanisms aimed at reducing the potential for conflict between the personal objectives of the managers and the objectives of the owners. Incurring agency costs has the potential effect of reducing the shareholder's value.

In the context of dividend policy, it implies that if a firm follows a liberal dividend policy, it would be forced to go to the capital markets to raise the additional funds required for expansion or new projects. We know that there are many regulations that have to be adhered to while issuing new equity. In addition to this, the investment community consisting of various players would scrutinize the firm's financial statements to decide about the worthiness of the company as an investment option. Such external scrutiny would reduce the agency costs because if the managers know that the firm will be regularly exposed to such examination they are less likely to indulge in actions, which are not in line with the objective of wealth maximization.

Hence, a liberal dividend policy by reducing the agency costs may lead to enhancement of the shareholder value.

Test Yourself

1. Explain the Walter model with its limitations.
2. What is agency cost theory?

Dividend Irrelevance Theory

This approach implies that dividend decisions are irrelevant in influencing the market price of share and, consequently, value of the firm. There are two components of the shareholder' returns:

1. Dividend yield (D/P_0).
2. Capital yield ($(P_1 - P_0)/P_0$).

Suppose a firm issues a ₹10 par value share at a premium of ₹90. In other words, the issue price is ₹100. If the firm declares a dividend per share of ₹3, the dividend yield is $D/P_0 = 3/100 = 0.03 = 3\%$. If the closing price during at the end of next year is ₹115, the capital yield is $(115 - 100)/100 = 15\%$. The total return to the shareholders is 18%.

The advocates of dividend irrelevance theories argue that it does not matter how the total yield is divided between these two yields. If the dividend yield is less, the shareholders would expect a higher capital yield and if the capital yield is relatively low they would expect a higher dividend yield. The price of the share depends on the overall yield and not on the individual yields. Hence, the dividend policy of the firm is not relevant.

The following theories support the above contention:

1. Residual theory.
2. Miller and Modigliani model.
3. Dividend clientele effect.
4. Rational expectations model.

Residual Theory

According to this theory, a firm will pay dividends only from the residual earnings, that is, from earnings left over after all the suitable investment opportunities have been financed. This is so because, retained earnings are the most important source of finance, as making a fresh issue of equity due involves cost. Let us recall the pecking order theory of capital structure discussed in the previous chapter. This would lead managers to adopt a residual approach towards dividend policy. This implies that the primary focus of the firm's management is on investment rather than on dividends. This does not mean that managers are not concerned with maximizing shareholder wealth. It only means that the management thinks that the value of the firm and the wealth of the shareholders will be maximized by investing earnings in appropriate investment projects rather than paying them out as dividends. The managers will thus seek out and invest the firm's earnings in all the acceptable projects which are expected to increase the firm's value. Dividends will be paid only when the retained earnings exceed the funds required to finance suitable investment projects. Dividend policy is thus a passive, rather than an active, decision variable.

Modigliani and Miller (MM) Model

This model, based on a few assumptions, sidelined the importance of the dividend policy and its effect thereof on the share price of the firm. According to this model, it is only the firms' investment policy that will have an impact on the share value of the firm, hence it should be given more importance.

Assumptions

1. Markets are perfect and investors are rational. In perfect market condition, there is easy access to information and there are no floatation and/or transaction costs. The securities are infinitely divisible, hence no single investor is large enough to influence the share value.
2. There are no taxes, implying that there are no differential tax rates for the dividend income and capital gains.
3. The firm follows a stable investment policy. Consequently, the risk composition and the required rate of return remain constant.
4. Investors are able to forecast the future earnings, the dividends, and the share value of the firm with certainty. This assumption was, however, dropped out of the model.

Based on these assumptions and using the process of arbitrage, Miller and Modigliani explained the irrelevance of the dividend policy.

As mentioned earlier, firms have two options for utilizing its after tax profits (i) to retain the earnings and plough them back for investment purposes (ii) distribute the earnings as cash dividends. If the firm selects the second option and declares dividend, then it will have to raise capital for financing its investment decisions by selling new shares. Here, the arbitrage process will neutralize the increase in the share value due to the cash dividends by the issue of additional shares. This makes the investor indifferent to the dividend earnings and the capital gains since the share value of the firm depends more on the future earnings of the firm, than on its dividend policy. Thus, if there are two firms having similar risk and return profiles, the market value of their shares will be similar in spite of different payout ratios.

The current market price of the share is equal to the discounted value of the dividend paid and the market price at the end of the period.

$$P_0 = \frac{1}{(1+k_e)}(D_1 + P_1)$$

where P_0 is the current market price of the share ($t=0$), P_1 is the market price of the share at the end of the period ($t=1$), D_1 is the dividends to be paid at the end of the period ($t=1$), and k_e is the cost of equity capital.

With no external financing, the total value of the firm will be as follows:

$$nP_0 = \frac{1}{(1+k_e)}(nD_1 + nP_1)$$

where n is the number of outstanding shares.

Now, if the firm finances its investment decisions by issuing n new shares at the end of the period ($t=1$), then the capitalized value of the firm will be the sum of the dividends received at the end of the period and the value of the total outstanding shares at the end of the period less the value of the new shares.

Symbolically,

$$nP_0 = \frac{1}{(1+k_e)}(nD_1 + (n+n_1)(P_1 - n_1 P_1))$$

Firms will have to raise additional capital to fund their investment requirements, if its investment requirement is more than its retained earnings, additional equity capital ($n_1 P_1$) after utilizing its retained earnings is as follows:

$$n_1 P_1 = I - (E - nD_1)$$

where I is the total investment required, nD_1 is the total dividends paid, and E is the earnings during the period, $(E - nD_1)$ = retained earnings.

Simplifying the above equation we get,

$$n_1 P_1 = I - E + nD_1$$

Substituting this value of the new shares in the above equation, we get

$$nP_0 = \frac{1}{(1+k_e)}\left[(nD_1 + (n+n_1)P_1 - I + E - nD_1)\right]$$

$$= \frac{nD_1 + (n+n_1)P_1 - I + E - nD_1}{(1+k_e)}$$

$$\Rightarrow nP_0 = \frac{(n+n_1)P_1 - I + E}{(1+k_e)}$$

Thus, according to the MM model, the market value of the share is not affected by the dividend policy and this is clear from the last equation above.

Illustration 3. The capitalization rate of AVON Ltd is 12%. This company has outstanding shares to the extent of 25,000 shares selling at the rate of ₹100 each. Anticipating a net income of ₹350,000 for the current financial year, AVON Ltd plans to declare a dividend of ₹3 per share. The company also has a new project, the investment requirement for which is ₹500,000. Show that under the MM model, the dividend payment does not affect the value of the firm.

Solution:

To prove that the MM model holds good, we have to show that the value of the firm remains the same whether the dividends are paid or not.

1. The value of the firm, when dividends are paid

Price per share at the end of year 1

$$P_0 = \frac{1}{(1+k_e)}(D_1 + P_1)$$

$$100 = \frac{1}{(1.12)}(3 + P_1)$$

$$P_1 = ₹109$$

The amount to be raised by the issue of new shares

$$n_1 P_1 = I - (E - nD_1)$$

$$= 500,000 - (350,000 - 75,000)$$

$$= ₹225,000$$

Number of additional shares to be issued

$$n_1 = \frac{2,25,000}{109} \text{ shares}$$

Value of the firm

$$nP_0 = \frac{(n+n_1)P_1 - I + E}{(1+k_e)}$$

$$= \frac{(25,000 + 2,25,000/109) - (5,00,000 - 3,50,000)}{1.12}$$

Value of the firm

$$nP_0 = ₹2,500,000$$

2. Value of the firm when dividends are not paid

Price per share at the end of the year 1

$$P_0 = \frac{1}{(1+k_e)}$$

$$100 = P_1/1.12$$

$$P_1 = ₹112$$

Amount to be raised from the issue of new shares

$$n_1 P_1 = (500,000 - 350,000) = ₹150,000$$

Number of new shares to be issued

$$n_1 = 150,000/112 \text{ shares}$$

Value of the firm

$$nP_0 = \frac{(n+n_1)P_1 - I + E}{(1+k_e)}$$

$$= \frac{(25,000 + 2,25,000/112)112 - (5,00,000 - 3,50,000)}{1.12}$$

Value of the firm

$$nP_0 = ₹2,500,000$$

Thus, the value of the firm, in both the cases remains the same.

Limitations

1. Clientele effect: Due to uncertainty, share prices tend to fluctuate, sometimes rather widely. When share prices fluctuate, conditions for conversion of current income into capital value and vice versa may not be regarded as satisfactory by the investors. Some investors who wish to enjoy more current income may be reluctant to sell a portion of their shareholding in a fluctuating market. Such investors would naturally prefer, and value more, a higher payout ratio. Some investors who wish to get less current income may be hesitant to buy shares in a fluctuating market. Such investors would prefer, and value a lower payout ratio.

2. Underpricing fresh equity: MM model assumes that a firm can sell additional equity at the current market price. In practice, firms following the advice and suggestions of merchant bankers offer additional equity at a price lower than the current market price. This practice of "under pricing", mostly due to market compulsions, *ceteris paribus,* makes a rupee of retained earnings more valuable than a rupee of dividends. This is because of the chain of causation shown in Figure 13.4.

Figure 13.4
Relationship between Dividend Payout and Value of Equity

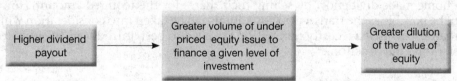

Source: Author.

3. Floatation costs: The MM irrelevance proposition is based on the premise that a rupee of dividend can be replaced by a rupee of external financing. This is possible when there is no issue cost. In the real world where issue cost is incurred, the amount of external financing has to be greater.than the amount of dividend paid. Due to this, other things being equal, its advantageous to retain earnings rather than pay dividends and resort to external finance.

4. Transaction costs: In the absence of transaction costs, current income (dividends) and capital gains are alike—a rupee of capital value can be converted into a rupee of current income and vice versa. In such a situation, if a shareholder desires current income (from shares) greater than the dividends received, he can sell a portion of his capital equal in value to the additional current income sought. Likewise, if he wishes to enjoy current income less than the dividends paid, he can buy additional shares equal in value to the difference between dividends received and the current income desired. In the real world, however, transaction costs are incurred. Due to this, capital value cannot be converted into an equal current income and vice versa. For example, a share worth ₹100 may fetch a net amount of ₹99 after transaction costs and ₹101 may be required to buy a share worth ₹100. Due to transaction costs, shareholders who have preference for current income, would prefer a higher payout ratio and shareholders who have preference for deferred income would prefer a lower payout ratio.

5. Differential taxation: MM model assumes that the investors are indifferent between a rupee of dividend and a rupee *of* capital appreciation. This assumption is true when the taxation is the same for current income and capital gains. In the real world, the effective tax on capital gains is lower than that for current income. Due to this difference, investors would prefer capital gains to current income.

Dividend Clientele Effect

According to this theory, dividend policy is irrelevant in determining the firm's value. Different firms may follow different dividend policies depending upon their own needs and circumstances. One may decide on a higher payout ratio whereas others may decide on lower dividend payout. Similarly, different shareholders may have different needs—some may prefer current dividends whereas others may be more interested in capital gains. Whatever dividend policy a firm follows, it will draw to itself shareholders whose requirements are in line with the dividend policy of the firm. Those investors who prefer current dividends would like to become shareholders in companies which declare generous dividends, whereas those investors who are more interested in capital gains would flock to companies having relatively lower payout ratios.

According to M and M, "each corporation would tend to attract itself a clientele consisting of those preferring its particular dividend payout ratio, but one clientele would be as good as another in terms of the valuation it would imply for firms."

If there is any sudden or dramatic change in the dividend policy of the firm, the clientele would also change and, consequently, it will result in a change in its share price.

M and M also argued that even if the shareholders desire more current income they could go for "home-made dividends" by selling their shares for the required amount. However, it may not be possible as the transaction costs are also to be taken into consideration while trading in shares. Now that a security transaction tax has also been introduced, the investors may not prefer this kind of action.

Rational Expectations Model

According to this model, there would be no effect of dividend declaration on the market price of the share as long as the dividend declared is in line with the expected dividends. If the dividend declared is different from the expected dividend then the market prices would adjust to account for this unexpected change. This is so because on the basis of information about the company from various sources, the market will form its expectations about the dividends and the prices will adjust accordingly before the actual declaration. When the dividend is subsequently declared by the company and is as per the market expectations, there will be no change in the market price as it has already discounted the expected dividends. However, if the dividends declared are different from the market expectations, the market price will change to account for the change in expected dividends. If the actual dividend is less than the expected, the market price will decline and if the actual dividend is more than the expected dividend the market price will move up to take into account the higher dividends.

Thus, insofar as the dividend declared ratifies the market expectations, the dividend policy is not relevant in determining the market price of the share and so also the market value of the firm.

Test Yourself

1. What is the essence of the MM theory?
2. Define the rational expectation model of dividend

Factors Affecting the Formulation of Dividend Policy

Profitability and Liquidity

The most important practical consideration influencing the dividend policy will be the firm's ability to generate adequate and stable income and cash flows. This is so because, as we shall see later, dividends are usually paid in cash. To pay cash dividends, the firm should have adequate cash inflows to pay for other operational and financial expenses before it can pay to the shareholders.

Legal Constraints

Usually, the law prohibits companies from paying out as cash dividends any portion of the firm's equity capital, which is measured by the par value of the common stock. These capital impairment restrictions are generally established to provide a sufficient equity base to protect the creditor's claims. Such legal constraints play an important role in formulating the dividend policy of the firm.

Contractual Constraints

Often, the firm's ability to pay cash dividends is constrained by restrictive provisions in a loan agreement. Generally, these constraints prohibit the payment of cash dividends until a certain level of earnings have been achieved, or they may limit dividends to a certain amount or a percentage of the earnings. Constraints on dividends help to protect creditors from losses due to the firm's insolvency. The violation of a contractual constraint is generally a ground for a demand of immediate payment by the funds supplier.

Growth Prospects

The firm's financial requirements are directly related to the anticipated degree of asset expansion. If the firm is in a growth stage, it may need all its funds to finance capital expenditures. Firms exhibiting little or no growth may never need to replace or renew the assets. A growth firm is likely to have to depend heavily on internal financing through retained earnings as dividends.

Owner Considerations

You know that in establishing a dividend policy, the firm's primary concern should be to maximize the shareholder's wealth. One such consideration, then, is the tax status of a firm's owners. Suppose that if a firm has a large percentage of wealthy stockholders who are in a high tax bracket, it may decide to pay out a lower percentage of its earnings to allow the owners to delay the payments of taxes until they sell the stock. Of course, when the stock is sold, the proceeds are in excess of the original purchase price, the capital gain will be taxed, possibly at a more favorable rate than the one applied to ordinary income. Lower-income shareholders who need dividend income will, however, prefer a higher payout of the earnings.

Market Considerations

We discussed the dividend signaling theory above where we said that dividends convey information about the future prospects of the company. A firm where the dividends fluctuate from period to period will be viewed as risky, and investors will require a high rate of return, which will increase the firm's cost of capital. So, the firm's dividend policy also depends on the market's probable response to certain types of policies. Shareholders are believed to value a fixed or increasing level of dividends as opposed to a fluctuating pattern of dividends.

Industry Practice

Different industries may have different patterns of cash flows, different investment requirements, etc., and hence may follow entirely different dividend policies. Firms in a particular industry are unlikely to deviate from the dividend policy followed by their peers in the industry.

Shareholders' Expectations

As discussed in the clientele effect, the shareholders will select a firm for investment if its dividend policies are in line with their preferences. Hence, the firm has to be cautious about the shareholders expectations. The shareholders may not view any sudden change in the dividend policy favorably. In such cases, they may even sell the shares causing the share prices to fall.

Test Yourself

1. What are the factors affecting dividend policy of the firm?

SUMMARY

1. Earnings which is distributable is called dividend. The percentage of earning which is distributed in the form of dividend is payout ratio. Dividend is paid on paid-up capital. If a company pays 20% dividend, it is 20% of paid-up capital.

2. Higher payout ratio denotes higher dividend and fewer amounts for expansion and growth. Lower dividend means fewer dividends to the shareholder and more amount for future projects.

3. Dividend will have an impact on market value of the firm.

4. Dividends are paid in two forms; cash dividend and stock dividend (bonus shares). Bonus shares are issued to the investor free of cost. Investor prefers cash dividend.

5. The company's ability to pay dividend depends on funds requirement for future projects. Amount of dividend depends on the shareholders desire and liquidity.

6. The company generally prefers stable dividend policy. Stable dividend does not mean constant dividend per share. But rather it means predictable dividend policy.

7. Walter model says that value of the firm depends on the future profitable opportunities. If the company's rate of return is greater than the cost of capital, company should invest rather than paying dividends. Conversely, the company should distribute 100% earnings in the form of dividend if the rate of return is less than the cost of capital.

$$P_0 = \frac{D + (E - D)r/k}{k}$$

8. Gordon model also emphasizes the same assumptions and considers relevance of dividend in affecting the value of the firm. It also suffers from the same limitation.

$$P = \frac{E(1-b)}{k_e - b_r}$$

9. **Dividend irrelevance theory:** These theories contend that there are two components of the shareholder' returns

Dividend yield (D/P_0)
Capital yield $((P_1 - P_0)/P_0)$

10. Miller and Modigliani model do not agree that dividends affect the market price. Share price will adjust according to the amount of dividend distributed. The shareholders neither get benefits nor are they worse off. The wealth of the shareholders would remain the same.

$$P_0 = \frac{1}{(1+k_e)}(D_1 + P_1)$$

11. Dividends signal future profitability and growth prospects of a firm.

12. There are various factors that affect dividend policy.

KEY TERMS

- Agency cost
- Cash dividend
- Declining firms
- Dividend
- Floatation cost
- High payout
- Payout ratio
- Retention ratio
- Underpricing

- Bird-in-hand theory
- Clientele effect
- Differential taxation
- Dividend signaling
- Growth firms
- Low payout
- Rational expectation
- Stock dividend
- Bird-in-hand theory

Learning Outcomes

Students would have appreciated different approaches to dividend and would be in a position to correlate rate of dividend, payment of dividend, and market price of shares.

CASE STUDY ON THE DIVIDEND POLICY OF HERO MOTOCORP LTD

Hero Motocorp Ltd (Formerly Hero Honda Motors Ltd) is the world's largest manufacturer of two-wheelers, based in India. In 2001, the company achieved the coveted position of being the largest two-wheeler manufacturing company in India and also, the "World No. 1" two-wheeler company in terms of unit volume sales in a calendar year. Hero Motocorp Ltd continues to maintain this position till date.

Vision

The story of Hero Honda began with a simple vision—the vision of a mobile and an empowered India, powered by its bikes. Hero Motocorp Ltd company's new identity, reflects its commitment toward providing world-class mobility solutions with renewed focus on expanding the company's footprint in the global arena.

Mission

Hero Motocorp's mission is to become a global enterprise fulfilling its customers' needs and aspirations for mobility, setting benchmarks in technology, styling, and quality so that it converts its customers into its brand advocates. The company will provide an engaging environment for its people to perform to their true potential. It will continue its focus on value creation and enduring relationships with its partners.

Strategy

Hero Motocorp's key strategies are to build a robust product portfolio across categories, explore growth opportunities globally, continuously improve its operational efficiency, aggressively expand its reach to the customers, continue to invest in brand building activities, and ensure customers' and shareholders' delight.

CERTAIN KEY RATIOS					
Particulars	2005–2006	2006–2007	2007–2008	2008–2009	2009–2010
Sales (numbers)	3,000,751	3,336,756	3,337,142	3,722,000	4,600,130
Growth in sales (numbers) (%)	14.5	11.2	0.01	11.53	23.59
Total net income	8,870	10,090	10,517	12,540	16,099
Growth in total income (%)	17.4	13.7	4.2	19.2	28.1
Profit before tax	1,412	1,246	1,410	1,781	2,832
Profit after tax	971	858	968	1,282	2,232
Share capital	39.94	39.94	39.94	39.94	39.94
Reserves and surplus	1,969	2,430	2,946	3,761	3,425
Total debt	186	165	132	78	66
Net fixed assets	994	1,355	1,549	1,694	1,707
Total assets (net)	2,195	2,635	3,118	3,879	3,531
Market capitalization	17,781	13,753	13,869	21,390	38,827

Dividend Policy for 2010–2011 and 2011–2012

Hero Motocorp has gone for stock split in 2001. The face value of the share has been reduced from ₹10 to ₹2. Over the years, the Company has consistently followed a policy of paying high dividends, keeping in mind the cash-generating capacities, the expected capital needs of the business, and strategic considerations. For 2010–2011, the board has recommended a dividend of 1,750%, higher than 1,500% declared in previous year, and has maintained a payout ratio of 42.1% vis-à-vis 31.3% in the previous year. Further, it has also declared a 3,500% interim dividend (previous year 4,000%). Given the strong financial position, your Company declared and paid an interim dividend of 3,500%, that is, ₹70 per equity share of the face value of ₹2 each, totaling ₹1,397.81 crores (exclusive of tax on dividend). Your directors are pleased to recommend a final dividend of 1,750%, that is, ₹35 per equity share of the face value of ₹2 per share, aggregating to ₹698.91 crores (exclusive of tax on dividend), for the financial year ended March 31, 2011 for your approval. The final dividend, if approved, will be paid to the eligible members well within the stipulated period.

Information Pertaining to Dividend

Particulars	2001–2002	2002–2003	2003–2004	2004–2005	2005–2006
EPS	23.2	29.1	36.5	40.6	48.6
DPS	17.0	18.0	20.0	20.0	20.0
Dividend payout ratio (%)	73.2	61.85	54.79	49.26	46.9
Dividend % of face value	850	900	1,000	1,000	1,000

Particulars	2006–2007	2007–2008	2008–2009	2009–2010	2010–2011
EPS	43	48.5	64.2	111.8	96.5
DPS	17	19	20	110	105.0
Dividend payout ratio (%)	46.3	45.9	36.5	98.38	108.80
Dividend % of face value	850	950	1,000	5,500	5,250

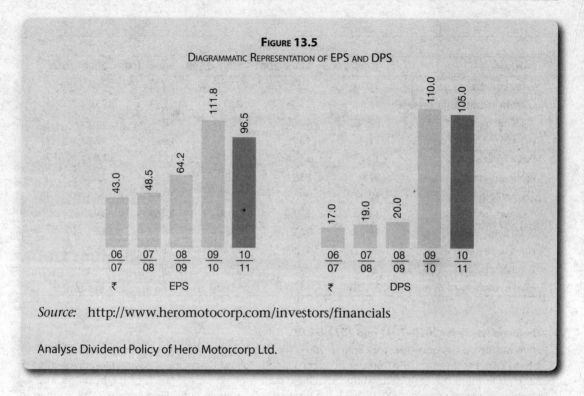

FIGURE 13.5
DIAGRAMMATIC REPRESENTATION OF EPS AND DPS

Source: http://www.heromotocorp.com/investors/financials

Analyse Dividend Policy of Hero Motorcorp Ltd.

SOLVED PROBLEMS

1. Abhishek Computers expects EBIT of ₹2,000,000 for the current year. The firm's capital structure consists of 40% debt and 60% equity, and its marginal tax rate is 40%. The cost of equity is 14%, and the company pays a 10% rate on its ₹5,000,000 of long-term debt. One million shares of common stock are outstanding. For the next year, the firm expects to fund one large positive NPV project costing ₹1,200,000, and it will fund this project in accordance with its target capital structure. If the firm follows a residual dividend policy and has no other projects, what is its expected dividend payout ratio?

Solution

EBIT	₹2,000,000
Interest	500,000
EBT	₹1,500,000
Taxes	600,000
NI	₹900,000
Project funding	720,000

₹1,200,000 project funded as follows:

$$0.60 \text{ equity} = ₹720,000$$

$$0.40 \text{ debt} = ₹480,000$$

Residual earnings payable as dividends ₹180,000

$$\text{Dividend payout ratio} = ₹180,000/₹900,000 = 20\%.$$

2. A firm has recently paid a dividend of ₹2.00 per share. The earnings per share of the company for the current year is ₹10 and the cost of equity capital of the company is 20%. It is assumed that the Walter's model on dividend policy is applicable to the company. The existing market price per share of the company is ₹60. Find out the market price per share of the company if the earnings per share is ₹12 and the payout ratio is 40%.

Solution

According to the Walter's model on dividend policy

$$P = \frac{D}{k_e} + \frac{r(E-D)/k_e}{k_e}$$

Given

$$\text{Existing market price per share, } P = ₹60$$

$$\text{Cost of equity capital, } k_e = 20\%$$

$$\text{Earnings per share, } E = ₹10$$

$$\text{Earnings per share, } E = ₹10$$

$$\text{Dividend per share, } D = ₹2$$

$$\therefore \quad 60 = \frac{2}{0.20} + \frac{r(10-2)/0.20}{0.20} = 10 + 200r$$

or

$$r = \frac{60-10}{200} = 0.25, \text{ i.e. } 25\%$$

If EPS = 12 and payout ratio = 40%, that is, 0.40, then

$$D = 12 \times 0.40 = ₹4.80$$

$$\therefore \quad P = \frac{4.80}{0.20} + \frac{0.25r(12-4.80)/0.20}{0.20} = ₹69$$

3. Malavika Steel has 1 lakh equity shares outstanding which are selling at ₹100 each. Its capitalization rate is 14%. The company is expecting ₹65 lakhs income for the current year and is planning to pay dividends amounting to ₹4 lakhs. The company wants to invest in a new project which will cost ₹75 lakhs. It is assumed that the Miller and Modigliani model on dividend policy is applicable to the company.

(a) Compute the price per share at the end of the current year and the number of shares to be issued for financing the investment when dividends amounting to ₹4 lakhs are paid.

(b) Compute the price per share at the end of the current year and the number of shares to be issued for financing the investment when dividends are not paid.

Solution

(a) According to the MM model

When dividends are paid

$$P_0 = \frac{1}{(1+k)}(D_1 + P_1)$$

$$P_0 = ₹100 \text{ per share (given)}$$

$$k = 0.14$$

$$D_1 = \frac{4}{1} ₹4.00 \text{ per share}$$

$$P_1 = ?$$

$$\therefore \quad 100 = \frac{4 + P_1}{1.14}$$

or

$$P_1 = 100 \cdot 1.14 - 4 = ₹110$$

Amount of additional investment required

$$= I - (E - n D_1)$$

$$= 75 - (65 - 1 \cdot 4.00) = ₹14 \text{ lakhs} = n_1 P_1$$

Number of equity shares to be issued additionally (n_1)

$$= \frac{14}{P_1} = \frac{14}{110} = 0.12727 \text{ lakh}$$

Thus, 12,727 shares have to be issued.

(b) When dividends are not paid

$$P_0 = \frac{1}{(1+k)}(D_1 + P_1)$$

$$D_1 = 0, P_0 = ₹(\text{given}) \, k = 0.14 \text{ (given)}$$

$$\therefore \quad 100 = \frac{0 + P_1}{1.14} = \frac{P_1}{1.14}$$

Or

$$P_1 = ₹114$$

Amount of additional investment required $= I - (E - nD_1)$

$$= 75 - (65 - 0)$$

$$= ₹10 \text{ lakhs}$$

$$= n_1 P_1$$

Number of equity shares to be issued additionally $= \frac{10}{114} = 0.08772 \text{ lakh}.$

$\therefore$ 8,772 equity shares have to be issued additionally.

4. The following information regarding the equity shares of M/s VNS Ltd is given:

EPS	=₹6.00
Dividend payout	=50%
Multiplier	=3.40

   What is the market price per share as per the traditional model?

   Solution

   The traditional approach to dividend policy establishes a relationship between the market price and the dividends in the following manner:

   $$P = m(D + E/3)$$

   where m is a multiplier, D is the dividend per share (DPS), and E is the earnings per share (EPS).

   Hence, $P = 3.4(3 + 6/3)$

   So, $P = ₹17$.

5. Consider the following information for a firm:

Profit before tax	=₹250,000
Tax rate	=40%
Retention ratio	=40%
Number of outstanding shares	=50,000
Equity capitalization rate	=12%
Rate of return on investment	=15%

   What should be the market price per share according to the Gordon's model on dividend policy?

   Solution

   Here, the profit after tax $= ₹2.50(1 - 0.40) = ₹1.50$ lakhs

   Amount of dividend paid $= ₹1.50$ lakhs $(1 - 0.40) = ₹0.90$ lakhs $= ₹90,000$

   Hence, the amount of dividend paid per share $= 90/50 = ₹1.80$

   According to the Gordon's capitalization model,

   $$\text{The share price } p = \frac{E(1-b)}{K_e - b_r}$$

   Here, $E(1-b) = ₹1.80$, $K_e = 12\%$, $r = 15\%$ and $b = 0.40$.

   $$P = \frac{1.80}{0.12 - 0.15 \times 0.4} = \frac{1.80}{0.06} = ₹30$$

   Hence, the share price will be $P = \dfrac{1.80}{0.12 - 0.15 \times 0.4} = \dfrac{1.80}{0.06} = ₹30$

6. A company has a total investment of ₹500,000 in assets and 50,000 outstanding shares of ₹10 each. Dividend Payout ratio is 50%. Its rate of return is 10%. Discount rate is 7%. Determine the price of share using Gordon's model. What shall happen to the price if payout ratio increases to 70%.

Solution

$$\text{Share price} = p = \frac{E(1-b)}{K_e - b_r}$$

Earnings available for distribution: $500,000 \times 10/100 = 50,000$

$$EPS = 50,000/50,000 = ₹1$$

$$P = 1.00\ (1-0.50)/(0.07-0.50 \times 0.10) = 1.00/0.02 = ₹50$$

At 70% payout ratio

$$P = 1.00\ (1-0.3)/(0.07-0.3 \times 0.10) = 0.70/0.04 = ₹17.5$$

The price fallen from ₹50 to ₹17.5 with increase in payout ratio. It justifies that when rate of return is greater than the cost of capital, optimum dividend policy is 0%.

7. Determine the market price of Zerox Ltd from the following information:

Earnings of the company	=₹1,000,000
Dividend paid	=₹600,000
Number of shares outstanding	=200,000
Price/earnings ratio	=8
Rate of return on investment	=15%

Are you satisfied with current dividend policy of the firm? If not, what should be the optimal dividend payout ratio using Walter's model.

Solution

$$\text{Price Earnings Ratio} = \frac{\text{Market Price}}{\text{EPS}}$$

$$8 = \frac{\text{Market Price}}{5}$$

$$\text{Market Price} = 8 \times 5 = ₹40$$

$$EPS = \frac{\text{Earnings available to the shareholders}}{\text{No. of outstanding shares}} = \frac{10,00,000}{2,00,000}$$

$$EPS = ₹5 \text{ per share}$$

$$DPS = \frac{\text{Dividend Paid}}{\text{No. of shares}} = \frac{6,00,000}{2,00,000}$$

$$DPS = ₹3$$

$$\text{Dividend Payout Ratio} = \frac{DPS}{EPS} \times 100 = \frac{3}{5} \times 100 = 60\%$$

Cost of equity is reciprocal of p/E ratio

$$K_e = \frac{1}{8} \times 100 = 12.5\%$$

Since, the rate of return on investment is 15% and cost of capital is 12.5%, the rate of return on investment is greater than the cost of capital. Therefore, the optimum dividend policy is 0%.

$$P = \frac{D}{k_e} + \frac{r(E-D)/k_e}{k_e}$$

$$P = \frac{3}{0.125} + \frac{\dfrac{0.15(5-0)}{0.125}}{0.125} = 40 + 8 = ₹48$$

ASSESS YOURSELF

Concept Review and Critical Thinking Questions

1. What are dividends? What is meant by the dividend policy? What are the various commonly used dividend policies? Is there any optimal dividend policy?
2. What do you mean by residual theory of dividends? How does it affect a firm's dividend payments? Discuss.
3. Can Walter's dividend model be used in practice to determine the dividend policy? Discuss.
4. What is bird-in-hand theory? Discuss the M&M bird-in-hand fallacy.
5. Discuss the M&M dividend irrelevancy theory. Illustrate your answer.
6. What do you mean by rational expectations hypothesis? Discuss.

STUDENT ACTIVITY

Student should collect data of select dividend-paying companies from the NSE and the BSE and should analyze relationship between dividend declaration and fluctuations in market price during 2014–2015.

SUGGESTED READINGS

Brealey, R.A., & Myers, S.C. (2002). *Principles of corporate finance* (7th ed.). New York: McGraw-Hill.
Horne, J.C.V. (2002). *Financial management & policy* (12th ed.). Singapore: Pearson Education.
Ross, S.A., Westerfield, R.W., & Jordan, B.D. (2002). *Fundamentals of corporate finance* (6th ed.). New Delhi: Tata McGraw-Hill.

CHAPTER 14

Corporate Restructuring

- To focus on the form of merger and acquisition.
- To explain the motives of merger and acquisition.
- To understand driver and valuation of merger and acquisition.

PRELUDE

How Mergers and Acquisitions Are Shaping Up India

The current economic environment suggests that there has to be size, volume, and presence of a high scale in order to grow and develop faster in the competitive market. When opportunities are fast drying up and resources are limited, perhaps mergers and acquisitions (M&A) is the only viable solution to retain and maintain an edge over competitors. Read the following to have a better understanding on how M&A are shaping up India.

M&A, in today's world, are the most fundamental elements of a corporate strategy, be it for a huge MNC in course of taking over a fast-growing gazelle company (the recent acquisition of Skype by the software giant Microsoft for a whopping $8.5 billion), or for two equals in the process of undergoing a merger (the merging of the then giant pharmaceuticals Glaxo Wellcome and SmithKline Beecham, to form a new pharmaceutical company, Glaxo Smith Kline Pharmaceuticals [GSK India]).

In simple terms, an acquisition is when one company takes over or purchases another company while a merger is a consensual situation wherein two companies agree to continue business operations and go forward as a single new company. By definition, a merger is generally a "merger of equals" (the firms are about the same size).

In recent years, India has been a very active player in the M&A transactions, both locally and globally. After a dismal 2009, 2010 proved to be just the year for M&As in India. According to an M&A global outlook survey by Bloomberg, companies in the Asia-Pacific region especially China and India were expected to be the most active buyers in 2011, which is what has exactly happened.

The volume of M&A deals in India had manifested three-folds to US$67.2 billion in 2010 from US$21.3 billion in 2009. Now, in 2011, M&As in India surged a whopping 270% in the first 3 months alone. Indeed, India has emerged into one of the top countries in the M&A deals. In addition, cross-border M&A were very rare in India till a couple of years ago. But now, news of Indian companies acquiring foreign businesses is quite common. The percentage of cross-border transactions has risen significantly. Cross-border deals in India have taken the form of both inbound and outbound transactions. The growth in inbound transactions can mainly be attributed to the fact that foreign companies have been increasingly interested in acquiring Indian firms in the IT and telecom sectors. As far as the outbound transactions are concerned, they too have increased significantly, with manufacturing companies acquiring the overseas companies. Two of the major acquisitions made by Indian companies worldwide are those of Tata Steel acquiring Corus Group plc (UK) for $12,000 million and that of Hindalco acquiring Novelis (Canada) for $6,000 million, both in the steel industries.

Whether it's Indian companies that are looking to expand by capturing foreign markets or foreign companies wishing to acquire market share in India, M&A have been used as means to achieve crucial growth and are becoming more and more accepted than ever as a tool for implementing business strategy. Major factors, such as favorable government policies, buoyancy in the economy, additional liquidity in the corporate sector, and dynamic attitudes of Indian entrepreneurs, have helped in facilitating the M&A transactions in India.

As George Bernard Shaw famously said, "We are made wise not by the collection of our past, but by the responsibility for our future"; and the future of India is definitely bright.

Source: http://www.youthkiawaaz.com/2011/06mergers-and-acquisitions-are-shaping-up-india/

Restructuring of business is an integral part of the new economic paradigm. As controls and restrictions give way to competition and free trade, restructuring and reorganization become essential. Restructuring usually involves major organizational change such as shift in corporate strategies to meet increased competition or changed market conditions. This activity can take place internally in the form of new investments in plant and machinery, research and development at product and process levels. It can also take place externally through M&A by which a firm may acquire other firm or by joint venture with other firms. This restructuring process has been mergers, acquisitions, takeovers, collaborations, consolidation, and diversification. Domestic firms have taken steps to consolidate their position to face increasing competitive pressures and MNCs have taken this opportunity to enter the Indian corporate sector.

Forms of Corporate Restructuring

Expansion

Following are the types of expansion:

Amalgamation: This involves fusion of one or more companies where the companies lose their individual identity and a new company comes into existence to take over the business of companies being liquidated. The merger of Brooke Bond India Ltd and Lipton India Ltd resulted in the formation of a new company Brooke Bond Lipton India Ltd.

Absorption: This involves fusion of a small company with a large company where the smaller company ceases to exist after the merger. The merger of Tata Oil Mills Ltd (TOMCO) with Hindustan Lever Ltd (HLL) is an example of absorption.

Tender Offer: This involves making a public offer for acquiring the shares of a target company with a view to acquire management control in that company. Takeover by Tata Tea of Consolidated Coffee Ltd (CCL) is an example of tender offer where more than 50% of shareholders of CCL sold their holding to Tata Tea at the offered price which was more than the investment price.

Asset Acquisition: This involves buying assets of another company. The assets may be tangible assets like manufacturing units or intangible like brands. HLL buying brands of Lakme is an example of asset acquisition.

Joint Venture: This involves the coming together of two companies whose ownership is changed. DCM Group and DAEWOO Motors entered into a joint venture to form DAEWOO Ltd to manufacture automobiles in India.

Contraction

There are generally the following types of contraction:

Spinoff: This type of demerger involves division of company into wholly owned subsidiary of parent company by distribution of all its shares of subsidiary company on pro-rata basis. By this way, both the companies, that is, holding as well as subsidiary company exist and carry on business. For example, Kotak Mahindra Finance Ltd formed a subsidiary called Kotak Mahindra Capital Corporation, by spinning off its investment banking division.

Split-ups: This type of demerger involves the division of parent company into two or more separate companies where parent company ceases to exist after the demerger.

Equity carve-out: This is similar to spin offs, except that same part of shareholding of this subsidiary company is offered to public through a public issue and the parent company continues to enjoy control over the subsidiary company by holding controlling interest in it.

Divestitures: These are sales of segment of a company for cash or for securities to an outside party. Divestitures involve some kind of contraction. It is based on the principle of "anergy" which says $5-3=3!$

Asset Sale: This involves sale of tangible or intangible assets of a company to generate cash. A partial sell-off, also called slump sale, involves the sale of a business unit or plant of one firm to another. It is the mirror image of a purchase of a business unit or plant. From the seller's perspective, it is a form of contraction.

From the buyer's point of view, it is a form of expansion. For example, when Coromandel Fertilizers Limited sold its cement division to India Cement Limited, the size of Coromandel Fertilizers contracted, whereas the size of India Cements Limited expanded.

Corporate Controls

Going Private: This involves converting a listed company into a private company by buying back all the outstanding shares from the markets. Several companies, such as Castrol India and Phillips India, have done this. A well-known example from the US is that of Levi Strauss & Company.

Equity Buyback: This involves the company buying its own shares back from the market. This results in reduction in the equity capital of the company. This strengthens the promoter's position by increasing his stake in the equity of the company.

Anti-takeover Defenses: With a high value of hostile takeover activity in recent years, takeover defenses both premature and reactive have been restored to by the companies.

Leveraged Buyouts (LBOs): This involves raising of capital from the market or institutions by the management to acquire a company on the strength of its assets.

Types of Business Combination

Amalgamation

Amalgamation is an arrangement or reconstruction. It is a legal process by which two or more companies are to be absorbed or blended with another. As a result, the amalgamating company loses its existence and its shareholders become shareholders of new company or the amalgamated company. In case of amalgamation, a new company may come into existence or an old company may survive while amalgamating company may lose its existence.

Amalgamation signifies the transfers of all or some part of assets and liabilities of one or more than one existing company or two or more companies to a new company.

The Accounting Standard, AS-14, issued by the Institute of Chartered Accountants of India has defined the term amalgamation by classifying (i) amalgamation in the nature of merger, and (ii) amalgamation in the nature of purchase.

1. Amalgamation in the Nature of Merger: As per AS-14, an amalgamation is called in the nature of merger if it satisfies all the following conditions:

- All the assets and liabilities of the transferor company should become, after amalgamation, the assets and liabilities of the other company.
- Shareholders holding not less than 90% of the face value of the equity shares of the transferor company (other than the equity shares already held therein, immediately before the amalgamation, by the transferee company or its subsidiaries or their nominees) become equity shareholders of the transferee company by virtue of the amalgamation.
- The consideration for the amalgamation receivable by those equity shareholders of the transferor company who agree to become equity shareholders of the transferee company is discharged by the transferee company wholly by the issue of equity share in the transferee company, except that cash may be paid in respect of any fractional shares.
- The business of the transferor company is intended to be carried on, after the amalgamation, by the transferee company.
- No adjustment is intended to be made in the book values of the assets and liabilities of the transferor company when they are incorporated in the financial statements of the transferee company except to ensure uniformity of accounting policies.
- Amalgamation in the nature of merger is an organic unification of two or more entities or undertaking or fusion of one with another. It is defined as an amalgamation which satisfies the above conditions.

2. Amalgamation in the Nature of Purchase: Amalgamation in the nature of purchase is where one company's assets and liabilities are taken over by another and lump sum is paid by the latter to the former. It is defined as the one which does not satisfy any one or more of the conditions satisfied above.

As per Income Tax Act 1961, merger is defined as amalgamation under Sec. 2 (1B) with the following three conditions to be satisfied.

1. All the properties of amalgamating company(s) should vest with the amalgamated company after amalgamation.
2. All the liabilities of the amalgamating company(s) should vest with the amalgamated company after amalgamation.
3. Shareholders holding not less than 75% in value or voting power in amalgamating company(s) should become shareholders of amalgamated companies after amalgamation.

Amalgamation does not mean acquisition of a company by purchasing its property and resulting in its winding up. According to Income Tax Act, exchange of shares with 90% of shareholders of amalgamating company is required.

Acquisition

Acquisition refers to the acquiring of ownership right in the property and asset without any combination of companies. Thus, in acquisition, two or more companies may remain independent, separate legal entity, but there may be change in control of companies. Acquisition results when one company purchases the controlling interest in the share capital of another existing company in any of the following ways:

1. Controlling interest in the other company. By entering into an agreement with a person or persons holding.
2. By subscribing new shares being issued by the other company.
3. By purchasing shares of the other company at a stock exchange.
4. By making an offer to buy the shares of other company, to the existing shareholders of that company.

Takeover

Acquisition can be undertaken through merger or takeover route. Takeover is a general term used to define acquisitions only and both terms are used interchangeably. A takeover may be defined as a series of transaction whereby a person, individual, group of individuals, or a company acquires control over the assets of a company, either directly by becoming owner of those assets or indirectly by obtaining control of management of the company.

Takeover is acquisition, by one company of controlling interest of the other, usually by buying all or majority of the shares. Takeover may be of different types depending upon the purpose of acquiring a company.

1. A takeover may be straight takeover which is accomplished by the management of the taking over company by acquiring shares of another company with the intention of taking over the operations as an independent legal entity.
2. The second type of takeover is where ownership of the company is captured to merge both companies into one and operate as a single legal entity.
3. A third type of takeover is takeover of a sick company for its revival. This is accomplished by an order of Board for Industrial and Financial Reconstruction (BIFR) under the provision of Sick Industrial Companies Act, 1985. In India, BIFR has also been active for arranging mergers of financially sick companies with other companies under the package of rehabilitation. These merger schemes are framed in consultation with the lead bank, the target firm, and the acquiring firm. These mergers are motivated and the lead bank takes the initiative and decides the terms and conditions of merger. The recent takeover of Modi Cements Ltd by Gujarat Ambuja Cement Ltd was an arranged takeover after the financial reconstruction of the Modi Cement Ltd. The fourth kind is the bail-out takeover, which is substantial acquisition of shares in a financially weak company not being a sick industrial company in pursuance to a scheme of rehabilitation approved by public financial institution which is responsible for ensuring compliance with provision of Substantial Acquisition of Shares and Takeover Regulations 1997 issued by SEBI, which regulates the bailout takeover.

Takeover Bid

This is a technique for affecting either a takeover or an amalgamation. It may be defined as an offer to acquire shares of a company, whose shares are not closely held, addressed to the general body of shareholders with a view to obtaining at least sufficient shares to give the offer or voting control of the company. Takeover bid is, thus, adopted by the company for taking over the control and management of affairs of the listed company by acquiring its controlling interest.

While a takeover bid is used for affecting a takeover, it is frequently against the wishes of the management of Offeree Company. It may take the form of an offer to purchase shares for cash or for share for share exchange or a combination of these two firms.

Where a takeover bid is used for effecting merger or amalgamation, it is generally by consent of management of both the companies. It always takes place in the form of share for share exchange offer, so that accepting shareholders of Offeree Company become shareholders of Offeror Company.

Types of Takeover Bids

There are three types of takeover bid:

1. Negotiated Bid
2. Tender Offer
3. Hostile Takeover Bid

Negotiated Bid: It is also called friendly merger. In this case, the management/owners of both the firms sit together and negotiate for the takeover. The acquiring firm negotiates directly with the management of the target company. So the two firms reach an agreement, the proposal for merger may be placed before the shareholders of the two companies. However, if the parties do not reach at an agreement, the merger proposal stands terminated and dropped out. The merger of ITC Classic Ltd with ICICI Ltd and merger of Tata Oil Mills Ltd with HLL were negotiated mergers.

However, if the management of the target firm is not agreeable to the merger proposal, then the acquiring firm may go for other procedures, that is, tender offer or hostile takeover.

Tender Offer: A tender offer is a bid to acquire controlling interest in a target company by the acquiring firm by purchasing shares of the target firm at a fixed price. The acquiring firm approaches the shareholders of the target firm directly to sell their shareholding to the acquiring firm at a fixed price. This offered price is generally kept at a level higher than the current market price in order to induce the shareholders to disinvest their holding in favor of the acquiring firm. The acquiring firm may also stipulate in the tender offer as to how many shares it is willing to buy or may purchase all the shares that are offered for sale.

In case of tender offer, the acquiring firm does not need the prior approval of the management of the target firm. The offer is kept open for a specific period within which the shares must be tendered for sale by the shareholders of the target firm.

Consolidated Coffee Ltd was takeover by Tata Tea Ltd by making a tender offer to the shareholders of the former at a price which was higher than the prevailing market price.

In India, in recent times, particularly after the announcement of new takeover code by SEBI, several companies have made tender offers to acquire the target firm. A popular case is the tender offer made by Sterlite Ltd and then counter offer by Alean to acquire the control of Indian Aluminium Ltd.

Hostile Takeover Bid: The acquiring firm, without the knowledge and consent of the management of the target firm, may unilaterally pursue the efforts to gain a controlling interest in the target firm, by purchasing shares of the latter firm at the stock exchanges.

Such case of M&A is popularly known as "raid." The Caparo Group of the UK made a hostile takeover bid to takeover DCM Ltd and Escorts Ltd. Similarly, some other NRIs have also made hostile bid to takeover some other Indian companies.

The new takeover code, as announced by SEBI, deals with the hostile bids.

Merger

Merger refers to a situation when two or more existing firms combine together and form a new entity. Either a new company may be incorporated for this purpose or one existing company (generally a bigger one) survives and another existing company (which is smaller) is merged into it. Laws in India use the term amalgamation for merger.

Merger through Absorption: Absorption is a combination of two or more companies into an existing company. All companies except one lose their identity in a merger through absorption. An example of this type of merger is the absorption of Tata Fertilizers Ltd (TFL). Tata Chemicals Ltd (TCL), an acquiring company (a buyer), survived after merger while TFL, an acquired company (a seller), ceased to exist. TFL transferred its assets, liabilities, and shares to TCL.

Merger through Consolidation: A consolidation is a combination of two or more companies into a new company. In this type of merger, all companies are legally dissolved and a new entity is created. In a consolidation, the acquired company transfers its assets, liabilities, and shares to the acquiring company for cash or exchange of shares. An example of consolidation is the merger of Hindustan Computers Ltd, Hindustan Instruments Ltd, and Indian Reprographics Ltd, to an entirely new company called HCL Ltd.

Merger is a marriage between two companies of roughly the same size. It is thus a combination of two or more companies in which one company survives in its own name and the other ceases to exist as a legal entity. The survivor company acquires assets and liabilities of the merged companies. Generally, the company which survives is the buyer which retires its identity and the seller company is extinguished.

Types of Mergers

There are four types of mergers as follows:

1. Horizontal Merger: It is a merger of two or more companies that compete in the same industry. It is a merger with a direct competitor and hence expands as the firms operate in the same industry. Horizontal mergers are designed to produce substantial economies of scale and result in the decrease in the number of competitors in the industry. The merger of Tata Oil Mills Ltd with the HLL was a horizontal merger. Coco Cola, Parle, Chevron, and Texaco are examples of horizontal mergers.

In the case of horizontal merger, the top management of the company being meted is generally replaced by the management of the transferee company. One potential repercussion of the horizontal merger is that it may result in monopolies and restrict the trade. M.A. Weinberg and M.V. Blank (1989, *Weinberg and Blank on takeovers and mergers*, 5th ed. London: Sweet & Maxwell) define horizontal merger as follows:

"A takeover or merger is horizontal if it involves the joining together of two companies which are producing essentially the same products or services or products or services which compete directly with each other (e.g., sugar and artificial sweetness). In recent years, the great majority of takeover and mergers have been horizontal. As horizontal takeovers and mergers involve a reduction in the number of competing firms in an industry, they tend to create the greatest concern from an anti-monopoly point of view, on the other hand horizontal mergers and takeovers are likely to give the greatest scope for economies of scale and elimination of duplicate facilities."

2. Vertical Merger: It is a merger which takes place upon the combination of two companies which are operating in the same industry but at different stages of production or distribution system. If a company takes over its supplier/producers of raw material, then it may result in backward integration of its activities. On the other hand, forward integration may result if a company decides to take over the retailer or the customer company.

Vertical merger may result in many operating and financial economies. The transferee firm will get a stronger position in the market as its production/distribution chain will be more integrated than that of the competitors. Vertical merger provides a way for total integration to those firms which are striving for owning of all phases of the production schedule together with the marketing network (i.e., from the acquisition of raw material to the relating of final products). "A takeover of merger is vertical where one of the two companies is an actual or potential supplier of goods or services to the other, so that the two companies are both engaged in the manufacture or provision of the same goods or services but at the different stages in the supply route (e.g., where a motor car manufacturer takes over a manufacturer of sheet metal or a car distributing firm). Here the object is usually to ensure a source of supply or an outlet for products or services, but the effect of the merger may be to improve efficiency through improving the flow of production and reducing stock holding and handling costs, where, however there is a degree of concentration in the markets of either of the companies, anti-monopoly problems may arise." Microsoft-Hotmail, Google and You Tube are examples of vertical integration.

3. Co-generic Merger: In these mergers, the acquirer and target companies are related through basic technologies, production processes, or markets. The acquired company represents an extension of product line, market participants, or technologies of the acquiring companies. These mergers represent an outward movement by the acquiring company from its current set of business to adjoining business. The acquiring company derives benefits by exploitation of strategic resources and from entry into a related market having higher return than it enjoyed earlier. The potential benefit from these mergers is high because these transactions offer opportunities to diversify around a common case of strategic resources. When a new product line allied to or complementary to an existing product line is added to the existing product line through merger, it is defined as product-extension merger. Similarly, market-extension merger helps to add a new market either through the same line of business or adding an allied field. Both these types bear some common elements of horizontal, vertical, and conglomerate merger. For example, merger between Hindustan Sanitary Ware Industries Ltd and associated Glass Ltd is a product-extension merger and merger between GMM Company Ltd and Xpro Ltd contains elements of both product-extension and market-extension merger.

4. Conglomerate Merger: These mergers involve firms engaged in unrelated type of business activities, that is, the business of two companies is not related to each other horizontally (in the sense of producing the same or competing products) nor vertically (in the sense of standing toward each other in the relationship of buyer and supplier or potential buyer and supplier). In a pure conglomerate, there are no important common factors between the companies in production, marketing, research and development, and technology. In practice, however, there is some degree of overlap in one or more of this common factor.

Conglomerate mergers are unification of different kinds of businesses under one flagship company. The purpose of merger remains utilization of financial resources, enlarged debt capacity, and also synergy of managerial functions. However, these transactions are not explicitly aimed at sharing these resources, technologies, synergies, or product market strategies. Rather, the focus of such conglomerate mergers is on how the acquiring firm can improve its overall stability and use resources in a better way to generate additional revenue. It does not have a direct impact on acquisition of monopoly power, and is thus favored throughout the world as a means of diversification.

Test Yourself

1. Define corporate restructuring. What are various forms of restructuring?
2. What is merger? Discuss various types of mergers.
3. What is acquisition? How is it different from takeover?
4. Explain the various types of takeover bid.

Drivers for Value Creation in Case of M&A

Drivers for value creation may be business synergies, inorganic growth, gain more competitive position, focus on core competencies, achieve economies of scale, state enhancement, greater control over assets and operations, exit, strategic alliances/partnerships, unlocking value as commercial logic and tax savings, reducing administrative and management costs, upstreaming cash, encashing value, cash infusion in operations, projecting stronger financials, organic growth, and larger dividends to promoters.

In the following, the above points are discussed in detail:

1. Diversification: Diversification destroys value. The degree of relatedness between the businesses of the buyer and seller is positively associated with returns. In particular, conglomerate deals (i.e., deals between firms with unrelated lines of business) are associated with the poorest returns. Diversifying (unrelated) mergers tend to be associated with worse performance than related mergers.

2. Synergy: Expected synergies are important drivers of the wealth creation through merger. Synergistic benefits in terms of enabling complementaries in marketing and production, gaining economies of scale and scope as well as improvement in risk management are appreciated. The market appears to discount the value of these benefits and applies a greater discount to revenue-enhancing synergies and a smaller discount to cost-reduction synergies.

3. Value acquiring pays, glamour acquiring does not. Study has found that post-acquisition underperformance by buyers was associated with "glamour" acquirers (companies with high book-to-market value ratios). Value-oriented buyers (low book-to-market ratios) outperform glamour buyers.

4. Market Power: M&A to build market power does not pay. Studies reveal that efforts to enhance market position through M&A yield no better performance, and sometimes worse.

5. Purchase Consideration: Paying with stock is costly; paying with cash is neutral. It has been found that stock-based deals are associated with significantly negative returns at deal announcements, whereas cash-based deals are zero or slightly positive. Thus, the announcement of the payment with shares (like an announcement of an offering of seasoned stock) could be taken as a signal that managers believe the firm's shares are overpriced.

6. Deployment of Excess Cash: M&A to use excess cash generally destroys value except when redeployed profitably. Cash-rich firms have a choice of returning the cash to investors through dividends, or reinvesting it through activities such as M&A. Studies 12 report value destruction by the announcement of M&A transactions by firms with excess cash. Before merger, buyers have more cash and lower debt ratios than non-acquirers. In addition, the return to the buyers' shareholders increases with the change in the buyer's debt ratio due to the merger.

7. Tender Offers: Tender offers create value for bidders. Mergers are typically friendly affairs, negotiated between the top management of buyer and target firms. Tender offers are structured as take-it-or-leave-it proposals, directly to the target firm shareholders. Quite often, tender offers are unfriendly. Research suggests that bypassing the target firm's management and appealing directly to target shareholders can pay. Several studies report larger announcement returns to bidders in tender offers, when compared with friendly negotiated transactions.

8. Stake of Managers: When managers have more at stake, more value is created. Studies suggest that returns to buyer firm shareholders are associated with larger equity interests by managers and employees. A related finding is that LBOs create value for buyers. The sources of these returns are not only from tax savings due to debt and depreciation shields, but also significantly from efficiency and greater operational improvements implemented after the LBO. In LBOs, managers tend to have a significant portion of their net worth committed to the success of the transaction.

9. Announcement Effect: The initiation of M&A programs is associated with creation of value for the buyers. Past studies report that when firms announce they are undertaking a series of acquisitions in pursuit of some strategic objectives, their share price rises significantly. That these kinds of announcements should create value suggests that M&A generally creates value, and that the announcement is taken as a serious signal of value creation.

10. Culture: Culture was identified as a very important element to consider as part of an acquisition decision. "Culture fit" between two organizations refers to a match between administrative, cultural practices, and personnel characteristics.

11. Due Diligence: The due diligence process has been identified as a driver to be undertaken once a decision has been made to acquire a firm. Furthermore, it has been identified as the most important activity or factor that affected the positive outcome of a specific acquisition. The due diligence process is also leveraged as one of the activities to help identify key associates within the target firm. There is no evidence that the due diligence scope included the following dimensions, efficiency of the target organization; quality and support of the target firm products/components; and effectiveness of the target organization (e.g., innovation capabilities). This represents a deviation from previous research and expectations. However, there are indications that the detailed due diligence might be difficult to implement due to confidentiality and competitive intelligence risks. It is possible that this level of due diligence was not executed.

12. Integration Strategy: The post-acquisition integration strategy for an acquiring firm can take two basic forms: low integration and high integration strategy. Low integration strategy would leave the target firm as standalone business unit with links to corporate strategy and administrative services to support a complementary strategy. High integration strategy would integrate functional departments of target firm within the acquiring firm in a relatively short time with the goal to gain economies of scale and to leverage the product innovation capabilities of the target firm (Table 14.1).

TABLE 14.1

INDUSTRY CHARACTERISTICS RELATED TO STRONG M&A PRESSURE

S. No	Industry	Characteristics
1.	Telecommunications	Technological change and deregulation
2.	Media	Technological change
3.	Financial services	Globalization
4.	Chemicals, pharmaceuticals	Technological change, increased risks due to competitive pressures
5.	Automotive, oil & gas, industrial machinery	Requirement of scale, volatility in price, supply instability
6.	Utilities	Deregulation
7.	Food, retailing	Expanding into new markets
8.	Natural resources, timber	Limited and exhausting sources of supply

Source: Author.

Valuation of M&A

Importance of Valuation

Valuation is a critical and the most important part of the merger process. A deal that may be sound from a business perspective may not appear so wise from a financial perspective if the bidder pays too much. The purpose of a valuation analysis is to provide a disciplined approach in arriving at a price. If the prospective buyer offers too little, the target company may resist, and since it is in play, it may attract other bidders. Remember what happened in Tata Steel's takeover of Corus, when midway during the process, CSN of Brazil also jumped into the fray and drove up the final offer price for Tata Steel. It was a fight "down to the wires." If the price is too high, the premium may never be recovered from the post-merger synergies.

In the context of acquisitions, there are several distinct concepts of value:

1. **Intrinsic Value:** This is based on the NPV of expected future cash flows completely independent of any acquisition.
2. **Market Value:** Commonly known as "current market capitalization," it is the same as share price. It reflects the market's valuation of a company.
3. **Purchase Price:** It is the price that a bidder anticipates having to pay to be accepted by the target company's shareholders.
4. **Synergy Value:** It is the NPV of expected future cash flows that will result from the combined operations and additional benefits expected to accrue.

5. **Value Gap:** The difference between the intrinsic value and the purchase price. Synergy value is expected to accrue on account of cost savings, revenue enhancements, process improvements, financial engineering, and tax benefits.

Estimating Merger Gains and Costs

Mergers increase value when the value of the combined entity is greater than the sum of the premerger values of the independent entities. There should be an economic gain from the merger for it to make sense. According to Brealey and Myers, "There is an economic gain *only if the two firms are worth more together than apart.*"

$$NPV_c = PV_{bt} - (PV_b + PV_t),$$

where NPV_c is the NPV increase or gain, PV_{bt} is the PV of the combined entity, PV_b is the PV of the bidder alone, PV_t is the PV of the target alone, and the cost is the cash paid $- PV_t$.

Decision Rule

The NPV to the bidder of a merger with a target company is measured by the difference between the gain and the cost. The bidder should go ahead with the merger only if its NPV, represented as given below, is positive.

$$NPV = Gain - Cost$$

$$= [PV_{bt} - (PV_b + PV_t)] - (Cash\ paid - PV_t)$$

Illustration

1. Assume the current market value of the bidding company is ₹40 crore, and that of the target company is also ₹40 crore. Then, the sum of the values as independent companies is ₹80 crore. Suppose, as a combined entity, due to synergistic effects, the value increases to ₹100 crore. The amount of value created is ₹20 crore.

2. How will the increase in value be shared or divided between the bidder and the target company? Targets usually receive a premium. If the bidder pays the target a premium of less than ₹20 crore, it will share the increase in the value. If the bidder pays ₹60 crore to the target, all gains will go to the target company. The bidder achieves no increase in the value for itself. On the other hand, if the bidder pays ₹70 crore to the target, the value of bidder will go down to ₹30 crore.

Test Yourself

1. Explain the various drivers of value creation for M&A.
2. How are economic advantages calculated in case of merger?

Methods of Valuation under M&A

In Discounted Cash Flow (DCF) valuation, the value of an asset is the PV of the expected cash flows on the asset. The basic premise in DCF is that every asset has an intrinsic value that can be estimated, based upon its characteristics in terms of cash flows, growth, and risk. Though the DCF valuation is one of the three approaches to valuation, it is essential to understand the fundamentals of this approach, as the DCF method finds application in the use of the other two approaches also. The DCF model is the most widely used standalone valuation model. To use DCF valuation, we need to estimate the following: the life of the asset, the cash flows during the life of the asset, and the discount rate to be applied to these cash flows to get the PV. The PV of an asset is arrived at by determining the PVs of all expected future cash flows from the use of the asset. Mathematically

$$\text{Value of an asset} = \sum_{i=1}^{i=n} \left[CF_i / (1+r)^i \right]$$

That is

$$\text{Value} = \frac{CF1}{(1+r)^1} + \frac{CF2}{(1+r)^2} + \ldots + \frac{CFn}{(1+r)^n}$$

where CF_i is the expected future net cash flow during period i, n is the life of the asset, and r is the rate of discount.

The expected future net cash flow is defined as after-tax cash flow from operations on an invested capital basis (excluding the impact of debt service) less the sum of net changes in working capital and new investments in capital assets. The discount rate should reflect the riskiness of the estimated cash flows. The rate will be higher for high-risk projects as compared to lower rates for safe or low-risk investments. The Weighted Average Cost of Capital (WACC) is used as the discount rate. The cost of capital with which the cash flows are discounted should reflect the risk inherent in the future cash flows.

The WACC is calculated using the following formula:

$$WACC = [(E/(D+E) \times C_E] + [(D/(D+E) \times C_D \times (1-T)]$$

where E is the market value of equity, D is the market value of debt, C_E is the cost of equity, C_D is the cost of debt, and T is the tax rate.

The first step in determining WACC is the assessment of capital structure, that is, how a company has financed its operations. It can thus be seen that the company's net cash flows are projected for a number of years and then discounted to the PV using the WACC. The expected cash flows earned beyond the projection period are capitalized into a terminal value and added to the value of the projected cash flows for a total value indication. The DCF model relies upon cash flow assumptions such as revenue growth rates, operating margins, working capital needs, and new investments in fixed assets for purposes of estimating future cash flows. After establishing the current value, the DCF model can be used to measure the value creation impact of various assumption changes and the sensitivity tested.

Importance of DCF

1. Business valuation is normally done to evaluate the future earning potential of a business, and involves the study of many aspects of a business, including anticipated revenues and expenses. As the cash flows extend over time in future, the DCF model can be a helpful tool, as the DCF analysis for a business valuation requires the analyst to consider two important components of:

   (a) Projection of revenues and expenses of the foreseeable future, and
   (b) Determination of the discount rate to be used.

2. Projecting the expected revenues and expenses of a business requires domain expertise in the business being valued. For example, a DCF analysis for a telecom company requires

knowledge of the technologies involved, their life cycle, cost advantages, and so on. Similarly, a DCF analysis of a proposed mine requires the expertise of geologists to ascertain the quality and quantity of deposits.

3. Selecting the discount rate requires consideration of two components:

  (a) The cost of capital, and

  (b) The risk premium associated with the stream of projected net revenues.

4. The cost of capital is the cost of funds collected for financing a project or purchasing an asset. Capital is a productive asset that commands a rate of return. When a business purchase is financed by debt, the cost of capital simply equals the interest cost of the debt. When it is financed by the owner's equity, the relevant cost of capital would be the "opportunity cost" of the capital, that is, the net income that the same capital would generate if committed to another attractive alternative.

5. The choice of discount rate must consider not only the owner's cost of capital, but also the risk of the business investment.

Advantages of DCF Valuation

1. As DCF valuation is based upon asset's fundamentals, it should be less exposed to market moods and perceptions.

2. DCF valuation is the right way to think about what an investor would get when buying an asset.

3. DCF valuation forces an investor to think about the underlying characteristics of the firm, and understand its business.

Limitations of DCF Valuation

1. Since DCF valuation is an attempt to estimate intrinsic value, it requires far more inputs and information than other valuation approaches.

2. The inputs and information are difficult to estimate, and can also be manipulated by a smart analyst to provide the desired conclusion.

3. It is possible in a DCF valuation model to find every stock in a market to be over-valued.

4. The DCF valuation has certain limitations when applied to firms in distress; firms in cyclical business; firms with unutilized assets, patents; firms in the process of reorganizing or involved in acquisition; and private firms.

Application of DCF Valuation

- DCF valuation approach is the easiest to use for assets or firms with the following characteristics:

  o Cash flows are currently positive.

  o The cash flows can be estimated with some reliability for future periods.

  o Where a proxy for risk that can be used to obtain discount rates is available.

- DCF approach is also attractive for investors who have a long time horizon, allowing the market time to correct its valuation mistakes and for price to revert to "true" value, or those who are capable of providing the needed thrust as in the case of an acquirer of a business.

Illustration 2.

Inputs		Time Relationships	
Base year revenues	₹8,658	Base year	2002
Revenue growth rate, initial period	15.50%	Initial year of projection	2003
Discount rate, initial period	10%	Last year of projection	2007
Discount rate, terminal period	12%		
Terminal period growth rate	0%		
Terminal period depreciation	5.00%		
Terminal period capital expenditures	5.00%		
Terminal period changes in working capital	0%		
Tax rate	40%		

			Years					
			1—2003	2—2004	3—2005	4—2006	5—2007	n+1—2008
Step 1: Initial Growth Period			₹	₹	₹	₹	₹	₹
1	Revenues		10,000	11,550	13,340	15,408	17,796	20,555
2	EBITDA	21%	2,100	2,425	2,801	3,236	3,737	3,737
3	Depreciation	5%	500	577	667	770	890	890
4	EBIT=NOI (2)−(3)	16%	1,600	1,848	2,134	2,465	2,847	2,847
5	Less: interest	3%	300	346	400	462	534	534
6	EBT (4)−(5)		1,300	1,501	1,734	2,003	2,314	2,314
7	Less: tax @40%	40%	520	601	694	801	925	925
8	Net income (6)−(7)		780	901	1,041	1,202	1,388	1,388
9	Add: [Interest×(1−T)] =(5)×(1 − T)		180	208	240	277	320	320
10	NOI'AT=(4)×(1−T)=(8)−(9)		960	1,109	1,281	1,479	1,708	1,708
10a.	Add: depreciation	5%	500	577	667	770	890	890
10b.	Less: capital expenditures	9%	900	1,039	1,201	1,387	1,602	890
10c.	Less: changes in working capital	4%	400	462	534	616	712	0
11	Free cash flow=10+(10a) −(10b)−(10c)		160	185	213	247	285	1,708
12	Discount factor @10%		0.909	0.826	0.751	0.683	0.621	
13	PV of free cash flow		145	153	160	168	177	
14	Sum of initial period PVs		804					

Step 2: Terminal Period

1	EBITDA of 2008	3,737
2	Free cash flow in 2008	1,708
3	Terminal period discount rate	12%
4	Terminal value in 2008	14,235
5	PVs factor $[1/(1+0.10)]^n$	0.6209
6	Present value of terminal period	8,839

Step 3: Calculation of Equity Value

1	Sum of initial period PVs	804
2	PV of terminal period	8,839
3	DCF enterprise value	9,642
4	Add: excess cash	0
5	Less: debt	3,000
6	Equity value	6,642
7	Number of shares outstanding	100
8	Value per share	66.42

Illustration 3. Chennai Limited and Kolkata Limited have agreed that Chennai Limited will take over the business of Kolkata Limited with effect from December 31, 2001. It is agreed that:

(i) A total of 1,000,000 shareholders of Kolkata Limited will receive shares of Chennai Limited. The swap ratio is determined on the basis of 26 weeks average market prices of shares of both the companies. Average prices have been worked out at ₹50 and ₹25 for the shares of Chennai Limited and Kolkata Limited, respectively.

(ii) In addition to (i) above, shareholders of Kolkata Limited will be paid cash based on the projected synergy that will arise on the absorption of the business of Kolkata Limited by Chennai Limited. A total of 50% of the projected benefits will be paid to the shareholders of Kolkata Limited. The following projection has been agreed upon by the management of both the companies.

Year	2002	2003	2004	2005	2006
Benefit	50	75	90	100	105

(in ₹ lakhs)

The benefit is estimated to grow at the rate of 2% from 2007 onward. It has been further agreed that a discount rate of 20% should be used to calculate the cash that the holder of each share of Kolkata Limited will receive.

(i) Calculate the cash that holder of each share of Kolkata Limited will receive.

(ii) Calculate the total purchase consideration.

Answer (i) PV of synergy gain:

$$= \frac{50}{(1.2)^1} + \frac{75}{(1.2)^2} + \frac{90}{(1.2)^3} + \frac{100}{(1.2)^4} + \frac{105}{(1.2)^5} + \frac{105(1.02)^1}{(1.2)^6} + \frac{105(1.02)^2}{(1.2)^7} + \cdots$$

$$= [(50)(0.833)] + [(75)(0.694)] + [(90)(0.579)] + [(100)(0.482)] + [(105)(0.402)]$$

$$+ \frac{105(1.02)/(1.2)^6}{1 - [(1.02)/(1.2)]} = 476.41$$

Cash for each shareholder of Kolkata = 0.50 (475.41L)/10L

$$= ₹23.77$$

$$\text{Cash} = ₹237.705L$$

5,00,000 shares of Chennai @ ₹50 = ₹250.000L

$$\text{Total PC} = ₹487.705$$

Reasons for Mergers

There are a number of reasons for mergers, why two companies may be worth more together than when they are apart. These are given below:

1. Economies of Scale: For all Oil and Gas companies, scale of operations has been a driving force. Consider the examples of mergers of Exxon and Mobil, BP and Amoco, Chevron and Texaco. The same is the case with the steel giants Arcelor and Mittal. Economies are stated to accrue in terms of sharing central services such as procurement, accounting, financial control, human resources management and development, and top-level management and control.

2. Economies of Vertical Integration: Organizations seek to attain economies by moving both forward (toward the customer) and backward (toward supplies of raw materials and inputs). Reliance Industries is a classic case, as it has set up its polymer plants to cater to its textile operations, moved back further to set up petroleum refinery, and then moved forward to set up its own outlets for petroleum products. The current trend of all metallurgical companies such as Tata Steel, SAIL, JSW Steel, Vedanta, and Hindalco to acquire mines across the globe is a classic example.

Tata Steel's acquisition of Corus in UK was stated to enable the company move up the value chain in terms of superior products. The rationale for Tata Motors' recent acquisition of Jaguar and Land Rover was stated to be on similar lines, that is, moving up the value chain. Tata's earlier acquisition of Tetley was to get access to the high tea-consuming Europe. Tata Chemicals recent acquisition of General Chemicals of US was due to a number of reasons:

GCIL has access to the world's largest and most economically recoverable trona ore deposits (which is converted into soda ash) in Wyoming in the US, said Mr Khusrokhan. After the buy, over 50% of Tata Chemicals' capacity would be through the natural route, providing both sustainability as well as a natural hedge against the commodity cycle, he said. As a thumb rule, natural soda ash is more economical and delivers higher margins, said Mr R. Mukundan, executive vice-president, Tata Chemicals.

Vertical integration facilitates better coordination and administration

This was the thinking of many auto companies earlier, when they manufactured all components in-house. The trend now is to outsource, and buy components from a host of dedicated suppliers, to achieve better cost efficiency. This was a major reason for General Motors to spin off its automotive parts into a separate entity called Delphi. Ford Corporation adopted a similar strategy by spinning off its auto parts business into Visteon.

3. Complementary Resources: When two companies have complementary resources, that is, each having what the other needs, they may see some logic to come together. The recently announced decision of HP to acquire EDS appears to be for these reasons. Read article given at the end of the chapter.

4. Investible Surplus Funds: When organizations have investible surplus funds that had not been distributed to the shareholders as higher dividends or bonus stocks, they look for investment opportunities. Organizations that have excess cash and do not payout to their shareholders or invest it through acquisitions may become targets of takeover.

5. Eliminating Inefficiencies: Organizations with unexploited opportunities to cut costs and improve revenues become takeover targets of organizations with better management.

Consider Tata Motors' recent acquisition of Jaguar and Land Rover: "The key here is the ability of Tata Motors to implement cost savings at JLR. What will help assess the long-term impact of the acquisition on the profitability of Tata Motors is how much of the marquee brands' component sourcing can actually be done from India...."

6. Increasing EPS: This is also called the "bootstrap" or "chain letter" game. Some organizations with high price-earnings ratio may purchase slow-growing businesses with low price-earnings ratios. This can lead to a dramatic increase in short-term EPS, although the long-term result will be a slower growth and a depressed price-earnings ratio. The higher EPS cannot come about year after year, and the plan will collapse one day.

7. Lower Financing Costs: Many a time, an argument is advanced that a merged entity can borrow more cheaply. This may be due to the debt being made less risky to the lenders due to mutual guarantees. However, the value to the shareholders is reduced.

Test Yourself

1. What are various reasons of M&A?
2. Explain DCF approach for valuation of M&A.

EXHIBIT NO. 1: GSK INDIA AND ITS CATCH-UP FORMULA

"GSK India is profitable and well run. It is also No. 4, and wants to be No. 1. Here is what the pharma major is trying out." P.B. Jayakumar

At GSK India's corporate office at Worli in Mumbai, Managing Director Hasit Joshipura desperately wants to get back to work now that the interview is over. He does not want to waste time posing for the B/W photographer. He is fretting about the fact that the number of GSK executives waiting to meet him is piling up.

"I don't believe in such publicity. What matters is how we create value for our shareholders, and offer new therapies to save lives," he says. Joshipura, who took charge in January 2007, is acutely aware that there is plenty of work left to be done in terms of creating more value for shareholders. (He was brought in from Johnson & Johnson with the mandate to shake things up.) It is not that GSK has been underperforming—indeed the stock has outperformed the BSE healthcare index over 5 years—but it has certainly lagged behind key rivals in terms of growing turnover and profits. In addition, from numero uno position in this market, it has slipped to the fourth spot now.

In 1997, when the Indian operations of Glaxo and Burroughs Wellcome were integrated as part of a global merger, the new entity—Glaxo (India)—became the largest pharma company in the domestic market with a combined market share of 7.2%. Glaxo's dominance in the market was further strengthened when Glaxo (India) and SmithKline Beecham Pharmaceuticals (India) were merged in 2001 to form GSK India—again as part of a global merger.

At that time, GSK India had a turnover of ₹1,097 crore (2001) with a net profit of ₹75 crore. Homegrown giant Cipla, one of the oldest Indian drug companies, was way behind it with ₹795 crore (2000–2001) sales, though it had a superior net profit of ₹133 crore. The then largest Indian drug company—Ranbaxy Laboratories—had sales of ₹1,741 crore (2000) with a net profit of ₹180 crore, thanks to its foray into exports. Roughly, ₹930 crore of the Ranbaxy turnover then came from the Indian market.

THE HEALTH SHEET

GSK INDIA'S PROFITS HAVE NOT GROWN SIGNIFICANTLY IN THE PAST 5 YEARS

	2006	2007	2008	2009	2010
Sales*	1,678	1,713	1,752	1,913	2,155
Net profit*	546	538	577	512	564
Employees	3,850	3,620	3,722	4,006	4,338

Source: GSK India.
Note: * in ₹ crore.

After a decade, GSK is way behind the trio. Abbott Laboratories, following its acquisition of Piramal Healthcare's formulation business, is the No. 1 in terms of market share. Ranbaxy, owned by Japan's Daiichi Sankyo, grew to a sales turnover of ₹8,550 crore with ₹1,496 crore net profit in 2010. Now, Cipla has global operations with ₹6,183 crore turnover and a ₹960-crore net profit (2010–2011). Compared to them, GSK India's turnover in 2010 was only ₹2,155 crore, with a net profit of ₹581 crore. Its market share has shrunk to 4.2% of the ₹58,842-crore Indian pharma market, according to drug sales tracking agency, IMS Health India.

Joshipura says it is unfair to compare a company that sells patented medicines with competitors who primarily rely on generics. GSK has six patented drugs (after India adopted a product-patent regime in 2005), and has a basket of around 250 off-patent generic and branded drugs. Compared to GSK, Cipla and Ranbaxy's product basket is over 600 generics. But Joshipura explains that 2001–2007 was a phase for consolidating the mergers. "We were focusing on optimising operational efficiencies and increasing profitability." Now, having achieved the efficiency goal to a large extent, GSK India wants to grow aggressively with restructured operations and smart marketing. In the past 2 years, the business has been regrouped under six divisions—mass market, mass specialty, dermatological, oncology, critical care, and vaccines. Soon, two more divisions will be added in cardiovascular and respiratory diseases. Joshipura says the future growth will be powered by new vaccines and medicines from its parent, in-licensing of drugs from other innovator firms, foray into off-patent branded generics, and, notably, through acquisitions.

He has the cash to acquire at least a few small firms. GSK India is sitting on a pile of ₹2,000 crore. "We are looking at assets that strategically fit our business," says Joshipura. Organically, the company cannot hope to grow faster than 12–16% annually and, hence, big-ticket jumps in turnover will have to come from a buyout. Analysts think restructuring has helped create a leaner GSK India. An Angel Broking analysis figures GSK's sales to grow 13.8% in 2011 and 14% in 2012, and net profit to be lesser by 21% in 2011 and a growth of 66.4% in 2012.

"The share of price-controlled products (which are of low margin) have come down from 30 per cent to 25 per cent in GSK's product basket and will go down further. This means GSK will grow above the industry average within a few years," says Ranjit Kapadia, senior vice-president of Centrum Broking.

Last year, GSK's net sales grew 13% and profitability was maintained at 35%. New products launched in the past 4 years contributed 7% of the overall prescription sales in 2010 with a growth of 26% over 2009.

Its flagship brand, anti-infectant Augmentin, has regained its position as the largest selling drug in India with sales of ₹244 crore for the 12 months ended June 2011, according to IMS Health India. Since antibacterials represent the largest anti-infective segment of the Indian market, this has been a welcome change.

The firm in-licensed two products last year—Mycamine injection (Micafungin) from Astellas Pharma and Parit D capsules from Japan's Eisai. Again, these are drugs meant for high-growth segments in the market. Its other popular brands have been doing well and it is adding to those with new launches. It launched Zemetril (an antibacterial drug) a few years ago, which has climbed to No. 1 in its category. Another popular brand—pain balm Iodex—grew 4% last year with sales of ₹88.2 crore.

Meanwhile, its oncology division, started in 2008 to launch breast cancer drug Tykerb, recently launched two more drugs—Revolade, a tablet for treating reduced blood platelet count, and the kidney cancer drug Votrient.

The division plans to launch at least one cancer drug every year from the parent's pipeline or through in-licensing, says C.T. Renganathan, vice-president of pharmaceuticals with GSK India.

Despite this, while GSK has beaten the broad pharma sector in terms of growth, so have its main rivals. Ranbaxy's sales grew by 16% last year, while Cipla's grew by 14%. Both the firms had a lower profitability than GSK, which has been a small consolation.

While restructuring and chasing efficiencies, GSK cut manpower too sharply which is the indicator of market getting more competitive by the day. GSK's manpower was more than 5,000 in 2001, and is now down to about 4,400. Out of these, 3,500 are sales representatives. Meanwhile, rivals have been adding more feet on street. Abbott has 7,000 medical representatives in the country, Cipla has over 5,000, and Ranbaxy, which has 4,300, is recruiting 1,500.

BIG LEAGUE
The top players in the ₹58,842-crore Indian pharmaceutical market

Rank	Company	Value (₹ crore)	Share
1	Abbott	4,038	6.9
2	Cipla	3,012	5.0
3	Ranbaxy	2,702	4.6
4	GSK India	2,551	4.3
5	Sun Pharma	2,284	3.9
6	Zydus Cadila	2,244	3.8
7	Alkem	1,932	3.3
8	Pfizer	1,881	3.2
9	Mankind Pharma	1,852	3.2
10	Lupin	1,636	2.8

Source: IMS Health India.
Note: For 12 months ended June 2011.

As GSK prepares for a flurry of launches, it realizes the need to hire more sales personnel. It plans to add about 800 sales people by the end of the fiscal. As part of GSK's global strategy of tier pricing (related to GDP growth of a developing country), the Indian arm is selling patented medicines at 35–70% less cost than its cost in developed markets. In India, Revolade is priced at ₹27,000 a month and Votrient at ₹58,000, almost 75% less than its US price. Other patented drugs such as breast cancer drug Tykerb and vaccines Rotarix and Cervarix are priced 25–40% less in India than in the US. This strategy, hopes GSK, will help it gain traction with its new drugs.

GSK has launched half a dozen drugs and vaccines in the past 2 years from the parent's product basket. It was forced to withdraw anti-diabetic drug Rosiglitazone (Windia) on safety issues 2 years ago, shaving off about ₹15 crore from annual sales. The withdrawal was a big blow given that the anti-diabetic market is growing rapidly and GSK has no presence here.

A large basket of vaccines has helped GSK emerge as the leader in the ₹210-crore Indian vaccine market. It cornered 19.86% market share, ahead of rivals Sanofi-Aventis (19.62%) and Novartis (10.77%) in 2010. Vaccines contribute about 10% of GSK's turnover and are expected to contribute 15% in a few years.

GSK has also changed its marketing strategies. It now focuses more on selling drugs to hospitals, directly to doctors, and tender orders. About 16% of its annual drug sales are through hospitals and doctors. Selling drugs in rural areas are another priority and GSK is implementing "Reach" program to tap rural India.

But all these are hygiene steps and GSK knows that it cannot play catch up in the league tables unless it does some acquisitions. But finding proper targets is no easy task. "I don't know when it will happen," says Joshipura candidly.

Source: http://www.businessworld.in/businessworld/businessworld/content/GSK-India-And-Its-Catch-Formula.html

Methods of Payment

The two main methods of financing an acquisition are cash and share exchange.

Cash: This method is generally considered suitable for relatively small acquisitions. It has two advantages: (i) the buyer retains total control as the shareholders in the selling company are completely bought out, and (ii) the value of the bid is known and the process is simple.

Illustration 4.

	Company A	**Company B**
Market price per share	₹75	₹15
Number of shares	100,000	60,000
Market value of the company	7,500,000	900,000

1. Assume Company A intends to pay ₹1,200,000 cash for Company B.
2. If the share price does not anticipate a merger:
   The share price in the market is expected to accurately reflect the true value of the company.

The cost to the bidder Company A = Payment – The market value of Company B

$$= ₹12\,lakhs - ₹9\,lakhs$$

$$= ₹3\,lakhs$$

Company A is paying ₹3 lakhs for the identified benefits of the merger.

3. If the share price includes a speculation element of ₹2 per share:

The cost to Company A = ₹300,000 + (60,000 × ₹2)

$$= ₹300,000 + ₹120,000$$

$$= ₹420,000$$

Worth of Company B = (₹15 – ₹2) × 60,000

$$= ₹13 × 60,000$$

$$= ₹780,000$$

This can also be expressed as ₹1,200,000 – ₹420,000 = ₹780,000.

Share Exchange: The method of payment in large transactions is predominantly stock for stock. The advantage of this method is that the acquirer does not part with cash and does not increase the financial risk by raising new debt. The disadvantage is that the acquirer's shareholders will have to share future prosperity with those of the acquired company.

Illustration 5. Suppose Company A wished to offer shares in Company A to the shareholders of Company B instead of cash:

Amount to be paid to shareholders of Company B = ₹1,200,000

Market price of shares of Company A = ₹75

Number of shares to be offered = ₹1,200,000/₹75

$$= 16,000$$

Now, shareholders of Company B will own part of Company A, and will benefit from any future gains of the merged enterprise.

Their share in the merged enterprise = 16,000/(100,000 + 16,000) = 13.8%

Further, now suppose that the benefits of the merger have been identified by Company A to have a PV of ₹400,000.

The value of the merged entity = ₹7,500,000 + (₹900,000 + ₹400,000) = ₹8,800,000

True cost of merger to the shareholders of Company A:

	Company A	Company B
Proportion of ownership in merged enterprise (%)	86.2	13.8
Market value: total = ₹8,800,000	7,585,600	1,214,400
Number of shares currently in issue	100,000	60,000
Market price per share	₹75.86	₹20.24

The above gives the value of shares in the company *before* the merger is completed, based on estimates of what the company will be worth *after* the merger. The valuation of each company also recognizes the split of the expected benefits which will accrue to the combined entity once the merger has taken place.

The true cost can be calculated as given as follows:

60,000 shares in Company B@ ₹20.24 = ₹1,214,400

Less: current market value = ₹900,000

Benefits being paid to shareholders of Company B = ₹314,400

Leveraged Buyouts

Leveraged buyouts, also referred to as LBO, refer to the acquisition of a business using mostly debt and a small amount of equity. The debt is secured by the assets of the business. In an LBO, the acquiring company uses its own assets as collateral for the loan in the hope that future cash flows will cover the loan payments. Management buyouts, also referred to as MBO, refer to a situation when the managers and/or executives of a company purchase a controlling interest in the business from existing shareholders. In most cases, the management will buy out all the outstanding shareholders because it feels it has the expertise to grow the business better if it controls the ownership. Quite often, management will team up with an investment bank, as this is a complicated process that requires significant business financing. It provides expert financial advisory services to clients considering an LBO, MBO, or reorganization. An LBO occurs when an entity primarily borrows money (sometimes 90% or more) in order to buy another company. Typically, the acquiring company uses as collateral the assets of the acquired business. Generally, repayments of the debt will be made from the yearly operating funds flow of the acquired company. An LBO may also be made when the acquiring company uses its own assets as security for the loan. It may also be used if a firm wishes to go private. In most cases, the stockholders of the acquired company will receive an amount greater than the current price of the stock. An LBO involves more risk than an acquisition done through the issuance of equity securities.

SEBI Guidelines for Takeovers: The salient features of the guidelines are as follows:

Disclosure of share acquisition/holdings: The SEBI (Substantial Acquisition of Shares and Takeovers) Regulations, 1997 has defined substantial quantity of shares or voting rights distinctly for two different purposes:

(I)   Threshold of disclosure to be made by acquirer(s):

1. **5% or more but less than 15% shares or voting rights:** A person who, along with person acting in concert (PAC), if any, (collectively referred to as "Acquirer" hereinafter) acquires shares or voting rights (which when taken together with his existing holding) would entitle him to exercise 5% or 10%, or 14% shares or voting rights of target company, is required to disclose the aggregate of his shareholding to the target company within 2 days of acquisition or within 2 days of receipt of intimation of allotment of shares.

2. **More than 15% shares or voting rights:** (a) Any person who holds more than 15% shares but less than 75% or voting rights of the target company, and who purchases or sells shares aggregating to 2% or more shall disclose such purchase/sale along with the aggregate of his shareholding to the target company and the stock exchanges within 2 working days. (b) Any person who holds more than 15% shares or voting rights of the target company or every person having control over the target company within 21 days from the

financial year ending March 31 as well as the record date fixed for the purpose of dividend declaration disclose every year his aggregate shareholding to the target company. The target company, in turn, is required to inform all the stock exchanges where the shares of the target company are listed, every year within 30 days from the financial year ending March 31 as well as the record date fixed for the purpose of dividend declaration.

(II) Trigger point for making an open offer by an acquirer.

1. 15% shares or voting rights: An acquirer who intends to acquire shares which along with his existing shareholding would entitle him to exercise 15% or more voting rights can acquire such additional shares only after making a public announcement (PA) to acquire at least additional 20% of the voting capital of the target company from the shareholders through an open offer.

2. Creeping acquisition limit: An acquirer who is having 15% or more but less than 75% of shares or voting rights of a target company can acquire such additional shares as would entitle him to exercise more than 5% of the voting rights in any financial year only after making a PA to acquire at least 20% shares of target company from the shareholders through an open offer.

3. Consolidation of holding: An acquirer, who is having 75% shares or voting rights of a target company, can acquire further shares or voting rights only through an open offer from the shareholders of the target company.

Public Announcement: A PA is an announcement made in the newspapers by the acquirer primarily disclosing his intention to acquire shares of the target company from existing shareholders by means of an open offer. The disclosures in the announcement include the offer price, number of shares to be acquired from the public, identity of the acquirer, purpose of acquisition, future plans of acquirer, if any, regarding the target company, change in control over the target company, if any, the procedure to be followed by acquirer in accepting the shares tendered by the shareholders, and the period within which all the formalities pertaining to the offer would be completed. The PA is made to ensure that the shareholders of the target company are aware of an exit opportunity available to them through ensuing open offer. The acquirer is required to make PA through the Merchant Banker (MB) within four working days of the entering into an agreement to acquire shares or deciding to acquire shares/ voting rights of target company or after any such change or changes as would result in change in control over the target company. In case of indirect acquisition or change in control, acquire can make PA within 3 months of consummation of acquisition or change in control or restructuring of the parent or the company holding shares of or control over the target company in India.

Open Offer: A letter of offer is a document addressed to the shareholders of the target company containing disclosures of the acquirer/PACs, target company, their financial justification of the offer price, the offer price, number of shares to be acquired from the public, purpose of acquisition, future plans of acquirer, if any, regarding the target company, change in control over the target company, if any, the procedure to be followed by acquirer in accepting the shares tendered by the shareholders, and the period within which all the formalities to the offer would be completed.

Offer Price: SEBI does not decide or approve the offer price. The acquirer/MB is required to ensure that all the relevant parameters are taken into consideration for fixing the offer price and that justification for the same is disclosed in the offer letter.

The relevant parameters are as follows:

(a) Negotiated price under the agreement which triggered the open offer.

(b) Highest price paid by acquirer or PACs with him for any acquisitions, including by way of allotment in public or rights or preferential issue during the 26-week period prior to the date of the PA.

(c) Average of weekly high and low of the closing prices of shares as quoted on the stock exchanges, where shares of the target company are most frequently traded during 26 weeks or average of the daily high and low prices of shares during the 2 weeks prior to the date of the PA. In case the shares of the target company are not frequently traded then instead of point (c) above, parameters based on the fundamentals of the company such as return on net worth of the company, book value per share, and EPS, are required to be considered and disclosed. Any amount paid in excess of 25% of the offer price toward non-complete agreement shall be added to the offer price.

Source: http://investor.sebi.gov.in/Reference%20Material/Guide-Substantial-E.pdf

Test Yourself

1. What are various payment methods of M&A? What is leverage buyout? Explain.

EXHIBIT NO. 2: TOP 10 M&A IN INDIA FOR 2014

1. Flipkart—Myntra
2. Asian Paints—Ess Ess Bathroom Products
3. RIL—Network 18 Media and Investments
4. Merck—Sigma Deal
5. Ranbaxy—Sun Pharmaceuticals
6. TCS—CMC
7. Tata Power—PT Arutmin Indonesia
8. Tirumala Milk—Lactalis
9. Aditya Birla Minacs—CSP CX
10. Sterling India Resorts—Thomas Cook India

SUMMARY

1. Acquisition refers to the acquiring of ownership right in the property and asset without any combination of companies. Thus, in acquisition, two or more companies may remain independent, separate legal entity, but there may be change in control of companies.

2. Merger refers to a situation when two or more existing firms combine together and form a new entity. Either a new company may be incorporated for this purpose or one existing company (generally a bigger one) survives and another existing company (which is smaller) is merged into it.

3. A takeover may be defined as a series of transaction whereby a person, individual, group of individuals, or a company acquires control over the assets of a company, either directly by becoming owner of those assets or indirectly by obtaining control of management of the company.

4. Horizontal merger is a merger of two or more companies that compete in the same industry. It is a merger with a direct competitor and hence expands as the firm's operations in the same industry. Horizontal mergers are designed to produce substantial economies of scale and result in decrease in the number of competitors in the industry.

5. Vertical merger is a merger which takes place upon the combination of two companies which are operating in the same industry but at different stages of production or distribution system. If a company takes over its supplier/producers of raw material, then it may result in backward integration of its activities. On the other hand, forward integration may result if a company decides to take over the retailer or the customer company.

6. Mergers increase value when the value of the combined entity is greater than the sum of the premerger values of the independent entities. There should be an economic gain from the merger for it to make sense. "There is an economic gain *only if the two firms are worth more together than apart.*" $NPV_c = PV_{bt} - (PV_b + PV_t)$

7. In DCF valuation, the value of an asset is the PV of the expected cash flows on the asset. DCF analysis is used to determine the value of the target company for the acquirer company.

8. An LBO occurs when an entity primarily borrows money (sometimes 90% or more) in order to buy another company. Typically, the acquiring company uses as collateral the assets of the acquired business. Generally, repayments of the debt will be made from the yearly operating funds flow of the acquired company.

KEY TERMS

- Absorption
- Amalgamation
- Conglomerate merger
- Discounted cash flow
- Equity carve-out
- Hostile takeover
- Share exchange ratio
- Split-up
- Takeover
- Value

- Acquisition
- Backward integration
- Consolidation
- Divestiture
- Horizontal merger
- Management buyout
- Spin off
- Synergy
- Tender offer

Learning Outcomes

Students may now connect with corporate restructuring along with few examples of recent M&A in India.

SOLVED PROBLEMS

1. X Ltd is intending to acquire B Ltd (by merger) and the following information is available in respect of the companies.

Particulars	X Ltd	B Ltd
No. of equity shares	500,000	300,000
Earnings after tax (₹)	2,500,000	900,000
Market value per share (₹)	21	14

(i) What is the present EPS of both the companies?

(ii) If the proposed merger takes place, what would be the new EPS for X Ltd (assuming that the merger takes place by exchange of equity shares and the exchange ratio is based on the current market prices).

(iii) What should be the exchange ratio, if B Ltd wants to ensure the same earnings to members as before the merger takes place?

Solution:

(i) **EPS** = Earnings after tax/Number of equity shares

$$\text{X Ltd.} = \frac{25,00,000}{5,00,000} = ₹5 \quad \text{B Ltd.} = \frac{9,00,000}{3,00,000} = ₹3$$

(ii) **Calculation of new EPS of X Ltd after merger (exchange ratio based on market prices)**

Particulars	X Ltd
Earnings after tax (₹)	2,500,000
No. of equity shares	500,000
Market value per share (₹)	21

Number of shares B Ltd shareholders will get in X Ltd based on market price of shares is as follows:

$$\frac{14}{21} \times 3,00,000 \text{ shares} = 2,00,000 \text{ shares}$$

For every three shares held in B Ltd, two shares of X Ltd are given.

Then, the total number of equity shares of X Ltd after merger is as follows:

$$= 500,000 + 200,000 = 700,000 \text{ shares}$$

Total earnings of X Ltd after merger = 2,500,000 + 900,000 = ₹3,400,000

The new EPS of X Ltd. after merger = $\dfrac{34,00,000}{7,00,000 \text{ Shares}}$ = ₹4.86

(iii) **Calculation of exchange ratio to ensure B Ltd to earn the same before the merger takes place**

Original EPS: X Ltd = ₹5; B Ltd = ₹3

The number of shares to be exchanged by X Ltd with B Ltd based on the EPS of the respective companies is as follows:

$$= \frac{3}{5} \times 3,00,000 = 1,80,000 \text{ shares}$$

Total number of shares of X Ltd after merger $= 500,000 + 180,000 = 680,000$ shares

$$\text{EPS after merger} = \frac{25,00,000 + 9,00,000}{6,80,000 \text{ Shares}} = ₹5$$

The total earnings in Q Ltd available to new shareholder of B Ltd

$$= 180,000 \text{ shares} \times ₹5 = ₹900,000$$

Recommendation: The exchange ratio based on market shares is beneficial to the shareholders of B Ltd.

2. X Ltd is considering the proposal to acquire Y Ltd and their financial information is given below:

Particulars	X Ltd	Y Ltd
No. of equity shares	1,000,000	600,000
Market price per share (₹)	30	18
Market capitalization (₹)	30,000,000	10,800,000

X Ltd intend to pay ₹14,000,000 in cash for Y Ltd, if Y Ltd's market price reflects only its value as a separate entity. Calculate the cost of merger: (i) when merger is financed by cash; (ii) when merger is financed by stock.

Solution:

(i) Cost of merger, when merger is financed by cash

$$= (\text{Cash} - MV_Y) + (MV_Y - PV_Y),$$

where MV_Y is the market value of Y Ltd and PV_Y is the true/intrinsic value of Y Ltd.

Then, $(14,000,000 - 10,800,000) + (10,800,000 - 10,800,000) = ₹3,200,000$

If the cost of merger becomes negative, then shareholders of X Ltd will get benefited by acquiring Y Ltd in terms of market value.

(ii) Cost of merger when merger is financed by exchange of shares in X Ltd to the shareholders of Y Ltd.

$$\text{Cost of merger} = PV_{XY} - PV_Y,$$

where PV_{XY} is the value in X Ltd that Y Ltd's shareholders get.

Suppose if X Ltd agrees to exchange 500,000 shares in exchange of shares in Y Ltd, instead of payment in cash of 14,000,000. Then, the cost of merger is calculated as follows:

$$= (500,000 \times ₹30) - ₹10,800,000 = ₹4,200,000$$

$$PV_{XY} = PV_X + PV_Y = 30,000,000 + 10,800,000 = ₹40,800,000$$

Proportion that Y Ltd's shareholders get in X Ltd's capital structure will be

$$= \frac{5,00,000}{10,00,000 + 5,00,000} = 0.333$$

True cost of merger $= PV_{XY} - PV_Y$

$$= (0.333 \times 40,800,000) - 10,800,000 = ₹2,800,000$$

The cost of merger, that is, ₹4,200,000 as calculated above is much higher than the true cost of merger, ₹2,800,000. With this proposal, the shareholders of Y Ltd will get benefited.

Notes:

(1) When the cost of merger is calculated on the cash consideration, then cost of merger is unaffected by the merger gains.

(2) But when merger is based on the exchange of shares, then the cost of merger depends on the gains, which has to be shared with the shareholder of Y Ltd.

3. East Co. Ltd is studying the possible acquisition of West Co. Ltd by way of merger. The following data are available in respect of the companies:

Particulars	X Ltd	B Ltd
Earnings after tax (₹)	200,000	60,000
No. of equity shares	40,000	10,000
Market value per share (₹)	15	12

(i) If the merger goes through by exchange of equity share and the exchange ratio is based on the current market price, what is the new EPS for East Co. Ltd?

(ii) West Co. Ltd wants to be sure that the earnings available to its shareholders will not be diminished by the merger. What should be the exchange ratio in that case?

Solution:

(i) Calculation of new EPS of East Co. Ltd.
No. of equity shares to be issued by East Co. Ltd of West Co. Ltd

$$= 10,000 \text{ shares} \times ₹12/₹15 = 8,000 \text{ shares}$$

Total no. of shares in East Co. Ltd after acquisition of West Co. Ltd

$$= 40,000 + 8,000 = 48,000$$

Total earnings after tax after acquisition $= 200,000 + 60,000 = ₹260,000$

$$EPS = \frac{2,60,000}{48,000 \text{ Equity Shares}} = ₹5.42$$

(ii) Calculation of exchange ratio which would not diminish the EPS of West Co. Ltd after its merger with East Co. Ltd.

Current EPS

$$\text{East Co. Ltd.} = \frac{2,00,000}{40,000 \text{ Equity Shares}} = ₹5$$

$$\text{West Co. Ltd.} = \frac{60,000}{10,000 \text{ Equity Shares}} = ₹6$$

Exchange ratio = 6/5 = 1.20

Number of new shares to be issued by East Co. Ltd to West Co. Ltd

= 10,000 × 1.20 = 12,000 shares

Total number of shares after acquisition = 40,000 + 12,000 = 52,000 shares

EPS after merger = ₹260,000/52,000 shares = ₹5

Total earnings of West Co. Ltd = Number of shares × EPS

= 12,000 × ₹5 = ₹60,000

4. Company R wishes to acquire company S. Company R's stock sells for ₹100 per share. Company S's stock sells for ₹40 a share. Due to merger negotiations, company R offers ₹50 a share. The acquisition is done through an exchange of securities. What is the ratio of exchange?

Solution:

$$\text{Exchange Ratio}: \frac{\text{Amount paid per share of the acquired company}}{\text{Market Price of the acquiring company s shares}} = ₹50/ ₹100 = 0.5$$

5. Burger Queen, a national hamburger chain, is considering a smaller chain, Johns Burger. Burger Queen's analysts project that the merger will result in the following incremental net cash flows (in millions of rupees):

Year 1	Year 2	Year 3	Year 4
1.5	2	3	5

Furthermore, Johns' cash flows are expected to grow at a constant rate of 5% after Year 4. Johns' post-merger beta is estimated to be 1.5, the risk-free rate is 6%, and the market risk premium is 4%. Calculate the value of Johns' Burger to Burger Queen.

Solution:

Johns' required rate of return = 6% + 1.5 × 4% = 12%

$$\text{So the terminal cash flow} = \frac{5(1+0.05)}{0:12-0:05} = 5.25/0.07 = ₹75$$

Year 4's NCF then is ₹5 + ₹75 = ₹80

NCF	PV Factor	PV
1. 5.0	0.8929	1.34
2. 2.0	0.7972	1.59
3. 3.0	0.7118	2.14
4. 80	0.6355	50.84
		55.91

NPV = ₹55.91 million.

SUGGESTED READINGS

Carney, William J. (2009). *Essentials mergers and acquisitions.* Aspen Publishers.

Gaughan, Patrick A. (2000). *Mergers, acquisitions and corporate restricting* (3rd ed.). Wiley.

Kothari, Rajesh. (2010). Financial services in India: Concepts application. SAGE India.

Sudarsanam, Sudi. (2010, January). *Creating value from mergers and acquisitions* (2nd ed.). Pearson Education.

PART IV
Operating Financial Decisions

CHAPTER 15

An Overview of Working Capital Management

Learning Objectives

- To understand the concept and types of working capital.
- To understand the various factors governing the level of investment in current assets.
- To understand the concept and significance of operating cycle.
- To identify and understand the nature of the sources of financing the investment in current assets.

PRELUDE

Working capital is an important operating decision as it reflects day-to-day, point-to-point, and level-to-level fluctuation in the quantity and components of working capital which is volatile and ever changing because of change in variables such as demand and supply, cost of funds, receipt and payment schedule, and of course regulatory mandate. To begin with, working capital is that optimum amount which will always be there in the organization to support operation. It encompasses current assets and current liabilities, their relationship and fluctuations. The following empirical paragraph may help you to know about working capital.

Financial Crisis Helped Companies Trim Working Capital by 2% as Sales Go Up by 20% (*The Economic Times*, February 19, 2010)

The global financial crisis has had positive fallout. Leading corporates have learnt to be more efficient in managing their finances. According to a study conducted by the management consultancy firm Booz & Co., companies reduced their working capital by 2% even as sales increased by 20% in 2008–2009. The companies that managed to bring down their working capital requirement did so by better management of inventory and receivables with some increase in payables. Significant reduction of average days of working capital from 37 days to 30 days effectively released ₹40,000 crore in cash sales of the same value. However, the success was not even with 60% of the companies covered under the study reporting a reduction in financing requirement, while 40% saw a small increase. The companies that were the most successful in reducing their capital requirement in a recessionary year included Indian Oil Corporation, Tata Motors, Sterlite, and UB holding. At a sector level, most sectors saw a reduction in net working capital except power, cement, construction, and retail, which saw a marginal increase.

It is a fact that a finance manager spends only 10% of his time on strategic financial decisions. Most of the times a finance manager goes toward operating financial decisions. Operating financial decisions are concerned with the day-to-day running of the business with the objective of ensuring liquidity and profitability. In other words, it means ensuring that bills are paid on time, adequate inventory is maintained for production and sales, ensuring that debtors pay on time, cash deficits are made good at a reasonable cost, and excess cash is invested on time to earn a suitable rate of return. Operating decisions are of repetitive nature; they are taken frequently and are of shorter duration.

Concept of Working Capital

We know that capital is the foundation stone of the business. When a business is started, the owners and investors contribute this capital. This capital is then invested in the long-term assets such as land, building, plant, and machinery. These fixed assets are of no use unless they are put to use. The capital, which makes the fixed assets work, is called the working capital. Fixed assets are like computer hardware, whereas working capital is like computer software. Hardware is dead without the software. Similarly, long-term assets of the business are of no use if there is no working capital. Working capital is that minimum amount which is always there in a business, that is used to meet payments as and when they become due, and is used to avoid technical insolvency arising out of nonpayment of routine bills.

There are two approaches for understanding the concept of working capital:

1. Static approach.
2. Dynamic approach.

Static Approach

The investment in the overall current assets is sometimes referred to as the gross working capital. In the process of managing current assets, current liabilities are also created. Current liabilities are the obligations arising out of business, which have to be paid for as they become due. The difference between current assets and current liabilities is the net working capital.

Symbolically, NWC = CA – CL

The data for determining working capital as per the static approach is obtained from the balance sheet of the company. The balance sheet merely indicates the financial position of a company as on a specific date and is, therefore, "static" in nature. Consequently, "working capital" as defined above provides a snapshot picture of current assets and current liabilities as on the balance sheet date. It fails to reflect the true dynamic nature of working capital, which can be captured by combining the data contained in both the balance sheet and profit and loss account of a company. In order to understand working capital better, it is imperative to know more about current assets and current liability.

Current Assets

Current assets are the result of operation, they keep changing shape and size, and they may be convertible in cash and vice versa.

The following items constitute the current assets of a firm:

1. **Inventories:** Inventories represent raw materials and components, work-in-process (WIP), and finished goods.

2. **Trade Debtors:** Trade debtors comprise credit sales.
3. **Prepaid Expenses:** Expenses have been paid for goods and services whose benefits are yet to be received.
4. **Loan and Advances:** They represent loans and advances given by the firm to other firms for a short period of time.
5. **Investment:** These assets comprise short-term surplus funds invested in government securities, shares, and short-terms bonds.
6. **Cash and Bank Balance:** This represents the cash in hand and at bank, which is used for meeting operational requirements.
7. **Accrued Income:** Income which has been due but not received till date.

Current Liabilities

They are short-term obligations to finance current assets such as bank overdraft.
　The following items comprise current liabilities:

1. **Sundry Creditors:** These liabilities stem out of purchase of raw materials on credit terms.
2. **Bank Overdrafts:** These include withdrawals in excess of credit balance standing in the firm's current accounts with banks.
3. **Short-term Loans:** Short-term borrowings by the firm from banks and others form part of current liabilities as short-term loans.
4. **Provisions:** These include provisions for taxation, proposed dividends, and contingencies.
5. **Outstanding Expenditures and Unearned Income** (or income received in advance) are current liabilities.

Dynamic Approach

According to this approach, working capital can be viewed as the amount of capital required for the smooth and uninterrupted functioning of the normal business operations of a company ranging from the procurement of raw materials, their conversion into finished products for sale, and realizing cash along with profit from the accounts receivables that arise from the sale of finished goods on credit. A company usually maintains some amount of liquid cash for transaction and precautionary and speculative purposes.

　Further, as the company extends credit to its customers, it can receive credit from its suppliers. Consequently, the drain on cash resources of the company can be delayed till the expiry of the credit period. Until such time, the amount will become "Accounts payable" of the company and as such provides a spontaneous source of credit.

Liquidity Versus Profitability Trade-off

One of the dilemmas faced in the management of current assets is to strike a balance between liquidity and profitability. They are inversely related. Profitability demands investment, whereas liquidity requires availability of cash (liquid resource), that is, sacrifice of investment. However, investment in current assets implies that to the extent resources are blocked up in current assets, they cannot be utilized in the business and hence the profitability is adversely affected. Further investment in current assets also entails some costs which also reduce the profitability. For example, when investment is made in inventories, ordering cost and carrying costs are incurred. On the other hand, if the financial manager decides to deploy fewer resources in current assets that would mean that though the profitability might be more the liquidity would be compromised.

A firm needs to invest in fixed assets as well as current assets to support a given level of output. Depending on their risk profile, different firms may deploy different levels of current assets for a given level of fixed assets to achieve a certain level of output. Three possible current asset policies are:

(a) Aggressive current asset policy.
(b) Moderate current asset policy.
(c) Conservative current asset policy.

Aggressive Current Asset Policy

A firm employs a lower level of current assets for a given level of fixed assets to achieve a certain level of sales. The relatively less investment in current assets helps in keeping greater amount of resources available for investment in business and thus increases profitability. Such a policy simultaneously reduces liquidity and increases the risk of insolvency.

Conservative Current Asset Policy

A firm employs a lower level of current assets for a given level of fixed assets to achieve a certain level of sales. The relatively less investment in current assets helps in keeping greater amount of resources available for investment in business and thus increases profitability. Such a policy simultaneously reduces liquidity and increases the risk of insolvency (Figure 15.1).

FIGURE 15.1

ALTERNATIVE CURRENT ASSET POLICIES

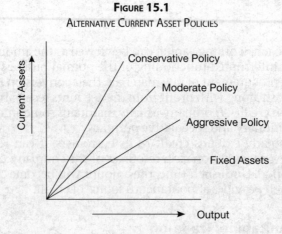

Source: Author.

Moderate Current Asset Policy

A firm employs a moderate level of current assets for a given level of fixed assets to achieve a certain level of sales. The moderate level of investment in current assets helps in keeping a sufficient amount of resources available for investment in business and simultaneously maintains adequate liquidity. It thus results in moderate level of risk for the business.

From the above discussion, it is apparent that management of current assets inevitably leads to a trade-off between "profitability" and "liquidity." An aggressive approach results in greater profitability but lower liquidity, while a conservative approach results in lower profitability but higher liquidity. This can be resolved to a certain extent by the management by following a moderate policy, which is neither highly aggressive nor highly conservative. Under this approach, some liquidity and some profitability have to be sacrificed so that the resultant figures of liquidity and profitability are reasonably satisfactory to the company.

Thus, a proper balancing between liquidity and profitability can be reached by considering alternatives along with their consequences on liquidity and profitability.

Under-trading and Over-trading

When the volume of sales is much less than the amount of assets employed, a situation of under-trading arises in a company. Under-trading indicates that funds of the company are locked up in current assets resulting in a lower turnover of the working capital. In other words, under-trading implies that a company is overcapitalized compared to the volume of sales. Unless the company takes some precautionary measures, the rate of return on equity is likely to come down as a result of which the market price of the company can be adversely affected. The precautionary measures may include change in the capital structure in order to reduce the debt–equity ratio, increase in the speed of the collection process, and reduce the level of inventory in relation to the sales forecast and production plans.

Over-trading is the opposite of under-trading. Over-trading means disproportionately high turnover of assets compared to the volume of sales. Over-trading thus implies undercapitalization. In the context of working capital, over-trading can be noticed from the high turnover of current assets. While increase in the turnover of current assets is generally considered to be a virtue, disproportionately high turnover is indicative of less amount of cash invested in current assets, which can create problems of liquidity. The problem of over-trading can be tackled by initially reducing the sales to a level commensurate with the amount of assets and the final solution lies in increasing the asset base through long-term financing.

Test Yourself

1. What is meant by gross working capital?
2. What are the implications of over- and under-trading?

Need for Working Capital

The ultimate objective of any firm is to optimize if not maximize the wealth of the shareholders. In order to do this, a firm should earn a suitable return from its operations. In order to earn sufficient returns, the firm should be able to generate sufficient sales. This requires adequate investment in current assets because all the sales do not get converted into cash immediately.

Operating Cycle

The cycle starting from cash and finally ending at cash is known as the operating cycle (Figure 15.2).

FIGURE 15.2
OPERATING CYCLE

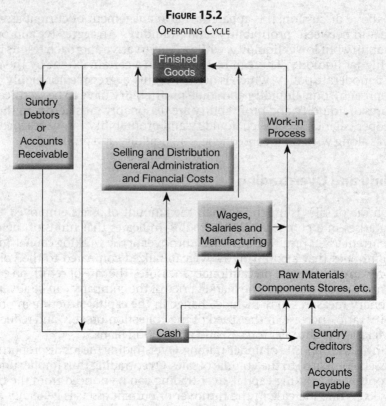

Source: Author.

The normal business operations of a manufacturing and trading company start with cash and go through the successive segments of the operating cycle, namely, raw material storage period, conversion period, finished goods storage period, and average collection period, before getting back cash along with profit. The total duration of all the segments mentioned above is known as the "gross operating cycle period." In case the company is in a position to sell its products for cash, then the total duration of the cycle gets reduced. In case advance payments are to be made for procuring materials, the operating cycle period increases. The purchase of raw materials, components, etc. is usually made on a credit basis, thereby giving rise to the spontaneous current liability, namely, accounts payable. When the average payment period of the company to its suppliers is deducted from the gross operating cycle (GOP) period, the resultant period is called the net operating cycle (NOC) period or simply the "operating cycle period." It becomes obvious that shorter the duration of the operating cycle period, faster will be the transformation of current assets into cash. The operating cycle approach is quite useful in both controlling and forecasting the working capital.

The length of the operating cycle for manufacturing is the sum of the inventory conversion period and receivables conversion period. The inventory conversion period is the time required for producing and selling the product. Inventory conversion period is the sum of the raw material storage period, WIP conversion period, and finished goods conversion period.

Raw Material Storage Period: The average time a raw material remains in stores before it is requisitioned for production.

WIP Conversion Period: The average time taken for converting raw materials into finished goods.

Finished Goods Storage Period: The average finished goods remain in the warehouse before they are sold.

Thus GOC=Inventory conversion period+Receivables conversion period.

Inventory conversion period=Raw material storage period+WIP conversion period+Finished goods storage period

GOC=Raw material storage period+WIP conversion period+Finished goods storage period+Receivables conversion period

NOC=GOC–Accounts payable period

Calculating the Various Components of Operating Cycle

Raw Material Storage Period

$$\text{Raw Material Storage Period} = \frac{\text{Average Stock of Raw Material}}{\text{Average Daily Consumption of Raw Material}}$$

$$\text{Average Daily Consumption of Raw Materials} = \frac{\text{Anual Consumption}}{360}$$

$$\text{Average Stock of Raw Materials} = \frac{\text{Opening Stock} + \text{Closing Stock}}{2}$$

WIP Conversion Period

$$\text{Average Conversion Period} = \frac{\text{Stock of Work-in-Process}}{\text{Average Daily Cost of Production}}$$

$$\text{Average Daily Cost of Production} = \frac{\text{Anual Cost of Production}}{360}$$

Annual cost of production=Opening stock of WIP+Consumption of raw materials+Other manufacturing costs such as wages and salaries and power and fuel+Depreciation–Closing WIP.

$$\text{Average Stock of work-in process} = \frac{\text{Opening W.I.P.} + \text{Closing W.I.P.}}{2}$$

Finished Goods Storage Period

$$\text{Finished goods storage period} = \frac{\text{Average Stock of Finished Goods}}{\text{Average Daily Cost of Sales}}$$

Annual cost of sales=Opening stock of finished goods+Cost of production+Excise duty+Selling and distribution costs+General administrative costs+Financial costs–Closing stock of finished goods.

$$\text{Average Daily Cost of Sales} = \frac{\text{Anual Cost of Sales}}{360}$$

$$\text{Average Stock of Finished Goods} = \frac{\text{Opening Stock Closing Stock}}{2}$$

Average Collection Period

$$\text{Average Collection Period} = \frac{\text{Average Balance of Sundry Debtors}}{\text{Average Daily Credit Sales}}$$

$$\text{Average Daily Credit Sales} = \frac{\text{Anual Credit Sales}}{360}$$

$$\text{Average Balance of Sundry Debtors} = \frac{\text{Opening Balance} + \text{Closing Balance}}{2}$$

Average Payment Period

$$\text{Average Payment Period} = \frac{\text{Average Balance of Sundry Cretors}}{\text{Average Daily Credit Sales}}$$

$$\text{Average Daily Credit Sales} = \frac{\text{Anual Credit Sales}}{360}$$

$$\text{Average Balance of Sundry Debtors} = \frac{\text{Opening Balance} + \text{Closing Balance}}{2}$$

Illustration 1. The following information pertains to Deccan Fertilizers Ltd (DFL) for the financial year 2010-2011: Income Statement

	(₹ in lakhs)
Sales	1,400
Increase in stocks	100
Other income	50
Revenues	1,550
Purchase of raw materials	700
Wages and salaries	150
Power and fuel	120
Depreciation	40
Excise duty	100
Advertising and promotional expenditure	100
Freight on finished goods	50
General administrative costs	80
Interest and finance charges	50
Expenses	1,390
Profit before tax	160
Tax	(40)
Profit after tax	120

Other Information

1. The opening stocks of raw materials, WIP, and finished goods are

	(₹ in lakhs)
Raw materials	105
WIP	30
Finished goods	134

2. The increase in stocks consists of the following changes:

	(₹ in lakhs)
Increase in the stock of raw materials	50
Increase in the stock of WIP	60
Decrease in the stock of finished goods	10

3. The sales are entirely on credit basis. The opening balance of sundry debtors was ₹180 lakhs. During the year, collections made from the sundry debtors amounted to ₹1,340 lakhs.
4. The purchases are entirely on credit basis. The opening balance of the sundry creditors was ₹160 lakhs. During the year, ₹740 lakhs was paid to the sundry creditors.
5. Wages and salaries as well as depreciation entirely relate to the manufacturing operations of the company.
6. Assume 1 year = 360 days.

What is the operating cycle of the company?

Solution:

A. Raw materials storage period

1. Annual consumption of raw materials

$$= \text{Opening stock of raw materials} + \text{Purchases} - \text{Closing stock of raw materials}$$

Closing stock = Opening stock + Increase in stock

$$= 105 + 50 = ₹155 \text{ lakhs}$$

Annual consumption of raw materials $= 105 + 700 - 155 = ₹650$ lakhs

2. Average daily consumption of raw materials $= \dfrac{650}{360}$

3. Average stock of raw materials $= \dfrac{\text{Opening Stock} + \text{Closing Stock}}{2}$

$$= \frac{105 + 155}{2} = ₹130 \text{ lakhss}$$

4. Raw materials storage period $= \dfrac{(3)}{(2)} = \dfrac{130}{\left(\dfrac{650}{360}\right)} = \dfrac{130 \times 360}{650} = 72$ days

B. WIP period

1. Average stock of work-in process $= \dfrac{\text{Opening Stock} + \text{Closing Stock}}{2}$

   Closing stock = Opening stock + Increase in stock

   $= 30 + 60 = ₹90$ lakhs

   Average stock of work-in-process $= \dfrac{30 + 90}{2} = ₹60$ lakhs

2. Annual cost of production = Opening stock of WIP + Consumption of raw materials + Wages and salaries + Power and fuel + depreciation − Closing stock of WIP

   $30 + 650 + 150 + 120 + 40 − 90 = ₹900$ lakhs

3. Average daily cost of production $= \dfrac{(2)}{360} = \dfrac{900}{360} = ₹2.5$ lakhs

4. Work-in-process period $= \dfrac{(1)}{(3)} = \dfrac{60}{2.5} = 24$ days

Finished goods storage period

1. Average stock of finished goods $= \dfrac{\text{Opening Stock} + \text{Closing Stock}}{2}$

   Closing stock = Opening stock − Decrease in stock

   $= 134 − 10 = ₹124$ lakhs

   Average stock of finished goods $= \dfrac{134 + 124}{2} = ₹129$ lakhs

2. Annual cost of sales = Opening stock of finished goods + Annual cost of production + Excise duty + Selling and distribution costs + General administrative expenses − Closing stock

   $= 134 + 900 + 100 + (100 + 50) + 80 + 50 − 124$

   $= ₹1,290$ lakhs

3. Average daily cost of sales $= \dfrac{(2)}{360} = \dfrac{1290}{360} = ₹43/12$ lakhs

4. Finished goods storage period $= \dfrac{(1)}{(3)} = \dfrac{129}{43/12} = 36$ days

Average collection period

1. Annual credit sales $= ₹1,400$ lakhs

2. Average daily credit sales $= \dfrac{1400}{360} = ₹35/9$ lakhs

3. Average balance of sundry debtors $= \dfrac{\text{Opening Stock} + \text{Closing Stock}}{2}$

   Closing balance = Opening balance + Annual credit sales − Collections

   $= 180 + 1,400 − 1,340 = ₹240$ lakhs

$$\therefore \text{Average balance of sundry debtors} = \frac{180 + 240}{2} = ₹210 \text{ lakhs}$$

4. $\text{Average collection period} = \frac{(3)}{(2)} = \frac{210}{(35/9)} = 54 \text{ days}$

Average payment period

1. Annual credit purchases = ₹700 lakhs

2. $\text{Average daily credit purchases} = \frac{700}{360} = ₹35/18 \text{ lakhs}$

3. $\text{Average balance of sundry creditors} = \dfrac{\text{Opening Stock} + \text{Closing Stock}}{2}$

$$\text{Closing balance} = \text{Opening balance} + \text{Credit purchases} - \text{Payments}$$
$$= 160 + 700 - 740 = ₹120 \text{ lakhs}$$

$$\therefore \text{Average balance of sundry creditors} = \frac{160 + 120}{2} = ₹140 \text{ lakhs}$$

4. $\text{Average payment period} = \frac{(3)}{(2)} = \frac{140}{(35/18)} = 72 \text{ days}$

$$\therefore \text{Operating cycle period} = A + B + C + D - E$$
$$= 72 + 24 + 36 + 54 - 72$$
$$= 114 \text{ days}$$

Application of the Operating Cycle

Monitoring the Working Capital

As mentioned earlier, the operating cycle approach proves quite useful as a technique for exercising control over working capital. Each segment of operating cycle can be compared with a pre-specific norm or with the corresponding figure in the previous accounting year or with the corresponding figure obtainable from the master budget of the company. Significant deviations call for closer scrutiny by the management. Once the reasons are known, remedial measures can be taken in respect of immediately controllable factors and the other factors may be accepted as constraints for the time being, pending long-term solutions. For example, frequent breakdown of plant may call for replacement of certain sections and/or modernization which cannot be implemented immediately but can be implemented say in about a year. Toward the end of exercising better control, the operating cycle may be calculated on a quarterly basis and/or on a product group basis.

In the case of seasonal industries such as the refrigeration industry, two sets of operating cycles may be calculated—one for the busy season and the other for the slack season—for exercising better control. As inter-temporal comparisons for monitoring working capital efficiency for a company are likely to be affected by the inflation factor, necessary adjustments can be made by the application of appropriately chosen price index. The comparisons made, after neutralizing the impact of inflation on both sales and working capital, are more likely to provide greater insight into the efficiency of working capital management across the years.

Estimating the Working Capital Requirement

Given the duration of various components of the operating cycle, the working capital needs can be estimated.

Illustration 2. Sunidhi Pens Pvt. Ltd plans to sell 100,000 units next year. The expected cost of goods sold is as follows:

Particulars	Unit Cost	Monthly Cost
Raw material cost	₹40	₹400,000
Manufacturing expenses	16	160,000
Selling, administration, and financial expenses	12	120,000
Total	**₹68**	**₹680,000**
The selling price per unit is expected to be ₹100		

(The monthly costs correspond to a monthly sales level of 10,000 units.)

The deviations at various stages of the operating cycle are expected to be as follows:

$$\text{Raw materials stage} = 3 \text{ months}$$
$$\text{WIP stage} = 1 \text{ month}$$
$$\text{Finished goods stage} = 1 \text{ month}$$
$$\text{Debtors stage} = 2 \text{ months}$$

Based on this information, estimate the working capital requirement of the firm if the minimum cash balance required by the firm ₹10 lakhs.

Solution:

INVESTMENT IN VARIOUS CURRENT ASSETS

(₹ in thousands)

Input	Period (in months)	Raw materials	WIP	Finished Goods	Debtors	Total
1. Raw material						
In stock	3	1,200				
In WIP.	1		400			
In finished goods	1			400		
In debtors	2				800	
						2,800

2. Manufacturing expenses					
In WIP.	½@	–		80	
In finished goods	1			160	
In debtors	2			320	
					560
3. Selling, administration and					
financial expenses					
In finished goods	1	–	–	120	
In debtors	2			240	
					360
4. Profit					
In debtors	2	–	–	–	240
					240
Total		1,200	480	680	1,600	3,960

Note: @Manufacturing expenses are expected to occur evenly. The WIP stage lasts for one month. Hence, on an average, the manufacturing expense component in WIP value will be equal to half month's manufacturing expenses.

The total investment in various assets=₹3,960 lakhs

To this sum, a desired cash balance of ₹10 lakhs may be added to get an estimate of the working capital.

Estimated working capital=₹3,960+₹10 lakhs=₹3,970 lakhs

Test Yourself

1. Why is working capital required?
2. What are the implications of operating cycle?

Types of Working Capital

Permanent Working Capital

This component represents the value of the current assets required on a continuous basis. Permanent working capital is the minimum amount of current assets, which is needed to conduct a business even during the dullest season. The minimum level of current assets is called permanent or fixed working capital as this part is permanently blocked in current assets. This amount varies from year to year, depending upon the growth of the company and the stage of the business cycle in which it operates. It is the amount of funds required to produce the goods and services necessary to satisfy demand at a particular point of time. It represents the current assets, which are required on a continuing basis over the entire year. It is maintained as the medium to continue the operations at any time.

Temporary Working Capital

Contrary to the above, temporary working capital represents a certain amount of fluctuations in the total current assets during a short period. These fluctuations are increased or decreased and are generally cyclical in nature. Additional current assets are required at different times during the operating year. Variable working capital is the amount of additional current assets that are required to meet the seasonal needs of a firm, and hence is also called as the seasonal working capital. For example, additional inventory will be required for meeting the demand during the period of high sales when the peak period is over and variable working capital starts decreasing or is very little during the normal period. It is temporarily invested in current assets. For example, a shopkeeper invests more money during winter season because he/she requires to keep more stock of woolen clothes. The same happens in a sugar factory where the factory manager buys more quantity of sugarcane during the harvesting season.

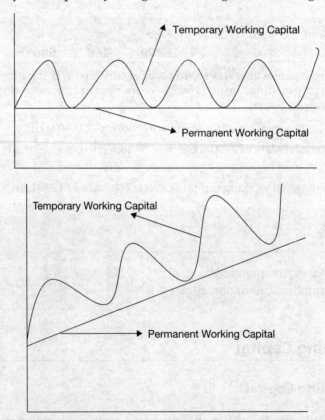

Zero Working Capital

Zero working capital is the state where the sum total of investment in total accounts receivable, accounts payable, and inventory is zero.

Inventory + Account receivables – Accounts payables = 0

Zero working capital tries to minimize the working capital deployed in the cash conversion cycle to the extent possible, and if possible, continuing the process without any working capital at all.

Zero working capital strategy diligently relates to the just-in-time practice. Both the concepts place importance on maintaining minimum stock or zero inventories to condense waste and to optimize the use of resources.

Financing Current Assets

The various sources of finance available to finance the current assets are:

1. Long-term sources such as ordinary share capital, preference share capital, debentures, and term loans.
2. Short-term sources such as working capital finances from banks, public deposits, and commercial paper.
3. Spontaneous sources such as trade credit and outstanding expenses.

The question that arises is which of these sources should be used and in what proportion for current asset financing? In this regard, there are three approaches that can be adopted by a firm:

1. Matching/hedging approach.
2. Conservative approach.
3. Aggressive approach.

Matching Approach

In this approach, the financial manager matches the maturity profiles of the assets with the maturity profile of the sources of finance. This is done in accordance with prudential principle of financing which says that long-term or fixed assets should be financed with long-term sources and short-term assets or current assets are to be financed with short-term sources. Thus in matching approach, the permanent component of working capital and fixed assets is financed using the long-term sources of financing, whereas the temporary component of current assets is financed using the short-term sources of finance.

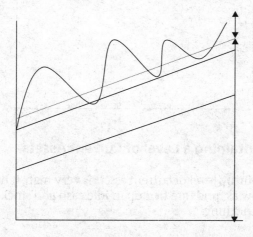

Conservative Approach

In conservative approach to financing, in its working capital, a firm depends on more of long-term funds. A firm finances its fixed/permanent working capital and also a part of its fluctuating working capital with long-term financing. Only a small portion of the temporary component is financed through short-term sources.

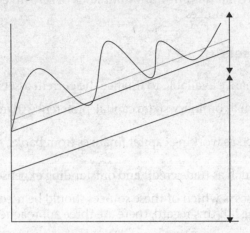

Aggressive Approach

When a firm uses more of short-term sources for financing working capital, it is said to be following an aggressive policy. In this approach, the temporary as well as a part of the permanent component of working capital is financed through the short-term sources. Some more aggressive firms, may in addition, finance a part of the fixed assets also through the shot-term sources.

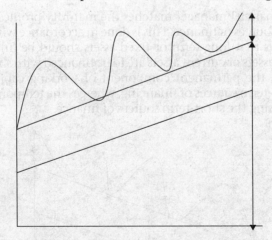

Costs Involved in Maintaining a Level of Current Assets

Costs of liquidity: If a firm's level of current assets is very high, it has excessive liquidity. Its return on assets will be low as funds are tied up in idle cash and stocks earn nothing and high level of debtors produces nothing.

Costs of Illiquidity: It is the cost of holding insufficient current assets. The firm will not be able to honor its obligations if it carries too little cash. This may force the firm to borrow at a high rate of interest.

In determining the optimum level of current assets, the firm should balance the profitability-solvency tangle by minimizing total costs—cost of liquidity and cost of illiquidity. This is shown in the Figure below:

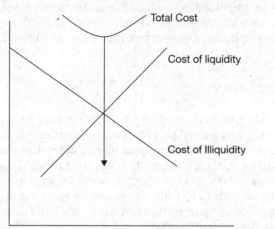

It is inferred that with the level of current assets, the cost of liquidity increases, while the cost of ill liquidity decreases and vice versa. A firm should maintain its current assets at that level where the sum of these two costs is minimized.

Test Yourself

1. What are the various approaches to manage working capital of a business?
2. How does the cost of liquidity and ill liquidity help in determining the optimum level of investment in current assets?

Factors Affecting the Composition of Working Capital

We have discussed the need for working capital along with its constituent elements in the case of atypical manufacturing and selling organization. But it is not necessary that every company should have the entire constituent elements considered earlier. For example, a purely trading company, which purchases finished products on credit basis and sells the same for cash will only have finished goods inventory and cash as current assets and accounts payable as current liabilities. As there is no manufacturing involved, the investment in fixed assets will be minimal. Consequently, working capital management assumes greater significance in such organizations. Some of the significant factors affecting the composition of working capital are as follows:

Nature of Business

As mentioned above, purely trading organizations will have only the finished goods inventory, accounts receivable, and cash as current assets and accounts payable as current liabilities.

On the other hand, manufacturing and trading companies will have a high proportion of current assets in the form of inventory of raw materials and WIP. Similarly, companies providing services such as telephony and IT-enabled services will have no inventory of raw materials or finished goods and the current assets will be in the form of cash or bills receivable. Similarly, organizations such as hotels and restaurants providing hospitality services will have some inventory (e.g. raw materials for food, housekeeping, etc.) and mostly have negligible accounts receivable, as services are provided on cash basis except for corporate clients. The prominent current asset in such organizations is undoubtedly cash. Thus, it is clear that depending on the nature of the business in which a company is, the composition and requirement of working capital will differ.

Nature of Raw Material Used

The nature of major raw materials used in the manufacture of finished goods will greatly influence the quantum of raw material inventory. For example, if the raw material is an agricultural product whose availability is seasonal in character, the proportion of raw material inventory to total current assets will be quite high. For example, sugarcane is the major raw material for sugar industry whose availability is seasonal in nature. Consequently, the percentage of raw material inventory to total current assets will be quite high compared to other items. Similarly, companies using imported raw materials with long lead time tend to have a high proportion of raw material inventory.

Manufacturing Process and Technology Used

In case the raw material has to go through several stages during the process of production, the WIP inventory is likely to be much higher than any other item of current assets. Similarly, the technology used for production will also determine the requirement of raw materials.

Nature of Finished Goods

The nature of finished goods greatly influences the amount of finished goods inventory. For example, if the finished goods have what is called a short life span or "shelf-life," the finished goods inventory will constitute a very low percentage of total current assets. For example, for a flower boutique finished goods inventory will be a small proportion of total current assets.

In the case of construction companies, which undertake work on a turnkey basis, as soon as the construction is completed the customer will take possession of it. Consequently, the finished goods inventory will be virtually insignificant and the WIP inventory (rather WIP) will be considerably high.

Sales and Demand Conditions

In the case of companies the demand for whose finished goods is seasonal in character, as in the case of fans, the inventory of finished goods will constitute a high percentage of total current assets. This is mainly because from the point of view of fixed costs to be incurred by the company, it would be more economical to maintain optimum-level production throughout the year than stepping up production operations during busy season.

In the case of reputed companies manufacturing consumer goods that enjoy growing demand over the years, the finished goods inventory need not be high as sales demand can be forecast with a reasonable degree of accuracy. However, in such companies the raw material inventory tends to be high in view of the large variety of products to be manufactured.

Credit Policy

The credit policy of a firm influences the amount of accounts receivable and hence affects the working capital requirement. If the credit policy of a firm is too lenient, it will result in more credit sales and more accounts receivable. If the collection is not efficient enough, it may also result in more bad debts. This would necessitate more investment in current assets and hence the working capital requirement would be higher. On the other hand, if the firm is following a reasonable credit policy, the credit will be extended only to the selected customers and hence the working capital requirement will be relatively less.

Availability of Credit

As discussed earlier, the working capital cycle is reduced if the credit period available to the firm from its suppliers is also considered. This implies that if credit is available to the firm from its suppliers, the credit terms of that credit will affect the working capital requirement of the firm. If credit is available for a longer time period and at a cheaper rate, to that extent the firm's investment in current assets will decline. You will recall that trade credit is a spontaneous source of finance for current assets.

Operational Efficiency

If a firm is operationally efficient, it will be in a position to check the time taken for production, control operating costs, and collect the receivables in time. All these actions will ultimately improve the utilization of current assets and reduce the investment in current assets.

Inflation

The behavior of the price level in the economy will have an impact on the costs associated with working capital management. Even if everything else remains constant, an increase in inflation would imply an increased investment in the working capital.

Evaluation of Working Capital Management Policy

The following criteria may be adopted for evaluating the working capital management of a company:

Liquidity

By and large, the current assets of a company are considered to be more liquid than fixed assets. Even among the current assets, some items are considered to be much more liquid than others. For instance, inventory is the least liquid, whereas cash is the most liquid asset.

The ultimate test of liquidity is the ability of a company to meet its current obligations. Although accounts receivables are generally considered to be liquid, the degree of liquidity depends upon the paying habits of customers and the collection efforts made by the company.

This implies that while judging the liquidity aspect both the qualitative and quantitative aspects have to be assessed. Consequently, if the firm is able to honor its financial obligations, its working capital management can be regarded as efficient. As we have already learnt, the criterion of liquidity can be quantitatively assessed by means of various financial ratios such as liquidity ratio and quick ratio.

Availability of Cash

Cash is an idle asset. If not invested suitably, it earns no returns. At the same time, unavailability of cash may lead to a crisis. In fact, many companies have failed because of cash crunch than because of any other reason. This duality in the nature of the asset requires that the financial manager should strike a balance between adequate and insufficient levels of cash.

Various factors that influence the proportion of cash in the total current assets include, among others, uncertainty associated with future cash flows, lack of synchronization between cash inflows and cash outflows, desired liquidity mix in terms of cash and bank balances and marketable securities, and attitude of management toward risk.

Inventory Turnover

Any type of inventory will represent the amount of cash locked up and the amount of carrying costs, which can be as high as 25% of the value of inventory, associated with the inventory. Too high a level of inventory and too low a level of inventory are not conducive to the financial health of a company as the former can create problems of liquidity, while the latter can affect profitability. Here again, the financial manager has to strike a balance between the two.

Credit Extended to Customers

If the credit policy of a firm is too lenient, it will result in more credit sales and more accounts receivable. If the collection is not efficient enough, it may also result in more bad debts. This would necessitate more investment in current assets and hence the working capital requirement would be higher. On the other hand, if a firm is following a reasonable credit policy, the credit will be extended only to the selected customers and hence the working capital requirement will be relatively less.

It is, therefore, necessary to ensure whether reasonable credit is provided to the customers as part of the evaluation of working capital management.

This can be measured in terms of the turnover of receivables or average collection period.

Credit Obtained from Suppliers

As discussed earlier, the working capital cycle is reduced if the credit period available to the firm from its suppliers is also considered. Working capital management should provide adequate flexibility to the purchase department so that they can shop around and obtain better terms for procurement of supplies. Further, regular payment habit on the part of the company can instill confidence in its suppliers. This can be measured in terms of the average payment period.

Profit Criterion for Working Capital

When we analyze whether to make an investment or not, we check whether the proposed investment will have a positive net present value (NPV). The NPV of a proposed investment is calculated by deducting the present value of the outflows from the present value of the inflows. Investment in working capital should also be evaluated on the same lines. Yet, there is a significant difference between other types of investments and investment in current assets. Investment in current assets is generally completely realizable at the time of liquidation.

For these types of investments, the profit per period criterion is equivalent to the NPV criterion.

The profit per year on current assets would be

$$P_r - P_k,$$

where P_r is the return for the year and P_k is the cost of funds for the year.

The NPV, assuming that the investment in the current asset continues for n years, will be

$$NPV = -P + P_r (PVIFA_{k,n}) + P (PVIF_{k,n})$$

On including the values of PVIFA and PVIF in the formula and solving further, we get

$$NPV = (P_r - P_k)$$

As the NPV criterion is a multiple of the profit per period criterion, it can be taken as equivalent. Hence, for the purpose of evaluating investment in working capital, the profit per period criterion can be used.

Test Yourself

1. What are the factors affecting the investment decisions in working capital?
2. "Inflation affects the level of working capital." Comment.
3. Elaborate profit criteria of working capital.

SUMMARY

1. Working capital means the total current assets of the business.
2. There are two approaches for understanding what constitutes working capital: static approach and dynamic approach.
3. Profitability and liquidity are inversely related. Profitability demands investment, whereas liquidity requires availability of cash (liquid resource), that is, sacrifices of investment.
4. Investment in current assets depends on the risk appetite of the firm. Therefore, a firm may adopt aggressive current asset policy, moderate current asset policy, or conservative current asset policy
5. The total duration of investments in the components of current assets is known as "gross operating cycle period."
6. Permanent working capital is the minimum amount of current assets, which is needed to conduct a business even during the dullest season of the year.
7. Temporary working capital represents a certain amount of fluctuations in the total current assets during a short period. These fluctuations are increased or decreased and are generally cyclical in nature.
8. Current assets may be financed through various sources such as

   - Long-term sources such as ordinary share capital, preference share capital, debentures, and term loans.

- Short-term sources such as working capital finances from banks, public deposits, and commercial paper.
- Spontaneous sources such as trade credit and outstanding expenses.

9. A firm may adopt three approaches to determine the proportion of each source of finance to meet its requirement of financing the current assets.

  - Matching/hedging approach
  - Conservative approach
  - Aggressive approach

10. Nature of business, nature of raw materials used, manufacturing process and technology used, nature of finished goods, demand and supply positions, operational efficiency, credit policy, and inflation are some of the factors affecting working capital of an organization.

KEY TERMS

- Gross working capital
- Net working capital
- Static approach
- Dynamic approach
- Liquidity
- Profitability
- Under-trading

- Over-trading
- Operating cycle
- Permanent working capital
- Temporary working capital
- Zero working capital
- Cost of liquidity
- Cost of illiquidity

Learning Outcomes

Students may have understood the concept and the different dimensions of working capital management policy as well as the factors affecting composition of working capital.

SOLVED PROBLEMS

1. The following details have been collected from the records of VXL Ltd. Income statement for the year ended March 31, 2004.

	(₹ in crore)
Sales	80
Other income	5
Revenues	85
Decrease in stocks	6

Purchase of raw materials and consumables stores	42
Wages and salaries	10
Power and fuel	4
Depreciation on manufacturing facilities	1
Excise duty	2
Sales promotion expenditure	3
Carriage and freight	2
Administrative expenses	2
Interest and financial charges	1
Expenses	73
Profit before tax	12
Provision for tax	4
Profit after tax	8

Other Information

1. The opening balances of raw materials, WIP, finished goods, sundry debtors, and sundry creditors are:

	(₹ in crore)
Raw materials and consumable stores	8
WIP	4
Finished goods	6
Sundry debtors	10
Sundry creditors	8

2. The decrease in stocks resulted from the following changes:

	(₹ in crore)
• Decrease in the stock of raw materials and consumable stores	4
• Increase in the stock of WIP	1
• Decrease in the stock of finished goods	3

3. The sales entirely consist of credit sales. During the year, the customers of the company paid ₹74 crore.
4. The purchases entirely consist of credit purchases. During the year, the company paid ₹36 crore to its suppliers.

5. Wages and salaries include ₹2 crore on account of salaries of general administrative staff of the company. The remaining amount of wages and salaries relate to the manufacturing operations of the company.
6. Carriage and freight entirely relate to the transportation expenditure of finished goods.
7. Power and fuel entirely relate to manufacturing operations of the company.
8. Assume 1 year = 360 days.

Calculate the duration of operating cycle of the company.

Solution:

Raw material storage period

1. Average stock of raw materials $= \dfrac{\text{Opening Stock} + \text{Closing Stock}}{2}$

    Opening stock = ₹8 crore (Given)

    Closing stock = Opening stock – Decrease in stock = 8 – 4 = ₹4 crore

    ∴ Average stock of raw materials $= \dfrac{8+4}{2} = ₹6$ core

2. Annual consumption of raw materials = Purchases + Decrease in stock

    $= 42 + 4 = ₹46$ crore

3. Average daily consumption of raw materials $= \dfrac{46}{360}$

4. Raw materials storage period $= \dfrac{6}{46/360} = \dfrac{6 \times 360}{46} \approx 46.96$ days.

WIP period

1. Average stock of work-in-process $= \dfrac{\text{Opening Stock} + \text{Closing Stock}}{2}$

    Opening stock = ₹4 crore (Given)

    Closing stock = Opening stock + Increase in stock = 4 + 1 = ₹5 crore

    ∴ Average stock of work-in-process $= \dfrac{4+5}{2} = 4.5$ crore.

2. Annual cost of production = Opening WIP + Annual consumption of raw materials + Manufacturing expenses + Depreciation – Closing WIP

    $= 4 + 46 + (10 - 2) + 4 + 1 - 5 = ₹58$ crore.

3. Averge daily cost of production $= \dfrac{58}{360}$

4. Work-in-process period $= \dfrac{4.5}{58/360} = \dfrac{4.5 \times 360}{58} \approx 27.93$ days.

Finished goods storage period

1. Average stock of finished goods $= \dfrac{\text{Opening Stock} + \text{Closing Stock}}{2}$

   Opening stock $= ₹6$ crore

   Closing stock $=$ Opening stock $-$ Decrease in stock $= 6 - 3 = ₹3$ crore

   $\therefore$ Average stock of finished goods $= \dfrac{6+3}{2} = ₹4.5$ crore

2. Annual cost of sales $=$ Opening stock of finished goods $+$ Annual cost of production $+$ Selling, administration, and financial expenses $+$ Excise duty $-$ Closing stock of finished goods

   $$= 6+58+3+2+2+1+2+2-3 = ₹73 \text{ crore}$$

3. Average daily cost of sales $= \dfrac{73}{360}$

4. Finished goods storage period $= \dfrac{4.5}{73/360} = \dfrac{4.5 \times 360}{73} = \approx 22.19$ days.

Average collection period

1. Average sundry debtors balance $= \dfrac{\text{Opening balance} + \text{Closing balance}}{2}$

   Opening balance $= ₹10$ crore (Given)

   Closing balance $=$ Opening balance $+$ Sales $-$ Payments made by customers

   $$= 10+80-74 = ₹16 \text{ crore}$$

   Average sundry debtors balance $= \dfrac{\text{Opening balance} + \text{Closing balance}}{2}$

2. Average daily sales $= \dfrac{\text{Annual Sales}}{360} = \dfrac{80}{360}$

3. Average collection period $= \dfrac{13}{80/360} = 58.5$ days.

Average payment period

1. Average sundry creditors balance $= \dfrac{\text{Opening Balance} + \text{Closing Balance}}{2}$.

   Opening balance $= ₹8$ crore (Given)

   Closing balance $=$ Opening balance $+$ Purchases $-$ Payments to sundry creditors

   $$= 8+42-36 = ₹14 \text{ crore}.$$

   Average balance of sundry creditors $= \dfrac{8+14}{2} = ₹11$ crore

2. Average daily purchases $= \dfrac{\text{Annual Purchases}}{360} = \dfrac{42}{360}$

3. Average payment period $= \dfrac{11}{42/360} \approx 94.29$ days.

$$\text{Operating cycle period} = A+B+C+D-E = 61.29 \approx 61 \text{ days}$$

4. If the average stock of WIP is ₹55.75 lakhs and the average conversion period is 3 days, what is the annual cost of production (assuming 360 days in a year)?

Solution:

$$\text{Average conversion period} = \dfrac{\text{Average stock of work-in-process}}{\text{Average daily cost of production}}$$

Average daily cost of production = 55.75 lakhs/3

Hence, annual cost of production = 360×55.75 lakhs/3 = ₹6,690 lakhs.

5. Consider the following data:

GOC	= 80 days
NOC operating cycle	= 55 days
Raw material storage period	= 40 days
Conversion period	= 2 days
Finished goods storage period	= 20 days

What is the average collection period?

Solution:

Average collection period = GOC − (RM storage period + Conversion period

+ FG storage period)

= 80 − (40 + 2 + 20) = 18 days

6. Consider the following data:

Raw material storage period = 50 days

Average stock of raw materials = ₹651,000

Average balance of trade creditors = ₹265,000

Assume 360 days in a year and all purchases are made on credit.

If the closing stock of raw materials is 10% higher than the opening stock of raw materials, what is the average payment period?

Solution:

$$\text{Raw material storage period} = \dfrac{\text{Average stock of raw materials}}{\text{Daily consumption of RMs}}$$

$$\text{Daily consumption of RMs} = \dfrac{6,51,000}{50} = ₹13,020$$

Annual consumption $= 13,020 \times 360 = ₹4,687,200$

Annual consumption $=$ Opening stock $+$ Purchases $-$ Closing stock

$$\text{Average stock of RMs} = \frac{\text{Opening} + \text{Closing}}{2}$$

where opening stock is S and closing stock is 1.1S

$$6,51,000 = \frac{S + 1.1S}{2}$$

$S = ₹620,000 =$ Opening stock

Closing stock $= ₹682,000$

Annual consumption $= 620,000 + P - 682,000$

$4,687,200 = 620,000 + P - 682,000$

$P = 4,749,200$

$$\text{Average payment period} = \frac{\text{Average balance of creditors}}{\text{Purchases}/360}$$

7. Consider the following data about Food Mart Ltd:

Opening stock of finished goods $= ₹650$ lakhs

Closing stock of finished goods $= ₹1,050$ lakhs

Cost of production $= ₹12,000$ lakhs

Selling, administration, and financial expenses $= ₹4,500$ lakhs

Customs and excise duties $= ₹35,000$ lakhs

Calculate the finished goods storage period (in days) for Food Mart.

Solution:

$$\text{Finished goods storage period} = \frac{\text{Average stock of finished goods}}{\text{Average daily cost of goods sold}}$$

$$\text{Average stock of Finished goods} = ₹\frac{(650 + 1050)\text{lakhs}}{2}$$

$$= ₹850 \text{ lakhs}$$

$$\text{Average daily cost of goods sold} = ₹\frac{650 + 12,000 + 4,500 + 35,000 + 1050 \text{ lakhs}}{360}$$

$$= ₹\frac{51,500}{360} \text{lakhs}$$

$$= ₹141.94 \text{ lakhs}$$

$$\text{Finished goods storage period} = \frac{850}{141.94} = 5.99 \text{ days} \approx 6 \text{ days}$$

Problems

1. Consider the following data about Flashlight Ltd:

GOC	124 days
NOC	105 days
Average collection period	40 days
Conversion period	3 days
Finished goods storage period	25 days
Average payment period	19 days

Calculate the raw material storage period.

2. The following information is related to the operations of a firm:

Raw material storage period	70 days
Average conversion period	8 days
Finished goods storage period	18 days
Average collection period	39 days
Average payment period	45 days

Calculate the operating cycle of the firm.

3. The following figures are collected from annual report of Deccan Mills:

	2003 (in ₹ 000s)	2004 (in ₹ 000s)
Raw materials inventory—closing balance	180	212
WIP inventory—closing balance	25	45
Purchases of raw materials during the year	1,085	1,192
Manufacturing expenses during the year	1,165	1,280
Depreciation	75	100

What should be the average conversion period of Deccan Mills for the year 2004? (Assume 360 days in a year)

4. The following figures are collected from the annual report of Jaipuria Sanitary Ltd:

	2003 (in ₹ 000s)	2004 (in ₹ 000s)
Raw materials inventory—closing balance	160	192
WIP inventory—closing balance	25	45
Finished goods inventory—closing balance	30	50

Purchases of raw materials during the year	1,135	1,242
Manufacturing expenses during the year	1,125	1,230
Depreciation	75	100
Selling, administration and financial expenses during the year	200	230
Excise duty paid during the year	120	150

What should be the average finished goods storage period of Jaipuria Sanitary for the year 2004?

5. Washer Man, a reputed washing machine manufacturer, plans to manufacture 12,000 sets of washing machines for the next year. The cost components are as follows:

Item	Unit Cost (₹)
Raw material	5,000
Manufacturing expenses	2,000
Selling, administrative and financial expenses	1,000

The selling price per unit is ₹10,000 and sales may be assumed to be uniform throughout the year while the manufacturing expenses are expected to be incurred evenly throughout the month. The duration at various stages of the operating cycle is given as follows:

Raw material stage	=2 months
WIP stage	=1 month
Finished goods stage	=1 month
Debtors stage	=3 months

If the minimum cash balance required is ₹1,000,000, what is the estimate for the working capital requirement of the company?

ACCESS YOURSELF

Concept Review and Critical Thinking Questions

1. Explain the concept of working capital. What are the different approaches toward working capital? Discuss.
2. What is profitability-liquidity trade-off in working capital management? Discuss.
3. Discuss the risk-return trade-off of different current asset financing policies.
4. What do you mean by operating cycle? Illustrate your answer.
5. "Working capital management deals with decisions regarding the appropriate mix and level of current assets and current liabilities." Elucidate the statement.

STUDENT ACTIVITIES

Identify three companies from different sectors:

- One with positive working capital
- One with negative working capital
- One with zero working capital

Perform the comparative analysis.

SUGGESTED READINGS

Brealey, R.A., & Myers, S.C. (2002). *Principles of corporate finance* (7th ed.). New York: McGraw-Hill.
Horne, J.C.V. (2002). *Management & policy* (12th ed.). Singapore: Pearson Education.
Ross, S.A., Westerfield, R.W., & Jordan, B.D. (2002). *Fundamentals of corporate finance* (6th ed.). New Delhi: Tata McGraw-Hill.

Inventory Management

- To optimize the firm's investment in inventory, striking a balance between cost of holding inventory and stock-out costs.
- To ensure adequate maintenance of supplies of raw material, store and spares, and finished goods so as to maintain production levels and meet the varying requirements of the customers.
- To learn about various types of inventory models.

PRELUDE

Inventory management consumes more than 50% of working capital and 85% of operating decision-making time. An effective inventory management provides a cutting-edge win over competitors. In contemporary market situation, managing inventory is a very dicey issue. Excess of inventory will eat up profit and insufficient inventory will take away opportunities. Read the following:

CWG Traffic Curbs: Retailers Rush to Pre-stock Inventory

The office goers are not the only ones who will fall victim to traffic mess during the Commonwealth Games (CWG). Large retailers in the Capital too are nervous about the movement of goods carriages that might affect the supply of their stocks in and around Delhi.

To ensure better security, the government has restricted the movement of commercial vehicles throughout the city. Commercial vehicles will not be allowed on some roads during the day, while they will be allowed to ply as usual at night. Markets around the venues will be asked to close early.

Brands, such as ITC's Wills Lifestyle, FabIndia, Future Group's Big Bazaar, LG, and Samsung, are rushing to pre-stock their inventory before the games.

Retailers also see the Games as a big business opportunity. Demand for Indian wears, handicrafts, and jewellery is likely to shoot up during the two weeks of the Games.

ITC Lifestyle, which retails the casual wear brand Wills Lifestyle, has started the process of pre-stocking fearing transportation and logistics problems. It plans to increase its inventory stock by 25% for October to ensure smooth supply. It expects the demand to grow by over 20% during the month compared to the average sales recorded in a festive season. "We are working out alternative transportation routes.

We anticipate a surge in demand in that period. We are stocking up all the stores in Delhi and NCR beforehand," ITC Lifestyle Retailing CEO Atul Chand said.

FabIndia, the ethic wear brand, has also stocked up its inventory to work around the traffic situation during CWG. "Usually we stock up a week before the festive season. We are doing it two weeks earlier this time due to CWG at all our 18 outlets in Delhi and NCR," FabIndia MD William Bissel said. The retailer expects a 30% increase in demand over the month.

Industry watchers feel retailers have no other option but to pre-stock outlets and do bulk supplies during the nights. "Shopping is bound to surge, as half the city will be on holiday. Visitors, athletes and delegates are also expected to shop and the retailers need to be prepared. It is a good opportunity for retailers," Harminder Sahni, MD of consultancy firm Wazir Advisors said.

Consumer durables major LG plans to hire additional warehouses in the areas where there are lower restrictions and which are close to the dealers within the Capital. It is looking for similar arrangements outside Delhi to ensure smooth supply to the NCR and nearby cities.

Source: Economic Times, September 21, 2010.

Inventories include raw material, work-in-process (W-I-P), and finished goods inventory. Although inventory management usually is not the direct operating responsibility of the finance manager, the investment of funds in inventory is an important aspect of financial management. Consequently, the finance manager must be familiar with ways to control inventories effectively, so that allocated capital may be used efficiently. **Inventory management is a dicey issue. If there is inventory, then the cost is there and if no inventory, then opportunity is lost.** The goal of effective inventory management is to optimize the total costs—direct and indirect—that are associated with holding inventories. At the same time, there is no loss of opportunity as well.

Need for Inventories

Inventory is needed as supplies for operations, raw materials, and work-in-progress for production, and finished goods for sale. Inventory does not earn interest, and is costly to store, order, insure, and protect. Inventories are needed for the following reasons:

1. **Avoiding Loss of Sales:** If the firm is not having enough stock of finished goods, it will result in a loss of sales normally unless the product is being made to order as per the specific requirements of the customer. In most cases, however, a firm must be in a position to deliver goods on demand. If the firm is not able to do so, it has to incur stock-out costs in the form of lost sales.

2. **Gaining Quantity Discounts:** Suppliers of raw material usually offer quantity discounts if purchases are made in bulk. These discounts will reduce the cost of goods sold and increase the profits earned on a sale. Thus, the firm would like to purchase the raw materials in quantities greater than its current requirements.

3. **Reducing Ordering Costs:** Each time a firm places an order, it incurs certain expenses, which are called as ordering costs. Forms have to be filled, approvals have to be obtained, and goods that arrive must be accepted, inspected, and counted. Later, an invoice must be processed and payment made. The greater the number of orders, the greater the ordering cost. By placing fewer orders, the firm can reduce its total ordering costs.

4. **Achieving Efficient Production Runs:** Each time a firm organizes workers and machines to produce an item, startup costs are incurred. These are then absorbed as production begins. Frequent setups will result in high startup costs; longer runs involve lower costs. This is because if the production run is longer, more numbers of units are produced and the total startup cost is spread over a larger number of units. Further, as the number of startups declines, the overall startup costs also declines.

5. Reducing Risk of Production Shortages: Once the production process starts, all the required raw materials and components should be made available to the production department without any delay. If any of these are missing, the entire production operation can come to a grinding halt, with consequent heavy expenses.

Types of Inventory

The inventory required by any firm would depend upon the nature of industry. For example, the inventory requirements of a trading firm would be different from the inventory requirement of a manufacturing firm. Similarly, a firm in the service industry will have different inventory requirements than a firm producing goods.

Usually, there are four types of inventories:

Raw Materials Inventory: It consists of those basic materials that are converted into finished goods through the manufacturing process. The purpose of maintaining raw material inventory is to separate the production function from the purchasing function so that delays, for example, in shipment of raw materials do not cause production delays.

Stores and Spares: It includes those products which are accessories to the main products produced for the purpose of sale. Examples of stores and spares items are bolts, nuts, clamps, and screws. These spare parts are usually bought from outside but sometimes they are manufactured in-house also.

W-I-P Inventory: These are semi-finished products. The longer and more complex the production process, the greater the W-I-P inventory will be. It helps in separating the various operations in the production process so that machine failures and work stoppages in one operation do not affect the other operations.

Finished Goods Inventory: These are completely manufactured products awaiting sale. The purpose of a finished goods inventory is to separate the production and sales functions so that sales can occur without any immediate dependence on production.

Costs Associated with Inventories

The effective management of inventory involves a trade-off between having too little and too much inventory. Costs associated with inventory management can be identified as three direct costs that are immediately connected to buying and holding goods and two indirect costs which are losses of revenues.

The costs associated with inventories are as follows:

Material Costs: These are the costs of purchasing the goods including transportation and handling costs.

Ordering Costs: Ordering costs refer to the costs associated with placing an order such as cost incurred for preparation of requisition forms by the user department, setup costs incurred by the manufacturing and transport departments, and inspection and handling at the warehouse by the user department. By and large, ordering costs remain more or less constant irrespective of the size of the order. But this is not going to significantly affect the behavior of ordering costs. As ordering costs are considered invariant to the order size, the total ordering costs can be reduced by increasing the size of the order.

A company can reduce its total ordering costs by increasing the order size, which in turn will reduce the number of orders. However, reduction in ordering costs is usually followed by an increase in carrying costs.

Carrying Costs: These are the expenses incurred for storing the inventories. These costs include insurance, rent/depreciation of warehouse, salaries of storekeeper, his assistants and security personnel, financing cost of money locked-up in inventories, obsolescence, spoilage, and taxes. Carrying costs are considered to be a given percentage of the value of inventory held in the warehouse, despite some fixed elements of costs, which comprise only a small portion of the total carrying costs. The greater the investment in inventory, the greater the carrying costs.

Cost of Funds Tied Up with Inventory: Whenever a firm commits its resources to inventory, it is using funds that otherwise might have been used in the business elsewhere. This implies that inventory has an opportunity cost associated with it. If more than required investment is made in inventories, this opportunity cost will also increase.

Cost of Stock-outs: These are costs associated with the inability to provide materials to the production department and/or inability to provide finished goods to the marketing department, as the requisite inventories are not available when demanded. There are qualitative as well as quantitative consequences associated with stock-outs. For example, when the raw materials are out of stock, production will be stopped. In order to resume production, materials may have to be purchased immediately; as a result, the quantity discounts may have to be foregone. Similarly, when finished goods are out of stock, it may result in creating a bad impression about the company in the market place, and if the customer switches over to some competing brand, it may result in a loss of sales.

Objectives of Inventory Management

The investment in inventory should strike a balance between efficient and smooth production/sales operations and profitability. This is so because both excessive and inadequate inventories are not desirable.

Excessive investment in inventories would ensure that there are no shortages in production/sales operations but it also entails an opportunity costs as excessive funds, which could be used elsewhere in the business when there are tied up in inventories. Further, this would also mean an increase in carrying costs. Not only profitability but also the liquidity of the firm is adversely affected, as inventories are not so liquid asset. It takes some time before they can be sold and cash realized.

On the other hand, inadequate investment in inventories is also not advisable as it also involves some costs. The production may get held up for the need of raw materials. If the raw materials are purchased in an emergency, the quantity discounts may not be available, thus increasing the purchase cost. As the production is held up, it also means an idling cost. Similarly, if the finished goods inventory is not adequate, it would mean that some sales would be lost if demand is there. This may also mean a loss of customer forever if he decides to switch over to a substitute product.

The optimum level of investment in inventories will lie somewhere between these two danger points. The objective of inventory management is to determine and maintain optimum level of inventory investment.

Inventory Management Techniques

As the order size increases, the total ordering costs decline, whereas the carrying costs increase. Since these costs behave in an opposite manner, there is a need to strike a proper balance between these two costs so as to minimize the total cost.

Likewise, if a company wants to avert stock-out costs, it has to maintain larger inventories of materials and finished goods, which will result in higher carrying costs.

Inventory Management Techniques	Solution
1. Overstocking and under stocking	Maximum and minimum levels, reorder quantity
2. Order quantity problem	EOQ, EOQ (quantity discount)
3. Stock-out problem	Safety stocks
4. Classification problem to determine the type of control required	ABC, VED, etc.

The following techniques are used for inventory management.

Economic Order Quantity

The economic order quantity (EOQ) refers to the optimal order size that will result in the lowest total of order and carrying costs for an item of inventory given its expected usage, carrying costs, and ordering cost. By calculating an EOQ, the firm attempts to determine the order size that will minimize the total inventory costs.

$$\text{Total inventory cost} = \text{Ordering cost} + \text{Carrying cost}$$

$$\text{Total ordering costs} = \text{Number of orders} \times \text{Cost per order (₹)}$$

$$= \frac{Q}{q} \times O$$

where Q is the annual quantity required, q is the quantity per order, and O is the fixed cost per order.

The total carrying costs = Average level of inventory × Price per unit × Percentage carrying cost

$$\text{Total carrying costs} = \frac{Q}{q} \times p \times c = \frac{qpc}{2}$$

where q is the quantity ordered, p is the purchase price per unit, and c is the carrying cost in %.

As the lead time (i.e., time required for procurement of material) is assumed to be zero, an order for replenishment is made when the inventory level reduces to zero. The level of inventory over time follows the pattern as shown in Figure 16.1.

Figure 16.1

Inventory Level and Order Point for Replenishment

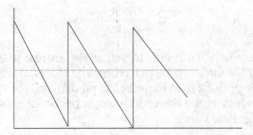

Source: Author.

From Figure 16.1, it can be noticed that the level of inventory will be equal to the order quantity (**q** units) to start with. It progressively declines (though in a discrete manner) to level **o** by the end of period 1. At that point, an order for replenishment will be made for **q** units. Since the lead time has been assumed to be zero, replenishment is immediate and the inventory level jumps to **q** and a similar procedure occurs in the subsequent periods. As a result of this, the average level of inventory will be **q/2** units.

As discussed above, as order size **q** increases, the total ordering costs will decrease, while the total carrying costs will increase.

The EOQ, denoted by **q'**, is that value at which the total cost of both ordering and carrying will be minimized.

$$\text{Total costs} = \text{Ordering Costs} + \text{Carrying Costs}$$

$$= ₹\frac{QO}{q} + \frac{qpc}{2}$$

FIGURE 16.2

BEHAVIOR OF COSTS ASSOCIATED WITH INVENTORY FOR CHANGES IN ORDER QUANTITY

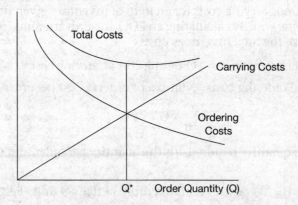

Source: Author.

From Figure 16.2, it can be seen that the total cost curve reaches its minimum at the point of intersection between the ordering costs curve and the carrying costs line. The value of **q** corresponding to it will be the EOQ, **q'**.

Symbolically

$$\frac{QC}{q} = \frac{qpc}{2}$$

$$2QC = q^2pc$$

$$q' = \sqrt{\frac{2QC}{pc}} \text{ units}$$

In the above formula, when "*Q*" is considered as the annual usage of material, the value of **q'** indicates the size of the order to be placed for the material which minimizes the total inventory-related costs. Suppose a firm expects a total demand for its product over the planning period to be 10,000 units, while the ordering cost per order is ₹800 and the carrying cost per unit is ₹4. Substituting these values

$$EOQ = \sqrt{\frac{4 \times 10,000 \times 800}{2}} = 4,000 \text{ units}$$

Thus, if the firm orders in 4,000 unit lot sizes, it will minimize its total inventory costs.

FIGURE 16.3
VALUE OF F FOR DIFFERENT STOCK OUT PERCENTAGE

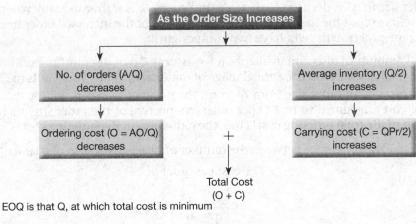

EOQ is that Q, at which total cost is minimum

EOQ = (2AO/C)$^{1/2}$

Source: Author.

The model is based on the following assumptions:

1. Demand remains constant throughout the planning horizon.
2. The purchase price ₹ **p** per unit of material will remain constant irrespective of the order size.
3. The carrying costs remain constant.
4. The ordering cost remains constant.
5. There is no lead time between placing an order and its delivery.

It is possible that these assumptions may not be practical. Therefore, the basic EOQ model has to be modified.

Modified EOQ to Include Varying Unit Prices: Bulk purchase discount is offered when the size of the order is at least equal to some minimum quantity specified by the supplier. The question that arises is whether the EOQ **q′** calculated on the basis of a price without discount will still remain valid even after taking discount into consideration.

In such cases, we can adopt the following procedure to determine the EOQ.

First, we calculate **q′**, that is, the EOQ without considering the discount. Let us suppose that **q*** is the minimum order size required for availing the discount. After calculating **q′**, the same will be compared with **q***.

Three possibilities may arise out of the comparison:

1. **q′>q***
2. **q′=q***
3. **q′<q***

If **q'** is greater than or equal to **q***, then **q'** will remain valid even in the changed situation caused by the quantity discount offered. This is because the company can avail itself of the benefit of quantity discount with an order size of **q'** as it is at least equal to **q***, the minimum order size for utilizing discount.

If **q'** is less than **q***, the need for the calculation of an optimal order size arises as the company cannot avail itself the discount with the order size of **q'**. An incremental analysis can be carried out to consider the financial consequences of availing oneself of discount by increasing the order size to **q***. A decision to increase the order size is warranted only when the incremental benefits exceed the incremental costs arising out of the increased order size.

The incremental benefits will have two components:

1. The total amount of discount available; if we assume ₹ d of discount per unit of material, then the total discount on the annual usage of material of Q units amounts to Qd.
2. With an increase in order size from **q'** to **q***, the number of orders will be reduced. If the ordering cost is assumed to be ₹ O per order irrespective of the order size, there will be a reduction in the total ordering cost. Thus, the reduction in the ordering cost is

= The difference between the number of orders with sizes of q' and q*

× The cost per order of ₹ O

$$= ₹\left[\frac{Q}{q^*} - \frac{Q}{q^*}\right] \times O$$

The total incremental benefits will be the sum of these two benefits.

Total incremental benefits $= ₹\, Qd + ₹\,\{Q/q' - Q/q^*\} \times O$

With an increase in the order size, there is likely to be an increase in the average value of inventory even after considering the discount. Increase in the average value of inventory will result in higher carrying cost, assumed to be **c**% of the average value of inventory.

Incremental carrying cost $= \dfrac{q^*(p-d)c}{2} - \dfrac{q^* pc}{2}$

The net incremental benefit of changing the order size to **q*** can be obtained by subtracting the incremental carrying cost from the total incremental benefits. This is given by the following expression:

Net Incremental Benefits $= ₹Qd + ₹\{Q/q' - Q/q^*\} \times O - \dfrac{q^*(p-d)c}{2} - \dfrac{q^* pc}{2}$

If the net incremental benefits are positive, then the optimal order quantity becomes **q***. Otherwise, **q'** will continue to remain valid even in a situation of bulk purchase discount.

Illustration 1. The annual usage of a raw material is 32,000 units for the Deccan Paints Ltd. The price of the raw material is ₹40 per unit. The ordering cost is ₹320 per order and the carrying cost 20% of the average value of inventory. The supplier has recently introduced a discount of 5% on the price of material for orders of 2,000 units and above. What was the company's EOQ prior to the introduction of discount? Should the company opt for availing the discount? What would be the optimal order size if the company opts to avail for itself the discount offered?

Solution: From the information given, we know

$$Q = 32,000 \text{ units}$$
$$O = ₹320 \text{ per order}$$
$$p = ₹40 \text{ per unit}$$
$$d = ₹2 \text{ per unit}$$
$$c = 0.20$$

EOQ without discount

$$q' = \sqrt{\frac{2QC}{pc}}$$

$$= \sqrt{\frac{2 \times 32,000 \times 320}{40 \times 0.2}}$$

$$= 1,600 \text{ units}$$

For utilizing discount, the minimum order size $q^* = 2,000$ units. As q' is less than q^*, we have to calculate the incremental benefits and incremental costs.

Total amount of discount available with an order size of 2,000 units.

$$= Q \times d = 32,000 \times 2.$$
$$= ₹64,000$$

Savings due to reduction in ordering costs

$$= ₹\left(\frac{Q}{q^*} - \frac{Q}{q^*}\right) \times O$$

$$= \left(\frac{32000}{1600} - \frac{32000}{2000}\right) \times 320$$

$$= (20 - 16 \times ₹320$$

$$= \text{Rs. } 1,280$$

Incremental carrying cost

$$= \frac{q^*(p-d)c}{2} - \frac{q^* pc}{2}$$

$$= \frac{2000 \times 38 \times 0.2}{2} - \frac{1600 \times 50 \times 0.2}{2}$$

$$= ₹7600 - ₹1600$$

$$= ₹6000$$

Net incremental benefits $(= 1 + 2 - 3)$

$$= ₹64,000 + ₹1,280 - ₹6,000 = ₹59,280$$

As the net incremental benefit is positive, the company should opt for availing the discount offered.

From the illustration, it is clear that although EOQ value of 1,600 units (q') is not relevant in the present situation of bulk purchase discount, the general framework of the EOQ model has provided the necessary basis for subsequent calculations and decision-making.

Reorder Point

In the EOQ model, we have assumed that the lead time for procuring material is zero. Consequently, the material/goods are reordered when the level of inventory drops down to zero. Since the inventory is replenished instantaneously, the level of inventory jumps to the original level from zero level. However, in real-life situations, one never encounters a zero lead time. There is always a time lag between the date of placing an order and the date on which materials are received. As a result, the inventory is to be reordered, before it drops down to zero level so that the new inventory arrives before the firm runs out of goods to sell. If there is no uncertainty with respect to supply of inventory in the lead time, the reorder level can be calculated as follows:

Reorder level = Average daily usage rate × lead time in days.

From the above formula, it can be easily deduced that an order for replenishment of materials is made when the level of inventory is just adequate to meet the needs of production during lead time.

In real life, it is quite possible that the actual time taken in receiving the supply will be more than the average lead time due to some unforeseen circumstances such as truckers strike. In such cases, it would be practical to include a buffer stock also to determine the reorder level. The reorder level can be calculated as the expected normal consumption during the lead time (delivery time stock) plus some buffer or safety stock to accommodate any delays in supply.

In other words, Reorder point = Normal consumption during lead time + Safety stock.

Since the delivery time stock is the expected inventory usage between ordering and receiving inventory, efficient replenishment of inventory would reduce the need for delivery time stock. The determination of level of safety stock involves a basic trade-off between the risk of stock-out and additional carrying costs.

Safety Stock

As said earlier, in real-life situations, one rarely comes across lead times and usage rates that are known with certainty. If usage rate and/or lead time behave stochastically, then the reorder level should naturally be at a level high enough to cater to the production needs during the procurement period and also to provide some measures of safety for at least partially neutralizing the degree of uncertainty.

How do we determine the magnitude of safety stock in such cases? There is no specific answer to this question. It depends, inter alia, upon the degree of uncertainty surrounding the usage rate and lead time. It is possible to a certain extent to quantify the values that usage rate and lead time can take along with the corresponding chances of occurrence, known as probabilities. Based on the above values and estimates of stock-out costs and carrying costs of inventory, it is possible to work out the total cost associated with different levels of safety stock.

The higher the quantity of safety stock, lower will be the stock-out cost and higher will be the incidence of carrying costs; estimating the reorder level will call for a trade-off between stock-out costs and carrying costs. The reorder level will then become one at which the total stock-out costs and the carrying costs will be minimized.

Illustration 2. Consider the following information for a firm:

Average Daily Usage Rate (units)	Probability	Lead Time (no of days)	Probability
200	0.25	12	0.25
500	0.50	16	0.50
800	0.25	20	0.25

The stock-out cost is estimated to be ₹10 per unit while carrying cost for the period under consideration is ₹3 per unit. What should be the reorder level based on financial considerations?

Solution:

The expected usage rate is nothing but the weighted average daily usage rate, where the weights are considered to be the corresponding probability values. Thus, the expected daily usage rate is

$$=200 \times 0.25 + 500 \times 0.5 + 800 \times 0.25$$
$$= 50 + 250 + 200$$
$$= 500 \text{ units}$$

Similarly, the expected lead time

$$= 12 \times 0.25 + 16 \times 0.5 + 20 \times 0.25$$
$$= 3 + 8 + 5 = 16 \text{ days}$$

Normal consumption during lead time can be obtained by multiplying the above two values.

Normal consumption during lead time

$$= 500 \text{ units per day} \times 16 \text{ days} = 8,000 \text{ units}$$

Since normal consumption during lead time has been obtained as 8,000 units, stock-outs can occur only if the consumption during lead time is more than 8,000 units.

Let us enumerate the situations with lead time consumption of more than 8,000 units, along with their respective probabilities of occurrence. This can be achieved by considering the possible levels of usage.

The possible levels of usage are as follows:

Daily Usage Rate		Lead Time in Days		Possible Levels of Usage	
Units	Probability	Units	Probability	Units	Probability
		12	0.25	2,400	0.0625
200	0.25	16	0.50	3,200	0.1250
		20	0.25	4,000	0.0625

(Continued)

(Continued)

Daily Usage Rate		Lead Time in Days		Possible Levels of Usage	
Units	Probability	Units	Probability	Units	Probability
		12	0.25	6,000	0.1250
500	0.5	16	0.50	8,000	0.250
		20	0.25	10,000	0.1250
		12	0.25	9,600	0.0625
800	0.25	16	0.50	12,800	0.1250
		20	0.25	16,000	0.0625

From the above table, it is clear that the situations with the lead time consumption of more than 8,000 units (normal usage) are 10,000 units with a probability of 0.1250, 9,600 units with 0.0625 probability, 12,800 units with 0.1250 probability, and 16,000 units with 0.0625 probability. In addition, the levels of stock-out are 2,000 units, 1,600 units, 4,800 units, and 8,000 units, respectively.

Thus, safety stock level can be maintained at any of the above levels and the stock-out cost and carrying cost associated with these various levels are shown in Table 16.1.

TABLE 16.1
LEVELS OF SAFETY STOCKS AND ASSOCIATED COSTS

Safety Stock (1)	Stock-outs (2)	Probability (3)	Expected Stock-out (4)=(2×3)	Expected Stock-out Cost (5)	Carrying Cost (6)	Total Cost (7)
8,000 units	0	0	0	0	₹24,000	₹24,000
4,800 units	3,200 units	0.0625	200 units	₹2,000	₹14,400	₹16,400
2,000 units	6,000 units	0.0625	375 units	₹7,250	₹6,000	₹13,250
	2,800 units	0.1250	350 units			
		725 units				
1,600 units	6,400 units	0.0625	400 units	₹8,500	₹4,800	₹13,300
	3,200 units	0.1250	400 units			
	400 units	0.1250	50 units			
		850 units				
0	8,000 units	0.0625	500 units	₹14,500	0	₹14,500
	4,800 units	0.1250	600 units			
	2,000 units	0.1250	250 units			
	1,600 units	0.0625	100 units			
		1,450 units				

Source: Author.

If the safety stock of the firm is 8,000 units, there is no chance of the firm being out of stock. The probability of stock-out is, therefore, zero. If the safety stock of the firm is 4,800 units, there is 0.0625 chance that the firm will be short of inventory.

If the safety stock of the firm is 2,000 units, there is stock-out of 6,000 units with a probability of 0.0625 and 2,800 units with a probability of 0.125 based on the possible usage of 16,000 units with probability of 0.0625 and 12,800 with a probability of 0.125 stock-out, and the probability of occurrence of stock-out at other levels is calculated in the same way.

Reorder Point Formula

Even in a relatively simple situation considered in the illustration above, the amount of calculations involved for arriving at the reorder level is large. In real-life situations, the assumption of independence in the probability distributions made in the illustration above may not be valid and the number of time periods may also be large. In such cases, the approach adopted earlier can become much more complex. That is the reason why one can adopt a much simpler formula which gives reasonably reliable results in calculating at what point in the level of inventory a reorder has to be placed for replenishment of stock. The formula along with its application is given below, using the notation developed earlier.

$$\text{Reorder point} = S \times L + F\sqrt{(S \times R \times L)}$$

where S is the usage in units per day, L is the lead time in days, R is the average number of units per order, and F is the stock-out acceptance factor.

The stock-out acceptance factor, "F," depends on the stock-out percentage rate specified and the probability distribution of usage (which is assumed to follow a Poisson distribution). For any specified acceptable stock-out percentage, the value of "F" can be obtained from Figure 16.4.

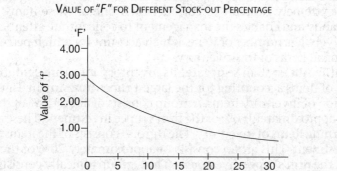

FIGURE 16.4
VALUE OF "F" FOR DIFFERENT STOCK-OUT PERCENTAGE

Source: Author.

Illustration 3. For Apex Company, the average daily usage of a material is 100 units, lead time for procuring material is 20 days, and the average number of units per order is 2,000 units. The stock-out acceptance factor is considered to be 1.3. What is the reorder level for the company?

Solution: From the data contained in the problem, we have

$$S = 100 \text{ units}$$
$$L = 20 \text{ days}$$
$$R = 2,000 \text{ units}$$
$$F = 1.3$$

$$\text{Reorder point} = S \times L + F\sqrt{(S \times R \times L)}$$
$$= 100 \times 20 + 1.3\sqrt{(100 \times 2,000 \times 20)}$$
$$= 2,000 + 1.3 \times 2,000 = 4,600 \text{ units}$$

Reorder for replenishment of stock should be placed when the inventory level reaches 4,600 units.

Test Yourself

1. Inventory carrying cost is directly proportional to the level of inventory. Explain.
2. If the carrying cost of inventory is more than stock-out cost, the company should produce and keep an inventory? Examine.
3. At the point of EOQ, inventory carrying cost and inventory ordering cost are equal.

ABC System

In the case of a manufacturing company of reasonable size, the number of items of inventory runs into hundreds, if not more. From the point of view of monitoring information for control, it becomes extremely difficult to consider each one of these items. The ABC analysis comes in quite handy and enables the management to concentrate attention and keep a close watch on a relatively less number of items which account for a high percentage of the value of annual usage of all items of the inventory.

A firm using the ABC system segregates its inventory into three groups—A, B and C. The A group consists of items accounting for the largest rupee investment. Figure 16.5 depicts the typical distribution of inventory items. A group consists of about 10% of the inventory items that account for approximately 70% of the firm's rupee investment. These are the most costly or the slowest turning items of inventory. The B group consists of the items accounting for the next largest investment. This group consists of approximately 20% of the items accounting for about 20% of the firm's rupee investment. The C group typically consists of a large number of items accounting for a small rupee investment. The C group consists of approximately 70% of all the items of inventory but accounts for only about 10% of the firm's rupee investment. Items such as screws, nails, and washers would be in this group.

Dividing its inventory into A, B, and C items allows the firm to determine the level and types of inventory control procedures needed. Control of the A items should be most intensive due to the high rupee investments involved, while the B and C items would be subject to correspondingly less sophisticated control procedures.

FIGURE 16.5

TYPICAL DISTRIBUTION OF INVENTORY ITEMS—ABC SYSTEM

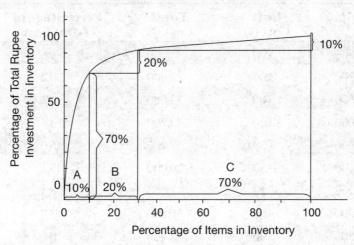

Source: Author.

The general procedure for categorization of items into "A," "B," and "C" groups is briefly outlined below followed by an illustration.

- All the items of inventory are to be ranked in the descending order of their annual usage value.
- The cumulative totals of annual usage values of these items along with their percentages to the total annual usage value are to be noted alongside.
- The cumulative percentage of items to the total number of items is also to be recorded in another column.
- An approximate categorization of items into A, B, and C groups can be made by comparing the cumulative percentage of items with the cumulative percentage of the corresponding usage values.

Illustration 4. From the following details, draw a plan of ABC selective control.

Item	Units	Unit Cost
1.	7,000	5.00
2.	24,000	3.00
3.	1,500	10.00
4.	600	22.00
5.	38,000	1.50
6.	40,000	0.50
7.	60,000	0.20
8.	3,000	3.50
9.	300	8.00
10.	29,000	0.40
11.	11,500	7.10
12.	4,100	6.20

Ranking of Items According to Their Usage Value

Item	Units	Unit Cost (₹)	Total Cost (₹)	Percentage of Total Cost	Ranking
1.	7,000	5.00	35,000	9.8	4
2.	24,000	3.00	72,000	20.2	2
3.	1,500	10.00	15,000	4.2	7
4.	600	22.00	13,200	3.7	8
5.	38,000	1.50	57,000	16.0	3
6.	40,000	0.50	20,000	5.6	6
7.	60,000	0.20	12,000	3.4	9
8.	3,000	3.50	10,500	3.0	11
9.	300	8.00	2,400	0.7	12
10.	29,000	0.40	11,600	3.3	10
11.	11,500	7.10	81,650	23.0	1
12.	4,100	6.20	25,420	7.1	5
			355,770	100.0	

The advantages of this system are as follows:

1. It ensures closer control on costly items in which a large amount of capital has been invested.
2. It helps in developing a scientific method of controlling inventories, clerical costs are reduced, and stock is maintained at optimum level.
3. It helps in achieving the main objective of inventory control at minimum cost. The stock turnover rate can be maintained at comparatively higher level through scientific control of inventories.

The system of ABC analysis suffers from a serious limitation. The system analyzes the items according to their value and not according to their importance in the production process. It may, therefore, sometimes create difficult problems. For example, an item of inventory may not be very costly and hence it may have been put in category C. However, the item may be very important to the production process because of its scarcity. Such an item as a matter of fact requires the utmost attention of the management though it is not advisable to do so as per the system of ABC analysis. Hence, the system of ABC analysis should not be followed blindly.

The required plan of ABC selective control can now be drawn as follows:

Items in Order of Ranking	Item Numbers	Percentage of Total Items	Value (₹)	Cumulative Value (₹)	Cumulative Percentage	Percentage of Total Value	Category
1.	3	25	81,650	81,650	23.0	59.2	A
2.			72,000	153,650	43.2		
3.			57,000	210,650	59.2		

Items in Order of Ranking	Item Numbers	Percentage of Total Items	Value (₹)	Cumulative Value (₹)	Cumulative Percentage	Percentage of Total Value	Category
4.	4	33.3	35,000	245,650	69.0	26.8	B
5.			25,420	271,070	76.2		
6.			20,000	291,070	81.8		
7.			15,000	306,070	86.0		
8.	5	41.7	13,200	319,270	89.7	14	C
9.			12,000	331,270	93.1		
10.			11,600	342,870	96.4		
11.			10,500	353,370	99.3		
12.	–	–	2,400	355,770	100.0	–	
Total	**12**	**100**	**355,770**			**100**	

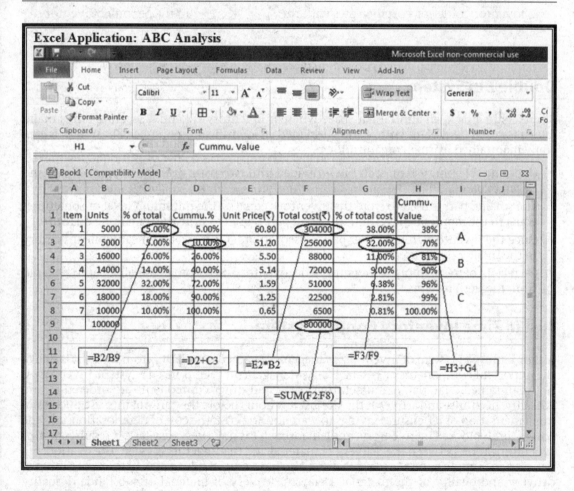

VED Analysis

Just like ABC analysis for classification of inventories, there is an inventory management technique called VED analysis for monitoring and controlling stores and spares inventory by classifying them into three categories, namely, vital, essential, and desirable. The mechanics of VED analysis are similar to those of ABC analysis.

Test Yourself

Fill in the blanks
1. _____ is the point, at which the firm should place an order to replenish the inventory. If annual demand is 12,000 units, order cost is ₹90 per order and inventory carry cost is ₹15 per annum. The EOQ will be _____.
2. In the situation of uncertainty, a firm keeps _____ to meet unexpected demand.
3. The formula of maximum level of inventory is _____.
4. Inventory ordering cost increases with the _____ in the per order inventory level.

Double Bin System

Bin refers to a rack, an almirah, or space wherein inventory is kept. A separate bin is maintained for each item of inventory and is assigned an identification number. Bin system is generally maintained by small organizations.

- Under double bin system, each bin is divided into two parts namely the smaller part and he larger part.
- The smaller part is used to store the inventory equal to the minimum level or sometimes equal to the reordering level and the larger part is used to store the remaining quantity.
- Once the inventory in the larger part is used, an order is made and meanwhile inventory in the smaller part is used.
- On receipt of fresh supply of inventory, the inventory used from the smaller part is replaced from the fresh receipts.

Just in Time Inventory Control System

Just in Time (JIT) system of inventory management gained popularity from Japan. It is one of the important components of Total Quality Management (TQM). In a JIT system, inventory is not maintained. Material, manufacturing parts, and other components are ordered as and when the need arise and arrives at the site just few hours before they are put into use. Successful implementation of JIT ensures savings in warehousing cost, the cost of deterioration, and the cost of funds blocked in inventory. Implementing JIT is not a very easy task. It requires perfect synchronization between the delivery of material and manufacturing cycle. The relationship between the supplier and the manufacturer also has a crucial role to play in terms of timing of delivery and quality of the material. Delay in delivery of material or substandard quality supply may result in stoppage of production. This system creates a lot of pressure on the manufacturer as well as on the supply and demand for a strong supply chain management.

Computer-based Inventory Control Systems

With the increasing business size and the nature of work, more and more companies have now started using computerized systems to control their inventory. A computerized system of inventory is an automatic system of taking an account for the flow of inventory. The computer system is programmed to identify the various levels of inventory such as the maximum level, minimum level, and the reorder level. As soon as the inventory reaches any of the above threshold limits, the computer program notifies the same and the storekeeper/operator may take necessary action to replenish the same. In case of large departmental stores/retail stores, computerized systems for inventory are must. In some advanced cases, computer systems of buyer and suppliers are linked. As soon as the supplier's computer receives order from the buyer's computer, the supply process is activated.

Outsourcing Inventory

Outsourcing inventory means procuring parts and components from outside rather than manufacturing them internally. Outsourcing decision involves cost-benefit analysis to be undertaken.

Stock Turnover Ratio

- It is a control technique.
- Gives the relationship between cost of material consumed and average stock held.
- **Formula:**
  Cost of material consumed during the year
  Cost of average stock held during the year
  where cost of material consumed = Opening stock + Purchases − Closing stock
- Average Stock $= \frac{1}{2}$(opening stock + closing stock)
- Inventory holding period = 365/Inventory turnover
- It indicates the speed with which the inventory is consumed.
- A too high and a too low ratio is a matter of concern.
- A satisfactory level of inventory should be maintained (intra-firm comparison and inter-firm comparison).

Nature of Stock	Meaning	Stock Turnover Ratio
Fast-moving stock	Stock in great demand	Very high
Slow-moving stock	Stock in low demand	Low
Dormant stock	Stock having no demand at present	Too low
Obsolete stock	Stock no longer in demand	Too low

SUMMARY

1. Inventory forms a major component in the total current assets of the company, especially in the manufacturing companies.
2. There are three motives of holding inventory, namely, transaction, speculation, and precautionary motives.
3. The main objective of inventory management is to achieve maximum efficiency in production and sales with the minimum investment in inventory.
4. Three types of costs are involved in management of inventory:

   - Ordering cost
   - Carrying cost
   - Stock-out cost

5. The firm should try to minimize its total cost of holding inventory by ordering at EOQ.
6. EOQ occurs at the point where the total cost is minimum (ordering cost + carrying cost).
7. Setting inventory levels enable the storekeeper to know the maximum and minimum levels of stock required to be maintained at all times.
8. The stock level at which the firm places an order to replenish the inventory is known as the reorder level or reorder point. Under perfect certainty, the reorder point is equal to lead time × usage rate.
9. Under uncertain conditions, a firm has to maintain a safety stock which serves as a cushion to meet contingencies. The reorder point under such conditions is calculated as safety stock + lead time × usage rate.
10. There are two systems of keeping the record of inventory: period system and the perpetual system.
11. A firm which carries a number of items of inventory that differs in value may follow a selective approach such as ABC analysis in managing its inventory.
12. There are many other techniques such as JIT, VED, and computerized system of managing inventories.

KEY TERMS

- ABC analysis
- Reorder point
- Lead time
- Economic production
- Setup cost
- Ordering costs
- Economic order quantity
- Carrying cost
- Safety stock
- Maximum level
- Quantity
- Economic order quantity

Learning Outcomes

Students would know the basic inventory model as well as other inventory management systems.

SOLVED PROBLEMS

1. Unichem Ltd uses copper for its manufacturing operations. The probability distributions for the daily usage rate and the lead time for the procurement of copper are given as follows:

Daily Usage Rate (tonnes)	Probability	Lead Time (days)	Probability
30	0.25	10	0.20
40	0.50	15	0.60
50	0.25	20	0.20

The stock-out cost is estimated to be ₹12,000 per tonne and the carrying cost is ₹2,000 per tonne.

(a) Calculate the probability of stock-out.
(b) Calculate the optimal level of safety stock.

Solution:

(a) Expected daily usage rate = 30 (0.25) + 40 (0.50) + 50 (0.25)

$$= 40 \text{ tonnes}$$

Expected lead time = 10 (0.20) + 15 (0.60) + 20 (0.20)

$$= 15 \text{ days}$$

Therefore, normal usage during lead time

$$= \text{Expected daily usage rate} \times \text{expected lead time}$$
$$= 40 \times 15 = 600 \text{ tonnes}$$

The possible levels of usage are as follows:

Daily Usage Rate		Lead Time (days)		Possible Usage Levels	
Tonnes	Probability	Days	Probability	Tonnes	Probability
		10	0.20	300	0.05
30	0.25	15	0.60	450	0.15
		20	0.20	600	0.05
		10	0.20	400	0.10
40	0.50	15	0.60	600	0.30
		20	0.20	800	0.10
		10	0.20	500	0.05
50	0.25	15	0.60	750	0.15
		20	0.20	1,000	0.05

Stock-out occurs in those situations when the usage level exceeds the normal usage, that is, 600 tonnes. The lead-time usages above 600 tonnes are 750 tonnes, 800 tonnes, and 1,000 tonnes.

Probability of stock-out = Probability of usage level of 750 tonnes + Probability of usage

level of 800 tonnes + Probability of usage level of 1,000 tonnes

= 0.15 + 0.10 + 0.05

= 0.30, i.e., 30%

(b) The levels of safety stock are 150 tonnes, 200 tonnes, and 400 tonnes.
Levels of safety stock and the related costs:

Safety Stock	Stock-out (tonnes)	Probability	Stock-out Cost (₹)	Expected Stock-out Cost (₹)	Carrying Cost (₹)	Total Cost (₹)
(1)	(2)	(3)	(4)=(2)×12,000	(5)=(3)×(4)	(6)=(1)×2,000	(7)=(5)+(6)
400	0	0	0	0	800,000	800,000
200	200	0.05	2,400,000	120,000	400,000	520,000
150	50	0.10	600,000	60,000		
	250	0.05	3,000,000	150,000	300,000	510,000
				210,000		
0	150	0.15	1,800,000	270,000		
	200	0.10	2,400,000	240,000		
	400	0.05	4,800,000	240,000	0	750,000
				750,000		

From the above table, we can find that the total cost is minimum for safety stock level of 150 tonnes, that is, ₹510,000.

Hence, the optimal level of safety stock is 150 tonnes.

2. Grace Tele-systems, a trading concern, had the following receipts of an item, coded PS7300, over the last quarter:

Month	January	February	March
Receipts (₹)	63,000	72,000	81,000

The opening balance of the item in January was ₹54,000 and the closing balance of the item in March was ₹90,000. The purchase price of the item is ₹18 per unit and the carrying cost is 25% of the average inventory value per annum. The cost for placing an order is fixed and it is ₹900 per order. The purchase price per unit of the item has not changed in the last quarter and it is not expected to change in the next 6 months which is the planning period. Their supplier, Vijay Systems Ltd, has offered a discount of 2.5% on order sizes of 6,000 units and above. It is assumed that the demand for the item is evenly distributed over the entire year.

(a) Determine the EOQ of the item.
(b) The optimal order size for the item.

Solution:

(a) $EOQ = \sqrt{\dfrac{2FU}{P.C}}$

Usage (U) during the planning period:

Usage in the last quarter = Opening balance + total receipts – closing balance

$$= 54,000 + (63,000 + 72,000 + 81,000) - 90,000$$
$$= ₹180,000$$

Usage in the last quarter (in units) $= \dfrac{1,80,000}{18} = 10,000$ units

Therefore, usage (U) in the planning period of next 6 months = $10,000 \times 2 = 20,000$ units

Fixed cost per order, $F = ₹900$ (given)

Unit price $P = ₹18$ (given)

Carrying cost for the entire year = 25%

Carrying cost for the planning period of six months, $C = \dfrac{25}{2} = 12.5\%$

$\therefore$ Economic Order Quantity (EOQ) $= \sqrt{\dfrac{2 \times 900 \times 20,000}{18(0.125)}}$

$$= 4,000 \text{ units}$$

(b) Let the EOQ be denoted as q'* and let the minimum required order size for getting the discount be denoted q*.

Net Incremental Benefits $= ₹Qd + ₹\{Q/q' - Q/q*\} \times O - \dfrac{q*(p-d)c}{2} - \dfrac{q*pc}{2}$

$q' = 4,000$ units (from above)

$q* = 6,000$ units (given)

Discount per unit

d = Price per unit × Percentage of discount

$$= \dfrac{18(2.5)}{100} = ₹0.45$$

Therefore, discount earned over the entire planning period = Qd = $20,000 \times 0.45$ = ₹9,000

Savings in ordering cost $= \{Q/q' - Q/q*\} \times O$

$$= \left[\dfrac{20,000}{4,000} - \dfrac{20,000}{6,000}\right] 900$$

$$= ₹1,500$$

$$\text{Increase in carrying cost} = \frac{q*(p-d)c}{2} - \frac{q*pc}{2}$$

$$= \frac{(6,000)(18-0.45)(0.125)}{2} - \frac{(4,000)(18)(0.125)}{2}$$

$$= ₹2,081.25$$

$$\therefore \text{Net incremental benefit} = 9,000 + 1,500 - 2,081.25$$

$$= ₹8,418.75 \text{ (gain)}$$

Thus, we find that there is a gain of ₹8,418.75. Hence, the optimal order size should be 6,000 units.

3. Consider the following data regarding a product:
   Total cost of ordering and carrying inventory ₹785
   Quantity per order 5,000 units
   Carrying cost of 2% of the purchase price
   Fixed cost per order ₹95
   Purchase price ₹10.
   What is the annual usage of the material?

Solution:

Total costs associated with inventory = Ordering cost + Carrying cost

$$\frac{QC}{q} = \frac{qpc}{2}$$

where Q is the annual usage, q is the quantity ordered, O is the fixed cost per unit, p is the purchase price per unit, and c is the carrying cost expressed as a percentage of the purchase price.

Hence

$$785 = \frac{Q \times 95}{5,000} + \frac{5,000 \times 10 \times 0.02}{2}$$

Hence, $Q = 15,000$ units.

4. F Ltd produces a product which has a demand of 4,000 units per month. The product requires a component X which is purchased at ₹20. For every finished product, one unit of component is required. The ordering cost is ₹120 per order and the holding cost is 10% per annum.

You are required to calculate

   i. EOQ
   ii. If the minimum lot size to be supplied is 4,000 units, what is the extra cost the company has to incur?

Solution:
The optimum production run is

(i) Determination of EOQ:

$$EOQ = \sqrt{\frac{2QC}{pc}} \text{ units}$$

$$EOQ = \sqrt{\frac{2 \times 48,000 \times 120}{2}} = 2,400 \text{ units}$$

(ii) Determination of extra cost when lot size is 4,000 units:

S. No.	Particulars	Cost When Lot Size Is	
		4,000	**2,400**
1.	Annual usage	48,000	48,000
2.	Size of the order	4,000	2,400
3.	Number of orders	12	20
4.	Cost per order	₹120	₹120
5.	Total ordering cost	1,440	2,400
6.	Carrying cost per unit per annum	2	2
7.	Average inventory size	2,000	1,200
8.	Total carrying cost	4,000	2,400
9.	Total cost	5,400	4,800

The extra cost to be incurred is ₹640 (5,440 – 4,800), when the order size is 4,000 units.

PROBLEMS

1. Shubhangi Enterprises has annual sales of 209,000 units at an average selling price of ₹19.95 per unit. The ordering costs are ₹80 per order and the carrying costs per year are ₹70.46 per unit. What is the optimal order quantity?

2. Sakthi Stabilizers maintains an average inventory of 129,000 items. The ordering costs are ₹160 each. The carrying costs per year are ₹25,400 per item. Sakthi Stabilizers sells about 49,000 items per year. What are the total ordering and carrying costs per year for Sakthi Stabilizers?

3. The production department of a company has provided the following information:

   Carrying costs per unit of inventory are ₹15.
   Fixed costs per order are ₹25.
   Number of units required per year is 36,000.

   ### Calculate

   i. The EOQ.
   ii. Total number of orders in a year.

4. Assume that the following quantity discount schedule for a particular product is available to a retail store:

Order Size (units)	Discount (%)
0–99	0
100–199	5
200–299	10
>300	15

The cost per unit of the product is ₹30. The annual demand is 350 units. Ordering cost is ₹15 per order and annual inventory carrying cost is ₹5 per unit. Determine the optimal order size, the corresponding total cost of inventory, and cost of purchase if storage is not possible.

5. A firm is purchasing an item costing ₹150 each in lots of 500 units. This supply is sufficient for 3 months. The ordering cost is ₹175 per order and the carrying cost is estimated at 20%.

   i. Determine the total annual cost of the existing inventory policy.

  ii. Determine the savings in cost if the order is placed in EOQs.

6. Consider the following information for a particular item of inventory of a firm:

Daily Usage (tonnes)	Probability	Lead Time (in days)	Probability
4	0.25	20	0.25
6	0.50	30	0.50
8	0.25	50	0.25

    If the carrying cost per year is ₹3,500 per tonne and the stock-out cost is ₹10,000 per tonne, calculate

   i. Optimum level of safety stock, and

  ii. Probability of stock-out.

7. Arshad & Co. maintains several items in its inventory. The average number of six of these as well as their unit costs is as follows:

Item	Average Inventory (units)	Average Costs Per Unit (₹)
1.	2,000	25
2.	5,000	9.50
3.	200	10.00
4.	3,200	3.50
5.	450	2.50
6.	3,000	2.60

The firm wishes to adopt an ABC inventory system. How would these items be classified into A, B, and C?

8. Krishna Industries manufactures medicines. On an annual basis, the industry requires 1,000 plastic bottles for packaging at a cost of ₹4 per unit. The company's differential cost of carrying items in the finished goods inventory is 20% of the inventory value per year and the ordering cost is ₹200 per order.
    What is the EOQ?

ACCESS YOURSELF

Concept Review and Critical Thinking Questions

1. Describe the objectives of inventory management and discuss its relevance in different types of organizations.
2. Enumerate and discuss different types of cost associated with inventory management.
3. "There are two extreme dangerous situations that management should avoid in controlling inventories." Explain.
4. Explain and illustrate the EOQ model with the help of a graph. Also examine the relationship between risk and cost with respect to inventories.

STUDENT ACTIVITY

Select any two manufacturing organizations from any sector and compare their inventory management process.

SUGGESTED READINGS

Brealey, R.A., & Myers, S.C. (2002). *Principles of corporate finance* (7th ed.). New York: McGraw-Hill.

Horne, J.C.V. (2002). *Financial management & policy* (12th ed.). Singapore: Pearson Education.

Ross, S.A., Westerfield, R.W., & Jordan, B.D. (2002). *Fundamentals of corporate finance* (6th ed.). New Delhi: Tata McGraw-Hill.

CHAPTER 17

Receivables Management

- To understand the concept and objectives of receivables management.
- To understand the application of incremental cost-benefit analysis in receivables management.
- To study the various components of credit policy in an organization.
- To study the techniques of credit evaluation employed in the organizations.

PRELUDE

The need of receivable management arises due to credit sales. If credit sale is documented, then there is the emergence of receivable management which deals with time and size of receivables along with the risk and returns attached to these components. Read on—"Dubai World CRISIS: L&T's $25 m Receivables at Stake" (*Economic Times*, November 28, 2009).

MUMBAI: Larsen & Toubro, India's largest engineering and construction company, has around $2,025 million (nearly ₹92,115 crore at current exchange rates) of receivables outstanding from clients in Dubai, mostly in civil construction.

The entire Gulf region—that includes Oman, Abu Dhabi, Kuwait, and other states—accounts for orders amounting to ₹5,000 crore out of a total order book of ₹90,000 crore. These contracts are in the electrical and water works segment while the real estate business has more or less come to a standstill since early 2008, said executive vice president Shankar Raman.

"The $20 million outstanding includes some receivables from Nakheel (Dubai's troubled real estate major), who have been very regular in making their payments," Mr Raman added. L&T got a ₹340 crore contract from Nakheel in 2005 for building a residential property called Mogul Gardens 2 on the Shaikh Zayed Road in Dubai. Some of the other projects include two 39-storied commercial and office buildings and two towers of a similar height.

Although Dubai is widely considered a financial services and trading hub, Indian engineering companies like L&T and some steel manufacturers have presence in that region's electricity, real estate, and oil pipeline sectors. "In transmission and distribution, the payments are based on progress of each phase of the contract and is through letters of credit that are opened for each stage," said Mr Raman, while explaining how the current financial problem in Dubai could have a limited impact.

Doubts about Dubai's financial health surfaced on Thursday after Dubai World, a large government-owned investment company, asked for a six-month breather for repaying its debts. Dubai World, which has a total debt of $59 billion, was due to repay $3.5 billion of its debt next month.

News about L&T's exposure in Dubai pulled down its shares on BSE, falling 4% in intraday trade to ₹1,564.95, before recovering to close at ₹1,586.50.

But the events at Dubai were not unexpected. "There have been clear indications of such happenings last year, and hence, many Indian firms had already made exit or had taken contingency measures," said KPMG executive director Arvind Mahajan. According to Deepak Jasani, head of retail research at HDFC Securities, "Under current circumstances, earnings and valuations of the companies exposed to Dubai will be impacted as markets tend to overreact. However, the intensity of the impact will depend on the order book exposure of the companies."

Once the goods and services are ready for consumption they have to be sold. However, it may not be possible for the firm to sell all the goods/services on cash basis. They have to provide some credit compulsorily due to many factors, such as competition, industry norms, need of consumers, higher sales, protect the market share, etc., thus, selling goods on credit is now almost compulsory despite unwillingness of the management to do so. Selling goods/services on credit results into the creation of account receivables or debtors or book debts.

Though selling goods and services through liberal credit policy may result in increasing sales and increasing earnings in the current account period, it may lead to a financial trouble. If the debtors do not pay in time or do not pay at all, the firm incurs losses. On the other hand, if the credit policy of the firm is stringent, it may lead to slow growth in sales as customers who are willing to and capable of paying are denied access to credit. So again a financial manager has to address the key issues, such as, what should be the credit terms of the firm? How many days of credit period should be allowed? Should the firm offer any cash discount for prompt payments? What should be the collection policy of the firm? What shall be the cost of investment?

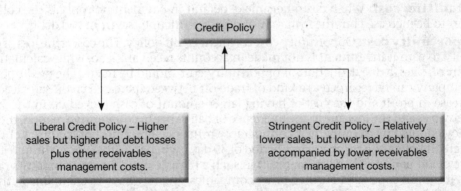

Objectives of Receivables Management

The main objective of receivables management is to strike a balance between the returns that the company gets from financing of receivables (in the form of increased sales and profits) and the cost that the company has to incur to fund these receivables. The other objectives are

- Increasing total sales.
- Increasing profits as a result of increase in sales.

- Accounts receivable may lead to increase in activities which may lead to sustained buying efficiency as the sales grows, there will be more demand of production and the entire cycle is on higher level.
- In order to meet increasing competition, the company may have to grant better credit facilities than those offered by its competitors.

Cost Consideration with Investment in Receivables

While formulating the credit policy of the firm, the financial manager has to analyze the incremental returns from extending credit against the incremental costs of investment in receivables. The various costs associated with receivables are:

1. **Additional Fund Requirement for the company:** When a firm maintains receivables, some of the firm's resources remain blocked in them because there is a time lag between the credit sale and receipt of cash from customers. To the extent that the firm's resources are blocked in its receivables, it has to arrange additional finance to meet its own obligations toward its creditors and employees, such as, payments for purchases, salaries, and other production and administrative expenses. Whether this additional funding is financed through its own resources or from outside, it involves a cost to the firm in terms of interest (if financed from outside) or opportunity costs (if internal resources which could have been put to some other use are taken).

2. **Administrative costs:** When a company maintains receivables, it has to incur additional administrative expenses in the form of salaries to clerks who maintain records of debtors, expenses on investigating the creditworthiness of debtors, etc.

3. **Collection costs:** These are costs that the firm has to incur for collection of the amount at the appropriate time from the customers.

4. **Defaulting cost:** When customers make default in payment not only is the collection effort to be increased but the firm may also have to incur losses from bad debts.

5. **Opportunity cost:** Opportunity cost is vital in credit policy. The cost is the loss of opportunity to earn if investment is not made in accounts receivables. So, while calculating the profit on sales, a due deduction of opportunity cost should be made. The credit policy of a company can be regarded as a kind of trade-off between increased credit sales leading to increase in profit and the cost of having larger amount of cash locked up in the form of receivables and the loss due to the incidence of bad debts. In competitive market, the credit policy adopted by a company is considerably influenced by a host of factors. A change in the credit policy of a company to a period of 30 days, when the other companies are following a credit period of 15 days can result in such a high demand for the company's product that it cannot cope with. Further, other companies also may have to fall in line in the long run. It is assumed generally that such factors have already been taken into consideration before making changes in the credit policy of a company.

The term credit policy thus encompasses the variables, such as, credit standards to be adopted, the period over which credit is extended to customers, any incentive in the form of cash discount offered, and the collection efforts made by the company. To be precise, the various components of credit policy are

1. credit standards,
2. credit period,
3. cash discount, and
4. collection policy.

All these variables underlying a company's credit policy influence sales, the amount locked up in the form of receivables, and some of the receivables turning sour and eventually become bad debts. While the various components of credit policy are interrelated, for the purpose of clarity in understanding, we shall follow what is technically known as **comparative static analysis** by considering each variable independently, holding some or all other constant, to study the impact of a change in that variable on the company's profit. It is also assumed that the company is making profits and has adequate unutilized capacity to meet the increased sales caused by a change in some variables without incurring additional fixed costs, such as wage and salaries, rent, etc.

Credit Standards

As indicated earlier, application of very stiff standards for the classification of customers to whom credit can be extended and to whom it cannot be extended is likely to result in a low level of sales but also less amount of funds locked up in receivables, virtually no bad debt losses, and less amount to be spent for collection. On the other hand, indiscriminate extension of credit without bothering much about the credit standards expected of the customers is likely to increase sales. But at the same time, the company is more likely to be saddled with a large quantum of funds blocked up in accounts receivable, higher incidence of bad debt losses, and increased administrative and collection expenses.

Credit Standards

1. Stiff standards (low sales, less amount locked up in receivables, less bad debts, and less collection expenditure).
2. Liberal standards (high credit sales, high investment in receivables, more amount locked up in receivables, more chances of bad debts, more collection expenses).

What standards should a business firm adopt?

Credit Rating

Credit rating can be done by the firm by assigning a credibility score to each customer on the basis of information provided by the customer about himself and using the past sales and credit collection data. The numerical credit scoring models, which are generally used are

1. ad hoc approach,
2. simple discriminate analysis, and
3. multiple discriminate analysis.
   (i) **Ad hoc Approach:** In this approach, the firm identifies a set of factors for determining the credit-worthiness of the customer and assign suitable weights to such factors depending on their importance. This information is used to calculate a numerical score for credit rating. The factors taken into consideration for determining the credit worthiness of the customers include age, income earning capacity, ownership of assets, such as, vehicles, house, property, marital status, etc.
   (ii) **Simple Discriminant Analysis:** In this method, the firm uses financial ratio, which discriminates between good and bad customers. A cutoff value of this ratio is selected to divide the customers into two categories with minimum number of misclassifications.

The cutoff point is selected by visual inspection. The firm can consider granting credit to those customers for whom the value of the financial ratio is greater than the cutoff rate.

(iii) **Multiple Discriminant Analysis:** In this method, the firm uses multiple factors to discriminate between good and bad customers. The process is similar to simple discriminate analysis except that more than one factor is used as the basis to differentiate between good and bad customers.

Illustration 1. ZMZ Ltd would like to segregate its client profile into the superior and inferior class on the basis of the current ratio and net operating income as a percentage of sales. Given below is the information relating to 12 accounts consisting of an equal number of good and bad customers.

Good Customers			Bad Customers		
Client Number	Current Ratio	NOI/Sales (%)	Client Number	Current Ratio	NOI/Sales (%)
1	2.00	20	7	0.86	22
2	1.65	18	8	0.66	8
3	1.50	15	9	0.49	4
4	1.72	22	10	0.52	11
5	1.90	14	11	0.72	−5
6	1.68	18	12	0.58	12

From the above information, you are required to estimate the discriminate function that best discriminates between superior and inferior clients.

Solution:

Let the discriminant function be $Z_i = aX_i + bY_i$, where Z_i is the discriminant score for the i-th account, X_i is the current ratio for the i-th account, Y_i is the NOI/sales ratio for the i-th account.

Account Number	X_i	Y_i	$(X_i - X_m)$	$(Y_i - Y_m)$	$(X_i - X_m)^2$	$(Y_i - Y_m)^2$	$(X_i - X_m)(Y_i - Y_m)$
Gr. I 1	2.00	20	0.81	6.75	0.6561	45.5625	5.4675
2	1.65	18	0.46	4.75	0.2116	22.5625	2.1850
3	1.50	15	0.31	1.75	0.0961	3.0625	0.5425
4	1.72	22	0.53	8.75	0.2809	76.5625	4.6375
5	1.90	14	0.71	0.75	0.5041	0.5625	0.5325
6	1.68	18	0.49	4.75	0.2401	22.5625	2.3275
Gr. II 7	0.86	22	−0.33	8.75	0.1089	76.5625	−2.8875
8	0.66	8	−0.53	−5.25	0.2809	27.5625	2.7825
9	0.49	4	−0.70	−9.25	0.4900	85.5625	6.4750
10	0.52	11	−0.67	−2.25	0.4489	5.0625	1.5075
11	0.72	−5	−0.47	−18.25	0.2209	333.0625	8.5775
12	0.58	12	−0.61	−1.25	0.3721	1.5625	0.7625
	14.28	159			3.9106	700.25	32.91

$X_m = 14.28/12 = 1.19$

$X_{m1} = $ Sum of X_i for Gr. I/6 $= 10.45/6 = 1.74$

$X_{m2} = $ Sum of X_i for Gr. II/6 $= 3.83/6 = 0.64$

$Y_m = 159/12 = 13.25$

$Y_{m1} = $ Sum of Y_i for Gr. I/6 $= 107/6 = 17.83$

$Y_{m2} = $ Sum of Y_i for Gr. II/6 $= 52/6 = 8.67$

$\sigma_x 2 = (1/n-1)\ \Sigma(X-X_m)2 = (1/11) \times 3.9106 = 0.355$

$\sigma_y 2 = (1/n-1)\ \Sigma(Y-Y_m)2 = (1/11) \times 700.25 = 63.659$

$\sigma_{xy} = (1/n-1)\ \Sigma(X-X_m)\ (Y-Y_m) = (1/11) \times 32.91 = 2.992$

$dx = X_{m1} - X_{m2} = 1.74 - 0.64 = 1.10$

$dy = Y_{m1} - Y_{m2} = 17.83 - 8.67 = 9.16$

$a = (\sigma_y 2\ dx - \sigma_{xy}\ dy)/(\sigma_x 2\sigma_y 2 - \sigma_{xy} 2)$

$= (63.659 \times 1.10 - 2.992 \times 9.16)/(0.355 \times 63.659 - 2.992 \times 2.992)$

$= (70.0249 - 27.4067)/(22.5989 - 8.9521) = 42.6182/13.6468 = 3.123$

$b = (\sigma_x 2\ dy - \sigma_{xy}\ dx)/(\sigma_x 2\sigma_y 2 - \sigma_{xy} 2)$

$= (0.355 \times 9.16 - 2.992 \times 1.10)/(0.355 \times 63.659 - 2.992 \times 2.992)$

$= (3.2518 - 3.2912)/(22.5989 - 8.9521) = -0.0394/13.6468 = -0.003$

Hence, the required discriminant function is $Z_i = 3.123X_i - 0.003Y_i$.

Credit standard also refers to amount of credit sales to the category of customers. "A" class customers mean unlimited credit and "D" class customers mean no credit. This classification is done on the basis of experience and requirements. Any change in the class and quantum will affect sales which will reflect the variation in the profit.

Test Yourself

1. What is meant by investment in receivables? Explain.
2. What factors should be considered while determining the optimal credit standards?

Credit Period

The credit period refers to the length of time allowed to the customers to pay for their purchases. It generally varies from 15 days to 60 days. If a firm allows, say, 45 days of credit with no discount to induce early payment, its credit terms are stated as net 45. Lengthening of the credit period pushes sales up by inducing existing customers to purchase more and attracting additional customers. At the same time it increases the incidence of bad debts loss. A shortening of credit period will tend to lower sales, as customers decrease investment in receivables, and reduce the incidence of bad debt loss.

1. It refers to length of time given to the customers to pay their purchases.
2. It generally varies from 15 days to 60 days.
3. Longer credit period (more sales, more investment in receivables, more chances of bad debts).
4. Shorter credit periods, low sales. Reduced investment in receivables, less chances of bad debts.

What will be the appropriate credit period?

Effect of Increase in Credit Period

Item	Direction of Change (Increase=I; Decrease=D)	Effect on Profits (Positive or Negative)
Sales volume	I	+
Average collection period	I	-
Bad debts expenses	I	-

Illustration 2. M/s Deccan Security Systems Ltd (DSSL) purchases components from M/s Softel Ltd (SEL) on the terms 1/10, net 45. DSSL has requested for an increase in the cash discount to 2%, the period of cash discount remaining unchanged. SEL has accordingly increased the cash discount and changed the credit period. On careful verification, DSSL realizes that because of change in the credit period, the cost of not paying within the discount period is now three times the cost before the change in terms. What is the new credit period?

Solution:

$$\text{Cost of trade credit} = \frac{\text{Discount}}{1 - \text{Discount}} \times \frac{360}{\text{Credit period} - \text{Discount period}}$$

$$= \frac{0.01}{0.99} \times \frac{360}{45 - 10} = 10.39\%$$

$$\text{New cost of trade credit} = 3 \times 10.39 = 31.17\%$$

$$= \frac{0.02}{0.98} \times \frac{360}{x - 10} = 31.17\%$$

$$\text{Solving } x = \frac{512.733}{15.2733} = 34 \text{ days}$$

3. Cash Discount

If the firm having a credit period of 45 days also allows a cash discount of say 2% if the payment is made in 10 days, the credit terms are stated as 2/10, net 45. That means, pay in 10 days and avail a cash discount of 2% else pay full in 45 days. Cash discount is offered to customers to induce prompt payment. This involves a cost to the company. At the same time, if a discount is also offered more customers may be attracted to make their purchases from the company. Thus, the rate of cash discount and the period for which it will be allowed has to be decided after considering its effect on the net incremental benefits.

Cash Discount

1. If offered results in prompt payment from customers.
2. If not offered chances that the payment will be received only on the last day.
3. Is it beneficial to have a longer discount period?
4. How much discount should a business firm offer to its customers?

Illustration 3. Currently, M/s Supreme Lubricants Ltd sells 30,000 units at an average price of ₹28,000 per unit. The variable cost is 90% of the selling price. The credit terms of the company are 1/20, net 30.10% of the customers avail the discount and the average collection period is 26 days. The bad debts to sales ratio is 0.015.

To increase the sales level, the finance manager has suggested to change the credit terms to 2/10, net 30. With the new policy, sales are expected to increase by 4,000 units and 40% of the old customers and 60% of the new customers are expected to avail the discount. The average collection period and bad debt to sales ratio are expected to remain the same. What is the net benefit of the new policy?

Solution:
Net benefit $=\Delta P-\Delta D$ is

$$\text{Increase in profit}=4,000\times0.1\times28,000=₹112\text{ lakhs}$$

$$\text{Cost of discount (old credit terms)}$$

$$1.1\times28,000\times30,000\times0.01=₹8.4\text{ lakhs}$$

$$\text{Cost of discount (new credit terms)}$$

$$0.4\times28,000\times30,000\times0.02+0.6\times28,000\times4,000\times0.02$$

$$=67.2+13.44=₹80.64\text{ lakhs}$$

$$\text{Net benefit}=₹112-80.64+8.4=₹39.76\text{ lakhs}$$

Collection Policy

Collection policy is an important component of credit policy because all the customers may not pay on time. Some customers may delay the payment whereas others may not pay at all resulting into bad debt loses. A collection policy is needed for prompt and efficient collection. Prompt collection facilitates fast turnover of working capital, keeps collection costs and bad debts within limits, and maintains collection efficiency.

Collection policy needs to establish in unambiguous terms. It should lay down the collection procedures clearly. It should also define the procedure for dealing with slow paying or non-paying customers. Some of these customers may be having some genuine financial problem, and hence in spite of their best intentions to pay, they may not be able to pay. Such cases should be dealt with very carefully and on merit basis. If they are also dealt with in a routine manner, it may antagonize such customers and they may in future switch over to other competitive brands.

The responsibility for collection and follow-up should be explicitly fixed. It may be entrusted to sales department or the accounts department or to a separate credit department. If the responsibility of collection is with the accounts department, it should consult the sales department before initiating any action against the customer. Similarly, the sales department should consult the accounts/credit department to obtain past information about a customer before granting credit. Such close coordination between the sales and accounts/credit department would ensure that slow paying and even non-paying customers make the payment or at least part payment and fresh credit is not granted to such customers.

Test Yourself

1. What do you understand by credit period?
2. Cash discount stimulates prompt payment. Comment.
3. What role does the collection policy play in determining the optimal credit policy? Explain.

Collection Policy

1. Objective of collection policy is to have fast recovery of funds locked up in receivables and to minimize the bad debt losses.

Effect of Increase in Cash Discount

Item	Direction of Change (Increase=I; Decrease=D)	Effect on Profits (Positive or Negative)
Sales volume	D	–
Average collection period	D	+
Bad debts expenses	D	+
Collection expenditure	I	–

Illustration 4. Shekhawati Tubes & Pumps is contemplating of relaxing its collection effort with a view to increase its sales. At present annual sales of the company are ₹200 lakhs, average collection period is 45 days, bad debt losses are 2% of sales, contribution to sales ratio is 20%, and cost of funds to the company is 15%. It is expected that once the collection effort is relaxed, the sales would increase by ₹50 lakhs, average collection period would increase to 60 days, and bad debt losses would increase to 4%. What is the net incremental benefit to the company?

Solution:
Increase in profit due to increase in sales

$$= 50 \times 0.2$$
$$= ₹10 \text{ lakhs}$$

Existing amount of receivables?

$$= \frac{200}{360} \times 45 = ₹25 \text{ lakhs}$$

Amount of receivables on existing sales after collection relaxation?

$$= \frac{200}{360} \times 60 = ₹33.33 \text{ lakhs}$$

So, increase in receivables on existing sales

$$= 33.33 - 25.00$$
$$= ₹8.33 \text{ lakhs}$$

Amount of receivables on additional sales?

$$= \frac{50}{360} = ₹8.33 \text{ lakhs}$$

Investment in the receivables on additional sales

$$= 8.33 \times 0.80 = 6.67$$

Incremental investment in receivables

$$= 8.33 + 6.67 = ₹15 \text{ lakhs}$$

Cost of financing additional investment in receivables at 15%

$$= 15 \times 0.15 = ₹2.25 \text{ lakhs}$$

Existing bad debts losses

$$= 200 \times 0.02 = ₹4 \text{ lakhs}$$

Bad losses after collection relaxation

$$= 250 \times 0.04 = ₹10 \text{ lakhs}$$

So, increase in bad debts losses

$$= 10 - 4 = ₹6.0 \text{ lakhs}$$

So, incremental costs

$$= 2.25 + 6.00 = ₹8.25$$

So, the net incremental benefit

$$= 10 - 8.25$$
$$= 1.75$$

The net incremental benefit is ₹1.75 lakhs.

Credit Evaluation of Individual Accounts

It is important that the firm lays down the guidelines and procedures for granting credit and collection of dues. However, all the customers cannot be treated equally for the purpose of extending credit. Each case has to be examined individually before extending any credit. The credit evaluation procedure for individual accounts involves the following steps:

- Collecting credit information
- Analyzing credit information
- Determining the credit limit
- Establishing collection procedures

Monitoring the Receivables

1. Collection period
2. Ageing schedule
3. Collection experience matrix

1. **Collection period:** Average collection period is defined as

$$ACP = \frac{Debtors \times 360}{Credit\ Sales}$$

The average collection period so calculated is compared with the credit period offered by the firm to see the efficiency of the collection effort. For example, if the credit period offered by the firm is 30 days and the average collection period is 45 days, it shows that the collection is not prompt. An extended collection period delays cash inflows, adversely affects the liquidity and increases the chances of nonpayment.

However, the method suffers from some limitations. First, the average collection period is based on aggregate data and thus provides an aggregate picture of the collection effort. For better control, specific information about the age of various accounts receivables is required. Second, as it is dependent on sales so it will vary depending on sales variations. Thus, it cannot provide meaningful information about the quality of outstanding receivables.

2. **Days sales outstanding (DSO):** The days sales outstanding tells us the size of the receivables in terms of the number of days of sales which is outstanding as receivables. It is calculated as

$$DSO = \frac{Average\ Receivables}{Average\ Daily\ Sales}$$

The result obtained can be compared with the credit period. If the number of days of sales outstanding is less than equal to the credit period followed by the company then the receivables are supposed to be within controllable range. If it is higher, it indicates that collection policy has to be strengthened as the debtors' turnover is low.

3. **Ageing schedule:** Ageing schedule classifies the outstanding receivables according to the time for which they are outstanding. It indicates the percentage of receivables that remain outstanding beyond the credit period. It helps to spot out the slow-paying customers. However, this method also suffers from the problem of aggregation and does not relate receivables to sales of the same period.

Outstanding Period (days)	Outstanding Amount (₹)	Percentage of Total Receivables (%)
0-30	500,000	45.45
31-45	350,000	31.82
46-60	150,000	13.63
Over 60	100,000	0.09
Total	1,100,000	100

4. **Collection experience matrix:** Collection experience matrix shows the pattern of collection of receivables, that is, how much or what percentage of the receivables were collected in the month of sales, one month after sales, two month after sales, and so on. From the collection pattern so obtained, we can judge whether the collection is improving or deteriorating or remains unchanged. If the percentage of sales collected in the month of sales and thereafter shows an increasing trend, it indicates an improving collection pattern whereas a decreasing trend indicates that collection has deteriorates over time.

Collection Experience Matrix

Percentage of Receivables Collected During the	January Sales	February Sales	March Sales	April Sales
Month of sales	5	10	15	12
First month after sales	40	45	50	30
Second month after sales	30	35	30	28
Third month after sales	20	10	5	10
Fourth month after sales	5	–	–	10

Factoring

Factoring helps in converting a nonproductive asset, that is, receivable into a productive asset, that is, cash, by selling receivables to a company that specializes in their collection and administration. Factoring is a continuing legal arrangement between a financial intermediary called a "Factor" and a "Seller" (also called a client) of goods or services whereby the factor purchases the client's accounts receivables and controls the credit extended to the customers and administers the sales ledger in relation to such accounts. It is to be noted that factoring is a continuous arrangement and not related to a specific transaction. This means that the factor handles all the receivables arising out of the credit sales of the seller company and not just some specific bills or invoices as is done in a bills discounting agreement.

Factoring Services

Based on the type of factoring, the factor performs the following services in respect of the accounts receivables arising from the sale of such goods or services:

- Purchases all accounts receivables of the seller for immediate cash.
- Administers the sales ledger of the seller.
- Collects the accounts receivable.
- Assumes the losses which may arise from bad debts.
- Provides relevant advisory services to the seller.

For rendering the services of collection and maintenance of sales ledger, the factor charges a commission which varies between 0.4–1% of the invoice value, depending upon the volume of operations. This service charge is collected at the time of purchase of invoices by the factor. For making an immediate part-payment to the client, the factor collects discount charges from the client. These discount charges are comparable to bank interest rates in that it is calculated for the period between the date of advance payment by the factor to the client and the date of collection by the factor from the customer. These are collected monthly. In developed countries, such as, USA, UK, etc., factors provide many other services, such as, providing information about prospective customers, assisting the client in managing liquidity, financing the purchase of inventories, etc.

Mechanics of Factoring

The factoring arrangement starts when the seller (client) concludes an agreement with the factor, wherein the limits, charges, and other terms and conditions are mutually agreed upon. From then onwards, the client will pass on all credit sales to the factor. When the customer places the order, and the client delivers the goods to the customer, the client sells the customers' account to the factor and also informs the customer that payment has to be made to the factor. A copy of the invoice is also sent to the factor. The factor purchases the invoices and makes prepayment, generally up to 80% of the invoice amount. The factor sends monthly statements showing outstanding balances to the customer, copies of which are also sent to the client. The factor also carries follow-up if the customer does not pay by the due date. Once the customer makes payment to the factor, the balance amount due to the client is paid by the factor.

FIGURE 17.1

TYPES OF CREDIT POLICY

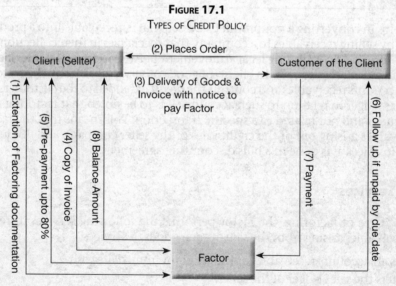

Source: Author.

Types of Factoring

Factoring can be classified into many types. This section covers only those forms of factoring which are more prevalent in India today.

1. Recourse Factoring: Under recourse factoring, the factor purchases the receivables on the condition that any loss arising out of irrecoverable receivables will be borne by the client. In other words, the factor has recourse to the client if the receivables purchased turn out to be irrecoverable.

2. Non-recourse or Full Factoring: As the name implies, the factor has no recourse to the client if the receivables are not recovered, that is, the client gets total credit protection. In this type of factoring, all the components of service, namely, short-term finance, administration of sales ledger, and credit protection are available to the client.

3. Maturity Factoring: Under this type of factoring arrangement, the factor does not make any advance or prepayment. The factor pays the client either on a guaranteed payment date or on the date of collection from the customer. This is as opposed to "Advance factoring" where the factor makes prepayment of around 80% of the invoice value to the client.

4. Invoice Discounting: Strictly speaking, this is not a form of factoring because it does not carry the service elements of factoring. Under this arrangement, the factor provides a prepayment to the client against the purchase of accounts receivables and collects interest (service charges) for the period extending from the date of prepayment to the date of collection. The sales ledger administration and collection are carried out by the client.

In terms of the services available to the client, these four types of factoring can be illustrated with the help of the following table:

The Service Types of Factoring	Short-term Finance	Sales Ledger Administration	Credit Protection
Recourse factoring	√	√	×
Non recourse factoring	√	√	√
Maturity factoring	×	√	×
Invoice discounting	√	×	×

There are also other types of factoring such as bank participation factoring, supplier guarantee factoring, and cross-border or international factoring which are beyond the scope of this chapter.

Test Yourself

1. Why is it necessary to monitor receivables?
2. What is factoring?

Factoring in India

While factoring, in the modern sense of the term, is more than three decades old in Europe and other developed countries, it came to India as a result of the recommendations of the 'Kalyansundaram Committee' a study group set up at the request of RBI, much later. The first two factoring companies in India, namely, SBI Factors and Commercial Services Ltd and Canbank Factors Ltd commenced operations in 1991. These companies provide only recourse factoring at present. Private financial companies are also planning to enter the factoring arena.

SOLVED PROBLEMS

1. Kunwar Ajay Sareés is a popular Indian name in the field of sarees. The existing annual sales of the company are ₹100 crore. Its existing credit terms are 1/10, net 30 days. Average collection period of the company is 25 days. It has been observed that 50% of the customers in term of sales revenue avail the cash discount incentive. To hasten the collection process, the company is contemplating of liberalizing its existing credit terms to 2/10, net 30 days. Sales are likely to increase by ₹15 crore and average collection period to decline to 15 days. Eighty per cent of the customers in terms of sales revenue are expected to avail the cash discount incentive under liberalization scheme. If the contribution to sales ratio is 20% and the cost of funds to the company is 12%, calculate the total incremental costs to the company due to this collection relaxation program.

Solution:
Existing cost of carrying receivables

$$= \frac{100}{360} \times 25 \times 0.12 = ₹0.8333 \text{ crore}$$

Cost of carrying receivables after liberalization

$$= \frac{115}{360} \times 15 \times 0.12 = ₹0.575 \text{ crore}$$

Saving in the cost of carrying receivables

$$= 0.833 - 0.575 = ₹0.258 \text{ crore} \qquad (A)$$

The cost of funds invested in the receivables arising out of new sales?

$$= \frac{15}{360} \times 15 \times 0.8 \times 0.12 = ₹0.0600 \text{ crore} \qquad (B)$$

Amount of discount presently paid

$$= ₹100 \times 0.01 \times \frac{50}{100} = ₹0.5 \text{ crore}$$

Amount of discount payable after liberalization

$$= 115 \times 0.02 \times 0.80 = ₹1.84 \text{ crore}$$

The additional amount of discount payable

$$= 1.84 - 0.50 = ₹1.34 \text{ crore} \qquad (C)$$

Thus, the total incremental cost $= B + C - A$

$$= 0.06 + 1.34 - 0.258$$
$$= ₹1.142 \text{ crore}$$

2. To reach the sales target quickly, the sales manager of Jaipur Golden is contemplating to take a liberal credit standard by offering discount of 5% on the selling price to those who

are buying cash. He is also considering reducing the collection effort. As a result, the sales volume is expected to go up by 25% from the present level of ₹300 lakh but the average collection period will be lengthened from 30 days to 45 days. While the amount of bad debt losses will increase from 3% to 5% of the total sales value. The contribution margin is 30%, the cost of funds is 14% and 20% of the customers are expected to make cash purchase under the new scheme. What is the incremental benefit? (Assume 360 days in a year)

Solution:

Present sales value=₹300 lakh	Expected sales=₹375 lakh
Bad debt losses=₹300 lakh × 0.03=₹9 lakh	Discount cost=₹375 × 0.20 × 0.05=₹3.75 lakh
	Bad debt losses=₹375 × 0.05=₹18.75 lakh

Incremental contribution=₹75 × 0.30=₹22.5 lakh

Incremental cost of funds=₹300 lakh × (45−30)/360 × 0.14+₹75 lakh × 45/360 × 0.80 × 0.14

$$=₹2.80 \text{ lakh}$$

Net incremental benefits=22.5−2.80−(18.75+3.75−9)=₹6.2 lakh

3. The finance manager of M/s. FinCorp Ltd is considering changing its credit terms of 2/10, net 30 to 2/10, net 45. With the change in the credit period it expects the sales to increase from ₹50 lakhs to ₹60 lakhs and average collection period from 36 days to 45 days. The contribution margin is 30% of the selling price.

   Assuming a cost of capital of 12% and 360 days in a year, what is the increase in the cost of funds locked in additional receivables?

Solution:
Cost of funds locked in additional receivables is

$$= (60-50) \times \frac{45}{360} \times 0.12 + 10 \times \frac{45}{360} \times 0.3 \times 0.12$$
$$= ₹19,500$$

4. M/s. Nippon Instruments Ltd (NIL) purchases components from M/s. Precision Electronics Ltd (PEL) on the terms 2/10, net 45. NIL has requested for an increase in the cash discount to 3%, the period of cash discount remaining unchanged. PEL has accordingly increased the cash discount and changed the credit period. On careful verification, NIL realizes that on account of change in the credit period, the cost of not paying within the discount period is now three times the cost before the change in terms. What is the new credit period?

Solution:

$$\text{Cost of trade credit} = \frac{\text{Discount}}{1-\text{Discount}} \times \frac{360}{\text{Credit period}-\text{Discount period}}$$
$$= \frac{0.02}{0.98} \times \frac{360}{45-10} = 20.99\%$$

New cost of trade credit = 3 × 20.99 = 62.97%

$$= \frac{0.03}{0.07} \times \frac{360}{x-10} = 62.97\%$$

$$\text{Solving } x = \frac{10.8}{0.611} + 10 = 27.67 \text{ days} = 28 \text{ days}$$

5. Star Ltd is considering the liberalization of existing credit terms to two of its big customers X and Y. The credit period and the likely quantity that will be purchased by the customers are as follows:

Credit Period (days)	Quantity Purchased (units)	
	X	Y
0	1,000	–
30	1,500	–
60	2,500	1,500
90	2,500	2,500

The selling price per unit is ₹9,000. The expected contribution is 20% of the selling price. If the cost of carrying debtors is 20% per annum, calculate the profit when credit period is extended for Y to 90 days.

Solution:

$$\text{Contribution} = (2,500 \times 9,000) \times 0.20 = ₹45 \text{ lakhs?}$$

$$\text{Cost of Investment in Debtors} = \left(\frac{\text{Total VC}}{\text{Debtors Turnoverd}}\right) \times 0.20 = \left(\frac{180}{360/90}\right) \times 0.20 \text{ lakhs}$$

$$\text{Profit} = \text{Contribution} - \text{Investment cost of receivables} = 45 - 9 = ₹36 \text{ lakhs}$$

6. Suppose a firm is contemplating an increase in credit period from 30 to 60 days. The average collection period at present 45 days is expected to increase to 75 days. It is also likely that the bad debt expenses will increase from the current level of 1-3% of sales. Total credit sales are expected to increase from the level of 30,000 units to 34,500 units. The present average cost is ₹8. The variable cost and sales per unit is ₹6 and ₹10, respectively. Assume that the firm expects a rate of return of 15%. Should the firm extend its credit policy?

Solution:

1. **Profit on additional sales:** (₹4 × 4,500) = ₹18,000
2. **Cost of additional investment in receivables:** Average investments with the proposed credit period, less average investments in receivables with the present credit period:

Proposed plan = cost of sales/turnover of receivables

$$= \{(8 \times 30,000) + (6 \times 4,500)\}/(360 \div 75)$$

$$= ₹55,625$$

Present plan $= (8 \times 30,000)/(360 \div 45)$

$$= ₹30,000$$

Additional investment in accounts receivables $= ₹55,625 - ₹30,000$

$$= ₹25,625$$

Cost of additional investment at 15% $= 0.15 \times 25,625 = ₹3,843.75$

3. **Additional bad debt expenses:** This is the difference between bad debt expenses with the proposed and present credit periods.

> Bad debts with proposed credit period = $0.03 \times 345,000 = ₹10,350$
>
> Bad debts with present credit period = $0.01 \times 300,000 = ₹3,000$
>
> Additional bad debt expense = $(₹10,350 - ₹3,000) = ₹7,350$

Thus, the incremental cost associated with the extension of the credit period is 11,193.75 (₹3,843.75 + ₹7,350). As against this, the benefits are ₹18,000. There is, therefore, a net gain of ₹6,806.25, that is, (18,000 − 11,193.75). The firm is well-advised to extend credit period from 30 to 60 days.

7. Price Mint Ltd has current sales of ₹600,000 per annum. To push up sales, Price Mint is considering a more liberal credit policy. The current average collection period of the company is 30 days. Proposed increase in collection period and their impact on sales and default rate (on total sales) is given below:

Credit Policy	Increase in Collection Period	Increase in Sales	Default Rate (%)
I	15 days	₹25,000	0.5
II	30 days	60,000	1.0
III	40 days	70,000	2.0

Price Mint Ltd is selling its product at ₹10 each. Average cost per unit at the current level is ₹8 and the variable cost is ₹6. If price mint requires an average rate of return of 20% on its investments, which credit policy do you recommend and why?

Solution:

Evaluation of proposed credit policies

Particulars	Present 30 Days	Proposed Number of Days		
		I (45)	II (60)	III (70)
Sales (units)	60,000	62,500	66,000	67,000
Sales revenue	₹600,000	₹625,000	₹660,000	₹670,000
Less: Variable cost	360,000	375,000	396,000	402,000
Less: Total fixed cost (60,000 × 2)	120,000	120,000	120,000	120,000
Less: bad debts	–	3,125	6,600	13,400
Less: cost of investment in debtors	8,000	12,375	1,7200	20,311
Profit	**112,000**	**114,500**	**120,200**	**114,289**

Policy II is recommended as it yields maximum profits.

8. The turnover of ST Ltd is ₹6,000,000 of which 80% is on credit. Debtors are allowed one month to clear off the dues. A factor is willing to advance 90% of the bills raised on credit for a fee of 2% a month + a commission of 4% on the total amount of debt. The company

will save ₹21,600 annually because of this arrangement and avoid bad debts at 1% on the credit sales.

A bank has come forward to make an advance equal to 90% of the debts at an annual interest rate of 18%. Its processing fee would be at 2% on the debts. What advice would you give the company whether it should accept factoring or the offer from the bank.

Solution:

	Cost of Factoring			
	Fee (0.02×0.90×₹400,000)			7,200
	Commission (0.04×₹400,000)			16,000
				23,200
A	Less: savings in cost			
	Management cost (21,600 ÷ 12)		1,800	5,800
	Savings in bad debts (0.01×₹400,000)		4,000	17,400
	Cost of bank advance			
	Interest (0.18×1/12×0.90×₹400,000			5,400
B	Processing Fee (0.02×₹400,000)			8,000
	Bad debts (0.01×₹400,000			4,000
	Net cost of bank advance			17,400

Since, costs of both the alternatives are equal, SL Ltd is indifferent between factoring and bank advance.

SUMMARY

1. Receivables have a substantial share in the total current assets of an organization.
2. The main objective of receivables management is to strike a balance between the returns that the company gets from financing of receivables (in the form of increased sales and profits) and the cost that the company has to incur to fund these receivables.
3. While formulating the credit policy of the firm, the financial manager has to analyze various costs associated with receivables, such as, additional fund requirement for the company, administrative costs, collection costs, defaulting cost and opportunity costs.
4. The term credit policy encompasses the variables, such as, credit standards, the period over which credit is extended to customers, any incentive in the form of cash discount offered, the period over which the discount can be utilized by the customers, and the collection efforts made by the company.
5. All the customers cannot be treated equally for the purpose of extending credit. Hence, each case has to be examined individually before extending any credit.
6. Credit evaluation procedure for individual accounts involves the following steps, namely, collecting credit information, analyzing credit information, determining the credit limit, and establishing collection procedures.

7. Following techniques, such as, collection period, ageing schedule, and collection experience matrix may be used for continuous monitoring of receivables.

8. Factoring helps in converting a nonproductive asset, that is, receivable into productive asset, that is, cash by selling receivables to a company that specializes in their collection and administration.

KEY TERMS

- Credit policy
- Collection cost
- Administration cost
- Opportunity cost
- Credit standards
- Credit limits
- Collection period

- Ageing schedule
- Collection experience matrix
- Day sales outstanding
- Recourse factoring
- Invoice discounting
- Maturity factoring
- Full factoring

Learning Outcomes

Student would have appreciated credit policy and its component as well as factoring.

PROBLEMS

1. A firm is selling a product priced at ₹50 per unit. The average cost of the product is ₹40 per unit and average cost is ₹27.50 per unit. The current sales are ₹15 lakhs per annum and the average collection period is 30 days. The firm is considering the following credit policies:

Credit Policy	Increase in Collection Period (days)	Increase in Sales (₹)
A	15	60,000
B	30	90,000
C	45	150,000
D	60	180,000
E	90	200,000

If the required rate of return is 20% and there are no bad debts, which of the above policies should the firm adopt?

2. Samsung Electronics is manufacturing color televisions and music systems. It is presently considering the liberalization of existing credit terms to three of its large distributors. The three distributors are expected to take off the following numbers of televisions and music systems under different credit periods:

Credit Period (days)	A		B		C	
	Television Sets	Music Systems	Television Sets	Music Systems	Television Sets	Music Systems
0	500	300	500	300	–	–
30	500	300	800	400	–	–
60	500	300	1,000	600	500	300
90	500	300	1,300	800	800	500

The selling price of the television set is ₹10,000 per set and that of the music system is ₹5,000. The contribution from television sets and music systems is expected to be 20% and 25%, respectively. The cost of debtors is 20% per annum.

What is the credit period to be allowed to each distributor? (Assume 360 days in a year.)

3. A company is currently selling 100,000 units of its product at ₹50 each unit. At the current level of production, the cost per unit is ₹45, variable cost being ₹40. The company is currently extending one month's credit to its customers. It is thinking of extending the credit period to two months in the expectation that sales will increase by 25%. If the required rate of return (before tax) is 30%, what is the net gain to the firm by changing the credit policy?

4. Consider the following information for Silver Syntex
   Annual sales: ₹2,400,000.
   Selling price: ₹10 per unit
   Variable cost to sales ratio is 70%.
   Annual collection expenditure: ₹50,000
   Bad debt losses: 3% of sales
   Average collection period: two months
   Silver Syntex is considering changing its credit policy. The consultants have recommended the following two programs—A and B.

	Program A	Program B
Average collection period (months)	1.5	1
Annual collection expenditure (₹)	75,000	150,000
Bad debt losses (%)	2	1

What is the operational cost of the programmes A and B?

5. Ultra White Ltd is considering of introducing a cash discount. The company's current credit terms are "net 40" and it would like to change it to 1/15, net 40. The current average collection period is 60 days and is expected to decrease to 30 days with the new credit terms. It is expected that 50% of the firm's customers will take advantage of the credit terms. The annual sales are ₹60 lakhs. If the required rate of return is 15%, calculate the net change in the firm's operating profit.

6. M/s Max Ltd is considering of introducing a cash discount. The company's current credit terms are "net 30" and it would like to change it to 1/10, net 30. It is expected that 50% of the firm's customers will take advantage of the credit terms. The annual sales are ₹50 lakhs. If the required rate of return is 12% and the net change in the firm's operating profit due to change in credit policy is ₹80,000, what is the incremental investment in receivables?

7. Express Ltd is considering pushing up its sales by extending credit to two more categories of customers—category A with 10% risk of default and category B with 30% risk of default. The incremental sales expected from category A customers is ₹40,000 while from category B it is ₹50,000. The costs of production and selling costs are 60% of sales while collection costs amount to 5% of sales in case of A category and 10% of sales in case of B category. Calculate the net benefit to the firm from extending credit to these two categories of customers.

8. Lakshya Corp., is a retailer that finances its purchases with trade credit under the following terms: 1/10, net 30 days. The company plans to take advantage of the free trade credit that is offered. After all the free trade credit is used, the company can either finance the clothing purchases with a bank loan that has an effective rate of 10% (on a 365-day year), or the firm can continue to use trade credit. The company has an understanding with its suppliers that within moderation, it is all right to "stretch out" its payments beyond 30 days without facing any additional financing costs. Therefore, the longer it takes the company to pay its suppliers, the lower the cost of trade credit. How many days would the firm wait to pay its suppliers in order for the cost of the trade credit to equal the cost of the bank loan?

ACCESS YOURSELF

Concept Review and Critical Thinking Questions

1. What is the objective of credit policy? Is there any optimum credit policy? Discuss.
2. Describe the costs and benefits associated with the extension of credit. How the financial manager needs to balance these costs and benefits in a credit policy? Discuss.
3. How are the receivables monitored? What are the various methods? Discuss the pros and cons of different methods.
4. What is factoring? How is it different from bill discounting and short-term financing? How a financial manager can use it in receivables management? Discuss.

STUDENT ACTIVITIES

Collect the financial data related to investment in receivables in various industries and perform a comparative analysis.

SUGGESTED READINGS

Brealey, R.A., & Myers, S.C. (2002). *Principles of corporate finance* (7th ed.). New York: McGraw-Hill.

Horne, J.C.V. (2002). *Financial management & policy* (12th ed.). Singapore: Pearson Education.

Ross, S.A., Westerfield, R.W., & Jordan, B.D. (2002). *Fundamentals of corporate finance* (6th ed.). New Delhi: Tata McGraw-Hill.

CHAPTER 18

Cash Management

Learning Objectives

- To understand the objectives of cash management.
- To study the factors affecting the requirement of cash and to understand the various strategies for cash management.
- To understand the models for determining optimal cash.

PRELUDE

Cash Is Not Only King, It Is Strategic

The global financial crisis and the resultant economic turbulence have dealt a double blow to companies. They are finding it more difficult to secure outside funding, just when cash flows are harder than ever to generate. Though not as battered by bankruptcies as corporate America, many companies in India Inc. are experiencing severe cash flow problems.

Airlines in India are prominent examples with Air India, Kingfisher, and Jet Airways facing heavy operating losses due to the slowdown and, as a result, are seeking government assistance such as reduced taxes on fuel.

Whether in India or elsewhere, the bottom line is that senior executives can no longer regard managing cash flow and liquidity as tactical and mundane. In today's brutally unforgiving environment, cash management has become strategic. Companies that manage cash and liquidity aggressively, and use the perspective and the data that come with it to gain forward visibility, have a big advantage in facing headwinds.

Walmart, for instance, is aggressively managing resources to take advantage of others' weaknesses. The company cut capital expenditures, halted a stock buyback program, and trimmed inventories. It shifted cash from opening new stores to remodeling existing ones. This has allowed Walmart to keep cutting prices and maintain a stable business amid the recession that has battered other retailers.

In India, Pantaloons Retail, the country's largest listed retailer, kept its ears to the ground early last year and prepared itself for a change in the business climate. It did so by cutting costs, redeploying existing staff to new stores, and outsourcing its IT function, among other steps. It called its program "Say with pride we are stingy." When the slowdown did hit later that year, Pantaloons was ready. And its "stinginess" paid.

The retailer's EBITDA surged over 43% in the tough October–December 2008 quarter to ₹1.57 billion year-on-year as it cut staff costs and rationalized administrative and selling costs, while its competitors struggled. Pantaloons managed this while continuing to expand, albeit at a slower pace.

In turbulence, scenario plans built from cash flow and liquidity measures can show management teams how much cash they need to preserve and protect the business under different conditions. But the immediate opportunity is to use cash and capital resources more efficiently.

Source: The Economic Times, September 23, 2009.

Cash is the most liquid asset of all and is vital for the existence of any business firm. Its efficient management is crucial to the solvency of the business. This is so because the cash inflows and outflows may not be always synchronized.

In a narrow sense, "cash" includes actual cash in the form of notes and coins and bank drafts held by a firm and the deposits' withdrawal on demand, whereas in a broader sense, it includes even marketable securities, which can be immediately sold or converted into cash. We have seen earlier that cash is embedded in different forms of current assets such as raw material inventory and accounts receivables, and comes back in the form of cash again along with profit after the operating cycle.

As it is the most liquid of all the current assets, larger cash and bank balances indicate high liquidity position of a company. It must, however, be noted that cash is also an idle asset as it fetches no return to the company unless it is kept in bank and suitably invested. Consequently, the higher liquidity position attained by holding a large amount of cash will result in lower profitability. Thus, cash management also involves a trade-off between liquidity and profitability as in the case of other current assets.

Why should companies, then, hold cash and bank balances when they know that it is an idle asset?

The need for holding cash arises from a variety of reasons such as:

1. **Transaction Motive:** Business is nothing but an array of transactions involving various parties. While some of these transactions may not result in an immediate inflow/outflow of cash (e.g., credit purchases and sales), other transactions cause immediate cash inflows and outflows. Hence, it is required that they always keep a certain amount as cash to deal with routine transactions where immediate cash payment is required.

2. **Precautionary Motive:** Business is full of uncertainties. Nobody can predict with 100% accuracy what will be the result of decisions taken by the managers/owners and what contingencies may arise. For example, there may be an unforeseen strike in the company, the suppliers may present the bills for payment earlier than expected, or there may be an accident in the factory. The company has to be prepared to meet these contingencies to minimize its losses. For this purpose, companies generally maintain some amount in the form of cash.

3. **Speculative Motive:** Firms also maintain cash balances in order to take advantage of opportunities that do not take place in the course of routine business activities. For example, there may be a sudden decrease in the price of raw materials which may not be expected to last long or the firm may want to invest in securities of other companies when the price is just right. These transactions are of a purely speculative nature for which the firms need cash.

4. **Lack of Synchronization between Cash Inflows and Outflows:** The cash outflows and inflows may not always take place at the same time. If that were possible, there would have been no need to hold excess cash. Consequently, companies are forced to hold more cash. The problem of lack of synchronization will be more pronounced in seasonal industries, such as sugar and jute.

5. **Resultant Asymmetry:** The finance manager is more worried about the consequences of a "cash deficit" than the opportunity cost of surplus cash lying idle in the bank. This is so

because the deficiencies in cash management are more likely to surface during a period of cash crunch than in a period of cash surplus. As the opportunity loss sustained by the company for keeping excess cash at bank is not likely to affect all sections of the business, while inability to meet expenses such as wages, salaries, and current liabilities do, the finance manager may keep more cash than required. This will result in surplus idle cash.

Objectives of Cash Management

The objective of cash management is to strike a balance between holding too much and too little cash. This is the focal point of the cash risk–return trade-off. A large cash balance minimizes the chances of default but penalizes the profitability of the firm. A small cash balance may free the excess cash balance for investment elsewhere in the business and thereby enhance the profitability as well as value of the firm, but increases simultaneously the chances of running out of cash. The goal of cash management is to reduce the amount of cash that is being used within the firm in order to increase profitability, but without reducing business activities or exposing the firm to undue risk in its financial obligations. In order to do so, the finance manager has to make short-term forecasts of cash position, find avenues for financing during periods when cash deficits are anticipated, and arrange for repayment/investment during periods when cash surpluses are anticipated with a view to minimizing idle cash as far as possible. Toward this end, short-term forecasts of cash receipts and payments are made in the form of cash budgets, information is monitored at appropriate intervals for the purpose of control, and suitable corrective measures are taken as warranted by the situation.

Test Yourself

1. Arrange the various components of current assets in the order of increasing liquidity.
2. What are the various motives of holding cash?

Factors Affecting the Cash Needs

It has already been said that the financial manager has to achieve a trade-off between liquidity and profitability and in doing so he should note that there are various factors, which will determine the amount of cash balance to be kept by the firm. Some of these factors are as follows:

1. **Cash Cycle:** The term cash cycle refers to the length of the time between the payment for purchase of raw material and the receipt of sales revenue. Hence, the cash cycle refers to the time that elapses from the point when the firm makes an outlay to purchase raw materials to the point when cash is collected from the sale of finished goods produced using that raw material. There may be different patterns of cash cycles and cash flows depending upon the nature of the business.

2. **Cash Inflows and Cash Outflows:** As already mentioned, every firm has to maintain cash balance because its expected inflows and outflows are not always synchronized. The timings of the cash inflows may not always match with the timings of the outflows. Therefore, a cash balance is required to fill up the gap arising out of differences in timings and quantum of inflows and outflows. If the inflows are appearing just at the time when cash is required for payment, then no cash balance will be required to be maintained by the

firm. But this seldom happens. So, the financial manager has to identify the timings and quantity by which the inflows will not be synchronized with the outflows and an arrangement must be made to fill the gap.

3. **Cost of Cash Balance:** Another factor to be considered while determining the minimum cash balance is the cost of maintaining excess cash or of meeting shortages of cash. There is always an opportunity cost of maintaining excessive cash balance. If a firm is maintaining excess cash, then it is missing the opportunities of investing these funds in a profitable way. Similarly, if the firm is maintaining inadequate cash balance, then it may be required to arrange funds on an emergency basis to meet any unexpected shortage. Even if the shortage is expected to continue only for a short period, yet the funds are to be arranged and there will always be a cost (may be more than normal cost) of raising fund.

Cash Management: Planning Aspects

In order to maintain an optimum cash balance, what is required is:

1. A complete and accurate forecast of net cash flows over the planning horizon.
2. Perfect synchronization of cash receipts and disbursements.

Thus, implementation of an efficient cash management system starts with the preparation of a plan of firm's operations for a period in future. This plan will help in preparation of a statement of receipts and disbursements expected at different points of time of that period. It will enable the management to pinpoint the timing of excessive cash or shortage of cash. This will also help to find out whether there is any expected surplus cash still unutilized or shortage of cash, which is yet to be arranged for. In order to take care of all these considerations, the firm should prepare a cash budget.

A cash budget is a summary of movement of cash during a particular period. There are three methods of preparation of cash budget. These are:

1. adjusted net income,
2. pro-forma balance sheet, and
3. cash receipts and disbursements.

In all these methods, the information with which the final cash budget is constructed is basically the same. However, they utilize different forecasting techniques; therefore, the information they provide to the financial manager is quite different.

1. **Adjusted Net Income Method** requires that a pro-forma income statement should be prepared for each desired interim period of the budget period. The net income figures for each period are then adjusted to a cash basis by deleting the transactions that are affecting the income statements but not the cash balance or the items, which affect the one without affecting the other. This adjusted figure is taken as cash profit (loss) during that period. This can be taken as net increase or decrease in cash balance during that period.

2. **Proforma Balance Sheet Method** requires the preparation of as many pro-forma balance sheets as there are interim periods in the cash budget. Each item of the balance sheet except cash is projected for each period, and the cash balance is ascertained in accordance with the accounting equation, that is, Total Assets = Total Liabilities + Capital. The balancing figure of the pro-forma balance sheet is taken as the cash balance. A negative cash balance or a cash balance falling below minimum desirable balance would, of course, indicate a need for borrowing funds or otherwise adjusting the flow to make up the anticipated shortages of cash.

Both these approaches to the preparation of cash budget tend to limit their use to those firms having stable earnings and sales, and also having cash surpluses. First, neither method produces an item-by-item forecast of cash receipts and disbursements and, consequently, it is difficult for the financial manager to plan the timing of the firm's payment closely with its anticipated receipts. Second, the lack of details also makes it difficult to locate an appropriate item for adjusting the timing of cash flows during the budget period.

3. **Receipts and Payments Method:** Cash budget, under this method, is a statement projecting the cash inflows and outflows (receipts and disbursements) of the firm over various interim periods of the budget period. For each period, the expected inflows are put against the expected outflows to find out if there is going to be any surplus or deficiency in a particular period. Surplus, if any, during a particular period may be carried forward to the next period or steps may be taken to make short-term investments of this surplus. Deficiencies, if any, must be arranged for within the same period from some short-term sources of finance such as bank credit.

The cash budget, under the receipts and payments method, may be prepared on a monthly basis or a quarterly or a half-yearly basis. For every month/quarter/half-year, there is an opening cash balance, expected inflows and expected outflows during that period, and a closing balance of cash at the end of that period. The cash inflows may be consisting of all receipts whether from cash sales, realization from debtors, income from investment or sale proceed of any investment or assets, any loan expected from bank, or a subsidy expected from the government. The cash outflows, on the other hand, may include payment for materials, labor and overheads, taxes dividends and interest, loan repayments, purchase of assets, statutory deposits, etc. The cash budget, as the name itself suggests, is prepared on a cash basis (against the accrual basis of accounting) and hence noncash items such as depreciation expense are ignored. Under the receipts and payments method of preparation of cash budget, first of all, the cash budget period is selected. A financial year is no doubt the overall period within which smaller interim periods, say a week or a month or a quarter is selected. Now, detailed cash inflows and outflows for each interim period are noted down. Beginning with the opening cash balance, the expected cash inflow during each period is added *to* it and from the total, the expected outflows *for* that period are deducted *to* find out the cash balance at the end of that period. This closing cash balance becomes the opening cash balance of the next period and so on. All types of expected cash inflows and outflows, that is, transaction cash flows, precautionary cash flows, and speculative cash flows, are incorporated because all these affect the cash balance required during a particular period; moreover, these cash flows are consistently changing from one period to another. The interaction among these three cash flows results in a need to identify the minimum cash balance, that is, desired at any point of time. While preparing the cash budget, this desired minimum cash balance is considered at the end of each of the cash budget period. If a firm is preparing monthly cash budget, then the cash balance at the end of each month must be equal to the desired cash balance. If not, then arrangements must be made/planned to increase the cash balance at that time by procuring funds from some or the other source.

Test Yourself

1. How does the length of cash cycle determine the liquidity of a firm?
2. What is the opportunity cost of maintaining cash balance?
3. Why do you think that proper planning is required for maintaining a certain amount of closing cash balance?

Factors for Efficient Cash Management

Cash reports help in monitoring actual data with the budgeted amounts, in understanding the reasons for the deviation between the two, and in controlling and revising the budget. The efficiency of cash management can be enhanced considerably by keeping a close watch on and controlling a few important factors briefly described below.

Prompt Billing

There is usually a time lag between the date of dispatching the goods and the date of preparing invoice documents and mailing the same to the customers. If this time gap can be minimized, early remittances can be expected. Accelerating the process of preparing and mailing bills will help reduce the delay in remittances and result in early realization of cash.

Collection of Checks and Remittance of Cash

Again, a delay in the receipt of checks and depositing the same in the bank will inevitably result in delayed cash realization. This delay can be reduced by taking measures to hasten the process of collecting and depositing checks or cash from the customers.

Centralized Purchases and Payments to Suppliers

The company can gain some advantages when purchases and payments to suppliers are centralized at the head office. The centralized purchases will result in a larger order size and so there will be enough scope to obtain bulk purchase discounts on certain items, which will reduce the cost.

Similarly, centralized cash collection will result in consolidation of cash receipts at the head office. This will help in implementing the disbursement schedule more effectively. The company can make an arrangement with suppliers so that the payment schedule matches with the schedule of cash receipts.

The company can also utilize the cash discounts on purchases, preferably by remitting checks on the last day for utilizing such facility. This will release cash within the discount period and the company can also avoid the implicit rate of interest underlying the failure to avail cash discount, as this rate will be considerably high.

Further, under the centralized purchase system, arrangements can be made with the suppliers for direct shipment of materials to the company's units located at different parts. This will reduce, to some extent, the total cost of transportation, handling, and storage.

Playing the Float

The basis for the concept of "float" arises from the practice of banks not to credit the customers' account in its books when a check is deposited by them and not to debit their account in its books when a check is issued by them until the check is cleared and cash is realized or paid, respectively. In the normal course of business, a company issues checks to the suppliers and deposits checks received from customers. It can take advantage of the concept of float while doing so. Let us see what float means.

Whenever checks are deposited with a bank, the credit balance increases in the company's books of account but not in the books of the bank until the checks are cleared and money realized. The amount of checks deposited by a company in the bank awaiting clearance is called "collection float." Similarly, the amount of checks issued by the company awaiting payment by the bank is called "payment float." The difference between "payment float" and "collection float" is called "net float." Obviously, when the net float is positive, the balance in the books of the company is less than that in the bank's books; when net float is negative, the book balance of the company is more than that in the bank's books.

When a company has a "positive net float," it may issue checks to the extent that the amount shown in the bank's books is higher than the amount shown in the company's books, even if the company's books indicate an overdrawn position. The company is then said to have been playing the float. This is illustrated by means of a numerical illustration before considering the merits and demerits of playing the float.

While a company can obtain greater mileage out of its cash balance by playing the float, there are certain inherent risks involved. When the clearing system operates much faster than anticipated, the checks issued may come for payment earlier than anticipated leading to financial embarrassment to the company. When the word goes around that the checks issued by the company to a supplier had bounced, the company's image will be at stake. In order to minimize the risks associated with playing the float, a company can take some of the following precautionary measures and obtain greater mileage out of its cash resources.

1. Maintain a minimum amount of cash balance with the bank.
2. Desist from using a larger proportion of the net float.
3. Have an overdraft arrangement with the bank.

Lockbox System

Under this system of collection, the company provides collection boxes at various centers such as banks or its own branches to expedite the collection process. A lockbox is a cash management system that helps you collect your funds quickly. Generally set up with the assistance of a big money center or a regional bank, lockboxes provide the company with a special zip code and, usually, quicker deliveries from regional post offices. They are especially important if you have clusters of customers in out-of-state locations and do not want to lose days waiting for their checks to arrive by long-distance mail.

Investment of Surplus Cash

Investing surplus cash involves:

 (i) Determination of surplus cash.
(ii) Determination of the avenues of investment.

Determination of Surplus Cash

The cash in excess of the firm's normal cash requirements is termed as surplus cash. Before determining the amount of surplus cash, the minimum cash balance required by the firm has to be accounted. This minimum level may be termed as a "safety stock of cash."

The determination of safety stock of cash is very similar to the determination of the safety stock of inventory. The safety stock of cash is determined by the finance manager separately for normal and peak period. In both the cases, the two basic factors to be decided are:

1. Desired days of cash: The number of days for which cash balance should be sufficient to cover payments.
2. Average daily cash outflows: The average amount of disbursements to be made daily.

   Once the above two items are known, the safety level of cash can be calculated as follows:

During Normal Periods

Safety level of cash = Desired days of cash × Average daily cash outflows.

Illustration 1. The finance manager feels that a safety level should provide sufficient cash to cover cash payments for a week and the firm's average daily cash outflows are ₹20,000. The safety level of cash will be ₹140,000 (i.e. 7 × 20,000).

During Peak Periods

Safety level of cash = Desired days of cash at the business period × Average of highest daily cash outflows.

Illustration 2. During the four busiest days in the month of October, a firm's cash outflows were ₹7,000, ₹8,000, ₹9,000, and ₹10,000. The finance manager desires sufficient cash to cover payments for 4 days during the peak periods. Calculate the safety level.

The average cash outflow is

$$= \frac{7,000 + 8,000 + 9,000 + 10,000}{4}$$

$$= ₹8,500$$

$$\text{Safety level} = 4 \times 8,500 = ₹32,000$$

Test Yourself

1. What is meant by efficient cash management?
2. What do you understand by the term float?

Determination of Avenues of Investment

Cash surplus may be of either a temporary or a permanent nature. Temporary cash surplus consists of funds, which are available for investment on a short-term basis, as they are required to meet regular obligations such as those of taxes and dividends. Permanent cash surplus consists of funds, which are kept by the firm to use in some unforeseen profitable opportunity of expansion or acquisition of some asset. Such funds are, therefore, available for investment for a period ranging from six months to a year.

In most of the companies, there are usually no formal written instructions for investing the surplus cash. It is left to the discretion of the finance manager. While exercising such discretion, he usually takes into consideration the following factors:

1. **Security:** This can be ensured by investing money in securities whose price remains more or less stable and a minimum return is guaranteed.

2. **Liquidity:** This can be ensured by investing money in short-term securities including short-term fixed deposits with the bank.

3. **Yield:** Most corporate managers give less emphasis to yield when compared to security and liquidity of investment. They, therefore, prefer short-term government securities for investing surplus cash. However, some corporate managers follow aggressive investment policies, which maximize the yield on their investments.

4. **Maturity:** Surplus cash is not available for an indefinite period. Hence, it is advisable to select securities according to their maturities keeping in view the period for which surplus cash is available. If such selection is done carefully, the finance manager can maximize the yield as well as maintain the liquidity of investments.

Liquidity and Liquidity Mix

Any company does not always keep the entire amount in the form of cash balance in the current account for the simple reason that the opportunity cost of idle cash is considerably high. That is why companies try to maintain, besides cash, other liquid assets which provide some return but at the same time can be converted into cash within a reasonably short time with relatively low risk.

The different forms in which cash may be kept are as follows:

Cash Balance in the Current Account

This is the most liquid form of cash; however, return on this account is nil. However, companies on an average maintain approximately 4–5% of their total assets.

Reserve Drawing Power under Cash Credit/Overdraft Arrangement

This form of liquidity appears to be quite attractive as it provides access to bank borrowing. However, constraints imposed by banks now make it much less attractive than what it once used to be.

Marketable Securities

These are short-term securities of government such as treasury bills and other gilt-edged securities whose default risk is zero and, for that very reason, the return is low.

Investment in Intercorporate Deposits

A company can invest money with other companies in the form of short-term deposits ranging from two or three months to five or six months at remunerative rates. However, these deposits being unsecured in nature are subject to considerable risk, unless the companies accepting such deposits have excellent antecedents with respect to their paying habits.

Money Market Mutual Funds

These are the portfolios of marketable securities managed by professionals. Immediate liquidity, competitive yields, and low transactions are some key features of these kinds of funds.

The choice of selecting the portfolio of cash and near-cash assets also depends on a variety of factors, which are as follows:

1. **Uncertainty Surrounding Cash Flow Projections:** Even if cash flow projections have been made with the utmost care, the general uncertainty can at times make the projections go haywire. However, the degree of uncertainty is more in certain types of industries than in others.

   Even within the same company, which is stable and growing certain types of cash flows, especially collections and payables tend to be more uncertain than others. When the degree of uncertainty is high as evidenced by the sensitivity of cash forecasts to adverse changes in some of the underlying assumptions, the company will do well to have the liquidity mix tilted largely toward cash balance and insofar as possible to the reserve drawing power under the cash credit/overdraft arrangement and to a less extent gilt-edged securities.

   On the other hand, certain types of industries such as synthetic fabrics and electrical appliances enjoy stable and growing demand. Once a company has established its image, the degree of uncertainty surrounding cash flow projections will be relatively less. Consequently, the liquidity mix of such companies will be tilted more toward marketable securities and intercorporate deposits.

2. **Management's Risk Profile:** If the management of the company has a higher risk appetite, it will attach greater importance to return than to liquidity. In such a case, the portfolio of liquid assets will have a higher proportion of aggressive instruments such as intercorporate deposits and a lower proportion of conservative marketable securities and cash balances.

   Whereas if the management has a conservative attitude, the liquidity mix tends to have a higher proportion of cash balance and marketable securities and a lower proportion of intercorporate deposits.

3. **Access to Nonbank Funds:** When a company is favorably placed in a position to have ready access to nonbank funds, it can afford to have less proportion of cash and more of intercorporate deposits and marketable securities. This kind of a situation arises mostly in the case of group companies. In the case of cash requirement, the cash may be transferred from one group company to another. Such a company need not maintain a large portion of its liquid assets in the form of cash.

Models for Determining Optimal Cash

Given the overall transactions and precautionary balances, the finance manager of a firm would like to consider the appropriate balance between cash and marketable securities. This is because optimal levels of cash and marketable securities would reduce and minimize the costs such as (a) transaction costs—costs incurred for transferring marketable securities to cash or vice versa, (b) inconvenience costs, and (c) opportunity costs—the interest earnings foregone on marketable securities for holding cash.

Baumol's Model

If future cash flows are known with certainty, the economic order quantity (EOQ) model is one of the simple models for determining the optimal average amount of transaction cash. In this model, the opportunity (carrying) cost of holding cash is balanced against the fixed costs associated with securities transactions to arrive at an optimal balance.

By using the EOQ formula, the firm attempts to determine the fund's transfer size that will minimize the total cash costs, that is, total transaction cost and total carrying (opportunity) costs.

Total cost = Transaction cost + Carrying (opportunity) cost

This cost can be expressed as $F(T/C) + I(C/2)$

where F is the fixed transaction cost associated with a transaction, T is the total demand for cash over the specified period, I is the interest rate on marketable securities for the period, and C is the cash balance for the period.

In the above formula, T/C reflects the number of transactions during the period. If we multiply T/C with F, that is, fixed cost per transaction, we get total fixed cost for the period. $C/2$ implies the average level of cash balance over the period of time involved and when it is multiplied with the interest rate (I), we will obtain the total carrying (opportunity) cost. From the above equation, we conclude that the larger the C or $C/2$, the smaller the total transaction cost $[F(T/C)]$ and higher the opportunity cost $[I(C/2)]$. Balancing the two costs can minimize total costs. The optimal level of cash can be determined using the underlying equation

$$C = \sqrt{\frac{2FT}{1}}$$

Illustration 3. Suppose ABC Ltd, a manufacturing firm, expects its total cash payments over the planning period (2 months) to be ₹1,000,000, while the fixed cost per transaction is ₹100 and the interest rate on marketable securities is 12% per annum, or 2.0% for the two-month period. Substituting these values, $C = \sqrt{2 \times 10,00,000 \times 100/2} = (100,000,000 = ₹10,000$. Thus, if the firm maintains an average cash balance of ₹10,000, it can minimize its total costs. It is noted that the limitations and assumptions of this model are similar to that of the EOQ inventory model.

Assumptions of Baumol's Model

1. The firm is able to forecast its cash need with certainty.
2. Cash payments occur uniformly over a period of time.
3. The opportunity cost of holding cash is known and it does not change over a period of time.
4. The firm will incur the same transaction cost whenever it converts its securities to cash.

Limitations of Baumol's Model

It does not allow the cash flows to fluctuate. Firms in practice do not use their cash balance uniformly nor are they able to predict daily cash inflows and outflows.

Miller and Orr Model

As the EOQ model assumes a constant demand for cash, this inventory model becomes inappropriate when the cash flows of the firms are relatively or reasonably unpredictable, and some other models must be employed to determine optimal cash balances. If cash balances fluctuate randomly, we can apply control theory to the problem. To apply this theory, assume that the cash flows are stochastic and random, and then set control limits such that when cash balance touches the upper bound, a conversion of cash into marketable securities is undertaken, and when it approaches the lower bound, a transfer from marketable securities to cash is activated. And, no transactions take place as long as the cash balance remains within these bounds.

Here, the question is how to set these boundaries (bounds) such that they should depend upon both fixed costs of a transaction and the opportunity cost of holding cash. For determining these limits, there are many control limit models; however, we study a relatively trouble-free one, the Miller–Orr model. This model specifies two bounds—h dollars as an upper bound and 0 (zero) dollars as a lower bound which are demonstrated in Figure 18.1, assuming that there is no underlying movement in the cash flows during the period.

FIGURE 18.1
MILLER AND ORR MODEL

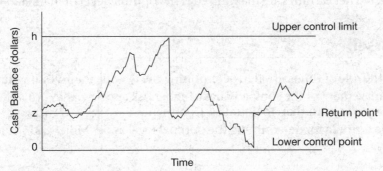

Source: Merton H. Miller and Daniel.

From Figure 18.1, we can observe that when the cash balance reaches the upper bound, h-z dollars (cash) are converted into marketable securities, and the new balance becomes z dollars (return point). When the cash balances hit the lower bound (zero dollars), z dollars of marketable securities are transferred to cash, and the new balance again becomes z dollars. And, as long as the cash balances stay within the bounds, no transaction is undertaken. Note that the lower bound (control limit) is taken as zero only for our better explanation, and can be set higher than zero.

The optimal value of return point z is

$$z = \sqrt[3]{\frac{3F\sigma^2}{4i}}$$

where "F" is the fixed transaction cost, "σ" is the variance of daily net cash balances, and "i" is the interest rate per day on marketable securities. The optimal value of "h" is $3z$. The model reduces the total fixed transaction cost and total opportunity cost by setting these bounds. However, the average cash balance recommended by the control-limit models will be higher than that of the EOQ model, as these models assume that cash flows are stochastic and unpredictable.

In practice, depending upon the nature of the business, the cash flows of a firm can be predictable within a range. Although the EOQ model assumes constant demand, when there is only moderate uncertainty, the model can be modified through the inclusion of safety (buffer) cash against uncertainty. And, for those cases where the uncertainty is large, the EOQ model becomes inappropriate. In contrast, when the cash flows of the firm are relatively or reasonably unpredictable, a stochastic model can be employed to make automatic transfers between cash and marketable securities. This is because when we employ this model in place of the EOQ model, we will always end up with a higher level of average cash balance, and this higher level of average cash balance is not appropriate for those firms whose cash flows are reasonably predictable.

For those firms, whose cash flows are neither reasonably predictable nor reasonably unpredictable, a probabilistic approach can be applied. To get a probability distribution, end-of-period cash balances are to be estimated for different cash flow outcomes. For more accuracy, the length of the period used should be short, say one week or less. This probabilistic information, together with information about the fixed (transaction) cost and interest earnings on investments in marketable securities, is required to estimate the initial balance between cash and marketable securities. Once the information is available, the expected net earnings (interest earned – [fixed transaction cost + opportunity cost]) associated with initial levels of marketable securities for different possible cash flow outcomes can be computed. The level at which expected net earnings are maximized is the optimal level of marketable securities.

Test Yourself

1. What is the role of time period in determining the avenue for investing surplus cash?
2. If the management of the company has a higher risk appetite, they will attach greater importance to return than to liquidity. Comment.
3. Write the formula for determining the optimal level as per Miller and Orr model.

SUMMARY

1. Cash is the most liquid asset of all and is vital for the existence of any business firm.
2. Businesses hold cash for three motives, namely, transaction motive, precautionary motive, and speculative motive.
3. Surplus idle cash results because business is more concerned about the consequences of a "cash deficit" than the opportunity cost of surplus cash lying idle in the bank.
4. Objective of cash management is to strike a balance between holding too much and too little cash.
5. Goal of cash management is to reduce the amount of cash that is being used within the firm in order to increase profitability, but without reducing business activities or exposing the firm to undue risk in its financial obligations.
6. Cash cycle refers to the time that elapses from the point when the firm makes an outlay to purchase raw materials to the point when cash is collected from the sale of finished goods produced using that raw material.
7. It is very important that the financial manager should identify the timings and quantity by which the inflows may not be synchronized with the outflows and an arrangement must be made to fill the gap.
8. Proper planning is required for implementation of efficient cash management system and it starts with the preparation of a plan of the firm's operations for a period in future. Cash budget is prepared to meet the above requirement.
9. A cash budget is a summary of movement of cash during a particular period.
10. There are three methods of preparation of cash budget, namely, adjusted net income, proforma balance sheet, and cash receipts and disbursements.
11. The efficiency of cash management can be enhanced considerably by keeping a close watch on and controlling a few important factors such as prompt billing, collection of

checks and remittance of cash, centralized purchases and payments to suppliers, playing the float, and lockbox system.

12. Decisions pertaining to investment of surplus cash involve two steps: (i) determination of surplus cash and (ii) determination of the avenues of investment.

13. Prior to determining the amount of surplus cash, the minimum cash balance required by the firm has to be accounted. This minimum level may be termed as a "safety stock of cash."

14. Security, liquidity, yield, and maturity are some of the factors which are taken into account while determining the avenues for investing surplus cash.

15. Cash balance in the current account, reserve drawing power under cash credit/overdraft arrangement, marketable securities, investment in intercorporate deposits, etc. are some of the avenues for keeping surplus cash balance.

16. The choice of selecting the portfolio of cash and near-cash assets also depends on a variety of factors such as uncertainty surrounding cash flow projections, management's risk profile, and access to nonbank funds.

17. According to Baumol's Model, a firm attempts to determine the funds transfer size that will minimize the total cash costs, that is, total transaction cost and total carrying (opportunity) costs.

$$\text{Total cost} = \text{Transaction cost} + \text{Carrying (opportunity) cost.}$$

This cost can be expressed as

$$F(T/C) + I(C/2)$$

where F is the fixed transaction cost associated with a transaction, T is the total demand for cash over the specified period, I is the interest rate on marketable securities for the period, and C is the cash balance for the period.

18. **Miller and Orr model** specifies two bounds—h dollars as an upper bound and 0 (zero) dollars as a lower bound—as control limits for cash balance.

KEY TERMS

- Transaction motive
- Precautionary motive
- Speculative motive
- Cash cycle
- Cash deficit
- Opportunity cost
- Playing the float
- Baumol's model

- Lockbox system
- Surplus cash
- Safety level of cash
- Cash credit
- Marketable securities
- Intercorporate deposits
- Economic order quantity
- Miller and Orr model

Learning Outcomes

Students would now be in a position to appreciate the concept of liquidity, significance of cash, and model for determining optimal level of cash.

SOLVED PROBLEMS

1. Rajasthan Electronics Ltd has planned its sales during January–March 2004 as follows:

Month	January	February	March
Sales (₹)	500,000	600,000	650,000

    The products are sold on credit where 50% is realized in the month of sale, whereas the rest is recovered by the next month. The purchases (amounting to 50% of the month's sales) are paid in the following month of purchase. Wages and administrative expenses per month amount to ₹150,000 and ₹80,000, respectively, and are paid in the following month in which they are incurred. Depreciation and amortization of preliminary expenses amount to ₹80,000 and ₹50,000, respectively. On January 1, a testing equipment worth ₹20,000 has been procured with a credit period of 45 days, while on December 31, a fixed deposit will mature (maturity value ₹150,000). If the opening cash balance at the end of January is ₹100,000, what is the closing cash balance by the end of the month of February?

Solution:

	February
(a) Opening balance	₹100,000
(b) Inflows:	
Sales realizations: Current month	₹300,000
Previous month	₹250,000
(c) Outflows:	₹250,000
Purchases	₹150,000
Wages	₹80,000
Administrative expenses	₹20,000
Payment for the equipment	₹500,000
Total	₹150,000

2. ABC Ltd requires ₹60 lakhs in cash to meet its transaction needs during the next three-month cash planning period. It holds marketable securities of an equal amount. The annual yield on these marketable securities is 20%. The conversion of these securities into cash entails a fixed cost of ₹3,000 per transaction. If the optimal lot size for conversion of securities into cash is ₹6 lakhs, calculate the total cost of conversion for the optimal lot size.

Solution:

    Number of conversions = 10

      Total conversion cost = ₹3,000 × 10 = ₹30,000

        Interest cost = 300,000 × 0.05 = ₹15,000

          Total cost = Conversion cost + Interest cost = ₹(30,000 + 15,000) = ₹45,000

3. Goyal Enterprises feels that a centralized collection system can shorten its accounts receivable collection by 3 days. The cost of the centralized collection system is ₹50,000. Credit sales are ₹360 lakhs per year billed on a continuous basis. If the opportunity cost of funds is 15%, what is the gain/loss from this arrangement?

Solution:

$$\text{Cash released by the lock box system} = \frac{360}{360} \times 3 = ₹\text{lakhs}$$

Savings	$= 0.15 \times 3 \text{ lakhs} = ₹45,000$
Cost of the lockbox system	$= ₹50,000$
Net loss from the lockbox system	$= ₹5,000$

4. Once each year, ABC Ltd purchases a perishable commodity. It processes and packages the commodity immediately and holds the cartons for sale a year later. Purchases have to be made in units of 100kg. The current purchase price is ₹60 per kg. Each 100kg yields sufficient output for a batch of 100 cartons and the processing and packaging of each 100kg costs ₹140. Storage costs excluding interest amount to ₹50 per 100 cartons per annum. It also incurs a fixed operating cost of ₹140,000 each year. The selling price next year for current output is estimated at ₹400 per 100 cartons. The probability of different volumes of sales has been estimated as shown below:

Cases of 100 Cartons	Probability
2,000	0.20
2,500	0.50
3,000	0.30

Assuming that the quantity purchased is 300,000kg, what is the expected value of annual cash flow?

Solution:
Purchase of 300,000kg

Demand (Cases)	Sales (₹)	Probability	Effective Sales (₹)
2,000	800,000	0.20	160,000
2,500	1,000,000	0.50	500,000
3,000	1,200,000	0.30	360,000
Total			**1,020,000**

Expected cash flows:
Number of cases purchased = 3,000

$$\text{Purchases at ₹60 per 100kg} = ₹180,000$$
$$\text{Processing cost at ₹140 per 100kg} = ₹420,000$$
$$\text{Storage cost at ₹50 per case} = ₹150,000$$
$$\text{Fixed operating cost} = ₹140,000$$
$$\text{Total cost} = ₹890,000$$
$$\text{Expected surplus} = 1,020,000 - 890,000 = ₹130,000$$

5. M/s. Regal Sports has forecast its sales to be as follows:

Month	July	August	September
Sales (₹)	500,000	600,000	400,000

Purchases amount to 70% of the following month's sales and are paid in the month following the month of purchase. Wages and administrative expenses per month amount to ₹50,000 and ₹60,000, respectively, and are paid in the month in which they are incurred. Depreciation and amortization of preliminary expenses amount to ₹70,000 and ₹30,000, respectively. If the opening cash balance during July is ₹50,000 and the receipts from sales during the months July and August are ₹450,000 and ₹500,000, respectively, calculate the closing cash balance at the end of the month of August.

Solution:

(₹)

	July	August
Opening balance	50,000	40,000
+ Receipts from sales	450,000	500,000
	500,000	**540,000**
– Wages and administration	110,000	110,000
– Purchases paid	350,000	420,000
Closing cash balance	**40,000**	**10,000**

Closing cash balance at the end of August=₹10,000.

6. The current assets of a company are ₹645 lakhs, current liabilities (other than bank borrowings) are ₹305 lakhs, and bank borrowings are ₹307 lakhs. Determine the Maximum Permissible Bank Finance (MPBF) under the methods I and II of the Tandon Committee.

Solution:
The MPBF as per the Method I of the Tandon Committee=0.75 (Current assets–Current liabilities other than bank borrowings)=0.75 (645–305)=₹255 lakhs. MPBF under the Method-II of the Tandon Committee=(0.75×Current assets)–Current liabilities=0.75× 645–305=₹178.75 lakhs.

7. Krishna Ltd feels that a lockbox system can shorten its accounts receivable collection period by 5 days. Credit sales are estimated at ₹400 lakhs per year, billed on a continuous basis. The firm's opportunity cost is 12%. The cost of lockbox system is ₹80,000.

   (a) Will you advise "Krishna Ltd" to go for lockbox system?

   (b) Will your answer be different if accounts receivable days are reduced by 8 days?

Solution:

(a) Cash released by lockbox system (₹400 lakhs/365 days=1.10 lakhs×5 days)

$$=₹5,500,00$$

$$\text{Savings (₹5.50 lakhs}\times0.12)=₹66,000$$

$$\textit{Less:}\text{Cost of lockbox system}=₹80,000$$

$$\text{Net loss}=26,000$$

It is not advised to go for lockbox system.

(b) Cash released by lockbox system (₹400 lakhs/365 days=1.10 lakhs×8 days)

$$=₹880,000$$

$$\text{Net loss}=26,000$$

$$\text{Savings (₹8.80 lakhs}\times0.12)=₹105,600$$

Less: Cost of lockbox system=₹80,000

$$\text{Net loss}=25,600$$

It is advised to go for lockbox system.

PROBLEMS

1. Currently, ECS Ltd is using a decentralized collection system whereby customers mail their checks to one of the firm's eight regional locations. Its annual sales are ₹95 million. Checks are deposited each business day in a local bank and the amount of the deposit is sent to the firm's concentration bank in Mumbai. The average time between deposit in the local bank and the availability of those funds, in Mumbai, to ECS is 6 days. ECS has determined that the use of electronic fund transfers would reduce the float by 4 days, but the transfer will cost ₹7.50. If transfers will be made on the 250 days that banks are open each year, should ECS switch to the electronic transfer system? Assume that ECS can earn 8% on the funds released through this more efficient transfer.

2. All For You Ltd writes checks averaging ₹15,000 a day, and it takes 5 days for these checks to clear. The firm also receives checks to the amount of ₹17,000 per day, but the firm loses 3 days while its receipts are being deposited and cleared. What is the firm's net float?

3. SCB bank has offered to set up a collection system to process credit card payments from customers of ABC Ltd for an annual fee of ₹150,000 plus ₹0.05 per payment. Total collections are ₹547.5 million annually—consisting of an average of 10 payments per year from 1,100,000 credit card customers. Average mailing time for customers would be reduced from 3.5 days currently to 2 days with the new system. Checks processing and clearing time also would be reduced from 5 days presently to 1.5 days with the new arrangement. Establishment of the new system would reduce annual payment processing costs at the Mumbai headquarters of SCB by ₹250,000 and reduce the compensating balance at its Mumbai bank by ₹500,000. The SCB bank will not require ABC Ltd to maintain a compensating balance if it establishes the new system. Funds released by the new arrangement can be invested elsewhere in the firm to earn 15% per annum pretax. Calculate the net pretax benefits to ABC Ltd of establishing the new system with the SCB bank.

4. Paras Dairy Products, located in Gurgaon, receives large remittances from its customers in New Delhi and Jaipur. If the firm deposits these checks in its local bank, two business days are required for the checks to clear and the funds to become usable by the firm. However, if it sends an employee to New Delhi or Jaipur and presents the check for payment at the bank upon which it is drawn, the funds are available immediately to the firm. The firm can earn 8% per annum on short-term investments and the cost of sending an employee to New Delhi or Jaipur to present the check for payment is ₹500. What is the net benefit to the firm of employing this special handling technique for a ₹50 lakhs check received on Tuesday.

5. The maximum permissible bank finance for ABC Ltd under method I of the Tandon Committee is 270 lakhs. If the current liabilities of the firm other than bank borrowings are ₹340 lakhs, then calculate the level of current assets maintained by the firm.

6. Gamma Enterprises has an annual turnover of ₹84 crores and the same is spread evenly over each of the 50 working weeks of the year. However, within each week, the daily sales on Mondays and Tuesdays are twice than experienced on the other 3 days of the week. The cost of banking per day is estimated at ₹2,500. It is suggested that banking should be done daily or twice a week on Tuesdays and Fridays when compared to the current practice of banking on Fridays. The firm always operates on overdraft and the current rate of interest is 15% per annum. The interest charge is applied by the bank on a daily basis. Calculate the total cost of banking twice a week.

7. The following table contains the amount of checks issued and the amount of checks deposited in the bank by Shanti Gems Pvt Ltd.

	Monday, August 23	Tuesday, August 24	Wednesday, August 25	Thursday, August 26	Friday, August 27	Saturday, August 28	Monday, August 30	Tuesday, August 31
Amount of check issued (?)	17,000	28,000	34,000	16,000	28,000	32,000	44,000	38,000
Amount of check deposited in bank (?)	23,000	33,000	50,000	40,000	25,000	15,000	21,000	35,000

On an average, a check issued by the company takes 5 days for actual payment and a check deposited by the company takes 5 days for realization. On the morning of August 23, the opening balance in company's books is ₹19,000, whereas it is ₹27,000 in the bank's book. The offices of the company were closed for some IR problem during the week between August 15, 2004 and August 21, 2004. Determine the net float available to the company at the end of June 30, 2004.

8. Chandak Corporation's budgeted monthly sales are ₹300,000. Forty percent of its customers pay in the first month and take the two percent discount. The remaining 60% pay in the month following the sale and do not receive a discount. Purchases for next month's sales are constant each month at ₹150,000. Other payments for wages, rent, and taxes are constant at ₹70,000 per month. Construct a single month's cash budget with the information given. Calculate the average cash gain/loss during a typical month for Chandak Corporation.

ACCESS YOURSELF

Concept Review and Critical Thinking Questions

1. What are the motives for holding cash? Discuss.
2. What are the objectives of cash management? Explain the risk–return trade-off with respect to cash management.
3. What is a cash budget? How is this prepared? What is the usefulness of a cash budget? Discuss.
4. What are the advantages of decentralized collection over centralized collections? Discuss.
5. What is a lockbox system? What are its advantages? Discuss.
6. What do you mean by "playing the float"? What are the risks involved in playing the float? Discuss.
7. "Cash is an idle asset but its management keeps the finance manager on his toes." Comment.

STUDENT ACTIVITIES

Collect the financial data related to investment in cash in various industries and perform a comparative analysis.

SUGGESTED READINGS

Brealey, R.A., & Myers, S.C. (2002). *Principles of corporate finance* (7th ed.). New York: McGraw-Hill.

Horne, J.C.V. (2002). *Financial management & policy* (12th ed.). Singapore: Pearson Education.

Ross, S.A., Westerfield, R.W., & Jordan, B.D. (2002). *Fundamentals of corporate finance* (6th ed.). New Delhi: Tata McGraw-Hill.

CHAPTER 19

Financing Current Assets

- To know the various sources of financing current assets.
- To understand the implications of cost–benefit analysis while taking various decisions pertaining to financing current assets.
- To know the statutory guidelines for taking bank credit and working capital loans.

Prelude

Financing current assets is a significant issue for the organization as such issues here are what shall be sources for financing the current assets? How long can we depend on permanent sources like equity capital and term loan, etc.? what is the relationship between cost of funds for financing current assets and expected return from current assets? It is believed that financing of current assets is the dicey issue. Unless a balance is struck, there is possibility of providing liquidity at the cost of profitability and vice versa.

There are two components of working capital—temporary and permanent, and the firm may adopt various approaches—**hedging approach, aggressive approach, or conservative approach**—to finance the current assets. In addition, there are various sources of financing the current assets such as long-term sources (e.g., ordinary share capital, preference share capital, debentures, and term loans) and short-term sources (e.g., bank finance, public deposits, commercial paper, spontaneous sources such as trade credit, outstanding expenses, and deferred payments (Figure 19.1).

Figure 19.1

Financing Current Assets: The Matching Principle

Financing Current Assets: The Matching Principle

The maturity of the sources of financing should match with the maturity of the assets being financed. It means that long-term assets and core current assets may be financed through long-term sources of finance like equity, term loans, preference shares, debentures, etc., whereas, fluctuating current assets must be supported by short-term sources of finance.

If a firm violates this principle it may be risky as well as troublesome. Hence, it makes sense to ensure that the maturity of the assets and the sources of financing are appropriately matched.

Source: Author.

Spontaneous Sources of Financing Current Assets

The sources of finance, which emerge during the normal course of business and as a result, are readily accessible to the firm, are called spontaneous sources of finance. These include outstanding expenses, provisions, trade credit, and guarantees resulting in deferred payment.

Outstanding Expenses

Those expenses, which have been incurred but not have been paid yet, are known as outstanding expenses. These are payable at some future date, for example, outstanding wages and salaries. It should be noted that "outstanding expenses" constitute a small proportion of current liabilities and its usefulness as a source of financing current assets is very much limited.

> **IS THERE A COST TO OUTSTANDING EXPENSES?**
>
> - They are free as no explicit interest is charged.
> - Though firms have little control over the level of outstanding expenses.

Provisions

These are the charges earmarked for an estimated expense such as provision for dividends, provision for taxes, and provision for payment of bonus. There is no immediate cash outflow on account of provisions; cash outflow occurs when the actual amount of liability is known and paid for. The usefulness of "provisions" as a source of financing current assets is very much limited.

Trade Credit

Trade credit or accounts payables or sundry creditors is an important spontaneous source for financing current assets. On an average, trade credit accounts for about 40% of current liabilities.

There are two important aspects of trade credit. Firstly, it instills confidence in suppliers by maintaining good relations supported by prompt payment. This will enable a company to obtain trade credit and also have continuous access to raw material even if the availability is limited. Secondly, trade credit is not free of cost and when the supplier offers some cash discount, the cost of trade credit reduces.

Obtaining Trade Credit

A company decides whether it should offer the facility of credit sales to its customers; similarly, the suppliers of raw materials will also consider whether or not to extend credit to its customers, that is, different firms. If the firm is credit worthy, it will be easy for the firm to obtain credit. Various factors, such as good track record of profitability and liquidity and record of prompt payment by the company to other suppliers will not only help in projecting a good image but also instill confidence in the potential suppliers. Trade credit helps in paying at the end of the credit period for supplies received now and prevents immediate cash drain.

Cost of Trade Credit

Whenever a company purchases materials on credit basis, the supplier stipulates the credit terms. If the credit period allowed is, say, net 30 days, then the company can pay on the 30th day for the purchases made now. By paying earlier than the stipulated 30-day period, the company is not going to gain anything. It is, therefore, advisable to defer payment till the last day of the credit period. The question that arises is whether or not the trade credit under the terms, say, net 30 days, is cost-free. As far as the explicit cost is concerned, it can be considered as cost-free. However, since the company can defer the payment till the 30th day, it implies that this cash can be used profitably in business or invested in short-term securities to earn some suitable return. This will result in some gain, thereby reducing the cost of trade credit.

When suppliers offer credit terms, such as 2/10, net 45, there is an implicit cost associated with not availing oneself of the cash discount of 2% offered for payment made on or before the 10th day of the sale. As payment made beyond the 10th day but on the 45th day will not entitle the company for cash discount, there is an implicit cost associated with "buying" time for 10 days for not making payment.

The implicit cost can be calculated as follows:

The company is losing at the rate of 2/98×100 or 2.041% for gaining 10-day period for payment by not availing the cash discount.

The implicit cost is thus

$$\frac{2.041 \times 360}{10} = 73.48\%$$

The above calculation can be summarized into a simple formula as shown as follows:

$$\frac{\text{Rate of discount}}{1 - \text{Rate of discount}} \times \frac{\text{Number of days in a year}}{(\text{Credit period} - \text{Discount period})}$$

In the above illustration, the implicit cost of not availing oneself of discount can be obtained as

$$\frac{0.02}{(1-0.02)} \times \frac{360}{(30-10)} = 36.73\%$$

The implicit cost of trade credit should be compared with the opportunity cost of cash. A decision to avail oneself of cash discount can be taken only when the cost of trade credit exceeds the opportunity cost of cash. If opportunity cost of cash exceeds implicit cost of trade credit, foregoing cash discounts are more advantageous.

It should be remembered that if a company could not avail itself of the cash discount facility during the stipulated time period, for some reason or the other, it is more advantageous to pay the amount only on the last date of expiry of the credit period. This strategy provides greater flexibility to cash without incurring any additional cost as payments made after the discount period but before the credit period will not result in any financial gain to the company.

Short-term Bank Finance

Traditionally, bank finance is an important source for financing the current assets of a company. Bank finance is available in different forms. The factors usually considered by bankers while granting such credit are the creditworthiness of the customer, the form of security offered, and the margin requirement on the assets provided as security.

ADVANTAGES AND DISADVANTAGES OF SHORT-TERM BANK FINANCE

- Advantages
  - Speediness
  - Flexibility
  - Cost advantage when compared with long-term debt
- Disadvantages
  - Changing interest expense
  - Risk of default during adverse economic conditions.

Bank finance may be either direct or indirect. Under direct financing, the bank not only provides the finance but also bears the risk of loss. Cash credit, overdraft, note lending, and purchase/discounting of bills come under the category of direct financing, whereas when a bank opens a Letter of Credit in favor of a customer, the bank assumes only the risk of default by the customer and the finance is provided by a third party; this is called indirect financing. Some forms of bank finance are as follows:

1. **Cash Credit:** Under the cash credit arrangement, the customer is permitted to borrow up to a pre-defined limit called the cash credit limit. The customer is charged interest only on the amount actually utilized, subject to some minimum service charge or maintaining some minimum balance (compensatory balance) in the cash credit account. The security offered by the customer is in the nature of hypothecation or pledge. As per the banking regulations, the margins are specified on different types of assets provided as security. From the operational view point, the amount that can be borrowed at any time is the minimum of the sanctioned limit and the value/asset as reduced by the required margin.

2. **Overdraft:** Under the overdraft arrangement, the customer is permitted to overdraw from his account up to a pre-defined limit. Interest is charged on the amount(s) overdrawn subject to some minimum charge. Both cash credit and overdraft accounts are running accounts and are frequently treated identical. However, there is a technical difference between these two arrangements. Cash credit account operates against security of inventory and accounts receivables in the form of hypothecation/pledge. Overdraft account operates against security in the form of pledge of shares and securities, assignment of life insurance policies, and sometimes even mortgage of fixed assets. While advances provided by banks in the form of cash credit or overdraft are technically repayable on demand, in actual practice it never happens. Cash credit/overdraft is only renegotiated for a further period.

3. **Note Lending:** Unlike cash credit/overdraft arrangements, which are running accounts, note lending is for a specified period ranging from 60 to 90 days. In this arrangement, the customer takes a loan against a promissory note. Interest is charged on the entire amount sanctioned as loan unlike cash credit/overdraft arrangement where interest is not charged on the undrawn portion within the sanctioned limit. This method is not very popular in our country.

4. **Purchasing/Discounting of Bills:** Under this arrangement, the bank provides finance to the customer either by outright purchase or discounting of the bills arising out of sale of finished goods. The purchased/discounted bills are collected by the bank on the due date. The bank charges some commission for providing this facility. From the point of view of the firm, it is beneficial as it helps in unlocking the funds blocked in receivables.

5. **Letter of Credit:** Letter of credit is opened by a bank in favor of its customer undertaking the responsibility to pay the supplier (or the supplier's bank) in case its customer fails to make payment for the goods purchased from the supplier within the stipulated time. Unlike in other types of finance where the arrangement is between the customer and bank and the bank assumes the risk of non-payment and also provides finance, under the letter of credit arrangement, the bank assumes the risk while the supplier provides the credit.

SECURITY IN BANK FINANCE

Before taking a decision to provide financial assistance to a company, the bank will consider the creditworthiness of the company and the nature of security offered. For providing accommodation toward financing the current assets of a company, the bank usually ask for security in the form of hypothecation pledge or mortgage.

Hypothecation

Under the hypothecation agreement, the goods hypothecated remain in the possession of the borrower and he can use the assets but he is under obligation to prominently display that the items are hypothecated. Usually, hypothecation is provided on movable assets such as vehicles and raw material inventory.

Pledge

In a pledge, the goods/documents in the form of share certificates, book debts, and insurance policies, which are provided as security will be in the possession of the bank lending funds but not with the borrowing company. In the event of default by the borrower either under hypothecation or pledge, the lender can sue the company that has borrowed funds and sell the items of security to realize the amount due. Now that Securitization Act 2002 is in force, the banks and financial institutions have got even more powers to enforce the security interest in assets of the borrower.

Mortgage

Assets are offered as collateral. The title and possessions are transferred to lenders. It is often applicable for immovable fixed assets.

6. **Public Deposits for Financing Current Assets:** Mobilization of funds from general public in the form of public deposits has become an important source. The deposits thus mobilized from public by non-financial manufacturing companies are popularly known as "Public Deposits" or "Fixed deposits." These are governed by the regulations of public deposits under the Companies (Acceptance of Deposits) Amendment Rules, 1978 and are covered by sections 58A and 58B of Indian Companies Act.

Salient Features of "Public Deposits"

A company cannot raise more than 10% of its "paid-up share capital" and "free-reserves." However, "capital redemption reserve" is treated as part of free reserves and "share premium account" is treated as part of paid-up share capital. This will allow a company to raise more money even within the 10% limit. Government companies can accept deposits up to 35% of their paid-up share capital and free reserves.

The maximum maturity period allowed for public deposits is 3 years, while the minimum permitted maturity period is 6 months. In certain cases, a maturity period of even 3 months also is allowed. By and large, companies invite public deposits with maturity periods of 1, 2, and 3 years.

A company inviting deposits from the public is required to issue an advertisement disclosing the details about its name, date of incorporation, business carried on by the company, management of the company, profits and dividends of the company over the preceding 3 years, financial position of the company, and a declaration that the company has complied with the acceptance of deposits guidelines. The advertisement has to be filed with the Registrar of Companies before releasing it to the press.

Evaluation of Public Deposits

From the point of view of the company, public deposits offer the following advantages:

1. The procedure involved is fairly simple, as it does not involve underwriting and related issue expenses are minimal.
2. No security is offered in the case of public deposits. Thus, the assets can be used in raising additional funds from banks/financial institutions.
3. The post-tax cost of public deposits is less than the post-tax cost of bank borrowing.
4. As public deposits with maturity periods of 2 and 3 years cannot be regarded as current liabilities, the calculation of "working capital gap" by the bankers to provide short-term finance is likely to be favorable from the company's point of view.
5. Public deposits have no restrictive covenants in respect of dividend payments and appointment of directors.

However, public deposits have following limitations:

1. The scope for mobilization of public deposits is limited.
2. With the maximum maturity period being limited to 3 years, debt servicing may be difficult.
3. Given so many instances of default by the companies in paying interest and repayment of principal on public deposits, the guidelines for raising public deposits have been made very strict and hence it may not be easy to tap this source of finance.

Regulation of Bank Credit

Traditionally, bank finance is an important source of financing the current assets of the companies. In order to regulate this important source of finance, RBI had appointed various committees at different points of time with the objective of streamlining the practices followed by banks in working capital finance. Though the recommendations given by these various committees are no longer applicable, still in order to gain an insight into various aspects of working capital finance, the major recommendations of some of the important committees set up by RBI are given below:

Tandon Committee

A study group to frame guidelines for the follow-up of bank credit programs was constituted by the RBI in July 1974 under the chairmanship of Shri P.L. Tandon. The study group submitted its report in August 1975, which is popularly referred to as the Tandon Committee Report.

Terms of Reference

1. To suggest guidelines for commercial banks to follow up and supervise credit to ensure proper end-use of funds and to keep a watch on the safety of the advances and to suggest the type of operational data and other information that may be obtained by banks periodically from such borrowers and by the RBI from the lending banks.
2. To make recommendations for obtaining periodical forecasts from borrowers of (i) business/production plans, and (ii) credit needs.
3. To make suggestions for prescribing inventory norms for different industries both in the private and public sectors and indicate the broad criteria for deviating from these norms.
4. To suggest criteria regarding satisfactory capital structure and sound financial basis in relation to borrowings.
5. To make recommendations regarding the sources for financing the minimum working capital requirements.
6. To make recommendations as to whether the existing pattern of financing working capital requirements by cash credit/overdraft system requires to be modified, and if so, to suggest suitable modifications.
7. To make recommendations on any other related matter as the group may consider germane to the subject of enquiry or any other allied matter which may be specifically referred to it by the RBI.

Summary of Recommendations

The recommendations of the Tandon Committee may be broadly grouped under the following four heads outlined below:

Norms for Inventory and Receivables

The Committee came out with a set of norms that represented the maximum levels for holding inventory and receivables in each of the 15 major industries, covering about 50% of industrial advances of the banks. Deviations from norms were permitted under extenuating circumstances, such as bunched receipt of raw materials including imports, power-cuts, strikes, and transport bottlenecks for usually short periods. Once normalcy was restored, the norms would become applicable. The norms were to be applied to all industrial borrowers with aggregate limits from the banking system in excess of ₹10 lakhs and extended to smaller borrowers progressively.

Approach to Lending

1. Bank should act as a supplemental source for financing the current assets.
2. The bank should finance a part of the working capital gap (the difference between total current assets and current liabilities other than bank borrowing is termed as working capital gap) and the balance should be financed through long-term sources comprising equity and long-term borrowings. Three alternative methods were suggested for calculating the maximum permissible bank borrowing.

    (a) **Method I:** In this method, the bank will finance at the most 75% of the working capital gap, that is, maximum permissible bank finance (MPBF)=0.75 (Current Assets − Current Liabilities). This method will ensure a minimum current ratio of 1:1.

(b) **Method II:** In the second method, the borrower will finance 25% of total current assets through long-term sources and the remaining of the working capital gap can be financed through bank borrowings, that is, maximum permissible bank finance = (0.75 Current Assets) – Current Liabilities. This method will ensure a current ratio of 1.33:1.

(c) **Method III:** In the third method, borrower will contribute 100% of core assets and 25% of the remaining current assets. The remaining working capital gap can be financed through bank borrowings. In other words, maximum permissible bank finance = 0.75 (Current Assets – Core Current Assets) – Current Liabilities.

Style of Credit

The committee suggested the following:

1. Bifurcation of the credit limit into a loan and a demand cash credit, which will be reviewed annually.
2. The irreducible minimum level of borrowing which is expected to be used throughout the year will comprise the loan component while the fluctuating part will be taken care of by the cash credit component.
3. As the intention of the proposed approach is to ensure financial discipline on the part of the borrower, the interest rate structure can be charged such that the rate of interest on loan component is lower than the rate of interest on cash credit component, while the rate of interest chargeable on excess borrowing converted into a term loan should carry a slightly higher interest rate than the cash credit component.
4. A part of the total eligible amount could also be provided by way of bill limits to finance the selling company's receivables, besides the cash credit and loan components. This is likely to ensure proper end-use of credit.

Information System

Another important recommendation of the Tandon Committee was related to the flow of information from the borrower to the bank. The information system suggested by the committee is intended to induce better planning of the credit needs by the borrowing company, ensure end-use of credit for the intended purpose, and ensure better monitoring of the borrower's credit situation by the banker. Keeping these aspects in view, the committee had recommended a quarterly budgeting-cum-reporting system. The following statements are to be submitted by the borrowing company:

1. Quarterly profit and loss statement giving details of previous year's actual, current year's budget, previous quarter's budget and actual, and current quarter's projections of revenues, costs, and profit.
2. Quarterly statement of current assets and current liabilities giving details of raw material inventory (imported and indigenous) work-in-process; finished goods and consumable stores; receivables; advances to suppliers; and other current assets and current liabilities.
3. Half-yearly proforma balance sheet and profit and loss statement within 2 months.
4. Annual audited accounts within 3 months, and
5. Monthly stock statement in required detail so as to enable the banker to reconcile stocks of raw materials and finished goods.

The Tandon Committee had identified the problems associated with cash credit system and recommended for the bifurcation of the credit limit into a loan component and a fluctuating cash credit component. The information system recommended by the committee is intended to ensure proper end-use of credit besides introduction of financial discipline on the part of borrowing companies.

Chore Committee[1]

Various committees constituted by the Reserve Bank of India including the Tandon Committee had pointed out the drawbacks of the cash credit system. Though the Tandon Committee had recommended for the bifurcation of the credit limit into a demand loan and a fluctuating cash credit component, the progress achieved in this respect had been very slow. Consequently, a small working group was set up by the RBI under the chairmanship of K.B. Chore in April 1979 with specific terms of reference outlined below:

Terms of Reference

1. To review the operation of the cash credit system in recent years, particularly with reference to the gap between sanctioned credit limits and the extent of their utilization;
2. In the light of the review, to suggest:
   (a) modifications to the system with a view to making the system more amenable to rational management of funds by commercial banks and/or
   (b) alternative types of credit facilities, which would ensure greater credit discipline and also enable banks to relate credit limits to increases in output or other productive activities; and
3. To make recommendations on any other related matter as the group may consider germane to the subject

The Working Group had analyzed the existing data in respect of cash credit/overdraft by the banking sector practices followed by other countries and submitted its report on 31 August 1979. The recommendations of the Chore Committee were accepted by the RBI and implemented by the commercial banks.

Summary of Recommendations

1. The advantages of the existing system of extending credit by a combination of the three types of lending, namely, cash credit, loan, and bill should be retained. At the same time, it is necessary to give some directional changes to ensure that wherever possible the use of cash credit would be supplanted by loans and bills. It would also be necessary to introduce necessary corrective measures to remove the impediments in the use of bill system of finance and also to remove the drawbacks observed in the cash credit system.
2. Bifurcation of cash credit limit into a demand loan portion and a fluctuating cash credit component has not found acceptance either on the part of the banks or the borrowers. Such bifurcation may not serve the purpose of better credit planning by narrowing the gap between sanctioned limits and the extent of utilization thereof. It is not likely to be voluntarily accepted nor does it confer enough advantages to make it compulsory.

---

[1] Compiled from various sources including https://www.scribd.com/document/265100971/Tandon-Chore-Committee and RBI Publications.

3. The need for reducing the overdependence of the medium and large borrowers—both in the private and public sectors—on bank finance for their production/trading purposes is recognized. The net surplus cash generation of an established industrial unit should be utilized partly at least for reducing borrowing for working capital purposes.

4. In order to ensure that the borrowers do enhance their contributions to working capital and to improve their current ratio, it is necessary to place them under the second method of lending recommended by the Tandon Committee, which would give a minimum current ratio of 1.33:1. As many of the borrowers may not be immediately in a position to work under the second method of lending, the excess borrowings should be segregated and treated as a working capital term loan which should be made repayable in installments. To induce the borrowers to repay this loan, a higher rate of interest should be charged. For the present, the group recommends that the additional interest may be fixed at 2% per annum over the rate applicable on the relative cash credit limits. This procedure should be made compulsory for all borrowers (except sick units) having aggregate working capital limits of ₹10 lakhs and over.

5. While assessing the credit requirements, the bank should appraise and fix separate limits for the "normal non-peak level" as also for the "peak level" credit requirements indicating also the periods during which the separate limits would be utilized by the borrower. This procedure would be extended to all borrowers having working capital limits of ₹10 lakhs and above. One of the important criteria for deciding such limits should be the borrowers' utilization of credit limits in the past.

6. If any ad hoc or temporary accommodation is required in excess of the sanctioned limit to meet unforeseen contingencies, additional finance should be given wherever necessary through a separate demand loan account or a separate "non-operable" cash credit account. There should be a stiff penalty for such demand loan or "non-operable" cash credit portion, at least 2% above the normal rate, unless Reserve Bank exempts such penalty. This discipline may be made applicable in cases involving working capital limits of ₹10 lakhs and above.

7. The borrower should be asked to give his quarterly requirement of funds before the commencement of the quarter on the basis of his budget, the actual requirement being within the sanctioned limit for the particular peak level and non-peak level periods. Drawings less than or in excess of the operative limit so fixed (with a tolerance of 10% either way) but not exceeding sanctioned limit would be subject to a penalty to be fixed by the Reserve Bank from time to time. For the time being, the penalty may be fixed at 2% per annum. The borrower would be required to submit his budgeted requirements in triplicate and a copy each would be sent immediately by the branch to the controlling office and the Head Office for record. The penalty would be applicable only in respect of parties enjoying credit limits of ₹10 lakhs and above, subject to certain exemptions.

8. The non-submission of the returns in time is partly due to certain features in the forms themselves. To get over this difficulty, simplified forms have been proposed. As the quarterly information system is part and parcel of the revised style of lending under the cash credit system, if the borrower does not submit the return within the prescribed time, he should be penalized by charging for the whole outstanding in the account at a penal rate of interest, 1% per annum more than the contracted rate for the advance from the due date of the return till the date of its actual submission.

9. Requests for relaxation of inventory norms and for ad hoc increases in limits should be subjected to close scrutiny by banks and agreed to only in exceptional circumstances.

10. The banks should devise their own check lists in the light of the instructions issued by the Reserve Bank for the scrutiny of data at the operational level.

11. Delays on the part of banks in sanctioning credit limits could be reduced in cases where the borrowers cooperate in giving the necessary information about their past performance and future projections in time.

12. As one of the reasons for the slow growth of the bill system is the stamp duty on usance bills and difficulty in obtaining the required denominations of stamps, these questions may have to be taken up with the state governments.

13. Banks should review the system of financing book debts through cash credit and insist on the conversion of such cash credit limits into bill limits.

14. A stage has come to enforce the use of drawee bills in the lending system by making it compulsory for banks to extend at least 50% of the cash credit limit against raw materials to manufacturing units whether in the public or private sector by way of drawee bills. To start this, discipline should be confined to borrowers having aggregate working capital limits of ₹50 lakhs and above from the banking system.

15. Banks should insist on the public sector undertakings/large borrowers to maintain control accounts in their books to give precise data regarding their dues to the small units and furnish such data in their quarterly information system. This would enable the banks to take suitable measures for ensuring payment of the dues to small units by a definite period by stipulating, if necessary, that a portion of limits for bills acceptance (drawee bills) should be utilized only for drawee bills of small-scale units.

16. To encourage the bill system of financing and to facilitate call money operations, an autonomous financial institution on the lines of the Discount Houses in the UK may be set up.

17. No conclusive data are available to establish the degree of correlation between production and quantum of credit at the industry level. As this issue is obviously of great concern to the monetary authorities, the Reserve Bank may undertake a detailed scientific study in this regard.

18. Credit control measures to be effective will have to be immediately communicated to the operational level and should be followed up. There should be a "Cell" attached to the Chairman's office at the Central Office of each bank to attend such matters. The Central Offices of banks should take a second look at the credit budget as soon as changes in credit policy are announced by the Reserve Bank and revise their plan of action in the light of the new policy and communicate the correct measures to the operational levels as quickly as possible.

19. Banks should give particular attention to monitor the key branches and critical accounts.

20. The communication channels and systems and procedures within the banking system should be toned up so as to ensure that minimum time is taken for collection of instruments.

21. Although banks usually object to their borrowers dealing with other banks without their consent, some of the borrowers still maintain current accounts and arrange bill facilities with other banks, which vitiate the credit discipline. Reserve Bank may issue suitable instructions in this behalf.

The Marathe Committee[2]

With a view to regulating the growth of bank credit to be more closely aligned to the requirements, the RBI advised all commercial banks to obtain its prior authorization before sanctioning credit limit to any single party which results in a limit of ₹1 crore or above from the entire

---

[2] *Source:* Report of the committee to review the working of the credit authorization scheme, Mumbai, RBI publications 1983.

banking sector. This was felt imperative as the economy was passing through a period of considerable stress during 1965 and the stipulation of the Reserve Bank provided an additional measure of credit regulation for ensuring greater alignment of bank credit to the requirements of the plan. This regulation of RBI is the genesis for what has come to be known more popularly as the Credit Authorization Scheme (CAS).

Since 1965, many environmental changes have taken place. These include the nationalization of banks in 1969; the fixing up of percentages of bank credit to priority sector borrowers such as small-scale industries (SSI), agriculture; the recommendations of Dehejia Committee report which highlighted the need for banks to take into consideration a broad view of the borrowers operations rather than be guided solely by security orientation; the recommendations of Tandon and Chore Committees which underlined the need for banks to switch over from security-oriented approach to "end-use" or "need-based" approach that called for greater financial discipline on the part of banks as well as borrowers; the Krishnaswamy Committee report of 1980 which provided guidelines for fixing sub-targets for "weaker" sectors in the wake of 20 Point Program in 1976 and Integrated Rural Development Program in 1979; and the recommendations of the Ghosh Committee report in 1982 which refined further the definitions and "Groups" needing special attention in lending operations. In the light of these changes, the CAS also underwent several changes. The credit limit originally fixed at ₹1 crore was progressively increased to ₹3 crore and later in certain cases to ₹5 crore. It is against this backdrop that the RBI set up a committee under the chairmanship of S.S. Marathe in November 1982 with the following terms of reference.

Terms of Reference

1. To examine the objectives, scope, and content of the scheme and make suggestions with regard to making modifications therein, if any, with regard to the changing economic situation.
2. To examine the adequacy or otherwise of the credit appraisal machinery/procedures in commercial banks, and based thereon, suggest modifications, if any, in the modalities in this behalf.
3. To study the existing setup for compliance with the requirements of the scheme within the commercial banks at the head and regional office levels and suggest any modifications therein considered necessary to facilitate proper appraisal and expeditious disposal of applications and monitoring thereof.
4. To examine the existing database relevant for making recommendations by banks to RBI for authorizing a given level of credit for a particular party and suggest modification/simplification, if any, in that behalf.
5. To examine the existing format for submitting applications by banks to RBI in respect of seeking authorization and suggest modifications therein, if necessary.
6. To study the desirability of introducing time-bound guidelines to be observed within commercial banks and Reserve Bank for speeding up the processing and disposal of applications.
7. To make any other recommendations which are germane to the scheme.

Summary of Recommendations

After making a thorough study of CAS in its historical perspective, the committee had followed broad-based objectives of CAS whose initial aim was to closely align the growth of bank credit with the requirements of the plan and use it as an additional measure of credit regulations. The enlarged objectives of CAS are as follows:

1. To ensure that additional bank credit is in conformity with the approved purposes and priorities and that the bigger borrowers do not preempt scarce resources;
2. To enforce financial discipline on the larger borrowers, where necessary, on uniform principles;
3. Whether a borrower is financed by more than one bank, to ensure that the customer's proposal is assessed in the light of the information available with all the banks; and
4. To bring about improvements in the techniques of credit appraisal by banks and their systems of follow-up.

Kannan Committee[3]

Kannan Committee headed by Bank of Baroda Chairman K. Kannan was formed on the suggestion of the RBI in January 1997 to examine the validity of the MPBF concept and to suggest what could replace it. The report submitted in March 1997 gave the following recommendations:

The report suggested doing away with the prescribed uniform formula for MPBF with the bank having the sole discretion to determine the borrowing limits of the corporate.

In a significant move, the committee has said that developing the modalities of working capital assessment of borrowers will be left to the banks, which may devise a flexible system. Corporate borrowers may be allowed to issue short-term working capital debentures of 12-18 months' maturity and banks may subscribe to such debentures as working capital assistance.

Alternatively, borrowers with working capital requirements of over ₹20 crore may be granted working capital facility in full by way of a demand loan. Borrowers with requirements of over ₹10 crore and up to ₹20 crore may have a loan component of 75%.

Interest rate incentives will be provided to borrowers availing full working capital finance by way of loan component. In addition, margin and holding level of stocks and book debts as security for working capital facility may entirely be left to the discretion of the financing bank. The current benchmark ratio of 1.33 and matters relating to the ideal debt–equity ratio of the borrower should also be left to the discretion of the financing bank. Borrowers have to obtain prior approval for investment of funds outside the business, such as inter-corporate deposits, investment in associate concerns, or in other investments.

The committee recognizes that the existing norms/guidelines as prescribed by the Tandon–Chore Committee in 1974 do not serve the needs of the productive sectors of the economy. It recommended that need-based working capital finance should be made available without sticking to an age-old rule which may have largely outlived its utility.

Nayak Committee

A committee headed by P.R. Nayak, Ex-Deputy Governor of RBI, was set up in December 1991 to look into the adequacy of the institutional credit to SSI sector, do modifications to the financing norms to SSI as per Tandon–Chore Committee norms, and revisions, if any, for the rehabilitation of sick SSI units. Among them, the relevant portions for the computation of working capital are that the working capital requirement of SSI should be worked out based

---

[3] Compiled from various sources including http://www.iibf.org.in/ and RBI publications.

on the projected turnover and the limit should be to the extent of 20% of such projected turn-over. This recommendation was accepted and the process of assessment of working capital requirement was made very simple and easy. But the onus lies with the bank to check up the genuineness of the projected turnover. If the request for working capital is from a new bor-rower who is starting the venture, the bank has to compare the projected turnover with the performance of the already existing entrepreneurs in the same industry. If the proposal is for a renewal of the existing limit of working capital, the projected enhanced turnover should be studied from the angle of previous years' performance and the possible trend that could be extrapolated.

As per the extant guidelines from the RBI, banks are advised to follow turnover method of assessment of working capital requirement mentioned above for limits up to ₹2 crore in the case of other than SSI borrowers and up to ₹5 crore for SSI borrowers. In respect of loans beyond these limits, banks have been given discretion to choose any method like MPBF method or cash budget method. Even while applying MPBF, the level of current ratio to be maintained has been left to the discretion of the individual bank.

In terms of the guidelines of RBI, the working capital limit is sanctioned to all bor-rowal accounts with fund-based working capital limit of ₹10 crore and above from the banking system wherein funds are to be disbursed as demand loan and cash credit in the ratio of 80:20. The demand loan portion of the working capital is called Working Capital Demand Loan which is repayable in minimum of six installments as per the directions of the RBI. The outer limit of repayment has been left to the discretion of the banks. This was brought in to introduce more discipline among the borrowers availing the working capital finance.

SUMMARY

1. There are two components of working capital—temporary and permanent working capital.
2. Long-term sources may be used for financing the permanent component of working capital, whereas temporary component is to be financed through short-term sources of finance.
3. Current assets may be financed through various sources such as outstanding expenses, provisions, trade credit, short-term bank finance, and Public Deposits.
4. Outstanding expenses constitute a small proportion of current liabilities and its useful-ness as a source of financing current assets is very much limited.
5. Provisions may also be used as a source to finance current assets but usefulness of "provisions" as a source of financing current assets is very much limited.
6. Trade credit accounts for the maximum proportion as a source of financing current assets.
7. The implicit cost of trade credit should be compared with the opportunity cost of cash. If opportunity cost of cash exceeds implicit cost of trade credit, foregoing cash discounts are more advantageous.
8. Bank finance is an important source for financing the current assets of a company.
9. Bank finance may be either direct or indirect. Under direct financing, the bank not only provides the finance but also bears the risk of loss. Cash credit, overdraft, note lending, purchase/discounting of bills come under the category of direct financing.
10. When a bank opens a Letter of Credit in favor of a customer, the bank assumes only he risk of default by the customer and the finance is provided by a third party; this is called indirect financing.

KEY TERMS

- Temporary working capital
- Outstanding expenses
- Trade credit
- Cash credit
- Note lending
- Letter of credit

- Permanent working capital
- Provisions
- Cost of trade credit
- Overdraft
- Bill discounting
- Public deposits

Learning Outcomes

Student would have appreciated how current assets are financed under the recommendation of different working groups.

ACCESS YOURSELF

Concept Review and Critical Thinking Questions

1. Describe the various spontaneous sources of current asset finance.
2. What are the different arrangements of bank financing which can be used for financing current assets?
3. "Kannan Committee recommendations have undone most of the recommendations of Tandon Committee and Chore Committee." Discuss.
4. Discuss the main forms of working capital advances by banks.

STUDENT ACTIVITIES

Prepare a report on the recommendations of various committees on working capital finance. In addition, give a comparative analysis of the recommendations given by various committees.

SUGGESTED READINGS

Gupta, L.C. (1978). *Banking and working capital finance*. Delhi: Macmillan India.
Moyer, R.C. (1980). *Financial management: A contemporary approach*. St. Paul: West Publishing Co.
Report of the Study Group to Frame Guidelines for Follow-up of Bank Credit. (1975). RBI Publication.
Report of the Working Group to Review the System of Cash Credit. (1979). RBI Publication.
Report of the Committee to Review the Working of the Credit Authorisation Scheme. (1983). RBI Publication.
Report of the Working Group on the Money Market. (1987). RBI Publication.

PART V
Long-term Financing

CHAPTER 20

Sources of Long-term Finance

Learning Objective

- To discuss various long-term sources of finance.

> **PRELUDE**
> Long-term finance is a foundational resource for an organization. Such resources set the structure of the organization. It includes resources with fairly long period of maturity such as equity shares (which are perpetual) and term loan and debentures (fix maturity and tenure). This chapter discusses the basic concept of shares and debentures as these two are crucial resources.

Equity Shares (Ordinary shares)

Issue of shares is the main source of long-term finance. Shares are issued by public limited companies. A company divides its capital into units of a definite face value, say of ₹10 each or ₹100 each. Each unit is called a share. Share is a fraction of a whole number. All shares added together will become a whole number. A person holding shares is called a shareholder. Equity shares are those shares which are ordinary in the course of a company's business. They are also called ordinary shares. These shareholders do not enjoy preference regarding payment of dividend and repayment of capital. Equity shareholders are paid dividend out of the profits made by a company in proportion of paid-up capital. The rate of dividend is not fixed. The board of directors decides the quantum of dividend in AGM. Higher the profits, higher dividend is expected; and lower the profits, lower may be the dividend. It is a variable income security. Payment of dividend is not mandatory. They are entitled for dividends after settling the claims of others. Ordinary shares are the permanent source of capital as they do not have a maturity date. In the case of winding up of a company, the equity share capital is refunded only after refunding the preference share capital. Equity shareholders have the right to take part in the management of the company. However, equity shares carry more risk.

Authorized share capital is that maximum amount of capital a company can legally raise from its shareholders. This number is specified in the memorandum of association. It can be changed later, with shareholders' approval and by altering memorandum of association. Authorized share capital may be divided into (i) issued capital is the portion of authorized capital which is offered to shareholders, (ii) subscribed capital represents the amount of issued capital which is duly accepted by shareholders, and (iii) paid-up capital represents the amount of subscribed capital which is paid up by the shareholders. Generally, subscribed capital and paid-up capital may be the same. Paid-up capital is used to calculate the amount of dividend which would be distributable to the shareholders. Shares can be issued at par, discount, and premium subject to guidelines issued by the regulator (Table 20.1).

TABLE 20.1

TATA STEEL SHARE CAPITAL AS ON MARCH 31, 2011

Particulars	Amount in Crore
Authorized 1,750,000,000 ordinary shares of ₹10 each	1,750.00
Issued 960,126,020 ordinary shares of ₹10 each	960.13
Subscribed 959,214,450 ordinary shares of ₹10 each fully paid up A	960.13
Reserve and surplus B	45,807.02
Total shareholders fund A+B	46,767.15

Source: www.tatasteel.com

Features of Equity Shares

1. **Fixed value or nominal value:** Every share has a fixed value or a nominal value. For example, if the price of a share is ₹10, it indicates a fixed value as well as a nominal value.
2. **Distinctive number:** Every share is given a distinct number just like a roll number for the purpose of identification.
3. **Attached rights:** A share gives its owner the right to receive dividend, the right to vote, the right to attend meetings, and the right to inspect the books of accounts. The shareholders have a right to control. The board of directors are elected to approve company policies and strategic decisions, whereas managers appointed by directors run day-to-day functions of the company. The shareholders have the right to appoint directors. Directors are elected at AGM through voting rights. Each equity share carries one voting right. A shareholder may vote in person or by proxy. A proxy gives the designated person a right to vote on behalf of shareholders. The ordinary shareholders have a right to control management of the company through voting rights.
4. **Return on shares:** Every shareholder is entitled to a return on shares. Ordinary shareholders have a residual ownership claim. They have claim on residual income which is left after paying expenses, interest, taxes, and preference share dividend. The income is categorized into two parts: dividend and retained earnings. The dividends are the part of profit which is distributed among shareholders in proportion to their holdings. It represents immediate cash inflow for shareholders.
5. **Transfer of shares:** Equity shares are easily transferable, that is, if a person buys shares of a particular company and he does not want them, he can sell those shares to others in secondary market, thereby transferring the shares in the name of that person.
6. **Benefit of right issue:** When a company makes fresh issue of shares, the equity shareholders are given certain rights in the company. The company has to offer the new shares first to the existing equity shareholders in proportion to their existing shareholding. In case they do not want to take up the shares offered to them, the same may be issued to

others. Thus, equity shareholders get the benefits of the right issue. Such rights are also known as preemptive rights.

7. **Benefit of bonus shares:** Public limited companies may issue bonus shares to their ordinary shareholders out of the reserve and surplus. These shares are issued free of cost in proportion to the number of existing equity shareholding.

8. **Irredeemable:** Equity shares are always irredeemable. This means equity capital is not returnable during the lifetime of a company. Shareholders have residual claim on assets of the company at the time of liquidation. Liquidation happens when a company fails. Out of the proceeds of assets, claims of debt holders and shareholders are satisfied. If any remaining balance is left, it is paid to ordinary shareholders.

9. **Limited liability:** Equity shareholders have limited liability up to their investment in shares. If shares are fully paid up, the shareholder is not required to contribute in cash of financial distress or liquidation. Unlike sole proprietor and partnership firm, they have limited liability. It may be noted that shareholders are not owners of the company, not even part owners.

EXHIBIT NO. 1

CHENNAI: Orchid Chemicals & Pharmaceuticals has proposed to raise long- term funds up to ₹1,000 crore through the issue of equity shares. The company informed stock exchanges after the board met on Wednesday that the funds would be raised from domestic and overseas capital market. The funds that may be raised through a combination offer of securities would be utilised for the redemption of the outstanding foreign currency convertible bonds due in February 2012 and for any other business purposes as may be required. Further, keeping in view the impending issue of shares for raising long term resources, the authorised share capital of the company is proposed to be increased from ₹100 crore to ₹125 crore.

Source: http://articles.economictimes.indiatimes.com/2011-05-18/news/29556170_1_net-profit-equity-ratio-fy10

Test Yourself

1. Define ordinary shares/equity shares.
2. What are the features of equity shares?

Methods of Issuing Equity Shares

An investor can apply offline or online to participate in a primary market to buy equity shares. The following methods are used to float new issue in the primary market:

1. **Initial Public Issue:** When a company issues shares to the public for the first time in order to get listed on the stock exchange, it is known as IPO. The issues are nowadays premium issues and oversubscribed.

2. **Offer for Sale:** When a company gives invitation to the general public by sponsoring an intermediary such as investment bank.

3. **A Follow-on Public Offering (Further Issue):** When an already listed company makes either a fresh issue of securities to the public or an offer for sale to the public, through an offer document.

4. **Rights Issue:** The rights issue involves selling of securities to the existing shareholders in proportion to their current holding. Rights issue is an inexpensive method of floatation of shares.

5. **Private Placement:** A private placement is a sale of securities privately by a company to a selected group of investors. The securities are normally placed, in a private placement, with the institutional investor, mutual funds, or other financial institutions. It is an inexpensive method of selling shares.

Initial Public Offerings Process

1. **Initialization:** In the initialization stage, a company appoints various intermediaries such as lead managers as book runners, bankers to issue, registrar to issue, and share and transfer agent.

2. **Pre-issue:** Issuing company and lead managers prepare draft offer documents, draft for IPO, and submit them to the SEBI for approval.

3. **Prospectus review:** SEBI reviews the draft offer document. If SEBI feels some changes are required, it suggests those changes, or otherwise it is approved. Draft offer document after approval becomes offer prospectus.

4. **Red herring prospectus:** Offer document is sent to SEBI, decision regarding issue date and price band is taken, and offer document is modified with respect to date and time. Now offer document is called red herring prospectus. Printing of red herring prospectus and application form is done.

5. **Bidding for the public issue—Investor:** Public issue open for investors' bidding; filling of application form by the investor; providing bidding information to The Bombay Stock Exchange (BSE)/National Stock Exchange (NSE); sending the checks collected to the registrar by syndicate members; revision of bid by investor, if any; updating stock exchanges with latest data; closing of public issue.

6. **Price fixing—Lead manager:** Lead managers evaluate the final issue price.

7. **Processing IPO applications—Registrar:** All checks and application forms are received by the registrar; applicant data are uploaded into systems; checks are sent for clearance; looking out for all bogus applications; finalizing the pattern for share allotment; preparing "Basis of Allotment"; transferring shares in the demat account of investors; refunding the remaining money through electronic check service (ECS) or checks.

8. **Stock listing—Lead manager:** After the completion of all the above processes, lead managers decide the listing date with stock exchanges followed by final listing of shares on the exchange.

Initial Public Issues Can Be Offered in Two Ways

- **Fixed Price Issue:** Here, shares are issued to public at a fixed price.
- **Book-building Process:** As per SEBI guidelines, "A Process when demand for the securities proposed to be issued by a body corporate is elicited and built up and price for such securities is assessed for the determination of the quantum of such securities to be issued by means of a notice, advertisement, offer document and circular."

The basic difference between book-building and fixed price issue: In case of fixed price, price is known to the investor in advance, whereas under the book-building mechanisms, investors bid for shares and price is determined for allotment of shares (Table 20.2).

TABLE 20.2
DIFFERENCE BETWEEN BOOK BUILDING AND FIXED PRICE ISSUES

Issue Type	Offer Price	Demand	Payment	Reservations
Fixed Price Issues	The price at which the securities are offered and would be allotted is made known in advance to the investors.	Demand for the securities offered is known only after the closure of the issue.	100% advance payment is required to be made by the investors at the time of application.	50% of the shares offered are reserved for applications below ₹1 lakh and the balance for higher amount applications.
Book-building Issues	A 20% price band is offered by the issuer within which investors are allowed to bid.	Demand for the securities offered, and at various prices, is available on a real-time basis on the BSE website during the bidding period.	10% advance payment is required to be made by the Qualified Institutional Bidders (QIBs) along with the application, while other categories of investors have to pay 100% advance along with the application.	50% of shares offered are reserved for QIBS, 35% for small investors, and the balance for all other investors.

Source: www.bseindia.com

Book-building Process

- The issuer company which offers IPO nominates lead merchant banker(s) as "**book runners**." The merchant banker maintains books of securities sold for a new issue.
- The issuer company must state the number of securities to be issued. The issuer company is required to indicate price band or a floor price in the prospectus. **Floor price** is the minimum price at which bids can be made. **Cap** is the highest price at which bid can be made. The spread between the floor and cap band shall not be more than 20%. In other words, cap should not be more than 120% of the floor price.
- The issuer company appoints syndicate members with whom orders are to be placed by the investors.
- The syndicate members input the orders into an "electronic book." This process is called "bidding" and is similar to open auction.
- The book normally remains open for a period of 5 days.
- Bids have to be entered within the specified price band.
- Bids can be revised by the bidders before the book closes.
- On the close of the book-building period, the book runners evaluate the bids on the basis of the demand at various price levels.

- The book runners and the issuer decide the final price at which the securities shall be issued. The determined price can be in the price band or any price above floor. The issue price is known as **cut-off price**.
- Generally, the number of shares is fixed; the issue size gets frozen based on the final price per share.
- Allocation of securities is made to the successful bidders. The rest get refund orders.

Test Yourself

1. What are methods for issue of shares?
2. What is book building? Explain its process.

Preference Shares

Preference share has combined features of equity shares and debenture. It is similar to equity shares because dividends are not deductible for tax purpose and nonpayment of dividend does not force company to insolvency. It is like debenture because (i) rate of dividend is fixed, (ii) they do not have voting right, (iii) they do not share residual income, and (iv) preference shares have claim on assets prior to ordinary equity shareholders. It is, therefore, termed as hybrid security. Preference shares are more flexible and have less burden of the company. The rate of dividend is less and generally less than equity shareholders. The redemption of preference share is also possible. The convertibility feature of preference share makes its more attractive and marketable.

Features of Preference Shares: Preference shares have the following features:

1. **Claim on income and assets:** Preference capital carries preference in payment of dividend and capital at the time of winding up of the company. They have prior claim on the company's assets and residual income in case of liquidation. But their claim is settled once the claim of debenture gets paid off. The preference share is less risky than equity shares. These shareholders cannot participate in extraordinary profits. They generally do not have voting rights.

2. **Fixed dividend:** Preference shares are known as fixed income security. The rate of dividend is fixed and expressed as a percentage of par value/face value of share. Preference share dividend is not tax deductible. The payment of preference share dividend is not a legal obligation. But a company can accumulate past year's unpaid dividend and pay in subsequent years (such are cases of cumulative preference shares). This acts as a protective feature for preference share. Since dividend payment is not a legal obligation for the company, this cumulative feature is necessary to protect the right of preference shareholders.

3. **Redemption:** Preference share can be categorized into redeemable or irredeemable. A redeemable preference share has a specific maturity period, whereas a perpetual or irredeemable share does not have any maturity date. In India, redeemable preference shares can be issued for a maximum of 20 years.

4. **Call feature:** Preference share can be issued with call feature. The call feature allows the company to buyback preference share after a stipulated time period at predetermined price. The call price is higher than par value/issue price. The difference between call price and issue price is known as call premium.

5. **Voting rights:** Preference shareholders normally do not have voting rights. They have contingent or conditional voting rights. In the case of cumulative preference share, if dividend is outstanding for two or more years, or preference share dividend is outstanding for a period of three or more years in preceding six months, a preference shareholder can nominate a member on the board of the company.

6. **Participative feature:** Generally, a preference shareholder does not have the participative right like ordinary shareholders. But in some cases, they could have this right. Due to this, they are entitled for additional profit like ordinary shareholders. Preference shareholder may also participate in residual assets in case of liquidation. In such a case, preference shares are known as participative preference shares.

7. **Convertibility:** A preference share may be convertible or nonconvertible. Nonconvertible shares are those preference shares which cannot be converted into equity shares or debenture. Convertible preference shares are convertible into equity or debenture after a given period of time at a specified price. For example, Andhra Cement converted its preference shares into debenture in the year 1985. To enhance the marketability of preference share, the Government of India introduced cumulative preference shares (Table 20.3).

TABLE 20.3

DIFFERENCE BETWEEN EQUITY SHARES AND PREFERENCE SHARES

Basis of Difference	Equity Shares	Preference Shares
1. Rate of dividend	Rate of dividend is not fixed and depends upon the decision of the board of directors.	Rate of dividend is fixed.
2. Payment of dividend	Dividend on these shares is paid after payment of dividend made to preference shareholders.	Dividend on these shares is paid before payment of dividend is made to the equity shareholders.
3. Refund of share capital on winding up of the company	On winding up of the company, equity shareholders get refund of capital only after preference shareholders have been paid off.	Preference shareholders have a preference over equity shareholders in regard to refund of capital in the case of winding up to the company.
4. Voting rights	Shareholders have voting rights in all matters.	Shareholders can vote only in special circumstances.
5. Redemption	Shares cannot be redeemed during the life of the company.	Shares can be redeemed as per terms of issue.

Source: Author.

Test Yourself

1. Define preference share. Explain what are preferences in preference shares?
2. Distinguish between equity share and preference shares.

Debenture

Whenever a company wants to borrow a large amount of fund for a long fixed period, it can borrow from the general public by issuing loan certificates called debentures. The total amount to be borrowed is divided into units of fixed amount, say of ₹100 each. These units are called debentures. These are offered to the public to subscribe in the same manner as is done in the case of shares. A debenture is issued under the common seal of the company. It is a written acknowledgment of money borrowed. It specifies the terms and conditions, such as rate of interest, time repayment, and security offered. A debenture is a promissory note for raising long-term capital. The firm promises to pay the interest and principal as stipulated. A debenture is a long-term, fixed-income security. Unlike equity shareholders and preference shareholders, debenture holders are lenders of funds for the company. Debentures are issued in different denominations.

Features

1. **Interest rate:** Interest on debenture is fixed and known and expressed as percentage value of par value/face value of debenture. Payment of interest is legally binding on the company. Debenture interest is tax deductible for computing tax liability of the company. Debenture interest is taxable in the hands of debenture holders. Interest charges are fixed charges due to which a company enjoys leverage. Interest charges also help the company in reaping the benefits of tax shield.
2. **Maturity:** Debentures are issued for a specific period. The maturity period generally ranges from 7 to 10 years. After the maturity period, the company is required to redeem the debenture.
3. **Redemption:** Debentures are redeemable. The debentures are redeemed after the maturity period. The debentures are redeemed either by buyback or by sinking fund method. Buyback (call option): The debentures are issued with call options which allow the company to redeem debenture before maturity period at a specified price. Call price is always higher than par value to make debenture more marketable. Sinking fund is a fund created periodically to retire debenture. The *fund* is kept under trustees who are responsible for redeeming debenture either by buy back or by calling them in an acceptable manner. After the maturity period, the company may face a temporary financial crunch. Repayment of huge principal would pose financial risk. In such a case, sinking fund reduces the amount required to redeem the debentures at the time of maturity.
4. **Claims on asset and income:** Debenture holders have a claim on the company's earnings and profit prior to the shareholders. Debenture interest is paid before paying dividends to preference shareholder and equity share holders. Payment of debenture interest is a legal obligation and nonpayment of it can force the company into bankruptcy. In case of liquidation, debenture holders have prior right on the assets of the company. But secured debentures have priority over unsecured debentures. Different types of debentures have hierarchy among themselves as their order of claims on the company's assets.
5. **Yield:** Yield of debenture is related to market price. Yield has two components: current yield and yield to maturity. Current yield is the ratio of annual interest to debenture current market price. Yield to maturity is the internal rate of return. It is the discount rate which equates present value of future interest and principal payments with current market price of debenture.
6. **Debenture trust deed:** It is a legal agreement between the company issuing debenture and the debenture trustee who represents the debenture holders. It is the responsibility of

the trustee to protect the debenture holder's interest by ensuring that the company should fulfill all the contractual obligations. Financial institutions, banks, and insurance companies act as trustees. A debenture trust deed consists of specification of debenture, rights of debenture holders, rights and responsibilities of issuing company, and responsibility of the trustee.

7. **Security:** Debentures can be secured or unsecured. A secured debenture has a right on the company's specific asset. Debenture has equitable mortgage which has a right on present and future immovable assets of the company. If the company defaults in making payment, trust can seize the assets. When debentures do not have any rights on any security, such debentures are known as unsecured debentures. The company finds difficulty in selling unsecured debentures. Secured debentures are considered to be most safe from an investor's point of view. Credit rating agency rates debentures to ensure timely payment of interest and principal. In India, various credit rating agencies, such as CRISIL, Investment Information and Credit Rating Agency of India Limited (ICRA), and CARE, are operating. Exhibit 2 shows nature of rating given by ICRA.

ICRA's Long-term Rating Scale

Long-term rating scale: All bonds, nonconvertible debentures (NCDs), and other debt instruments (excluding public deposits) with original maturity exceeding 1 year.

AAA Instruments with this rating are considered to have the highest degree of safety regarding timely servicing of financial obligations. Such instruments carry lowest credit risk.

AA Instruments with this rating are considered to have high degree of safety regarding timely servicing of financial obligations. Such instruments carry very low credit risk.

A Instruments with this rating are considered to have adequate degree of safety regarding timely servicing of financial obligations. Such instruments carry low credit risk.

BBB Instruments with this rating are considered to have moderate degree of safety regarding timely servicing of financial obligations. Such instruments carry moderate credit risk.

BB Instruments with this rating are considered to have moderate risk of default regarding timely servicing of financial obligations.

B Instruments with this rating are considered to have high risk of default regarding timely servicing of financial obligations.

C Instruments with this rating are considered to have very high risk of default regarding timely servicing of financial obligations.

D Instruments with this rating are in default or are expected to be in default soon.

Types of Debenture

The different types of debentures are:

- **Registered Debentures:** These are debentures which are registered in the register of the company. The names, addresses, and particulars of holdings of debenture holders are entered in a register kept by the company. Such debentures are treated as non-negotiable instruments and interest on such debentures is payable only to registered holders of debentures. Registered debentures are also called as debentures payable to registered holders.

- **Bearer Debentures:** These are debentures which are not registered in the register of the company. Bearer debentures are like a bearer check. They are payable to the bearer and are deemed to be negotiable instruments. They are transferable by mere delivery. No formality of executing a transfer deed is necessary. When bearer documents are transferred, stamp duty need not be paid. A person transferring a bearer debenture need not give any notice to the company to this effect. The transferee who acquires such a debenture in due course bona fide and for available consideration gets good title not withstanding any defect in the title of the transferor. Interest coupons are attached to each debenture and are payable to the bearer.
- **Secured Debentures:** These are debentures which are secured against the assets of the company which means if the company is closing down its business, the assets will be sold and the debenture holders will be paid their money. The charge or the mortgage may be fixed or floating and they may be fixed mortgage debentures or floating mortgage depending upon the nature of charge under the category of secured debentures. In case of fixed charge, the charge is created on a particular asset such as plant and machinery. These assets can be utilized for payment in case of default. In case of floating charge, the charge is created on the general assets of the company.

The assets which are available with the company at present as well as the assets in future are charged for the purpose. A mortgage deed is executed by the company. The deed includes the term of repayment, rate of interest, nature and value of security, dates of payment of interest, and right of debenture holders in case of default in payment by the company. The deed may give a right to the debenture holder to nominate a director as one of the board of directors. If the company fails to pay the principal amount and the interest thereon, they have the right to recover the same from the assets mortgaged.

- **Unsecured Debentures:** These are debentures which are not secured against the assets of the company which means when the company is closing down its business, the assets will not be sold to pay off the debenture holders. These debentures do not create any charge on the assets of the company. There is no security for repayment of principal amount and payment of interest. The only security available to such debenture holders is the general solvency of the company. Therefore, the position of these debenture holders at the time of winding up of the company will be like that of unsecured debentures. That is, they are considered the ordinary creditors of the company.
- **Convertible Debentures:** These are debentures which can be converted into equity shares. These debentures have an option to convert them into equity or preference shares at the stated rate of exchange after a certain period. If the holders exercise the right of conversion, they cease to be the lenders to the company and become the members. Thus, convertible debentures may be referred as debentures which are convertible into shares at the option of the holders after a specified period. The rate of exchange of debentures into shares is also decided at the time of issue of debentures. Interest is paid on such debentures until their conversion. Prior approval of the shareholders is necessary for the issue of convertible debentures. It also requires sanction by the central government.
- **NCD:** These are debentures which cannot be converted either into equity shares or into preference shares. They may be secured or unsecured. Non-convertible debentures are normally redeemed on maturity period which may be 10 or 20 years.
- **Redeemable Debentures:** These debentures are issued by the company for a specific period only. On the expiry of that period, debenture capital is redeemed or paid back. Generally, the company creates a special reserve account known as "Debenture Redemption Reserve Fund/Sinking Fund" for the redemption of such debentures. The company makes

the payment of interest regularly. Under Section 121 of the Indian Companies Act, 1956, redeemed debentures can be re-issued.

- **Irredeemable Debentures:** These debentures are issued for an indefinite period which are also known as perpetual debentures. The debenture capital is repaid either at the option of the company by giving prior notice to that effect or at the winding up of the company. The interest is regularly paid on these debentures. The principal amount is repayable only at the time of winding up of the company. However, the company may decide to repay the principal amount during its lifetime.

Term Loans

Fixed-term business loan with a maturity of more than 1 year provide an organization with working capital to acquire assets or inventory, or to finance plant and equipment generating cash flow. The term loan is the most common form of intermediate-term financing arranged by commercial banks, and there is wide diversity in how it is structured. Maturities range from 1 year to 15 years, although most term loans are made for 1- to 5-years period. Term loans are paid back from profits of the business, according to a fixed amortization schedule. Term loans may be secured or unsecured, and carry a rate based on the lender's cost of funds. Loan interest normally is payable monthly, quarterly, semiannually, or annually.

Most business loans contain both affirmative and restrictive covenants that impose certain conditions on the borrower that permit acceleration of the maturity if the loan conditions are violated. The lender may, for example, restrict cash dividends paid and loans taken out by corporate officers, and usually will require the borrower to maintain the business in good order, keep adequate insurance, and file quarterly financial statements with the bank. Larger borrowings often are financed by several banks through a syndication arrangement.

Features of Term Loans

1. **Maturity:** The maturity period of term loans is typically longer. In the case of financial institutions, loan ranges from 6 to 10 years in comparison to 3–5 years of bank advances. However, they are rescheduled to enable corporate borrowers tide over temporary financial exigencies. In some cases, a 2-year grace period (moratorium) is also allowed.

2. **Negotiated:** The term loans are negotiated loans between the borrowers and the lenders. They are akin to private placement of debentures in contrast to their public offering to investors. The main benefits of private placement are ease of negotiation and low cost of raising loan. Loan helps the firm in saving underwriting commission and other flotation costs.

3. **Security:** Term loans typically represent secured borrowings. Usually, assets, which are financed with the proceeds of the term loan, provide the prime security. Other assets of the firm may serve as collateral security. All loans provided by financial institutions, along with interest, liquidated damages, commitment charges, expenses, etc., are secured by way of:

   (a) First equitable mortgage of all immovable properties of the borrower, both present and future, for the entire institutional loan including commitment charges, interest, liquidated damages, and so on; and

   (b) Hypothecation of all movable properties of the borrower, both present and future, subject to prior charges in favor of commercial banks for obtaining working capital finance/advance.

4. **Interest Payment and Principal Repayment:** The interest on term loans is a definite obligation that is payable irrespective of the financial situation of the firm. To the general category of borrowers, financial institutions charge an interest rate that is related to the credit risk of the proposal, subject usually to a certain minimum prime lending rate (PLR)/floor rate. Financial institutions impose a penalty for defaults. In the case of default of payment of installments of principal and/or interest, the borrower is liable to pay by way of liquidated damages additional interest calculated at the rate of 2% per annum for the period of default on the amount of principal and/or interest in default.

In addition to interest, lending institutions levy a commitment fee on the unutilized loan amount. The principal amount of a term loan is generally repayable over a period of 6–10 years after the initial grace period of 1–2 years. Typically, term loans provided by financial institutions are repayable in equal semiannual installments, whereas term loans granted by commercial banks are repayable in equal quarterly installments.

With this type of loan amortization pattern, the total servicing burden declines over time, the interest burden also declines, and principal repayment remains constant. In other words, the common practice in India to amortized loan is repayment of principal in equal installments (semiannual/annual) and payment of interest on the unpaid/outstanding loans.

5. **Loan Covenants:** To protect the surety of their loans, banks also require covenants in loan agreements. Loan covenants are of two primary types. Affirmative covenants describe actions that a firm agrees to take during the term of the loan. These include such activities as providing financial statements and cash budgets, carrying insurance on assets and against insurable business risks, and maintaining minimum levels of net working capital. Negative covenants describe actions that a firm agrees not to take during the term of the loan. These may include agreements not to merge with other firms, not to pledge assets as security to other lenders, or not to make or guarantee loans to other firms. Another common restriction, especially with closely held companies, is a limit on officers' compensation. The covenants in private lending agreements often modify generally accepted accounting principles. For example, off-the- balance-sheet debt may be included in calculating the debt-to-equity ratio.

Test Yourself

1. Define debenture. Explain the various types of debentures.
2. What is the significance of debenture ratings?

Mortgage Loan

The word *mortgage* is a term from the French law meaning "dead pledge," apparently meaning that the pledge ends (dies) either when the obligation is fulfilled or the property is taken through. A **mortgage loan** is a loan secured by real property through the use of a mortgage note which evidences the existence of the loan and the encumbrance of that realty through the granting of a mortgage which secures the loan.

A home buyer or builder can obtain financing (a loan) either to purchase or to secure against the property from a financial institution, such as a bank, either directly or indirectly through intermediaries. Features of mortgage loans such as the size of the loan, maturity of the loan, interest rate, method of paying off the loan, and other characteristics can vary considerably. The scheme is for people engaged in trade, commerce, and business and also for professionals and self-employed, proprietary firms, partnership firms, companies, NRIs, and individuals with high net worth including salaried people, agriculturists, and staff members. This scheme provides loan/overdraft facility against mortgage of property at low rate of interest. The product provides an opportunity to the customers to borrow against a fixed asset (mortgage of property) at a short notice without much paperwork/attendant hassles.

Mortgage loan is available for the following purposes:

- To meet the credit needs of trade, commercial activity, other general business, profession, and also for their bona fide requirements.
- To meet marriage or medical or educational expenses of the family members including near relatives.
- To undertake repairs/renovation/extension to the residence/commercial property.
- Purchase of consumer durables.
- To purchase/construct house/flat, purchase of plot.
- To purchase 2-/4-wheeler vehicles.
- For going on pilgrimage/tours/excursions, etc.
- Repayment of existing loans from other banks/FIs.

Reverse Mortgage[1]

Old age without proper financial support can be a very bad experience. The rising cost of living, health care, and other amenities compound the problem significantly. No regular incomes, a dwindling capacity to work and earn livelihood at this age can make life miserable. A constant inflow of income, without any work would be an ideal solution, which can put an end to all such sufferings. The reverse mortgage scheme offered by some of the leading banks in India could bring the required answers to the suffering senior citizens. Most of the people in the senior age groups, either by inheritance or by virtue of building assets, have properties in their names, but they are not able to convert them into instant and regular income streams due to their illiquid nature. The Union Budget 2007–2008 had a great proposal which introduced the "Reverse Mortgage" scheme.

The concept is simple, a senior citizen who holds a house or property, but lacks a regular source of income can mortgage his property with a bank or housing finance company (HFC), and the bank or HFC pays the person a regular payment. The good thing is that the person who "reverse mortgages" his property can stay in the house for his whole life and continue to receive the much-needed regular payments. So, effectively the property now pays for the owner that you can continue to stay at the same place and also get paid for it. Where is the catch? In case of reverse mortgage, the bank will have the right to sell off the property after the incumbent passes away or leaves the place to recover the loan. It passes on any extra amount to the legal heirs.

The whole idea is entirely opposite to the regular mortgage process where a person pays the bank for a mortgaged property. Hence, it is called reverse mortgage. This concept is particularly popular in the West.

The draft guidelines of reverse mortgage in India prepared by RBI have the following salient features:

- Any house owner over 60 years of age is eligible for a reverse mortgage.

---

[1] http://www.rupeetimes.com/article/home_loans/reverse_mortgage_in_india_your_property_pays_you_a_regular_income_1129.html

- The maximum loan is up to 60% of the value of residential property.
- The maximum period of property mortgage is 15 years with a bank or HFC.
- The borrower can opt for a monthly, quarterly, annual, or lump-sum payments at any point, as per his discretion.
- The revaluation of the property has to be undertaken by the bank or HFC once every 5 years.
- The amount received through reverse mortgage is considered as loan and not income; hence, the same will not attract any tax liability.
- Reverse mortgage rates can be fixed or floating and hence will vary according to market conditions depending on the interest rate regime chosen by the borrower.

The lender will recover the loan along with the accumulated interest by selling the house after the death of the borrower or earlier, if the borrower leaves the mortgaged residential property permanently. Any excess amount will be remitted back to the borrower or his heirs. Reverse mortgage, thus, is very beneficial for senior citizens who want a regular income to meet their everyday needs, without leaving their houses.

Private Investment in Public Entity (PIPE)

A private investment firm's mutual fund or other qualified investors purchase the stock in a company at a discount to the current market value per share for the purpose of raising capital. There are two main types of PIPEs: traditional and structured. A traditional PIPE is one in which stock, either common or preferred, is issued at a set price to raise capital for the issuer. A structured PIPE, on the other hand, issues convertible debt. PIPE investments take a sizable position in publicly traded companies whose valuations have dropped since they went public and now are seeking new sources of cash infusion. Private investors want deals with a longer investment period and companies established business models that have recently discovered a new market. Basically, they are looking for a huge return on their investment in the shortest time possible. This feat is only attainable by a select number of businesses and other companies with less-than-stellar growth potential need to look elsewhere.

Private investors would like to get at least a 30% return on their investment, and if a business model cannot seem to guarantee that, then they typically will not lend the money. They consider many factors when making their final decisions including what your product or service can offer the marketplace, and how unique your product or service offering is. Another factor considered is the competition.

PIPE DEALS

New Delhi|Mumbai: Private equity (PE) funds, which mostly invest in unlisted companies, are buying more shares in listed firms trading at attractive prices on the bourses. The downturn in stock markets in the past few months has brought down valuations of companies throwing up significant investment opportunities for PE firms to invest in listed enterprises, termed as PIPE deals.

"India's equity markets have corrected dramatically," said Rob Chandra, managing partner at Bessemer Venture Partners that recently raised a $1.6 billion fund, of which a quarter is dedicated for the Indian market The fund which has been investing in India for 7 years now has a listed portfolio that is currently around 30% of its total activity.

This includes companies such as Shriram EPC and Orient Green Power. As per data available with Venture Intelligence, a research firm that tracks PE investments and mergers and acquisitions in India, the period between January and June saw 27 PIPE deals worth $1.05 billion (about ₹4,739 crore) vis-à-vis 16 deals amounting to $0.27 billion (about ₹1,219 crore) in the same period last year.

Private equity funds are opting for PIPE (private investment in public equity) deals in mostly semi-large and mid-cap companies across sectors.

"We find valuations in public markets to be far more reasonable than private equity markets, although it tends to vary by sector and by year depending on the amount of capital chasing a few sectors which are 'in favor' at any given point," said K.P. Balaraj, MD at West Bridge Capital Partners, who is part of a team of PE managers raising a new fund for investments in public enterprises that is due to launch by the end of this year.

Range-bound equities provide an easy turf for PE funds to pick stocks from the secondary market. PE fund managers expect the trend to continue if markets hold on to current levels for some more time.

"It is only in India where you will find so many small-scale companies in the listed space. These companies are not tracked by most analysts. If one digs a bit deeper, there are many good companies in the listed space where PE funds can make investments," said Raja Kumar, Founder, Ascent Capital. "PIPE valuations or secondary market valuations are much more attractive than private space valuations currently," he added.

In PIPE deals, a PE fund purchases a certain percentage of the shareholding in a listed company at market price or at a discount to the market value. In some of the large ticket transactions sealed in the listed space this year, Apax Partners invested $375 million iGATE in January, while Kolkata-based non-banking finance company Magma Fincorp raised close to $100 million from KKR and IFC. ChrysCapital, India's homegrown private equity biggie, picked up around 10 per cent stake in Pune-based IT consulting firm KPIT Cummins Infosystems Limited for over $25 million in February.

Source: http://articles.economictimes.indiatimes.com/2011-07-09/news/29755818_1_pefund-pipe-deals-private-equity

Loan against Shares (Securities)

Loan against shares is available in the form of an overdraft facility against the pledge of financial securities such as shares/units/bonds. These shares can be owned by you (the borrower) or your immediate relatives (third-party pledgers). The loan limit depends on the valuation of the security, applicable margin, your ability to service and repay the loan, and other conditions as applicable from time to time. The shares held by you have to be in the physical form or in the demat form.

Features/Advantages

- Finance against shares enables instant liquidity against shares without selling them.
- It takes care of all your investment as well as personal needs, meets contingencies, subscribing to primary issues, rights issues.
- Best for interim (short-term) funding.
- Loan amount ranges from ₹1 lakh to ₹10 lakhs (for physical) and up to ₹20 lakhs (for demat).
- For demat, usually 65% of the scrip pledged is available as overdraft and 50% if shares are physical.
- Generally, physical shares are accepted in market lots only.
- There is a minimum and maximum number of scrip which are accepted by banks. It ranges from 1 to 20, although for few banks there is no maximum limit.

Overdraft Facility against Pledge of

- Equity shares—Demat shares up to 50% of the value.
- Mutual fund units—Mutual funds up to 50% of net asset value (NAV).
- Gold Exchange Traded Funds (ETFs).
- National Bank for Agriculture and Rural Development's (NABARD) Bhavishya Nirman Bonds.
- RBI Bonds (8% Savings Bonds 2003 (Taxable)).
- Life insurance policies issued by LIC and select private insurance companies.
- National Savings Certificate (NSC).
- Kisan Vikas Patra (KVP).
- Gold Deposit Certificates (GDCs).
- NCDs.

Test Yourself

1. What is reverse mortgage loan?
2. Explain private placement in PE.
3. Discuss mortgage loan and loan against security.

SUMMARY

1. Equity shares, preference shares, debentures, and term loans are important long-term sources of funds.
2. Equity shares are those shares which are ordinary in the course of a company's business. They are also called ordinary shares. These shareholders do not enjoy preference regarding payment of dividend and repayment of capital. Equity shareholders are paid dividend out of the profits made by a company.
3. Equity shareholders have the right to take part in the management of the company and elect board of directors. However, equity shares also carry more risk.
4. Preference share has combined features of equity shares and debenture. It is similar to equity shares because dividends are not deductible for tax purpose and nonpayment of dividend does not force the company to insolvency. It is like debenture because (1) rate of dividend is fixed, (2) they do not have voting right, (3) they do not share residual income, and (4) preference shares have a claim on assets prior to ordinary equity shareholders. It is therefore termed as hybrid security.
5. A debenture is a promissory note for raising long-term capital. The firm promises to interest and principals stipulated. A debenture is a long-term, fixed-income security. Unlike equity shareholders and preference shareholders, debenture holders are lenders of funds for a company. Debentures are issued in different denominations.
6. Fixed-term business loan with a maturity of more than one year provides an organization with working capital to acquire assets or inventory, or to finance plant and equipment generating cash flow. The term loan is the most common form of intermediate-term financing arranged by commercial banks.

KEY TERMS

- Bond
- Convertible debenture
- Current yield
- Dividend
- Hybrid security
- Initial public offering
- Mortgage
- Preference shares
- Residual earnings
- Sinking fund
- Underwriting

- Book building
- Covenants
- Debenture
- Equity shares
- Hypothecation
- Irredeemable
- Preemptive rights
- Private placement
- Reverse mortgage
- Term loan
- Yield to maturity

Learning Outcome

Students would have experienced the concept of long-term sources such as shares and debentures in detail.

ASSESS YOURSELF

Concept Review and Critical Thinking Questions

1. What is equity share? What is the process of issuing shares to the shareholders in the primary market?
2. Differentiate between book building and fixed price issue.
3. Why is preference share known as hybrid security? Justify.
4. What are the types of debentures?

STUDENT ACTIVITY

Student should visit yearbook of SEBI 2015 and observe trends in resources mobilization from primary market.

Appendix I: Guidelines for Issuing Shares and Debentures

(a) Shares

IPO

IPO is a process through which an unlisted company can be listed on the stock exchange by offering its securities to the public in the primary market. The object of an IPO may be related to the expansion of existing activities of the company or setting up of new projects or any other object as may be specified by the company in its offer document or just to get its existing equity shares listed by diluting the stake of existing equity shareholders through offer for sale.

New Listing

New Listing is a process through which a company which is already listed on other stock exchange(s) approaches the exchange for listing of its equity shares. The companies fulfilling the eligibility criteria prescribed by the exchange from time to time are listed on the exchange.
Qualifications for listing IPOs are:

(i) Paid-up Capital

The paid-up equity capital of the applicant shall not be less than ₹10 crore (for this purpose, the post-issue paid-up equity capital for which listing is sought shall be taken into account) and the capitalization of the applicant's equity shall not be less than ₹25 crore (for this purpose, capitalization will be the product of the issue price and the post-issue number of equity shares). In respect of the requirement of paid-up capital and market capitalization, the issuers shall be required to include, in the disclaimer clause of the exchange required to put in the offer document, that in the event of the market capitalization (product of issue price and the post-issue number of shares) requirement of the exchange not being met, the securities would not be listed on the exchange.

Source: http://sebi.gov.in

(ii) Conditions Precedent to Listing

The issuer shall have adhered to conditions precedent to listing as emerging from inter alia from Securities Contracts (Regulations) Act 1956, Companies Act 1956, Securities and exchange Board of India Act 1992, any rules and/or regulations framed under foregoing statutes, as also any circular, clarifications, guidelines issued by the appropriate authority under foregoing statutes.

(iii) At least 3-years' track record of either:

- the applicant seeking listing,
- the promoters/promoting company, incorporated in or outside India, or
- partnership firm and subsequently converted into a company (not in existence as a company for 3 years) and approaches the exchange for listing. The company subsequently

formed would be considered for listing only on fulfillment of conditions stipulated by SEBI in this regard.

For this purpose, the applicant or the promoting company shall submit annual reports of three preceding financial years to NSE and also provide a certificate to the exchange in respect of the following:

- The company has not been referred to the Board for Industrial and Financial Reconstruction (BIFR).
- The net worth of the company has not been wiped out by the accumulated losses resulting in a negative net worth.
- The company has not received any winding up petition admitted by a court.

Promoters means one or more persons with minimum 3 years of experience in the same line of business and holding at least 20% of the post-issue equity share capital individually or severally.

(iv) The applicant desirous of listing its securities should satisfy the exchange on the following:

- No disciplinary action by other stock exchanges and regulatory authorities in the past 3 years.
  There shall be no material regulatory or disciplinary action by a stock exchange or regulatory authority in the past 3 years against the applicant company. In respect of promoters/promoting company(ies), group companies, companies promoted by the promoters/promoting company(ies) of the applicant company, there shall be no material regulatory or disciplinary action by a stock exchange or regulatory authority in the past 1 year.
- Redressal Mechanism of Investor Grievance
  The points of consideration are:
  1. The applicant, promoters/promoting company(ies), group companies, companies promoted by the promoters/promoting company(ies) track record in redressal of the investor's grievances.
  2. The applicant's arrangements envisaged are in place for servicing its investor.
  3. The applicant, promoters/promoting company(ies), group companies, companies promoted by the promoters/promoting company(ies) general approach and philosophy to the issue of investor service and protection.
  4. Defaults in respect of payment of interest and/or principal to the debenture/bond/fixed deposit holders by the applicant, promoters/promoting company(ies), group companies, companies promoted by the promoters/promoting company(ies) shall also be considered while evaluating a company's application for listing. The auditor's certificate shall also be obtained in this regard. In the case of defaults in such payments, the securities of the applicant company may not be listed until such time it has cleared all pending obligations relating to the payment of interest and/or principal.
- **Distribution of Shareholding**
  The applicant's/promoting company(ies) shareholding pattern on March 31 of the last three calendar years separately showing promoters and other groups' shareholding pattern should be as per the regulatory requirements.

- **Details of Litigation**

  The applicant, promoters/promoting company(ies), group companies, companies promoted by the promoters/promoting company(ies) litigation record, the nature of litigation, status of litigation during the preceding 3-years' period need to be clarified to the exchange.

- **Track Record of Director(s) of the Company**

  In respect of the track record of the directors, relevant disclosures may be insisted upon in the offer document regarding the status of criminal cases filed or nature of the investigation being undertaken with regard to alleged commission of any offence by any of its directors and its effect on the business of the company, where all or any of the directors of issuer have or has been charge-sheeted with serious crimes such as murder, rape, forgery, and economic offences.

Note:

(a) In the case a company approaches the exchange for listing within six months of an IPO, the securities may be considered as eligible for listing if they were otherwise eligible for listing at the time of the IPO. If the company approaches the exchange for listing after six months of an IPO, the norms for existing listed companies may be applied and market capitalization will be computed on the basis of the period from the IPO to the time of listing.

An issuer has to take various steps prior to making an application for listing its securities on the NSE. These steps are essential to ensure the compliance of certain requirements by the issuer before listing its securities on the NSE. The various steps to be taken include:

1. **Submission of Memorandum and Articles of Association:** Rule 19(2)(a) of the Securities Contracts (Regulation) Rules, 1957, requires that the Articles of Association of the issuer wanting to list its securities must contain provisions as given hereunder.

   The Articles of Association of an issuer shall contain the following provisions:

   (a) that there shall be no forfeiture of unclaimed dividends before the claim becomes barred by law;

   (b) that a common form of transfer shall be used;

   (c) that fully paid shares shall be free from all lien and that in the case of partly paid shares, the issuer's lien shall be restricted to money called or payable at a fixed time in respect of such shares;

   (d) that registration of transfer shall not be refused on the ground of the transferor being either alone or jointly with any other person or persons indebted to the issuer on any account whatsoever;

   (e) that any amount paid up in advance of calls on any share may carry interest but shall not in respect thereof confer a right to dividend or to participate in profits;

   (f) that option or right to call of shares shall not be given to any person except with the sanction of the issuer in general meetings; and

   (g) permission for subdivision/consolidation of share certificate.

Note: The relevant authority may take exception to any provision contained in the Articles of Association of an issuer which may be deemed undesirable or unreasonable in the case of a public company and may require inclusion of specific provisions deemed to be desirable and necessary. If the issuer's Articles of Association is not in conformity with the provisions as stated above, the issuer has to make amendments to the Articles of Association. However, the securities of an issuer may be admitted for listing on the NSE on an undertaking by the issuer that the amendments necessary in the Articles of Association to bring Articles of Association in conformity with Rule 19(2)(a) of the Securities Contract (Regulation) Rules 1957 shall be made in the next AGM meeting and in the meantime the issuer shall act strictly in accordance with prevalent provisions of Securities Contract (Regulation) Act 1957 and other statutes.

It is to be noted that any provision in the Articles of Association which is not in tune with sound corporate practice has to be removed by amending the Articles of Association.

2. **Approval of Draft Prospectus:** The issuer shall file the draft prospectus and application forms with NSE. The draft prospectus should have been prepared in accordance with the statutes, notifications, circulars, guidelines, etc., governing preparation and issue of prospectus prevailing at the relevant time. The issuers may particularly bear in mind the provisions of Companies Act, Securities Contracts (Regulation) Act, the SEBI Act, and the relevant subordinate legislations thereto. NSE will peruse the draft prospectus only from the point of view of checking whether the draft prospectus is in accordance with the listing requirements, and therefore any approval given by NSE in respect of the draft prospectus should not be construed as approval under any laws, rules, notifications, circulars, guidelines, etc. The issuer should also submit the SEBI acknowledgment card or letter indicating observations on draft prospectus or letter of offer by SEBI.

3. **Submission of Application**

4. **The Listing Fee Applicable is as Follows:**

Particulars	Amount (₹)
Initial listing fees	50,000
Annual listing fees (based on paid-up share, bond, and/or debenture capital) up to ₹5 crore	18,000
Above ₹5 crore and up to ₹10 crore	31,500
Above ₹10 crore and up to ₹20 crore	57,500
Above ₹20 crore and up to ₹30 crore	90,000
Above ₹30 crore and up to ₹40 crore	100,000
Above ₹40 crore and up to ₹50 crore	105,000
Above ₹50 crore and up to ₹100 crore	175,000
Above ₹100 crore and up to ₹150 crore	200,000
Above ₹150 crore and up to ₹200 crore	240,000
Above ₹200 crore and up to ₹250 crore	275,000
Above ₹250 crore and up to ₹300 crore	310,000
Above ₹300 crore and up to ₹350 crore	340,000
Above ₹350 crore and up to ₹400 crore	375,000
Above ₹400 crore and up to ₹450 crore	435,000

- Companies which have a paid-up share, bond and/or debenture and/or debt capital, etc., of more than ₹500 crore will have to pay a minimum fees of ₹500,000 and an additional listing fees of ₹3,400 for every increase of ₹5 crore or part thereof in the paid-up share, bond and/ debenture and/or debt capital, etc.

- Companies which have a paid-up share, bond and/or debenture and/or debt capital, etc., of more than ₹1,000 crore will have to a pay minimum fees of ₹850,000 and an additional listing fees of ₹3,700 for every increase of ₹5 crore or part thereof in the paid-up share, bond and/or debenture and/or debt capital, etc.
- The listing fee depends on the paid-up share capital of the company.
- Please draw your checks/demand drafts favoring **NSE of India Limited** payable at Mumbai.

Listing Conditions and Requirements

- All issuers whose securities are listed on the NSE shall comply with the listing conditions and requirements contained in the Listing Agreement Form appearing in Appendix F to this Regulation or such other conditions and requirements as the relevant authority may from time to time prescribe in addition thereto or in modification or substitution thereof.

(b) Debentures

Eligibility Criteria

The security proposed for listing on the Wholesale Debt Market (WDM) segment of NSE should comply with the requirements as indicated hereunder:

Issuer	Eligibility Criteria for Listing	
	Public Issue	**Private Placement**
Corporate (public limited companies and private limited companies)	Paid-up capital of ₹10 crore	
	or	
	Market capitalization of ₹25 crore	
	(In the case of unlisted companies net worth is more than ₹25 crore)	
	Credit rating	
Public sector undertaking, statutory corporation established/constituted under Special Act of Parliament/ State Legislature, local bodies/ authorities	Credit rating	
Mutual funds:	Qualifies for listing under SEBI's regulations	
Units of any SEBI-registered mutual fund/scheme:		
• Investment objective to invest predominantly in debt or		
• Scheme is traded in secondary market as debt instrument		

Issuer	Eligibility Criteria for Listing	
	Public Issue	**Private Placement**
Infrastructure companies	Qualifies for listing under the respective acts, rules, or regulations under which the securities are issued	
• Tax exemption and recognition as infrastructure company under related statutes/regulations	Credit rating	
Financial Institutions u/s. 4A of Companies Act, 1956 including industrial development corporations	Qualifies for listing under the respective acts, rules, or regulations under which the securities are issued	Credit rating
Banks	Scheduled banks	Scheduled banks
	Net worth of ₹50 crore or above	Net worth of ₹50 crore or above
	Qualifies for listing under the respective acts, rules, or regulations under which the securities are issued	Credit rating

An issuer shall ensure compliance with SEBI circulars/guidelines and any other law, guidelines/directions of the central government, other statutory or local authority issued on regulating the listing of debt instruments from time to time.

Procedure and Conditions for Listing

- All listings are subject to compliance with bylaws, rules, and other requirements framed by the exchange from time to time in addition to the SEBI and other statutory requirements.
- The issuer of security proposed for listing has to forward an application in the format prescribed in Annexure I of this booklet.
- Every issuer, depending on the category and type of security has to submit along with application such supporting documents/information as specified and as prescribed by the exchange from time to time.
- On getting an in-principle consent of the exchange, the issuer has to enter into a listing agreement in the prescribed format under its common seal.
- Upon listing, the issuer has to comply with all requirements of law, any guidelines/directions of the central government, other statutory or local authority.
- The issuer shall also comply with the post-listing compliance as laid out in the listing agreement and shall also comply with the rules, bylaws, regulations, and any other guidelines of the exchange as amended from time to time.
- Listing on WDM segment does not imply a listing on Capital Market (CM) segment also or vice versa.
- If the equity shares of an issuer are listed on other stock exchanges but not listed on CM segment of the exchange, though eligible, then the debt securities of the said issuer will not be permitted to be listed on the WDM segment.

- The exchange reserves the right to change any of the requirements indicated in this book-let/document without prior notice.

The Listing Fee Depends on the Issue Size:

Particulars	Amount (₹)
Initial listing fees	7,500
Annual listing fees issue size:	
Of ₹1 crore	2,100
Above ₹1 crore and up to ₹5 crore	4,200
Above ₹5 crore and up to ₹10 crore	7,000
Above ₹10 crore and up to ₹20 crore	14,000
Above ₹20 crore and up to ₹50 crore	21,000
Above ₹50 crore	35,000

- Issuers who have applied for listing of issue size more than ₹50 crore would be charged an additional listing fees of ₹700 for every increase of ₹5 crore or part thereof in the issue size (in ₹) subject to a maximum of ₹50,000.
- Annual listing fee payable by an issuer is limited to a maximum of ₹7.50 lakhs.

Listing Conditions and Requirements

- All issuers whose securities are listed on the NSE shall comply with the listing conditions and requirements contained in the Listing Agreement Form appearing in Appendix F to this Regulation or such other conditions and requirements as the relevant authority may from time to time prescribe in addition thereto or in modification or substitution thereof.

RESOURCES MOBILIZED FROM THE PRIMARY MARKET

Year	Total		Category-wise				Instrument-wise							
			Public		Rights		Equities				CCPS		Bonds (₹ in crore)	
							At Par		At Premium					
	No.	Amt	No.	Amt	No.	Amt	No.	Amt	No.	Amt	No.	Amt	No.	Amt
1	2	3	4	5	6	7	8	9	10	11	12	13	14	15
2010-2011	91	67,609	68	58,105	23	9,503	2	50	78	57,617	1	490	10	9,451
2011-2012	71	48,468	55	46,093	16	2,375	4	104	47	12,753	0	0	20	35,611
2012-2013	69	32,455	53	23,510	16	8,945	4	571	45	14,902	0	0	20	16,982
2013-2014	90	55,652	75	51,075	15	4,576	19	824	36	12,445	0	0	35	42,383
Apr. 14 to Dec. 14	63	11,545	51	8,732	12	2,813	6	42	37	3,191	1	1,000	19	7,312

Source: SEBI Year Book 2015.

CHAPTER 21

Lease and Hire Purchase

Learning Objectives

- To understand the meaning of leasing.
- To elucidate the role and importance of lease financing in the economic development of a country.
- To distinguish between the various types of leases.
- To describe the meaning of hire purchase.
- To distinguish between leasing and hire purchase.

PRELUDE

Mercedes Benz starts car-leasing business in India

German luxury car maker Mercedes Benz on Tuesday started car-renting business in India with the launch of Star Lease that will make available its complete range of cars for hire.

According to the new scheme, customers would have the option of leasing a Mercedes car on a monthly rental for a period ranging between 12 and 36 months.

Commenting on the development, Mercedes Benz India's Director, Sales and Marketing, Debashis Mitra said, "Consumers shall now have an option to drive away a Mercedes without any initial investment and just pay affordable rentals which shall cover all insurance and maintenance costs for three years."

The customers who lease a car would also have an option to buy the car after three years, he added.

The lease would be provided through Daimler Financial Services India, a subsidiary of Daimler Financial Services AG that was launched in July 2011, under the Mercedes Benz Financial branding.

The company would offer the Star Lease from its dealerships in Delhi, Mumbai, Pune, Bangalore, and Chennai.

Leasing is the grant of use of a vehicle where the customer pays for only what he uses. Under a leasing contract the customer can use a vehicle over a period of time for a fixed monthly lease rate.

"The Indian consumer's appetite for luxury vehicles has been voracious and we foresee this growing in the future," Daimler Financial Services India's Managing Director, Sidhartha Nair, said.

Source: PTI, October 11, 2011.

Concept of Lease Financing

Lease financing denotes procurement of assets through lease. Leasing has developed as a full-size industry in the USA and UK and spread to other countries during the present century. In India, the concept was pioneered in 1973 when the First Leasing Company was set up in Madras and the 1980s has seen a rapid growth of this business. Lease as a concept involves a contract whereby the ownership, financing, and risk taking of any equipment or asset are separated and shared by two or more parties. Thus, the lessor may finance and the lessee may accept the risk through the use of it while a third party may own it. Alternatively, the lessor may finance and own it while the lessee enjoys the use of it and bears the risk. There are various combinations in which the above characteristics are shared by the lessor and the lessee.

Meaning of Lease Financing

A lease transaction is a commercial arrangement whereby an equipment owner or manufacturer conveys to the equipment user the right to use the equipment in return for a rental. In other words, lease is a contract between the owner of an asset (the lessor) and its user (the lessee) for the right to use the asset during a specified period in return for a mutually agreed periodic payment (the lease rentals). The important feature of a lease contract is the separation of the ownership of the asset from its usage. Lease financing is based on the observation made by Donald B. Grant, "Why own a cow when the milk is so cheap? All you really need is milk and not the cow".

Importance of Lease Financing

Leasing industry plays an important role in the economic development of a country by providing money incentives to the lessee. The lessee does not have to pay the cost of asset at the time of signing the contract of leases. Leasing contracts are more flexible, so the lessees can structure the leasing contracts according to their needs for finance.

Who is a Lessee?	Who is a Lessor?
- Business customers with very high credit ratings	- Specialized leasing companies
- Public sector undertakings	- Banks and bank subsidiaries
- Mid-market companies	- Specialized financial institutions
- Consumers	- One-off lessors
- Car customers	- Manufacturer lessors
- Commercial vehicle customers	
- Earth-moving machinery customers	
- Government departments	

Types of Lease Agreements

Classification of equipment lease transaction depends on the various factors such as

1. transfer of risk and ownership,
2. number of parties to the transaction,
3. domicile of the equipment manufacturer, and
4. parties to the contract, that is, the lessor and the lessee.

Based on the above parameters, lease may be classified as:

1. Financial lease: It is a commitment on part of the lessee to make a series of payments to the lessor for the use of asset. Financial lease, also known as full payout lease or capital lease, is a type of lease wherein the lessor transfers substantially all the risks and rewards related to the asset to the lessee. Generally, the ownership is transferred to the lessee at the end of the economic life of the asset. The lease term is spread over the major part of the asset life. Here, the lessor is only a financier. Important features of financial lease are:

1. It contains a condition wherein, the lessor agrees to transfer the title of the asset to the lessee at the end of the lease period at a nominal cost.
2. Lessee must get an option to purchase the asset at the end of lease period.
3. The lease agreement is irrevocable.
4. Lessee bears the cost of maintenance, insurance and repairs, only title deed remains with the lessor.
5. Example of a finance lease is big industrial equipment.

2. Operating lease: On the contrary, in operating lease, risk and rewards are not transferred completely to the lessee. The term of lease is very small compared to financial lease. The lessor depends on many different lessees for recovering his cost. Ownership along with its risks and rewards lies with the lessor. Here, the lessor is not only acting as a financier but he also provides additional services required in the course of using the asset or equipment. Example of an operating lease is music system leased on rent to the respective technicians.

The main characteristics of an operating lease are thus

1. Lease may be canceled by the lessee prior to the lease period at a short notice.
2. Maintenance and upkeep cost is to be borne by the lessor.
3. This kind of lease is generally for a smaller period.
4. Lessor has an option to lease out the asset again to another party.

Test Yourself

1. Identify lease business in your surroundings.
2. Differentiate between financial and operating lease.

3. Sale and lease back: Under this type of lease agreement, the lessee first buys the asset from the market and sells it to the lessor. The lessor then leases out the same asset to the lessee. This option may also be exercised in case of an old asset already in use by the lessee. The lessor gets a tax credit for depreciation.

The advantage of this agreement is that the lessee may satisfy himself regarding the quality of asset as he himself has purchased the same. This arrangement is different from simple lease where the asset is either owned by the lessor or he acquires it.

4. Direct lease: Direct lease is a contract which is not the sale and leaseback agreement. Direct lease may be categorized into bi-party lease and tri-party lease. Two parties are involved in a bi-party lease, whereas in case of tripartite agreement three parties, namely, the supplier, lessor, and the lessee are involved.

5. Leveraged lease: Under this type of lease arrangement, three parties are involved

1. lessor,
2. lessee, and
3. financier.

The lessor undertakes only to finance a part of the funds required to purchase the asset. Remaining is agreed to be financed through a financier. There are two agreements under this arrangement, one is between the lessor and the lessee and the other one is between the lessor and the financier. This agreement enables the lessor to expand its leasing business by employing a limited amount of capital.

It is different from the single investor lease in the sense that there is a direct connection of the financier with the lessee, and in case of default by the lessor, the lender is also entitled to receive money from the lessee. Such transactions are generally routed through a trustee.

6. International lease: International lease are of two types—import lease and cross-border lease. When the lessor and the lessee reside in the same country and the equipment supplier stays in a different country, the lease arrangement is called import lease. When the lessor and the lessee are residing in two different countries, irrespective of where the equipment supplier stays, the lease is called a cross-border lease.

When all the parties of the lease agreement reside in the same country, it is called a domestic lease.

Effect of Lease Agreement on Financial Statements

1. **Profit and loss account:** Accounting profit is higher in the case of lease financing as compared to loan financing. This is so because in case of loan financing, both the interest and depreciation are expenses and are charged from the profit and loss account, whereas in case of lease financing, the lease payments are charged to profit and loss account.

2. **Balance sheet:** Level of total assets appearing in the balance sheet has generally been lower under a lease agreement than a loan agreement. All loans appear in the balance sheet as a source of finance and all assets purchased appear as the part of total assets.

Tax Effects of Lease Agreement

Tax effects of a lease transaction are different for the lessor and the lessee and may be discussed as follows:

1. **From a lessee's point of view:** The full amount of annual lease payment is eligible for deduction while calculating the taxable income.

2. **From lessor's point of view:** The lessor is entitled to claim depreciation and the lease rentals are included in calculating the taxable income.

EVOLUTION OF LEASING

Leasing activity was initiated in India in 1973. The first leasing company of India, named First Leasing Company of India Ltd, was set up in that year by Farouk Irani, with the industrialist A.C. Muthiah. For several years, this company remained the only leasing company in the country until 20th Century Finance Corporation was set up—this was around 1980.

By 1981, the trickle started and Shetty Investment and Finance, Jaybharat Credit and Investment, Motor and General Finance, Sundaram Finance, etc., joined the leasing game. The last three names, already involved with hire purchase of commercial vehicles, were looking for a tax break and leasing seemed to be the ideal choice.

The industry entered the third stage in the growth phase in late 1982, when numerous financial institutions and commercial banks either started leasing or announced plans to do so. ICICI, prominent among the financial institutions, entered the industry in 1983, giving a boost to the concept of leasing. Thereafter, the trickle soon developed into a flood, and leasing became the new gold mine. This was also the time when the profit-performance of the two doyen companies, First Leasing and 20th Century had been made public, which attracted many more companies to the leasing industry. In the meantime, International Finance Corporation announced its decision to open four leasing joint ventures in India. To add to the leasing boom, the Finance Ministry announced strict measures for enlistment of investment companies on stock exchanges, which made many investment companies to turn overnight into leasing companies.

As per RBI's records, by March 31, 1986 there were 339 equipment leasing companies in India whose assets leased totaled ₹2,395.5 million. One can notice the surge in number—from merely 2 in 1980 to 339 in six years.

Subsequent swings in the leasing cycle have always been associated with the capital market—whenever the capital markets were more permissive, leasing companies have flocked the market. There has been an appreciable entry of first-generation entrepreneurs into leasing, and, in retrospect, it is possible to say that specialized leasing firms have done better than diversified industrial groups opening a leasing division.

Another significant phase in the development of Indian leasing was the Dahotre Committee's recommendations based on which the RBI formed guidelines on commercial bank funding to leasing companies. The growth of leasing in India has distinctively been assisted by funding from banks and financial institutions.

Banks themselves were allowed to offer leasing facilities much later—in 1994. However, even to date, commercial banking machinery has not been able to gear up to make any remarkable difference to the leasing scenario. The post-liberalization era has been witnessing the slow but sure increase in foreign investment into Indian leasing. Starting with GE Capital's entry, an increasing number of foreign-owned financial firms and banks are currently engaged or interested in leasing in India.

Source: www.india-financing.com (accessed on June 7, 2016).

Decision-Making—Lease or Buy

To evaluate lease or buy decision, the net present value method is generally used.

1. While evaluating buying decisions, the initial cost and residual value of the asset, depreciation allowance, corporate taxation rate, and the after-tax borrowing cost at discount rate are considered.

2. While evaluating a lease transaction, discounting of lease payments using the after-tax cost of borrowing and any rebate, for example, a percentage of the salvage value which accrues to the lessee is calculated.

Illustration 1. Kajal Enterprises is planning to install a machine at its plant. The finance manager is asked to evaluate the alternatives either to purchase or acquire machine on the lease basis

Buying	Initial cost ₹100,0000	Residual value ₹320,000
Leasing for five years	Annual lease rental ₹300,000	Residual value ₹180,000 returned to lessee in five years

Depreciation is charged at 20% p.a. on written-down value. Corporate tax rate is 40%. After-tax cost of debt is 14%. The time gap between the claiming of tax allowance and receiving the benefit is one year.

Evaluate the lease or buy decision based on the above information.

Solution:

Buying Decision

Year	Cost or WDV	Depreciation at 20%	Corporate Tax at 40%
1	1,000,000	200,000	80,000
2	800,000	160,000	64,000
3	640,000	128,000	51,200
4	512,000	102,400	40,960
5	409,600	–	
Less: Residual value	320,000	–	
	89,600	89,600	35,840

Calculation of Net Present Value

Year	Cost (₹)	Tax Advantage (₹)	Net Cash Flow (₹)	PV Factor 14%	Present Value (₹)
0	1,000,000	Nil	-1,000,000	Nil	-1,000,000
1		Nil	Nil	0.8772	
2		80,000	80,000	0.7695	61,560
3		64,000	64,000	0.675	43,200
4		51,200	51,200	0.5921	30,316
5	320,000	40,960	360,960	0.5194	187,483
6		35,840	35,840	0.4556	16,329
Net present value					**-661,113**

Leasing

Year	Lease Rentals (₹)	Tax Advantage (₹)	Net Cash Flow (₹)	PV Factor 14%	Present Value (₹)
0	-300,000	Nil	-300,000	Nil	-300,000
1	-300,000	Nil	-300,000	0.8772	-263,158
2	-300,000	120,000	-180,000	0.7695	-138,510
3	-300,000	120,000	-180,000	0.675	-121,500
4	-300,000	120,000	-180,000	0.5921	-106,578
5	180,000	120,000	300,000	0.5194	155,820
6		120,000	48,000	0.4556	21,869
		-72,000			
Net present value	**-752,057**				

Conclusion

The net present value of cash outflows is greater in the case of lease decision as compared to the buy decision. The company should go for purchasing the machine instead of acquiring it on lease.

Hire Purchase

Hire purchase is a method of purchasing assets through making installment payments over a period of time.

The contract allows one party (hirer) to acquire possession of goods belonging to another party by paying an initial deposit and then paying the remaining sum in installments. Under this transaction, the hire purchaser acquires the property (goods) immediately on signing the hire purchase agreement but the ownership or title of the same is transferred only when the last installment is paid.

The hire purchase system is regulated by the Hire Purchase Act 1972. This Act defines a hire purchase as "an agreement under which goods are let on hire and under which the hirer has an option to purchase them in accordance with the terms of the agreement and includes an agreement under which

1. the owner delivers possession of goods thereof to a person on condition that such person pays the agreed amount in periodic installments,
2. the property in the goods is to pass to such person on the payment of the last of such installments, and
3. such person has a right to terminate the agreement at any time before the property so passes."

Difference between Lease and Hire Purchase

Basis	Lease Financing	Hire Purchase
Meaning	A lease transaction is a commercial arrangement, whereby lessor (asset owner) conveys to the equipment user (lessee) the right to use the equipment in return for a rental.	It is a type of installment credit under which the hire purchaser agrees to take the goods on hire at a stated rental, which is comprehensive of the repayment of principal with interest, with an option to purchase.
Option	Lessee has no option to buy the asset on lease.	There is an option to the user to buy asset.
Nature of Expense	Lease rental paid by the lessee is a tax deductible item.	Only the interest element in the hire purchase installment is the tax-deductible item for the user.
Depreciation	Depreciation is claimed by the lessor	Depreciation is claimed by the user.

EVOLUTION OF HIRE PURCHASE

The British concept of hire purchase has, however, been there in India for more than six decades. The first hire purchase company is believed to be Commercial Credit Corporation, successor to Auto Supply Company. While this company was based in Madras, Motor and General Finance and Installment Supply Company were set up in North India. These companies were set up in the 1920s and the 1930s.

Development of hire purchase took two forms: consumer durables and automobiles.

Consumer durables' hire purchase was promoted by the dealers in the respective equipment. Thus, Singer Sewing Machine company, or Murphy Radio dealers would provide installment facilities on hire purchase basis to the customers of their products.

The other side that developed very fast—hire purchase of commercial vehicles. The dealers in commercial vehicles as well as pure financing companies sprang up. The value of the asset being good and repossession being easy, this branch of financing activity flourished fast, although until recently, most of automobile financing business was in the hands of family-owned businesses.

Source: www.india-financing.com (June 7, 2016).

Contents of Valid Hire Purchase Agreement

Hire purchase agreement should be in writing and signed by both the parties, as it is a conditional contract. They must clearly contain the following information:

1. A clear description of goods.
2. Cash price of the goods.
3. The hire purchase price.
4. The deposit.
5. The monthly installments.
6. A comprehensive statement of the parties' rights.

SUMMARY

1. A lease transaction is a commercial arrangement whereby an equipment owner or manufacturer conveys to the equipment user the right to use the equipment in return for a rental.

2. Leasing industry plays an important role in the economic development of a country by providing money incentives to lessee. The lessee does not have to pay the cost of asset at the time of signing the contract of leases.

3. Classification of equipment lease transaction depends on the various factors such as

   - transfer of risk and ownership,
   - number of parties to the transaction,
   - domicile of the equipment manufacturer, and
   - parties to the contract, that is, the lessor and the lessee.

4. Commitment on part of the lessee to make a series of payments to the lessor for the use of asset is known as finance lease or full payout lease or capital lease. The lessor transfers substantially all the risks and rewards related to the asset to the lessee, whereas in operating lease, risk and rewards are not transferred completely to the lessee. The term of lease is very small compared to finance lease.

5. Under sale and leaseback arrangement, the lessee first buys the asset from the market and sells it to the lessor. The lessor then leases out the same asset to the lessee. This option may also be exercised in the case of an old asset already in use by the lessee. Lessor gets a tax credit for depreciation.

6. Another type of lease agreement is leveraged lease. This agreement enables the lessor to expand its leasing business by employing a limited amount of capital. There are three parties to the agreement, namely, the lessor, the lessee, and the financier.

7. International lease are of two types—import lease and cross-border lease.

8. Lease agreement affects both the profitability and the valuation of assets of the lessor and the lessee.

9. The full amount of annual lease payment is eligible for deduction while calculating the taxable income in the books of the lessee.

10. The lessor is entitled to claim for depreciation and the lease rentals are included in calculating the taxable income.

11. While evaluating buying decisions, the initial cost and residual value of the asset, depreciation allowance, corporate taxation rate, and after-tax borrowing cost at the discount rate are considered and while evaluating lease transaction, discounting of lease payments using the after-tax cost of borrowing and any rebate, for example, a percentage of the salvage value which accrues to the lessee is calculated.

12. Hire purchase is a method of purchasing assets through making installment payments over a period of time.

13. The contract allows one party (hirer) to acquire possession of goods belonging to another party by paying an initial deposit and then paying the remaining sum in installments.

KEY TERMS

- Lease financing
- Lessee
- Operating lease
- Leveraged lease
- Cross-border lease
- Net present value

- Lessor
- Financial lease
- Sale and leaseback
- Import lease
- Taxable income
- Hire purchase

Learning Outcomes

Students would learn the concept of lease and hire purchase.

PROBLEMS

1. Fair Finance, a leasing company, has been approached by a prospective customer intending to acquire a machine whose cash down price is ₹3 crores. The customer, to leverage his tax position, has requested for a quote for a three-year lease with rental payable at the end of each year but in a diminishing manner such that they are in the ratio of 3:2:1.

   Depreciation can be assumed to be on straight line basis and Fair Finance's marginal tax rate is 35%. The target rate of return for Fair Finance on the transaction is 10%.

   Required
   Calculate the lease rents to be quoted for the lease for three years.
   (C.A. Final Nov. 2004)
   (**Ans.** Year 1: ₹191.54 lakhs, Year 2: ₹127.69 lakhs, Year 3: ₹63.85 lakhs.)

2. ABC Leasing Ltd has been approached by a client to write a five years' lease on an asset costing ₹1,000,000 and having estimated salvage value of ₹100,000 thereafter. The company has an after-tax required rate of return of 10% and its tax rate is 50%. It provides depreciation at 33.22% on a written-down value of the asset. What lease rental will provide the company its after-tax required rate of return?
   (C.A. Final, May 2006)
   (**Ans.** ₹308,530)

3. ABC Ltd, is a lease company and has decided to lease out an equipment to XYZ company. Cost of the equipment is ₹2,000,000. The equipment is expected to have an economic life of six years. Its scrap value is ₹200,000. Corporate tax rate is 35% and required rate of return is 10%. Determine the lease rentals assuming depreciation rate to be 30% on WDV.
   (**Ans.** ₹493,578 p.a.)

4. From the following information suggest whether the lease proposal is feasible or not (using NPV method. Investment ₹15,000,000, economic life of the equipment is five years, scarp value at the end being ₹160,000. Required rate of return is 12%. Tax rate is 100%. Depreciation is 20%. Lease rent per year is ₹5,000,000.
   (**Ans.** NPV of leasing is ₹232,040, therefore, it is better to lease)

ACCESS YOURSELF

Concept Review and Critical Thinking Questions

1. Explain the concept of lease financing.
2. What are the various types of lease agreement? Explain their applicability in the industry.
3. Explain the concept of hire purchase agreement.
4. Differentiate between lease and hire purchase agreement.
5. What are factors taken into consideration for lease or buy decisions?

STUDENT ACTIVITIES

1. Collect the data of leading lease and hire purchase companies in India and perform a comparative analysis. Also, identify the sectors having scope of development of lease and hire purchase practice.
2. Visit a dealer and find how they provide lease finance.

SUGGESTED READINGS

Brealey, R.A., & Myers, S.C. (2002). *Principles of corporate finance* (7th ed.). New York: McGraw-Hill.
Kothari, Rajesh. (2010). *Financial services in India, concept and application* (I ed.). SAGE India.

CHAPTER 22

Venture Capital Financing

Learning Objectives

- To understand the concept of venture capital.
- To learn venture capital investment process.
- To discuss the stages of venture capital assistance.
- To focus on exit strategy of venture capital.

PRELUDE

For the past 7 years, a small group of people has been working round-the-clock to shape a unique investment asset class in India—VC or money that is invested in early-stage and high-risk companies. The group is an odd mix of former first-generation entrepreneurs, career executives, and investment professionals. They helm the country's most active VC firms and their goal is to entrench risk investing in the emerging world's second-largest startup economy. The hard work seems to be paying off. During 2004–2010, venture capitalists invested $3.96 billion in Indian startup. Another $621 million has been invested this year, according to Chennai-based research firm Venture Intelligence. There is an established line of VC firms who have consistently invested through this period. Some are local arms of Silicon Valley firms such as Norwest Venture Partners (NVP) and Draper Fisher Jurvetson. Others, such as Helion Venture Partners and Inventus Capital Partners, are independent startups themselves. By 2015, total investments will touch $10 billion through projects by Bangalore-based VC firms such as IDG Ventures India.

Source: http://www.businessworld.in/businessworld/businessworldcontent/VCs-Next-Phase.html

Venture Capital plays a vital role in financing small and medium enterprises and highly technical and risky projects. It has taken a shape in developed countries and now has penetrated into developing countries. It is a financial innovation of the twentieth century. VC finance is associated with early-stage financing in risky projects. A venture capitalist finances a project based on the potentialities of a new innovative project unlike conventional security-based financing. The main drive is to develop new ideas or technological innovations. Finance is being provided not only for "start up" but also for "development capital" by the financial intermediary.

VC deals with investment in an enterprise that offers the probability of profit along with the possibility of loss. Indeed, VC is also known as risk capital. It provides capital cushion to startup firms and small businesses with perceived, long-term growth potential. This is a very important source of finance for startups that do not have access to capital markets. Such firms have a high risk for the investor, but they have the potential for above-average returns. Finance may be required for the startup, development/expansion, or purchase of a company. VC firms invest funds on a professional basis, often focusing on a limited sector of specialization (e.g., IT, infrastructure, health, life sciences, and clean technology). Venture capitalists act as mentors and aim to provide support and advice on production, management, human resource sales, and technical issues to assist the company to develop its full potential.

Features of venture Capital

VC has the following features:

- It provides long-term equity finance which provides a solid capital base for future growth. The objective is to make capital gain by selling off the investment on exit.
- The venture capitalist is a business partner, sharing both the risks and rewards.
- The venture capitalist is able to provide practical advice and assistance to the company based on past experience with other companies which were in similar situations.
- The venture capitalist also has a network of contacts in many areas that can add value to the company, such as in recruiting key personnel, providing contacts in international markets, introductions to strategic partners, and if needed co-investments with other VC firms when additional rounds of financing are required.
- The venture capitalist may be capable of providing additional rounds of funding should the company require financial growth. It is a long-term source of investment ranging from 5 to 10 years.

VC is quite different from traditional bank loan. The bankers usually do not fund risky projects. They play safe and ask for security. They do not participate in day-to-day affairs of the company. Securities and Exchange Board of India regulates VC firms. It provides guidelines pertaining to operation of VC funds. VC firms may be structured as a company, firm, or trust to raise finances through loans, donations, issue of securities or units, and to make investment in new ventures according to SEBI guidelines.

Stages of Venture Capital Financing

Earlier, VC assistance was associated with early-stage financing. The main objective was to provide seed fund (see Exhibit No. 1) to highly technical risky projects. But notion of VC has extended to different stages of project life cycle. VC assistance cannot be confined to early stages only. There are various stages where enterprises need financing. These stages are early stage, expansion, development, and buyout strategy. Venture capitalist also provides turn-around finance to revive sick units to foster growth and development in India. Different stages in VC assistance are shown in Table 22.1.

TABLE 22.1

STAGES IN VC FINANCING

Early-stage financing	• Seed financing for supporting a concept or idea. • R&D financing for product development. • Startup capital for initiating the operations and developing prototype. • First-stage financing for full-scale production and marketing.
Expansion financing	• Second-stage financing for working capital and initial expansion. • Development financing for major expansion. • Bridge financing for facilitating public issue.
Acquisition/Buyout financing	• Acquisition financing for acquiring another firm for further growth. • Management buyout financing for enabling operating group to acquire firm or part of its business. • Turnaround financing for turning around a sick unit.

Source: Author.

EXHIBIT: SEEDFUND: THE SWEET SPOT

Tuesday afternoons are usually a good time to visit the Seedfund Office, tucked away in a by-lane off the Mahalaxmi Racecourse in mid-town Mumbai. Gandhi, Murthy, and team members Anand Lunia and Paula Mariwala can be found poring over monthly reviews of portfolio companies or talking deals. Sometimes, Bharati Jacob, the firm's Bangalore-based Managing Partner, joins in. Tuesday is also when the team catches up with each other's lives. They mostly work from home or are in the field the rest of the week. It is a throwback to the informal way many VC firms worked when "dotcom" was not a bad word. "It was a good experience for this country as it chastened a lot of people. The true entrepreneur — driven by passion and willing to make sacrifices — began to emerge after that," says Gandhi, referring to the excesses that marked the era.

Yet, it did not change the way Gandhi and Murthy saw VC investing. In 2006, when they raised Seedfund's $15 million maiden fund, they had no doubt that they would back only pre-revenue startups. "There was enough money above us. So we picked the seed stage as our sweet spot," he says. This is where firms need that critical $50,000 (up to $1 million) to build a prototype and test their idea in the market. The strategy was validated last November when German media company Axel Springer bought majority control in automobiles classifieds portal CarWale. Seedfund had picked up 25% in the firm for $6,90,000 in 2006 and made a profit of $25 million on exit. When the firm invested in CarWale, it had not even raised its first fund. "They wrote us a personal cheque of ₹30-odd lakhs," recalls Mohit Dubey, Founder and CEO of CarWale.

Firms, such as CarWale, fitted nicely in Gandhi's own sweet spot. Gandhi has never enjoyed investing in mature firms with proven business models. An active angel investor since 1996 and an early-stage investor with Delhi's Infinity Ventures, he continued to back ground-up startups well after the crash. In Murthy, who earlier ran early-stage fund Passion Fund, he found a kindred soul. While Murthy used the void left by the dotcom crash to start digital advertising firm Pinstorm, he continued to engage with startups as a mentor. "At one point, we were practically running every business plan contest in India," he jokes.

The exposure to startups of different hues had a big role in firming up the belief that there was a clear need for a specialist seed-stage fund. This unique approach, which mirrors the classical VC style of investing in the US Silicon Valley, has led to 16 deals so far. The first 12 have come from Fund I, which is now fully invested and already in exit mode. Another four have come from Fund II, which the firm raised with a $55 million corpus this February. "We will announce three more deals," says Lunia, Executive Director at Seedfund. While a larger fund will allow the firm to put more money to work, the investment thesis will remain the same. "We try to invest in ideas we think will become sector leaders, often creating new sectors," says Lunia.

So far, this thesis has been borne out by most of the firm's investments. Vaatsalya, founded by doctors Ashwin Naik and Veerendra Hiremath, is now the acknowledged pioneer of affordable hospitals for smaller towns. It has just raised a $10 million round of funding from Singapore's Aquarius Capital and is surging toward 20 hospitals by the end of 2011. Online bus ticketing portal redBus has notched up ₹120 crore revenues and 3.6 million users.

Education solutions startup ThinkLABS Technosolutions now has a presence in 25 schools and 10 colleges. It expects to reach ₹10 crore revenues by March. "When we met Seedfund in 2007, we did not even know what VC was. It played a big role in helping us become a full-fledged business," says Gagan Goyal, Founder and CEO of ThinkLABS.

Seedfund has had a few other exits too. It sold its 54.5% stake in online financial services startup Rupeetalk to Delhi-based NetAmbit. It had invested $9,40,000 in the company in November 2007. It has also partially exited personal health records portal Healthizen and sold off its stakes in SaaS startup Uhuroo and social networking startup Lifeblob (bought by Printo). Not all the exits have been successful, though the investment in each has been under $1 million. "We realised early that some would not make it, and it made sense to cut losses," says Lunia.

Source: www.businessworld.in/businessworld/businessworld/bw/seed-fund

Test Yourself

1. Explain the concept of VC?
2. What are the various stages of VC financing?

The Business Plan

The first step for entrepreneur to approach VC funds is to prepare a business plan for projects. Business plan should be self-explanatory, such that venture capitalist firms get convinced that the project is very promising. Business plan should explain the nature of project, what it wants to achieve, and how it is going to do it. Venture capitalists view hundreds of business plans every year. The business plan must therefore convince the venture capitalist that the company and the management team have the ability to achieve the goals of the company within the specified time. The company's management should prepare the plan and they should set challenging but achievable goals. The length of the business plan depends on the particular circumstances but, as a general rule, it should be no longer than 25–30 pages. It is important to use plain English, especially if you are explaining technical details. Aim the business plan at non-specialists, emphasizing its financial viability.

Essential Elements of Business Plan[1]

Executive Summary: This is the most important section and is often best written last. It summarizes your business plan and is placed at the front of the document. It is vital to give this summary significant thought and time as it may well determine the amount of consideration the VC investor will give to your detailed proposal. It should be clearly written and powerfully persuasive, yet balance "sales talk" with realism in order to be convincing. It should be limited to no more than two pages and include the key elements of the business plan.

Background of the Company: The business plan should provide a summary of the fundamental nature of the company and its activities, a brief history of the company, and an outline of the company's objectives.

The Product or Service: The business should explain the company's product or service. This is especially important if the product or service is technically orientated. A non-specialist must be able to understand the plan. The plan should emphasize the product or service's competitive edge or unique selling point. It should describe the stage of development of the product or service (seed, early stage, and expansion). Is there an opportunity to develop a second-generation product in due course? Is the product or service vulnerable to technological redundancy? It should suggest wherever legal protection on the product is required, such as patents attained, pending, or required. It should also assess the impact of legal protection on the marketability of the product.

Market Analysis: The plan needs to convince the VC firm that there is a real commercial opportunity for the business and its products and services. It should provide the reader a combination of clear description and analysis, including a realistic "SWOT" (strengths, weaknesses, opportunities, and threats) analysis. The plan should define your market and explain in what industry sector your company operates. What is the size of the whole market? What are the prospects for this market? How developed is the market as a whole, that is, developing, growing, mature, and declining? How does your company fit within this market? Who are your competitors? For what proportion of the market do they account? What is their strategic positioning? What are their strengths and weaknesses? What are the barriers to new entrants?

Plan should highlight the distribution channels. Who are your customers? How many are there? What is their value to the company now? Comment on the price sensitivity of the market. Explain the historic problems faced by the business and its products or services in the market. Have these problems been overcome, and if so, how? Address the current issues, concerns, and risks affecting your business and the industry in which it operates. What are your projections for the company and the market? Assess future potential problems and how they will be tackled, minimized, or avoided?

Marketing: Having defined the relevant market and its opportunities, it is necessary to address how the prospective business will exploit these opportunities. Outline your sales and distribution strategy. What is your planned sales force? What are your strategies for different markets? What distribution channels are you planning to use and how do these compare with your competitors? Identify overseas market access issues and how these will be resolved. What

---

[1] *Source:* http://www.indiavca.org/ven_business_plans.aspx

is your pricing strategy? How does it fare compared with your competitors? What are your advertising, public relations, and promotion plans?

The Management Team: The plan should demonstrate that the company has the quality of management to be able to turn the business plan into reality. The senior management team ideally should be experienced in complementary areas, such as management strategy, finance, and marketing, and their roles should be specified. The special abilities each member brings to the venture should be explained. Concise curriculum vitae should be included for each team member, highlighting the individual's previous track record in running, or being involved with, successful businesses. The plan should identify the current and potential skills gaps and explain that they aim to fill them. VC firms will sometimes assist in locating experienced managers where an important post is unfilled—provided they are convinced about the other aspects of your plan. The plan should list advisers and board members and include an organizational chart.

Financial Projections: The business plan should realistically assess sales, costs (both fixed and variable), cash flow, and working capital. It should produce a profit and loss statement and balance sheet. It must ensure these are easy to update and adjust. It should assess your present and prospective future margins in detail, bearing in mind the potential impact of competition. It explains the research undertaken to support these assumptions. The plan should demonstrate the company's growth prospects over, for example, a 3- to 5-year period. What are the costs associated with the business? What are the sale prices or fee-charging structures? What are your budgets for each area of your company's activities? It must present different scenarios for the financial projections of sales, costs, and cash flow for both the short- and long-term. Ask "what if?" questions to ensure that key factors and their impact on the financing required are carefully and realistically assessed. For example, what if sales decline by 20%, or supplier costs increase by 30%, or both? How does this impact the profit and cash flow projections? If it is envisioned that more than one round of financing will be required (often the case with technology-based businesses in particular), identify the likely timing and any associated progress "milestones" or goals which need to be achieved. Keep the plan feasible. Avoid being overly optimistic. It must highlight challenges and show how they will be met. Relevant historical financial performance should also be presented. The company's historical achievements can help give meaning, context, and credibility to future projections.

Amount and Use of Finance Required and Exit Opportunities: The business should state how much finance is required by business and from what sources (i.e., management, VC, banks, and others) and explain the purpose for which it will be applied. It should also consider how the VC investors will exit the investment and make a return. Possible exit strategies for the investors may include floating the company on a stock exchange or selling the company to a trade buyer.

Test Yourself

1. Define a business plan. What are the elements of business plan?

The Process of VC Financing

The VC investment activity is a sequential process involving five steps:

1. **Deal Origination:** A continuous flow of deals is essential for the VC business. Deals may originate in various ways: (i) referral system, (ii) active search, and (iii) intermediaries. Referral system is an important source of deals. Deals may be referred to the VCs through their parent organizations, trade partners, industry associations, and friends. The VC industry in India has become quite proactive in its approach to generating the deal flow by encouraging individuals to come up with their business plans. Consultancy firms, such as Mckinsey and Arthur Anderson, have come up with business plan competitions on an all-India basis through the popular press as well as direct interaction with premier educational and research institutions to source new and innovative ideas. The shortlisted plans are provided with necessary expertise through people who have experience in the industry.

2. **Screening:** VCFs carry out initial screening of all projects on the basis of some broad criteria. For example, the screening process may limit projects to areas in which the venture capitalist is familiar in terms of technology, or product, or market scope. The size of investment, geographical location, and stage of financing could also be used as the broad screening criteria.

3. **Evaluation or Due Diligence:** Once a proposal has passed through initial screening, it is subjected to a detailed evaluation or due diligence process. Most ventures are new and the entrepreneurs may lack operating experience. Hence, a sophisticated, formal evaluation is neither possible nor desirable. The VCs thus rely on a subjective but comprehensive evaluation. VCFs evaluate the quality of the entrepreneur before appraising the characteristics of the product, market, or technology. Most venture capitalists ask for a business plan to make an assessment of the possible risk and expected return on the venture.

4. **Deal Structuring:** Once the venture has been evaluated as viable, the venture capitalist and the investment company negotiate the terms of the deal, that is, the amount, form, and price of the investment. This process is termed as deal structuring. The agreement also includes the protective covenants and earn-out arrangements. Covenants include the venture capitalists right to control the investee company and to change its management if needed, buy back arrangements, acquisition, and making IPOs. Earn-out arrangements specify the entrepreneur's equity share and the objectives to be achieved.

   Venture capitalists generally negotiate deals to ensure protection of their interests. They would like a deal to provide for a return commensurate with the risk, influence over the firm through board membership, minimizing taxes, assuring investment liquidity, and the right to replace management in case of consistent poor managerial performance.

   The investee companies would like the deal to be structured in such a way that their interests are protected. They would like to earn reasonable return, minimize taxes, have enough liquidity to operate their business, and remain in commanding position of their business. There are a number of common concerns shared by both the venture capitalists and the investee companies. They should be flexible, and have a structure, which protects their mutual interests and provides enough incentives to both to cooperate with each other.

5. **Post-investment Activities and Exit:** Once the deal has been structured and agreement finalized, the venture capitalist generally assumes the role of a partner and collaborator. He also gets involved in shaping of the direction of the venture. This may be done via a formal representation of the Board of Directors, or informal influence in improving the quality of marketing, finance, and other managerial functions. The degree of the venture capitalists involvement depends on his policy. It may not, however, be desirable for a venture capitalist to get involved in the day-to-day operation of the venture. If a financial or managerial crisis occurs, the venture capitalist may intervene, and even install a new management team.

Venture capitalists typically aim at making medium-to-long-term capital gains. They generally want to cash out their gains in 5-10 years after the initial investment. They play a positive role in directing the company toward particular exit routes. A venture capitalist can exit in four ways:

- IPOs
- Acquisition by another company
- Repurchase of the venture capitalists share by the investee company
- Purchase of the venture capitalists share by a third party

Selection of VC Fund

After the business plan is completed, the next step is to select the VC fund, which is suitable to your proposal. The entrepreneur should first ascertain as to the investment strategy of the VC with regard to the sector in which the VC is interested as well as the stage at which he chooses to fund the project. Based on this information, the entrepreneur should shortlist the suitable VCs who match his requirement and then approach them.

It is normally advisable to approach more than one VC firm simultaneously for funding as there is a possibility of delay due to the various queries put by the VC. If the application for funding is finally rejected, then approaching another VC at that point and going through the same process would cause delay. If the business plan is reviewed by more than one VC, this delay can be avoided as the probability of acceptance will be much higher. The only problem with the above strategy is the processing fee required by a VC along with the business plan. If you are applying to more than one VC, then there would be a cost escalation for processing the application. Hence, a cost–benefit analysis should be done into before using the above strategy.

Normally, the review of the business plan would take a maximum of 1 month and disbursal for the funds to reach the entrepreneur would take a minimum of 3 months to a maximum of 6 months.

Once the initial screening and evaluation is over, it is advisable to have a person with finance background like a finance consultant to take care of the details like negotiating the pricing and structuring of the deal. Of course, alternatively, one can involve a financial consultant right from the beginning particularly when the entrepreneur does not have a management background.

Test Yourself

1. Explain the process of VC financing. How is due diligence carried out?

Methods of Venture Financing[2]

VC is typically available in three forms in India, they are as follows:

- **Equity:** All VCFs in India provide financial assistance in the form of equity but their contribution does not exceed 49% of the total equity capital, and therefore, effective control and ownership of the firm remain with the entrepreneur. When venture capitalists acquire equity stake in a firm, he becomes entitled for profit and liable to bear loss. There is no compulsion to pay dividends to VC funds. They buy shares of firm with an intention to ultimately sell them off to make capital gains.

- **Conditional Loan:** It is repayable in the form of a royalty once the venture starts generating sales. No interest is paid on such loans. In India, VCFs change royalty ranging between 2% and 15%; the actual rate depends on other factors of the venture such as gestation period, cost flow patterns, riskiness, and other factors of the enterprise.

- **Income Note:** It is a hybrid security which combines the features of both conventional loan and conditional loan. The entrepreneur has to pay both interest and royalty on sales, but at substantially low rates. VCFs provide unsecured loans at a lower rate of interest during the development phase. After the development phase gets over, a high rate of interest is charged. Along with it, company requires to pay royalty on sales.

- **Participating Debenture:** A few venture capitalists, particularly in the private sector, have started introducing innovative financial securities like participating debentures, introduced by TCFC is an example. Such security carries charges in three phases. In the startup phase, before the venture attains operations to a minimum level, no interest is charged; after this, low rate of interest is charged, up to a particular level of operation. Once the venture is commercial, a high rate of interest is required to be paid.

- **Quasi-equity:** Quasi-equity instruments are converted into equity at a later date. Convertible instruments are normally converted into equity at the book value or at certain multiple of EPS, that is, at a premium to par value at a later date. The premium automatically rewards the promoter for their initiative and hard work. Since it is performance related, it motivates the promoter to work harder so as to minimize dilution of their control on the company. The different quasi-equity instruments are as follows:

  o Cumulative convertible preference shares.
  o Partially convertible debentures.
  o Fully convertible debentures.

Disinvestment Methods

Venture capitalists generally want to cash out their gains in 5-10 years after the initial investment. They play a positive role in directing the company toward particular exit routes. A venture may exist in one of the following ways:

- Initial Public Offer (IPO)
- Repurchase of venture capitalists share by promoters
- Purchase of venture capitalists share by a third party

Promoters Buyback

The most popular disinvestment route in India is promoters buyback. This method keeps the ownership and control of the promoter integral. The major limitation is that market value of venture firm's stake would have depreciated after some years. The question which arises is whether the promoter would be in a financial position to buy them back?

In India, the promoters are given the first option to buy back equity of their enterprise. SBI Capital Markets ensures through examining the personal assets of the promoters and their associates, which buyback would be a feasible option. GV would make disinvestment, in consultation with the promoter, usually after the project has settled down, to a profitable level and the entrepreneur is in a position to avail finance under conventional schemes of assistance from banks or other financial institutions.

Initial Public Offers (IPOs)

The benefits of disinvestments via the public issue route are improved marketability and liquidity, better prospects for capital gains, and widely known status of the venture as well as market control through public share participation. This option has certain limitations in the Indian context. The promotion of the public issue would be difficult and expensive since the first-generation entrepreneurs are not known in the capital markets. Further, difficulties will be caused if the entrepreneurs business is perceived to be an unattractive investment proposition by the investors. In addition, the emphasis by the Indian investors on short-term profits and dividends may tend to make the market price unattractive. Yet another difficulty in India until recently was that the Controller of Capital Issues (CCI) guidelines for determining the premium on shares took into account the book value and the cumulative average EPS till the date of the new issue. This formula failed to give due weightage to the expected stream of earning of the venture firm. Thus, the formula would underestimate the premium. The government has now abolished the Capital Issues Control Act, 1947 and consequently, the Office of the Controller of Capital Issues. The existing companies are now free to fix the premium on their shares. The initial public issue for disinvestment of VCFs holding can involve high transaction costs because of the inefficiency of the secondary market in a country like India. In addition, this option has become far less feasible for small ventures on account of the higher listing requirement of the stock exchanges.

Sale on the OTC Market

An active secondary capital market provides the necessary impetus to the success of the VC. VCFs should be able to sell their holdings, and investors should be able to trade shares conveniently and freely. In the US, there exist well-developed OTC markets where dealers trade in share on telephone/ terminal and not on an exchange floor. This mechanism enables new, small companies which are not otherwise eligible to be listed on the stock exchange, to enlist on the OTC markets, and provides liquidity to the investors. The National Association of Securities Dealers Automated Quotation System (NASDAQ) in the US daily quotes over 8,000 stock prices of companies backed by VC.

The OTC Exchange in India was established in June 1992. The Government of India had approved the creation for the Exchange under the Securities Contracts (Regulations) Act in 1989. It has been promoted jointly by UTI, ICICI, SBI Capital Markets, Can Bank Financial Services, GIC, LIC, and IDBI. The OTCEI should perform better. The other disinvestment mechanisms such as the management buyouts or sale to other venture funds are not considered to be appropriate by VCFs in India.

Test Yourself

1. What is conditional loan? How is it different from conventional loan?
2. What is quasi-equity? What are the methods of disinvestment? Explain.

Development of VC Industry in India

The first major analysis on risk capital for India was reported in 1983. It indicated that new companies often confront serious barriers to entry into capital market for raising equity finance which undermines their future prospects of expansion and diversification. It also indicated that on the whole there is a need to review the equity cult among the masses by ensuring competitive return on equity investment. This brought out the institutional inadequacies with respect to the evolution of VC.

In India, the IFCI initiated the idea of VC when it established the Risk Capital Foundation in 1975 to provide seed capital to small and risky projects. However, the concept of VC financing got statutory recognition for the first time in the fiscal budget for the year 1986–1987.

The VC companies operating at present can be divided into four groups:

- Promoted by all-india development financial institutions.
- Promoted by state-level financial institutions.
- Promoted by commercial banks.
- Private venture capitalists.

The IDBI started a VC in 1976 as per the long-term fiscal policy of the Government of India, with an initial of ₹10 crore which was raised by imposing a cess of 5% on all payment made for the import of technology know-how. Projects requiring funds from ₹5 lakhs to ₹2.5 crore were considered for financing. Promoter's contribution ranged from this fund was available at a concessional interest rate of 9% (during gestation period) which could be increased at later stages.

The ICICI provided the required impetus to VC activities in India. In 1986, it started providing VC finance; in 1998, it was promoted, along with the Unit Trust of India (UTI) Technology Development and Information Company of India (TDICI), as the first VC company registered under the Companies Act, 1956. The TDICI may provide financial assistance to VC undertaking which are set up by technocrat entrepreneurs, or technology information and guidance services.

The risk capital foundation, established by the Industrial Finance Corporation of India (IFCI) in 1975, was converted in 1988 into the Risk Capital and Technology Finance Company (RCTC) as a subsidiary company of the IFCI. The rate provides assistance in the form of conventional loans, interest free and conditional loans on a profit and risk-sharing basis, or equity participation in extended financial support to high technology projects for technological upgradations. The RCTC has been renamed as IFCI Venture Capital Funds Ltd (IVCF).

Promoted by State-level Financial Institutions

In India, the State-level Financial Institutions in some states, such as Madhya Pradesh, Gujarat, and Uttar Pradesh, have done an excellent job and have provided VC to a small-scale enterprise. Several successful entrepreneurs have been the beneficiaries of the liberal funding environment. In 1990, the Gujarat Industrial Investment Corporation promoted the Gujarat Venture Financial Ltd (GVFL) along with other promoters such as the IDBI and the World Bank. The GVFL provides financial assistance to business in the form of equity, conditional loans, or income notes for technologies development and innovative products. It also provides finance assistance to entrepreneurs.

The Government of Andhra Pradesh has also promoted the Andhra Pradesh Industrial Development Corporation (APIDC) Venture Capital Ltd to provide VC financing in Andhra Pradesh.

Promoted by Commercial Banks

Canbank VC Fund, State Bank VC Fund, and Grindlays Bank VC Fund have been set up at the respective commercial banks to undertake VC activities. The State Bank VC funds provide financial assistance for bought-out deal as well as new companies in the form of equity which it disinvests after the commercialization of the project.

Canbank VC Funds provide financial assistance for proven but yet to be commercially exploited technologies. It provides assistance both in the form of equity and conditional loans.

Private VC Funds

Several private sector VC funds have been established in India such as the 20th Century Venture Capital Company, Indus Venture Capital Funds, Infrastructure Leasing and Financial Services Ltd, Sequoia Capital Ltd, Matrix Partners India, and Light Speed Ventures Ltd.

Future of VC in India

Rapidly changing economic environment accelerated by the high technology explosion, emerging needs of new generation of entrepreneurs in the process, and inadequacy of the existing VC funds/schemes are indicative of the tremendous scope for VC in India and pointers to the need for the creation of a sound and broad-based VC movement in India.

There are many entrepreneurs in India with a good *project* idea but no previous entrepreneurial track record to leverage their firms and handle customers and bankers. VC can open a new window for such entrepreneurs and help them to launch their projects successfully.

With rapid international march of technology, demand for newer technology and products in India has gone up tremendously. The pace of development of new and indigenous technology in the country has been slack in view of the fact that several process developed in laboratories are not commercialized because of unwillingness of the people to take entrepreneurial risks, that is, risk their *funds* as also undergo the ordeal of marketing the products and process. In such a situation, *venture* financing assumes more significance. It can act not only as a financial catalyst but also provide strong impetus for entrepreneurs to develop products involving newer technologies and commercialize them. This will give a boost to the development of new technology and would go a long way in broadening the industrial base, creation of jobs, provide a thrust to exports, and help in the overall enrichment of the economy.

Another type of situation commonly found in our country is where the local group and a MNC may be ready to enter into a joint *venture* but the former does not have sufficient *funds* to put up its share of the equity and the latter is restricted to a certain percentage. For the personal reasons or because of competition, the local group may not be keen to invite any one in its industry or any major private investor to contribute equity and may prefer a VC company, as a less intimately involved and temporary shareholder. *Venture* capitalists can also lend their expertise and standing to the entrepreneurs.

In service sector, which has immense growth prospects in India, *venture* capitalists can play a significant role in tapping its potentiality to the full. For instance, *venture* capitalists can provide *capital* and expertise to organizations selling antique, remodeled jewellery, builders of resort hotels, baby and healthcare market, retirement homes, and small houses.

In view of the above, it will be desirable to establish a separate national VC fund to which the financial institutions and banks can contribute. In scope and content, such a national VC fund should cover:

1. All the aspects of VC financing in all the three stages of conceptual, developmental, and exploitation phases in the process of commercialization of the technological innovation, and

2. As many of the risk stages—development, manufacturing, marketing, management, and growth—as possible under Indian conditions. The fund should offer a comprehensive package of technical, commercial, managerial and financial assistance, and services to building entrepreneurs and be in a position to offer innovative solutions to the varied problems

faced by them in business promotion, transfer, and innovation. To this end, the proposed national VC fund should have at its command multidisciplinary technical expertise. The major thrust of this fund should be on the promotion of viable new business in India to take advantage of the oncoming high technology revolution and setting up of high growth industries so as to take the Indian economy to commanding heights.

Test Yourself

1. Discuss the development of VC in India. What is the role of VC Funds in the success story?

SUMMARY

1. VC provides capital cushion to startup firms and small businesses with perceived, long-term growth potential. This is a very important source of finance for startups that do not have access to capital markets.
2. Finance is sanctioned for the startup, development/expansion, or purchase of a company.
3. The venture capitalist is capable of providing additional rounds of funding should it be required to finance growth. It is a long-term source of investment ranging from 5 to 10 years.
4. The first step for entrepreneur to approach VC funds is to prepare a business plan for projects. Business plan should be self-explanatory such that venture capitalist firms get convince that the project is very promising. Business plan should explain the nature of the project, what it wants to achieve, and how it is going to do it.
5. VC assistance is available in the form of equity, conditional loan, income notes, and quasi-equity.
6. Buyback by promoters, IPO, and sales on OTC are various disinvestment strategies of VC funds.
7. IVCAs mission is to promote the development of VC and private equity industry in India and to support entrepreneurial activity and innovation.

KEY TERMS

- Business plan
- Convertible loan
- Early-seed financing
- Initial public offerings
- Over the counter market
- Buyout financing
- Disinvestment
- Participating debenture
- Conditional loan
- Due diligence
- Income notes
- Venture capital
- Turnaround financing
- Exit
- Quasi-equity

ASSESS YOURSELF

Concept Review and Critical Thinking Questions

1. Define VC. Explain its features.
2. What are the various methods of venture financing with stages?
3. Explain briefly VC investment process.
4. Discuss the disinvestment methods of VC firms.

CASE STUDY: DRUVA SOFTWARE

Druva Software Raises $5 Million from Sequoia

Funds will be used to set up sales offices in US and Europe

Druva Software, a Pune-based startup that makes proprietary backup software solutions for laptops, has raised $5 million in Series A funding (funding that follows seed funding) from Sequoia Capital India and Indian Angel Network (IAN). The stake picked up by the VC investors was not disclosed. The money will be used to expand the 3-year-old company's marketing and sales footprint overseas, including in Europe and the US. So far, it has relied largely on Web-based channels to sell its products in those markets.

"We will now have offices in the UK, mainland Europe, Singapore and the US," says Jaspreet Singh, co-founder and CEO of Druva. Singh teamed up with Ramani Kothandaraman, Chairman and Managing Director, and Milind Borate, Chief Technology Officer, in 2007 to set up the company. "We noticed that across companies, 80 per cent of data is duplicated," he says. Druva, therefore, developed a software that would allow companies to cut out this duplication and enable laptops to work faster as well as increase storage capacity. It claims 400 corporate customers across 23 countries. Globally, the laptop backup software market is estimated at $350 million annually, according to Singh.

Druva had earlier raised seed funding from the Delhi-based IAN and Hong Kong-based Accord International. With the latest round of funding, the total raised by the company so far stands at $5.2 million, says Singh. "India is traditionally an IT services country. When we saw that Druva was developing a continuous data protection product, which is the next level of back-up technology, we decided to fund them," says Rehan Yar Khan, who represents IAN on the Druva board. Sequoia could not be reached for comments.

The idea for Druva was born when the founders were colleagues at the former Veritas Software (merged with Symantec in 2005) operations in Pune. There have been some hiccups along the way. Druva Replicator, the company's first product, which provides real-time server replication software, did not find any takers. But Druva inSync, which is the laptop backup product, clicked. "We found that clients were willing to experiment with a new brand for their laptops but did not want to take similar risks with their servers," says IAN's Khan. Some of the company's earliest clients include NASA and the US Marine Corps. Druva Phoenix, Khan says, is now beginning to gain traction in the market.

Analyze the case.

Source: Author (compiled from various sources including www.druva.com).

KEY TERMS

- Arbitrage
- Bid-ask price
- Derivative
- Forward
- Option
- Swap
- Direct quote
- Indirect quote
- Cross rate
- Transaction exposure

- Operational exposure
- Exchange rate
- Fisher effect
- Hedging
- Forward premium
- Interest rate parity
- Purchasing power parity
- Law of one price
- Translation exposure
- Spot exchange rate

ASSESS YOURSELF

1. Describe international finance management.
2. What is foreign exchange market? Who can participate in a foreign exchange market?
3. Discuss the four international parity relationships.
4. What is foreign exchange risk? How this foreign exchange risk can be hedged?

Appendix I: SEBI's Guidelines for Registration of VC Funds in India

How to Get Registered as a VC fund

The Applicant for grant of registration as a VC Fund under SEBI (VC Funds) Regulations, 1996 should make an Application to SEBI in Form A along with all the necessary documents. Generally on receipt of Application, the applicant will receive a reply from SEBI within 21 working days. The time taken for registration, however, depends on how fast the requirements are complied with by the applicant. The applicant is advised to go through the SEBI (VC Funds) Regulations, 1996 for checking the eligibility criteria and such other details which may help expedite the registration process. As an integral part of the registration process, the applicant must submit:

1. Form A along with the Application fees of ₹1,00,000 and documents as under:

   (a) Copy of Memorandum and Articles of Association in case the applicant is set up in the form of a Company (Reg. 4(a)) *or* Copy of Registered Trust Deed in case the applicant is set up in the form of a trust (Reg. 4(b)) *or* Copy of Main objective of constitution in case the applicant is set up in the form of a body corporate (Reg. 4(c)).

   (b) Copy of Investment Management Agreement (only if applicable). Apart from the above documents/declarations as required under Form A, the applicant will also be required to submit the details/information as under:

2. Details of the Sponsor/Settlor.

   2.1. Write up on the activities of the Sponsor/Settlor, its shareholding pattern/profile of the directors. In case of an individual, please state whether the individual is a director/ employee of any entity registered with SEBI.

   2.2. State whether the Sponsor/Settlor has floated VC funds previously, which are registered with SEBI. If so details. Also state whether they (sponsor or their directors) were refused a certificate by the Board or its certificate has been suspended under regulation 30 or cancelled under regulation 31.

   2.3. State whether the Sponsor/Settlor is registered with SEBI, RBI, or any other regulatory authority in any capacity along with the details of its registration.

   2.4. State whether any of its group companies are registered with SEBI, RBI, or any regulatory authority along with the details of its registration.

   2.5. State whether Sponsor/Settlor or its holding company is listed on any of the recognized stock exchanges in India. If so details thereof.

   2.6. State whether the Sponsor/Settlor or its directors are involved in any litigation connected with the securities market and any order passed against them for violation of securities laws. If so details.

3. Details of the Trustees/Trustee Company.

   3.1. Write up on the activities of the Trustee Company/Profile of Trustees.

   3.2. Shareholding pattern and the write up on profile of the Directors.

   3.3. State whether the Trustee Company is registered with SEBI, RBI, or any other regulatory authority in any capacity along with the details of its registration.

4. Details of the Investment Manager/Investment Adviser/Asset Management Company (AMC).

   4.1. Write up on the activities of the Investment Manager/Investment Adviser/AMC.

   4.2. Shareholding pattern along with the profile of the Directors.

   4.3. State whether the Investment Manager/Adviser/AMC is registered with SEBI, RBI, or any other regulatory authority in any capacity, along with the details.

   4.4. Details of Key Personnel/Management Team. Also state whether they are also the employees of any SEBI registered entity. If so details.

5. State whether the applicant is registered with SEBI in any capacity or has applied for registration in any other capacity with SEBI.

6. List of all the associates registered with SEBI along with their Registration No. Please, refer to Reg. 2(aa) of SEBI (VC Funds) Regulations, 1996 for the definition of the "associate company".

7. Investment Strategy: Disclose in detail the investment strategy of the fund (Reg. 12(a)). Investment strategy should disclose the investment style or pattern, preferred sectors/ industries for investment, proposed corpus, the class of investors, life cycle of the fund, and any other information.

8. Declarations to be submitted by the applicant:

   8.1. An undertaking under Regulation 11(3) of SEBI (VC Funds) Regulations, 1996.

   8.2. Undertaking under Third Schedule to SEBI (VC Funds) Regulations, 1996.

   8.3. Declaration in respect of "Fit and Proper Person" criteria as per regulation 4A of the SEBI (VC Funds) Regulation, 1996 and as specified under Schedule II of the Securities and Exchange Board of India (Intermediaries) Regulation, 2008.

Grant of Certificate of Registration

Once all requirements including the Fit and Proper Person criteria have been complied with and on intimation from SEBI for payment of Registration fees of ₹5,00,000 as per Second Schedule to Regulations, SEBI will grant the applicant certification of registration as a SEBI Registered VC Fund. Please note the following:

- "The applicant" means the entity seeking registration as a VC Fund.
- Application which is incomplete or without the necessary documents/information/declarations would not be accepted and would be treated as not filed. However, intimation to this effect will be addressed to the applicant within a reasonable period of time.

Appendix II: Active Venture Capital Funds in India: A Brief Review

Helion Venture Partners

Investing in technology-powered and consumer service businesses, Helion Ventures Partners is a $605 million Indian-focused, an early-to-mid-stage venture fund participating in future rounds of financing in syndication with other venture partners.

Accel Partners

Accel Partners founded in 1983 has a global presence in Palo Alto, London, New York, China, and India. Typical multistage investments in Internet technology companies are made by Accel Partners.

Blume Ventures

VC firm, Blume Venture Advisor funds early-stage seed, startups, pre-series A, series B, and late-stage investments. Blume backs startups with both funding as well as active mentoring and support.

Sequoia Capital India

Sequoia Capital India specializes in investments in startup seed, early, mid, late, expansion, public, and growth-stage companies.

Nexus Venture Partners

Nexus Venture Partners is a VC firm investing in early-stage and growth-stage startups across sectors in India and US.

Inventus Capital Partners

With the sole goal of making new entrepreneurs successful, Inventus is a VC fund managed by entrepreneurs and industry-operating veterans.

IDG Ventures

Having a global network of technology venture funds with more than $4 billion, IDG Ventures India is a leading India-focused technology VC fund specialized in investments in startups, early-stage, growth-stage, and expansion-stage companies.

Fidelity Growth Partners

Fidelity Growth Partners India is the private equity arm of Fidelity International Limited focused on investing in India. Since 2008, FGPI has made several investments across sectors including Healthcare and Life Sciences, Technology, Consumer, and Manufacturing.

Naspers

Naspers is a leading multinational media group, incorporated in 1915 as a public limited liability company and was listed on the Johannesburg Stock Exchange (JSE) in September 1994. The group's principal operations are in Internet platforms (focusing on commerce, communities, content, communication, and games), pay-television, and the provision of related technologies and print media (including publishing, distribution, and printing). The group's most significant operations are located in South Africa and elsewhere in Africa, China, Central and Eastern Europe, India, Brazil, Russia, Thailand, and the Netherlands.

Steadview Capital

Steadview is a leading alternative asset manager based in Hong Kong. The firm makes concentrated long-term investments across multiple industries

Jungle Ventures

Jungle Ventures is a Singapore-based, entrepreneur-backed venture firm that funds and helps startups scale across Asia Pacific. It invests in global startups that are solving problems relevant to Asia-Pacific markets. It currently has investments in US, Singapore, India, Australia, Thailand, Malaysia, and the Philippines.

Zodius Capital

Operational since 2011, Zodius typically develops one company every 6 months and works intensively with its portfolio company teams to "speed up" and "shape up" for exceptional growth and profitability.

Qualcomm Ventures

Qualcomm Ventures is the investment arm of Qualcomm Inc. (NASDAQ: QCOM), a Fortune 500 company with operations across the globe.

Warburg Pincus

Warburg Pincus is a leading global private equity firm focused on growth investing. The firm has more than $37 billion in assets under management. Its active portfolio of more than 120 companies is highly diversified by stage, sector, and geography.

Canaan Partners

Global VC firm investing in people with visionary ideas, Canaan Partners specializes in all stages of development, seed financing, startups, growth- and early-stage investments, typically Series A and B financing.

SAIF Partners

Investing in India since 2001, SAIF Partners specializes in private equity and VC across Asia.

Ascent Capital Advisors

Ascent Capital, an India-focused independent private equity firm, is among the most experienced teams on ground with over 150+ years of collective experience in Indian capital markets.

Axon Partners Group

Specialized in global emerging markets, the Group prefers to invest in technology-focused companies in countries such as Latam, Spain, and India.

Bain Capital Private Equity

Bain Capital professionals in aggregate is the largest investor in every fund raised. Bain Capital, along with management teams, provides the strategic and analytic resources needed to build and grow great companies.

Basil Partners

It is a VC fund involved in early-stage venture investments focusing on investing in India besides investing in North America, Europe, and Asian Countries.

Battery Ventures

Battery Ventures is based in Boston, Silicon Valley and invests in technology-driven companies. With over 30 years of experience, this VC fund has deep pockets.

Bessemer Venture Partners

With great experience in investing, this 1911 founded company operates on a global scale with offices located in Israel, India, and both coasts in the US.

Catamaran Investment Pvt Ltd

Founded in 2010 Catamaran Investment is a private investment office headquartered in Bangalore, India and London, UK. It is a ₹600 crore multistage, multisector fund.

Forum Synergies (India) PE Fund

The company's vision and mission is to be a unique, ethical private equity fund management model in India that provides investors with a best-in-class private equity model.

Fulcrum Venture India

Founded in 2000, Fulcrum is a private equity investor which focuses on the SME business opportunities. They prefer to invest in like-minded entrepreneurs with solid principles and objectives.

General Atlantic LLC

Founded in 1980, General Atlantic is a leading global growth equity firm providing capital and strategic support for growing companies. It does early-stage venture, later-stage venture, and private equity investments.

India Quotient

Launched in 2012, India Quotient is an early-stage fund with a corpus of ₹30 crore.

Intel Capital

The firm focuses on mergers, acquisitions, and equity investments related to tech startups. Till date, it has invested $10.7 billion in over 1,250 companies in 52 countries.

IvyCap Ventures

Guided by an entrepreneur-centric investment approach, IvyCap focuses on high-quality professional entrepreneurs from premier education institutions of the country.

Kae Capital

Kae Capital invests in those companies which bring out innovative solutions for existing gaps in the markets. They believe in identifying and building large companies even from a concept.

Kalaari Capital

With a strong advisory team in Bangalore, Kalaari is a $160 million VC fund investing in early-stage technology-oriented companies in India. They seek companies that are capable of capturing new markets, providing innovative solutions, and creating new wealth for India and beyond.

Lightbox Management Ltd

India-based Lightbox Management Ltd with an investment horizon of 7-8 years is a new $100 million tech fund focused on early-stage consumer technology businesses.

Lightspeed Venture Partners

Founded in 2000, Lightspeed Venture Partners investment company engages in consumer, enterprise, technology, and cleantech markets.

Lok Capital Group

Gurgaon-based Lok Capital initiative launched at the end of 2000 with support of a grant from the Rockefeller Foundation specializes in bottom-of-pyramid customer segment investments.

Matrix Partners India

Mumbai-based Matrix Partners was founded in 1977, and is committed to build long-term relationships. With capital over ₹3,000 crore, they invest across sectors in India.

Mayfield Fund

One of the oldest VC firms focusing on early-stage to growth-stage investments in information technology companies, in particular on enterprise software, Internet consumer & media services, and communications.

New Enterprise Associates

It is one of the largest and most active VC firms which helps entrepreneurs to build transformation businesses across multiple stages, sectors, and geographies.

New Path Ventures, LLC

New Path Ventures, LLC is a VC firm which specializes in seed stage, startups, and early-stage investments. They prefer to invest in technology-based startups in India and US.

Nirvana Venture Advisors

Nirvana Venture Advisors invests in early-stage and market-leading companies in the fast-growing Indian Internet and mobile segments.

Norwest Venture Partners

NVP is an India-centric multistage investment firm that has partnered with entrepreneurs to build great businesses for more than 50 years.

Ojas Venture Partners

India-based VC Ojas Venture Partners believes that for young startups to become successful, it is imperative for them to have the guidance of experienced professionals with in-depth understanding of the marketplace.

Seedfund

This VC fund recognized the need for an early-stage investment ecosystem in India and hence focuses on investing in Indian startups.

SIDBI Venture Capital Limited

It focuses on life sciences, clean technology, retailing, light engineering, food processing, information technology, infrastructure-related services, healthcare, logistics and distribution, water and sanitation, agriculture, and education sectors.

Unitus Seed Fund

Unitus Seed Fund is a seed-stage venture fund based in Bangalore and Seattle which invests in developing markets with primary focus on rural startups focusing on low-income groups.

Utthishta

A firm that seed funds for software, web, mobile, and cloud computing-based Indian startups and also claims to provide a unique experience for entrepreneurs.

Ventureast Fund Advisors India Limited

It is India's longest standing VC firm investing in innovative businesses across seed, early, and growth stages.

Trifecta Capital Partners

It is a ₹300 crore venture debt fund which is expected to be closed in the next 3–6 months. It is also technically India's first venture debt fund.

Orios Venture Partners

It is a ₹300 crore and a 7-year, high-risk high-return fund, which is typically in early-stage investing. Software product startups are one of the key themes that Orios will be investing in.

Unilazer

It is a Mumbai-based private equity and venture fund specializing in early-stage and late-stage investments.

SUGGESTED READINGS

Kothari, Rajesh. (2010). *Financial services in India: Concept and application.* SAGE India.
Madura, Jeff. (2009). *International financial management* (10th ed.). Cengage Publishing.
Shapiro, A.C. (1996). *Multinational financial management* (5th ed.). Prentice Hall.
Vyuptakesh, Sharan. (2009, June). *International financial management* (5th ed.). Prentice Hall India.

PART VI
Contemporary Issues in Financial Management

CHAPTER 23

Foreign Exchange Management: An Introduction

Learning Objectives

- To understand foreign exchange market operations.
- To discuss international parity relationship.
- To learn about foreign exchange risk.
- To understand how to hedge foreign exchange exposures.

PRELUDE

With globalization being intensified, the role of foreign exchange management has become very significant. All economies in the world do pay much-needed attention to foreign exchange management, especially to exchange rate mechanism and to maintain the stability of currency. The salient aspects of foreign exchange management are discussed in the following empirical write-up (http://economictimes.indiatimes.com/tech/ites/wikileaks-why-infosys-gave-up-its-china-plans/articleshow/9895257.cms).

Why Infosys Gave Up Its China Plans

Bangalore: Infosys' plan to expand in China was hampered by clients' concerns about China's poor intellectual property protection. This was what Infosys co-founder N.R. Narayana Murthy told US diplomats in 2007 as per a cable from the Consulate in Chennai released by WikiLeaks. "In a wide ranging discussion with us, Murthy discussed the state of Infosys, with particular emphasis on its expansion plans outside of India. He admitted that the expansion plans hadn't been going as well as he hoped. Murthy said his clients, particularly European and American ones, are reluctant to have their work done in China due to their concerns about China's poor intellectual property protections," the cable stated.

The cable dated December 14, 2007, is titled "Infosys founder on IPR in China, hiring in US." It is classified as "unclassified/for official use only."

"I Can Get It"

Murthy said he understood the misgivings of his clients and narrated his experience in China to show how rampant piracy was. Stepping out of his central Beijing hotel to go for a stroll with Peter

Bonfield, then CEO of British Telecom, they encountered a sidewalk vendor selling pirated Microsoft and Windows products. Bonfield jokingly asked the vendor if he had Finacle (an Infosys banking software product), and the vendor replied: "I can get it for you tomorrow." Murthy further explains how the company has to spell out all the locations where the clients' work will be done in the master agreement and that clients were initially reluctant to allow China to be included.

"Chinese the Best"

Murthy, however, was optimistic about the long-term potential of China. As per the cable, he stated: "There is nobody better than the Chinese at solving a problem once they are serious about it." Murthy said it would take 4–5 years for the Chinese to overcome that reluctance.

There were other concerns for Infosys to expand in China. Murthy told the diplomats that though qualified graduates were available, those with sufficient English skills commanded a high premium. He said retention was more difficult in China than in India, as Chinese professionals are more willing to leave their job for a higher salary, whereas Indian professionals value institutions a bit more.

Expansion in US

During the interaction, Murthy is said to have talked about how Infosys planned to dramatically expand its hiring of US graduates from 300 per year to 3,000 in 2008. He said 95% of the US hires would work in the US, with a small number sent to work in other countries. Murthy was philosophical when discussing the effect of rupee appreciation on Infosys. He acknowledged that the appreciation of the Indian rupee had hurt his company, but did not appear overly concerned.

He admitted that it has a negative impact on the company's profitability, but said: "One of our founding principles is to focus on things that you can control"; the currency appreciation is a "macroeconomic effect, which we have to live with."

Foreign exchange management includes all business activities on which management should take financial decisions taking into account simultaneously the conditions prevailing in two or more financial markets, regulatory and institutional barriers to the international movement of funds, and changes in the exchange rate of national economies.

Foreign Exchange Management: Scope of Operation

- Foreign exchange market
- Foreign exchange rate
- International parity relationship
- Foreign exchange risk and hedging

The importance of MNCs and the globalization of production are now well recognized. MNCs have become central actors of the world economy and in linking foreign direct investment, trade, technology, and finance they are a driving force of economic growth. As the world is reduced to an electronic village and global finance has become a reality, in a contemporary global corporation, financial capital is one of the most fungible assets to cross national boundaries. The determinants of the way in which transnational corporations acquire, organize, and manage those assets are of critical importance, not only to the success of those corporations but also to the development and industrial restructuring of nation-states. The task of international financial manager is to make the best possible tactical decision that the market has to offer on liabilities, within the strategic funding constraints set by currency denomination, maturity, and capital structure.

Foreign Exchange Market

The market for foreign exchange involves the purchase and sale of national currencies. A foreign exchange market exists because economies employ national currencies. If the world economy used a single currency, there would be no need for foreign exchange markets. In Europe, 11 economies have chosen to trade their individual currencies for a common currency. But the euro will still trade against other world currencies. For now, the foreign exchange market is a fact of life. The foreign exchange market is extremely active. It is primarily an over-the-counter (OTC) market, the exchanges trade futures and option (more below) but most transactions are OTC. It is difficult to assess the actual size of the foreign exchange market because it is traded in many markets.

Globally, operations in the foreign exchange market started in a major way after the breakdown of the Bretton Woods System in 1971, which also marked the beginning of floating exchange rate regimes in several countries. Over the years, the foreign exchange market has emerged as the largest market in the world. The decade of the 1990s witnessed a perceptible policy shift in many emerging markets toward reorientation of their financial markets in terms of new products and instruments, development of institutional and market infrastructure, and realignment of regulatory structure consistent with the liberalized operational framework. The changing contours were mirrored in a rapid expansion of foreign exchange market in terms of participants, transaction volumes, decline in transaction costs, and more efficient mechanisms of risk transfer.

The foreign exchange market in India started in earnest less than three decades ago, when in 1978 the government allowed banks to trade foreign exchange with one another. However, it was in the 1990s that the Indian foreign exchange market witnessed far-reaching changes along with the shifts in the currency regime in India. The exchange rate of the rupee that was pegged earlier was floated partially in March 1992 and fully in March 1993 following the recommendations of the Report of the High Level Committee on Balance of Payments. The unification of the exchange rate was instrumental in developing a market-determined exchange rate of the rupee. Today, over 70% of the trading in foreign exchange continues to take place in the inter-bank market. The market consists of over Authorized Dealers (mostly banks) who transact currency among themselves and come out "square" or without exposure at the end of the trading day. Trading is regulated by the Foreign Exchange Dealers' Association of India (FEDAI), a self-regulatory association of dealers. Since 2001, clearing and settlement functions in the foreign exchange market have been largely carried out by the Clearing Corporation of India Limited (CCIL). The liberalization process has significantly boosted the foreign exchange market in the country by allowing both banks and corporations greater flexibility in holding and trading foreign currencies. The Sodani Committee set up in 1994 recommended greater freedom to participating banks, allowing them to fix their own trading limits, interest rates on deposits, and the use of derivative products.

The two main functions of the foreign exchange market are to determine the price of the different currencies in terms of one another and to transfer currency risk from more risk-averse participants to those more willing to bear it. As in any market, essentially the demand and supply for a particular currency at any specific point in time determines its price (exchange rate) at that point. However, as the value of a country's currency has significant bearing on its economy, foreign exchange markets frequently witness government intervention in one form or another to maintain the value of a currency at or near its "desired" level. Interventions can range from quantitative restrictions on trade and cross-border transfer of capital to periodic trades by the central bank of the country or its allies and agents to move the exchange rate in the desired direction. It is safe to say that over the years since liberalization, India has allowed restricted capital mobility and followed a "managed float"-type exchange rate policy. The main sources of foreign exchange are export earnings from goods and services, remittances from overseas, direct investment flows, and private and official loan inflows. The owners of these receipts are the fundamental suppliers in the market, that is, they sell foreign exchange to licensed foreign exchange dealers who are then able to sell to other institutions and individuals who need to buy foreign exchange.

Participants in Foreign Exchange Market

Speculation is the activity guided by profit making. A speculator takes risk to earn profit from exchange rate fluctuation. Speculators take a position to "speculate" the direction of exchange rates. A speculator takes on a foreign exchange position on the expectation of a favorable currency rate change. That is, a speculator does not take any other position to reduce or cover the risk of this open position.

Hedging is a way to transfer part of the foreign exchange risk inherent in all transactions, such as an export or an import, which involves two currencies. That is, by contrast to speculation, hedging is the activity of covering an open position. A hedger makes a transaction in the foreign exchange market to cover the currency risk of another position.

Arbitrage refers to the process by which banks, firms, or individuals attempt to make a risk/profit by taking advantage of discrepancies among prices prevailing simultaneously in different markets.

The players in the foreign exchange markets are speculators, corporations, commercial banks, currency brokers, and central banks. Corporations enter into the market primarily as hedgers; however, corporations might also speculate. Central banks tend to be speculators, that is, they enter into the market without covering their positions. Commercial banks and currency brokers primarily act as intermediaries; however, at different times, they might be also speculators, arbitrageurs, and hedgers. All the parties in the foreign exchange market communicate through traders or dealers.

Test Yourself

1. What is foreign exchange market?
2. Who can participate in foreign exchange market? Explain.

Foreign Exchange Rate

Foreign exchange rate is the value at which a country's currency unit is exchanged for another country's currency unit. For example, the current foreign exchange rate for Euros is 100 EUR = USD 130. Currently, domestic banks will determine their exchange rates based on international financial markets. There are two common ways to quote exchange rates: direct and indirect quotation.

Direct Quotation: This is also known as price quotation. The exchange rate of the domestic currency is expressed as equivalent to a certain number of units of a foreign currency. It is usually expressed as the amount of domestic currency that can be exchanged for 1 unit or 100 units of a foreign currency. The more valuable the domestic currency, the smaller the amount of domestic currency needed to exchange for a foreign currency unit and this gives a lower exchange rate. When the domestic currency becomes less valuable, a greater amount is needed to exchange for a foreign currency unit and the exchange rate becomes higher. Under the direct quotation, the variations in the exchange rates are inversely related to the changes in the value of the domestic currency. When the value of the domestic currency rises, the exchange rates fall, and when the value of the domestic currency falls, the exchange rates rise. For example, the price of one INR is $0.02102607. It can be written as US$0.02102607/INR.

Indirect Quotation: This is also known as the quantity quotation. The exchange rate of a foreign currency is expressed as equivalent to a certain number of units of the domestic currency. This is usually expressed as the amount of foreign currency needed to exchange for 1 unit or 100 units of domestic currency. The more valuable the domestic currency, the greater the amount of foreign currency it can exchange for and the lower the exchange rate. When the domestic currency becomes less valuable, it can exchange for a smaller amount of foreign currency and the exchange rate drops. Under indirect quotation, the rise and fall of exchange rates are directly related to the changes in the value of the domestic currency. When the value of the domestic currency rises, the exchange rates also rise, and when the value of the domestic currency falls, the exchange rates fall as well.

Direct Quotation	Indirect Quotation
USD/JPY = 134.56/61	EUR/USD = 0.8750/55
USD/HKD = 7.7940/50	GBP/USD = 1.4143/50
USD/CHF = 1.1580/90	AUD/USD = 0.5102/09

There are two implications for the above quotations:

1. Currency A/Currency B means the units of Currency B needed to exchange for 1 unit of Currency A.
2. Value A/Value B refers to the quoted buy price and sell price. As the difference between the buy price and sell price is not large, only the last two digits of the sell price are shown. The two digits in front are the same as the buy price.

Cross Rate: A cross rate is the currency exchange rate expressed by a currency pair in which none of the currencies involved is the official currency of the country in which this quotation is made. For example, if the currency exchange rate between a Japanese yen (JPY) and a British pound is quoted in a US newspaper, this would be called a cross rate as none of the currencies of this pair is the US dollar (USD). However, if the same rate is quoted in a Japanese newspaper, it would not be a cross rate, as Japan's official currency is involved in this pair.

At a more general level, the exchange rates expressed by any currency pair that does not involve the USD are called cross rates. Thus, this broader definition implies that the exchange rate of the currency pair GBP/JPY would be a cross rate, regardless of the country in which this quotation is being made.

How Does a Cross Rate Work? A cross rate is often used as a tool in currency trading by investors. The comparison of the current value of one foreign currency to the value of another foreign currency is considered as an extremely important indicator for currency trades. This indicator provides investors a helpful method of tracking the impact of various events on the value of the currencies that are being traded.

The basic formula always works like this: $A/B \times B/C = C/B$. The cross rate should equal the ratio of the two corresponding pairs, therefore, EUR/GBP = EUR/USD divided by GBP/US, just like GBP/CHF = GBP/USD × USD/CHF.

Spot Exchange Rate: In finance, an exchange rate (also known as the foreign exchange rate, forex rate, or FX rate) between two currencies is the rate at which one currency will be exchanged for another. It is also regarded as the value of one country's currency in terms of another currency. (i) For example, an inter-bank exchange rate of 91 Japanese yen (JPY, ¥) to the USD means that ¥91 will be exchanged for each US$1 or that US$1 will be exchanged for each ¥91. Exchange rates are determined in the foreign exchange market, (ii) which is open to a wide range of different types of buyers and sellers where currency trading is continuous. The spot exchange rate refers to the current exchange rate. The forward exchange rate refers to an exchange rate that is quoted and traded today but for delivery and payment on a specific future date.

Forward Market: In conjunction with spot trading, there is also a forward foreign exchange market. The forward market involves contracting today for the future purchase or sale of foreign exchange. The forward price may be the same as the spot price, but usually it is higher (at a premium) or lower (at a discount) than the spot price. Forward exchange rates are quoted on most major currencies for a variety of maturities. Bank quotes for maturities of 1, 3, 6, 9, and 12 months are readily available. Quotations on nonstandard or broken-term maturities are also available. Maturities extending beyond 1 year are becoming more frequent, and for good bank customers, a maturity extending out to 5, and even as long as 10 years, is possible. To learn how to read forward exchange rate quotations, let us consider the following example. Notice that forward rate quotations appear directly under the spot rate quotations for five major currencies (the British pound, Canadian dollar, JPY, Swiss franc, and euro) for 1-, 3-, and 6-month maturities. As an example, the settlement date of a 3-month forward transaction is three calendar months from the spot settlement date for the currency. That is, if today is Friday, January 4, 2011, and spot settlement is January 8 then the forward settlement date would be April 8, 2011, a period of 91 days from January 8. In this textbook, we will use the following notation for forward rate quotations. In general, $F N(j/k)$ will refer to the price of one unit of currency k in terms of currency j for delivery in N months. N equaling 1 denotes a 1-month maturity based on a 360-day banker's year. Thus, N equaling 3 denotes a 3-month maturity. When the context is clear, the simpler notation F will be used to denote a forward exchange rate. Forward quotes are either direct or indirect, one being the reciprocal of the other. From the US perspective, a direct forward quote is in American terms. As an example, let us consider the American term Swiss franc forward quotations in relationship to the spot rate quotation for Friday, January 4, 2011.

$$S (\$/SF) = 0.9036$$

$$F1 (\$/SF) = 0.9052$$

$$F3 (\$/SF) = 0.9077$$

$$F6 (\$/SF) = 0.9104$$

From these quotations, we can see that in American terms, the Swiss franc is trading at a premium to the dollar, and that the premium increases out to 6 months. Thus, according to the forward rate, when the Swiss franc is trading at a premium to the dollar in American terms, we can say the market expects the dollar to depreciate, or become less valuable, relative to the Swiss franc. Consequently, it costs more dollars to buy a Swiss franc forward. European term forward quotations are the reciprocal of the American term quotes. In European terms, the corresponding Swiss franc forward quotes to those stated above are:

$$S\,(SF/\$)=1.1067$$
$$F1\,(SF/\$)=1.1047$$
$$F3\,(SF/\$)=1.1017$$
$$F6\,(SF/\$)=1.0984$$

From these quotations, we can see that in European terms, the dollar is trading at a discount to the Swiss franc and that the discount increases out to 6 months; further, the forward maturity date is from January 4. Thus, according to the forward rate, when the dollar is trading at a discount to the Swiss franc in European terms, we can say the market expects the Swiss franc to appreciate or become more valuable relative to the dollar. Consequently, it costs fewer Swiss francs to buy a dollar forward. This is exactly what we should expect, as the European term quotes are the reciprocals of the corresponding American term quotations.

Forward Premium: It is common to express the premium or discount of a forward rate as an annualized percentage deviation from the spot rate. The forward premium (or discount) is useful for comparing against the interest rate differential between two countries. The forward premium or discount can be calculated using American or European term quotations, as shown in the example.

The formula for calculating the forward premium or discount for currency j in American terms is

$$f_{NJ} = \frac{FN(\$/j) - S(\$/j)}{S(\$/j)} \times 360\,/\,\text{days}$$

Test Yourself

1. How are exchange rates quoted in forward market?
2. What is forward market?

International Parity Relationship

International parity relationships starting with the Law of One Price (LOP) are extended to **Purchasing Power Parity (PPP)** and **Interest Rate Parity (IRP)**. These parity relationships help us to understand (i) how ex-rates are determined and (ii) how to forecast ex-rates. International Parity is based on efficient market hypothesis (**EMH**). Foreign exchange/securities markets are efficient when (i) securities/FX are priced efficiently reflecting all currently available information and (ii) no arbitrage opportunities exist.

Arbitrage: Arbitrage is riskless profit making opportunity by exploiting price differences. Simultaneously buying and selling mispriced securities/FX to make a guaranteed, riskless profit **without** any investment. "Picking up dimes with a bulldozer." For example, triangular arbitrage. International parity conditions exist when there are no arbitrage opportunities and markets are in equilibrium.

Law of One Price (LOP): $P_D = S\,(\$/£)\,P_F$,

where P_D is the Domestic Price (\$), P_F is the Foreign Price (£), and $S\,(\$/£)$ is the Spot ex-rate.

Example: Gold in US is $579.50/oz., gold in UK is £305, and S is $1.9000/£.

In USD: £305 × $1.9000/£ = $579.50, Gold is sold in both countries for the same price in USD.

In BP: $579.50/oz. ÷ $1.9000 = £305/oz., Gold is sold in both countries for the same price in BP.

If LOP (price equalization principle) did not hold, arbitrage would be possible, and would quickly restore parity. For example, what if gold in UK was $575? What if gold in US was £300?

The following four international parity relationships exist:

Interest Rate Parity: Interest rate parity is a no-arbitrage condition representing an equilibrium state under which investors will be indifferent to interest rates available on bank deposits in two countries. (i) Two assumptions central to IRP are capital mobility and perfect substitute of domestic and foreign assets. The IRP condition implies that the expected return on domestic assets will equal the expected return on foreign currency assets due to an equilibrium in the foreign exchange market resulting from changes in the exchange rate between two countries. (ii) Interest rate parity takes on two distinctive forms: **uncovered interest rate parity** refers to the parity condition in which exposure to exchange rate risk (unanticipated changes in exchange rates) is uninhibited, whereas **covered interest rate parity** refers to the condition in which a forward contract has been used to *cover* (eliminate exposure to) exchange rate risk. Each form of the parity condition demonstrates a unique relationship with implications for the forecasting of future exchange rates: the forward exchange rate and the future spot exchange rate. It states that the exchange rate of two countries will be affected by their interest rate differential. In other words, the currency of a high-interest-rate country will be at a forward discount relative to the currency of a low-interest-rate country and vice versa. This implies that the exchange rate (forward and spot) differential will be equal to the interest rate differential between the two countries.

That is, interest differential = exchange rate (forward and spot) differential

$$\frac{(1+r_F)}{(1+r_D)} = \frac{f_{F/D}}{s_{F/D}}$$

- IRP is a "no-arbitrage" condition.
- If IRP did not hold, then it would be possible for an astute trader to make unlimited amounts of money, exploiting the arbitrage opportunity.
- As we do not typically observe persistent arbitrage conditions, we can safely assume that IRP holds.

Purchasing Power Parity: In absolute terms, PPP states that the exchange rate between the currencies of two countries equals the ratio between the prices of goods in these countries. Further, the exchange rate must change to adjust to the change in the prices of goods in the two countries. In relative terms, purchasing power states that the exchange rate between the currencies of the two countries will adjust to reflect changes in the inflation rates of the two countries. In formal terms, it implies that the expected inflation differential equals to the current spot rate and the expected spot rate differential.

Thus, inflation rate differential = current spot rate and expected spot rate differential, that is,

$$\frac{(1+i_F)}{(1+i_D)} = \frac{E(s_{F/D})}{s_{F/D}}$$

Thailand and South Korea are running annual inflation rates of 5 and 7%, respectively. The current spot exchange rate is won 18.50/baht. What should be the value of the Thai baht in 1 year?

If PPP holds, then the expected spot rate after 1 year will be won 18.85/baht.

$$\frac{1.07}{1.05} = \frac{E(s_{W/B})}{18.5}$$

$$E(s_{W/B}) = 18.5 \times \frac{1.07}{1.05} = 18.85$$

Expectation Theory of Forward Rates: The expectation theory of forward exchange rates states that the forward rate provides the best and unbiased forecast of the expected future spot rate. In formal terms, it means that the forward rate and the current rate differential must be equal to the expected spot rate and the current spot rate differential. Thus, forward and current spot rate differential = expected and current spot rate differential, that is,

$$\frac{f_{F/D}}{s_{F/D}} = \frac{E(s_{F/D})}{s_{F/D}}$$

International Fisher Effect: In formal terms, the **International Fisher Effect** states that the nominal interest rate differential must be equal to the expected inflation rate differential in two countries.

Thus, nominal interest rate differential = expected inflation rate differential, that is,

$$\frac{(1+r_F)}{(1+r_D)} = \frac{E(1+i_F)}{E(1+i_D)}$$

Test Yourself

1. Discuss international parity relationship.
2. What is interest rate parity?
3. Elaborate on purchasing power parity.

Foreign Exchange Risk and Hedging

Firms dealing in multiple currencies face a risk (an unanticipated gain/loss) on account of sudden/unanticipated changes in exchange rates, quantified in terms of exposures. Exposure is defined as a contracted, projected, or contingent cash flow whose magnitude is not certain at the moment and depends on the value of the foreign exchange rates. The process of identifying risks faced by the firm and implementing the process of protection from these risks by financial or operational hedging is defined as foreign exchange risk management. Foreign exchange exposures may be classified into three broad categories:

- Transaction exposure
- Translation exposure
- Operating exposure

Transaction Exposure

This exposure arises on account of having receivables and payables denominated in foreign currency. The risk arising out of fluctuation in the exchange rate and its impact on the value of receivables and payables in local currency is known as transaction exposure.

Exporters and importers are affected by the transaction exposure. For example, if an Indian exporter has bills receivable of $200,000 to be realized at the end of 4 months hence and meanwhile rupee appreciates, the exporter will suffer loss on account of converting the amount due at a lower rate. Similarly, on depreciation of rupee vis-à-vis dollar, the exporter will record a gain.

Translation Exposure

This exposure arises in case of foreign subsidiaries. For the purpose of consolidation, the accounts of foreign subsidiary need to be converted into the home currency of the holding company at the exchange rates prevailing on the dates of consolidation. If the value of foreign currency changes between two dates, the translation gains or losses arise.

Operating Exposure

Operating exposure is characterized by evaluating real exchange gains or losses. It is prospective and long term in nature. The essence of operating exposure is that exchange rate changes significantly alter the cost of a firm's input and prices of its output and thereby influence its competitive position significantly.

Managing Foreign Exchange Exposure

It is often found that there is a lack of coordination of foreign exchange management among a company's subsidiaries and an absence of proper reporting system. The traditional approach to foreign exchange exposure management essentially encompasses the following steps:

- Determining and consolidating the net exposure of the international group.
- Determining and projecting the future movements in the currency to which the company is exposed and their possible impact on the company's financial position.
- Considering hedging alternatives and their relative costs.
- Selecting the hedging alternative which minimizes the company's exposure to the minimum possible extent.

Apart from traditional approaches, international companies prefer to maintain an internationally diversified portfolio of foreign currencies to minimize the risk of foreign currency exposure.

Hedging Instruments

There is a spectrum of opinions regarding foreign exchange hedging. Some firms feel hedging techniques are speculative or do not fall in their area of expertise and hence do not venture into hedging practices. Other firms are unaware of being exposed to foreign exchange risks. There are a set of firms which only hedge some of their risks, while others are aware of the various risks they face, but are unaware of the methods to guard the firm against the risk. There is yet another set of companies which believes that shareholder value cannot be increased by hedging firm's foreign exchange risks as shareholders can themselves individually hedge against the same using instruments such as forward contracts available in the market or diversify such risks out by manipulating their portfolio. There are some explanations backed by theory about the irrelevance of managing the risk of change in exchange rates. For example, the International Fisher Effect states that exchange rate changes are balanced out by interest rate changes; the PPP theory suggests that exchange rate changes will be offset by changes in relative price indices/inflation as the LOP should hold. Both these theories suggest that exchange rate changes are evened out in some form or the other.

A derivative is a financial contract whose value is derived from the value of some other financial asset, such as a stock price, a commodity price, an exchange rate, an interest rate, or even an index of prices. The main roles of derivatives are that they reallocate risk among financial market participants and help to make financial markets more complete. This section outlines the hedging strategies using derivatives with foreign exchange being the only risk assumed.

Forwards: A forward is a made-to-measure agreement between two parties to buy/sell a specified amount of a currency at a specified rate on a particular date in the future. The depreciation of the receivable currency is hedged against by selling a currency forward. If the risk is that of a currency appreciation (if the firm has to buy that currency in future say for import), it can hedge by buying the currency forward. For example, if Reliance Industries Limited (RIL) wants to buy crude oil in USD 6 months hence, it can enter into a forward contract to pay INR and buy USD and lock in a fixed exchange rate for INR–USD to be paid after 6 months regardless of the actual INR–dollar rate at the time. In this example, the downside is an appreciation of dollar which is protected by a fixed forward contract. The main advantage of a forward is that it can be tailored to the specific needs of the firm and an exact hedge can be obtained. On the downside, these contracts are not marketable, they cannot be sold to another party when they are no longer required, and are binding.

Futures: A futures contract is similar to the forward contract but is more liquid because it is traded in an organized exchange, that is, the futures market. Depreciation of a currency can be hedged by selling futures and appreciation can be hedged by buying futures. Advantages of futures are that there is a central market for futures which eliminates the problem of double coincidence. Futures require a small initial outlay (a proportion of the value of the future) with which significant amounts of money can be gained or lost with the actual forwards price fluctuations. This provides a sort of leverage. The previous example for a forward contract for RIL applies here also except that RIL will have to go to a USD futures exchange to purchase standardized dollar futures equal to the amount to be hedged as the risk is that of appreciation of the dollar. As mentioned earlier, the tailor ability of the futures contract is limited, that is, only standard denominations of money can be bought instead of the exact amounts that are bought in forward contracts.

Options: A currency option is a contract giving the right, not the obligation, to buy or sell a specific quantity of one foreign currency in exchange for another at a fixed price, called the exercise price or strike price. The fixed nature of the exercise price reduces the uncertainty of exchange rate changes and limits the losses of open currency positions. Options are particularly suited as a hedging tool for contingent cash flows, as is the case in bidding processes. Call options are used if the risk is an upward trend in price (of the currency), while put options are used if the risk is a downward trend. Again, taking the example of RIL which needs to purchase crude oil in USD in 6 months, if RIL buys a call option (as the risk is an upward trend in dollar rate), that is, the right to buy a specified amount of dollars at a fixed rate on a specified date, there are two scenarios. If the exchange rate movement is favorable, that is, the dollar depreciates, then RIL can buy them at the spot rate as they have become cheaper. In the other case, if the dollar appreciates compared to today's spot rate, RIL can exercise the option to purchase it at the agreed strike price. In either case, RIL benefits by paying the lower price to purchase the dollar.

Swaps: A swap is a foreign currency contract whereby the buyer and seller exchange equal initial principal amounts of two different currencies at the spot rate. The buyer and seller exchange fixed or floating rate interest payments in their respective swapped currencies over the term of the contract. At maturity, the principal amount is effectively re-swapped at a predetermined exchange rate so that the parties end up with their original currencies. The advantages of swaps are that firms with limited appetite for exchange rate risk may move to a partially or completely hedged position through the mechanism of foreign currency swaps, while leaving the underlying borrowing intact. Apart from covering the exchange rate risk, swaps also allow firms to hedge the floating interest rate risk. Consider an export-oriented company that has entered into a swap for a notional principal of USD 1 million at an exchange rate of 42/dollar. The company pays US 6months LIBOR to the bank and receives 11.00% p.a. every 6 months on January 1 and July 1, for 5 years. Such a company would have earnings in dollars and can use the same to pay interest for this kind of borrowing (in dollars rather than in rupee) thus hedging its exposures.

Foreign Debt: Foreign debt can be used to hedge foreign exchange exposure by taking advantage of the International Fischer Effect relationship. This is demonstrated with the example of an exporter who has to receive a fixed amount of dollars in a few months from the present. The exporter stands to lose if the domestic currency appreciates against that currency in the meanwhile; hence, to hedge this, he could take a loan in the foreign currency for the same time period and convert the same into domestic currency at the current exchange rate. The theory assures that the gain realized by investing the proceeds from the loan would match the interest rate payment (in the foreign currency) for the loan.

Test Yourself

1. What are the various types of foreign exchange exposures?
2. What are the various hedging strategies available to overcome exposure?
3. Define options, forwards, and swaps.

SUMMARY

1. International financial management deals with multiple currencies, interest rate, inflation rate, foreign exchange, and political risks.
2. Foreign exchange rate is the price of one currency in terms of other currency.
3. Spot rate is the rate that is used for immediate delivery of currency.
4. Forward rate is the price determined today for delivery in the future.
5. There is a relationship between interest rate, inflation rate, and exchange rate. Such a relationship is known as international parity.

$$\frac{1+r_f}{1+r_D} = \frac{1+i_f}{1+i_d} = \frac{E(s_{f/d})}{s_{f/d}} = \frac{f_{f/d}}{s_{f/d}}$$

KEY TERMS

- Arbitrage
- Derivate
- Option
- Direct quote
- Cross rate
- Operational exposure
- Fisher effect
- Forward premium
- Purchasing power parity
- Translation exposure

- Bid-ask price
- Forward
- Swap
- Indirect quote
- Transaction exposure
- Exchange rate
- Hedging
- Interest rate parity
- Law of one price
- Spot exchange rate

Learning Outcomes

Students would be in the position of understanding foreign exchange management.

ASSESS YOURSELF

Concept Review and Critical Review Questions

1. Describe international finance management.
2. What is foreign exchange market? Who can participate in a foreign exchange market?
3. Discuss the four international parity relationships.
4. What is foreign exchange risk? How can this foreign exchange risk be hedged?

STUDENT ACTIVITY

Students should conduct a sample study of fluctuation in Indian rupee v/s USD and explain the reason for fluctuation.

SUGGESTED READINGS

Madura, Jeff. (2009). *International financial management* (10th ed.). Cengage Publishing.
Shapiro, A.C. (1996). *Multinational financial management* (5th ed.). Prentice Hall.
Vyuptakesh, Sharan. (2009, June). *International financial management* (5th ed.). Prentice Hall India.

CHAPTER 24

Derivatives

- To learn about derivatives and its role in the Indian economy.
- To overview derivative markets in India and the instruments available for trading.
- To explain the features of forwards and futures and their usefulness in hedging.
- To study the fundamentals of options contract and basic investment strategies using options.

PRELUDE

BRIC Bourses Form Alliance to Cross-list

Benchmark Equity Index Derivatives

Stock exchanges in Brazil, Russia, India, and China (BRIC) have formed an alliance to cross-list benchmark equity index derivatives on one another's boards. It was decided at the 51st annual general meeting (AGM) of the World Federation of Exchanges in Johannesburg that the alliance will also develop innovative products tracking these exchanges.

The initiative brings together Brazil's Bovespa, Russia's MICEX, Hong Kong Exchanges & Clearing (HKEx), Johannesburg Stock Exchange (JSE), and India's National Stock Exchange and Bombay Stock Exchange BSE. These exchanges represent a combined listed market capitalisation of $9.02 trillion, equity market trading value of $422 billion per month and 9,481 listed companies.

The second phase of this project will include development of products combining exposures to equity indices of all alliance partner exchanges. The third phase may include product developments and cooperation in additional asset classes and services.

Source: Economic Times, October 13, 2011.

Derivatives

"Mr X has purchased the shares of Company XYZ at a price of ₹500 per share. He wants to liquidate his position after two months, but fears that the market price will be below ₹500 per share after two months".

This situation is faced by many of us in real life, where we are bound to think of some alternate trading strategy which may either reduce or cover the risk to which our investments are exposed.

There are two types of risks to which an investment is exposed:

1. Diversifiable.
2. Non-diversifiable.

Diversifiable risks are those risks which may be reduced by an investor by including different categories of assets in his investment portfolio. Still, the investments are exposed to certain risks which cannot be reduced. These non-diversifiable risks should be given a cover, that is, investor suffers the loss, but then that loss is compensated by the profit on an alternative investment, specifically made to cover the losses arising out of non-diversifiable risks.

Derivatives are a means to provide cover to the systematic (non-diversifiable) risk on an investment. Derivative is a contract which derives its value from another contract. In financial terms, a derivative is a contract which derives its value from an underlying asset. Underlying asset may be anything, such as, weather, performance of a cricketer in a cricket match, price of a commodity, fluctuations in the interest rates on bonds/debentures, currencies and, for our reference, it may be even shares of the companies in which the funds are invested or even the fluctuations in the market indices, such as, Sensex and S&P CNX Nifty.

If an investor wants to invest in the cash segment of financial markets there are different instruments available, such as, equity shares, debentures, Government securities, mutual funds, real estate and commodities. Similarly, if an investor wants to invest in derivatives segment of the financial markets, there are different instruments available, such as, futures, options, swaps, forwards, etc.

In India, stock futures, stock options, and index option instruments are available for trading on the BSE, NSE, and the United Stock Exchange.

Development of Derivatives Market in India

Derivatives trading commenced in India in June 2000 after SEBI granted the final approval to this effect in May 2001. SEBI permitted the derivative segments of two stock exchanges, NSE and BSE, and their clearing house/corporation to commence trading and settlement in approved derivatives contracts. To begin with, SEBI approved trading in index futures contracts based on S&P CNX Nifty and BSE-30 (Sensex) index. This was followed by approval for trading in options based on these two indexes and options on individual securities.

The trading in BSE sensex options commenced on June 4, 2001 and the trading in options on individual securities commenced in July 2001. Futures contracts on individual stocks were launched in November 2001. The derivatives trading on NSE commenced with S&P CNX Nifty Index futures on June 12, 2000. The trading in index options commenced on June 4, 2001 and trading in options on individual securities commenced on July 2, 2001.

Single stock futures were launched on November 9, 2001. The index futures and options contract on NSE are based on S&P CNX.

NSE introduced the currency derivatives in August 2008 and interest rate futures in August 2009 as one of the move to strengthen the Indian capital market. Currency futures are available on Euro, Pound, Dollar, and Yen.

Growth in Derivatives Segment

Trading and settlement in derivative contracts is done in accordance with the rules, byelaws, and regulations of the respective exchanges and their clearing house/corporation duly approved by SEBI and notified in the official gazette. Foreign institutional investors (FIIs) are permitted to trade in all exchange-traded derivative products.

Derivatives Market: Functions

The derivatives market performs a number of economic functions:

1. **Risk transfer:** It transfers risk from risk-adverse investors to risk-prone investors.
2. **Price discovery:** A well-developed derivatives market reflects the perception of investors about the future and thus leads the prices to the perceived future level.
3. **Increased trading volume:** Due to the introduction of the derivatives, the volume of trading of the underlying asset increases as more and more investors participate, who otherwise may not due to lack of risk transfer facilities.
4. **Trading catalyst:** A well-developed financial market cannot flourish without a sound derivatives market. Derivatives markets calls for new entrepreneurial activities, employment opportunities, and development of various innovative financial products. Thus, it acts as a catalyst in the overall economic development.

Trading Motives of an Investor

Arbitration

Arbitration activity may be defined as a trading activity wherein investor attempts to earn abnormal return (after adjusting brokerage cost) with a net investment of ₹"0". In simpler words, arbitrage involves buying an asset at a low price in one market and selling the same at a higher price in another market and booking an abnormal profit due to mismatch in the price of an asset in different markets.

Arbitrage profits cannot be earned on permanent basis. Due to the presence of arbitragers in the market, the demand and supply of an asset forces the prices to reach at the level of equilibrium.

In stock markets, arbitragers keep a watch on the share price movements at various stock exchanges in the country. As and when they find a situation wherein the same share is being traded at different prices on two exchanges, they take the buy position where it is traded at low prices and sell position where it is being traded at higher prices, and later on square off their positions, booking an abnormal profit equal to the difference in prices (after adjusting for the brokerage cost). Introduction of online trading has reduced the profits of arbitragers as the information of each and every second is available to crores of investors at the same time. It is only due to this reason that one can observe that the shares of a particular company are traded at more or less the same price on various stock exchanges. The minor difference in the prices is generally less than the brokerage cost and hence does not call for an arbitrage activity.

Speculation

Speculation involves taking buying and selling positions on the shares merely on the basis of intuition. Based upon the market awareness, investors may be categorized as informed and uninformed investors. The trading activities of uninformed investors may be termed as speculative activities. Increase in the trading activities of the uninformed investors increases volatility in the market.

Hedging

Derivatives are often used to hedge risk. Hedge means "to cover." As discussed in the previous chapters, systematic risk cannot be diversified but they can be adequately hedged by the rational use of derivative contracts.

An example of a hedge would be if you owned a stock, and you are not sure about how the market will move in the near future, hence, you sold a futures contract stating that you will sell your stock at a set price, therefore, avoiding market fluctuations. Investors use this strategy when they are unsure of what the market will do. A perfect hedge reduces your risk to nothing (except for the cost of the hedge).

Derivative Instruments in India

A wide variety of instruments are available on both the NSE and the BSE. The following table summarizes the contract specifications of the various F&O contracts available on the NSE:

Parameter	Index Futures	Index Options	Futures on Individual Securities	Options on Individual Securities	Mini Index Futures	Mini Index Options	Long-term Index Options
Underlying	Five indices*	Five indices	202 securities	202 securities	S&P CNX Nifty	S&P CNX Nifty	S&P CNX Nifty
Security descriptor							
Instrument	FUTIDX	OPTIDX	FUTSTK	OPTSTK	FUTIDX	OPTIDX	OPTIDX
Underlying symbol	Symbol of underlying index	Symbol of underlying index	Symbol of underlying security	Symbol of underlying security	MINIFTY	MINIFTY	NIFTY
Expiry date	DD-MM-YYYY	DD-MM-YYYY	DD-MM-YYYY	DD-MM-YYYY	DD-MM-YYYY	DD-MM-YYYY	DD-MM-YYYY
Option type	-	CE/PE	-	CA/PA	-	CE/PE	CE/PE
Strike price	-	Strike price	-	Strike price	-	Strike price	Strike price
Trading cycle	Three-month trading cycle - the near month (one), the next month (two), and the far month (three)						Three quarterly expiries (March, June, September, and December cycle) and next eight half-yearly expiries (June, December cycle)
Expiry day	Last Thursday of the expiry month. If the last Thursday is a trading holiday, then the expiry day is the previous trading day.						
Strike price intervals	-	Depending on underlying price	-	Depending on underlying price	-	Depending on underlying price	Depending on underlying price
Permitted lot size	Underlying specific	Underlying specific	Underlying specific	Underlying specific	20	20	Underlying specific
Price steps	₹0.05	₹0.05	₹0.05	₹0.05	₹0.05	₹0.05	₹0.05
Price bands	Operating range of 10% of the base price	A contract-specific price range based on its delta value is computed and updated on a daily basis	Operating range of 20% of the base price	A contract-specific price range based on its delta value is computed and updated on a daily basis	Operating range of 10% of the base price	A contract-specific price range based on its delta value is computed and updated on a daily basis	A contract-specific price range based on its delta value is computed and updated on a daily basis

Source: NSE.

BSE also offers similar instruments for trading in derivatives segment.

Test Yourself

1. Derivatives are a means to reduce unsystematic risk. Comment.

Futures

Futures contract is a derivative instrument, in which two or more parties agree to buy or sell an underlying asset at an agreed price, at a specific date in future, with an intermediation of an exchange.

Futures are primarily traded in three primary areas

1. Agricultural commodities
2. Metals and oils
3. Financial assets, such as, indices, stocks, interest rates, and currencies.

Futures	Forwards
Traded on an exchange	Traded over the counter
Standardized contracts	Non-standardized contracts
Daily settlement on the basis of mark to market margin	Only final settlement, no margin required
Counterparty risk assumed by the exchange	Counterparty risk present

Types of Futures Contracts

1. **Commodity Futures:** Underlying asset is a commodity, such as, gold, metal, oil, wheat, soyabean, rice, etc. In India, commodity futures are available on Multi Commodity Exchange (MCX) and National Commodity Exchange (NCDEX).
2. **Index Futures:** Underlying asset is an index. In India, index futures are available on the NSE and the BSE.
3. **Stock Futures:** Underlying asset is an individual stock. In India, stock futures are available at the NSE and the BSE.
4. **Currency Futures:** Underlying asset is a currency. In India these are traded on the NSE.
5. **Interest Rate Futures:** Underlying asset is an interest rate bond. These are available on the NSE.

Investors are attracted towards the futures market mainly because it provides leverage to the small investors. Leverage means having control over large cash amount of an underlying asset with a comparatively less amount of capital. In other words, an investor may enter into a futures contract that is much more than what he/she has to pay initially.

The smaller the amount of margin as compared to cash value, higher is the leverage. By high leverage, we mean that even a small change in the futures price may translate into huge gains or losses. (Margin system has been discussed in the chapter on risk management.)

Futures Market

There are two ways by which an investor may enter a futures market:

1. **Long position:** Going long on futures contract means an investor is buying a futures contract. A long investor is bullish about the market, hence he locks the purchase price of the underlying assets by means of a futures contract. If the market turns as per his expectations, he earns a profit by closing his position at a higher price (buy-sell strategy).

2. **Short position:** Taking a short position on a futures contract is also referred to as sell-buy strategy. An investor who is bearish about the market may open his position as a seller. If the market goes as per his anticipation he books a profit by squaring off his position as a seller.

Role of Beta in Trading of Futures

It is widely known that futures are used to hedge your risk of investment in cash markets. The general problem which arises is whether the position of an investor in the futures provides a complete hedge against the probable risks. This problem generally arises in case the stock futures for any individual stock are not available. In that situation, investor has to take a position on index futures. This problem may be resolved by knowing and implementing the concept of beta. Beta may be defined as the factor sensitivity of returns on individual stocks towards the movement in the index.

The value of futures contract which has to be taken by an investor may thus be determined with help of the following formula:

Futures contract value = investment value of the asset to be hedged/beta value of the stock.

Test Yourself

1. Differentiate between forwards and futures.
2. What is the role of beta in hedging systematic risk?

Standardization of Futures Contract

A futures contract is a forward contract, which is traded on an exchange. NSE commenced trading in index futures on June 12, 2000. The index futures contracts are based on the popular market benchmark S&P CNX Nifty index.

NSE defines the characteristics of the futures contract such as the underlying index, market lot, and the maturity date of the contract. The futures contracts are available for trading from introduction to the expiry date.

CONTRACT SPECIFICATIONS

To understand, let us discuss the contract specification of futures contract on S&P CNX Nifty.

Security Descriptor

The security descriptor for the S&P CNX Nifty futures contracts is

1. market type: N,
2. instrument type: FUTIDX,
3. underlying: NIFTY,
4. expiry date: date of contract expiry,
5. instrument type represents the instrument, that is, futures on index,
6. underlying symbol denotes the underlying index which is S&P CNX Nifty, and
7. expiry date identifies the date of expiry of the contract.

Underlying Instrument

The underlying index is S&P CNX NIFTY.

Trading Cycle

S&P CNX Nifty options contracts have three consecutive monthly contracts, additionally three quarterly months of the cycle March/June/September/December and eight following semi-annual months of the cycle June/December would be available, so that at any point in time, there would be options contracts with at least a five-year tenure available. On expiry of the near month contract, new contracts (monthly/quarterly/half-yearly contracts as applicable) are introduced at new strike prices for both call and put options, on the trading day following the expiry of the near month contract.

Expiry Day

S&P CNX Nifty futures contracts expire on the last Thursday of the expiry month. If the last Thursday is a trading holiday, the contracts expire on the previous trading day.

TRADING PARAMETERS

Contract Size

The value of the futures contracts on Nifty may not be less than ₹2 lakhs at the time of introduction. The permitted lot size for futures contracts and options contracts shall be the same for a given underlying or such lot size as may be stipulated by the exchange from time to time.

Price Steps

The price step in respect of S&P CNX Nifty futures contracts is ₹0.05.

Base Prices

Base price of S&P CNX Nifty futures contracts on the first day of trading would be theoretical futures price. The base price of the contracts on subsequent trading days would be the daily settlement price of the futures contracts.

Price Bands

There are no day minimum/maximum price ranges applicable for S&P CNX Nifty futures contracts. However, to prevent erroneous order entry by trading members, operating ranges are kept at +/−10%. In respect of orders which have come under price freeze, members would be required to confirm to the exchange that there is no inadvertent error in the order entry and that the order is genuine. On such confirmation, the exchange may approve such an order.

Quantity Freeze

Orders which may come to the exchange as quantity freeze shall be such that have a quantity of more than 15,000. However, in exceptional cases, the exchange may, at its discretion, not allow the orders that have come under quantity freeze for execution for any reason whatsoever including nonavailability of turnover/exposure limit. In all other cases, quantity freeze orders shall be canceled by the exchange.

Order Type/Order Book/Order Attribute

1. regular lot order,
2. stop loss order,
3. immediate or cancel, and
4. spread order.

Source: www.nseindia.com (June 7, 2016).

Options

An option is a security that gives the holder the right to buy or sell a particular asset at a specified price, on or before, a specific date. Depending on the parties and types of assets involved, options can take on many different forms. Certain features are common to all options.

1. With every option contract there is a right, but not the obligation, either to buy or to sell.
2. A call is the right to buy a specific asset or security.
3. A put is the right to sell a specific asset or security.
4. Every option contract has a buyer and a seller.
5. The option buyer is referred to as the holder and has a long position in the option.
6. The holder buys the right to exercise or evoke the terms of the option claim.
7. The seller often referred to as the writer, has a short position and is responsible for fulfilling the obligations of the option if the holder exercises.
8. Every option has an option price, an exercise price, and an exercise date.
9. The price paid by the buyer to the writer is referred to as the option premium.
10. The exercise price or strike price is the price specified in the option contract at which the underlying asset can be purchased or sold.
11. The exercise date is the last day the holder can exercise.
12. A European option is one that can be exercised only at the exercise date, while an American option can be exercised at any time on or before the exercise date.

Underlying Cash Assets

Option contracts are traded on two types of underlying assets

1. One type of asset is a cash or spot asset such as shares of stock, indexes, currencies, and bonds.
2. The other type is a futures contract.

Commodity Derivatives

Commodity futures contracts: A futures contract is an agreement for buying or selling a commodity for a predetermined delivery price at a specific future time.

For example, suppose a farmer is expecting his crop of wheat to be ready in two months time, but is worried that the price of wheat may decline in this period. To minimize his risk, he can enter into a futures contract to sell his crop in two months' time at a price determined now. This way he is able to hedge his risk arising from a possible adverse change in the price of his commodity.

Commodity options contracts: Like futures, options are also financial instruments used for hedging and speculation. The commodity option holder has the right, but not the obligation, to buy (or sell) a specific quantity of a commodity at a specified price on or before a specified date. There are two types of commodity options: a "call" option gives the holder a right to buy a commodity at an agreed price, while a "put" option gives the holder a right to sell a commodity at an agreed price on or before a specified date (called expiry date). For example, suppose a farmer buys a put option to sell 100 quintals of wheat at a price of ₹100 per quintal and pays a "premium" of ₹2 per quintal. If the price of wheat declines to say ₹90 before expiry, the farmer will exercise his option and sell his wheat at the agreed price of ₹100 per quintal. However, if the market price of wheat increases to say ₹110 per quintal, it would be advantageous for the farmer to sell it directly in the open market at the spot price, rather than exercise his option to sell at ₹100 per quintal.

Need of Commodity Derivatives

India is among the top producers of most of the commodities, in addition to being a major consumer of bullion (gold, silver, etc.) and energy products. Agriculture contributes about 20% to the GDP of the Indian economy. Agriculture sector is an important factor in achieving a GDP growth of 8-10%. All this indicates that India can be promoted as a major center for trading of commodity derivatives. In India, commodity derivatives are traded at Multi Commodity Exchange of India Limited (MCX) and National Commodity & Derivatives Exchange Limited (NCDEX).

Test Yourself

1. Which is more risky: options or futures?
2. An investor is highly bullish about the market and does not possess the asset. What investment strategy would you suggest?

Trading Strategies

Speculation using index futures: If a speculator is bearish about the index, he/she may speculate by adopting the buy-sell strategy on index futures. He opens his position as a seller at higher index value and squares off at a lower value, thus booking a speculative profit. Similarly, if a speculator is bullish about the index, he may adopt a buy-sell strategy to book speculative profits.

Hedging using stock futures: Suppose an investor has a portfolio of stocks for which he has invested for the long term. Recent market anticipations are that the market may fall down in next six months. But the investor is not willing to sell the shares at this point of time and buy them again at a lower price in the next few months as it may entail the cost. Here, he may go short on a stock index future to hedge his portfolio against adverse movements in the stock market. If the stock market ends up falling over the next six months (as the investor expected), the profit from the futures contract should help to offset the losses from his stock portfolio. In this way, he has used the futures market to hedge his portfolio in the near term.

Basic Option Strategies

1. **Long call:** Suppose an investor buys a call option on ABC stock with an exercise price (X) of ₹50 at a call premium (C) of ₹3. In simple terms, this option gives the holder the right, but not the obligation, to buy ABC stock for ₹50.

   The following table shows the payoff to the investor due to this strategy:

Stock Price, ₹	Exercise?	Premium, ₹	Profit from Exercing	Net Profit
40	No	3	0	–3
45	No	3	0	–3
50	Yes/no	3	0	–3
45	Yes	3	55–50=5	2
60	Yes	3	60–50=10	7
65	Yes	3	65–50=15	12

The same can be explained graphically.

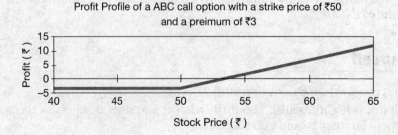

Profit Profile of a ABC call option with a strike price of ₹50 and a preimum of ₹3

2. **Naked short call:** An investor who is bearish about the market knows that if the market goes down, the holder of the call option will not exercise the contract, and thus, he will enjoy the amount of premium on the contract. The payoff of the writer of the call option is exactly opposite to the payoff of the holder of the call option.

Stock Price, ₹	Holder Exercise?	Premium Received, ₹	Action from writer	Writers Profit/Loss
40	No	3	Nothing	3
45	No	3	Nothing	3
50	Yes/No	3	Nothing	3
45	Yes	3	Buy ABC for ₹55 sell at ₹50	3−5=−2
₹60	Yes	₹3	Buy ABC for ₹60 sell at ₹50	3−10=−7
₹65	Yes	₹3	Buy ABC for ₹65 sell at ₹50	3−15=−12

Profit profile for the writer of an ABC call option with a strike price of ₹50 and a premium of ₹3

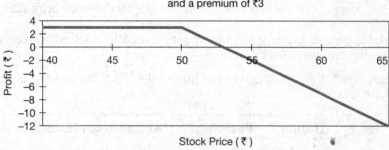

Profit profile for the writer of an ABC call option with a strike price of ₹50 and a premium of ₹3

3. **Covered call write:** This is one of the most popular option strategies to write a call on a stock already owned. For example, an investor who bought ABC stock at ₹50 sometime ago and who did not expect its price to appreciate in the near future, might sell a call on ABC stock with an exercise price of ₹50.

The profits/losses of this strategy are detailed in the following table:

Stock Price	Profit on Uncovered Call Write	Profit on Stock Purchased at ₹50	Total
40	3	−10	−7
45	3	−5	−2
50	3	0	3
45	−2	5	3
60	−7	10	3
65	−12	15	3

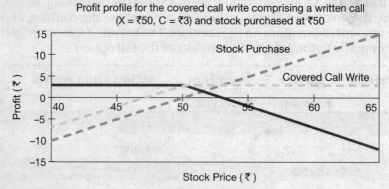

Profit profile for the covered call write comprising a written call
(X = ₹50, C = ₹3) and stock purchased at ₹50

Features of the covered call write strategy

1. If ABC stock is ₹50 or more, the covered call writer loses the stock when the holder exercises.
2. This leaves the writer with only the premium of ₹3.
3. The benefit of the covered call write occurs when the stock price declines. For example, if ABC stock declined to ₹40, then the writer would suffer an actual loss of ₹10 (by virtue of selling a stock he bought for ₹50 for only ₹40).
4. The ₹3 premium received from selling the call, though would reduce this loss to just ₹7.
5. Thus, the covered call offers partial insurance against the stock price falling.

4. **Long put:** Suppose an investor buys a put option on ABC stock with an exercise price (X) of ₹50 at a call premium (C) of ₹3.

In simple terms, this option gives the holder the right, but not the obligation, to sell ABC stock for ₹50.

Stock Price, ₹	Holder Exercise?	Premium Paid, ₹	Action from Holder	Holder Profit/Loss
40	Yes	3	Buy stock for 40 sell at ₹50	3+10=7
45	Yes	3	Buy stock for ₹45 sell at ₹50	3+5=2
50	Yes/No	3	Nothing	−3
45	No	3	Nothing	−3
60	No	3	Nothing	−3
65	No	3	Nothing	−3

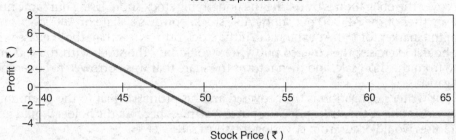

Profit profile to the holder of an ABC Put Option with a strike price of ₹50 and a premium of ₹3

Thus, similar to a call purchase, a long put position provides the buyer with potentially large profit opportunities (not unlimited, since the price can never be below zero), while limiting the losses to the amount of the premium. Unlike the call purchase strategy, the put purchase position requires the stock price to decline before profit is realized.

5. **Naked short put:** The exact opposite to a put purchase (in terms of profit or loss and stock price relations) is the sale of a put, known as a naked put write. This positions profit and loss figures are shown below.

| Stock Price (₹) | Exercise Put | Premium | Action by Writer | Put Writers |
	Yes/No?	Paid/ Received (₹)		Profit
40	Yes	₹3	Buy Stock for ₹50 (real value 40)	+3+40−50=−7
45	Yes	3	Buy Stock for ₹50 (real value ₹45)	+3+40−45=−2
50	No/yes	3	Nothing	3
45	No	3	Nothing	3
60	No	3	Nothing	3
65	No	3	Nothing	3

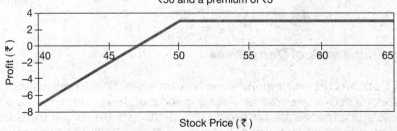

Profit profile to the writer of an ABC put option with a strike price of ₹50 and a premium of ₹3

Covered short put: This strategy requires the seller of a put to cover her position. Because a put writer is required to buy the stock at the exercise price if the holder exercises, the only way she can cover the obligation is by selling the underlying stock short. Using our same numbers, suppose a writer of the ABC 50 put shorts ABC stock: borrows a share of ABC stock and then sells it in the market for ₹50. At expiration, if the stock price is less than the exercise price and the put holder exercises, the covered put writer would buy the stock with the ₹50 proceeds obtained from the short sale, and then returns the share that was borrowed to cover the short sale obligation.

The put writer's obligation is thus covered and his profit is equal to the premium. If the stock price rises above the strike price the put is worthless because the holder would not exercise, but losses would occur from covering the short sale.

Stock Price	Naked Put Profit/Loss	Profit on Stock Sold at ₹50	Combined
40	-7	10	3
45	-2	5	3
50	3	0	0
45	3	-5	-3
60	3	-10	-7
65	3	-15	-12

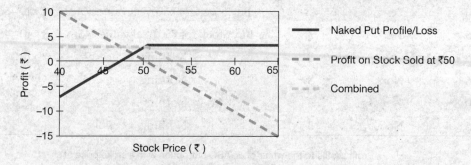

Profit profile for a covered put write (X = ₹50, P = ₹3)

Regulatory Framework of Derivatives

L.C. Gupta Committee was appointed on November 18, 1996 to cultivate suitable regulatory framework for derivatives trading. The main focus of the committee was on the development of a regulatory framework for financial derivatives with special focus on the equity derivatives. The committee submitted its report in March 1998. The same was approved in March 1998 and was approved by SEBI in May 1998.

THE GUIDING PRINCIPLES

Regulatory Objectives

1. The Committee believes that regulation should be designed to achieve specific, well-defined goals. It is inclined towards positive regulation designed to encourage healthy activity and behavior. It has been guided by the following objectives:

    (a) **Investor protection:** Attention needs to be given to the following four aspects:
    (b) **Fairness and transparency:** The trading rules should ensure that trading is conducted in a fair and transparent manner. Experience in other countries shows that in many cases, derivatives brokers/dealers failed to disclose potential risk to the clients. In this context, sales practices adopted by dealers for derivatives would require specific regulation. In some of the most widely reported mishaps in the derivatives market elsewhere, the underlying reason was inadequate internal control system at the user–firm itself so that overall exposure was not controlled and the use of derivatives was for speculation rather than for risk hedging. These experiences provide useful lessons for us for designing regulations.

    - **Safeguard for clients' moneys:** Moneys and securities deposited by clients with the trading members should not only be kept in a separate clients' account but should also not be attachable for meeting the broker's own debts. It should be ensured that trading by dealers on own account is totally segregated from that for clients.

    - **Competent and honest service:** The eligibility criteria for trading members should be designed to encourage competent and qualified personnel so that investors/clients are served well. This makes it necessary to prescribe qualification for derivatives brokers/dealers and the sales persons appointed by them in terms of a knowledge base.

    - **Market integrity:** The trading system should ensure that the market's integrity is safeguarded by minimizing the possibility of defaults. This requires framing appropriate rules about capital adequacy, margins, clearing corporation, etc.

For full report logon to http://www.sebi.gov.in/commreport/lcgupta.html (accessed on June 7, 2016).

Some F&O Pointers

Rollover of Contracts

The near-month F&O contract expires on the last Thursday of the month. Rollover figures become an important indicator of the market sentiment. Rollover is applicable to future contracts and not options. If an investor is holding a position in futures, he will close his position in the near month or in the current month and take a fresh position in the next month contract.

Rollover of contracts involves certain costs to the investors. Apart from the brokerage cost involved, investor has to bear an additional cost equal to the difference between the futures price at which the existing position is canceled (squared off) and the price at which a new position is taken.

Suppose an investor is long on, say, 10 contracts of Nifty futures in July. To rollover, he sells these 10 contracts and simultaneously buy 10 contracts with expiry in August 2010. If the Nifty futures expiring in July 2010 are trading at 5,520, the investor will find the Nifty futures with expiry in August 2010 trading at a slight premium above 5,520. Suppose, the Nifty futures expiring in August 2010 are trading at 5,530, he will have to bear the difference of 10. Further, the investor will have to bear transaction-related expenses such as brokerage.

% of Outstanding Positions Rolled Over	Market Mood/Sentiment
Higher	1. Symbolizes bullish sentiment
	2. If the market is in a bull phase, market would remain firm or move up further in the near future
	3. If the market is in extreme bear phase, troublesome situation as the bears are convinced that the market will fall in the future
	1. Bearishness
Lower	2. The contract is not active in the market
	3. Prices may find a strong resistance in the near future
	4. Symbolizes bullish sentiment

Open Interest Positions

Open interest is the total number of contracts—futures or options—that remain open at the end of the day. It can also be defined as the number of contracts that are still to be squared off or to be delivered at the end of the day.

Open interest increases by the value "1" for every buy and sell open position.

Simply speaking, 1 open buy + 1 open sell = 1 open interest

Day	Investor "A"	Investor "B"	Investor "C"	Investor "D"	Open Interest	Volume
1	Buy 100, RIL 1,800 call				100	100
2	Sell 50, RIL 1,800 call	Buy 50, RIL 1,800 call			100	50
			Buy 25, RIL 1,800 call	Sell 25, RIL 1,800 call		

Understanding the implications of change in open interest

1. If prices are rising and open interest is increasing—this is a bullish sign. More participants are entering the market, involving additional buying.
2. Rising prices and a decline in open interest is bearish. This condition indicates that people are covering their short positions and fundamental demand is not contributing to the increase in prices. Consequently, when the short covering is done, market prices will decline.
3. If prices are declining and the open interest rises, this indicates that new short positions are being opened. As long as this process continues it is a bearish factor, but once the shorts begin to cover it turns bullish.
4. A decline in both price and open interest indicates liquidation by discouraged traders with long positions. As long as this trend continues, it is a bearish sign. Once open, interest stabilizes at a low level, the liquidation is over and prices are then in a position to rally again.

Premium or Discount with Respect to Cash Market Prices

Trading of indices and stocks at premium or discount in the derivatives segment is also used to gauge the bullish, bearish, or irresolute sentiments of the market. Suppose stock futures or index futures are trading at a premium compared with the underlying stock or index. This points to a bullish trend in the cash market. But a stock or an index trading at a discount in the futures market indicates a bearish market.

Beta of the Stock

Beta of a stock plays an important role in hedging the risk of individual stocks with the help of index options. Lower beta stocks tend to react proportionately less than the movement in the market index. Higher beta stocks tend to react more viz-a-viz the market index. Thus, the aggressive stocks sometimes betray the investors when the market suddenly takes a sudden dip, whereas the low beta stocks have fewer tendencies to overreact.

Put–Call Ratio

The put–call ratio is calculated by dividing the daily or weekly traded volume of put options by the daily or weekly traded volume of call options. Higher the number of call options traded; higher are the chances of the market turning bullish in future. If put options are more popular, bears could dominate the market.

An increasing ratio over a period of time means investors are putting more money in put options, implying the broad market outlook is bearish. Thus, the market can be expected to move south or witness a sell-off. This could also be the case of investors trying to hedge their portfolios. On the other hand, a declining put–call ratio indicates investors are showing more interest in buying call options and the market is likely to move up in the near future.

This can also be termed as a contrary indicator. An extremely high value of this ratio is considered a buying opportunity as traders start covering their short positions. On the contrary, too many call options or a low put–call volume ratio signifies that the market has reached an overbought level and a correction is likely. In short, a very high put–call ratio indicates the bear phase is likely to end, while a very low ratio means bulls could lose the grip over the market and a market correction is likely.

Put–Call Open-Interest Ratio

The put–call open-interest ratio is also one of the key indicators of possible futures movement in the spot market. The put–call open-interest ratio is calculated by dividing the total open interest of put options by the total open interest of call options. For instance, if the open interest for put options is nine and the same figure for the call options is 10, the put–call open-interest ratio would be 0.90. A put–call open-interest ratio of more than one means put options have a higher open interest compared with the call options and, thus, the future price trend is likely to be bearish. A low put–call open-interest ratio means bullish sentiments are likely to continue in future. Investors can monitor periodical changes in the put–call open-interest ratio to gauge future market outlook.

Volatility Index

Volatility is the prime factor that reflects risk. Volatility index (VI) is a measure of the market's expectation of volatility over the near term. Volatility is defined as the rate and magnitude of changes in prices. Volatility index measures the amount by which an underlying index is expected to fluctuate in the near term. Volatility index is based on the order book of the underlying index options and is calculated as annualized volatility denoted in percentage. In the domestic market, India VIX = VI developed by the NSE is a VI based on the Nifty 50 index option prices. From the best bid-ask prices of Nifty 50 options contracts, a volatility figure is calculated, indicating the expected market volatility over the next 30 calendar days.

Volatility index indicates expected stock market volatility over a specified time period. An investor can get a sense of market volatility by simply looking at one number: VI. A rising VI means increase in volatility and vice a versa. As the VI is calculated on a real-time basis and is continuously disseminated throughout the trading session, it can aid "buy" or "sell" decisions.

Retail Participation in Derivatives Market

Considering the downtrend in the stock market since the beginning of 2008, there has been a rapid decline in the retail participation. Retail investors, considered to be the "weak hands" in the derivatives segment because of their limited capital base, were hit the hardest when stock prices plunged in January. Retail investors have limited knowledge about the working of F&O segment, hence they generally prefer to hedge their portfolios through the route of mutual funds and generally avoid taking directional calls in the market.

Till January 2008, market was moving in one direction, that is, upwards, hence it was easy for investors to take a directional call by going long on Nifty futures. But the scenario just became topsy-turvy after January 2008. The possibilities of market moving in either direction made retail investors to withdraw themselves from the market.

Lack of retail participation causes lesser liquidity in the F&O segment. Hence, to bring back the interest of the retail investors, SEBI has taken certain steps, such as, introduction of mini derivative contracts, providing more leverage to the retail investors by reducing the exposure margin requirements to 5% from 10% etc.

Snap quote of index Futures on S&P CNX Nifty

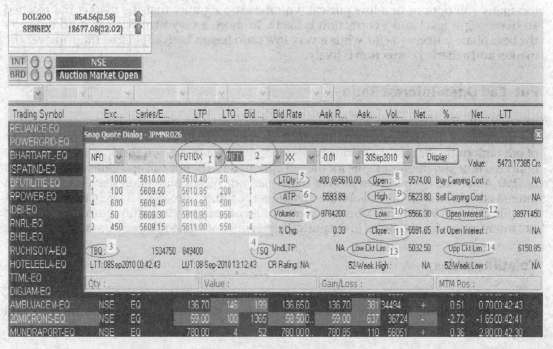

Symbol of index futures

1. Underlying index is S&P CNX Nifty
2. Total buy quantity
3. Total sell quantity
4. Last traded quantity
5. Average traded price
6. Volume traded
7. Open
8. High
9. Low
10. Close
11. Open interest
12. Low circuit limit
13. Upper circuit limit

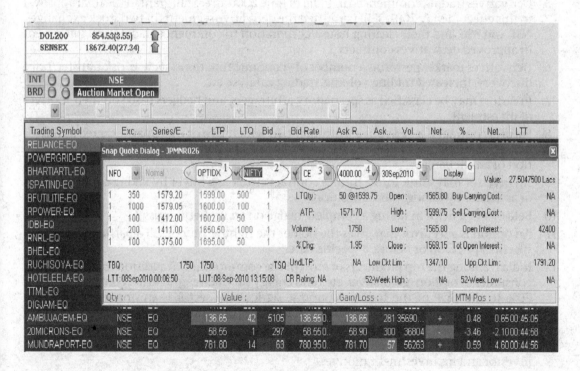

Snap quote of index option on S&P CNX Nifty

1. Symbol of index options
2. Underlying asset is S&P CNX Nifty
3. European call option
4. Exercise price
5. Exercise date

SUMMARY

1. There are two types of risk to which an investment is exposed

   - diversifiable, and
   - non-diversifiable.

2. Diversifiable risks are those risks which may be reduced by an investor by including different categories of assets in investment portfolio.

3. Derivatives are a means to provide cover to the systematic (non-diversifiable) risk on an investment.

4. Derivative is a contract which derives its value from another contract. In financial terms, a derivative is a contract which derives its value from an underlying asset. Underlying asset may be anything, such as, weather, performance of a cricketer in a cricket match, price of a commodity, fluctuations in the interest rates on bonds/debentures, currencies and for our reference, it may be even shares of the companies in which the funds are invested or even the fluctuations in the market indices, such as, Sensex and S&P CNX Nifty.

5. Derivatives trading commenced in India in June 2000 after SEBI granted the final approval to this effect in May 2001. SEBI permitted the derivative segments of two stock exchanges, NSE and BSE, and their clearing house/corporation to commence trading and settlement in approved derivatives contracts.

6. Derivatives market performs a number of economic functions, such as, risk transfer, price discovery, increased trading volume, trading catalyst, etc.

7. Investors may be classified as speculators, arbitragers, and hedgers based on their motives of investment.

8. Futures contract is a derivative instrument, in which two or more parties agree to buy or sell an underlying asset at an agreed price, at a specific date in future, with an intermediation of an exchange.

9. An investor may enter into a futures contract either as a buyer by taking a long position or as a seller by taking a short position.

10. Beta of stock helps in taking a complete hedge on an underlying asset.

11. An option is a security that gives the holder the right to buy or sell a particular asset at a specified price, on or before, a specific date.

12. India is among the top producers of most of the commodities, in addition to being a major consumer of bullion (gold, silver, etc.) and energy products. Agriculture contributes about 20% to the GDP of the Indian economy. Agriculture sector is an important factor in achieving a GDP growth of 8-10%. All this indicates that India can be promoted as a major center for trading of commodity derivatives.

13. Trading strategies involving futures and options depend upon the risk return profile of an investor and his investment motives.

KEY TERMS

- Systematic risk
- Risk transfer
- Trading catalyst
- Speculation
- Over the counter

- Unsystematic risk
- Price discovery
- Arbitration
- Hedging
- Mark to market

- Counterparty risk
- Put options
- Open interest
- Volatility index

- Call options
- Rollover of contracts
- Put-call ratio
- Put-call open interest ratio

Learning Outcomes

Students would appreciate the concept of derivatives, futures, options, and trading strategy.

PROBLEMS

1. A call option with an exercise price of ₹300 can be bought at a premium of ₹6. A put option with an exercise price of ₹295 is available at a premium of ₹8. How can you combine these options to form a portfolio? What will be your payoff at the expiration?

2. The equity shares of HLL are being sold at ₹138. April call option is available for a premium of ₹4 and April put option is available at a premium of ₹7.45 per share. Find the net payoff of the holder of the call and put option given that strike price in both the cases is ₹140 and the share price on the day of exercise is ₹120 or ₹130 or ₹140 or₹150 or ₹160.

3. Equity shares of ABC Ltd are being currently sold for ₹100 per share. Both the call and put options for a three-month period are available at a strike price of ₹105 a premium of ₹3 and ₹2 per share, respectively. An investor wants to create a straddle position in this share. Find out his net payoff at the expiration of the option period if the share price on that day happens to be ₹97 or ₹112.

4. A call option with an exercise price of ₹100 can be bought at a premium of ₹5. Prepare the payoff both for the buyer and the writer of the call option if the prices on the day of expiration are ₹90 or ₹92 or ₹95 or ₹98 or ₹100 or ₹105 or ₹108.

5. A put option with an exercise price of ₹200 can be bought at a premium of ₹10. Prepare the payoff both for the buyer and the writer of the call option if the prices on the day of expiration are ₹180 or ₹192 or ₹195 or ₹198 or ₹200 or ₹205 or ₹218.

ASSES YOURSELF

Concept Thinking and Critical Review Questions

1. What are derivative contracts? What is the need of derivative contract?
2. Explain forward contracts.
3. Define and explain futures contract. How do they differ from the forward contracts?
4. What are option contracts?
5. Enumerate and discuss the differences between options and futures.
6. Discuss the basic option strategies.
7. What is the role of beta in futures trading?
8. Discuss some pointers in futures and options market.

STUDENT ACTIVITIES

Students should observe trading volume in derivatives securities in India and should also assess the impact of merger of FMC with SEBI. Collect the Call option and put option contract details on S&P CNX Nifty and prepare various option strategies on the basis of bullish and bearish nature of the investors.

SUGGESTED READING

Hull, John C., et al. (2010). *Option future and other derivatives* (7th ed.). Pearson.

WEB RESOURCES

www.nseindia.com (accessed on June 7, 2016.)
www.sebi.gov.in

CHAPTER 25

Share Value and Corporate Governance

- To understand shareholders' value creation.
- To discuss economic value added and market value added measures.
- To explain the balance scorecard as performance measurement system, and focus on corporate governance.

PRELUDE

Contemporary environment has also redefined the objective of financial management. Value creation and adherence to corporate governance have also emerged as new focus areas. Value creation and wealth creation may be seen as two sides of a coin. Good corporates are engaged in value creation for their stakeholders, thereby enjoying support of the investors. Total value creation, not just dividend, would attract the stakeholders.

Creating shareholder value is the main goal of the firm. Investors or shareholders invest their money in the companies. The main concern is that the money should be invested in the right direction and should be beneficial from both the company's and the investor's perspectives. Companies will either retain the money or return the money in the form of dividend to the investors. Most of the companies will like to retain the money, which will be reinvested on the behalf of shareholders to give them a better return on their investment. Such a strategic decision leads to increase in the market price of shares. Hence, creating the value for shareholders would lead to increased profitability which in turn will enhance the growth of the firm. The impact of profitability on shareholder value is significant. This is the organic strategy which leads to value creation for the shareholder. Organic strategies refer to internal growth strategies that focus on growth by the process of asset replication, adaptation of technology, better customer relationship, and innovation of new technology and products to fill the gaps in the marketplace. It is a gradual growth process spread over a few years.

Value creation occurs where the returns on the investment exceed the returns required. This investment bears a positive net present value; the investor's wealth grew higher than was required. The investor must be very happy. **Value conserved** is when investment returns equal the required returns. Shareholders get just what they required. The investment has a net present value of zero; it breaks even in present value terms. Economically speaking, the investor earns "normal" returns. **Value destroyed** is where the investment returns are less than required returns. The investor could have done better by investing in another opportunity of similar risk.

Shareholder Value

Shareholder value analysis is the process of analyzing how a business decision affects the economic value. The economic value is measured by discounting the expected cash inflows with the cost of capital. It is a yardstick for measuring the performance of the shareholder value.

Shareholder value = market value of the firm – market value of the debt.

Shareholder value creation can be used to evaluate the consequences of strategies pursued by the company. The SVC approach helps to strengthen the competitive position of the firm by focusing on wealth creation. It provides an objective and consistent framework of evaluation and decision-making across all functions, departments, and units of the firm. The focus should be on maximizing the overall shareholder value rather than treating business units as absolutely autonomous and working at cross-purposes.

Shareholder value creation can be analyzed with the help of free cash flow method. Free cash flow (FCF) represents the cash that a company is able to generate after laying out the money required to maintain or expand its asset base. Free cash flow is important because it allows a company to pursue opportunities that enhance shareholder value. Without cash, it is tough to develop new products, make acquisitions, pay dividends, and reduce debt.

FCF is calculated as

EBIT (1 – tax rate) + depreciation and amortization – change in net working capital

– capital expenditure

It can also be calculated by taking operating cash flow and subtracting capital expenditures. When value of business is calculated over planning horizon, then an estimate of terminal cash flows will be made. The firm is expected to grow at a higher rate during planning horizon and thereafter, firm grows at a lower rate. Terminal value reflects the value of the firm after planning cash flows. Therefore, economic value of a firm is equal to present value of FCFs and present value of terminal value. Weighted average cost of capital is used to discount FCFs.

$$V = \sum_{t=1}^{n} \frac{FCF_t}{(1 + WACC)} + \frac{TV^n}{(1 + WACC)^n}$$

Test Yourself

1. Define the concept shareholder value creation.
2. What is the FCF method? Explain.

Market Value Added

Market value added is the difference between the company's market and book value of shares. If the total market value of a company is more than the amount of capital invested in it, the company has managed to create shareholder value. If the market value is less than capital invested, the company has destroyed shareholder value.

$$\text{Market value added} = \text{company's total market value} - \text{capital invested}$$

Or

$$\text{Market value added} = \text{enterprise value} - \text{money invested}$$

$$\text{Enterprise value} = \text{market capitalization} + \text{debt} - \text{cash equivalents}$$

$$\text{Market capitalization} = \text{current market price} * \text{number of outstanding shares}$$

$$\text{Money invested} = \text{shareholders equity} + \text{debt} + \text{other liabilities}$$

Market value added tells us how much value the company has added to, or subtracted from, its shareholders investment. Successful companies add their MVA and thus increase the value of capital invested in the company.

Whether a company has positive or negative MVA depends on the rate of return compared to the cost of capital. To determine whether management has created or destroyed value, the market value of the firm's capital (both equity and debt capital) may be compared to the capital invested by shareholders and lenders (the capital employed in the firm). A positive MVA implies that value has been created whereas a negative MVA means that value has been destroyed.

Market-to-Book Value

A most common measure of the shareholder value creation is the comparison between the market value and book value per share. When the market value exceeds the book value, the shareholder value is created and when the book value exceeds the market value, the shareholder value is destroyed.

A firm is said to create shareholder value when its market value per share (M) is greater than its book value per share (B). The market-to-book value (M/B) analysis implies the following:

1. **Value creation:** If M/B > 1, the firm is creating value of shareholders.
2. **Value maintenance:** If M/B = -1, the firm is not creating value of shareholders.
3. **Value destruction:** If M/B < 1, the firm is destroying value of shareholders.

A simple valuation model that can be used to make predictions about the relationship between profitability and growth and shareholder value is the constant growth model. The market value of a share (M) is given as follows:

$$M = \frac{\text{DPS}}{\text{ke} - \text{g}} = \frac{\text{EPS}(1 - \text{b})}{\text{ke} - \text{g}}$$

This model assumes that dividends grow at a constant rate in perpetuity. Dividend per share (DPS) is equal to earnings per share (EPS) multiplied by one minus retention ratio (b). EPS depends on the firm's return on equity (ROE) and the equity investment, expressed as book value of per equity share (B). The equation can be rewritten as follows:

$$M = \frac{B \times \text{ROE}(1 - \text{b})}{\text{ke} - \text{g}} = \frac{B(\text{ROE} - \text{b} \times \text{ROE})}{\text{ke} - \text{g}}$$

$$\frac{M}{B} = \frac{\text{ROE} - \text{g}}{\text{ke} - \text{g}}$$

The shareholder value will be created when M/B ratio is greater than 1, and value will be destroyed if it is less than 1. M/B will be greater than 1 if ROE exceeds ke; that is, the spread, ROE – ke, is positive. Hence, a firm will be creating value for its shareholders when it undertakes investments that generate positive spread; which is, ROE exceeding the cost of equity (ROE > ke).

Determinants of M/B Ratio

Growth (g) is the sustainable growth based on a firm's financial policies. The sustainable growth for each year is calculated as follows:

$$g = [ROA + (ROA - i) \, D/E](1 - \text{payout ratio})$$

$$ROA = \text{after-tax return on assets;}$$

$$i = \text{after-tax interest rate on debt;}$$

$$D/E = \text{debt-equity ratio and}$$

$$(1 - \text{payout}) = \text{retention ratio}$$

Simplifying the equation, the sustainable growth is equal to ROE multiplied by retention ratio, that is, g = ROE (1 – payout).

Economic profitability (spread) is defined as the difference between ROE and cost of equity (ROE – ke). ROE is calculated as profit net of all expenses and taxes and excluding all extraordinary items divided by the net worth (book value equity). Cost of equity (ke) is calculated using the capital assets pricing model (CAPM). The estimation of the equity beta is based on the daily closing share prices.

Test Yourself

1. What is M/B value? Explain. Discuss the importance of M/B approach.

Economic Value Added (EVA)

Economic value added (EVA) was developed by a New York consulting firm, Stern Steward & Co in 1982 to promote value-maximizing behavior in corporate managers. It is a single, value-based measure that was intended to evaluate business strategies, capital projects, and to maximize long-term shareholders' wealth. Value that has been created or destroyed by the firm during the period can be measured by comparing profits with the cost of capital used to produce them. Therefore, managers can decide to withdraw value-destructive activities and invest in projects that are critical to shareholder's wealth.

Economic value added sets managerial performance target and links it to reward systems. EVA focuses on ends and not means as it does not state how a manager can increase company's value as long as the shareholders' wealth is maximized.

Economic value added is a financial measure based on accounting data and is therefore historical in nature. It has the same limitations as other traditional accounting measures and cannot adequately replace all measures within the company, especially the nonfinancial ones. Due to the historical nature of EVA, a manager can benefit in terms of rewards or be punished by the past history of the organization.

Stern Stewart describes four main applications of EVA:

1. **Measurement:** EVA is the most accurate measure of corporate performance over any given period. EVA is a measure of "total factor productivity" whose growing popularity reflects the new demands of the information age.
2. **Management system:** The EVA system covers the full range of managerial decisions, including strategic planning, allocating capital, pricing acquisitions or divestitures, setting annual goals, and even day-to-day operating decisions.
3. **Motivation:** To instill both the sense of urgency and the long-term perspective of an owner, Stern Stewart designs cash bonus plans that cause managers to think and act like owners because they are paid like owners.
4. **Mind-set:** The EVA framework is, in effect, a system of internal corporate governance that automatically guides all managers and employees and propels them to work for the best interests of the owners. The EVA system also facilitates decentralized decision-making because it holds managers responsible for and rewards them for delivering value.

The EVA Concept of Profitability

Economic value added is based on the concept that a successful firm should earn at least its cost of capital. Firms that earn higher returns than financing costs benefit shareholders and account for increased shareholder value. In its simplest form, EVA can be expressed as the following equation:

$$EVA = \text{net operating profit after tax (NOPAT)} - \text{cost of capital}$$

Net operating profit after tax is calculated as net operating income after depreciation, adjusted for items that move the profit measure closer to an economic measure of profitability. Adjustments include such items as: additions for interest expense after taxes (including any implied interest expense on operating leases); increases in net capitalized R&D expenses; increases in the LIFO (last in first out) reserve; and goodwill amortization. Adjustments made to operating earnings for these items reflect the investments made by the firm or capital employed to achieve those profits.

Measurement of EVA

Measurement of EVA can be made using either an operating or financing approach. Under the operating approach, NOPAT is derived by deducting cash operating expenses and depreciation from sales. Interest expense is excluded because it is considered as a financing charge. Adjustments, which are referred to as equity equivalent adjustments, are designed to reflect economic reality and move income and capital to a more economically based value. These adjustments are considered with cash taxes deducted to arrive at NOPAT. Economic value added is then measured by deducting the company's cost of capital from the NOPAT value. The amount of capital to be used in the EVA calculations is the same under either the operating or financing approach, but is calculated differently.

The operating approach starts with assets and builds up to invested capital, including adjustments for economically derived equity equivalent values. The financing approach, on the other hand, starts with debt and adds all equity and equity equivalents to arrive at invested capital. Finally, the weighted average cost of capital, based on the relative values of debt and equity and their respective cost rates, is used to arrive at the cost of capital which is multiplied by the capital employed and deducted from the NOPAT value. The resulting amount is the current period's EVA.

Advantages of EVA

Economic value added is more than just performance measurement system and it is also marketed as a motivational, compensation-based management system that facilitates economic activity and accountability at all levels in the firm.

Stern Stewart reports that companies that have adopted EVA have outperformed their competitors when compared on the basis of comparable market capitalization.

Several advantages claimed for EVA are

- EVA eliminates economic distortions of GAAP (generally accepted accounting principles) to focus decisions on real economic results.
- EVA provides for better assessment of decisions that affect balance sheet and income statement or tradeoffs between each through the use of the capital charge against NOPAT.
- EVA decouples bonus plans from budgetary targets.
- EVA covers all aspects of the business cycle.
- EVA aligns and speeds decision-making, and enhances communication and teamwork.

Evaluation of M/B and EVA Approaches

1. Both M/B and EVA approaches focus on economic profitability rather than on accounting profitability. The M/B approach defines economic profitability as the spread between the ROE and the cost of capital, while in the EVA approach it is the spread between the return on total capital and the cost of total capital. The spread in both the approaches are value added to the shareholders. Thus, they are essentially the same approach. From the accounting perspective, a firm is profitable if its ROE is positive. However, from an economic perspective, the firm is profitable if the ROE exceeds the cost of equity, or return on capital employed exceeds the overall cost of the total capital employed. It is economic, and not accounting, profitability that determines the capability of wealth creation on the part of the firm. It is perfectly possible that a company is in the black, and yet its market value is way below its book value, which means that, from economic point of view, its resources would be more profitable if deployed in an alternative investment of similar risk.

2. Both the approaches are an improvement over the traditional accounting measures of performance. But both do suffer from the limitation that they are partially based on accounting numbers. In the M/B approach, ROE is an accounting number (profit after tax and book value of shareholders investment) while the cost of equity is market determined. Similarly, the EVA approach uses the accounting-based net operating profit after tax while the cost of capital is market determined. Both ROE and EVA are biased because they use accounting earnings (NOPAT or PAT) which are based on arbitrary assumptions, allocations and accounting policy changes.

3. They also do not include changes in working capital and capital expenditures.

4. Both approaches do not fully and explicitly recognize risk and time value of money. In the EVA approach, a short-term perspective is taken. It is, therefore, doubtful that the application of these approaches in project/business evaluation and, particularly, in strategic analysis and planning will lead to an increase in the shareholder value.

Balance Scorecard

It was developed by Dr Robert Kaplan and David Norton as a performance measurement framework that added strategic nonfinancial performance measures to traditional financial metrics to give managers and executives a more "balanced" view of organizational performance.

It provides a clear prescription as to what companies should measure in order to "balance" the financial perspective.

Kaplan and Norton describe the innovation of the balanced scorecard (Figure 25.1) as follows:

> The balanced scorecard retains traditional financial measures. But financial measures tell the story of past events, an adequate story for industrial age companies for which investments in long-term capabilities and customer relationships were not critical for success. These financial measures are inadequate, however, for guiding and evaluating the journey that information age companies must make to create future value through investment in customers, suppliers, employees, processes, technology, and innovation.

FIGURE 25.1

VALUE CREATION THROUGH BALANCE SCORE CARD

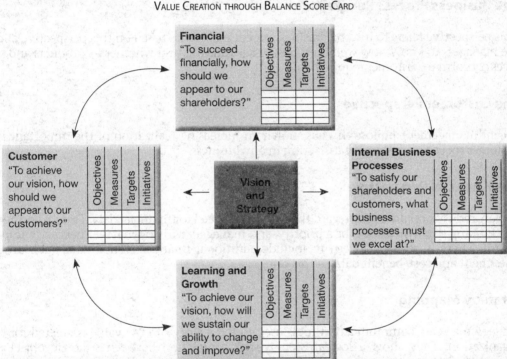

Source: Adapted from Kaplan, Robert S., & Norton David, P. (1996). Using the balanced scorecard as a strategic management system. *Harvard Business Review,* January–February, 76.

The aim of the balanced scorecard is to direct, help, manage, and change in support of the longer-term strategy in order to manage performance. The scorecard reflects what the company and the strategies are all about. It acts as a catalyst for bringing in the "change" element within the organization. This tool is a comprehensive framework which considers the following perspectives and tries to get answers to the following questions:

1. Financial perspective—How do we look at shareholders?
2. Customer perspective—How should we appear to our customers?
3. Internal business processes perspective—What must we excel at?
4. Learning and growth perspective—Can we continue to improve and create value?

Perspectives

The balanced scorecard suggests that an organization is viewed from four perspectives.

The Learning and Growth Perspective

This perspective includes employee training and corporate cultural attitudes related to both individual and corporate self-improvement. In a knowledge-worker organization, people—the only repository of knowledge—are the main resource. In the current climate of rapid technological change, it is becoming necessary for knowledge workers to be in a continuous learning mode.

The Business Process Perspective

This perspective refers to internal business processes. Metrics based on this perspective allow the managers to know how well their business is running, and whether its products and services conform to customer requirements.

The Customer Perspective

Recent management philosophy has shown an increasing realization of the importance of customer focus and customer satisfaction in any business.

The Financial Perspective

Kaplan and Norton do not disregard the traditional need for financial data. Timely and accurate funding data will always be a priority, and managers will do whatever necessary to provide it. There is perhaps a need to include additional financial-related data, such as risk assessment and cost–benefit data, in this category.

Strategy Mapping

Strategy maps are communication tools used to tell a story of how value is created for the organization. They show a logical, step-by-step connection between strategic objectives (shown as ovals on the map) in the form of a cause-and-effect chain. Generally speaking, improving performance in the objectives found in the learning and growth perspective (the bottom row) enables the organization to improve its internal process perspective objectives (the next row up), which in turn enables the organization to create desirable results in the customer and financial perspectives (the top two rows).

Implementing a Balanced Scorecard[1]

The following conditions are necessary for the successful implementation of the balanced scorecard:

- Top management commitment and support
- Determine the critical success factors (CSFs)

---

[1] Kaplan and Norton. (1996). "Using the Balanced Score Card as a Strategic Management System." *Harvard Business Review*, January-February.

- Translate CSFs into measurable objectives (metrics)
- Link performance measures to rewards
- Install a simple tracking system
- Create and link the balanced scorecards at all levels of the organization
- Communication
- Link strategic planning, balanced scorecard, and budgeting process

Test Yourself

1. What do you understand from balance scorecard?
2. Briefly explain the four perspectives of balance scorecard.

7S McKinsey Model

The 7S McKinsey model is essentially a value-based management (VBM) model that is intended to provide a company with a framework with the intent generate value within its overall organization. The model considers the organization of a company as a mix of six dimensions that function around a seventh one, that is, *the Shared Values* of a company (see Figure 25.2).

The six dimensions are *strategy, structure, systems, style, staff, and skills*

The *strategy* is the only dimension that takes into consideration the external environment like competition and customers although it could be argued that at least the *structure* dimension should (could) reflect the external ambient as well. The other five dimensions focus on the internal organization of the company and especially how the units (divisions, departments etc.) are structured and which systems and processes they adopt. Interestingly human resource (HR) components such as skills, staff, and style are contemplated here.

FIGURE 25.2

THE SHARED VALUE OF A COMPANY

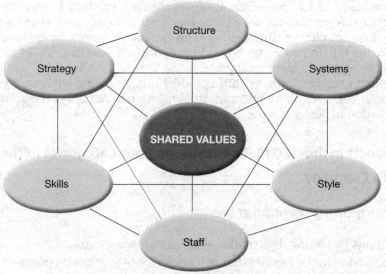

Source: http://www.mckinsey.com/business-functions/strategy-and-corporate-finance/our-insights/enduring-ideas-the-7-s-framework (accessed on June 7, 2016).

Dimension

1. **Strategy:** the plan devised to maintain and build competitive advantage over the competition.
2. **Structure:** the way the organization is structured and who reports to whom.
3. **Systems:** the daily activities and procedures that staff members engage in to get the job done.
4. **Shared values:** called "super ordinate goals" when the model was first developed, these are the core values of the company that are evidenced in the corporate culture and the general work ethic.
5. **Style:** the style of leadership adopted.
6. **Staff:** the employees and their general capabilities.
7. **Skills:** the actual skills and competencies of the employees working for the company.

BCG Matrix

The Boston Consulting Group (BCG) matrix (Figure 25.3), also called BCG model, relates to marketing. BCG matrix is often used to prioritize which products within company product mix get more funding and attention. The BCG matrix model is a portfolio planning model developed by Bruce Henderson of the Boston Consulting Group in the early 1970s. The BCG model is based on classification of products (and implicitly also company business units) into four categories based on combinations of market growth and market share relative to the largest competitor. Each product has its product life cycle, and each stage in product's life cycle represents a different profile of risk and return. In general, a company should maintain a balanced portfolio of products. Having a balanced product portfolio includes both high-growth products as well as low-growth products. A high-growth product is, for example, a new one that we are trying to get to some market. It takes some effort and resources to market it, to build distribution channels, and to build sales infrastructure, but it is a product that is expected to bring the gold in the future.

A low-growth product is, for example, an established product known by the market. Characteristics of this product do not change much, customers know what they are getting, and the price does not change much either. This product has only limited budget for marketing. It is like the milking cow that brings in the constant flow of cash. An example of this product would be regular Colgate toothpaste.

The BCG matrix reaches further behind product mix. Knowing what we are selling helps managers to make decisions about what priorities to assign to not only products but also company departments and business units.

Placing Products in the BCG Matrix Results in Four Categories in the Portfolio of a Company

BCG Stars (high growth, high market share)

1. Stars are defined by having high market share in a growing market.
2. Stars are the leaders in the business but still need a lot of support for promotion and placement.
3. If market share is kept, stars are likely to grow into cash cows.

BCG Question Marks (high growth, low market share)

1. These products are in growing markets but have low market share.
2. Question marks are essentially new products where buyers have yet to discover them.
3. The marketing strategy is to get markets to adopt these products.
4. Question marks have high demands and low returns due to low market share.
5. These products need to increase their market share quickly or they become dogs.
6. The best way to handle question marks is to either invest heavily in them to gain market share or to sell them.

BCG Cash Cows (low growth, high market share)

1. Cash cows are in a position of high market share in a mature market.
2. If competitive advantage has been achieved, cash cows have high profit margins and generate a lot of cash flow.
3. Because of the low growth, promotion and placement investments are low.
4. Investments into supporting infrastructure can improve efficiency and increase cash flow more.
5. Cash cows are the products that businesses strive for.

BCG Dogs (low growth, low market share)

1. Dogs are in low growth markets and have low market share.
2. Dogs should be avoided and minimized.
3. Expensive turnaround plans usually do not help.

FIGURE 25.3

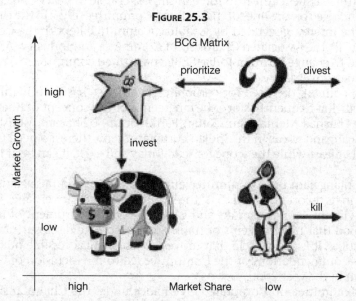

Source: https://www.bcgperspectives.com/content/articles/corporate_strategy_portfolio_manage
ment_strategic_planning_growth_share_matrix_bcg_classics_revisited/ (accessed on June 7, 2016).

Test Yourself

1. Explain the 7S Model.
2. What is BCG matrix?

Corporate Governance

Corporate governance is the set of processes, customs, policies, laws, and institutions affecting the way a corporation (or company) is directed, administered, or controlled. Corporate governance also includes the relationships among the many stakeholders involved and the goals for which the corporation is governed. In contemporary business corporations, the main external stakeholder groups are shareholders, debt-holders, trade creditors, suppliers, customers, and communities affected by the corporation's activities, internal stakeholders are the Board of Directors, executives, and other employees.

Underlying Principles

(a) Rights and equitable treatment of shareholders
(b) Interests of other stakeholders
(c) Role and responsibilities of the Board
(d) Integrity and ethical behavior
(e) Disclosure and transparency

Corporate governance has been a hotly debated issue in USA and Europe over the last decade. In India, these issues came into force in the last couple of years. The corporate governance code was modeled on the lines of the Cadbury Committee (1992) in the United Kingdom. On account of the interest generated by Cadbury Committee Report, the Confederation of Indian Industry (CII), the Associated Chambers of Commerce and Industry (ASSOCHAM) and the Securities and Exchange Board of India (SEBI) constituted committees to recommend initiatives in corporate governance.

In the Indian context, the need for corporate governance has been highlighted because of the scams occurring frequently since the emergence of the concept of liberalization from 1991 such as the Harshad Mehta Scam, Ketan Parikh Scam, UTI Scam, Vanishing Company Scam, Bhansali Scam and so on. In the Indian corporate scene, there is a need to induct global standards so that at least while the scope for scams may still exist, it can be at least reduced to the minimum.

The Kumara Mangalam Birla Committee aims to promote and raise standards of corporate governance in its report observed that "the strong Corporate Governance if indispensable to resilient and vibrant capital markets and is an important instrument of investor protection. It is the blood that fills the veins of transparent corporate disclosure and high quality accounting practices. It is the muscle that moves a viable and accessible financial reporting structure". The recommendations of the Committee led to the inclusion of Clause 49 in the listing Agreement in the year 2000.

The second Committee on Corporate Governance under the Chairmanship of Shri N.R. Narayana Murthy was constituted in October 2002 by SEBI and based on the recommendations of it, SEBI issued a circular on August 26, 2003 revising Clause 49 of the Listing Agreement, to review the progress of the corporate sector in meeting the norms of corporate governance and to determine the role of companies in responding to rumor and other price-sensitive information circulating in the market. It enabled the mechanism of working of transparency and integrity of the market players and participants.

Theories of Corporate Governance

Agency theory: The main objective of the firm is to maximize the shareholder's wealth. The shareholder's wealth maximization model may not work because of existence of agency problem. Agency problem arises because of separation of ownership and control. The shareholders own the company and managers, being agents, manage it. It is possible that managers may not work to maximize owner's value. Agency theory helps in resolving agency problems through monitoring, observing the behavior, and performance of agents; making the arrangements that penalize agents for acting in ways that violate the interests of principals or reward them for achieving principal's goals and having contracts between agents and principals specifying the monitoring and bonding arrangements.

Stewardship theory: Stewardship theory argues that shareholder interests are maximized by shared incumbency of these roles. This theory considers managers as stewards whose interests are aligned with that of the owners. This theory assumes that managers are basically trustworthy and attach significant value to their own personal reputations. It defines situations in which managers are stewards whose motives are aligned with the objectives of their principles. Given a choice between self-serving behavior and pro-organizational behavior, a steward's behavior will not depart from the interests of his/her organization.

Stakeholder theory: This theory is a synthesis of economics, behavioral science, business ethics, and the stakeholder concept. The theory considers the firm as an input–output model by explicitly adding all interest groups—employees, customers, dealers, government, and the society at large—to the corporate mix. It is grounded in many normative, theoretical perspectives including ethics of care, the ethics of fiduciary relationships, social contract theory, theory of property rights, etc. This theory explains that managers should aim at maximizing the wealth of all the stakeholders. The corporate governance norms empower stakeholders to ensure that their interest must be aligned with the shareholders.

Corporate Governance in Listed Companies—Recommendations of K.M. Birla Committee

1. Board of directors: The board of a company provides leadership and strategic guidance, objective judgment independent of management to the company and exercises control over the company, while remaining at all times accountable to the shareholders. The measure of the board is not simply whether it fulfills its legal requirements but, more importantly, the board's attitude and the manner it translates its awareness and understanding of its responsibilities. An effective corporate governance system is one, which allows the board to perform these dual functions efficiently.

2. Composition of the board of directors: The board of a company must have an optimum combination of executive and nonexecutive directors with not less than 50% of the board comprising the nonexecutive directors. The number of independent directors would depend on the nature of the chairman of the board. In case a company has a nonexecutive chairman, at least one-third of board should comprise of independent directors and in case a company has an executive chairman, at least half of the board should be independent.

3. Nominee directors: Institutions should appoint nominees on the boards of companies only on a selective basis where such appointment is pursuant to a right under loan agreements or where such appointment is considered necessary to protect the interest of the institution. When a nominee of the institutions is appointed as a director of the company, he should have the same responsibility, be subject to the same discipline, and be accountable to the shareholders in the same manner as any other director of the company. In particular, if he reports to any department of the institutions on the affairs of the company, the institution should ensure that there exist Chinese walls between such department and other departments which may be dealing in the shares of the company in the stock market.

4. Chairman of the board: The role of the chairman is to ensure that the board meetings are conducted in a manner which secures the effective participation of all directors, executive and nonexecutive alike, and encourages all to make an effective contribution, maintain a balance of power in the board, make certain that all directors receive adequate information, well in time and that the executive directors look beyond their executive duties and accept full share of the responsibilities of governance.

5. Audit committee: The need for having an audit committee grows from the recognition of the audit committee's position in the larger mosaic of the governance process, as it relates to the oversight of financial reporting. A proper and well-functioning system exists therefore, when the three main groups responsible for financial reporting—the board, the internal auditor, and the outside auditors—form the three-legged stool that supports responsible financial disclosure and active and participatory oversight. The audit committee has an important role to play in this process, since the audit committee is a subgroup of the full board and hence the monitor of the process. The committee's job is clearly one of oversight and monitoring and in carrying out this job it relies on senior financial management and the outside auditors.

6. Remuneration committee of the board: The board should set up remuneration committee to determine on their behalf and on behalf of the shareholders with agreed terms of reference, the company's policy on specific remuneration packages for executive directors including pension rights and any compensation payment.

7. Disclosures of remuneration package: All elements of remuneration package of all the directors, that is, salary, benefits, bonuses, stock options, pension, etc., has to be disclosed to the shareholders.

8. Accounting standards and financial reporting: Reporting on accounting based on accounting standards. Reporting should include consolidated accounts in respect of all its subsidiaries in which they hold 51% or more of the share capital. Segment reporting is a must where a company has multiple lines of business. It is important that financial reporting in respect of each product segment should be available to the shareholders and the market to obtain a complete financial picture of the company.

9. Management: The management is subservient to the board of directors and must operate within the boundaries and the policy framework laid down by the board.

10. Responsibilities of shareholders: The General Body Meetings provide an opportunity to the shareholders to address their concerns to the board of directors and comment on and demand any explanation on the annual report or on the overall functioning of the company. It is important that the shareholders use the forum of general body meetings for ensuring that the company is being properly stewarded for maximizing the interests of the shareholders.

11. Shareholders' rights: Half-yearly declaration of financial performance including summary of the significant events in last six months, should be sent to each household of the shareholders. A board committee under the chairmanship of a nonexecutive director should be formed to specifically look into the redressing of the shareholder complaints like transfer of shares, non-receipt of balance sheet, non-receipt of declared dividends, etc. The committee believes that the formation of such a committee will help focus the attention of the company on shareholders' grievances and sensitize the management to redress of their grievances. To expedite the process of share transfers, the board of the company should delegate the power of share transfer to an officer, or a committee or to the registrar, and share transfer agents. The delegated authority should attend to share transfer formalities at least once in a fortnight.

12. Institutional shareholders: The institutional shareholders take active interest in the composition of the board of directors, be vigilant, maintain regular and systematic contact at senior level for exchange of views on management, strategy, performance, and the quality of management, ensure that voting intentions are translated into practice, and evaluate the corporate governance performance of the company.

Test Yourself

1. Discuss the concept corporate governance and explain the theories of corporate governance also.

SUMMARY

1. Value creation occurs where the returns on the investment exceed the returns required. This investment bears a positive net present value; the investor's wealth grew higher than was required.

2. Shareholder value analysis is the process of analyzing how business decision affects the economic value. The economic value is measured by discounting the expected cash inflows with cost of capital. It is a yardstick for measuring the performance of the shareholder value. Shareholder value creation can be used to evaluate the consequences of strategies pursued by the company.

   Shareholder value = market value of the firm – market value of debt

3. Free cash flow is calculated as, EBIT(1 – tax rate) + depreciation and amortization – change in net working capital – capital expenditure.

4. Market value added is the difference between the company's market and book value of shares. If the total market value of a company is more than the amount of capital invested in it, the company has managed to create the shareholder value. If the market value is less than the capital invested, the company has destroyed the shareholder value.

   Market value added = company's total market value – capital invested

5. A firm is said to create shareholder value when its market value per share (M) is greater than its book value per share (B). The M/B value analysis implies the following: value creation if M/B > 1, the firm is creating value of shareholders; value maintenance if M/B = –1, the firm is not creating value of shareholders; value destruction if M/B < 1, the firm is destroying value of the shareholders.

6. Economic value added is based on the concept that a successful firm should earn at least its cost of capital. Firms that earn higher returns than financing costs benefit shareholders and account for increased shareholder value. In its simplest form, EVA can be expressed as the following equation:

$$\text{EVA} = \text{net operating profit after tax (NOPAT)} - \text{cost of capital}$$

7. Balance scorecard was originated by Dr Robert Kaplan (Harvard Business School) and David Norton as a performance measurement framework that added strategic nonfinancial performance measures to traditional financial metrics to give managers and executives a more "balanced" view of organizational performance.

8. Corporate governance is the set of processes, customs, policies, laws, and institutions affecting the way a corporation (or company) is directed, administered, or controlled. Corporate governance also includes the relationships among the many stakeholders involved and the goals for which the corporation is governed.

KEY TERMS

- Agency problem
- Corporate governance
- Economic value added
- Growth
- Market value added
- Stewardship stakeholders
- Weighted average cost of capital
- Balance scorecard
- Economic profitability
- Free cash flow
- Market-to-book value
- Shareholder value creation
- Terminal value

Learning Outcomes

Students would have understood value creation as reward to investors.

ASSESS YOURSELF

Concept Review and Critical Thinking Questions

1. What is shareholder value analysis? How value can be created?
2. What is market value added? How is it calculated?
3. Discuss economic value added. How is it different for market value added approach?
4. What is balance scorecard? How is it implemented in an organization?
5. Discuss BCG matrix and 7S Model of McKinsey for value creation.
6. Define corporate governance. Discuss the recommendations of Kumar Managlam Committee.

STUDENT ACTIVITY

Students should take a few listed companies and see whether annual reports mention corporate governance with full disclosures.

SUGGESTED READINGS

Chandra, Prasanna. (2004). *Financial management: Theory & practice* (6th ed.). TMH.

Kumar Manglam Birla Committee. Report on corporate governance. http://www.sebi.gov.in/commreport/corpgov.html (accessed on June 7, 2016).

Pandey, I.M. (2005). What drives the shareholder value. *Asian Academy of Management Journal of Accounting and Finance, 1*(1), 105–120.

Sinha, Abhijit. (2006). Balance scorecard: A strategic management tool. *Vidyasagar University Journal of Commerce, 11*(3), 71–81.

Thenmozhi, M. (2000). Market value added and share price behaviour: An empirical study of BSE sensex companies. *Delhi Business Review, 1*(1).

Glossary

ABC analysis An approach to inventory control where the items are categorized on the basis of usage and value. The most valuable items used being rated as a category.

Accounting rate of return The return on investment on a project which is measured as the project's average accounting profits on its average investment.

Acid test ratio A liquidity measure which is defined as: (current assets – inventories + prepaid expenses)/current liabilities.

Acquisitions When a firm takes over or acquires another firm, it is called acquisition; this also involves a change in management.

ADR American depository receipt. A negotiable instrument representing receipts of depository. It is used in USA.

Agency costs The costs that arise as a result of conflict of interest between the owners of the firm and its agents, that is, managers.

Aging schedule A statement showing age-wise distribution of accounts receivables.

Amalgamation When two firms—A and B merge with each other and form a firm "C"

Annuity A cash flow stream of equal amount to be paid or received at constant interval of time.

Arbitrage The process of taking advantage of difference in prices of the same scrip in different markets.

Average collection period The ratio of receivables to average credit sales per day.

Bear market A market dominated by operators who believe that prices of shares are expected to come down. So, sell today, buy tomorrow.

Bearer security A security for which physical possession is the primary evidence of ownership.

Beta
It measures the risk of one security vis-à-vis overall changes in market. A security having five beta would reflect 50% change on price of the security as compared to change in the market price.

Bond
A generic term for a long-term debt security issued to borrow money from the market. It may be secured or unsecured.

Bonus issues
It is known as capitalization of profit, reserve, and surplus. It is conversion of profit, reserve, and surplus into a capital. By bonus issues, the net worth of the company remains the same but the number of shares increases, thereby reducing book value per share. There is no direct cost of bonus issue to investor as investors are not required to pay anything to the company.

Book value
In respect of assets—it is original cost minus depreciation. Also known as written-down value. In respect of liability side, it is net worth divided by number of shares outstanding. It represents cumulative earnings per share.

Book value weights
The proportion of different sources of financing in the overall financial structure of the firm as reflected by the balance sheet values.

Business risk
The risk arising from operating in a given economic system and a given industry. Often, it reflects variation in EBIT because of change in sales.

Call option
A contractual agreement which gives the buyer the option to exercise the option or let it expire.

Call provision
A stipulation in a bond or preferred stock contract enabling the issuing firm to call back (repurchase) the outstanding bonds or preferred stock at a predetermined price.

Capital
It is a foundational resource in which a company is incorporated and which lasts forever. In a company kind of organization there are authorized share capital (maximum amount of capital that a company can raise without changing its capital clause as mentioned in memorandum of association), issued capital (a part of authorized share capital, offered to investors), subscribed capital (response to issued capital), and paid-up capital (the actual amount paid by investors). For calculation of dividend, right issue, bonus issues of shares, paid-up capital is taken as a base.

Capital gain (loss)
If the current market price of a capital asset is greater (less) than its original cost or book value, it results into a capital gain (loss).

Capital budgeting
Planning and execution of capital expenditure decisions for acquiring long-term investment or assets.

Capital employed
It means net working capital plus fixed assets or total assets minus current liability.

Capital market
A part of financial market where resources for long-term are mobilized through securities like shares, debentures, etc.

Capital structure	The composition of a firm's long-term finances consisting of equity, preference capital, and long-term debt.
Cash budget	A statement showing the forecast of cash receipts and disbursements, and net cash balance over a period of time on a rollover basis.
Cash conversion cycle	The time for which cash remains tied up starting from the purchase of raw materials and ending with realization of sales receipts.
Cash credit	An arrangement whereby the bank allows the borrower to borrow up to a certain limit.
Certainty equivalent	The cash flows which the decision-maker would be ready to accept for certain, in place of uncertain/risky, cash flows.
Collection float	The amount of checks deposited in the bank but not cleared.
Convertible debt	Debt, which offers the holder the option to convert the debt into equity at some point of time in future at a prespecified price and at a prespecified ratio.
Cost of capital	The minimum rate of return the firm must earn on its investments in order to satisfy the expectations of the investors who provide the long-term funds to the firm. It is often measured as the weighted arithmetic average of the cost of various sources of finance tapped by the firm.
Coupon rate	The rate of interest on a bond or loan expressed as a percentage and payable on the face value.
Coverage ratios	Ratios that measure a firm's ability to meet its recurring fixed charge obligations, such as interest on long-term debt, lease payments, and/or preferred stock dividends.
Credit period	The length of time customers are allowed to make payment for their credit purchases.
Credit risk	The risk that a customer or borrower will not pay their financial obligations.
Currency risk	The risk arising from the effect of changes in foreign exchange rates.
Current yield	Annual interest or dividend currently received divided by the current market price.
Days sales outstanding	The ratio of receivables outstanding to average daily sales.
DCF analysis	Discounted cash flow analysis used in capital budgeting. It has two approaches—present value and future value.
Debenture	A long-term debt divided into small units issued by companies to borrow from investors. It may be secured or unsecured, convertible or nonconvertible, etc.

Debt capacity
The maximum amount of debt that a firm can raise in relation to equity at a given point of time.

Debt–asset ratio
Ratio that reflects the proportion of assets financed through debt.

Default risk
The uncertainty associated with future payments to the security owner by the security issuer. Treasury securities are considered to be default-free.

Degree of financial leverage
The percentage change in earnings per share (EPS) as a result of a 1% change in earnings before interest and tax (EBIT).

Degree of operating leverage
The percentage change in earnings before interest and taxes (EBIT) as a result of 1% change in sales.

Degree of total leverage
The percentage change in earnings per share (EPS) as a result of 1% change in sales.

Depository receipt
A negotiable certificate issued by a depository bank which represents the beneficial interest in shares or underlying security, issued by a company.

Derivative instruments
Instruments derived from conventional direct dealings in securities, currencies, and commodities, that is, security which is derived from underlying security.

Direct quote
Exchange-rate-expressed units of home currency per unit of foreign currency.

Discounting
Process of finding the present value of a future cash flow or a series of future cash flows by applying an appropriate discount rate often known as interest rate or cost of fund.

Diversifiable risk
That component of total risk associated with an asset which can be reduced or eliminated by holding the asset in a portfolio. Also known as firm-specific or unique risk.

Diversification
Spreading out

Dividend
It is profit sharing by the company. It is paid as a fraction of the paid-up capital, say, a company pays a 20% dividend, it means that the company would pay 20% of the paid-up capital. A company can pay dividend out of the current years' profit, from accumulated profit, free reserves and surplus, etc.

Dividend capitalization model
A share valuation model, which discounts the expected dividends from equity shares at shareholders required rate of return to determine the intrinsic value of the share.

Dividend yield
The dividend per share divided by the market price per share.

Earnings per share (EPS)
The profit available to each equity share after deduction of tax, extraordinary items, and preference dividends. This is the earning for current year.

Economic order quantity (EOQ)	The quantity of goods per order, which minimizes the total inventory holding costs (that is, the sum of inventory ordering cost and inventory carrying cost).
Economic risk	The risk due to the effect of changes in foreign exchange rates on the value of their future cash flows.
Equity	It means net worth or shareholders fund, that is, paid-up share capital + reserves and surplus – fictitious reserve.
Exchange rate	The rate at which one currency is converted into another currency.
Exercise price	The price at which a specified underlying asset or security can be bought or sold by the option holder. It is also referred to as the strike price.
Expected return	The arithmetic mean or average of all possible outcomes where those outcomes are weighted by the probability that each will occur.
External funds	Funds acquired from external sources by borrowing or issuing additional equity or preference stock.
Factoring	A method of financing offered by the subsidiaries of major banks or other specialized companies (factors) where they purchase the accounts receivables of the company with or without recourse basis.
Financial institutions	Institutions working as catalyst, that is, developer, initiators, and risk takers like IDBI.
Financial intermediaries	Institutions or individuals who act as a conduit between borrowers and lenders.
Financial lease	A non-cancellable contractual commitment where the firm leasing the asset (the lessee) makes a series of payments to the firm that actually owns the asset (the lessor) for the use of the asset.
Financial leverage	Refers to the use of debt or other fixed cost source of funds in capital structure of the firm.
Financial risk	Risk that arises from the use of debt or long-term loan. It refers to payment of interest.
Financial structure	The composition of total both short-term as well as long-term sources of finance used by a firm.
Float	Funds represented by checks, which have been issued, but which have not been collected.
Floatation costs	The legal, printing, postage, underwriting brokerage, and other costs associated with the issuing securities.
Floating charge/ lien	A general lien against a company's assets.

Foreign exchange rate risk	The risk arising due to adverse movements in exchange rate between currencies.
Futures	A futures contract is a form of forward contract, which conveys an agreement to exchange a specific amount of a commodity or financial instrument on a stipulated future date at a particular price which is agreed now.
GDR	Global depository receipts—a negotiable instrument, which represents publicly traded equity shares of a foreign company other than USA market.
Gearing	The ratio of debt finance to equity finance in a company's financial structure.
Hedgers	Institutions or individuals specializing in hedging.
Hedging	Process or techniques adopted to reduce the exposure to risk.
Hurdle rate	The minimum acceptable rate of return on a project.
Incremental cash flows	The difference in the cash flows of a firm with and without investment in a project.
Indenture	A formal agreement between the issuer and purchasers of a bond.
Indirect quote	Exchange rate expressed as units of foreign currency per unit of home currency.
Inflation premium	A premium for anticipated inflation that investors require in addition to the pure rate of interest.
Internal rate of return (IRR)	The rate of discount at which the net present value of cash inflow and outflow is equal.
Intrinsic value	The intrinsic value of an asset is the present value of the stream of benefits expected from it. It is also referred to as the fair value or reasonable value or investment value.
Inventory turnover	The ratio of net sales to inventory suggesting how fast inventory is converting into sales.
Letter of credit	A letter from a bank mentioning that it has established a line of credit in favor of a certain party and the bank will pay on behalf of the client.
Leverage	Represents the change in one financial variable because of change in other related financial variable.
Line of credit	An agreement under which a financial institution agrees to provide credit up to a specified limit during a given period.
Liquid assets	Cash or other assets, which can be easily converted into cash like marketable securities.
Liquidity	Access to cash. Also the ease with which assets can be converted into cash without any significant loss in value.

Marginal cost of capital	The cost of capital that represents the weighted cost of each additional rupee of financing from all sources, debt, preferred stock, and common stock.
Market risk	That part of an asset's risk which cannot be reduced or eliminated through diversification.
Market risk premium	It is the additional return which the investors require over and above the risk free rate of return to hold a highly diversified portfolio called the market portfolio.
Market-value weights	The percentage of financing provided by different capital sources, measured by the current market prices of the firm's bonds and preferred and common stock.
Merger	When a firm merges with other and loses its identity like ICICI merged with ICICI Bank.
Money markets	Financial markets for trading in short-term securities.
Net present value (NPV)	The difference between the discounted present values of future cash inflows and the present value of the cash outflow associated with an investment project where discounting is done using firm's cost of capital.
Net profit margin	A ratio that measures the net income of the firm as a percentage of sales.
Net working capital	The difference between total current assets and total current liabilities.
Operating cycle	The time between the delivery of raw materials/finished goods and realization of cash from the sale of such finished goods/finished goods made from the same raw material. It represents time taken between the procurement of raw material and realization of sales.
Operating lease	A lease contract, which is not a financial lease. It is usually for a shorter time period and is cancelable at a short notice without any significant penalty.
Operating leverage	The proportion of fixed operating costs in the total operating costs of the firm. The greater the operating leverage, the greater the variability of the firm's earnings before interest and taxes to changes in sales. It measures operating risk which arises out of variation in EBIT because of change in sales.
Operating profit	It measures the operational efficiency. Higher operating profit means higher efficiency. It is calculated by subtracting interest and depreciation from the gross profit.
Opportunity cost	The benefit that one foregoes by selecting the next best alternative.
Opportunity cost of capital	The rate of return foregone by the investor when he selects the next best alternative at a given level of risk.

Optimal capital structure
Capital structure that minimizes (optimizes) the firm's composite cost of capital and consequently maximizes the value of the firm.

Options
A contractual agreement that confers the right, but not an obligation to the buyer of the contract to buy or sell an underlying asset like stock, currency, commodity, financial instrument, or a futures contract before a specific expiry date at a price agreed upon today.

Overdraft system
A financial arrangement between a bank and its client where the borrower is allowed to overdraw on his current account with the banker up to a certain specified limit during a given period.

Overtrading
Carrying on business at a level of activity for which sufficient funds are not available.

Payback period
Time required for an asset to generate cash flows just enough to cover the initial investment, that is, duration during which investment is recovered.

Payment float
The amount of checks issued by the firm but not paid for by the bank, that is, the time gap between issue of check and realization of the payment.

Payout ratio
The proportion of earnings paid out by way of dividends.

Perpetuity
A constant periodic cash flow that occurs perpetually.

Present value
The value of cash flows expected to occur at some point of time in future expressed in terms of money of current purchasing power.

Price/earnings (P/E) ratio
The ratio of market price per share to earnings per share. This ratio indicates how the earnings of the firm are valued in the market.

Primary market
The market in which financial securities are issued by the firm to raise capital. Also known as new issue market comprising of initial public offer and further public offer.

Processing float
Funds tied up during the time required for the firm to process remittance checks before they can be deposited in the bank.

Profitability index
Also called benefit–cost ratio, it measures the present value per rupee of outlay.

Public deposit
Unsecured deposit obtained by a company from public at large. It is governed by Section 58 A & B of Indian Companies Act, 1956 in India.

Put option
An option contract where the buyer gets the right to sell a given security at a price agreed upon today before some specific expiry date.

Receivables turn-over ratio
The ratio of net sales to receivables.

Reinvestment rate
The rate of return at which the intermediate cash inflows of a project may be reinvested.

Required rate of return	Rate of return required by investors on their investment. It is cost of capital to the company and return on investment to the investors.
Restrictive covenants	Provisions in the loan agreement that place restrictions on usage of funds by the borrower and demand a certain level of financial performance. The objective is to safeguard the interests of the lender.
Right issue	Existing shareholders enjoy pre-emptive rights in subsequent public issue offered by the company. A right issue may be offered at par or at premium.
Risk	Risk refers to variability or uncertainty regarding return. It is measured in general as the variance of returns.
Risk-adjusted discount rate	The discount rate applicable to a risky investment. It is equal to the risk-free rate of return plus a risk premium reflecting the risk characterizing the investment.
Risk premium	The additional return required by the investors for undertaking additional risk.
Risk-free rate	The rate of return on risk-free investments, such as the interest rate on short-term government securities.
Return on equity (ROE)	Measures the return being earned on the funds provided by the shareholders. It is calculated by dividing the profit after tax by shareholders' funds.
Return on investment (ROI)	Measures the overall return generated by the firm on its total assets. It is calculated by dividing profit before interest and taxes by capital employed (total assets – current liabilities). Also referred as the return on capital employed.
Safety stock	Inventories carried to protect against variations in sales, production, and procurement time.
Sale and leaseback	An arrangement arising when a firm sells land, buildings, or equipment that it already owns and simultaneously enters into an agreement to lease the property back for a specified period, under specific terms.
Salvage value	The value realized from the disposal of an asset.
Secondary market	A market where subsequent purchase and selling of listed securities takes place, popularly known as stock exchange or stock market. There are 23 stock exchanges in the country.
Sensitivity analysis	A technique of risk analysis which tests the responsiveness of a project's expected outcome like net present value or internal rate of return to changes in underlying factors like sales volume, sales price, quantity sold, etc.

Shares	One fraction of a whole number. Share capital is fraction capital, that is, capital divided into small parts of capital where one part (fraction) is equal to other. There are basically three types of shares available (i) equity shares, (ii) preference shares, and (iii) CCP shares. An equity share is one which carries no fixed rate of dividend; payment of dividend is optional, and it is the very first resource of capital so much so that unless there is equity share capital, there cannot be any other form of capital. The equity share is also known as ordinary or common stock. A preference share is one enjoying preference to equity shares in respect of dividend payment and redemption of capital in case of liquidation. Preference share carries a fixed rate of dividend. A cumulative convertible preference (CCP) share—is a hybrid between equity share and preference share. It is issued as a preference share carrying a fixed rate of dividend of 10% with maturity of 10 years. From 6 years, 20% of CCP shares are converted into equity shares every year.
Simulation	A statistical approach to project risk analysis, which makes use of random numbers and preassigned probabilities to simulate a project's return.
Speculators	Traders who enter the futures or options contract, with a view of making profit from the subsequent price movements.
Spontaneous financing	The trade credit and other accounts payable that arise spontaneously in the firm's day-to-day operations.
Spot rate	Exchange rate which applies to "on the spot" delivery of the currency—in practice it means delivery two days after the day of trade.
Subscription price	Price at which the issue of a security can be subscribed to by the investors.
Systematic risk	Risk that cannot be diversified away. It is also referred to as market risk or non-diversifiable risk.
Technical insolvency	Situation in which the firm is not in position to honor its normal and routine financial obligations because of liquidity crisis. Although its assets may exceed its total liabilities, thereby indicating a positive net worth, the company simply does not have sufficient liquidity to pay its debts.
Term loan	A loan which is generally repayable in more than one year.
Term structure of interest rates	The relationship between interest rates and the term to maturity, where the risk of default is held constant.
Time value of money	The basic concept underlying financial analysis, which says that money has time value, that is, a rupee today is worth more than a rupee after one year.
Trade credit	Inter-firm credit arising from credit sales. It is recorded as an account receivable by the seller and as an account payable by the buyer.

Transit float	Funds tied up during the time necessary for a deposited check to clear through the commercial banking system and become usable funds to the company.
Unsystematic risk	Risk that can be diversified away. It is also referred to as unique risk, specific risk, residual risk, or diversifiable risk.
Venture capitalists	Investors interested in supplying capital to particularly high-risk situations, such as start-ups or firms denied conventional financing.
Warrant	A call option to buy a stated number of shares.
Warrant price	The exercise price of a warrant is what the holder must pay to purchase the stated number of shares.
Weighted average cost of capital (WACC)	The weighted average of the costs of various sources of finance being used by the firm. The weights being the proportion in which various sources of finance are used by the firm.
Working capital	The capital that makes the fixed assets work is called working capital. There are two measures of working capital—gross working capital and net working capital. Gross working capital is the total of current assets. Net working capital is the difference between the total of current assets and the total of current liabilities.
Yield	It measures relationship between dividend and earning with market price. It is of two types (a) earning yield—it measures relationship between EPS and (market price of share) MPS, and (b) dividend yield—it measures relationship between dividend per share and market price of shares.

Financial Calculation: Ready Reckoner

Financial Forecasting

1. External financing requirement

$$EFR = \frac{A}{S}(\Delta S) - \frac{L}{S}(\Delta S) - mS_1(1-d)$$

where EFR is the external financing requirement, A/S is the current assets and fixed assets as a proportion of sales, ΔS is the expected increase in sales, L/S is the spontaneous liabilities as a proportion of sales, m is the net profit margin, S_1 is the projected sales for next year, and d is the dividend payout ratio.

2. Sustainable growth rate

$$g = \frac{m(1-d)A/E}{A/S_0 - m(1-d)A/E},$$

where g is the sustainable growth rate with internal equity.

$$A/E = \frac{\text{Total Assets}}{\text{Equity}}$$

= current and fixed assets as proportion of **value of money**

3. Future value of a lump sum (single flow)

$$FV_n = PV(1+k)^n,$$

where FV_n is the future value of the initial flow n years hence, PV is the initial cash flow, k is the annual rate of interest and n is the life of investment.

4. Effective rate of interest

$$r = \left(1 + \frac{k}{m}\right)^m - 1,$$

where r is the effective rate of interest, k is the nominal rate of interest, and m is the frequency of compounding per year.

5. Future value interest factor of annuity

$$\text{FVIFA}_{(k,n)} = \frac{(1+k)^n - 1}{k},$$

where k is the rate of interest and n is the time horizon.

$$\text{Sinking fund factor} = \frac{1}{\text{FVIFA}_{(k,n)}}$$

6. Present value interest factor of annuity

$$\text{PVIFA}(k,n) = \frac{(1+k)^n - 1}{k(1+k)^n},$$

where k is the rate of interest and n is the time horizon.

$$\text{Capital recovery factor} = \frac{1}{\text{FVIFA}_{(k,n)}}$$

where k is the rate of interest and n is the time horizon.

7. Present value interest factor of a perpetuity

$$P_\infty = 1/k$$

where k is the rate of interest.

Risk and Return

1. Rate of return is calculated as

$$k = \frac{D_t + (P_t - P_{t-1})}{P_{t-1}},$$

where k is the rate of return, P_t is the price of security at time "t", that is, at the end of the holding period. P_{t-1} is the price of the security at time "t−1," that is, at the beginning of the holding period or purchase price and D_t is the income or cash flows receivable from the security at time "t."

2. Expected rate of return $(\bar{k}) = \sum_{i=1}^{n} p_i k_i$,

where k_i is the rate of return from the i-th outcome, p_i is the probability of the i-th outcome, and n is the number of possible outcomes.

3. Variance of an asset's rate of return

$$\text{VAR}(k) = \sum_{i=1}^{n} P_i \left(k_i - \bar{k}\right)^2,$$

where VAR (k) is the variance of returns, P_i is the probability associated with i-th possible outcome, k_i is the rate of return from the i-th possible outcome, $\bar{k}$ is the expected rate of return, and n is the number of years. Standard deviation

$$\sigma = \sqrt{VAR(k)}$$

The notations are same as those used in variance.

4. CAPM model

$$k_j = r_f + \beta_j (k_m - r_f),$$

where k_j is the expected or required rate of return on security "j," r_f is the risk-free rate of return, β_j is the beta coefficient of security "j," and k_m is the return on market portfolio.

$$\beta_i = \frac{Cov_{im}}{\sigma_m^2},$$

where Cov_{im} is the covariance of security i with true market and $\sigma_m 2$ is the variance of return on the market index.

5. Required return $R(r_i)$

$$= r_f + \beta_{im} [E(r_m) - r_f]$$

$$r_f = \text{risk-free interest rate}$$

$$[E(r_m) - r_f] = \text{slope of SML}$$

$$\alpha = E(r_i) - R(r_i)$$

$$= E(r_i) - [r_f + \beta_{im} (E(r_m) - r_f)]$$

6. Systematic risk of security i

$$\beta_{im}^2 \sigma_m^2 = \frac{\rho_{im}^2 \sigma_i^2 \sigma_m^2}{\sigma_m^2} = \rho_{im}^2 \sigma_i^2$$

$$= R_{im}^2 \rho_i^2$$

$$\text{since } R_{im}^2 = \rho_{im}^2$$

where ρ_{im}^2 is the correlation coefficient and R_{im}^2 is the coefficient of determination between the security i and the market portfolio.

7. Unsystematic risk $(\sigma_{ei}^2) = \sigma_i^2 - \beta_{im}^2 \sigma_m^2$
   Or

$$= \sigma_i^2 - \rho_{im}^2 \sigma_i^2$$

$$= \sigma_i^2 (1 - \rho_{im}^2) = \sigma_i^2 (1 - R_{im}^2)$$

where σ_i^2 is the variance of security I and β_{im} is the beta of security i

Valuation of Securities

1. Equity valuation
2. Dividend discount model

$$P_0 = \sum_{t=1}^{n} \frac{D_t}{(1 + k_e)^t} + \frac{P_n}{(1 + k_e)^n}$$

where P_0 is the current market price of the equity share or intrinsic value of the share, D_t is the expected equity dividend at time t, P_n is the expected price of the equity share at time n, and k_e is the expected rate of return or required rate of return.

The value of equity share when there is constant growth

$$P_0 = \frac{D_0(1+g)}{k_e - g}$$

where D_0 is the current dividend per share and g is the expected constant growth rate in dividends.

3. H model

$$P_0 = \frac{D_0\left[(1+g_n) + H(g_a - g_n)\right]}{r - g_n}$$

where P_0 is the intrinsic value of the share, D_0 is the current dividend per share, r is the required rate of return, g_n is the normal long-run growth rate, g_a is the current growth rate, and H is the one half of the period during which g_a will level off to g_n.

4. Bond valuation

(a) The intrinsic value or the present value of a bond V_0 or P_0

$$= I(PVIFA_{kd, n}) + F(PVIF_{kd, n}),$$

where V_0 is the intrinsic value of the bond, P_0 is the present value of the bond, I is the annual interest payable on the bond, zn is the maturity period of the bond and k_d is the cost of capital or required rate of return.

(b) Current yield $= \dfrac{\text{Coupon interest}}{\text{Prevailing market price}}$

(c) Yield to maturity is r in the equation

$$P_0 = \sum_{t=1}^{n} \frac{I}{(1+r)^t} + \frac{F}{(1+r)^n}$$

(d) Realized yield is r in the equation

$$P_0 (1+r)^n = \text{total cash flows received by the investor.}$$

(e) Nominal rate = risk-free rate + inflation rate

(f) Duration $= \dfrac{1C.PVIF_{r,1} + 2C.PVIF_{r,2} + \ldots + n[C + F]PVIF_{r,n}}{P_0}$

where C is the coupon interest payments, r is the promised yield to maturity, n is the number of years to maturity, and F is the redemption value.

(g) Simplified formula for duration

$$D = \frac{r_c}{r_d} PVIFA(r_{d,n}) \times (1+r_d) + \left[1 - \frac{r_c}{r_d}\right] n,$$

where r_c is the coupon yield and r_d is the YTM.

(h) When bond is selling at par, (that is, $r_c = r_d$) duration $(D) = PVIFA(r_{d,n}) \times (1+r_d)$

(i) Duration of a perpetual bond is

$$D = \frac{1+r}{r},$$

where r is the current yield

(j) Limiting value of duration is given by $\dfrac{1+\text{YTM}}{\text{YTM}}$

(k) Interest rate elasticity, $IE = \dfrac{\Delta P_0 / P_0}{\Delta \text{YTM} / \text{YTM}}$

(l) Approximate method of calculating interest rate elasticity is given by $IE = D_{it} \times \dfrac{\text{YTM}}{1+\text{YTM}}$,

where D_{it} is the duration

(m) Interest rate risk which measures change in price of bond for a change in the YTM is given by

$$\frac{\Delta P_0}{P_0} = IEit \times \frac{\Delta \text{YTM}}{\text{YTM}}$$

(n) Modified duration

$$D_{mod} = \frac{D}{1 + \dfrac{\text{YTM}}{f}},$$

where f is the discounting periods per year, D is the Macaulay's duration, YTM is the yield to maturity in decimal form.

(o) Percentage price volatility is $\dfrac{\Delta P}{P} \times 100 = -D_{mod} \cdot \Delta y$

(p) Duration of equity based on dividend discount model $= \dfrac{1}{k-g}$

(q) Duration of equity $= \dfrac{1}{\text{Dividend yield}} = \dfrac{\text{Market price}}{\text{Dividend}}$

5. Valuation of a convertible

(a) The value of convertible is $\displaystyle\sum_{t=1}^{n} \frac{C}{(1+r)^t} + \frac{(P_n) \times \text{Conversion ratio}}{(1+r)^n}$,

where C is the coupon amount, r is the required rate of return, P_n is the expected price of equity share on conversion, n is the number of years to maturity.

(b) Percentage of downside risk

$$= \frac{\left(\begin{array}{l}\text{Market Price of convertible Security} - \text{Price of an equivalent} \\ \text{non-convertible security}\end{array}\right)}{\text{Price of an equivalent non convertible security}} \times 100$$

(c) Conversion premium $= \dfrac{\text{Market Price} - \text{Conversion Value}}{\text{Conversion Value}}$

(d) Conversion parity price $= \dfrac{\text{Bond price}}{\text{Number of shares on convesion per warrant}}$

(e) Break even period $= \dfrac{\text{Conversion premium}}{\text{Interest income Dividend}}$

(f) Payback period $= \dfrac{\dfrac{\%\text{ premium}}{1+\%\text{ premium}}}{\text{Current yield} - \dfrac{\text{Dividend yield}}{1+\%\text{ premium}}}$

Financial Analysis

1. Liquidity ratios

   (a) Current ratio = current assets/current liabilities

   (b) Quick Ratio $= \dfrac{\text{Current Assets} - \text{Inventories}}{\text{Current Liabilities}}$

   (c) Bank finance to working capital ratio $= \dfrac{\text{Short-term bank borrowings}}{\text{Working capital gap}}$

2. Leverage ratios

   (a) Long-term debt-equity ratio $= \dfrac{\text{Long-term debt}}{\text{Net worth}}$

   (b) Total debt-equity ratio $= \dfrac{\text{Total Debt}}{\text{Net Worth}}$

   (c) Debt–asset ratio $= \dfrac{\text{Total Debt}}{\text{Total Assets}}$

3. Coverage ratios

   (a) Interest coverage ratio $= \dfrac{\text{EBIT}}{\text{Interest}}$

   (b) Cash flow coverage ratio $= \dfrac{\text{EBILT} + \text{D}}{\text{I} + \text{L} + \dfrac{\text{LR}}{(1-t)} + \dfrac{\text{P}}{(1-t)}}$,

   where EBILT is the earnings before interest, lease payments, and taxes, D is the depreciation, I is the interest charges, L is the lease payments, t is the marginal tax rate, LR is the loan repayment, and P is the preference dividend.

   (c) Debt service coverage ratios

   $$= \left(\dfrac{\text{PAT} + \text{Depreciation} + \text{Other non} - \text{cash charges} + \text{Interest on term loan}}{\text{Interest on term loan} + \dfrac{\text{Repayment of the term loan}}{1-t}} \right)$$

4. Turnover ratios

(a) Inventory turnover $= \dfrac{\text{Cost of goods sold}}{\text{Average Inventory}}$

(b) Accounts receivables turnover $= \dfrac{\text{Net credit sales}}{\text{Average accounts receivable}}$

(c) Total assets turnover $= \dfrac{\text{Net sales}}{\text{Average Total Assets}}$

5. Profitability ratios

(a) Gross profit margin $= \dfrac{\text{Gross Profit}}{\text{Net Sales}}$,

(b) Net profit margin $= \dfrac{\text{Net Profit}}{\text{Net Sales}}$

(c) Return on investment (earning power) $= \dfrac{\text{EBIT}}{\text{Average total assets}}$

(d) Return on net worth $= \dfrac{\text{Profit after tax}}{\text{Average net worth}}$

6. Altman's Z Score Model (to identify the financial distress of the firm)

$$Z = 1.2X_1 + 1.4X_2 + 3.3X_3 + 0.6X_4 + 1.0X_5,$$

where Z is the discriminant score, X_1 is the working capital/total assets, X_2 is the retained earnings/total assets.

$X_3 = $ EBIT/total assets

$X_4 = $ market value of equity/book value of debt

$X_5 = $ sales/total assets.

Leverages

1. $\text{DOL} = [Q(S-V)] / [Q(S-V) - F]$

2. DFL $\text{DFL} = \dfrac{\text{EBIT}}{\text{EBIT} - I - \dfrac{D_p}{(I-T)}}$

3. $\text{DTL} = \text{DOL} \times \text{DFL} = \dfrac{Q(S-V)}{Q(S-V) - F - I - \dfrac{D_p}{(I-T)}}$

4. Overall breakeven point

5. $Q = \dfrac{F + I + \dfrac{D_p}{(I-T)}}{S-V}$

6. Operating breakeven point $Q = \dfrac{F}{(S-V)}$

7. Financial break-even point $EBIT = I + \dfrac{D_p}{(I-T)}$

Cost of Capital

1. Cost of term loans $= I(1-T)$,
   where I is the interest rate, T is the tax rate.
2. Cost of debentures

$$P = \sum_{t=1}^{n} \frac{I(1-t)}{(1+k_d)^t} + \frac{F}{(1+k_d)^n},$$

where k_d is the post-tax cost of debenture capital, I is the annual interest payment per debenture capital, t is the corporate tax rate, F is the redemption price per debenture, P is the net amount realized per debenture, and n is the maturity period.

3. Cost of preference capital

$$P = \sum_{t=1}^{n} \frac{D}{(1+k_p)^t} + \frac{F}{(1+k_p)^n}$$

where k_p is the cost of preference capital, D is the preference dividend per share payable annually, F is the redemption price, P is the net amount realized per share, and n is the maturity period.

4. Cost of equity capital
5. Dividend forecast approach

$$P_e = \frac{D_1}{k_e - g},$$

where P_e is the price per equity share, D_1 is the expected dividend per share at the end of one year, k_e is the rate of return required by the equity shareholders and g is the growth rate of dividends.

6. Cost of external equity

$$k_e' = \frac{D_1}{P_0(1-f)} + g, \text{ (Method 1)}$$

where k_e' is the cost of external equity, D_1 is the dividend expected at the end of year 1, P_0 is the current market price per share, g is the constant growth rate applicable to dividends, and f is the floatation costs as a percentage of the current market price.

$$k_e' = \frac{D_1}{P_0(1-f)} + g \text{ (Method 2)}$$

7. Weighted average cost of capital

$$= k_e\left(\frac{E}{E+P+D}\right) + k_p\left(\frac{P}{E+P+D}\right) + k_d(1-T)\left(\frac{D}{E+P+D}\right),$$

where E is the market value of equity, P is the market value of preference capital, and the D is the market value of debt.

Capital Structure

1. Overall Capitalization Rate of the Firm

$$k_0 = k_d \frac{B}{B+S} + k_e \frac{S}{B+S},$$

where k_d is the cost of debt, B is the market value of the outstanding debt, S is the market value of equity, k_e is the cost of equity, k_0 is the weighted average cost of capital.

2. Present value of a tax shield of interest payments
   (a) When debt is perpetual $= t_c B$,
       where t_c is the tax rate on corporate income and B is the market value of the debt.
   (b) When corporate taxes are considered the value of the levered firm =

   $$V = \frac{O(1-t_c) + t_c B}{k}$$

   (c) If the personal tax rate is t_p the tax advantage of debt $= t_c B (1-t_p)$
   (d) When the tax rate on stock income (t_{ps}) differs from the tax rate on debt income (t_{pd}) the tax advantage of debt capital

   $$= 1 - \frac{(1-t_c)(1-t_{ps})}{(1-t_{pd})} \times B$$

3. Relation between EBIT and EPS

   $$EPS = \frac{(EBIT - I)(1-t)}{n},$$

   where EBIT is the earning before interest and tax, EPS is the earning per share, I is the interest payment, t is the tax rate, and n is the number of shares.

4. EBIT–EPS indifference point

   $$\frac{(EBIT - I_1)(1-t)}{n_1} = \frac{(EBIT - I_2)(1-t)}{n_2},$$

   where EPS is the earnings per share.

   I_1 & I_2 = interest payment under alternative one and interest payment under alternative two, respectively

5. Relation between ROI and ROE

   $$ROE = \{ROI + (ROI - k_d) D/E\} (I - t),$$

   where ROE is the return on equity, ROI is the return on investment, k_d is the cost of debt (pre-tax), D is the debt component in the total capital, E is the equity component in the total capital, and t is the tax rate.

Dividend Policy

1. Traditional model (Graham–Dodd model)

$$P = m(D + E/3),$$

where P is the market price per share, m is the multiplier, D is the dividend per share, and E is the earnings per share.

2. Walter model

$$P = \frac{D + (E - D)r/k_e}{k_e},$$

where P is the market price per share, D is the dividend per share, E is the earnings per share, r is the internal rate of return, and k_e is the cost of equity capital.

3. Gordon model
The model is expressed as

$$P_0 = \frac{Y_0(1 - b)}{k_e - br},$$

where P_0 is the market price per share at the beginning of period 0, Y_0 is the earnings per share for period 0, b is the retention ratio (retained earnings/total earnings), r is the return on investments, and k_e is the cost of equity capital or (cost of capital of firm).

4. MM approach

$$P_0 = \frac{D_1 + P_1}{1 + k_e},$$

where P_0 is the market price per share at the beginning of period 0, D_1 is the expected dividend per share for period 1, P_1 is the market price per share at the end of period 1, and k_e is the cost of equity capital.

5. Corporate dividend behaviour (Lintner model)

$$D_t = cr\, EPS_t + (1 - c)\, D_{t-1},$$

where D_t is the dividend per share for the time period t, c is the weightage given to current earnings by the firm, r is the target payout rate, EPS_t is the earnings per share for the time period t, and D_{t-1} is the dividend per share for the time period $(t-1)$.

Working Capital Management

1. Working capital management

(a) Raw material storage period $= \dfrac{\text{Average Stock of Raw Material and Stores}}{\text{Average Raw Materials and Stores consumed per day}}$

(b) Work-in-process period $= \dfrac{\text{Average Work-in-process inventory}}{\text{Average daily cost of production}}$

(c) Finished goods storage period $= \dfrac{\text{Average finished good inventory}}{\text{Average daily cost of sales}}$

(d) Average collection period $= \dfrac{\text{Average accounts receivable}}{\text{Average daily credit sales}}$

(e) Average payment period $= \dfrac{\text{Average accounts receivable}}{\text{Average credit purchases per day}}$

2. Net operating cycle period $= A + B + C + D - E$

3. Weighted operating cycle $=$

$$D_{woc} = W_{rm} D_{rm} + W_{wip} D_{wip} + W_{fg} D_{fg} + W_{ar} D_{ar} - W_{ap} D_{ap}$$

where D_{woc} is the duration of weighted operating cycle, W_{rm} is the weight of raw material expressed as a percentage of raw material cost to sales, D_{rm} is the duration of raw material, W_{wip} is the weight of work-in-progress expressed as a percentage of work-in-progress cost to sales, D_{wip} is the duration of work-in-progress, W_{fg} is the weight of finished goods expressed as a percentage of cost of goods sold to sales, D_{fg} is the duration of finished goods, W_{ar} is the weight of accounts receivables expressed as a percentage of sales to sales, D_{ar} is the duration of accounts receivables, W_{ap} is the weight of accounts payables expressed as a percentage of raw material cost to sales, and D_{ap} is the duration of accounts payables.

Inventory Management

1. Economic order quantity

$$EOQ = \sqrt{\dfrac{2UF}{PC}} \text{ units,}$$

where U is the annual usage rate, F is the ordering cost, C is the carrying cost, and P is the price per unit.

2. Reorder point $= S \times L + F\sqrt{S \times R \times L}$,
    where S is the usage in units, L is the lead time in days, R is the average number of units per order, and F is the stock out acceptance factor.

Receivables Management

1. Effect of relaxing the credit standards on profit

$$\Delta P = \Delta S(1 - V) - k \, \Delta I - b_n \, \Delta S,$$

where ΔP is the change in profit, ΔS is the increase in sales, V is the variable costs to sales ratio, k is the cost of capital, and ΔI is the increase in investment in receivables

$$= \dfrac{\Delta S}{360} \times \text{average collection period} \times V$$

$$b_n = \text{bad debts loss ratio on new sales}$$

$$1 - V = \text{contribution to sales ratio}$$

2. Effect of increasing the credit period on profit

$$\Delta P = \Delta S(1 - V) - k \, \Delta I - b_n \, \Delta S$$

The components of the formula are same except

$$\Delta I = (ACP_N - ACP_O)\frac{S_o}{360} + V(ACP_N)\frac{\Delta S}{360},$$

where ΔI is the increase in investment in receivables, ACP_N is the new ACP (after increasing credit period), ACP_O is the old ACP, V is the ratio of variable cost to sales, and ΔS is the increase in sales.

3. The effect on profit for a change in cash discount rate

$$\Delta P = \Delta S (1-V) + k\Delta I - \Delta\, DIS,$$

where ΔS is the increase in sales, V is the ratio of variable cost to sales, k is the cost of capital, ΔI is the savings in investment in receivables.

$$= \frac{S_o}{360}(ACP_O - ACP_N) - V\frac{\Delta S}{360}(ACP_N)$$

DIS is the increase in discount cost

$$= p_n\,(S_o + \Delta S)d_n - p_o\,S_o\,d_o,$$

where p_n is the proportion of discount sales after liberalizing, S_o is the sales before liberalizing, ΔS is the increase in sales, d_n is the new discount percentage, p_o is proportion of discount sales before liberalizing, and d_o is the old discount percentage.

ACP_o = average collection period before increasing cash discount

ACP_N = average collection period after increasing cash discount.

4. Effect of decreasing the rigor of collection program on profit

$$\Delta P = \Delta S(1-V) - k\Delta I - \Delta BD,$$

where ΔP is the change in profits, ΔS is the increase in sales, V is the variable costs to sales ratio, k is the cost of capital, and ΔI is the increase in investment in receivables.

$$= \frac{S_o}{360}(ACP_N - ACP_O) + \frac{\Delta S}{360}(ACP_N \times V)$$

ΔBD = increase in bad debts cost

$$= b_n\,(S_o + \Delta S) - b_o\,s_o$$

where ACP_O is the average collection period before relaxing collection effort, ACP_N is the average collection period after relaxing collection effort, b_o is the proportion of bad debts to sales before relaxing collection effort, and the b_n is the proportion of bad debts to sales after relaxing collection effort.

Cash Management

1. Baumol model

$$TC = I\,(C/2) + b\,(T/C),$$

where TC is the total costs (total conversion costs + total holding costs), I is the interest rate on marketable securities per planning period, C is the amount of securities liquidated per batch, T is the estimated cash requirement over the planning period.

The point where total costs are minimum

$$C = \sqrt{\frac{2bT}{I}}$$

2. Miller and Orr model

$$RP = \sqrt[3]{\frac{3b\sigma^2}{4I}} + LL \text{ and,}$$

$$UL = 3 RP - 2 LL,$$

where LL is the lower control limit, RP is the return point, UL is the upper control limit, b is the fixed conversion cost, I is the interest rate per day on marketable securities, and σ^2 is the variance of daily changes in the expected cash balance.

Capital Expenditure Decisions

1. Cash flow as per long-term point of view

   $$= PAT + depreciation + interest on long-term (1 - t)$$

2. Cash flow as per equity funds point of view

   $$= PAT + depreciation - repayment of long-term borrowings - repayment of short-term$$
   $$bank borrowings$$

3. Accounting rate of return

   Accounting rate of return (ARR) = average profit after tax/average book value of the investment.

4. Net present value (NPV)

   $$NPV = \sum_{t=1}^{n} \frac{CF_t}{(1+k)^t} - I_o$$

   where k is the cost of funds, CF is the cash flows, and I_o is the initial investment.

5. Benefit—cost ratio (BCR)

   $$BCR = \frac{PV}{I},$$

   where BCR is the benefit-cost ratio, PV is the present value of future cash flows, I is the initial investment.

6. Net-benefit-cost ratio

   $$NBCR = \frac{NPV}{I}$$

7. Internal rate of return (IRR)

$$0 = \sum_{t=1}^{n} \frac{CF_t}{(1+k)} - I_o$$

where k is the IRR, CF is the cash flow, and I_o is the initial investment.

8. Expected NPV and standard deviation of NPV

(a) In perfectly correlated cash flows

$$\text{Expected NPV}\left(\overline{NPV}\right) = \sum_{t=1}^{n} \overline{A}_t / (1+i)^t - I$$

$$\text{S.D. of the NPV} = \sum_{t=1}^{n} \sigma_t^2 / (1+i)^t$$

(b) In uncorrelated cash flows

$$\text{Expected NPV}\left(\overline{NPV}\right) = \sum_{t=1}^{n} \overline{A}_t / (1+i)^t - I$$

$$\text{S.D. of the NPV} = \left[\sum_{t=1}^{n} \sigma_t^2 / (1+i)^{2t} \right]^{1/2},$$

where $\overline{A}_t$ is the expected cash flows for a time period t, i is the risk free discount rate, n is the life of the project, $\overline{NPV}$ is the the expected net present value, σ_t is the standard deviation of the cash flows for a time period t, and I is the initial investment.

9. Modified net present value

$$NPV_n = \frac{TV}{(1+k)^n} - 1,$$

where NPV_n is the modified net present value, TV is the terminal value, k is the cost of capital, and I is the investment outlay.

$$TV = \sum_{t=1}^{n} CF_t (1+r')^{n-t},$$

where CF_t is the cash inflow at the end of the year t and r' is the reinvestment rate applicable to the cash inflows of the project.

10. Modified internal rate of return

$$r^* = \left[\frac{TV}{I} \right]^{1/n} - I,$$

where I is the initial investment, r* is the modified IRR, n is the project life, and TV is the terminal value.

$$I(1+r^*)n = TV$$

11. Asset beta

$$\beta_A = \beta_E \left(\frac{E}{E+D} \right) + \beta_D \left(\frac{E}{E+D} \right),$$

where β_A is β_E E D, β_A is asset beta, β_E is equity beta, and B_D is debt beta.

Additional Problems and Solutions

Time Value of Money

1. AML Motors Ltd, currently pays a dividend of ₹2 per share and this dividend is expected to grow at the rate of 15% for next three years, then at the rate of 10% for next three years after which the growth rate will decline to 5% and remain at that level forever.
   You are required to determine

   1. the value of the company's stock if the required rate of return is 18%, and
   2. whether the value will be different if the investor is expected to hold the stock only for three years.

   ### Solution

   (a)

End of Year	Dividend Per Share (₹)	PVIF (18, n)	Present Value of Dividends (₹)
1	2.00 (1.15)=2.30	0.847	1.95
2	2.30 (1.15)=2.64	0.718	1.90
3	2.64 (1.15)=3.04	0.608	1.85
4	3.04 (1.10)=3.35	0.515	1.73
5	3.35 (1.10)=3.68	0.437	1.61
6	3.68 (1.10)=4.05	0.370	1.50
		Total	10.54

   The dividend per share in the seventh year is expected to be ₹4.05 (1.05)=₹4.25.
   The market price per share at the end of the sixth will be

   $$\frac{D_1}{k_e - g} = \frac{4.65}{0.18 - 0.05} = ₹32.69$$

   The present value of this price at time period t=0, will be=32.69×PVIF (18, 6)=32.69× 0.370=₹12.095

Value of company's stock if the required rate of return is 18%

$$=10.54+12.095=₹22.635\cong₹22.64$$

(b) If the investor expects to hold the stock for three years only, the market value of the stock at the end of three years will depend on the expected dividends in the fourth, fifth, and the sixth year and the market price expected to prevail at the end of sixth year

Present value of market value of AML's stock at the end of three years $=1.73+1.61+1.50+12.095=₹16.935$

The value of stock at t=0, will be=PV of dividends expected in the first, second, and the third year+PV of market price at the end of three years

$$=1.95+1.90+1.85+16.935=₹22.635\cong₹22.64$$

Thus, the value remains unchanged even if the holding period is different.

2. Mr Jitendra Agarwal is planning to purchase a house which costs ₹800,000. He has contacted two housing finance companies, that is, Grihalaxmi Housing Finance Ltd (GHFL) and Deccan Housing Finance Ltd (DHFL). GHFL has offered for 100% financing for a period of seven years. Mr Agarwal has to repay the loan along with the interest in equated monthly installments of ₹18,500 each, payable at the end of every month over a period of seven years.

DHFL has offered to provide 90% finance for a period of eight years. Mr Agarwal has to bring in 10% of the cost of the house at the time of purchase. He will borrow the amount of his contribution from one of his relatives and will pay back his relative ₹40,000 and ₹50,000 (which include the amount borrowed and the interest) at the end of the first year and the second year, respectively. The amount borrowed from DHFL has to be repaid along with interest in equated monthly installments of ₹12,800 each, payable at the end of every month over a period of eight years.

You are **required** to find out the effective rates of interest for both the financing alternatives and advise Mr Agarwal accordingly.

Solution

$$\text{Cost of house}=₹800,000$$

Financing by GHFL
Let the interest rate per month be "r"
Number of months for which payments have to be made to GHFL$=7\times12=84$
Amount payable at the end of every month to GHFL$=₹18,500$

$$\therefore 8,00,000 = 18,500\,\text{PVIFA}\,(r,\,84)$$

$$\Rightarrow \text{PVIFA} = \frac{800,000}{18,500} = 43.243$$

$$\text{For,}\quad r = 1.7\%,\,\text{PVIFA} = \frac{(1.017)^{84} - 1}{0.017(0.017)^{84}} = 44.548$$

$$\text{For,}\quad r = 1.8\%,\,\text{PVIFA} = \frac{(1.018)^{84} - 1}{0.018(0.018)^{84}} = 43.141$$

$$\therefore\quad r = 1.7 + \frac{1.8 - 1.7}{43.141 - 44.548} \times (43.141 - 44.548) = 1.793\%$$

Effective interest rate $= (1+r)12 - 1 = (1.01793)12 - 1 = 23.77\%$ p.a. (approx.)

Financing by DHFL and relative of Mr Agarwal

Let the interest rate be "r".

Amount of finance from DHFL $= 800,000 \times 0.90 = ₹720,000$

Amount of finance from relative $= ₹80,000$

Total amount of financing $= ₹720,000 + ₹80,000 = ₹800,000$

Amount payable at the end of every month to DHFL $= ₹12,800$

Number of months for which payments have to be made to DHFL $= 8 \times 12 = 96$ months

Amount payable to relative

At the end of one year (i.e., 12 months) $= ₹40,000$

At the end of two years (i.e., 24 months) $= ₹50,000$

$$\therefore 8,00,000 = 12,800 \, \text{PVIFA}(r, 96) + \frac{40,000}{(1+r)^{12}} + \frac{50,000}{(1+r)^{12}}$$

Let, $r = 1.2\%$,

$$\therefore \text{RHS} = 12,800 \times \frac{(1.012)^{96} - 1}{0.012(1.012)^{96}} + \frac{40,000}{(1.012)^{12}} + \frac{50,000}{(1.012)^{2}}$$

$$= 12,800 \times 56.818 + 34,665.2 + 37,552.4 = ₹799,488$$

$$r = 1.1\%$$

$$\therefore \text{RHS} = 12,800 \times \frac{(1.011)^{96} - 1}{0.011(1.011)^{96}} + \frac{40,000}{(1.011)^{12}} + \frac{50,000}{(1.011)^{2}}$$

$$= 12,800 \times 59.104 + 35,078.9 + 38,454.1 = ₹830,064.2$$

$$r = 1.1 + \frac{(1.2 - 1.1)}{(799,488 - 83,0064.2)} \times (800,000 - 83,0064.2) = 1.198$$

$\therefore$ Effective interest rate per annum $= (1+r)12 - 1 = (1.01198)12 - 1 = 0.1536$, that is, 15.36%.

We find from above that if Mr Agarwal borrows 90% of the cost of the house from DHFL and borrows the remaining amount from his relative, he faces a lesser effective rate of interest (15.36% per annum) than the effective rate of interest (23.77% per annum) he faces if he borrows 100% of the cost of the house from GHFL. Hence, he should borrow 90% of the cost of the house from DHFL and the remaining amount from his relative.

Risk and Return

3. The equity shares of Ice Spice, an ice cream manufacturing and marketing company, are presently trading at ₹96 per share. The company has recently paid a dividend of ₹3.00 per share. The next year's market price dividend per share of Ice Spice and the market return have been projected as follows:

Scenario	Optimistic	Normal	Pessimistic
Probability	0.30	0.40	0.30
Market price per share (₹)	₹110	₹105	₹99
Dividend per share (₹)	₹4.00	₹3.00	₹3.00
Return on market index	15%	12%	8%

You are **required** to determine

1. the expected return and risk for the equity shares of the company,
2. the expected return and risk for the market, and
3. the beta coefficient for the equity shares of the company and state its implication.

Solution

1.

Scenario	Optimistic	Normal	Pessimistic
Projected rate of return $\dfrac{D_1 + P_1}{P_0} - 1$	$\dfrac{110 + 4}{96} - 1 = 0.1875$ that is, 18.75%	$\dfrac{105 + 3}{96} - 1 = 0.125$ that is, 12.5%	$\dfrac{99 + 3}{96} = 0.0675$ that is, 6.25%
Probability	0.30	0.30	0.30

Expected rate of return from the share $= \Sigma p_i k_i$

$$= 18.75\,(0.30) + 12.5\,(0.40) + 6.25\,(0.30)$$
$$= 12.5\%$$

Risk for the share $\left[\Sigma p_i \left(k_i - \bar{k} \right)^2 \right]^{1/2}$

$$= [(18.75 - 12.50)2\,(0.30) + (12.50 - 12.50)2\,(0.40) + (6.25 - 12.50)2\,(0.30)]1/2$$
$$= [11.719 + 0 + 11.719]1/2$$
$$= 4.84\%$$

2. Expected return from the market $= \Sigma p_i k_m$

$$= 15\,(0.30) + 12\,(0.40) + 8\,(0.30)$$
$$= 11.70\%$$

Risk for the market, $\sigma_m = [\Sigma p_i (k_i - \bar{k})^2]^{1/2}$

$$= [(15 - 11.70)2\,(0.30) + (12 - 11.70)2\,(0.40) + (8 - 11.70)2\,(0.30)]1/2$$
$$= [3.267 + 0.036 + 4.107]1/2$$
$$= (7.41)1/2 = 2.72\%.$$

3. $\beta = \dfrac{\text{Cov}(i,m)}{\sigma_m^2}$

$$\text{Cov}(i, m) = \Sigma P_i (k_i - \overline{k}_i)(k_m - \overline{k}_m)$$
$$= (0.30)(18.75 - 12.50)(15 - 11.70) + (0.40)(12.50 - 12.50)$$
$$(12 - 11.70) + (0.30)(6.25 - 12.50)(8 - 11.70)$$
$$= 13.125$$
$$\sigma_m^2 = 7.41$$
$$\therefore \quad \beta = \frac{13.125}{7.41} = 1.77$$

Implication: A beta of 1.77 indicates that if market returns change by 1% then returns on the share will change by 1.77% in the same direction.

4. Mr Mahendra Reddy wants to follow the market index and hence has invested 100% of his holdings in the market portfolio. However, with a view to increasing his return per unit of risk, he is considering the following two options:

   Option 1: Increase his current position in the market portfolio by 1% through financing at risk-free rate.

   Option 2: Add to current position in the market portfolio by investing 1% in the Hind Motors' stock, which is to be financed at risk-free rate.

   The following information is available regarding the market index, Hind Motors and Treasury Bills:

Particulars	Return (%)	Standard Deviation (%)
Market index	15	20
Hind Motors	13	18
Treasury bills	6	–

If the correlation between the returns of market index and Hind Motors is 0.8, you are **required** to determine

1. the incremental risk premium per unit of incremental risk under Plan A,
2. the incremental risk premium per unit of incremental risk under Plan B, and
3. whether the market is in equilibrium? If not, what could be the reasons for it? Explain.

Solution

1. Return under option 1

$$= W_m R_m + W_f R_f$$
$$= 1.01 \times 15\% + (-0.01) \times 6\% = 15.09$$

Risk premium $= 15.09 - 6 = 9.09\%$

Risk premium under present position $= 15 - 6 = 9\%$

Incremental risk premium $= 9.09\% - 9\% = 0.09\%$

Risk under plan A

$$= W_m 2 \; \sigma_m 2 + W_f 2 \; \sigma_f 2 + 2 W_m W_f \; \sigma_m \; \sigma_f \; \rho_{mf}$$
$$= 1.012 \times 202 + (-0.01)\,2 \times (0)\,2 + 2 \times (1.01) \times (-0.01) \times (20) \times (0) \times (0)$$
$$= 408.04 (\%) 2$$

Standard deviation $= 20.2$

Incremental risk $= 20.2 - 20 = 0.2\%$

Incremental risk premium per unit of risk $= \dfrac{0.09}{0.2} = 0.45\%$

2. Return under option 2

$$= W_m R_m + W_{\text{Hind Motors}} R_{\text{Hind Motors}} + W_f R_f$$
$$= 1 \times 15\% + (0.01) \times 13\% + (-0.01) \times 6\% = 15.07\%$$

Risk premium $= 15.07 - 6 = 9.07\%$

Incremental risk premium $= 9.07\% - 9\% = 0.07\%$

Risk under plan B

$$= W_m^2 \; \sigma_m^2 + W^2_{\text{Hind Motors}} \sigma^2_{\text{Hind Motors}} + W_f^2 \; \sigma_f^2 + 2 W_m W_{\text{Hind Motors}} \; \sigma_m \sigma_{\text{Hind Motors}} \rho_{m\prime\text{Hind Motors}}$$
$$+ 2 W_{\text{Hind Motors}} W_f \sigma_{\text{Hind Motors}} \sigma_f \; \rho_{\text{Hind Motors},f} + 2 W_m W_f \; \sigma_m \; \sigma_f \rho_{m,f}$$
$$= 12 \times 202 + (0.01)2 \times 182 + (-0.01)2 \times (0)2 + 2(1) \times (0.01) \times 20 \times 18 \times 0.8 + 2 \times 0.01 \times -0.01$$
$$\times 18 \times 0 \times 0 + 2 \times 1 \times -0.01 \times 18 \times 0 \times 0$$
$$= 405.7924 (\%) 2$$

Standard deviation $= 20.144$

Incremental risk $= 20.144 - 20 = 0.144$

Incremental risk premium per unit of risk $= \dfrac{0.07}{0.144} = 0.486$

3. The market is not in equilibrium, as the incremental return per unit of incremental risk under both the options is not equal. In other words, in equilibrium, the marginal price of risk of Hind Motors stock must be equal to that of the market portfolio. Otherwise, if the marginal price of risk of Hind Motors is greater than the market's, investors can increase their portfolio reward for bearing risk by increasing the weight of Hind Motors in their portfolio. Until the price of Hind Motors stock rises relative to the market, investors will keep buying Hind Motors stock. The process will continue until stock prices adjust so that marginal price of risk of Hind Motors equals that of the market. The same process, in reverse, will equalize marginal prices of risk when Hind Motors's initial marginal price of risk is less than that of the market portfolio.

5. Jane Foods' stock had a beta of 0.95 in March 2003. The interest rate on T-bills at the time was 5%, and the interest rate on long-term government paper was 7.5%. The firm had debt outstanding of ₹17 crore and a market value of equity of ₹150 crore. The relevant market risk premiums for short-term and long-term investors are 8% and 5%, respectively. The tax rate applicable to the company is 36%.

    You are **required** to estimate the

1. expected return on the stock for a short-term investor in the company,
2. expected return on the stock for a long-term investor in the company,
3. unlevered beta of the company, and
4. estimate the cost of equity for the company.

Solution

1. The expected rate of return for the short-term investors $= Rf + \beta (Rm - Rf)$

$$= 5 + 0.95 \times 8$$

$$= 12.60\%$$

2. The expected rate of return for the long-term investors $= Rf + \beta (Rm - Rf)$

$$= 7.5 + 0.95 \times 5$$

$$= 12.25\%$$

3. Unlevered beta of the company $= \dfrac{\beta}{(1 + (1 - T)D/E)}$

$$= \dfrac{0.95}{(1 + (1 - 0.36)170/150)} = 0.55$$

4. The cost of equity will be equal to the rate of return required by the long-term investors. In this case, it is 12.25% and so that is the cost of equity.

6. A security analyst has estimated the characteristic line of AML's stock as follows:

$$R_{AML} = 0.5\% + 1.2\ R_M$$

The variance of return on AML's stock and on the market index are 50 (%)2 and 20 (%)2, respectively. The historical market risk premium has been 8%. During the last one year, the following changes have taken place in the market:

1. The risk-free rate has declined from 5% to 3%.
2. The market price of AML's stock has gone down ₹54 per share to ₹50 per share.
3. The dividend per share on AML's stock was ₹2.00 last year and is expected to be ₹2.50 next year.
4. The market index has gone down 8% over the last year, with a dividend yield of 3%.

You are **required** to determine

1. the expected return on AML's stock over the next year,
2. the market price of AML's stock one year from now,
3. the expected return on AML's stock be over the last year, and
4. the actual returns on AML's stock over the last year.

Solution

1. Expected return $= Rf + \beta (Rm - Rf)$

$$= 3\% + 1.2\ (8.0\%) = 12.60\%$$

2. Expected price appreciation $=$ expected return $-$ expected dividend yield

$$= 0.126 - (2.50/50) = 0.076 = 7.60\%$$

Expected price one year from today $= 50\ (1.076) = ₹53.80$

3. Expected returns on AML's stock over last year = 5% + 1.20 (−5%−5%) = −7.00%

    Return on the market index over last year $(Rm) = -8\% + 3\% = -5\%$

4. Actual returns over last year = $(P_1 - P_0 + D_0)/P_0$

    $$= (50 - 54 + 2)/54 = -3.70\%$$

Valuation

7. La Belle, a beauty care company reported EPS of ₹2.10 in 2005, on which it paid dividends per share of ₹0.69. Earnings are expected to grow 15% a year from 2006 to 2010, during which period the dividend payout ratio is expected to remain unchanged. After 2010, the earnings growth rate is expected to drop to a stable 6%, and the payout ratio is expected to increase to 65% of earnings. The firm has a beta of 1.40 currently, and it is expected to have a beta of 1.10 after 2010. The risk-free rate is 6.25% and the market risk-premium is 5.5%. You are **required** to determine

    1. the expected price of the stock at the end of 2010, and
    2. the value of the stock, using the two-stage dividend discount model.

Solution

1. Expected earnings per share in 2011 = ₹2.10 × (1.15)5 × (1.06)1 = ₹4.48

    Expected dividends per share in 2011 = ₹4.48 × 0.65 = ₹2.91

    Cost of equity after 2011 = 6.25% + 1.1 × 5.5% = 12.30%

    Expected price at the end of 2010

    $$= \text{Expected DPS in 2010}/(ke - g)$$
    $$= ₹2.91/(0.1230 - 0.06) = ₹46.19$$

2.

Year	EPS (₹)	DPS (₹)
2006	2.42	0.79
2007	2.78	0.91
2008	3.19	1.05
2009	3.67	1.21
2010	4.22	1.39

Cost of equity = 6.25% + 1.40 × 5.5% = 13.95%

Present value of the stock will be equal to the present value of dividends and expected market price at the end of 2010 discounted at the rate of 13.95%.

$P_0 = 0.79 \times \text{PVIF}(13.95, 1) + 0.90 \times \text{PVIF}(13.95, 2) + 1.05 \times \text{PVIF}(13.95, 3) + 1.21 \times \text{PVIF}(13.95, 4) + 1.39 \times \text{PVIF}(13.95, 5) + 46.19 \times \text{PVIF}(13.95, 5)$

$$= ₹27.59$$

8. Mangatrai Pearls, a leader in the cultured pearls market, reported earnings per share of ₹2.02 in 2005 and paid nil dividends. These earnings are expected to grow 14% a year for five years (2006-2010) and 7% per year after that. The firm reported depreciation of ₹20 lakhs

in 2005 and capital spending of ₹42 lakhs and had 70 lakhs shares outstanding. The working capital is expected to remain at 50% of revenues, which were ₹1,060 lakhs in 2005 and are expected to grow 6% a year from 2006 to 2010 and 4% a year after that. The firm is expected to finance 10% of its capital expenditures and working capital needs with debt. Mangatrai had a beta of 1.20 in 2005 and this beta is expected to drop to 1.10 after 2010. The risk-free rate is 7%.

1. Estimate the expected free cash flow to equity from 2006 to 2010, assuming that capital expenditures and depreciation grow at the same rate as earnings.
2. Estimate the terminal price per share (at the end of 2010). Stable firms in this industry have capital expenditures that are 150% of revenues, and maintain working capital at 25% of revenues.
3. Estimate the value per share today, based upon the FCFE model.

Solution

1.

Year	EPS (₹)	CapEx (₹)	Depreciation (₹)	Change in WC (₹)	FCFE (₹)	Terminal Price (₹)
1	2.30	0.68	0.33	0.45	1.57	
2	2.63	0.78	0.37	0.48	1.82	
3	2.99	0.89	0.42	0.51	2.11	
4	3.41	1.01	0.48	0.54	2.45	
5	3.89	1.16	0.55	0.57	2.83	52.69
6	4.16	0.88	0.59	0.20	3.71	

Note: Net capital expenditures (CapEx − depreciation) and working capital change is offset partially by debt (10%). The balance comes from equity. For instance, in year 1: FCFE = 2.30 − (0.68 − 0.33) × (1 − 0.10) − 0.45 × (1 − 0.10) = 1.57

2. Terminal price = 3.71/(0.1305 − 0.07) = ₹52.69
3. Present value per share = 1.57/1.136 + 1.82/1.136² + 2.11/1.136³ + 2.45/1.136⁴ + (2.83 + 52.69)/1.136⁵ = ₹35.05

Capital Budgeting

9. There are three mutually exclusive projects with the following cash flows

Year	Project A	Project B	Project C
0	−₹10,000	₹5,000	−₹15,000
1	₹8,000	₹5,000	₹10,000
2	₹7,000	−₹8,000	₹10,000

The cost of capital is 12%. You are required to select one of these projects.

1. Which project would you pick using the NPV rule?
2. Which project would you pick using the IRR rule?
3. Is there any conflict in ranking? How would you explain the conflict?

Solution

Year	A	B	C
0	−10,000	5,000	−15,000
1	8,000	5,000	10,000
2	7,000	−8,000	10,000

1. NPV of project A $=-10,000+8,000\times$ PVIF $(12, 1)+7,000\times$ PVIF $(12, 2)=₹2,723$

   NPV of project B $=5,000+8,000\times$ PVIF $(12, 1)-8,000\times$ PVIF $(12, 2)=₹3,086.73$

   NPV of project C $=-15,000+10,000\times$ PVIF $(12, 1)+10,000\times$ PVIF $(12, 2)=₹1,900.51$

   So, on the basis of NPV, project B is the best as it is giving the highest NPV >

2. IRR for project A $=32.74\%$

   IRR for project B $=-13.99\%$

   IRR for project C $=21.53\%$

   On the basis of IRR, project A is the best project.

3. The reasons for the conflict can be attributed to differences in scale, and difference in reinvestment rate assumptions. The strange pattern of cash flows on B also throws off the IRR rule. The IRR rule is devised with the idea that cash flows go from negative to positive, not the other way around.

10. Mr Anil Sharma is considering setting up a software development business. To set up the enterprise, Mr Sharma anticipates that he will need to acquire computer hardware costing ₹100,000 (the lifetime of this hardware is five years for depreciation purposes, and straight line depreciation will be used). In addition, Mr Sharma will have to rent an office for ₹50,000 a year. Mr Sharma has also estimated that he will need to hire five software specialists at ₹50,000 a year to work on the software and that marketing and selling costs will be ₹100,000 a year. He expects to price the software at ₹100 per unit and to sell 6,000 units in the first year. The actual cost of materials used to produce each unit is ₹20. The number of units sold is expected to increase 10% a year for the remaining four years, and the revenues and costs are expected to increase at 3 per cent a year, reflecting inflation. The actual cost of materials used to produce each unit is ₹20, and you will need to maintain working capital at 10% of revenues (assume that the working capital investment is made at the beginning of each year). The tax rate will be 40%, and the cost of capital is 12%.

    1. Estimate the cash flows each year on this project.
    2. Should Mr Sharma accept the project?

Solution (₹)

1.

	1	2	3	4	5
Revenues	600,000	679,800	77,0213	872,652	988,714
−Rent	50,000	51,500	53,045	54,636	56,275
−Salaries	250,000	257,500	265,225	273,182	281,377
−Marketing Cost	100,000	103,000			
−Material	120,000	135,960	106,090	109,273	112,551
−Depreciation (₹)	20,000	20,000	154,043	174,530	197,743
Taxable income (₹)	60,000	111,840	20,000	20,000	20,000
Taxes	24,000	44,736	171,811	241,031	320,768
Net income	36,000	67,104	68,724	96,412	128,307
+Depreciation	20,000	20,000	103,086	144,618	192,461
−Change in WC	7,980	9,041	20,000	20,000	20,000
After tax cash flows	48,020	78,063	10,244	11,606	-

2. NPV of project

$$PV \text{ of } ATCF = 42,875 + 62,231 + 80,319 + 97,242 + 120,556 = ₹403,223$$

$$NPV = -₹160,000 + ₹403,223 + 98,871/(1.12)5 = ₹299,325$$

Capital Structure

11. Nasdaq Ltd, an unlevered firm, has expected earnings before interest and taxes of ₹20 lakhs per year. Nasdaq's tax rate is 40%, and the market value is V = E = ₹120 lakhs. The stock has a beta of 1, and the risk free rate is 9%. T`he market risk pre [Assume that E (Rm) − Rf = 6%]. Management is considering the use of debt; debt would be issued and used to buy back stock, and the size of the firm would remain constant. The default-free interest rate on debt is 12%. The firm's analysts have estimated that the present value of any bankruptcy cost is ₹80 lakhs and the probability of bankruptcy will increase with leverage according to the following schedule:

Value of Debt (₹ lakhs)	Probability of Failure
25	0.00%
50	8.00%
75	20.5%
80	30.0%
90	45.0%
100	52.5%
125	70.0%

1. What is the cost of equity and WACC at this time?
2. What is the optimal capital structure when bankruptcy costs are considered?
3. What will the value of the firm be at this optimal capital structure?

Solution

1. Cost of equity = 9% + 6% = 15%
   Since it is an all-equity financed firm, the cost of capital is equal to the cost of equity.
2.

Value of Debt (₹ lakhs)	Increase in Debt (₹ lakhs)	Incremental Tax Benefits (₹ lakhs)	Incremental Exp. Bankruptcy Cost (₹ lakhs)
25	25	10	0
50	25	10	6.40
75	25	10	10.00
80	5	2	7.60
90	10	4	12.00
100	10	4	6.00
125	25	10	14.00

Every marginal increment past ₹75 lakhs has expected cost > expected tax benefits! Optimal debt is between ₹50 lakhs and ₹75 lakhs.

3. Value of firm at optimal = current firm value + sum of incremental tax benefits − sum of incremental bankruptcy costs = 120 + 30 − 16.40 = ₹133.60 lakhs.

12. Deccan Paints Ltd (DPL) has come to you for some advice on how best to increase their leverage over time. In the most recent year, DPL had EBITDA of ₹30 crore, owed ₹100 crore in both book value and market value terms, and had a net worth of ₹200 crore (the market value was twice the book value). It had a beta of 1.30, and the interest rate on its debt is 8% (the risk-free rate is 7%). If it moves to its optimal debt ratio of 40%, the cost of capital is expected to drop by 1%. The market risk premium is 5.5%.

1. How should the firm move to its optimal? In particular, should it borrow money and take on projects or should it pay dividends/repurchase stock?
2. Are there any other considerations that may affect your decision?

Solution

1. Current return on capital = EBIT $(1-t)/(D+E) = 30 (1-0.4)/(100+200) = 6.00\%$

   Current cost of equity = $7\% + 1.30 (5.5\%) = 14.15\%$

   Cost of capital = $14.15\% (400/500) + 8\% (1-0.4) (100/500) = 12.28\%$

   Given that the return on capital is less than the cost of capital, DGF Corporation should try to increase its debt ratio by buying back stock or paying dividends, unless it expects future projects to earn more than its expected cost of capital (11.28%)—that is, 1% less than the current cost of capital.

2. One should consider future investment opportunities and the volatility of operating income in making this decision. If one expects future projects to be better than existing projects, one should be more inclined towards recommending borrowing money/ taking projects.

Appendix: Time Value Tables

TABLE A1

FUTURE VALUE INTEREST FACTOR (FVIF K_{1n}) $= (1+k)n$

n/k	1%	2%	3%	4%	5%	6%	7%	8%	9%	10%	11%	12%	13%
0	1.000	1.000	1.000	1.000	1.000	1.000	1.000	1.000	1.000	1.000	1.000	1.000	1.000
1	1.010	1.020	1.030	1.040	1.050	1.060	1.070	1.080	1.090	1.100	1.110	1.120	1.130
2	1.020	1.040	1.061	1.082	1.102	1.124	1.145	1.166	1.188	1.210	1.232	1.254	1.277
3	1.030	1.061	1.093	1.125	1.158	1.191	1.225	1.260	1.295	1.331	1.368	1.405	1.443
4	1.041	1.082	1.126	1.170	1.216	1.262	1.311	1.360	1.412	1.464	1.518	1.574	1.630
5	1.051	1.104	1.159	1.217	1.276	1.338	1.403	1.469	1.539	1.611	1.685	1.762	1.842
6	1.062	1.126	1.194	1.265	1.340	1.419	1.501	1.587	1.677	1.772	1.870	1.974	2.082
7	1.072	1.149	1.230	1.316	1.407	1.504	1.606	1.714	1.828	1.949	2.076	2.211	2.353
8	1.083	1.172	1.267	1.369	1.477	1.594	1.718	1.851	1.993	2.144	2.305	2.476	2.658
9	1.094	1.195	1.305	1.423	1.551	1.689	1.838	1.999	2.172	2.358	2.558	2.773	3.004
10	1.105	1.219	1.344	1.480	1.629	1.791	1.967	2.159	2.367	2.594	2.839	3.106	3.395
11	1.116	1.243	1.384	1.539	1.710	1.898	2.105	2.332	2.580	2.853	3.152	3.479	3.836
12	1.127	1.268	1.426	1.601	1.796	2.012	2.252	2.518	2.813	3.138	3.498	3.896	4.335
13	1.138	1.294	1.469	1.665	1.886	2.133	2.410	2.720	3.066	3.452	3.883	4.363	4.898
14	1.149	1.319	1.513	1.732	1.980	2.261	2.579	2.937	3.342	3.797	4.310	4.887	5.535
15	1.161	1.346	1.558	1.801	2.097	2.397	2.759	3.172	3.642	4.177	4.785	5.474	6.254
16	1.173	1.373	1.605	1.873	2.183	2.540	2.952	3.426	3.970	4.595	5.311	6.130	7.067
17	1.184	1.400	1.653	1.948	2.292	2.693	3.159	3.700	4.328	5.054	5.895	6.866	7.986
18	1.196	1.428	1.702	2.026	2.407	2.854	3.380	3.996	4.717	5.560	6.544	7.690	9.024
19	1.208	1.457	1.754	2.107	2.527	3.026	3.617	4.316	5.142	6.116	7.263	8.613	10.197
20	1.220	1.486	1.806	2.191	2.653	3.207	3.870	4.661	5.604	6.728	8.062	9.646	11.523
25	1.282	1.641	2.094	2.666	3.386	4.292	5.427	6.848	8.623	10.835	13.585	17.000	21.231
30	1.348	1.811	2.427	3.243	4.322	5.743	7.612	10.063	13.268	17.449	22.892	29.960	39.116

n/k	14%	15%	16%	17%	18%	19%	20%	24%	28%	32%	36%	40%
0	1.000	1.000	1.000	1.000	1.000	1.000	1.000	1.000	1.000	1.000	1.000	1.000
1	1.140	1.150	1.160	1.170	1.180	1.190	1.200	1.240	1.280	1.320	1.360	1.400
2	1.300	1.322	1.346	1.369	1.392	1.416	1.440	1.538	1.638	1.742	1.850	1.960
3	1.482	1.521	1.561	1.602	1.643	1.685	1.728	1.907	2.097	2.300	2.515	2.744
4	1.689	1.749	1.811	1.874	1.939	2.005	2.074	2.364	2.684	3.036	3.421	3.842
5	1.925	2.011	2.100	2.192	2.288	2.386	2.488	2.392	3.436	4.007	4.653	5.378
6	2.195	2.313	2.436	2.565	2.700	2.840	2.986	3.635	4.398	5.290	6.328	7.530
7	2.502	2.660	2.826	3.001	3.185	3.379	3.583	4.508	5.629	6.983	8.605	10.541
8	2.853	3.059	3.278	3.511	3.759	4.021	4.300	5.590	7.206	9.217	11.703	14.758
9	3.252	3.518	3.803	4.108	4.435	4.785	5.160	6.931	9.223	12.166	15.917	20.661
10	3.707	4.046	4.411	4.807	5.234	5.695	6.192	8.594	11.806	16.060	21.647	28.925
11	4.226	4.652	5.117	5.624	6.176	6.777	7.430	10.657	15.112	21.199	29.439	40.496
12	4.818	5.350	5.936	6.580	7.288	8.064	8.916	13.215	19.343	27.983	40.037	56.694
13	5.492	6.153	6.886	7.699	8.599	9.596	10.699	16.386	24.759	36.937	54.451	79.372
14	6.261	7.076	7.988	9.007	10.147	11.420	12.839	20.319	31.961	48.757	74.053	111.120
15	7.138	8.137	9.266	10.539	11.974	13.590	15.407	25.196	40.565	64.359	100.712	155.568
16	8.137	9.358	10.748	12.330	14.129	16.172	18.488	31.243	51.923	84.954	136.969	217.795
17	9.276	10.761	12.468	14.426	16.672	19.244	22.186	38.741	66.461	112.139	186.278	304.914
18	10.575	12.375	14.463	16.879	19.673	22.901	26.623	48.039	85.071	148.023	253.338	426.879
19	12.056	14.232	16.777	19.748	23.214	27.252	31.948	59.568	108.890	195.391	344.540	597.630
20	13.743	16.367	19.461	23.106	27.393	32.429	38.338	73.864	139.380	257.916	468.574	836.683
25	26.462	32.919	40.874	50.658	62.669	77.388	95.396	216.542	478.905	1033.590	2180.081	4499.880
30	50.950	66.212	85.850	111.065	143.371	184.675	237.376	634.820	1645.504	4142.075	10143.019	24201.432

TABLE A2
FUTURE VALUE INTEREST FACTOR FOR AN ANNUITY (FVIFA) $= \dfrac{(1+k)^n - 1}{k}$

n/k	1%	2%	3%	4%	5%	6%	7%	8%	9%	10%	11%	12%	13%
1	1.000	1.000	1.000	1.000	1.000	1.000	1.000	1.000	1.000	1.000	1.000	1.000	1.000
2	2.010	2.020	2.030	2.040	2.050	2.060	2.070	2.080	2.090	2.100	2.110	2.120	2.130
3	3.030	3.060	3.091	3.122	3.152	3.184	3.215	3.246	3.278	3.310	3.342	3.374	3.407
4	4.060	4.122	4.184	4.246	4.310	4.375	4.440	4.506	4.573	4.641	4.710	4.779	4.850
5	5.101	5.204	5.309	5.416	5.526	5.637	5.751	5.867	5.985	6.105	6.228	6.353	6.480
6	6.152	6.308	6.468	6.633	6.802	6.975	7.153	7.336	7.523	7.716	7.913	8.115	8.323
7	7.214	7.434	7.662	7.898	8.142	8.394	8.654	8.923	9.200	9.487	9.783	10.089	10.405
8	8.286	8.583	8.892	9.214	9.549	9.897	10.260	10.637	11.028	11.436	11.859	12.300	12.757
9	9.369	9.755	10.159	10.583	11.027	11.491	11.978	12.488	13.021	13.579	14.164	14.776	15.416
10	10.462	10.950	11.464	12.006	12.578	13.181	13.816	14.487	15.193	15.937	16.722	17.549	18.420
11	11.567	12.169	12.808	13.486	14.207	14.972	15.784	16.645	17.560	18.531	19.561	20.655	21.814
12	12.683	13.412	14.192	15.026	15.917	16.870	17.888	18.977	21.141	21.384	22.713	24.133	25.650
13	13.809	14.680	15.618	16.627	17.713	18.882	20.141	21.495	22.953	24.523	26.212	28.029	29.985
14	14.947	15.974	17.086	18.292	19.599	21.015	22.550	24.215	26.019	27.975	30.095	32.393	34.883
15	16.097	17.293	18.599	20.024	21.579	23.276	25.129	27.152	29.361	31.772	34.405	37.280	40.417
16	17.258	18.639	20.157	21.825	23.657	25.673	27.888	30.324	33.003	35.950	39.190	42.753	46.672
17	18.430	20.012	21.762	23.698	25.840	28.213	30.840	33.750	36.974	40.545	44.501	48.884	53.739
18	19.615	21.412	23.414	25.645	28.132	30.906	33.999	37.450	41.301	45.599	50.396	55.750	61.725
19	20.811	22.841	25.117	27.671	30.539	33.760	37.379	41.446	46.018	51.159	56.939	63.440	70.749
20	22.019	24.297	26.870	29.778	33.066	36.786	40.995	45.762	51.160	57.275	64.203	72.052	80.947
25	28.243	32.030	36.459	41.646	47.727	54.865	63.249	73.106	84.701	98.347	114.413	133.334	155.620
30	34.785	40.568	47.575	56.805	66.439	79.058	94.461	113.283	136.308	164.494	199.021	241.333	293.199

n/k	14%	15%	16%	17%	18%	19%	20%	24%	28%	32%	36%	40%
1	1.000	1.000	1.000	1.000	1.000	1.000	1.000	1.000	1.000	1.000	1.000	1.000
2	2.140	2.150	2.160	2.170	2.180	2.190	2.200	2.240	2.280	2.320	2.360	2.400
3	3.440	3.473	3.506	3.539	3.572	3.606	3.640	3.778	3.918	4.062	4.210	4.360
4	4.921	4.993	5.066	5.141	5.215	5.291	5.368	5.684	6.016	6.362	6.725	7.104
5	6.610	6.742	6.877	7.014	7.154	7.297	7.442	8.048	8.700	9.398	10.146	10.946
6	8.536	8.754	8.977	9.207	9.442	9.683	9.930	10.980	12.136	13.406	14.799	16.324
7	10.730	11.067	11.414	11.772	12.142	12.523	12.916	14.615	16.534	18.696	21.126	23.853
8	13.233	13.727	14.240	14.773	15.327	15.902	16.499	19.123	22.163	25.678	29.732	34.395
9	16.085	16.786	17.518	18.285	19.086	19.923	20.799	24.712	29.369	34.895	41.435	49.153
10	19.337	20.304	21.321	22.393	23.521	24.709	25.959	31.643	38.592	47.062	57.352	69.814
11	23.044	24.349	25.733	27.200	28.755	30.404	32.150	40.238	50.399	63.122	78.998	98.739
12	27.271	29.002	30.850	32.824	34.931	37.180	39.580	50.985	65.510	84.320	108.437	139.235
13	32.089	34.352	36.786	39.404	42.219	45.244	48.497	64.110	84.853	112.303	148.475	195.929
14	37.581	40.505	43.672	47.103	50.818	54.841	59.196	80.496	109.612	149.240	202.926	275.300
15	43.842	47.580	51.660	56.110	60.965	66.261	72.035	100.815	141.303	197.997	276.979	386.420
16	50.980	55.717	60.925	66.649	72.939	79.850	87.442	126.011	181.868	262.356	377.692	541.988
17	59.118	65.075	71.673	78.979	87.068	96.022	105.931	157.253	233.791	347.310	514.661	759.784
18	68.394	75.836	84.141	93.406	103.740	115.266	128.117	195.994	300.252	459.449	700.939	1064.697
19	78.969	88.212	98.603	110.285	123.414	138.166	154.740	244.033	385.323	607.472	954.277	1491.576
20	91.025	102.44	115.380	130.033	146.628	165.418	186.688	303.601	494.213	802.863	1298.817	2089.206
25	181.871	212.793	249.214	292.105	342.603	402.042	371.981	898.092	1706.803	3226.844	6053.004	11247.199
30	356.787	434.745	530.321	647.439	790.948	966.712	1181.882	2640.916	5873.231	12940.859	28172.276	60501.081

TABLE A3
PRESENT VALUE INTEREST FACTOR $(PVIF, k, n) = \left(\dfrac{1}{1+k}\right)^n$

n/k	1%	2%	3%	4%	5%	6%	7%	8%	9%	10%	11%	12%	13%
0	1.000	1.000	1.000	1.000	1.000	1.000	1.000	1.000	1.000	1.000	1.000	1.000	1.000
1	0.990	0.980	0.971	0.962	0.952	0.943	0.935	0.926	0.917	0.909	0.901	0.893	0.885
2	0.980	0.961	0.943	0.925	0.907	0.890	0.873	0.857	0.842	0.826	0.812	0.797	0.783
3	0.971	0.942	0.915	0.889	0.864	0.840	0.816	0.794	0.772	0.751	0.731	0.712	0.693
4	0.961	0.924	0.889	0.855	0.823	0.792	0.763	0.735	0.708	0.683	0.659	0.636	0.613
5	0.951	0.906	0.863	0.822	0.784	0.747	0.713	0.681	0.650	0.621	0.593	0.567	0.543
6	0.942	0.888	0.838	0.790	0.746	0.705	0.666	0.630	0.596	0.564	0.535	0.507	0.480
7	0.933	0.871	0.813	0.760	0.711	0.665	0.623	0.583	0.547	0.513	0.482	0.452	0.425
8	0.923	0.853	0.789	0.731	0.677	0.627	0.582	0.540	0.502	0.467	0.434	0.404	0.376
9	0.914	0.873	0.766	0.703	0.645	0.592	0.544	0.500	0.460	0.424	0.391	0.361	0.333
10	0.905	0.820	0.744	0.676	0.614	0.558	0.508	0.463	0.422	0.386	0.352	0.322	0.295
11	0.896	0.804	0.722	0.650	0.585	0.527	0.475	0.429	0.388	0.350	0.317	0.287	0.261
12	0.887	0.788	0.701	0.625	0.557	0.497	0.444	0.397	0.356	0.319	0.286	0.257	0.231
13	0.879	0.773	0.681	0.601	0.530	0.469	0.415	0.368	0.326	0.290	0.258	0.229	0.204
14	0.870	0.758	0.661	0.577	0.505	0.442	0.388	0.340	0.299	0.263	0.232	0.181	0.205
15	0.861	0.743	0.642	0.555	0.481	0.417	0.362	0.315	0.275	0.239	0.209	0.183	0.160
16	0.853	0.728	0.623	0.534	0.458	0.394	0.339	0.292	0.252	0.218	0.188	0.163	0.141
17	0.844	0.714	0.605	0.513	0.436	0.371	0.317	0.270	0.231	0.198	0.170	0.146	0.125
18	0.836	0.700	0.587	0.494	0.416	0.350	0.296	0.250	0.212	0.180	0.153	0.130	0.111
19	0.828	0.686	0.570	0.475	0.396	0.331	0.276	0.232	0.194	0.164	0.138	0.166	0.098
20	0.820	0.673	0.554	0.456	0.377	0.312	0.258	0.215	0.178	0.149	0.124	0.104	0.087
25	0.780	0.610	0.478	0.375	0.295	0.233	0.184	0.146	0.116	0.092	0.074	0.059	0.047
30	0.742	0.552	0.412	0.308	0.231	0.174	0.131	0.099	0.075	0.057	0.044	0.033	0.026

n/k	14%	15%	16%	17%	18%	19%	20%	24%	28%	32%	36%	40%
0	1.000	1.000	1.000	1.000	1.000	1.000	1.000	1.000	1.000	1.000	1.000	1.000
1	0.877	0.870	0.862	0.855	0.847	0.840	0.833	0.806	0.781	0.758	0.735	0.714
2	0.769	0.756	0.743	0.731	0.718	0.706	0.694	0.650	0.610	0.574	0.541	0.510
3	0.675	0.658	0.641	0.624	0.609	0.593	0.579	0.524	0.477	0.435	0.398	0.364
4	0.592	0.572	0.552	0.534	0.516	0.499	0.482	0.423	0.373	0.329	0.292	0.260
5	0.519	0.497	0.476	0.456	0.437	0.419	0.402	0.341	0.291	0.250	0.215	0.186
6	0.456	0.432	0.410	0.390	0.370	0.352	0.335	0.275	0.227	0.189	0.158	0.133
7	0.400	0.376	0.354	0.333	0.314	0.296	0.279	0.222	0.178	0.143	0.116	0.095
8	0.351	0.327	0.305	0.285	0.266	0.249	0.233	0.179	0.139	0.108	0.085	0.068
9	0.308	0.284	0.263	0.243	0.226	0.209	0.194	0.144	0.108	0.082	0.063	0.048
10	0.270	0.247	0.227	0.208	0.191	0.176	0.162	0.116	0.085	0.062	0.046	0.035
11	0.237	0.215	0.195	0.178	0.162	0.148	0.135	0.094	0.066	0.047	0.034	0.025
12	0.208	0.187	0.168	0.152	0.137	0.124	0.112	0.076	0.052	0.036	0.025	0.018
13	0.182	0.163	0.145	0.130	0.116	0.104	0.093	0.061	0.040	0.027	0.018	0.013
14	0.160	0.141	0.125	0.111	0.099	0.088	0.078	0.049	0.032	0.021	0.014	0.009
15	0.140	0.123	0.108	0.095	0.084	0.074	0.065	0.040	0.025	0.016	0.010	0.006
16	0.123	0.107	0.093	0.081	0.071	0.062	0.054	0.032	0.019	0.012	0.005	0.007
17	0.108	0.093	0.080	0.069	0.060	0.052	0.045	0.026	0.015	0.009	0.005	0.003
18	0.095	0.081	0.069	0.059	0.051	0.044	0.038	0.021	0.012	0.007	0.004	0.002
19	0.083	0.070	0.060	0.051	0.043	0.037	0.031	0.017	0.009	0.005	0.003	0.002
20	0.073	0.061	0.051	0.043	0.037	0.031	0.026	0.014	0.007	0.004	0.002	0.001
25	0.038	0.030	0.024	0.020	0.016	0.013	0.010	0.005	0.002	0.001	0.000	0.000
30	0.020	0.015	0.012	0.009	0.007	0.005	0.004	0.002	0.001	0.000	0.000	0.000

TABLE A4
PRESENT VALUE INTEREST FACTOR FOR AN ANNUITY

$$PVIFA_{(k,n)} = \frac{1 - \dfrac{1}{1+k^n}}{k}$$

n/k	1%	2%	3%	4%	5%	6%	7%	8%	9%	10%	11%	12%	13%
0	1.000	1.000	1.000	1.000	1.000	1.000	1.000	1.000	1.000	1.000	1.000	1.000	1.000
1	0.990	0.980	0.971	0.962	0.952	0.943	0.935	0.926	0.917	0.909	0.901	0.893	0.885
2	1.970	1.942	1.913	1.886	1.859	1.833	1.808	1.783	1.759	1.736	1.713	1.690	1.668
3	2.941	2.884	2.829	2.775	2.723	2.673	2.624	2.577	2.531	2.487	2.444	2.402	2.361
4	3.902	3.808	3.717	3.630	3.546	3.465	3.387	3.312	3.240	3.170	3.102	3.037	2.974
5	4.853	4.713	4.580	4.452	4.329	4.212	4.100	3.993	3.890	3.791	3.696	3.605	3.517
6	5.795	5.601	5.417	5.242	5.076	4.917	4.767	4.623	4.486	4.355	4.231	4.111	3.998
7	6.728	6.472	6.230	6.002	5.786	5.582	5.389	5.206	5.033	4.868	4.712	5.564	4.423
8	7.652	7.325	7.020	6.733	6.463	6.210	5.971	5.747	5.535	3.335	5.146	4.968	4.799
9	8.566	8.162	7.786	7.435	7.108	6.802	6.515	6.247	5.995	5.759	5.537	5.328	5.132
10	9.471	8.983	8.530	8.111	7.722	7.360	7.024	6.710	6.418	6.145	5.889	5.650	5.426
11	10.368	9.787	9.253	8.760	8.306	7.887	7.499	7.139	6.805	6.495	6.207	5.938	5.687
12	11.255	10.575	9.954	9.385	8.863	8.384	7.943	7.536	7.161	6.814	6.492	6.194	5.918
13	12.134	11.348	10.635	9.986	9.394	8.853	8.358	7.904	7.487	7.103	6.750	6.424	6.122
14	13.004	12.106	11.296	10.563	9.899	9.295	8.745	8.244	7.786	7.367	6.982	6.628	6.302
15	13.865	12.849	11.938	11.118	10.380	9.712	9.108	8.559	8.061	7.606	7.191	6.811	6.462
16	14.718	13.578	12.561	11.652	10.838	10.106	9.447	8.851	8.313	7.824	7.379	6.974	6.604
17	15.562	14.292	13.166	12.166	11.274	10.477	9.763	9.122	8.544	8.022	7.549	7.120	6.729
18	16.398	14.992	13.754	12.659	11.690	10.828	10.059	9.372	8.756	8.201	7.702	7.250	6.840
19	17.226	15.678	14.324	13.134	12.085	11.158	10.336	9.604	8.950	8.365	7.839	7.366	6.938
20	18.046	16.351	14.877	13.590	12.462	11.470	10.594	9.818	9.129	8.514	7.963	7.469	7.025
25	22.023	19.523	17.413	15.622	14.094	12.783	11.654	10.675	9.823	9.077	8.422	7.843	7.330
30	25.808	22.397	19.600	17.292	15.373	13.765	12.409	11.258	10.274	9.427	8.694	8.055	7.496

n/k	14%	15%	16%	17%	18%	19%	20%	24%	28%	32%	36%	40%
0	1.000	1.000	1.000	1.000	1.000	1.000	1.000	1.000	1.000	1.000	1.000	1.000
1	0.877	0.870	0.862	0.855	0.847	0.840	0.833	0.806	0.781	0.758	0.735	0.714
2	1.647	1.626	1.605	1.585	1.566	1.547	1.528	1.457	1.392	1.332	1.276	1.224
3	2.322	2.283	2.246	2.210	2.174	2.140	2.106	1.981	1.868	1.766	1.674	1.589
4	2.914	2.855	2.798	2.743	2.690	2.639	2.589	2.404	2.241	2.096	1.966	1.849
5	3.433	3.352	3.274	3.199	3.127	3.058	2.991	2.745	2.532	2.345	2.181	2.035
6	3.889	3.784	3.685	3.589	3.498	3.410	3.326	3.020	2.759	2.534	2.339	2.168
7	4.288	4.160	4.039	3.922	3.812	3.706	3.605	3.242	2.937	2.678	2.455	2.263
8	4.639	4.487	4.344	4.207	4.078	3.954	3.837	3.421	3.076	2.786	2.540	2.113
9	4.946	4.772	4.607	4.451	4.303	4.163	4.031	3.566	3.184	2.868	2.603	2.379
10	5.216	5.019	4.833	4.659	4.494	4.339	4.193	3.682	3.269	2.930	2.650	2.414
11	5.453	5.234	5.029	4.836	4.656	4.486	4.327	3.776	3.335	2.978	2.683	2.438
12	5.660	5.421	5.197	4.988	4.793	4.611	4.439	3.851	3.387	3.013	2.708	2.456
13	5.842	5.583	5.342	5.118	4.910	4.715	4.533	3.912	3.427	3.040	2.727	2.469
14	6.002	5.724	5.468	5.229	5.008	4.802	4.611	3.962	3.459	3.061	2.740	2.478
15	6.142	5.847	5.575	5.324	5.092	4.876	4.675	4.001	3.483	3.076	2.750	2.484
16	6.265	5.954	5.669	5.405	5.162	4.938	4.730	4.033	3.503	3.088	2.758	2.489
17	6.373	6.047	5.749	5.475	5.222	4.990	4.775	4.059	3.518	3.097	2.763	2.492
18	6.467	6.128	5.818	5.534	5.273	5.033	4.812	4.080	3.529	3.104	2.767	2.494
19	6.550	6.198	5.877	4.584	5.316	5.070	4.844	4.097	3.539	3.109	2.770	2.496
20	6.623	6.259	5.929	5.628	5.353	5.101	4.870	4.110	3.546	3.113	2.772	2.497
25	6.873	5.464	5.097	5.766	5.467	5.195	4.948	4.147	3.564	3.122	2.776	2.499
30	7.003	6.566	6.177	5.829	5.517	5.235	4.979	4.160	3.569	3.124	2.778	2.500

Index